proper

> BA rehearsal? Ask BA director

Brecht in/und Asien

Das Brecht-Jahrbuch 36

Redaktion des Bandes:
Markus Wessendorf

Geschäftsführender Herausgeber:
Friedemann J. Weidauer

Redaktions-Assistenz:
Ute Bettray

Mitherausgeber:
Stephen Brockmann, Jürgen Hillesheim,
Karen Leeder, Astrid Oesmann, Marc Silberman,
Vera Stegmann, Antony Tatlow, Carl Weber

Die Internationale Brecht-Gesellschaft
Vertrieb: University of Wisconsin Press

Brecht in/and Asia

The Brecht Yearbook 36

Guest Editor:
Markus Wessendorf

Managing Editor:
Friedemann J. Weidauer

Editorial Assistant:
Ute Bettray

Editorial Board:
**Stephen Brockmann, Jürgen Hillesheim,
Karen Leeder, Astrid Oesmann, Marc Silberman,
Vera Stegmann, Antony Tatlow, Carl Weber**

The International Brecht Society
Distribution: University of Wisconsin Press

Copyright ©2011 by the International Brecht Society. All rights reserved. No parts of this book may be reproduced without formal permission.

Produced at the University of Connecticut—Storrs, Storrs, Connecticut, USA.
Distributed by the University of Wisconsin Press, 1930 Monroe Street, Madison, WI 53711, USA.

www.wisc.edu/wisconsinpress/brecht.html

ISSN 0734-8665
ISBN 978-0-9718963-9-0

Printed in Canada

Front Cover:
D'neka Patten (Okichi) and Ryan Wuestewald (Saito) in *The Judith of Shimoda*, directed by Paul Mitri at Kennedy Theatre Honolulu in April 2010. Photo courtesy of Kennedy Theatre Honolulu. Photographer: Chesley Cannon.

Back Cover:
Kymberly Vanclute (Nakamura), Nicholas Atiburcio (Inoue), Daniel D. Randerson (Heusken) and James Schirmer (Townsend Harris) in *The Judith of Shimoda*, directed by Paul Mitri at Kennedy Theatre Honolulu in April 2010. Photo courtesy of Kennedy Theatre Honolulu. Photographer: Chesley Cannon.

Submissions
Manuscripts in either English or German should be submitted to The Brecht Yearbook via email as attachments, or via snail mail on compact discs. Hard-copy submissions are also acceptable, but they should be accompanied by an electronic file. For English language submissions, American spelling conventions should be used, e.g."theater" instead of "theatre," "color" instead of "colour," etc. Submissions in German should use the new, not the old, spelling conventions. Endnote or footnote format should be internally consistent, preferably following The Chicago Style Manual. Specific guidelines for the Yearbook in both English and German can be found at the website address listed on the next page. Address contributions to the editor:

> Friedemann Weidauer, Department of Modern and Classical Languages, University of Connecticut, Storrs, CT 06269, USA.
> Email: friedemann.weidauer@uconn.edu

Inquiries concerning book reviews and conference participation should be addressed to:

> Marc Silberman, Department of German, 818 Van Hise Hall, University of Wisconsin, Madison, WI 53706, USA.
> Email: mdsilber@wisc.edu

Officers of the International Brecht Society

Hans Thies Lehmann, President, Institut für Theater-, Film-und Medienwissenschaft, Johann Wolfgang Goethe-Universität, Grüneburgplatz 1, 60323 Frankfurt/M., Germany.
Email: H.T.Lehmann@tfm.uni-frankfurt.de

Günther Heeg, Vice-President, Universität Leipzig, Institut für Theaterwissenschaft, Ritterstr. 16, 04109 Leipzig, Germany.
Email: guenther.heeg@gmx.de

Paula Hanssen, Secretary/Treasurer, Dept. of International Languages and Cultures, Webster University, 470 E. Lockwood, Saint Louis, MO, 63119, USA. Email: hanssen@webster.edu

Norman Roessler, Editor, *Communications,* Intellectual Heritage Program, Temple University, Philadelphia, PA, 19122, USA.
Email: nroessler@temple.edu

Internet Website address
http://www.brechtsociety.org

Internet Website Communications from the IBS:
http://ecibs.org/new/index.php

Internet Website The Digital Brecht Yearbook Vols. 1 – 30:
http://digicoll.library.wisc.edu/German/subcollections/BrechtYearbookAbout.html

Membership
Members receive The Brecht Yearbook and the annual journal Communications of the International Brecht Society. Dues should be sent in US$ to the Secretary/Treasurer or in Euro to Deutsche Bank Düsseldorf, Konto Nr. 76-74146, BLZ 300 700 24, IBAN — DE53 3007 0024 0767 4146 00, BIC bzw. Swift Code: DEUTDEDBDUE.

Student Member (up to three years)	$30.00	€30
Low income and emeritis faculty	$30.00	€30
Regular Member (full-time employed)	$40.00	€40
Sustaining Member	$50.00	€50
Institutional Member	$50.00	€50
Lifetime (retirees only)	$200.00	€200

Online credit card payment is possible at the IBS website listed above; click on "membership" for instructions.

The International Brecht Society

The International Brecht Society has been formed as a corresponding society on the model of Brecht's own unrealized plan for the Diderot Society. Through its publications and regular international symposia, the society encourages the discussion of any and all views on the relatioship of the arts and the contemporary world. The society is open to new members in any field and in any country and welcomes suggestions and/or contributions in German, English, Spanish or French to future symposia and for the published volumes of its deliberations.

Die Internationale Brecht-Gesellschaft

Die Internationale Brecht-Gesellschaft ist nach dem Modell von Brechts nicht verwirklichtem Plan für die Diderot-Gesellschaft gegründet worden. Durch Veröffentlichungen und regelmäßige internationale Tagungen fördert die Gesellschaft freie und öffentliche Diskussionen über die Beziehungen aller Künste zur heutigen Welt. Die Gesellschaft steht neuen Mitgliedern in jedem Fachgebiet und Land offen und begrüßt Vorschläge für zukünftige Tagungen und Aufsätze in deutscher, englischer, spanischer oder französischer Sprache für *Das Brecht-Jahrbuch*.

La Société Internationale Brecht

La Société Internationale Brecht a été formée pour correspondre à la société rêvée par Brecht, "Diderot-Gesellschaft". Par ses publications et congrès internationaux à intervalles réguliers, la S.I.B. encourage la discussion libre des toutes les idées sur les rapports entre les arts et le monde contemporain. Bien entendu, les nouveaux membres dans toutes les disciplines et tous les pays sont accueillis avec plaisir, et la Société sera heureuse d'accepter des suggestions et des contributions en français, allemand, espagnol ou anglais pour les congrès futurs et les volumes des communications qui en résulteront.

La Sociedad Internacional Brecht

La Sociedad Internacional Brecht fué creada para servir como sociedad corresponsal. Dicha sociedad se basa en el modelo que el mismo autor nunca pudo realizar, el plan "Diderot-Gesellschaft". A través de sus publicaciones y los simposios internacionales que se llevan a cabo regularmente, la Sociedad estimula la discusión libre y abierta de cualquier punto de vista sobre la relación entre las artes y el mundo contemporáneo. La Sociedad desea, por supuesto, la participación de nuevos miembros de cualquier área, de cualquier país, y accepta sugerencias y colaboraciones en alemán, inglés, francés y español para los congresos futuros y para las publicaciones de sus discusiones.

Contents

Editorial

Markus Wessendorf — xi

Silvia Schlenstedt (1931-2010) — 1

Brecht in India / Brecht in Indien

Richard Schechner (New York) — 5
Malleable Brecht: The Performance Group's *Mother Courage* in India, 1976

Amal Allana (Delhi) — 27
Brecht: A Participant in the Process of Nation-Building

Boris Daussà-Pastor (New York) — 45
Estrangement in *Kathakali*

Contemporary Japanese Theater / Japanisches Gegenwartstheater

Michiko Tanigawa (Tokyo) — 57
Die Stellung des Black Tent Theaters in der japanischen Brecht-Rezeption

Joachim Lucchesi (Berlin) — 73
Jan-Jan-Oper und Osaka Rap Teil 1: Brecht-Nachklänge im Theater *Ishinha*

Akira Ichikawa (Osaka) — 85
Jan-Jan-Oper und Osaka Rap Teil 2: Yukichi Matsumotos *Mizumachi* und *Keaton*

The "Chinese" Brecht / Der "chinesische" Brecht

Andreas Aurin (Sydney) — 95
Towards a Taoist Reading of the *Lehrstück The Horatians and the Curiatians*

Weijia Li (Macomb) — 107
Braveness in Non-Action: The Taoist Strategy of Survival in Bertolt Brecht's *Schweyk* and Anna Seghers' *Transit*

Zheng Jie (Singapore) — 115
Brecht's *Good Person* and Traditional Humanistic Chinese Philosophy: Towards an Ethical Subject

Günther Heeg (Leipzig) — 135
Brechts chinesische Wendungen: *Me-ti* und die Praxis kultureller Flexionen

Yuan Tan (Wuhan)   151
Unter der chinesischen Maske: Neue Studien zu Brechts "Sechs chinesischen Gedichten"

Eberhard Fritz (Altshausen)   165
Die Großmutter, der Pietismus und die Missionare: Neue biografische Erklärungsansätze in Bezug auf Brechts "chinesisches Werk"

Friedemann Weidauer (Storrs)   189
Brecht's (Brush with) Maoism

Tradition — Brecht — Political Theater / Tradition — Brecht — Politisches Theater

Farzana Akhter (Dhaka)   201
Performing Brecht in Bangladesh: Making the Unfamiliar Familiar

Parichat Jungwiwattanaporn (Bangkok)   211
Brechtian Theater Meets Buddhist Aesthetics: Kamron Gunatilaka's *The Revolutionist*

Jan Creutzenberg (Seoul)   225
The Good Person of Korea: Lee Jaram's *Sacheon-ga* as a Dialogue between Brecht and *Pansori*

Brecht between Imperialism and Postcolonialism, Orient and Occident / Brecht zwischen Imperialismus und Postkolonialismus, Orient und Okzident

Marc Silberman (Madison)   241
A Postcolonial Brecht?

Melissa Dinsman (Notre Dame)   249
Imperial Brecht? Bertolt Brecht's Complex Portrayal of Empire in *Mann ist Mann*

Gudrun Tabbert-Jones (Santa Clara)   265
The "Lord of the South See" and His "Maori Woman:" The Function of the Tahiti Metaphor in Brecht's Early Works

Martin Revermann (Toronto)   277
Brecht's Asia vs. Brecht's Greece: Cultural Constructs and the Explanatory Power of a Binary

Fritz Bennewitz's Intercultural Brecht Productions / Fritz Bennewitz' interkulturelle Brecht-Inszenierungen

Rolf Rohmer (Leipzig)   291
Annäherungen an den Interkulturalismus mit Brecht: Fritz Bennewitz' Theaterarbeit in Asien

Joerg Esleben (Ottawa)   303
From Didactic to Dialectic Intercultural Theater: Fritz Bennewitz and the 1973 Production of the *Caucasian Chalk Circle* in Mumbai

David G. John (Waterloo) 315
Fritz Bennewitz's Islamic *Chalk Circle* in the Philippines

Brecht('s) Adaptations / Brecht(s) Bearbeitungen

Dennis Carroll (Honolulu) 329
Wuolijoki, Brecht, "Well Made" Dramaturgy, and *The Judith of Shimoda*

Markus Wessendorf (Honolulu) 337
"Fear and Misery" Post-9/11: Mark Ravenhill's *Shoot/Get Treasure/Repeat*

Conspectus

Antony Tatlow (Dublin) 353
Brecht's East Asia

Book Reviews 371

Books Received 399

Contributors 401

Editorial

Markus Wessendorf

The following 26 essays are based on presentations given at "Brecht in/ and Asia," the 13th Symposium of the International Brecht Society (IBS), which was held at the University of Hawai'i at Mānoa (UHM) from May 19 to 23, 2010. More than 90 Brecht scholars from 17 countries participated in the event. Ong Keng Sen, Haiping Yan, and Richard Schechner gave keynote lectures. The symposium also included a Brecht Theater Festival, featuring Robyn Archer and Michael Morley (German Cabaret Songs), the *Threepenny Opera* at Army Community Theatre (certainly one of the first Brecht productions on an American military base!), the first English-language production of Brecht/Wuolijoki's *The Judith of Shimoda* at Kennedy Theatre, the *Mahagonny Songspiel* by the Hawaii Opera Theatre, an original production by the Honolulu-based The Red Rockets (*Mor Is Mor*), and Tremayne Tamayose's *The Hilo Massacre* at Kumu Kahua Theatre.

The idea to dedicate a symposium to "Brecht in/and Asia" was born in 2006, during a breakfast conversation between Hans-Thies Lehmann and myself, while we both attended a conference on "Drama and/after Postmodernism." The last time the IBS had dealt specifically with Asia had been in 1986, when Antony Tatlow organized the 7th IBS Symposium in Hong Kong. Since then Asia had undergone many changes, from the emergence of post-Soviet states in Central Asia to the political and economic ascendency of China and India to the U.S.-led "War on Terror" in the Islamic parts of West, South and Southeast Asia. These developments called for a reassessment of the complex interrelationships between Brecht's work and various Asian cultures from a 21st-century perspective. And UHM seemed a suitable location for a conference like this—considering Hawai'i's role as a meeting-place of East and West: geographically, demographically, culturally, and spiritually.

Admittedly, it would be difficult to find more than tangential evidence for a link between Brecht and Hawai'i. Even though Brecht occasionally refers to the Pacific in his early work (the poem "Tahiti"), and even though Mahagonny could have been modeled after Waikiki, there are no references to Hawai'i in his writings. The most popular Western theater genres in the Island State are musicals and conventional realism, even though the expropriation of Hawaiians since the 19th century, the 20th-century plantation history of Hawai'i, and the race relations resulting from both developments often cry out for a Brechtian treatment (which they have received on occasion, for example in Victoria Nālani Kneubuhl's *The Conversion of Ka'ahumanu*, the already-mentioned *Hilo Massacre*, and Dennis Carroll's *Massie/Kahahawai*). One could point to Charles Lindbergh, the dubious protagonist of Brecht's "Lehrstück" *Flight of the Lindberghs*, who is buried outside of Hāna on Maui, with his grave overlooking the ocean. Or one could mention that Brecht's actor-friend Peter Lorre, after his emigration to the United States, played the Japanese secret agent Mr. Moto in a series of Hollywood films—including the 1937 film, *Think Fast, Mr. Moto*, in which Lorre's character stops by in Honolulu on his way to Shanghai. One could also point out that Robert Louis Stevenson, whose writings Brecht considered a precursor of filmic montage, visited Hawai'i repeatedly and left many traces on the islands. If Brecht would have visited Honolulu, he might have been interested in the fact that the Chinese revolutionary and political leader Sun Yat-sen spent his teenage years in Honolulu. As the author of an unfinished play on the *Life of Confucius* (also known by its alternative title, *The Bowl of Ginger*) he might have been amused to find a statue of the great Chinese thinker in the center of a food court in Chinatown. But these are minor facts.

Hawai'i's links to Asia and Asian theater, however, cannot be questioned. More than 40% of Hawai'i's residents today are of Asian descent. Asian performance traditions were first introduced to the islands by immigrants from China, Japan, the Philippines and other countries in the early 20th century. In the 1920s and 1930s, a Jingju (or Beijing opera) troupe performed continuously at Maunakea Street in Chinatown, while the Kabuki actor Shusui Hisamatsu toured the Pacific Coast with his Shinsei Gekidan theater company while being based in Hawai'i. Also, the theater department hosting the symposium is home to the oldest academic program in Asian theater in the Western hemisphere. (*The Vengeful Sword* in spring 2011, for example, was the 31st Kabuki production at UHM in 87 years!)

The great variety of academic papers presented at the symposium allowed for intellectually stimulating debate throughout the duration of the event. The following proceedings, however, only represent a sample of the topics that were discussed. Richard Schechner, in his keynote lecture, examines the varying critical reception that his production of *Mother Courage* with The Performance Group received during their India tour in 1976. Surprisingly, three conference participants from India were able to comment on their actual experience of seeing the production during the Q&A session following Schechner's presentation. Amal Allana provides a short history of Brecht's influence on Indian theater since the 1950s, with particular regard to developments in folk theater as well as feminist and postcolonial aesthetics. Boris Daussà-Pastor contrasts Brecht's *Verfremdungseffekt* with the traditional strategies of estrangement in *kathakali*, a South Indian form of dance-drama. Michiko Tanigawa discusses the Brechtian aesthetics of the Japanese theater company Black Tent Theater since the late 1960s, whereas Joachim Lucchesi and Akira Ichikawa analyze the key themes and visual leitmotifs of more recent productions by Yukichi Matsumoto's theater group Ishinha. A number of essays scrutinize Brecht's engagement with Chinese culture. While Andreas Aurin and Weijia Li examine specifically Taoist elements in Brecht's work and Günther Heeg interrelates Brecht's "cultural flexions" with the Mohist tradition, Zheng Jie analyses Brecht's interest in humanistic Chinese philosophy more broadly. Yuan Tan provides an in-depth comparison of Brecht's "Six Chinese Poems" with Arthur Waley's sources and the original Chinese poems (which Brecht didn't know). Eberhard Fritz suggests that Brecht was first introduced to Chinese culture by the publications of foreign mission societies that his Pietist grandmother subscribed to. Friedemann Weidauer, finally, examines Brecht's critical engagement with Maoism in the 1950s. Several essays also examine the intermediate role of the Brecht reception between national performance tradition and progressive political theater. Farzana Akhter surveys the history of Brecht productions and adaptations in Bangladesh since the mid-1970s. Parichat Jungwiwattanaporn reads one of the most radical productions in modern Thai theater, Kamron Gunatilaka's *The Revolutionist* (1986), as a deconstruction of the hegemonic narrative of Thai-style democracy. Jan Creutzenberg discusses the recent staging of *The Good Person of Szechwan* in *pansori* style as an attempt to address contemporary social issues in Korea by recourse to traditional form. A few articles also interrogate the ambiguities of Brecht's work with regard to empire, colonialism, and orientalism: Marc Silberman questions the postcolonial credentials of Brecht's work, Melissa Dinsman deconstructs the representation of empire in *Man Equals Man*, Gudrun Tabbert-Jones examines the Tahiti metaphor in Brecht's early plays and poetry, and Martin Revermann sheds new light on the structural opposition between (rejected) Aristotelianism and (embraced) Asian theater aesthetics in Brecht's work. One entire section is dedicated to Fritz Bennewitz's intercultural stagings of Brecht plays in Asia. While Rolf Rohmer locates Bennewitz's work in a more general intercultural context, Joerg Esleben and David G. John discuss specific productions: the 1973 staging of *The Caucasian Chalk Circle* in Mumbai and the 1977-1978 production of the same play in Manila, respectively. Dennis Carroll highlights Hella Wuolijoki's contributions to her and Brecht's adaptation of *The Judith of Shimoda* (based on Yamamoto Yūzō's 1929-play *The Sad Tale of a Woman, the Story of Chink Okichi* in Glenn Shaw's English translation from 1935). Markus Wessendorf interprets Mark Ravenhill's "Epic Cycle of Short Plays" *Shoot/Get Treasure/Repeat* (2008) as an updated version of *Fear and Misery of the Third Reich* for the post-9/11 era. Antony Tatlow, last but not least, provides a retrospective assessment of Brecht's reception in China and other East Asian countries over the past decades.

I am grateful to all participants, speakers, and contributing artists who made the symposium a success. Both the symposium and this volume would have been impossible without the generous support and dedicated help of many institutions and individuals. At UHM, I would like to thank Dennis Carroll, the Chair of the Department of Theatre and Dance, Thomas Bingham, the Dean of Arts and Humanities, Gary Ostrander, the Vice Chancellor for Research and Graduate Education, as well as the Department of Political Science and the Center for South Asian Studies for their financial assistance. The Hawai'i Council for the Humanities, the Hawai'i State Foundation on Culture and the Arts, the Deutscher Akademischer Austauschdienst (DAAD), the Sidney Stern Memorial Trust, and the International Brecht Society also provided vital funding. The theater students who staffed the information desk, provided technical support, and created a hospitable cafeteria environment deserve the wholehearted gratitude from all symposium participants. One student in particular, Ronald Gilliam, spent countless hours designing the conference website and other publicity materials. If the production of *The Judith of Shimoda* turned into the cultural high point of the symposium, this is only due to the efforts of my director-colleague Paul Mitri and the professional commitment of all student performers, designers, and crew. Without the efforts of fiscal officer Colleen Young and the departmental secretaries Tana Marin and Lori Chun the symposium would not have happened. I would also like to thank my many colleagues from other departments at UHM who, to my pleasant surprise, volunteered to chair panels. Of my fellow conference organizers, Marc Silberman in particular provided helpful advice every step of the way. I also enjoyed the efficient collaboration with managing editor Friedemann Weidauer on this volume. My thanks, finally, go to Ute Bettray for her diligent work on the editing and formatting of the final version of this volume.

Markus Wessendorf

Honolulu, May 2011

Conference poster design courtesy of Ronald Gilliam.

Silvia Schlenstedt (1931-2010)

With permission of Dieter Schlenstedt.

Silvia Schlenstedt passed away in Berlin on March 16, 2010, just one month short of her eightieth birthday. Born in 1931 into a Jewish family in Wuppertal, she fled with them in 1934 first to Spain, then France, and finally Switzerland. She returned with her family to Frankfurt am Main in 1946, and moved with them to East Berlin in 1950, where she studied German literature at the Humboldt Universität and completed her doctoral dissertation on Brecht's exile poetry collection "Svendborger Gedichte" in 1959. After teaching for several years at her alma mater, she took up a position at the Zentralinstitut für Literaturgeschichte (in the GDR Academy of Sciences) where she completed her habilitation in 1976 (*Wegscheiden: deutsche Lyrik im Entscheidungsfeld der Revolutionen von 1917 und 1918*). In the following decades her research and publications were focused mainly on anti-fascist German exile writers and contemporary lyric poetry. Most recently she edited two volumes in the new Anna Seghers edition (Aufbau Verlag). The International Brecht Society mourns the loss of this internationally recognized scholar and extends condolences to her surviving husband, Dieter Schlenstedt, and their children and grandchildren.

The following text by poet and dramatist Volker Braun appeared in the *Berliner Zeitung* on April 9, 2011, and is reprinted here with his permission.

EIN STEIN FÜR SILVIA SCHLENSTEDT

In die Hand, der es schwerfällt, diese Zeilen zu schreiben, nehme ich immer wieder den Stein, den ich beim Abstieg vom südlichsten Felsen Afrikas aufhob, um ihn ihr mitzubringen, ein Bruchstück gelb und roten Sandsteins, dessen Abrieb an den Fingern haftet. Den Stein vom Kap der Guten Hoffnung, den ich in ihre Hand legen, den ich ihrer Hand gönnen wollte, ihrem Blick vermachen, das greifbare, faßliche Material der Poesie, die ihr Lebensstoff war. Ich weiß nicht, wie mir der Gedanke kam; die grandiose Natur, die umkämpfte Gesellschaft, ich hatte auf der Reise Blyde River und Treur River gesehen, den Trauer- und Freudenfluß. Ihr lebenslanger Zuspruch: wer schreibt, handelt... *Um nun die Empfindung des Lebens wiederzugewinnen, die Dinge wieder zu fühlen, den Stein steinern zu machen*, wie Viktor Schklowski sagte. Ich nahm ihn mit im Handgepäck, so kostbar wurde er mir im Gedanken an sie, ich trug ihn ans andere Ende der Welt, nicht ahnend, daß sie nicht mehr am Leben war, daß ihre Reise geendet hatte. Das Meer lag unerwartet ruhig, die Sonne schien warm am Cape Point, Exil der Hoffnung, daß es kein Schwarz und Weiß mehr gäbe, aber die vielfarbne Menschheit. Sie hat Exile gekannt, sie kam da her, ihr Ernst, ihr Wissen, ihre Anmut; und ging wohl wieder da hin.

Der formbare Brecht: Die *Mutter Courage* der Performance Group in Indien, 1976

Richard Schechner

Vom 10. Februar bis 6. April 1976 gastierte die New Yorker von Richard Schechner gegründete und geleitete Performance Group (TPG) mit ihrer Vorjahresinszenierung der brechtschen *Mutter Courage und ihrer Kinder* in fünf Städten und einem Dorf in Nord- und Zentralindien. In New York erlaubte die Performing Garage—eine flexible Studiobühne—der Gruppe eine Inszenierung im Stil des "environmental theater." In Indien versuchte TPG, die für die New Yorker Inszenierung charakteristische räumliche Integration von Darstellern und Zuschauern weitestgehend beizubehalten. In Indien wurde *Mutter Courage* in Neu-Delhi, Lucknow, Kalkutta (jetzt Kolkata), Singjole (ein Dorf in der Nähe von Kalkutta), Bhopal und Bombay (jetzt Mumbai) aufgeführt. Die Produktion wurde von der indischen Presse und Öffentlichkeit überwiegend enthusiastisch aufgenommen, obwohl einige Kritiker und Zuschauer sich über mangelnde "Werktreue" beklagten. Davon abgesehen, dass der Marketenderwagen der Courage in der TPG-Inszenierung fehlte, trugen die Darsteller moderne amerikanische Kleidung, dem Publikum wurde (nach dem dritten Akt) Essen serviert, und auf eine Proszeniumsbühne wurde ganz verzichtet.

From February 10 through April 6, 1976, the New York-based Performance Group (TPG), founded and directed by Richard Schechner, toured its 1975 production of Brecht's *Mother Courage and Her Children* to five cities and one village in North and Central India. In New York, the group's Performing Garage—a flexible black-box theater—allowed for a fully "environmental theater" production. In India TPG tried to maintain the environmental character of the production as much as possible. *Mother Courage* in India was performed in New Delhi, Lucknow, Calcutta (now Kolkata), Singjole (a village near Calcutta), Bhopal, and Bombay (now Mumbai). The production was generally enthusiastically received by both the Indian press and public, though some critics and spectators thought TPG did not "accurately" produce Brecht's play. TPG's production—in addition to doing away with Courage's wagon—costumed the characters in modern American dress, served supper to the audience (after scene 3), and completely abandoned the proscenium stage.

Malleable Brecht: The Performance Group's *Mother Courage* in India, 1976[1]

Richard Schechner

Scene 3 in New Delhi. The Cook (James Griffiths) cleans a chicken—represented by a single block of wood which will also be Swiss Cheese's cash box—as Courage (Joan MacIntosh) talks to spectators. Photo Courtesy of Richard Schechner. (above)

Scene 3 in New Delhi. Courage (Joan MacIntosh) stares directly at the camera...a spectator... as the Cook (James Griffiths) thinks his own thoughts. Photo Courtesy of Richard Schechner. (right)

Brecht in/and Asia // Brecht in/und Asien

From New Delhi's Hindi weekly *Dinman* (21-27 March 1976):

...when you get a ticket for Brecht's *Mother Courage and Her Children* by The Performance Group (New York), you do not go to see *Mother Courage* — you enter the world and environment of *Mother Courage* — the world of the wagon and of children, of war-torn Europe, of bargaining and haggling. It is not a regular theatre you go to but the space of a gymnasium at the Modern School, New Delhi. Jim Clayburgh's environmental design gives you a more or less central longish space, surrounded on all sides by scaffolding of angle irons supporting two levels of platforms for seating — the upper one reaches almost to the ceiling...As you walk in, checked in by Richard Schechner, the play's director, who stands by the cash register, you are told to sit anywhere and you choose your little space — on the floor level, or the second tier or on the third, on the projected platforms or on the wagon steps. Ropes dominate the scene; hooked on to the ceiling, on sides, on the scaffolding...The performers move around, checking props, smiling and waving or talking to you. The whole place seems full of a strange kind of energy and has a dynamic quality...As the action of *Mother Courage* proceeds, you soon discover that the central space is not the only space — the two projections on either side, the stationary wagon...the painted pit, the ladder, the right hand corner as you enter, outside the door into the street — are all spaces that are exploited. The spectator moves according to action, even during action, to find his own space and his own view, in the different circles of spaces (there is *no* demarcation between audience-space and performance-space)...Sitting through the play, one experiences this oneness with the performers, the immediacy of the action, the flow of energy. Initially, so used is one to the separateness and holiness of stage illusion, that as a spectator one may feel embarrassed or uncomfortable. As you watch — you are watched, too — full lights on performer and spectator alike. Their changing costumes in view of the audience, setting up props, each in turn announcing the scene, mingling with the audience in the supper break, present them dually as persons that are non-performers and characters in the play. Having watched the play a number of times, I realize that there is no lack of interest on my part in seeing them as performers nor any lack of concentration on their part when they performed. The performer and the spectator form one unit — the confrontation between them brings each nearer to the other. The dynamism of the form then lies in this participatory act, which is as old as theatre itself in which we have our roots — but which we seem to have forgotten in our urban setting under the influence of 19th century Western theatre. To convey the feeling of movement and flux of continuing war

Scene 3 in Bombay. Yvette (Elizabeth LeCompte) counting her money as she rides a soldier. More soldier-clients wait on the right, while the audience looks on. Photo Courtesy of Richard Schechner.

> with its attendant desolation and exploitation, which forms the basic rhythm of the play, four elements contribute to create the total effect: the use of ropes in the environment, the use of sound and silence, scenic transpositions and extensions, and of course the physical elements of voice and gesture of the performers. Ropes are used symbolically—as harness, yoke, the moving wagon, the hangman's rope. Functionally, to demarcate and sectionalize areas, as territorial definitions…Except for Joan MacIntosh as Mother Courage and Leeny Sack as dumb Kattrin, each performer plays more roles than one—especially Elizabeth LeCompte in two entirely different roles of the General (male) and Yvette the prostitute. Whatever role the performer plays the focus is on a kind of distilled pure quality in performance—on the essential with no frills. Yet the character is not presented as flat. Voice and physical action contribute to the rhythm and movement of the play. (Translator unknown.)

Another Indian opinion, this one from Calcutta's (Kolkata) *Theatre Bulletin* (March 1976):

> Schechner has no right to distort Brecht's epic theatre…I feel nearly all the Brecht-lovers of Calcutta were disappointed by seeing his "Mother Courage." The people who were not disappointed were those who do not know what "pure" Brecht

is about and those who went to see what Brecht's play looked like in Environmental Theatre...The worst part of *Mother Courage* was the sex scene of Yvette (a prostitute). That they need not have been shown so vividly is what *Statesman* and lots of other papers said...This many regard as an attack on modesty. Because of these sex scenes, outside the gates there was a crowd for tickets. These sex scenes are thought of in such a way that either the spectators laugh or they are frightened or they find it disgusting, which is something that does not happen during the times of war.

And finally a few words from the Bombay (Mumbai) *Times of India*, April 5, 1976:

Fantastic! Never before has a Bombay audience been exposed to such an enriching theatrical experience...It has everything. Action, activity (often frenetic and bewildering, often physically stunning), laughter, pathos, tension, ribaldry, humor, music, biting remarks against war and injustice. A summative statement on drama; an unforgettable event...Through it all, through the words and the action and the noise and the novelty and the enormous planning and intellection behind it Brecht's deep humanism emerges...*Mother Courage* is Man [sic] confronting the absurd. As performed she is vigorous, harsh, pragmatic, tender, defiant, raw as a scoop of earth, ineluctably human. I came away from it, walking from the starkness of what happened into the stillness of midnight, prodded to thought, a little more involved in this incredible thing called life.

Brecht was as much an adapter of other people's plays as he was an "original playwright" (if that moniker means anything substantive). In this, he is like Shakespeare and the ancient Greeks and Romans. *Threepenny Opera, Coriolanus, Don Juan, The Tutor (Der Hofmeister), Antigone, The Duchess of Malfi*...the list can go on and on. So why should anyone insist on doing Brecht as Brecht did Brecht? Here, in regard to The Performance Group's[2] *Mother Courage and Her Children*, which opened in New York in 1974 and toured north India in 1976, I am speaking not of an adaptation of text (the default meaning of the term adaptation) but of the mise-en-scene, setting, and interpretation of roles. This is of special interest with regard to *Mother Courage* because Brecht's staging, Helene Weigel's acting, and the iconic presence of Courage's wagon haunt every production since the Berlin Ensemble's of 1949. The Ensemble production, enshrined by the *Mother Courage Modellbuch* (even more than the film) eclipsed the 1941 world premiere in Zurich, directed by Leopold Lindtberg and featuring Therese Giehse.

In 1974 I challenged this orthodoxy by doing away with the wagon, superimposing a 1970s American woman on Brecht's 17th century European, and offering an environmental theater staging that included the audience. Brecht posits an interaction among business, war, and dehumanization. Joan MacIntosh's Courage was both a middle class American woman sinking into poverty and desperation and Brecht's "hyena of the battlefield" feeding off the detritus of late American capitalism. Because no full-scale war has been fought on North American soil since the Civil War and the wars against Native Americans, I decided to emphasize business and through it make manifest the whole system. The south wall of The Performing Garage was plastered with super-market ads and armed forces enlistment posters. Spectators entering paid in cash at an old-fashioned cash register. No tickets were sold in advance. Throughout the performance, each time money was taken, exchanged, or mentioned the register's bell rang: from the first spectator to buy a ticket to when Courage gives the Peasant Woman money to bury Kattrin. TPG's manager-drummer counted the night's receipts at his desk near his drum-set and wrote the night's take on a chalkboard. Real cash was used as props with about $50 in circulation. Yvette was paid real money for her make-believe prostitution. In addition to cash, a "silver brick" iconized the items Courage accumulates and sells, and was also used as Swiss Cheese's cash box. After the death of Swiss Cheese in scene 3, the actors sold and served soup, apples, bread, and cheese to spectators, converting the Performing Garage into Courage's canteen. During supper Courage sang the "Song of the Great Capitulation" as a cabaret number. In many ways, the life of TPG and its audience was interwoven with Brecht's narrative highlighted by Paul Dessau's music. The underlying idea of TPG's production was coherently Brechtian: a good woman who, in identifying herself with the rich, the military, and the capitalists, makes choices against her own class interests. Blind to the system that is oppressing her and which she serves, Courage is ground down, defeated and transformed into an animal—at the play's end, she is hitched to her canteen wagon, hauling her world with her. On her way down, she plunders corpses, sells to both sides in an endless war, cheats, haggles, and does what she has to do in order to save her own skin. But through all this, and Brecht knew it, Courage displays grit, keeps her sense of irony and humor, aims wise-cracks against the generals and priests, kings and popes. As in *The Caucasian Chalk Circle* and *The Good Person of Szechwan*, in *Mother Courage* Brecht shows why good people must act bad in order to survive in bad times; that the only good person in bad times is a bad person like Azdak. What the audience experiences is not a bad person getting worse—that has no educative value and contradicts Brecht's fundamental optimism—but a good person forced to act inhumanly in order to survive. When in scene 3 Courage "bargains too long" letting her son Swiss Cheese be executed, she is not being stingy. She is forced to choose between her son's life and her (and his) living. Brecht intends the audience to comprehend and condemn the system that forces such choices on people.

Scene 1 in Lucknow. In the foreground, Eilif (Jim Clayburgh) and Swiss Cheese (Spalding Gray) pull Courage's "office wagon." Holding the reins is Courage (Joan MacIntosh) and next to her Kattrin (Leeny Sack). Director Richard Schechner is seated cross-legged at the foot of the steps. Photo Courtesy of Richard Schechner.

Scene 1 in New Delhi. On the left, back to the camera, Swiss Cheese (Spalding Gray). On the right, facing the camera, Eilif (Jim Clayburgh). Photo Courtesy of Richard Schechner.

Richard Schechner

We brought as much of this as we could to India where we played from February to April 1976 in New Delhi, Lucknow, Calcutta, the village of Singjole near Calcutta, Bhopal, and Bombay.³ In each place, TPG adapted our mise-en-scene to the given circumstances. Overall, *Mother Courage* was not only received differently in India than in New York but became something different than it was. This is the interesting, if obvious, theoretical point: that location and reception as much as the work "in itself" determine what a work is. That there is no "work in itself," but only given instances of a piece's productions. For the most part, TPG kept to Brecht's text as translated from the German by Ralph Manheim. But even the spoken and sung text, especially in Singjole, collapsed and became something else under the pressure of circumstances. Despite these changes, I would argue that TPG did *Mother Courage and Her Children* in as authentic a way as any production—that, in fact, if we are to use the word "authentic" at all, we must redefine it so that it comprises a bundle or family of versions with no Platonic or Aristotelian ideal at its core. I fear that Brecht, anti-Aristotelian by self-proclamation, is too often performed as if there were a set play and mise-en-scene that all productions must be "of" and judged "in terms of." This notion of "setness," I reject.

Before returning to this theoretical provocation, I will offer a thick description⁴ of what happened in India. What I will barely touch on here are the profound effects the India tour had on TPG—contributing to the reformation of the Group leading to the emergence of The Wooster Group.⁵

We arrived in Delhi on the morning of February 3rd, twelve of us on the Air India weekly charter from Amsterdam. Only Joan MacIntosh and I had been to India before, in 1971. Greeting us at the airport were Suresh Awasthi who originated the idea of the *Courage* tour, Rajinder Nath, leader of our Delhi sponsor the Abhiyan Theatre group, and V. Ramamurthy (Murti), our Indian tech director. An immediate plunge into work: we accept the old gym at the Modern School in New Delhi as our venue. We decide to erect structures we can dismantle and haul around India rather than build from scratch at each site. We open on February 10th to a full house, but by the end about one-third of the audience was gone. Language was one problem and the four-hour length of the show another. But the most important factor was the environmental theater style so unfamiliar to modern Indian theater-goers (not to villagers or those familiar with folk or ritual theater) requiring spectators to sit on hard wooden planks, or on the floor, or to move about. My own immediate reactions as recorded in my notebook:

> Environment too long for its width. Acoustics bad. One-third of the audience left at intermission; one-third very appreciative. They rushed up to the performers and me after the show and

showered us with congratulations. Mostly authentic, some just being polite. The show itself was slow and ragged.

And MacIntosh wrote in her notebook:

> I was rolling in dirt. I breathed dirt, dry earth dirt. I strained my voice between a dirt-clogged throat and bad acoustics. I felt like I could have been anywhere on tour doing *MC* not in India…I was exhausted, hungry, sick to my stomach. The wheelbarrow—used as a market basket—didn't work. I slipped and fell on the wagon steps. I spilled a bucket of water on an audience member in scene 3. And yet the Indians loved it. One man squeezed my hand so hard I thought he had broken my knuckles. Scene 12 [the final scene] took on a special meaning to me here of an Indian peasant woman beggar tromping through the dusty countryside, stumbling, enduring…During the show I was not at all nervous, only angry or concentrated on what needed to be done: keeping the story clear. The audience's reaction was pleasing, but being a perfectionist I wasn't satisfied. It could've been better.

It got better. It takes a great audience to make a great performance. On Friday February 13, people kept pushing in until there were too many, probably about 350 in a space designed for 200. The performers bitched, but again and again I've seen that when something unexpected and hard happens: too big a house, a sudden error, a part of the environment that fails, etcetera—the performance either collapses or overcomes the challenge luminously. The audience needs something so badly that they will it into existence. This can happen in sports too, in any live event actually.

In Delhi too the first inklings of the "sex problem" appeared. In scene 3, Yvette and three soldiers perform a stylized mimicry of copulation while on the other side of the space Courage smears Kattrin's face with mud in order to make her unattractive to rapacious soldiers. The meaning is clear: in war a safe face is one smeared with filth, and love is business. Two days after we opened Principal M. N. Kapur of the Modern School told me that this scene had repercussions among the governing board of the school. He also felt that it distorted our production—some people came to the performance just to see what was usually banned while others stayed away because of the scene. I discussed the issue with the Group.

We came to the conclusion that TPG hadn't come to India to show Indians how Indians would stage *Mother Courage* but how Americans did. I felt torn because Kapur had been exceedingly generous to us. Then, just before the performance when I was about to make some modifications to

Scene 2 in Lucknow. Eilif (Jim Clayburgh) — a hero because he killed a peasant family during a battle — sings about his exploits for the General (Elizabeth LeCompte) seated to the rear. Next to the General is the Chaplain (Stephen Borst). Photo Courtesy of Richard Schechner.

Scene 3 in Calcutta. Courage (Joan MacIntosh) scolds Swiss Cheese (Spalding Gray) as he sits on the toilet. Photo Courtesy of Richard Schechner.

the scene, Kapur came up to me and said: "No, don't change anything. Do what is right for your work."

When we got to Lucknow we began working in the garage where the environment was being set up. They were ready for us because on October 10th, 1975 I wrote a detailed letter to all our sponsors emphasizing that,

> TPG does not perform in a proscenium theatre or in any way separate the audience from the performers. As the enclosed photographs show, the audience sits among the performers, or stands around them…Thus instead of a regular theatre we need a large room for our performance…Also we can perform in a gymnasium or a large banquet hall. In every case we need large quantities of scaffolding to build up the theatre.

The Lucknow environment was extraordinary, a garage where amid piles of tires, broken down cars, and steel girders *Mother Courage* took place. We didn't use the whole 100- by 200-foot space but lashed slotted angles to girders. Despite the efforts of our Indian technical staff and TPG's members, the Lucknow audience was confused. They held back. Raj Bisaria, our sponsor, explained that few people in Lucknow know English, especially the American dialect. And despite my expounding the parallels between environmental theater and traditional Indian theater, audiences coming to *Mother Courage* often didn't get what we were trying to do. That's because a gap had opened between modern Indian theater and Indian traditional forms. More recently, from the late 1970s onward, the "roots movement" forged links between the traditional and the modern, but we were too early to benefit from this. In fact, TPG's presence and my activism in India and collaboration with Suresh Awasthi during this period contributed to the "Theatre of Roots" movement. The issue was and continues to be complex because although the traditional forms are exciting theatrically they are often ideologically and socially conservative. The problem facing modern theater makers was how to use the forms without adhering to their reactionary mythopoesis. For me, the answer lay in writers, designers, and actors learning folk forms and then "forgetting" what they've learned. It is at the level of body consciousness, integration of music and rhythmic movement, environmental staging, and direct contact with the audience that modern artists can benefit from the traditional theater.

In Lucknow for the first time on tour, poor people came to the show. At first about 75 farmers and laborers stood outside and peered at the performance through the side of the garage that had no wall. There was space inside, so during a scene change I gestured for the poor to come in. Most of the adults held back but the kids swarmed. They found places on the floor and in the corners of the environment. Then about 50 people scampered across the roof, peering down through the opening between the peaked roof and the horizontal walls. Paying spectators ignored this new group, or moved away slightly.

Our next stops after Bhopal were Calcutta the megapolis and Singjole the village. We performed in Calcutta at the unfinished Abhinav Bharati theater off Shakespeare Sarani. The audience entered through piles of junk and scraps from sets. They passed over a plank-boardwalk to the stage where we'd set up *Mother Courage*. The environment combined folk and modern elements—the lighting grid and platform railings were of bamboo. Everything went smoothly in Calcutta because of the superb organizational skills of Shyamanand Jalan and Bishu Sureka. Also in Calcutta we resumed our relationship with playwright and theater visionary Badal Sircar who'd come to North America and worked with TPG during the summer of 1972. Performances in Calcutta went smoothly except for the "sex issue" which came to a head after an unsigned review in the Hindi paper, *Vishvamitra*, proclaimed:

> The most daring use of this environment is made when the actors, both male and female, in full view of the audience and in full illumination strip down completely and change their costumes. In this manner they educate the audience — acting out everything, even the way a woman is disgraced as the soldiers fornicate with her. (Translator unknown.)

The reviewer was seeing things: there was no nakedness either in the performance or in the visible green room. But there was simulated sex onstage; and performers were briefly in their underwear in the green room.

The day this review appeared we were besieged by men offering me up to 100 rupees for a ticket while women with tickets stayed away. Men fought on the street in front of the theater in order to gain places. At interval I said, "The sex scene is over, so if that's what you came for, eat your supper and go." Many left, maybe forty men. Suddenly, for one scene at least, and for maybe 25% of the audience, *Mother Courage* was not at all what I intended or what Brecht intended. The "sex issue" exploded in Calcutta but, as noted, it was there earlier in the tour. Granted that standards varied greatly from the USA to India at that time, *Mother Courage* is not a sex show. The green room is visible for the same reason that TPG showed every aspect of the production—the drama, the business of the theater, and the technical work. But not only was no one naked, there was absolutely no connection between the Yvette part of scene 3 and the costume changes. The scene itself compares Yvette's primping and unbuttoning her blouse to arouse the soldiers with Courage's smearing mud on Kattrin's face making her ugly. Unwittingly, the males who stormed the Abhinav Bharati played the role of the soldiers in scene 3.

Scene 3 in Calcutta. Yvette (Elizabeth LeCompte) worries that the battle might totally ruin her business. She couldn't be more wrong. War is great for business. Photo Courtesy of Richard Schechner.

Scene 3 in Bombay. Courage (Joan MacIntosh) performs her "silent scream" at the moment when Swiss Cheese is executed. Standing behind her, the Chaplain (Stephen Borst). Photo Courtesy of Richard Schechner.

On the last night's performance in Calcutta signs appeared outside the theater: "Schechner Has No Right to Destroy Brecht's Epic Theatre," "We Want Brecht Not Environmental Theatre," "Environmental Theatre Is a Deliberate Distortion of Brecht's Philosophy of Theatre," "Long Live Bertolt Brecht, the Dramatist of the People," "Brecht Dealt with War, Schechner Deals with Orgasm," "Schechner Preaches Community Involvement by Making You Pay for It," "Brecht Spoke of Reality and Struggle, Schechner Deals with Gags, Stunts and Sexual Perversion." I carried the signs inside the theater making them part of the environment by pasting them on the walls and hanging them on the scaffolding.

On March 18th, with arrangements made by Sircar and Barin Saha, we performed *Mother Courage* in Singjole, a village about three hours outside of Calcutta. We played Singjole even though one of our Calcutta sponsors (not Jalan or Sureka) opposed it. On January 5th 1976, shortly before leaving the USA for India, I got this letter from Calcutta:

> I would strongly suggest, after consulting people in the theatre field, not to produce the play in any village as it will not only cost a huge amount of money and hard work, but also it will be very difficult to attract the required audience, as the atmosphere in our villages has not yet reached the standard to appreciate productions like yours. Please clarify the situation immediately.

I wrote back on 16 January:

> It is very important to us to be able to play in villages — we want our work to reach the people who live in the villages, no matter how difficult that may be. We are willing to adjust our staging to suit village conditions: outdoors spaces, courtyards, bad lighting or no stage lighting at all. It is most important to us that we perform for a cross-section of the Indian public. This is the other reason why we insist on trying to perform, for no charge, in a village near Calcutta.

The production cost almost nothing because we set up under two large trees using them as the grid for our rope system; a trench was dug that came very close to the pit we had in New York; we lit the show with Petromax kerosene lanterns; a harmonium substituted for the piano; the audience sat on the ground all around; there was no interval and no supper.

Instead of the 800 people we'd expected — two times the most we'd ever played *Mother Courage* for — about 2,000 people eagerly attended. As elsewhere in Indian folk theater, the women and young children sat in one place and the men and older boys other places. Most of the audience stayed for about three of the four hours (we began at 7:30pm), by the end about 750 people were left. Speaking Bengali, Sircar introduced the play and before each scene he outlined its action. But TPG's actors weren't skilled at projecting their voices through the open air to such a large crowd; and *Mother Courage* isn't the kind of play that can be suddenly shouted. I wrote in my notebook:

> Aesthetics went out the window. We adjusted our staging and made it broad: telling the story through big actions…We didn't contact this audience so much through our work as simply by our presence. People in the audience chatted throughout the performance; they pointed at the actors; they laughed; they wandered to and from the performance paying attention only to what interested them. I've seen this behavior at performances of Chhau, Raslila, and Ramlila. For much of the evening, *Mother Courage and Her Children* was entertainment at a mela, an Indian country fair. But when Kattrin was shot, and Courage stripped off her last child's outer clothes in order to sell them, then hooked herself up to all the ropes and pulleys and tugged her tired body toward the grave-pit, silence ruled.

Improvising as we went along, we cut large sections of scenes 6 and 8, and all of 9 and 10. Group members found the performance "liberating." Freed from the restraint of a closely attentive audience, the actors went as far as possible in physicalizing their roles, playing the words-as-sounds rather than as cognitive speech. The morning after, I went around Singjole with Saha who translated for me talking to people. They liked the performance. "What did you like?" "The songs, the falling, the fighting, the killing. The girl who couldn't talk. The way Mother tried to save her children." More than a few villagers identified Mother Courage with Mother Teresa.[6] A Bengali director who saw the performance said, "They were being polite. The only reason they didn't bust up the show was because you are white." I think both opinions are true. Definite contact was made with some of the villagers who never before (or since?) played host to an American troupe or were respected enough to be offered city art except for the cinema.

After the surging crush of people in Calcutta and Singjole, Bhopal was emptiness itself. We set up on the stage of Bhopal's city theater, the Ravindra Bhawan with the theater's large load-in back door open. It was hot and to encourage a breeze we left the front curtain open but permitted no one to sit in the auditorium. The audience moved from the stage to a sloping lawn for scenes 9 through 12. The two performances at Bhopal went so smoothly that we invited technical director Benu Ganguly to come with us to Bombay. As it turned out, we needed all his skills.

If Calcutta is India's New York, then Bombay is her Los Angeles, Bollywood and all. TPG just slid into Bombay's luxury like falling into velvet. Except for one night at a Tamasha I saw nothing of Bombay's other side, its grinding poverty, its communal clashes between Muslim and Hindu, Maharashtran and Gujarati. We performed *Mother Courage* in the posh Cathedral School's magnificent courtyard surrounded on three sides by galleried buildings. We expanded our environment to the large space making room for 500 spectators, and another 150 (at reduced prices) up in the galleries. I watched some of each show from up top: it was like looking at a terrain map on which figures made dance patterns, the sound rose splendidly so all the dialogue was heard. Everything arranged for us by Narayana Menon and K. K. Suvarna of the National Centre for the Performing Arts was first-rate. The shows were near perfect—we'd learned from Singjole to physicalize more than in America, to slow down, and to eliminate extraneous gestures. Most of the audience understood English and many knew Brecht's works.

A year before I started directing *Mother Courage*, I theorized the distinctions among drama, script, theater, and performance.[7] To summarize my theory: The drama is a play, score, scenario, instruction, plan, or map that can be archived and accessed and that can exist separate from any embodiment. The script is the embodiment of a drama as it is invented and transmitted from person to person. There can be any number of scripts of the same drama. The work of rehearsals is to devise a script. The theater is a specific single enactment of a script by a specific performer or group of performers; the theater changes sometimes slightly, sometimes greatly with each enactment. A performance is the constellation of events taking place from the time the first person (artist, worker, spectator, box office person, etc.) enters the venue where the theater takes place until the last person leaves. The drama is the domain of archivists, scholars, dramaturges, and literary analysts; the script is the domain of directors collaborating with performers and other theater artists and producers (money people); the theater is the domain of directors, performers, designers, and spectators; the performance is the domain of performers, spectators, and workers. Obviously, these domains overlap and interact. The mechanics, quality, and intensity of those interactions comprise performances both as art and as social-political events.

During our India tour of *Mother Courage* TPG played with Brecht's drama, as directed by me and interpreted by my colleague artists. But several times—in Calcutta when the protesters arrived, in Singjole for almost the whole night—the audience strongly intervened asserting the strength of the performance over the theater and the script. Brecht's drama was untouched because by definition a drama is a Platonic-Aristotelian ideal, and as such a culture-specific Western category. Brecht's drama was untouched but the event titled *Mother Courage and Her Children* changed vastly from instance to instance. In my view, the "play itself," the drama, is a component of the whole complex comprising a performance. It may or may not be the starting point of any given script, theater, or performance.

To return to the question of whether or not TPG's *Mother Courage* was "true to Brecht." Theoretically, because the drama is a Platonic ideal, one cannot be true or false to it. As an ideal, no one can access it directly. It is known only by its existence as a script, indirectly, by means of its various transmissions and interpretations. To bring my argument down to earth, I don't think fidelity matters much, even if it could be determined. Most of the time an author's intentions aren't known. What did Sophocles, Kalidasa, or Shakespeare intend? And when intentions are known — as with garrulous Shaw who wrote introductions almost as long as his plays — these do not limit what theater people do, or how audiences react or interact. Audiences are the determining factor. Ought Greek tragedies be performed as intended, outdoors in semicircular theaters seating 17,000 spectators who attend as part of yearly ritual-civic celebrations comprised of three tragedies followed by a satyr play? If so, tell me also how to recreate the Athenian city-state. And so on for every epoch, culture, and locale. Hybridity, promiscuity, and creative theft is the name of the theater game.

I have long taken the position, and hold it now, that a text is a skeleton, an outline, a plan, a map — but that the body, picture, structure, and territory of a play can be actualized only in performance, at the immediate and unique encounter of performers and spectators; and that rehearsal is a research process for unfolding and discovering what the performance will be. As for "changing the text," there are times when that's appropriate and other times when it's not. A classic text such as *Mother Courage* is in no danger of being forgotten; it is open to retelling, especially if it is being performed in translation, which is already a retelling. As a matter of fact, except in Singjole, TPG made no text changes to Manheim's translation of *Mother Courage* except to cut all of scene 4 up to the "Song of the Great Capitulation."

But the objections, and praise, were based not on text changes but on tone — on a sense that TPG didn't do Brecht as Brecht would have done Brecht, and therefore we did it wrong. *Mother Courage* is not one of Brecht's hardline plays like *The Measures Taken*. It belongs to a later period along with *The Caucasian Chalk Circle* and *The Good Person of Szechwan*. *Mother Courage* is as much an anti-war play as a condemnation of capitalist greed. Despite Brecht's own intentions, the character of Courage is one audiences identify with. In her, Brecht internalized the dialectical conflict which makes Shen Te (in *The Good Person*) invent a second self, Shui Ta: Courage is loving and cruel, generous and stingy, wise and stupid, the

Scene 12 in New Delhi. Courage (Joan MacIntosh) looks on as Kattrin (Leeny Sack) is about to be dragged off to the grave-pit. Courage has stripped her daughter down to her underclothes. Courage needs to sell Kattrin's clothes and possessions. Note Kattrin's drum: It once alerted the town of the advancing soldiers — now it is just another item for sale. Photo Courtesy of Richard Schechner.

Scene 12 in the village of Singjole, West Bengal. At the end of the play, Courage (Joan MacIntosh) is attached to all the ropes and preparing to move on ... to the grave-pit. Photo Courtesy of Richard Schechner.

best humanity has to offer and an animal. At the end she is neither a hero nor a hyena, but both. That's why I staged her stripping the clothes off the corpse of her dead daughter Kattrin. Anna Fierling can't let valuable goods go to waste. And that's why Courage hooks herself up to all the ropes and pulleys: she is suspended and trapped both in an external system and in a device of her own making. Brecht's own Berlin Ensemble production ends sentimentally with Courage and her wagon alone on the empty stage. Fierling/Weigel lifts the heavy yoke, hitches herself to it, and hauls the vehicle two full times around the floor of the revolving stage. I don't criticize Brecht for this choice which points up Courage's humanity, grief, and (pardon) courage. This final action is balanced by others showing Courage's bitterness, contempt, cynicism, and brutality. But I point out that Brecht the director knew different than Brecht the author.

At another level altogether, TPG was "true" to Brecht the author even when we differed with Brecht the director. There is no rolling wagon, but instead a store which is more in the American tradition; we serve supper; the final scenes were played outdoors or with the theater open to the street. Signs indicate dates from the 17th century, but everything else was staged as "now." Actors wore no makeup making visible the gap between their ages and the age of the characters whose gestures and words they conveyed. We "out-Brechted" Brecht by showing not only the play but how the theater workers were making the play. Scene and costume changes, music, serving food, everything was enacted in full view of the spectators — our embodiment of the *Verfremdungseffekt*. What is a better Verfremdungseffekt than MacIntosh playing Mother Courage playing the flute while Spalding Gray playing Swiss Cheese hangs suspended in ropes over the small orchestra? Or watching Stephen Borst playing the Chaplain set the ropes between scenes? These choices, and other choices like them, were made on the basis of mise-en-scenic efficiency, on how to get the play across to our audiences, and in terms of the environmental theater I advocate as thoroughly as Brecht advocated his Epic Theatre. The underlying politics of TPG's production (in New York as well as in India) was the same as Brecht's: a good woman who, in identifying herself with the military-industrial complex, makes choices against her own class interest. If the production succeeded, the audience both sympathized with Courage's cruel dilemmas and condemned the small-time capitalism and the larger system of which Courage — and everyone else in the play — is a part. What kind of system makes a mother choose between her livelihood and a bribe to ransom her son? But choose she does, and then she must deny that the corpse lying on the ground in front of her is that of someone she knows.[8] What's more, the play goes on for nine more scenes.

Every TPG member except Joan MacIntosh and I left India by the end of June. MacIntosh stayed until early fall. Together we saw many traditional Indian performances. Alone during the summer I studied Kathakali in

Kerala at the Kalamandalam. I undertook initiation rites as a Hindu but did not disavow my Judaism. Even today I am not sure exactly how the experiences with *Mother Courage* fed into the other things I did in India and elsewhere in Asia that year and in years to come. But I know that when I returned to New York in February 1977, I was not the same, my life had changed.

Scene 12 in New Delhi. At the end of the play, Courage (Joan MacIntosh), pulling the whole theater environment, a spider caught in her own web, trudges ever onwards...toward the line of the dead standing to her right. Photo Courtesy of Richard Schechner.

Endnotes

1   This essay in a slightly different version appeared in Richard Schechner, *Performative Circumstances: From the Avant Garde to Ramlila* (Calcutta: Seagull Books, 1983), pp. 31-54, and in Richard Schechner, *Over, Under, and Around* (Calcutta and New Delhi: Seagull Books, 2004), pp. 73-100.
2   Hereafter abbreviated as TPG.
3   The names of two of these cities have changed, but I have retained the names as they were in 1976. At present, Calcutta is Kolkata and Bombay is Mumbai.
4   Clifford Geertz's term for situating an event in terms of as many of its generating and operating circumstances as possible. See Geertz's Preface to Clifford Geertz, *Interpretation of Cultures* (New York: Basic Books, 1973), pp. 3-30.
5   The changes within TPG reached a critical stage during our India tour. Two rhythms interacted: (i) as individuals and as a theater we met audiences, sponsors, and the multiplicity called India, itself undergoing stress and change during the Emergency; (ii) within each of us and as TPG we began to work through—by means of two sets of talks, one in Calcutta in March and one at Juhu Beach near Bombay right after the tour's end in April—our past relationships, present circumstances, future arrangements. There's no doubt that the high of the tour—we were praised even when our work fell short— mixed with its difficulties brought on the crisis within TPG.
6   The Albanian-born Roman Catholic nun who from 1948 to her death in 1997 ministered to Kolkata's orphaned, sick, and dying. Some of the residents of Singjole identified Mother Courage with Mother Teresa because Courage, in the words of one villager, "did her best to save her children, and cried for them when they died." That both women were called "mother" probably added to the identification.
7   See Richard Schechner, "Drama, Script, Theatre, and Performance," *The Drama Review* 17, 3 (1973): pp. 5-36.
8   The parallel with Peter three times denying Jesus is obvious and, I believe, intended. All four Gospels recount the denial; see especially Luke chapter 22.

Brecht: Ein Mitwirkender im Prozess der Nationsbildung

Amal Allana

Dieser Aufsatz versucht den geschichtlichen Verlauf des brechtschen Einflusses auf indische Theaterpraktiken und Inszenierungen von den 1960er bis 1990er Jahren nachzuzeichnen. Als die Theater Nord- und Westindiens vor allem damit beschäftigt waren, ihr kulturelles Kolonialerbe aufzulösen, wurde Brecht ihnen zu einem wichtigen Werkzeug in der Wiederherstellung einer postkolonialen, indigenen und indischen Identität in dieser Region. Seine Strategien standen im Einklang mit volkstümlichen Aufführungstraditionen, die seit den 1960er Jahren neu erfunden wurden, um nun einem nationalistischen Imperativ zu dienen. Im Osten Indiens hingegen halfen Brechts Ideen in den 1970er Jahren, eine politische Ästhetik des Widerstandes für das Gegenwartstheater zu formulieren, als die Anzeichen eines versagenden demokratischen Systems mit zunehmender Intensität offensichtlich wurden. Später, in den 1990er Jahren, lebte das Interesse an Brecht wieder auf, als Regisseurinnen sich mit Fragen der Demontage und Rekonstruktion von Geschlechteridentitäten zu beschäftigen begannen.

This paper seeks to describe the trajectory of Brecht's impact on Indian theater practice and performance from the 1960s to the 1990s. While the theater in North and West India was in the process of dismantling its colonial legacy, Brecht became an important tool in the reconstruction of a postcolonial indigenous Indian identity in this part of the country. His strategies resonated with folk performing traditions, which were being reinvented from the 1960s onwards to serve a nationalist imperative. In the East, on the other hand, through the better part of the 1970s, Brecht helped define a political aesthetic of resistance for contemporary theater, as the signs of a malfunctioning democracy began to surface with greater intensity. Later, in the 1990s, there was a rekindled interest in Brecht, as women directors engaged in issues relating to the dismantling and reconstruction of gender identities.

Brecht: A Participant in the Process of Nation-Building

Amal Allana

After Brecht's death in 1956, his work became extremely well known internationally, especially in countries where great changes were taking place: Latin America, Egypt, Africa, India, and many parts of South East Asia. Most of these countries had been colonized and had gained their freedom after fighting fascism in its imperialist garb. As newly emerging postcolonial cultures, they were searching for their own, indigenous identities. In this context India's reception of Bertolt Brecht is an interesting and significant phenomenon, particularly with regard to the development of contemporary Indian theater during the post-independence period.

Among the first Indians to see Brecht's work in Berlin a few years before his death in August 1956 was the eminent Punjabi playwright and director Balwant Gargi. He describes a memorable evening in February 1955, when the famous curtain of the Berliner Ensemble, painted with the Picasso dove, rose on Brecht's powerful anti-war play, *Mother Courage*.

> On the revolving stage, two young men yoked to a wagon walked with heavy steps. Mother Courage (Helene Weigel) in a full-length skirt and padded grey jacket, a pewter spoon tucked in her pocket, stands in a wagon singing a marching song in her bugle-like voice…Some scenes still stand out in my memory: Mother flirts with the soldiers to hide her identity, refusing to recognize the body of her son. As the soldiers bend forward to examine the face of her son, Mother lets out a silent cry, a dumb wail…Finally, as the soldiers shoot [her daughter] down, she gives one final beat with her limp hand, and collapses… Mother—dehumanized, stubborn, mean, foolish, a beast—learns nothing from the experience. She reminded me of my own mother. I continued to sit in my chair, overpowered by emotion. [My interpreter] Kitty tapped my shoulder. "Get up, it's over."[1]

The following year, in 1956, Habib Tanvir, a young director at the time, was returning to India after studying theater at RADA, in England. He writes about his experience in Berlin:

> From Prague I finally went to Berlin…but the thing is, when I arrived in Berlin, Brecht had died a few weeks before. That was very disappointing. But his productions were all there, and I saw them all…I saw the rehearsals done by two very eminent directors who directed together, special disciples of Brecht. I was in Berlin for eight months, met all the actors and actresses,

sat in their canteen, discussed many things, saw *Caucasian Chalk Circle*, some Chinese one-act plays, *Mother Courage*, the whole gamut...Of course, I did meet Elisabeth Hauptmann and also Helene Weigel. She was doing the role of the Mother. I made lots of friends and traveled all over East Germany. At that time there was no division, no wall, many people were working in the East and living in the West.[2]

In India, the 1950s were a time when the trauma and bloodbath of the Partition of the country into India and Pakistan, which had caused the displacement of hundreds of thousands of people, was still vivid in the memory. This was followed by the most tragic loss of all time for Indians, the assassination of the Father of the Nation, Mahatma Gandhi, by fundamentalist right-wing forces. Communal strife between Hindus and Muslims continued for some time, all of which left India's first Prime Minister, Jawaharlal Nehru, with a truly disturbing legacy.

Nehru took on the problem of binding India together with missionary zeal. His slogan became "unity in diversity," and he made the notion of one state, as one indivisible whole, a national agenda to be realized. To achieve this goal, Nehru propagated a pan-Indian identity—that is, a single, unified cultural identity—for a basically diverse people whose languages, religions and ethnic differences were already beginning to manifest themselves in different ways. But Nehru was a dreamer and idealist who believed that a strong, unified India was not a distant or impossible dream, and he quickly embarked on several projects of nation-building. One of the key areas he tackled was culture. He recognized the crucial role artists could play in cultivating an integrated identity for a new India. For this massive enterprise he began to draw on the support of the most eminent musicians, dancers, painters, cinema directors, writers and theater persons of the day.

A wave of euphoria swept the newly liberated, post-independence generation of artists such as Tanvir and Gargi, who willingly committed themselves to supporting Nehru and his grand plans. They were confident and proud to be part of the nation-building process he advocated through creating a pan-Indian as well as "modern Indian" culture by linking city to village, past to present, and by attempting to synthesize India's vast storehouse of traditions with a contemporary artistic sensibility.

A playwright/director like Balwant Gargi, for example, was energized to undertake a massive journey across the country, in an effort to have a first-hand experience of all the existing folk performing traditions of the country. Documenting traditional performances through photographs and making copious notes and sketches in his diary, Gargi compiled material for what came to be regarded as the first comprehensive book on the subject, *The Folk Theatre of India*.[3]

Equally fervent and committed was Habib Tanvir, who at this time in the late 1950s was a member of the Hindustani Theater, a theater group set up in Delhi under the guiding spirit of Begum Qudsia Zaidi. Driven by a strong desire to stage a Sanskrit classic in a *new* way, Habib chose *The Little Clay Cart* for his first production after his return to India from England and Europe.

The choice of Shudraka's Sanskrit classic was not merely an aesthetic one. It was part of the creed of the postcolonial artist to do Indian plays in an attempt to reforge his identity in relation to his own culture. However, at this juncture the problem was that no guidelines were available on how to stage a classic, other than those set out in the *Natya Shastra*. After looking for other performative sources of inspiration, Tanvir ultimately turned to our existing folk traditions:

> I have come to this conclusion, that if you want to interpret Sanskrit drama you must go back to your folk theater traditions and draw from them, even take folk actors to introduce these techniques, and you'll get somewhere. The two together, the folk and the classical, are going to give to our modern type of Indian producers lots of ideas, lots of inspiration. Everything new, and yet Indian, can, in my belief, flow from this kind of a background.[4]

Seeing Brecht's plays during his travels in Europe, Tanvir recognized the influence of popular theater as well as Eastern performance traditions on Brecht:

> If you analyze it, I should think there is this distinguishing feature in Brecht that he has assimilated influences from all periods of dramatic history, also from all countries…[T]he folk elements are very strong in Brecht. Then he received influences from American jazz and Negro blues, the Chinese theater, Indian and Burmese (theater)…Now the amalgamation of these and the reaction against what was going on in Germany and Europe…he was fed up with it…which resulted in him and his collaborators experimenting and developing the theory of epic theater.[5]

Seeing how Brecht himself had used and synthesized diverse folk elements and popular traditions into a modern/post-modern aesthetic, Tanvir was excited and stimulated enough to extend his stay in Berlin. What he saw was the emergence of a new dramaturgy, derived from international traditions and physicalized into an entirely new mode of theatrical expression. Brecht's "epic" theater took realism to a new level, challenging the naturalistic mode that had so far held sway internationally. Even for Indian theater practitioners like Tanvir, naturalism as a genre had outlived its efficacy.

Strangely enough, in a fundamental sense what my observation of the European theater did to me, was precisely to turn me back to India even more intensely and much more vigilantly. I concentrated mostly on Bertolt Brecht's dramas at the Berliner Ensemble. As you are aware, Brecht already had imbibed so much from the Eastern theater traditions, including the Indian. So it made me look back at Indian traditions in a new light.[6]

M. S. Sathyu, who later became the well-known filmmaker of *Garam Hawa* and was a young member of Hindustani Theater at the time, notes:

I think it was way back in the late 50's when Habib Tanvir returned from Germany after his training at Royal Academy of Dramatic Arts, that he spent some time in Germany, in Berlin. He saw some of Brecht's plays and he was quite enthused about them. When he came back, we were going to stage *Mitti ki Gadi/ The Little Clay Cart*, the Sanskrit classic of Shudraka. It was in this production that he wanted to use Brechtian techniques. Whatever he explained to us about Brecht seemed very interesting. So we did *Mitti ki Gadi* as our first Brecht-style play.[7]

Eventually Hindustani Theater in Delhi produced *Mitti ki Gadi* in 1958 in Hindi. The production was conceived of as a blend of folk forms and Brechtian modes of narrative dramaturgy. Using folk artists from Chhattisgarh for the proletarian characters such as the gambler and the thief, the influence of Brecht on this production basically lay in the manner in which Tanvir structured the central love story to be set against the political uprising. Sharvilak the rogue, like Brecht's Azdak, cunningly agitates for a better world. At the end of the play the hostile masses, which have hovered in the background so far, take center stage, becoming the focal and climactic point of the narrative. Masks were used for certain characters in order to distance them. Songs, using melodies from Chhattisgarh, were sung both by the Narrator and the characters in the play, as a means to interpret the fable as well as a comment on the action.[8] Some of Tanvir's experiments in this production of *Mitti ki Gadi* were, perhaps, carried out for the first time: the presentation of a classical Sanskrit text using conventions and techniques of folk traditions; the combination of classical and folk traditions using Brechtian narrative devices; the reorganization and reshaping of the text so as to focus on its political dimensions, compelling the audience to make social choices (again a fallout of the Brechtian encounter); the updating of an older text to make it more contemporary and relevant to the present; and the blending of folk and urban actors in the same production. Forging the contemporary through classical and folk traditions, aided by a Brechtian approach, this production of *The Little Clay Cart* very much served as a template, or module, for other directors and playwrights to follow and develop over the decades to come.

Indian Encounters with Brecht

From the mid 1960s Brecht's Asian aspects began to be discussed at seminars and symposiums, especially in New Delhi. For example, Dr. Lothar Lutze from Heidelberg University gave a talk on "Indian Classical Drama in the Light of Bertolt Brecht's Dramatic Theory and Practice" at the Max Mueller Bhavan in Delhi.

In the early 1960s the International Theater Institute (ITI) and the Bharatiya Natya Sangh organized an East/West Theater Seminar in Delhi, which was attended by an authority on contemporary German theater, Dr. Käthe Rülicke-Weiler. The international delegates also included Joan Littlewood of *Oh! What A Lovely War* fame. A student at the National School of Drama (NSD) at the time, I vividly remember this seminar where she graphically demonstrated Brechtian acting techniques, generously sharing her experiences of adopting Brechtian techniques into her own work. Important seminar participants from India included Ebrahim Alkazi, then Director of the NSD, Dr. Kapila Vatsyayan, Kamaladevi Chattopadyay and others. The discussions at the seminar concluded in a series of contractual agreements between the Indian and the GDR governments, leading to the establishment of cultural exchange programs.

Brecht in Bengal

Bengali theater practitioners with leftist leanings were excited by Brecht early on. Brecht enthusiasts in Bengal were comprised of the most progressive elements of contemporary Bengali theater; many had been erstwhile members of the Indian People's Theater Association (IPTA), the cultural wing of the Communist Party in India that had done pioneering work in the 1940s during the fight against British imperialism and international fascism.

IPTA's efforts had helped establish theater as a platform for political debate, giving modern Bengali theater its strong political orientation. Summing up the impact of Brecht in Bengal, the critic Samik Bandyopadhyay writes that although the early years of IPTA's work were not affected by Brecht, translations of Brecht published in Moscow had begun to circulate in Calcutta. After a hiatus of nearly two decades, that is, by the early 1960s, information regarding Brecht began to be available in India in English through, for example, *Brecht on Theatre* and *The Messingkauf Dialogues*, both translated by John Willett.

From 1961 onwards translations of Brecht's plays into Bengali also began to appear on the scene. One of the earliest Brecht plays to be staged in Bengal was *The Life of Galileo* in 1964 at the University of Burdwan, translated by the well-known film director Ritwik Ghatak, who followed this up with a translation of *The Caucasian Chalk Circle*. The same year saw the establishment of the Brecht Society of India, founded in Calcutta with Satyajit Ray as the President and Shova Sen, the brilliant actress/wife of Utpal Dutt, as its Secretary. Dutt himself, who spoke and wrote fluent German, edited the magazine of the Brecht Society of India, aptly calling it *Epic Theatre*, with the cover designed by Ray himself. From 1967 onwards the magazine began to serialize *Himmatbai*, Dutt's adaptation of *Mother Courage* into Bengali. All this led to a growing critical interest in Brecht in Bengal.

One of the first landmark productions was Ajitesh Bannerjee's adaptation of *The Threepenny Opera* in 1969, which transported the action to Calcutta in 1876. Speaking at a seminar on Brecht in Calcutta in 1978, Banerjee recounted his desperate and mainly futile efforts in the early 1960s to learn more about Brecht and his theater. A new methodology seemed to be required in approaching a Brecht text:

> Half-educated people told us there was no scenery in Brecht, that the acting was stylized, the same gesture was repeated continuously, the same music was used throughout.[9]

However, when he saw *Mother Courage* on film, it proved they were wrong. Production stills of Brecht's own productions as well as Brecht's own theoretical writings clarified doubts further. Finally, Satyajit Ray, who had recently returned from abroad, physically acted out a scene from *Arturo Ui* that he had seen, followed by Utpal Dutt who acted out the same scene even better! All of this was very helpful to Banerjee, who has made the following salient point about handling Brecht as an Indian director:

> When I came to do *The Threepenny Opera* in 1969, I tried to bring it *as close* to the Bengali experience as possible. Adaptation is only possible if one knows one's own country. I would like to know Brecht through my *own* tradition. I am not interested in a *German* presentation of Brecht.[10]

Brecht at the National School of Drama

These were individual responses of receptive Indian directors. However, further north, in Delhi, there was an *institutional* response to Brecht's teachings and practice by the NSD, India's premier institution for theater training, which led to the methodical study, understanding, and absorption of Brecht into Indian mainstream thinking and, eventually, theater practice. The participation of NSD director Alkazi in the Brecht-Dialog in East Berlin in 1968, organized by the ITI and the Brecht-Zentrum, now facilitated the Indian reception of Brecht on a larger institutional level.

Amal Allana

At the NSD Brecht was initially performed under the direction of German experts, in *Modellbuch* productions, which closely followed the original Brecht productions of the Berliner Ensemble. In 1968 Carl Weber, whose visit was supported by the Goethe Institute and who stood out because he had been a first-generation assistant to Brecht at the Berliner Ensemble, directed *The Caucasian Chalk Circle* at the NSD, with a new Indian score composed by Vanraj Bhatia. This was followed in 1970 by *The Threepenny Opera*, directed by Fritz Bennewitz, a second-generation student of Brecht and, at the time, artistic director of the National Theater at Weimar, GDR. Both productions were in Hindi, the former translated by Razia Sajjad Zaheer, the latter by Surekha Sikri. Earlier the same year I had met Bennewitz in Weimar, where I was studying Brecht, and he had asked me to be the assistant director and costume designer on *Threepenny Opera*, to which I readily agreed. Under the guidance of these Brechtian experts, Brecht began to be taught systematically at the NSD, allowing student actors to gain a direct insight and experience of how to approach a Brechtian role, using techniques of alienation. Weber gave a series of lectures on Brechtian drama, while Bennewitz, concurrently with his rehearsals of *Threepenny Opera*, taught an eight-week course on Brecht to the students.

The incorporation of Brecht into the syllabus of the NSD was not arbitrary on the part of the NSD director Alkazi. Even though he was laying the foundations of a national institution based on both traditional and contemporary Indian theater, it was quite clear to him that the students also required an international dimension. Alkazi sums up Brecht's relevance to Indian theater in an interview with Nissim Ezekiel:

> Of all Western playwrights we believe that Brecht has the greatest relevance to the Indian theater today, not only on account of the content of his plays but particularly because of their form. He has broken away from the closed three-act play and, chiefly as a result of his intense study of the classical Indian, the Chinese and the Japanese theaters, he has evolved the loose epic style. He has used such devices of our own ancient theaters as the narrator, the chorus, song, music and poetry, to bring back color and vitality to the insipid prose theater of today.[11]

To Alkazi the Brecht connection was contiguous with his own interest in developing a cultural relationship between Indian and other traditional forms of Asian Theater. He felt that an exposure to various international legacies could provide a springboard that would propel contemporary practice into exciting directions of creating a new Indian modernism, contextualized within Asia. Therefore, at the NSD Brecht began to be taught in conjunction with Kabuki and Noh traditions. Shozo Sato was invited to do *Ibaragi*, while Alkazi himself directed the students in a new version of Dharamvir Bharati's *Andha Yug* (The Age of Blindness) in 1976, a contemporary take on the *Mahabharata*, in a spectacular production mounted against the historic ruins of the Old Fort/Purana Quila, in Delhi.

Culling many elements of his presentational style from Kabuki, Noh and Brechtian theater, Alkazi introduced a formal Kabuki-like chorus, painted the faces of the characters with Kabuki and Kathakali-inspired makeup, and dressed the characters in costumes that were an eclectic mix of traditional Indian and Japanese styles.

It was during these very years that the study of Indian folk theater was also introduced into the NSD curriculum. Yakshagana gurus like Kota Shivaram Karanth were invited to direct the students in traditional productions, while Shanta Gandhi, an ex-IPTA person herself and teacher of Sanskrit drama, staged a landmark production of *Jasma Odan* with the NSD students. Using the Bhavai tradition of Gujarat, Gandhi reinvented an old folk play, contemporizing the choices made by Jasma, the central woman character.

Between 1968 and 1977, the NSD was a veritable cauldron, a laboratory where an extraordinary amount of study, research and practical experimentation was underway with folk theater, Brechtian and Asian theater all being explored for contemporary use. In this way Alkazi, while compiling a canon for a national/Hindi theater, was simultaneously allowing and preparing the ground for a new movement in Indian modernism to take shape.

Brecht in Maharashtra

The phenomenal success of both *The Threepenny Opera* and *The Caucasian Chalk Circle* in Delhi prompted Alkazi to travel with these productions to Mumbai, Pune, Hyderabad and Bangalore. Using straight translations, and following the *Modellbuch* treatments, these productions went a long way in acquainting both theater practitioners and audiences alike with an "authentic" rendition of the Brechtian performance style. As theatrical experiences they opened doors to a new dimension of, and approach to, contemporary theater per se.

In Mumbai Vijaya Mehta, responsible for nurturing a new wave of Marathi experimental theater, had just directed Venkatesh Madgulkar's adaptation of *The Good Person of Szechwan* as *Devajeena Karuna Keli*, in Marathi. She describes why Indian theater practitioners like herself were responding favorably to Brecht:

> I felt that was the period when all of us, the directors, were trying to know what is Indian theater's identity in terms of world

theater. Whatever we were doing, it was tailored on British heritage, which stayed with us. And we all were in search of trying to belong to the Indian soil. We were all urban people. We separately tried to understand what our roots were. What we did at that time was not folk theater, it was an urban mind exposing itself to the various traditions, which were rooted in the soil, and having those traditions reflect in our work. Sorry to say, but at that time Brecht came in very handy, because he talked of Asian theater, he talked of *Total* Theater, something that our researchers were also leading us towards. Here was a European mind talking of a very contemporary idiom of Total Theater, that's why I feel we found Brecht attractive.[12]

However, Bennewitz, the director of *The Threepenny Opera* at the NSD, was not completely satisfied with his maiden venture. As he wrote in his article "How the Story of the Indian Chalk Circle Happened:" "The results of this work remain limited, because to a large extent it has remained a production transmitted to the Indian stage from *our* theatrical traditions and *our* habits of play."[13]

However, the cultural agreement between India and the GDR allowed for yet another opportunity in 1973. This time Bennewitz's venture was a collaborative one, namely to co-direct, along with veteran Vijaya Mehta, C. T. Khanolkar's *Ajab Nyaya Vartulacha/The Caucasian Chalk Circle*, in Marathi, in Mumbai, for the Mumbai Marathi Sahitya Sangha. Bennewitz felt that,

> [i]n order for Brecht to be fully absorbed into the fabric of India, it is necessary for us to have more comprehension of their history and culture in theater, an experience of the vitality of grass roots Indian theater is necessary…It is my conviction that our knowledge and experience can be communicated more profitably on both sides by a certain amount of *adaptation* of the text to the Indian context and traditions.[14]

Mehta has commented on her collaboration with Bennewitz:

> We worked, to start with, on the basis that it will be an adaptation. We got a person, who was the greatest poet Maharashtra ever had, to do the translation, Khanolkar. He did not read a word of English. There were seven or eight drafts…I used to go to Germany, get it looked at by Bennewitz. The division of work was basically that he will watch out for the content and allow me the freedom to go to town as far as actors and the whole form was concerned…He would be my guru and I would be the director. And he would work with me on each scene and he would

attend rehearsals every four to five days to see whether those ideas were reflected in the performance or not. Working with an equally talented mind like Khanolkar's, a man who did not read English—forget German—he was able to capture even the meter of Brecht!...There were no cypress trees, there was "champa ki dali!"[15] There were mango groves! If there was christening there, it was "Ganga Tirth"[16] in our version, but the whole thing blended so beautifully that I think, without our having to believe in Brechtian ideology and thought, we delivered the goods.[17]

Although Indian audiences were becoming familiar with Brecht, there was trenchant criticism regarding the "Indianization" of this and other productions of Brecht's plays. D. G. Nadkarni,[18] a well-respected critic, argued that the productions were "formal exercises that had lost interest in Brecht's radical politics," while Arun Naik, a young playwright, complained in *Enact* that by "Indigenizing the content of Brecht we had made him too familiar, so that the element of alienation or 'estrangement,' so intrinsic to Brecht, had vanished."[19]

New Writing

Throughout this period from the mid-1960s until the mid-1970s, when the Brechtian impact was consolidating itself, a remarkable spate of plays by Indian writers like Dharamvir Bharati, Mohan Rakesh, Girish Karnad, Vijay Tendulkar, and Adya Rangacharya exploded onto the scene, giving voice, for the first time, to the volatile and unstable conditions that began to prevail, especially in the urban metropolises. What linked these plays together was that they were peopled by alienated, disturbed, practically schizophrenic characters living in the grand, new megapolises built by Nehru. Urban reality with all its uncertainties registered an angst and existential questioning that found unparalleled expression in the explicit violence characterizing this new writing, all of which disturbed and shocked spectators.

Writing in their own mother tongue, these playwrights were still highly influenced by the Euro/American tradition of realistic playwriting. However, with the growing number of Brecht translations and performances, as well as in-depth research into folk performing traditions, writers were becoming increasingly familiar with various aspects of epic dramaturgy and were tentatively beginning to explore non-linear narrative modes.

The Emergency

By the mid 1970s, it was clear that the honeymoon with Nehruvian ideals and dreams of a strong unified nation under a powerful and centrally controlled Congress Government were over. Massive migrations to the cities, unemployment, a shift in the equations of caste, class and gender politics, together with growing regional aspirations, reflected a society in transition. Events took a turn for the worse with widespread unrest among students and workers, which ultimately provoked the Socialist leader, Jayprakash Narayan, to call for a total revolution. The mounting pressure forced the next Prime Minister, Indira Gandhi, to declare a national state of Emergency in 1975. Opposition leaders were arrested, civil liberties suspended, censorship of the press and mass media enforced, with the Prime Minister assuming the executive authority to overrule the law.

Alarmed and seized by a sense of betrayal and loss of idealism, all kinds of artists found themselves in a similar predicament and in a sense began to produce work that could be considered a part of independent India's first self-conscious and dissenting subculture. Playwrights like Badal Sirkar, Mahesh Elkunchwar and Satish Alekar, filmmakers like Mani Kaul, Shyam Benegal, Govind Nihilani, Adoor Gopalakrishnan, Mrinal Sen, painters like Bhupen Khakkar, Gulam Mohammad Sheikh, Sudhir Patwardhan, Gieve Patel were radical in their political views and broadly postmodernist in their aesthetic. Their work bore testimony to an India that was shaping itself within the horizons of the present.

Asserting their Third World status and location, they imported the local environment, its look, feel, its explicit and encoded histories, onto the stage, screen, and canvas. Discarding myth, history or folklore as a peg to talk about contemporary issues, dramatists now turned their attention to their local environment, in plays like *Aadhe Adhure, Khamosh! Adalat Jari Hai, Giddhare, Wada Chirebandi, Kamala,* and others.

The implications of this maneuver were momentous. Characters began to lose their significance as symbols with universal qualities and began to acquire a specificity of class, occupation, region, and ethnicity. Described in this way, the characters spoke viscerally of situations of dominance and enslavement, presenting themselves in their everyday *avtars* as ordinary, middleclass women, clerks, and lawyers. These characters carried their habitats with them into the new theatrical space; the metropolis, the suburbs, satellite townships, and small towns began to be drawn into the orbit of scrutiny. Ordinary characters and locations had never been memorialized on the modern Indian stage before. They now took center stage. More importantly, these playwrights redefined their roles of poets and seers to those of social agents and participants in the process of self-definition, constructing for themselves through their practice a vantage point from which to relate to their own social and political realities.

At this juncture, when there was a complete disillusionment with the idea that the new cities of India represented a hope for the future, when they had been revealed instead to be veritable jungles of corruption and dung heaps of dirty politics, the city plays of Brecht became particularly meaningful and powerful. Productions of such plays as *The Good Person of Szechwan* or *Threepenny Opera* were staged in a number of regional languages, making this perhaps the most intensive period of Brecht appropriations in India, in the form of full-scale cultural adaptations.

It was against this background of feverishly pitched avant-garde work that P. L. Deshpande, an eminent Marathi writer/actor, and Jabbar Patel, a young director from the Progressive Dramatic Association (PDA) in Pune, collaborated on a production of *The Threepenny Opera*, adapted as *Teen Paishacha Tamasha*. An established satirist, Deshpande saw the pursuit of money as a dehumanizing and corrupting force and made this the central thematic impulse of the play. Combining presentational elements of Tamasha, the secular folk performing tradition of Maharashtra, with Brechtian dramaturgy, Deshpande created a new text that bristled with social critique, political satire, while contextualizing the play within the framework of India's Emergency, a fact that got the play instant attention and publicity. As Aparna Dharwadker writes:

> With the event of the Emergency as his immediate referent, Deshpande launched into a multipronged attack on politics and nationhood, spheres that are still idealized in India...The experience of the Emergency with its suspension of constitutional rights and the large number of secret arrests had given the already menacing figure of the policeman, for example, an entirely new dimension in Indian political and public life. The Sutradhar/Narrator in the play, therefore, emphasizes the predatory connotations of Police Chief Tiger Bhandare/Brown's nickname and reacts with exaggerated terror whenever Bhandare and his men appear. The complicity of spies and informants during the Emergency also gives new meaning to Tiger's betrayal of his old friend, Macheath. When the men in Mackie's gang object to a business like theirs being conducted by a woman, Polly/Malan strong-arms them into agreeing that *only* a woman can carry on such a business! In the following scenes Polly/Malan begins to mimic the physical appearance and mannerisms of Indira Gandhi, with the distinctive white streak in the hair, and the habit of covering her head with her *sari*. Her metamorphosis and draconian control over the gang become a satiric re-enactment of the Emergency.[20]

The eclectic musical score by Bhaskar Chandavarkar was a pastiche of semi-classical and popular Indian musical traditions ranging from *gazals* and Natya Sangeet to Bollywood and western pop music; the casting of a young pop singer in the role of Macheath and the highly politicized landscape of the Emergency against which the play was set gave a cutting-edge quality to this dissonant production that utilized Brecht to describe a frantic and displaced urban Indian landscape. In my view all these aspects catapulted Brecht out of the practically pastoral prettiness of some earlier folk-inspired Brecht productions, truly reinventing him as our contemporary.

My Work

This paper would not be complete without my sharing the deep and abiding impact that Brecht has had on my own directorial work, both in relation to the plays of his that I have staged as to his ideas that have shaped the fundamental philosophy of my work.

Born after Independence, I, too, was searching for an identity but, unlike the generation of Tanvir, Mehta, Alkazi, B. V. Karanth and others before me, it was not a *pan-Indian* identity on "behalf" of the whole nation nor a *national* identity of any kind that I was looking for, but one more personal and close to me, the more autobiographical identity of being a postcolonial at this point. In a 1998-interview I said:

> Brecht was indeed one of the first inter-culturists, an approach which is the core of our postmodern culture, a fact that both interests me and pertains to my context. By virtue of the fact that I am a postcolonial, a product of two cultures, both Indian and Western, I don't and cannot lay claim or subscribe to a single, monolithic, "Indian" identity, as those before me in the 60's felt compelled to do in order to reassert their identity as Indians. I am no true, blue, "traditional" Indian, I don't hail from some remote village in India. I am of mixed parentage. Arab and Indian. I was born and brought up in Mumbai. I went to a Protestant School and I speak English at home. So...I have a hybrid, bastardized identity! Like millions of other urbanized Indians, I have plural identities because I respond to and interact with more than one tradition, more than one culture, a phenomenon which is being experienced increasingly by India's diaspora, all over the world, as greater migrations occur, as technology makes the world a smaller and smaller place, etc. These are facts of my birth and my circumstances. So am I not to be regarded as a true "Indian?"[21]

As a postcolonial director then, what I needed to construct for myself was a performance language that would reflect my cultural *instability*, the instability of the postcolonial, my in-betweenness, my *lack* of belonging to any culture/language/ethnic group specifically. In theatrical terms this ultimately translated into my attempt to create a constantly *shifting, vacillating identity* on stage, one that would dynamically reflect my constant state of *uprootedness*. So, unlike those before me who were searching for rootedness, I needed to assert my *lack* of it. And although my very first play on my return to India after two years of studying Brecht in the GDR was about the identity of Galy Gay in *Man Is Man* and how it was blotted out, it was not until much later that I realized that there were autobiographical connotations in my choice of this play.

What I found compelling and intriguing about *Man Is Man* was that besides the powerful political statement we were made to witness the transformation of an individual's identity. Here the character had not been conceived of as a fixed psychological entity, with unalterable traits, but as something that could be taken apart and remodeled at will. This struck me as an entirely new formulation of character. It was the death of character in the old sense.

The lack of fixity of character was a theme I was to take up two years later, again with a play by Brecht, *The Good Person of Szechwan* (produced in 1973 and 1982). Here the transformation of identity is treated in a more complex manner. Unlike Brecht's earlier play, where Galy Gay moves categorically from point A to B, here Shen Te, the central character, moves continuously back and forth between performing female and male. There is no respite for Shen Te if she wishes to survive, except to be in a constant state of flux between male and female genders. It has become her permanent state of being, her condition.

An Androgynous Being: *Himmat Mai*

> Eleven years later, in 1993, I was to return to the same theme, the paradox of dual gender which finds its most powerful and mature formulation in the central protagonist of Brecht's best known play, a chronicle of the 30-years war that ravaged Europe, *Mother Courage*. Brecht's contention can be simply stated — the female (Mother), if she wants to survive (in this case, the condition of war), requires a degree of maleness (Courage) to protect herself and her children. Here Brecht crystallizes the male and female into a single identity. Mother Courage does not suffer the schizophrenia of Shen Te, rather, in her the disparate identities have grown into one another so that the sharp demarcations of gender are no longer visible. The split is not evident. Mother Courage is both male and female at once and simultaneously. The warring identities have congealed, as blood into stone, which results in a character of savage and brutal mien. The dynamics of her ambivalent split gender have given rise to a character who is both repulsive as well as one to whom we are compassionately drawn. Mother Courage's sexuality, then, is an expression of her toughened will to survive. Brecht's concern

> is with the havoc war can play with human nature, brutalizing and desensitizing the human being to the point where he begins to resemble a grotesque creature, half man/half woman, a practically deformed androgynous being. It is this "unnatural" mother that the casting of a man in a woman's role sought to represent in my production.[22]

Another reason why Brecht appealed to me and my condition as a postcolonial subject was the manner in which he treated his material. Breaking the linearity of the narrative through several means, Brecht applied the treatment of collage, assemblage and bricolage by combining fragments of texts or statistics with songs or clowning routines, thereby coupling multiple media with the performative skills of the actor and creating out of the material a complex web of dynamically imparted information that energized the audience into what he called alert, *complex seeing*.

Despite applying, modifying and reinventing many of his strategies to the treatment of all my following work, I was never really concerned with recreating any particularly "Brechtian" style, but Brecht's ideas propelled me to construct and explore for myself new methods of approaching any material, any text. My effort is to always construct a performative dramaturgy through which I can dynamically perform the narrative, on multiple levels, through multiple means. Of late this has been expressed through creating, for example, a continuously shifting stage picture that becomes a continuously moving, fluid, unstable vantage point, through which the spectator is required to read/view the drama. I believe that my work achieves its energy and rhythm from the creation of such fluid, shifting registers, through which the performance, in a sense, is filtered.

Conclusion

As a woman director, one of the problematic areas for me has been the fact that most plays, whether western or Indian, have been written by men. Although male playwrights can give us a profound and sympathetic insight into a woman's psyche and world, their works are often, albeit unwittingly, dominated by the male gaze. Suffice to say here that Brecht's "Verfremdung" has helped me gain a neutral perspective and vantage point into drama. Such a vantage point constantly shuttles between the polarities of the subjective and objective, between character and actor, between the emotional and the distanced, which in terms of gender could be read as the male and female. This is the liminal space I have chosen to explore, that twilight zone between sleep and waking, the thin dividing line that separates the conscious from the unconscious, illusion from reality, where experiences of both may overlap, and where moments of clarity as well as ill-definition co-exist.

In my search to evolve my own language of theatrical articulation, I have been constantly drawn to study and explore older performance traditions of India and other parts of Asia, in conjunction with the theoretical premises on which Brecht formulated a new theater for the scientific age. These, as well as cinema, are invaluable storehouses of possible narrative modes through which stories and characters can travel along several trajectories simultaneously. I would like to describe my work, then, as "experiential." My attempt is to relate directly to the senses, without the mediation of the mind, so that colors, sounds and images "evoke" meanings, rather than use words to describe them. What is important to me is to "experience" theater, both as thought and feeling. This undoubtedly relates to my experience of being both an Indian and a woman.

Endnotes

1 Balwant Gargi, "Meeting Brecht in Person," in Nissar Allana, ed., *A Tribute to Bertolt Brecht 1993* (Delhi: Theatre and Television Associates, 1993), p. 25.
2 Anjum Katyal and Biren De, "It Must Flow: A Life in Theatre" [Interview with Habib Tanvir], *Seagull Theatre Quarterly* 10 (1996), p. 15.
3 Balwant Gargi, *Folk Theatre of India* (Seattle: University of Washington Press, 1966).
4 Habib Tanvir, "The Crisis of Identity and the Question of Authenticity in Theatre," paper presented at a symposium on *Perspectives of Contemporary Indian Theatre* by the Sangeet Natak Academy, December 1984 (reprinted in Pratibha Aggarwal and Natya Shodh Sansthan, eds., *Habib Tanvir ek Vyaktitva* [Kolkata: Natya Shodh Sansthan]), p. 210.
5 Amal Allana, interview with Habib Tanvir (TV documentary), Door Darshan, 1998.
6 Rajinder Paul, interview with Habib Tanvir, *Enact*, 1974 (reprinted in Pratibha and Sansthan, p. 179).
7 Amal Allana, interview with M. S. Satyu, *Brecht in India* (TV documentary), Door Darshan, 1998.
8 See Vasudha Dalmia, *Poetics, Plays and Performances: The Politics of Modern Indian Theatre* (Oxford and New York: Oxford University Press, 2008), p 261.
9 Ajitesh Banerjee quoted in *Bertolt Brecht '80, 1898-1978*, Samik Bandyopadhaya's account of a seminar held in Kolkatta and organized by Max Mueller Bhawan and ICCR, p. 41.
10 Ibid.
11 Nissim Ezekiel, interview with Ebrahim Alkazi, *Indian Express*, 17 Jan. 1971.
12 Amal Allana, interview with Vijaya Mehta, *Brecht in India* (TV documentary), Door Darshan, 1998.
13 Fritz Bennewitz, "The Story of Indian Chalk Circle," *Rangavarta* 55 (Nov. 1994), p. 21.
14 Ibid., p. 22.
15 Branches of the *champa* tree.
16 Ritual bathing in the River Ganga on auspicious occasions.
17 Amal Allana, interview with Vijaya Mehta, *Brecht in India* (TV documentary), Door Darshan, 1998. (The interview was conducted in English.)
18 D. G. Nadkarni, "The Search for Form," *Enact* 118/119 (Oct./Nov. 1976), p. 16.
19 Arun Naik, "Brechtian Experiment in Marathi," *Enact* 145/146 (Jan./Feb. 1979), p. 13.

20 Aparna Bhargava Dharwadker, *Theatres of Independence: Drama, Theory, and Urban Performance in India since 1947* (Iowa City: University of Iowa Press, 2005), pp. 379, 380.
21 Interview by Amal Allana, *Brecht in India* (TV documentary), Door Darshan, 1998.
22 Amal Allana, "Gender Relations and Self Identity," in Lakshmi Subramanyam, ed., *Muffled Voices: Women in Modern Indian Theatre* (Delhi: Har-Anand Publications, 2002), p. 301.

Verfremdung in *Kathakali*

Boris Daussà-Pastor

Dieser Aufsatz untersucht, ob man zu Brechts Verfremdungseffekt Parallelen im *Kathakali* finden kann, einer Form von Tanz-Drama aus Süd-Indien. Das Ziel ist nicht die Idee der Verfremdung durch eine vergleichende Analyse zu bestätigen, sondern neue Interpretationen dieses Konzepts anzubieten. Zusätzlich könnte die Analyse des *Kathakali* im Licht der Verfremdung als eine Einführung in die Theorien der ästhetischen Würdigung im klassischen indischen Theater dienen. Der Aufsatz bietet einen Überblick über die derzeitige Forschung zu Brecht und dem indischen Theater und legt dar, dass die Entfremdung bei Brecht das Ziel hatte, eine bekannte Situation fremd erscheinen zu lassen, während *Kathakali* das Gegenteil zu sein scheint, nämlich den Zweck verfolgt, eine unvertraute Situation vertraut zu machen. In beiden Fällen findet man eine Situation der Entfremdung vom Publikum vor aber *Kathakali* versucht die Entfremdung zu überbrücken, indem es die Vorführung der emotionalen Welt des Publikums näher bringt.

This paper investigates if Brecht's notion of *Verfremdungseffekt* finds any parallel in *kathakali*, a form of dance-drama from South India. The objective is not to validate the idea of estrangement through a comparative analysis, but to provide new interpretations for this concept. In addition, the analysis of *kathakali* in the light of estrangement may serve as an introduction to theories of aesthetic appreciation in classical Indian theater. The paper surveys the current scholarship on Brecht and Indian theater and argues that estrangement as proposed by Brecht had the objective of rendering a familiar situation unfamiliar, whereas the process in *kathakali* seems to be the opposite, namely to render an unfamiliar situation familiar. In both cases there is a situation of estrangement from the audience, but *kathakali* tries to bridge this estrangement by bringing the performance closer to the emotional world of the audience.

Estrangement in *Kathakali*

Boris Daussà-Pastor

Introduction

Can we apply the Brechtian concept of estrangement to *kathakali*? I admit that starting this article with such a question may seem a bit off-putting to hardened readers of Brechtian scholarship. Is this another effort of exegesis in Brechtian theory? Is this a new corrective of Brecht's mistaken interpretation of Chinese acting? Is this a bold attempt to bring Brecht's concept back to Asia, to a theater practice that predates Brecht? It is none of the above. This article does not intend to re-interpret or validate Brecht's theories; it aims at providing additional shades of meaning to the concept of estrangement. Rather than trying to read Brechtian estrangement forcefully in the performance practice of *kathakali*, I will describe how *kathakali* may effect in the audience a particular form of estrangement of its own accord. This comparison between Brechtian estrangement and estrangement in *kathakali* is meant not only to expand the idea of estrangement, but also to provide a deeper understanding of some aspects of Indian theater of the *Natyasastric* tradition to those who may be conversant with the theories of Brecht but not necessarily with the theories of Indian theater. However, before introducing the structure of the project in more detail I would like to make a short detour that will show that the current effort of placing *kathakali* in a conversation with a foreign practice is germane to already existing trends in the scholarship and practice of this art form.

Kathakali is perhaps best known outside of India for its codified language of hand gestures and facial expressions, for the visual appeal of its elaborate costumes and makeup, and for the complexity of a training system that starts at a young age and lasts for some six to ten years of intensive instruction. It is probably less known that *kathakali* is still a quite lively performance tradition today, one that deals actively with the challenges and changes that an increasingly globalized society poses to *kathakali*'s long-held conventions. The *kathakali* community has been well aware of the need for adaptation as its only means for survival since the traditional systems of patronage crumbled about a hundred years ago under a new socio-economic order.[1] Examples of changes in *kathakali* conventions under modern socio-economic structures include the formation of an all-female professional troupe in what is supposed to be an all-male performance tradition, the institutionalization of training into school-based systems that contrast with the traditional master-student relationship, the numerous intercultural experiences—including *kathakali* adaptations of Shakespeare's plays—or even the commoditization of *kathakali* in TV commercials or as the trademark image of the state of Kerala.[2] Certainly, the *kathakali* community still treasures its distinct cultural identity and performance conventions, but it has grown sensitive to the socio-economic and cultural realities of an increasingly globalized society. The fact that the community has embraced to a greater or lesser degree all the innovations described above is testament to its adaptability.

Rather than remaining a fossilized system impermeable to change, since the early twentieth century *kathakali* has been transforming its means of support, its training methods, and its performance structure to ensure survival. During the 1960s the academic discourse on *kathakali* also started to change, introducing concepts and narratives that were foreign to the original cultural framework that saw its birth. This global turn of *kathakali* practice and scholarship developed as an interesting double-edged process: on one side Western artists approached *kathakali* for artistic inspiration while Western scholars provided some understanding of the art form to Western audiences; on the other side local *kathakali* artists embarked on unprecedented intercultural projects and international tours, while Indian scholars turned to Western ideas in their discussion of this local art form.[3] The current paper can be placed at the intersection of the Indian and Western lines of *kathakali* scholarship: it intends to generate a better understanding among Western audiences of the aesthetic processes in *kathakali*, such as Western scholarship has tended to do, but it draws upon a Western idea (namely, estrangement) to explore these aesthetic processes in *kathakali* from a renewed perspective, a strategy more typical of Indian writings on the subject.

Having concluded this detour on the permeability of *kathakali*, the structure of the project can finally be laid out. The following section provides some general context and presents the peculiarities and limitations of the scholarship comparing Indian theater to Brechtian theory. The essay then turns specifically to *kathakali*, a form of dance-drama particular to South India, describing how local scholars have considered it in the light of Brechtian theories of theater. After a review of this scholarly discourse, the article focuses briefly on what has been called the representation of the "non-worldly," an aspect of *kathakali* that may complicate the comparison with the principles proposed by Brecht. Finally, the paper discusses the Brechtian idea of *Verfremdungseffekt* or estrangement in the spectator, exploring the question if a similar process may be taking place in *kathakali*. For this discussion, I briefly mention some basic aspects of *rasa* theory, a theory based on the *Natyasastra*, which is generally regarded as the basic model for aesthetic appreciation in *kathakali*.

Scholarship on Brecht and Indian Theater

Most frequently Western scholars have compared specific aspects of Brecht's theories to some characteristics of Indian theater and performance, coming to some fragmentary and often seemingly contradictory conclusions. For example, theater scholars Farley Richmond, Darius Swann and Phillip Zarrilli suggest: "there are in some Indian theater forms the equivalents of Brecht's alienation devices, which keep the spectators aware of the distinction between real life and the stage."[4] However, they also explain that the classical Indian theories of aesthetic appreciation in drama focus greatly on emotion and that "the savoring of the sentiment may be contra-Brechtian."[5] They seem to acknowledge that a fragmentary comparison of a particular aspect of Brechtian theory such as estrangement seems promising at first, but the comparison falls apart because Indian theater only conforms to some of the characteristics of Brechtian estrangement, not to all of them.

Such partial fulfilling of Brechtian principles hints at the problem that a blunt comparative analysis poses: it so happens that many elements of Indian theater seem to be somewhat Brechtian but, more often than not, we encounter some particular detail that tells us it cannot be considered *fully* Brechtian. Apparently, Brechtian theory is useful for approaching some aspects of Indian theater from a Western perspective, but it cannot provide a fully satisfactory explanation. In addition, any attempt to validate an entire theory on account of the other seems inadequate, since this strategy carries the uncomfortable notion that the model created in one culture is superior to that of the other culture. Hence, a straight comparison may end up being more misleading than helpful. Perhaps this will only reveal the fact that both Brechtian and Indian dramatic theory are highly developed and articulated systems that can stand fully on their own.

Aware of the impossibility of comparing the entire Brechtian model to Indian theater, Richmond, Swann, and Zarrilli enumerate specific Brechtian principles that can be observed in the latter:

> There are at least three other ways in which Brechtian principles can be observed in Indian plays. (1) Simple stereotypical characters can be effectively used…(2) Like Brecht's, many Indian plays are given to moralizing. Generally, their teaching undergirds traditional social values but some forms…make use of satire to expose and correct social ills…(3) The potential of theater for social commitment and political agitation became particularly evident in the struggle for freedom from British rule.[6]

The list of Brechtian characteristics provided by the authors could be subject to debate, but there is no doubt that the comparison is centered on the Brechtian model rather than the Indian one. None of the characteristics they mention are central to Indian theories of theater. It is clearly an effort to provide some understanding of Indian theater theories to those who may already be acquainted with Brecht's ideas.

It is worth noting that such comparisons to Brecht are not exclusive to Western scholars. The principles of Brechtian theater are also discussed within the Indian academic discourse on theater and performance. Brecht has been—and still is today—a particularly important influence on forms of theater activism in India, but his relevance certainly goes beyond that. For classical forms of theater, which are largely based on gestural stylization and codified and presentational acting, Brechtian principles have been applied to validate the local tradition in terms of Western discourse. For the new Indian theater that developed during the twentieth century, the Brechtian body of work has also been a particularly useful theoretical and practical tool. It is worth noting that Indian culture willingly accepts the artifice of theater and is not particularly concerned with a realistic reproduction of the world. Brechtian theories helped justify the exploration of a particular performative style that is often far removed from Western realism.

However, as we will see in the case of *kathakali*, the Brechtian model is tempting but insufficient. It falls short when it comes to explaining the mechanisms of aesthetic distance and appreciation in the theater of the *Natyasastric* tradition. The *rasa* theory based on the *Natyasastra* implies that the intellectual understanding and appreciation of a play is necessarily linked to a complex emotional experience.[7]

The reason why Brechtian theories are somewhat inadequate may be related to the fact that Western and Indian thought tend to regard the relationship between the intellectual, the emotional, and the transcendental in different terms. John Glynn argues in his unpublished dissertation on aesthetic processes among *kathakali* audiences that this difference is key in framing the discourse of appreciation, and he adds: "The aesthetic experience…described in terms of *both* emotions *and* cognition…is more conducive to an understanding of Indian aesthetics."[8] Later in his dissertation he explains: "the correlatives that might be useful in achieving the necessary shift from Western thinking into Indian will then be among those that provide for the transcendental within the aesthetic experience."[9] Indeed, the idea of the transcendental, or what in *kathakali* scholarship has sometimes been called the "non-worldly,"[10] is central to the distinction that I am intending to make between Brechtian estrangement and the comparable process that operates in *kathakali*. Before we finally move to the core of my argument let's briefly introduce some of the ideas raised by local scholars regarding *kathakali* and Brechtian theories.

Brecht and *Kathakali* in Indian Scholarship

Among the Indian scholars that have discussed the ideas of Brecht, we find the work of the former secretary of Delhi's *Sahitya Academy* (Literary Academy), Malayali poet and literary scholar Prof. K. Satchidanandan. In his book *The Art of Bertolt Brecht,* Satchidanandan discusses several aspects of Brechtian theory and relates them to Indian literary and dramatic theory.[11] Satchidanandan introduces his consideration of *kathakali* by stating bluntly: "one should not misconstrue as found out by a theater-scholar here that 'epic theater is a Marxist Kathakali.' Save a superficial and solely technical similarity, epic theater and Kathakali are binary opposites."[12] In conversation with Kaladharan Viswanath, I learned that this statement was directed to address former claims on the nature of *kathakali* by Prof. K. Aravindkshaw, a leftist scholar, literary critic, and theater activist from Kerala.[13] As a side note, it is worth pointing out that Kerala, the home state of *kathakali,* has a long tradition of communist political activism since its first democratic elections in 1957. Communists are still a major political force today and are often elected to local and state government, alternating with some of the other major political parties of the region (the Communist Party is currently in power at the state level). This is particularly relevant since this communist tradition led many artists from Kerala to study the theories developed by theater artists commonly associated with socialist and Marxist thought, such as Brecht.

Satchidanandan continues with his criticism, adding that the intellectual process at play in *kathakali* is different from that of Brechtian epic theater. He explains: "Instead of enabling the spectators to think, Kathakali makes them consumers of certain known incidents and perspectives."[14] These incidents and perspectives come from the classical Indian epics, the *Mahabharata,* the *Ramayana,* and the *Puranas* from which *kathakali* borrows its storylines. The world of the Indian epics is frozen in time and depicts an imaginary society of superhuman creatures, filled with universal values of transcendental significance that reflect the established perspectives of Hindu society with little room for individual interpretations outside of the given ideals. As Satchidanandan notes, this is quite different from the Brechtian project: "The new theater movement [that is represented by Brecht's approach] discards the degenerated, primordial and subjective terrains of emotions and gives way to the new, multi-faceted, social and creative emotions of a new age."[15] This difference between the socially and historically specific referents of Brechtian theater and the static and transcendental situations presented in *kathakali* is essential and needs further explanation. In fact, *kathakali* depicts on stage what has been called "the realm of the non-worldly."[16]

Kathakali: The Art of the Non-Worldly

The world of *kathakali* is clearly different from that of the audience; it is the transcendental realm of the "non-worldly," inhabited by mythical creatures that perform legendary deeds. The reality presented on the *kathakali* stage is of a fabulous nature and has its natural place in the common imaginary of Hindu culture and spirituality. It is a reality that has no direct connection with the tangible world of everyday interactions and cannot be perceived in the regular activities of daily life. The characters inhabiting the *kathakali* stage are themselves superhuman creatures detached from quotidian reality; they are the living and breathing representation of non-worldly creatures. Through *kathakali*, the spectator finds him- or herself directly facing a representation of this intangible world: a world that is estranged from the one the audience inhabits since it is not bound by time or space, a world that human beings can only perceive through representation and performance and that would be impossible to experience otherwise. More particularly, it is through the aesthetic experience or *rasa* that the spectator bridges the gap between the realm of worldly experience and the immutable transcendental world.

Through the savoring of *rasa*, a complex experience of emotions, this seemingly esoteric realm becomes an embodied experience. Certainly, the audience already knows beforehand the stories of the Indian epics, including all the deeds that the creatures of the non-worldly are going to perform as well as the main interpretations and meanings that these stories may have. Nevertheless, the combination of sensory and emotional experiences achieved in performance trigger an empathic response that eventually links the existing intellectual understanding of the stories and meanings contained in the Indian epics with an embodied experience felt by the spectator. What was merely an intellectual perception before the performance gains an additional level of meaning when associated with emotional and sensorial experiences.

Now that we understand that the world depicted on the *kathakali* stage is ahistorical, universal, superhuman, and transcendental, and the world presented on Brecht's stage is historically and culturally specific, reflects on the human condition, and focuses on the particularities of distinct situations, we can move on to considering how estrangement may operate in each approach to theater.

Brecht's Estrangement and Estrangement in *Kathakali*

For Brecht, the devices of epic theater were meant to render a familiar situation somewhat unfamiliar. Witnessing the reenactment of a situation that may be familiar to the spectator could generate some sort of unconscious reaction, a judgment that is more related to the spectator's own feelings towards this seemingly familiar act than to the actual circumstances of the particular situation of the play. For example, if we present a factory manager punishing a factory worker for having manufactured some defective pieces, an audience member who happens to be a factory worker may feel that the manager is too harsh, but a spectator who happens to be a factory manager may feel that the worker is endangering the viability of the business, thus jeopardizing the jobs of all other factory workers. In each case, the audience member reacts according to her or his preconditioned empathic response rather than to an objective understanding of all conditions presented. By distancing spectators from perfectly realistic depictions of actions on stage, Brecht could expect to detach the spectator's intellectual understanding of the situation from the empathic feeling that any personal identification may have triggered. Thus, using the device of Brechtian estrangement, the spectator's understanding is not always predetermined by the particular feeling that he or she usually associates with the situation but should be bound to the understanding of the specific conditions that determine the particular circumstances presented on stage.

Following the example given above, in an ideal situation the spectator would be presented with all the circumstances that lead to the defective manufacture of the piece in order to determine the origin of the problem and any possible solutions. The action of the manager punishing the factory worker could then be viewed as appropriate or inappropriate regardless of the personal background of the spectator once it has been determined if this action is actually going to address the cause of the problem (for example, if we discover that the factory worker is a careless worker we may view the punishment as an appropriate corrective, but if we discover that the manager is exploiting the workers asking for an unusual increase in production, we may view the punishment as unfair and inappropriate). By making both the factory worker and the manager objects of our observation instead of vehicles for our empathic response, each person in the audience should be able to see the punishment of the worker presented on stage with a renewed perspective based on an intellectual understanding of the situation. Rather than responding with a set of preconditioned responses, the audience should eventually be able to judge according to the social, historical, and circumstantial conditions presented on stage. It is important to note that this reasoning presupposes that a strong emotional response affects intellectual understanding, but also that intellectual understanding can be detached from human emotions. In the case of Brecht's estrangement, it is necessary to create an aesthetic distance that will allow the spectator to reflect with detachment on a situation that would otherwise be perceived as normal and familiar, and therefore unquestionable.

In the case of *kathakali* there is a certain element of estrangement, but it operates at a different level than the one proposed by Brecht. In fact, *kathakali* works basically the other way around: it presents a world that is known to the audience but turns out to be clearly unfamiliar at an experiential level. Since the spectator cannot recognize him- or herself in the mythical situations presented, these situations do not automatically trigger an emotional empathic response. There is no need to estrange the audience from the action because the audience is already estranged from it to begin with. A *kathakali* performance is meant to achieve the opposite: by generating an emotional response in the audience, this unfamiliar world gains a greater level of familiarity. Although the audience remains always aware that those presented on stage belong to the realm of the "non-worldly," by the end of the performance each spectator can relate to the characters in a very personal way, informed by his/her experience of the sentiments savored during the performance.

Indeed, estrangement exists in *kathakali*, but it exists in order to be bridged. I would claim that all the presentational and non-realistic features of this art form, of which there are many, reflect the non-worldly condition of the stories and characters presented. These stories could not be performed in a realistic way, among other reasons because they do not reflect the so-called "real," the world that the audience inhabits in their everyday interactions. It is precisely through the familiar and worldly process of feeling emotions that this estranged, non-worldly reality can finally be fully grasped. After all, it is through sensorial perception that we mediate between the world and its meanings. Research in cognitive science in the last twenty years points towards an inextricable connection between emotion and cognition, leading to the idea that all intellectual processes are inevitably linked to some sort of emotional response.

In the light of this interpretation, it seems quite possible that the Indian model of aesthetic appreciation, in which intellectual understanding is complemented by a complex combination of sentiments eliciting a pleasurable response in the audience, is perhaps closer to our current understanding of the process of cognition than any approach that intends to detach emotion from cognition. Rather than thinking of estrangement as a situation of emotional detachment, it would probably be more accurate to think of Brechtian estrangement as a situation in which the emotional response is different from any expected precondition. Rendering the familiar unfamiliar is obviously a process that elicits some emotional response, perhaps not an empathic one, but at least one of surprise and possibly bewilderment.

Conclusion:

If Brecht intended to render the familiar unfamiliar, making us reflect on the particularities of the social, cultural and historical determinants that inform a particular act, *kathakali* tries to render the unfamiliar familiar, making the generalized, transcendental, and universal features of the Indian epics a personal, specific, and particularly meaningful experience for each member of the audience.

Both Brecht's *Verfremdungseffekt* and *kathakali*'s bridging of the estrangement between the real and the non-worldly contribute to a better understanding of a particular situation. In the case of the *Verfremdungseffekt*, it is the possibility for us to reflect on something and to consider its social, cultural and historical context, allowing us to shed our preconditioned disposition towards the event. In the case of *kathakali*, the performance aims at a deeper personal understanding of the transcendental world, unmediated by the teachings and interpretations imposed by others and clearly linked to our individual understanding of it.

Earlier in this article I cautioned against blunt comparisons of dramatic theory across cultures, although this essay could be characterized precisely as a comparative analysis. I hope it will be clear by now that this piece of writing does not seek to validate any particular theory by establishing points of congruence. The intention has been to further a mutual understanding of the discourses on both sides of the comparative analysis. For those already acquainted with the theoretical principles proposed by Brecht, the analysis of the differences we encounter in the case of *kathakali* may have served as a basic introduction to some of the Indian principles of aesthetic appreciation in the theater. In addition, the discussion of Brecht's concept of *Verfremdungseffekt* and *kathakali*'s bridging of the estrangement between the real and the non-worldly may have led to a refined understanding of *kathakali* in its own cultural context. Finally, the particular notion of estrangement in *kathakali* may not only contribute to a renewed understanding of this notion but also, if productively re-applied to its original context, complement and further the existing discourse on Brecht's *Verfremdungseffekt*.

Endnotes

1   Phillip B. Zarrilli, *Kathakali Dance-Drama: Where Gods and Demons Come to Play* (London and New York: Routledge, 2000). See, particularly, chapter 2 "A Social History of *Kathakali* Patronage, Connoisseurship, and Aesthetics," pp. 17-38.
2   The above-mentioned all-female troupe is the Tripunithura Kathakali Kendram Ladies Troupe, commonly known as TKK. See Diane Daugherty and Marlene Pitkow, "Who Wears the Skirts in Kathakali?" *TDR: The Drama Review: A Journal of Performance Studies* 35.2 (Summer, 1991): pp. 138-156; the transition to school-based instruction started with the establishment of the Kerala Kalamandalam in 1930 and today includes a number of state-sponsored and private schools; although there have been a number of *kathakali* adaptations of Western plays, the best known on the international stage is probably *Kathakali King Lear*; see Diane Daugherty, "The Pendulum of Intercultural Performance: Kathakali King Lear at Shakespeare's Globe," *Asian Theatre Journal* 22.1 (Spring 2005): pp. 52-72.
3   Certainly the interest of Westerners in *kathakali* and the beginning of international *kathakali* tours predate the decade of the 1960s. For the purpose of this general introduction it is only relevant to point out that it was during the 1960s that international forays into *kathakali* gained momentum.
4   Farley P. Richmond, Darius L. Swann, and Phillip B. Zarrilli, eds., *Indian Theatre: Traditions of Performance* (Honolulu: University of Hawaii Press, 1990), p. 464.

5   Ibid.
6   Ibid.
7   For an English annotated translation of the *Natyasastra* see, for example: Bharatamuni, *The Natyasastra: English Translation with Critical Notes*, Adya Rangacharya, ed. and trans. (New Delhi: Munshiram Manoharlal Publishers, 1996); for an article dealing specifically with *rasa* see S. K. Saxena, "The Rasa Theory: An Essay in Understanding," *Sangeet Natak* 91 (1989): pp. 3-30; for an additional resource in dealing with *rasa* in intercultural theorization see Rosa Fernández Gómez,"The *Rasa Theory*: A Challenge for Intercultural Aesthetics," in Antoon van den Braembussche, Heinz Kimmerle, and Nicole Note, eds., *Intercultural Aesthetics: A Worldview Perspective* (Dordrecht: Springer, 2009), pp. 105-118.
8   John Glynn, "Kathakali: A Study of the Aesthetic Processes of Popular Spectator and Elitist Appreciators Engaging with Performances in Kerala," Diss. University of Sidney, 2001. Print. p. 30.
9   Ibid., p. 31.
10 D. Appukattan Nair and K. Ayyappa Paniker, ed., *Kathakali: The Art of the Non-worldly* (Bombay: Marg Publications, 1993).
11 Koyamparambath Satchidanandan, *The Art of Bertolt Brecht* (Wayanad, Kerala: Phoenix Publishers 1989 [revised 2007]). I am indebted to *kathakali* scholar and senior officer of the Kalamandalam, Mr. Viswanath Kaladharan, for pointing me to this book and for helping me access its contents, since my knowledge of Malayalam is still very limited. The quotes provided here are Mr. Kaladharan's translations from the original Malayalam version.
12 Ibid., p. 108.
13 Personal interview with V. Kaladharan in Cheruthuruthy, Kerala (January 2010).
14 Satchidanandan, p. 109.
15 Ibid.
16 Nair and Paniker, *Kathakali: The Art of the Non-worldly*.

The Role of the Black Tent Theatre in the Japanese Brecht Reception

Michiko Tanigawa

Since the mid-1950s Brecht has evidently played an important role in Japan. Using the example of the Black Tent Theatre, this paper summarizes the Japanese reception of Brecht especially in the last 30 years.

It is well-known that at the end of the 1960s the underground theater movement was formed in opposition to Shingeki ("new theater"), which had existed since the Meiji-era and was mainly based on the reception of Western theater. This underground theater generation probably marks a turning point in Japanese theater history after World War II.

Whereas most of the general underground theater groups intentionally turned their back on European drama — and especially on Brecht — and staged their original Japanese plays, Sato Makoto with BTT attempted to bring Brecht to the stage and to also absorb his dramaturgy productively. This is examined by way of example of the "Brecht-Renaissance" (since 1989), while the paper also attempts to demonstrate the status of the BTT in the Japanese Brecht reception.

Seit Mitte der 1950er Jahre hat Brecht in Japan eine wichtige Rolle gespielt. Hier soll die japanische Brecht-Rezeption besonders der vergangenen 30 Jahre am Beispiel des Black Tent Theaters (BTT) zusammengefasst werden.

Bekannterweise entstand Ende der 60er Jahre die Bewegung des Untergrundtheaters als Opposition gegen das seit der Meiji-Ära bestehende Shingeki ("neues Theater"), welches hauptsächlich auf der Rezeption des westlichen Theaters beruhte. Vermutlich markiert diese Untergrund-Theatergeneration einen Wendepunkt in der japanischen Theatergeschichte der Nachkriegszeit.

Während die meisten Gruppen des Untergrundtheaters absichtlich dem europäischen Drama—und insbesondere Brecht—den Rücken kehrten und zumeist ihre originären japanischen Stücke auf die Bühne brachten, versuchte Sato Makoto mit dem BTT Brecht auf die Bühne zu bringen und auch in seine Dramaturgie produktiv aufzunehmen. Dies wird am Beispiel seiner "Brecht-Renaissance" (seit 1989) in Augenschein genommen und damit zugleich der Stellenwert des BTT in der japanischen Brecht-Rezeption aufgezeigt.

Die Stellung des Black Tent Theaters in der japanischen Brecht-Rezeption[1]

Michiko Tanigawa

In Japan setzte die Brecht-Rezeption, wie bekannt,[2] bereits sehr früh ein, nämlich vor dem Zweiten Weltkrieg und fast zeitgleich mit Europa. So wurde zum Beispiel im Jahr 1929 *Trommeln in der Nacht* ins Japanische übersetzt und drei Jahre später, 1932, *Die Dreigroschenoper* in einer Bearbeitung aufgeführt. Aber auch nach dem Zweiten Weltkrieg vollzog sich die Rezeption fast gleichzeitig mit der in europäischen Ländern. Seit Mitte der 1950er Jahre hat Brecht in Japan eine wichtige Rolle gespielt. Hier soll die japanische Brecht-Rezeption besonders der vergangenen 30 Jahre am Beispiel des Black Tent Theaters (BTT) zusammengefasst werden. Diese Rezeption kann grob in folgende fünf Phasen eingeteilt werden:

1. 1953-1966: Shingeki und die "Blütezeit" Brechts in Japan
2. 1966-1976: Die Bewegung des Untergrund-Theaters und das BTT
3. Die 1980er Jahre: "Brecht-Müdigkeit" und das BTT
4. Die 1990er Jahre: "Brecht-Renaissance" und "Brecht Re-Lektüren" am BTT
5. Das 21. Jahrhundert: Drei neuere Produktionen der *Mutter Courage* und andere Brecht-Inszenierungen.

1. 1953-1966: Shingeki und die "Blütezeit" Brechts in Japan

In den 1950er Jahren erlebte das Shingeki ("Neues Theater"), das seit der Meiji-Ära als Hauptströmung des modernen japanischen Theaters hauptsächlich auf der Rezeption des westlichen Theaters in japanischer Übersetzung beruhte, durch neuere Impulse des westlichen Theaters einen Wendepunkt. Dabei spielten drei Faktoren eine zentrale Rolle. Erstens: französische existenzialistische Dramen etwa von Albert Camus, Jean-Paul Sartre und Jean Anouilh, die die Entscheidung von Menschen in extremen Situationen thematisieren, aber insofern eine Fortsetzung des frühen modernen (und das heißt: realistischen) Theaters darstellen, als sie das Einfühlungsvermögen seitens der Zuschauer nach wie vor voraussetzen. Zweitens: das "absurde Theater" etwa von Samuel Beckett und Eugène Ionesco, das die Absurdität des menschlichen Daseins von innen her betrachtet und *un*dramatische Situationen hervorhebt, in denen die Sprache als Kommunikationsmittel nicht mehr taugt. (In diesem Sinne markiert das absurde Theater auch den Beginn des Antitheaters.) Drittens: Brecht als der Erneuerer des gegenwärtigen Theaters, mit seinem epischen Theater und dem Verfremdungseffekt in Theorie und Praxis. Auf seine Weise brachte Brecht das Dramatische wieder ins Theatralische zurück. Sein "nicht-aristotelisches Theater" richtete sich gegen das gesamte moderne Theater.

Dabei spielte Senda Koreya (1904-1994) eine große Rolle. Er spielte schon vor dem Zweiten Weltkrieg im "Tsukiji-kleinen-Theater" als Schauspieler bei Aufführungen expressionistischer Dramen viele Hauptrollen. Danach (1929 bis 1932) ging er nach Deutschland, wo er in enger Beziehung zur damaligen Arbeitertheaterbewegung stand. Nach seiner Rückkehr brachte er, wie gesagt, 1932 Brechts *Dreigroschenoper* unter dem Titel *Kojiki Shibai* ("Bettlertheater") auf die Bühne. In der Nachkriegszeit entwickelte er die Gruppe "Haiyuza" zu einem eigenständigen Theater und bildete an der angegliederten Schauspielschule Nachfolger aus. So leistete er einen großen Beitrag sowohl zur Entwicklung des Shingeki der Nachkriegszeit als auch zur Brecht-Rezeption in Japan.

In den 1950er und 1960er Jahren übersetzten Koreya, Iwabuchi und andere viele Dramen Brechts, stellten diese theoretisch vor und führten Stücke wie etwa *Das Leben des Galilei* und *Mutter Courage und ihre Kinder* auf. Damals wurden Brechts Dramen nicht nur von professionellen Truppen sondern auch von Amateurgruppen häufig gespielt. Ferner wurden viele andere Dramatiker wie etwa Arnold Wesker, Harold Pinter, Friedrich Dürrenmatt, Max Frisch und Peter Weiss ins Japanische übersetzt und aufgeführt. Diese Zeit gilt als die Blütezeit des Shingeki der Nachkriegszeit. Darüberhinaus war die Zeit um 1968 eine Zeit des politischen Protestes. Brecht wurde nicht nur als Theater-Vorbild (mit möglichst genauen Nachinszenierungen anhand seiner Modellbücher), sondern auch im politischen Sinne mit seinen sozialistischen Ideen—aber entgegen der sozialistisch-realistischen Tendenz—aufgenommen.

Diese Brecht-Rezeption hatte auf das japanische Theater tiefgreifende Wirkungen. Sie stellte das herkömmliche Shingeki, das in der Tradition des modernen realistischen Theaters stand, in Frage. Obwohl zu jener Zeit viele andere westliche Dramatiker eine Rolle spielten, galten vor allem jedoch Brecht und Beckett als Inbegriff des Antitheaters. Vor allem Brechts Dramaturgie beeinflusste die neuen japanischen Dramatiker: seine Antihelden, die künstlerische und künstliche Verfremdung des Alltäglichen, die offene Form des epischen Theaters ohne Anfang und Ende, und die Frage nach dem Volkstümlichen. Diese Merkmale lassen sich auch in den Dramen von Yoshiyuki Fukuda, Kobo Abe, Hisashi Inoue, Makoto Sato und Minoru Betsuyaku finden. Viele japanische Dramatiker, die eher in der Traditionslinie des Shingeki standen, gerieten methodisch, stilistisch und thematisch unter den Einfluss Brechts. Der vor kurzem verstorbene Hisashi Inoue (1934—2010)[3] hat einmal erwähnt, dass er 1965 bewußt damit angefangen hätte, für seine Dramaturgie-Studien Brecht gründlich und vollständig zu lesen.[4] Brecht war für diese Dramatiker ein Katalysator oder Erneuerer, wobei die Versuche, die Inszenierungen des Berliner Ensembles zu kopieren, als Lernprozess nützlich waren. Die 1960er und 1970er Jahre (die ersten beiden Phasen der Brecht-Rezeption) waren in Japan nicht nur eine Blütezeit des Shingeki, sondern auch eine Blütezeit Brechts.

2. 1966-1976: Die Bewegung des Untergrund-Theaters und das BTT

Bekannterweise war es die Bewegung des Untergrund-Theaters,[5] die Ende der 1960er Jahre als Opposition zum Shingeki aufkam. Vermutlich stellt die Generation des Untergrund-Theaters einen Wendepunkt in der japanischen Theatergeschichte der Nachkriegszeit dar und entspricht in vielerlei Hinsicht der "68er Generation" in Westdeutschland, wie sie unter anderen Peter Stein und Claus Peymann, oder die Bewegung der "Freien Theater" vertraten. Das Untergrund-Theater setzte sich mit Problemen der japanischen Modernisierung seit der Meiji-Ära thematisch, dramaturgisch und auch systematisch auseinander, und entwickelte sich gleichzeitig abseits des etablierten Systems als Form des "freien Theaters" (wie zum Beispiel die verschiedenen Zelttheater-Gruppen).

Die Mitglieder des BTT beim Aufschlagen ihres schwarzen Zeltes, 1985. © BTT

Nicht nur auf der dramatischen und konzeptionellen Ebene lassen sich Parallelen zwischen den jungen japanischen Theatermenschen und Brecht finden. In den 1930er Jahren versuchte Brecht, abseits der "offiziellen Theater-Ordnung" eine neue freie Theaterform wie etwa das "Lehrstück" zu entwickeln. Auch die Bewegung des "Untergrund-Theaters," in der Opposition gegen das Shingeki, ist als Suche nach einer neuen Theaterform zu verstehen, die über den herkömmlichen Theaterrahmen hinausgeht.

Verschiedene "Untergrund-Theater" traten auch international auf. Shuji Terayamas Gruppe "Tenjo Sajiki" ("Galerie") zum Beispiel zeigte eigene Stücke wie *Inugami* ("Hundegott") und *Marie im Pelzmantel* auf westlichen Theaterfestivals wie der "Experimenta 3" (1969) und ging in Europa auf Tournee. Mit eigenen Werken öffnete sich Juro Karas Ensemble "Aka Tento" ("Rotes Zelt") der arabischen Welt, und Satos Gruppe "Kuro Tento" ("Schwarzes Zelt") der asiatischen. Suzuki Tadashi und seine Truppe "Waseda Kleines Theater" veranstalteten mit ausländischen Theatermachern, die Terayama auf seiner Auslandstournee kennengelernt hatte, ein internationales Theaterfest in dem Dorf Toga. Viele von ihnen waren Dramatiker, Regisseure, Organisatoren und Schauspieler zugleich. Dass sie sich mit ihren eigenen Stücken thematisch wieder Japan zuwendeten, aber gleichzeitig mit ihren Theatergruppen im Ausland auftraten, stellt lediglich zwei Seiten derselben Medaille dar. Im Verlaufe dieser Entwicklung traten später Tadashi Suzuki, Yukio Ninagawa und andere als Regisseure in der internationalen Theaterszene in Erscheinung und stellten jeweils auf ihre eigene Weise ein anderes, nicht auf Noh oder Kabuki reduzierbares, japanisches Theater vor.

Für viele Künstler war diese "Rückkehr nach Japan" ein Anlass, das Verhältnis des modernen japanischen Theaters zum einheimischen traditionellen Theater neu zu überdenken. Auch Brecht hatte sich einst mit dem asiatischen Theater—insbesondere Noh und Kabuki— auseinandergesetzt, als er seine eigene Theaterform über den Rahmen des modernen westlichen Theaters hinaus zu konzipieren versuchte. Koreya Senda sagte einmal, dass er erst durch die Auseinandersetzung mit Brecht die Möglichkeit erhalten habe, sowohl das japanische Gegenwartstheater als auch das traditionelle Noh- oder Kabuki-Theater wie aus der Perspektive des internationalen Theaters neu wahrzunehmen.[6] Nun sahen die japanischen Theaterleute sich veranlasst, gleichsam "agonale" Beziehungen zwischen dem modernen und dem traditionellen Theater Japans, die im Zuge der Rezeption des westlichen Theaters fast abgebrochen waren, wieder ins Auge zu fassen. Damit begann die zweite Phase.

Während die meisten Gruppen des Untergrund-Theaters absichtlich den europäischen Dramen, und insbesondere Brecht, den Rücken kehrten und meistens ihre eigenen japanischen Stücke auf die Bühne brachten, versuchte Makoto Sato (1943-), der eigentlich an der Haiyuuza-Schauspielschule von Senda studiert hatte, mit seinem Black Tent Theater (BTT) Brecht auf seine Weise in seine Dramaturgie aufzunehmen, obwohl das BTT damals nicht direkt Brechts Stücke aufführte. Aber Satos Tätigkeit als japanischer Dramatiker zeigt deutlich seine methodologischen Anleihen von Brecht. Sein aus fünf Stücken bestehender Zyklus *Diebmaus Jirokichi* (1969-71)[7] behandelt einen Macheath in der *Dreigroschenoper* vergleichbaren, mythischen Räuber der Edo-Zeit, und mit der Trilogie

Die Welt der Showa-Zeit ("Abe Sadas Hunde," "Kinema und das Phantom" und "Die Ermordung Blanquis im Shanghaier Frühling;" 1972-1979) versuchten Sato und das BTT das Japan der Showa-Ära (1926-1989), also das Japan des 20. Jahrhunderts zu historisieren, wobei viele Aspekte und Methoden Brechts bewusst benutzt wurden, und auch die Musik von Kurt Weill sehr effektiv eingesetzt wurde.

3. Die 1980er Jahre: "Brecht-Müdigkeit" und das BTT

Vergleichbar mit der Situation in der BRD ist seit den 1980er Jahren bei der jungen Generation in Bezug auf die Brechtrezeption fast eine Art "Brechtmüdigkeit" eingetreten. Dies hat mehrere Gründe: einerseits wurden die Werke von Brecht immer weniger auf die Bühne gebracht, andererseits war der politische Kontext verschwunden, der die bisherige Brechtrezeption unterstützt hatte. Auch in Japan gab es "eine Tendenzwende." Gleichzeitig kamen neuartige Theatermoden auf und es entstanden viele kleinere Truppen, die als Generation des "Klein-Theaters" bezeichnet werden und für ausländische Dramen weniger Interesse hatten und haben. Für sie war die Generation des Untergrund-Theaters das große Vorbild.

Inzwischen hatte aber das BTT seit 1978 die Zusammenarbeit mit der philippinischen Theaterorganisation PETA (Philippine Educational Theater Association) und anderen asiatischen Gruppen begonnen und Brecht neu im Kontext des "asiatischen Gegenwartstheaters" entdeckt. Sato hat einmal geäußert, dass er sehr davon überrascht war, wie natürlich und selbstverständlich sich das thailändische Studententheater auf Brecht bezog.[8] 1978 begann das BTT ein zehnjähriges Projekt zum asiatischen Theater mit dem Schlagwort "Theater für die kämpfende Masse." Gleichzeitig wurden auch zwei neue Programme gestartet: das "Rote Kabarett" als ein mobiles Theater und das "Rote Klassenzimmer" als politisches Schul(ungs)theater. Seitdem unterhält Sato enge Beziehungen zu anderen asiatischen Theaterleuten und organisiert auch außerhalb des BTT, zum Beispiel als Intendant des Setagaya-Public Theater oder des Za-Koenji-Theater, verschiedene gemeinsame Projekte mit anderen asiatischen Theatergruppen.

In dieser Situation hat das BTT eine ganze Reihe von Brecht-Stücken bearbeitet und inszeniert, jedoch nicht die eher für das Shingeki geeigneten Stücke, sondern seine Lehrstücke mit ihrem eher experimentellen und politischen Kabarettstil: *Die Maßnahme oder über die Maßnahme* im Roten Kabarett mit nachfolgender Publikumsdiskussion (1980): *Der Jasager und der Neinsager* mit Elementen des Noh-Stils, eine Gemeinschaftsinszenierung von Sato, Tadashi Kato und dem Noh-Darsteller Hideo Kanze, am Goethe-Institut Tokyo aufgeführt (1981); *Brecht-Wettkampf: Ein "Flüchtlingsgespräche"-Konzert*, konzipiert, komponiert und gesungen von dem Schauspieler Haruhiko Saito und dem Komponisten Hikaru Hayashi, ebenfalls am Goethe-Institut Tokyo aufgeführt (1981); das "Theater im August"-Konzert *Die Ballade vom toten Soldaten*, konzipiert und realisiert von Hayashi und Kiyokazu Yamamoto am Haiyuuza-Theater (1982), und die "Theater im August"-Revue mit Liedern aus dem *Mahagonny Songspiel*, inszeniert von Sato, ebenfalls am Haiyuza-Theater (1985). Dies waren alles eigenständige Versuche der Gruppe, einen neuen Zugang zu Brecht und zur Theaterarbeit allgemein zu finden.

Die "Theater im August"-Revue des BTT mit Liedern aus dem *Mahagonny Songspiel*, konzipiert und inszeniert von Makoto Sato am Haiyuza-Theater, 1985. © BTT

Im Vergleich zu den anderen Untergrund-Theatern zeichnet sich das BTT durch folgende Eigentümlichkeiten aus:

1. Starker Gruppencharakter, aber als ein ständig in Bewegung bleibender Körper, sogar unter kollektiver Leitung. (Eigentlich wurde das BTT von drei Theatergruppen zunächst als "Theater Zentrum 1968" gegründet).

2. Seit 1970 begann die Gruppe mit seinem schwarzen Zelt als eine Art Wandertruppe überall in Japan aufzutreten, und 1971 benannte sie sich in "Black Tent 68/71" um. In 20 Jahren gastierte die Truppe an 120 Orten und nutzte dabei bis 1990 zwei Zelte ab.

3. Seit 1990 nennt sich die Gruppe "Black Tent Theater" (BTT) und ist seitdem in Zelten, in großen Theatern, im eigenen Studio, im Freien, aber auch auf Auslandstourneen in Asien (Hongkong Art Festival) oder in

Europa (Avignon Off-Festival) aufgetreten. Sato hat dazu geäußert: "Die Reise ist schon fast ein Teil unseres Körpers geworden."[9]

4. Zum Theater gehören im Grunde drei Regisseure: Sato, Yamamoto und Kato. Jeder von ihnen ist Dramatiker, Regisseur und Organisator zugleich und alle arbeiten auf verschiedene Weise zusammen. Gleichzeitig geht jedes Mitglied der Gruppe auch außerhalb des BTT seiner eigenen Tätigkeit nach — als Dramatiker, Regisseur, Fernsehschauspieler oder Musiker, oder, im Falle Satos, auch als Universitätsprofessor und Intendant des Setagaya Public Theater (SePT) oder Za-Koenji-Theaters.

5. Aber nicht nur Regisseure und Schauspieler, sondern auch Dramaturgen und Herausgeber arbeiten im BTT zusammen, wie der Verleger Kaitaro Tsuno, der Romanist Ryuko Saeki oder der Japanologe David Goodmann, die in den frühen Jahren der Gruppe dramaturgisch, theoretisch und redaktionell tätig waren und später alle Universitätsprofessoren wurden. Das BTT ist seit jeher eine hochintellektuelle Theatergruppe.

6. Das Repertoire der Gruppe ist ebenfalls sehr vielseitig und schließt neben Sprechtheater und Musiktheater auch Revues, Konzerte und Liederabende ein. Außerdem gibt das BTT eine Zeitschrift heraus und produziert Poster und Kataloge. Heute hat das seit 40 Jahren bestehende BTT 40 Mitglieder, die einerseits fest angestellt sind, andererseits aber locker wie ein Freundeskreis organisiert sind. Allerdings versucht das BTT zur Zeit einen Generationswechsel zu vollziehen.

7. Bei all dem spielen im Grunde der theatralische Gedanke und die Methode Brechts eine zentrale Rolle. Das BTT ist sicherlich die japanische Theatergruppe, auf die Brecht den größten Einfluss ausgeübt hat, obwohl sich das nicht an der Zahl der Brecht-Produktionen und -Aufführungen ablesen lässt.

4. Die 1990er Jahre: "Brecht-Renaissance" und "Brecht Re-Lektüren" am BTT

1989 läutete eine Reihe von szenischen "Re-Lektüren" eine "Brecht-Renaissance" am BTT ein, und zwar unter folgenden Schlagworten: "Brecht soll interessant sein," "Wir müssen Brecht auf amüsante Weise auf die Bühne bringen," "Brecht ist ein Volksstückschreiber!"[10] Der Versuch, mit Brecht die eigene Geschichte zu reflektieren und die eigene Theatertätigkeit zu popularisieren, war eine Reaktion darauf, dass Brecht zu diesem Zeitpunkt für die junge Generation nicht mehr so interessant war.

Der erste Versuch war *Die Dreigroschenoper à la BTT* (1989), in Yamamotos Bearbeitung und Satos Inszenierung. Die Handlung wurde an den Anfang der Meiji-Ära in Tokyo verlegt, einer Zeit großer Umwälzungen Japans auf dem Weg zur Modernisierung. Bettler, Gangster und Prostituierte treten in einer Punk-Oper über Habgier und Liebschaften auf, die aber nicht als vergangene, sondern als zukünftige Geschichte erzählt wird. Die Charaktere fragen implizit, ob und wie sich Japan seit Beginn der Meiji-Zeit verändert hat und sich in Zukunft verändern wird. Macheath wird als "Saheiji Messer" von Saito gespielt und gesungen und von einer Live-Band begleitet. Die Produktion wurde im neuen schwarzen Zelt auf dem Hof des Tsukiji-Honganji Tempels aufgeführt und ging danach auf Tournee durch ganz Japan. Amüsant, lebendig, kitschig und kritisch, war diese Inszenierung ein guter Anfang der "Brecht-Renaissance" des BTT, mit guter Resonanz beim Publikum.

BTT: *Die Dreigroschenoper à la BTT*, in Kiyokazu Yamamotos Bearbeitung und Makoto Satos Inszenierung, 1989. © BTT

1992 folgte *Herr Hazama ["zwischen"] und Fräulein Sumi ["Ecke"]* nach *Der gute Mensch von Sezuan*, erneut in der Bearbeitung Yamamotos und in Satos Inszenierung. *Herr Hazama* wurde im großen Honda-Theater aufgeführt und tourte danach ebenfalls durch Japan. 1993 folgte dann *Im Dickicht der Städte*, bearbeitet und inszeniert von Kato, und mit neuer Musik und Choreographie. Diese Inszenierungen fanden aber nicht so großen Anklang wie die *Dreigroschenoper à la BTT*.

Danach folgten verschiedene Bearbeitungen klassischer und moderner Stücke im Geiste Brechts: Satos *Warten lassen auf Gogo – drei Kluge aus dem Osten* nach Becketts *Warten auf Godot* (1991); Yamamotos *Der schalkhafte Kaufmann in Nagasaki à la Oper* nach Shakespeares *Kaufmann von Venedig* (1994); *Eunuch* von Kuo Pao Kun, einem bekannten Dramatiker aus

Singapur, von Sato bearbeitet und inszeniert (1996); Shakespeares *Romeo und Julia* als Zusammenarbeit mit PETA, von Yamamoto und Rody Vera bearbeitet und sowohl auf den Philippinen als auch in Japan aufgeführt (1997); *Dickicht* nach Brecht, von Sato bearbeitet und inszeniert; sowie eine Wiederaufnahme von Büchners *Woyzeck*, von Sato bearbeitet und inszeniert (1998), und viele mehr.

2002 brachte das BTT als besondere Produktion der "Brecht-Renaissance" am BTT *Mutter Courage in der verborgenen Festung* auf die Bühne, von Yamamoto bearbeitet und von Sato inszeniert. Danach wurde 2004 wieder *Die Dreigroschenoper* im schwarzen Zelt des BTT am Ikegamihonganji-Tempel aufgeführt, mit Yamamotos Text, aber in einer Neuinszenierung von Sato. (Auf diese Inszenierung wird im folgenden eingegangen.) Man kann aus der Aufführungsgeschichte des BTT folgern, dass die "Brecht-Renaissance" immer noch andauert, der Überzeugung Satos entsprechend, dass Brechts Theaterinnovationen immer noch neue Anregungen bieten.

Diese Auffassung teilen nach meinem Eindruck inzwischen auch andere Theaterleute in Japan. Aus Anlass des 100. Geburtstags und 50. Todesjahres von Brecht hat es verschiedene Versuche auch innerhalb der jungen japanischen Generation von Theatermachern gegeben, Brecht neu zu überdenken und seine Stücke auf die Bühne zu bringen. Brecht ist wohl auch in Japan, zumindest teilweise, ein Klassiker geworden.

1999 wurde z.B. sogar eine von dem Dramatiker Ren Saito geschriebene und von Sato inszenierte *Brecht-Oper* am Neuen Nationaltheater in Tokyo uraufgeführt und dann überall in Japan gezeigt. In dieser Oper erscheinen Brecht, Walter Benjamin, Helene Weigel, Elisabeth Hauptmann, Margarete Steffin und Asja Lacis, also Brecht und seine Frauen, als Charaktere auf der Bühne. Das Leben Brechts wurde aus verschiedenen Blickwinkeln repräsentiert: aus der Perspektive seines dänischen Exils in Svendborg, dem retrospektiven Rückblick auf seinen Lebenslauf, aber auch im Blick auf die Zukunft.[11] Diese Oper ist, als erste japanische Brecht-Oper, ein gutes Beispiel dafür, wie tief Brecht schon Wurzeln in Japan geschlagen hat.

5. Das 21. Jahrhundert: Drei neuere Produktionen der *Mutter Courage* und andere Brecht-Inszenierungen

Im Folgenden werden drei neuere *Mutter Courage*-Aufführungen vorgestellt, um die japanische Theatersituation zu veranschaulichen. Zunächst soll auf *Mutter Courage in der verborgenen Festung* (BTT 2002) eingegangen werden.

So wie der Titel dem Film *Die verborgene Festung* (1958) von Akira Kurosawa entliehen wurde, wurde auch die ursprüngliche europäische Handlung, die während des Dreißigjährigen Krieges spielt, in die Nagoya-

BTT: *Mutter Courage in der verborgenen Festung*, in Kiyokazu Yamamotos Bearbeitung und Makoto Satos Inszenierung, 2002. © BTT

Gegend (Zentraljapan) im Kriegszeitalter des 16. Jahrhunderts (der "Zeit der streitenden Reiche" in Japan) verlegt. Die Gegenspieler sind General Nobunaga Oda und die religiöse Fraktion der Ikkō Sekte, und alle Charaktere tragen Kimono-Kostüme wie in einem historischen Drama. Die Inszenierung wurde im schwarzen Zelt auf dem West-Marktplatz Kitasenjyu in Nord-Tokyo aufgeführt. Am Anfang, als der Zeltvorhang aufgezogen wurde, konnte man den in Dämmerlicht getauchten Vorplatz des Zeltes sehen. Aus der Ferne kam, begleitet von Pauken und Trompeten, ein Lastwagen, in dessen Mitte die in Oraku umbenannte Mutter Courage saß. Sie kam mit ihrer Kapelle vom Raku-Markt, hinter dem man die realen Häuser der Unterstadt im herbstlichen Abendlicht sehen konnte. Dies alles wirkte wie eine Revue aus dem Kriegszeitalter. Die Oraku, die Mutter Courage, wird hier von einem Mann gespielt, Saito, dem Hauptschauspieler des BTT. Für Oraku ist auch der Krieg ein Geschäft, Geschosse und Granaten sind lediglich Handelsware, wenngleich verbunden mit Lebensgefahr. Im Zelt entwickelt sich ein zugleich lustiges und schmerzliches bürgerliches Drama zwischen Mutter und Kindern, aber als am Ende der Zeltvorhang wieder aufgeht, entschwindet Oraku, diesmal allein, begleitet von munterer Musik in die Ferne. Die Außenwelt, die für sie früher ein Marktplatz war, auf dem sie vom Kriegszeitalter profitieren konnte, ist jetzt zu einem kalten Schlachtfeld im Lebenskampf verkommen. Dies alles wird als amüsante, aber bittere Gegenwartskomödie wahrgenommen.

Die Geschichte ist fast dieselbe wie bei Brecht. Aber ist das Brecht? Nein. Eine Kopie? Auch nicht! Was ist es dann? Es ist ein Werk Yamamotos. Geschrieben und auch inszeniert "nach Brecht," aber ein Werk des BTT—so behauptet das BTT. Deswegen ist das Stück auch nicht in der japanischen Aufführungsliste von Brechts *Mutter Courage* registriert, auch seine *Dreigroschenoper* nicht, obwohl beide in der japanischen Brecht-Rezeption als bahnbrechend eingeschätzt werden. "Brecht ist ein Volksstückschreiber, so müssen wir auch unser Volksstück auf die Bühne bringen," war sicher eine Grundidee des BTT dabei. Dahinter steckt nicht nur eine methodologische Frage (Brecht hatte auch John Gays *The Beggar's Opera* verarbeitet oder "plagiiert"), sondern auch die Frage nach der Autorenschaft. Wie sieht es jetzt nach dem 50. Todesjahr Brechts eigentlich damit aus?

Das ist auch ein Grund, warum man die jetzige Zeit als die fünfte Phase der japanischen Brecht-Rezeption bezeichnen kann. Doch nicht nur deswegen. Seit Beginn des 21. Jahrhunderts wurden auch viele andere Brechtstücke in Japan aufgeführt, unter anderem mehrmals *Mutter Courage*, vermutlich weil wir immer noch im Kriegszeitalter leben. In den letzten Jahren habe ich selbst über zehn neue *Mutter Courage*-Inszenierungen gesehen. Zwei davon möchte ich noch als Beispiele anführen, da ich an der Neuübersetzung beteiligt war.

Die zweite *Mutter Courage* wurde, mit der beliebten Starschauspielerin Shinobu Ohtake in der Titelrolle, im Neuen Nationaltheater 2005 von Tamiya Kuriyama im Zusammenhang mit dem "Deutschlandjahr in Japan" inszeniert. Hier sollen nur einige wenige Dinge benannt werden: Mutter Courage wurde als alleinstehende Mutter und Karrierefrau in den besten Jahren dargestellt (wobei Ohtake selbst so alt ist wie die Mutter Courage bei Brecht, nämlich Mitte vierzig; darüberhinaus ist sie anmutig und beliebt). Das Stück wurde als Gegenwartsstück in heutiger Sprache und in schnellem Tempo gespielt, aber nicht als Antikriegsdrama, sondern als Kriegsdrama, weil die Charaktere alle vom und für den Krieg leben. Paul Dessaus Musik wurde neu arrangiert, und das Bühnenbild erinnerte an den Irakkrieg oder an "Ground Zero" nach dem 11. September, 2001. Am Ende der Aufführung wurden die Namen der geschichtlichen Epochen von 1636 bis über 2005 hinaus auf eine Leinwand projiziert.

Die dritte Produktion wurde 2010 vom "The Bird Theater" inszeniert. Diese junge Theatergruppe hat 2006 in Tottori in Westjapan ihre Theatertätigkeit neu begonnen, nachdem sie zuvor in Tokyo und Shizuoka ansässig war. Die Mitglieder der Gruppe haben die alte große Sporthalle der ehemaligen Volksschule in Tottori in ein Theater mit 180 Publikumsplätzen umgebaut und dort auch *Mutter Courage* aufgeführt.

The Bird Theater: *Mutter Courage und ihre Kinder*, inszeniert von Makoto Nakashima in Tottori/Westjapan, 2010. © The Bird Theater

Diese Inszenierung zeichnet sich durch folgende Merkmale aus: der junge Regisseur Makoto Nakashima (1972-) hat dem Brecht-Drama eine Rahmenstruktur gegeben, indem er Brecht selbst auf der Bühne als Kommentator erscheinen und von einer Schauspielerin als Drahtzieher der gesamten Veranstaltung spielen läßt. Dadurch wird die geschichtliche und räumliche Distanz des Publikums zum Stück deutlich, aber am Ende wird auch klar gemacht, dass der Krieg immer noch auf dieser Welt andauert, indem gegenwärtige Kriegsszenen als Videomontage hintereinander gezeigt werden. Als Musik werden vertraute japanische Kriegs- und Soldatenlieder benutzt, die man immer noch in Pachinko-Spielhallen hören kann.

Diese drei Inszenierungen haben alle Brechts *Mutter Courage* neu übersetzt, interpretiert, bearbeitet oder umgearbeitet, je nach Standpunkt. Gleichzeitig ließe sich noch auf andere neue Tendenzen der "Brecht-Rezeption" hinweisen.

Ein gutes Beispiel für die postdramatische Brecht-Rezeption in Japan ist die Duo-Performance *Bre. Brecht* von Yoko Tawada als Autorin/Performerin und Aki Takase als Jazzpianistin, die im Herbst 2003 beim "Brecht-Theaterfest in Brechtmanier" im Theater X aufgeführt wurde. Wie es der Titel schon andeutet, ist diese Performance sowohl ein Wort- als auch ein Assoziationsspiel mit Brecht, bei dem die einzelnen Wörter mit anderen Wörtern in immer stärkere Verbindung gebracht werden, bis sie miteinander verflochten sind: "bureru" ("verwackeln"), "zureru" ("sich verschieben"), "swing suru" ("schwingen"), "break" im Englischen, "brechen" im Deutschen, sowie "prä-." Ausgehend vom Terminus "Post-Brechtisches Theater" wird aber nicht etwa "Prä-Brecht," sondern "Bre-Brecht" assoziiert. Diese "Verwacklungsweise" charakterisiert die ganze Performance. In der Tat gibt es in Tawadas Texten[12] oft Stellen, wo man denkt: "Daher kommt das also," natürlich unter der Prämisse, dass man sich gut bei Brecht auskennt. Wenn man diesen Zusammenhang erkennen kann, findet man die Verbindungen Tawadas noch lustiger. Tawadas Rückgriff auf Brecht ist jedoch kein Verfahren, bei dem sie einen Dialog mit Brecht führt oder sich auf Brecht stützt. Vielmehr spielt sie mit Brecht, sie usurpiert ihn, wickelt ihn um den Finger, zeigt ihm manchmal sogar die Zunge und macht sich über ihn lustig. Ist diese Verfahrensweise im wirklichen Sinne intertextuell? Tawada selbst hat geäußert, dass ihre Vorliebe für Brecht bei weitem nicht so groß ist wie man vermuten könnte, was für sie aber gerade deshalb ein Grund für ihre rebellische Haltung ist.

Aber die "Brecht-Theaterfeste in Brechtmanier" 2003 und 2004 im Theater X waren selbst voll von einem post-dramatischen und post-Brechtischen, um nicht zu sagen, einem anderen Brecht-Geist erfüllt. Symbolisch war die Anfangs-Aufführung "Eine Stunde und 20 Minuten am 1. und 2. Oktober beim Brecht-Theaterfest in Brechtmanier im Theater X," die als freie Adaptation der "Lehrstücke" Brechts von Akira Takayama (1969-) und der Theatergruppe Port B konzipiert und inszeniert waren. Der Regisseur Takayama schreibt:

> In the "Lehr-stücke" [sic] ("exemplary plays") by B. Brecht, the matter which occurred on the stage itself was not the essence of the work. But rather the relation between the matters on the stage and the audience that should have decided the quality of the work. Brecht critically dealt with the way of "reception" by the public in a mass, that was: they *consume* the *products* on the stage. Over fixed division between producers and consumers, he indicated a theater that the audience would also be a producer/critic simultaneously, not just remaining as a consumer. After this conversion, the substance of the "reception" by audiences became so creative/critical that it became a matter of "how I connect with a world" = "how I create a world, *me*, or *myself*." If a theater works in such way as occurs with those conversions, certainly it would be worth calling "exemplary plays" as *educational* and *political* at the same time. And if we search for possibilities of "exemplary plays" in our time, it will be necessary first to "alienate" such concepts as educations or politics in a sense mentioned above, rather than to deal with these concepts in capital letters which tends to be easily consumed. If we realize the "Lehrstücke" today, the result will completely different from "Lehrstücke" of Brecht.

The point at issue is not Brecht himself, but is our attitude how and what we receive from Brecht's "Lehrstücke", and to show a new way of "reception" before audiences in our time now and here, and that is our essential intention in this play.[13]

Dabei wurden aber nicht Szenen aus Brechts "Lehrstücken," sondern Texte aus Brechts früher Gedichtsammlung *Hauspostille* unter dem Titel "Eine Stunde und 20 Minuten am 1. und 2. Oktober beim Brecht-Theaterfest in Brechtmanier im Theatre X" frei konzipiert, bearbeitet und benutzt. Man könnte sagen, dass Brechts "Lehrstück"-Theorie in vielerlei Variationen das theaterkonzeptionelle Rückgrat von Port B bildet.

Was die "Brecht-Nachklänge" in Japan betrifft, lassen sich viele verschiedene Aspekte und Beispiele finden. Akira Ichikawa und Joachim Lucchesi berichten in diesem Band zum Beispiel über die japanische Theatergruppe Ishinha. Ich denke, mit diesen drei Essays werden die Hauptlinien der jetzigen japanischen Brecht-Rezeption im Überblick dargestellt.

Anmerkungen

1   Was die japanische Brecht-Rezeption betrifft, wurde u.a. die Bibliographie "Die japanische Brecht-Rezeption bis 1984" (auf Japanisch) von Michiko Tanigawa und Hirokazu Akiba in der Zeitschrift der Japanischen Gesellschaft für Germanistik (JGG) *Doitsu-Bungaku (Deutsche Literatur*") in drei Teilen 1985-1986 veröffentlicht, insgesamt 87 Seiten (mit Aufführungsliste).
2   Was die japanische Brecht-Rezeption im Einzelnen betrifft, vergleiche Tatsuji Iwabuchi, "Brecht-Reception in Japan," in Antony Tatlow und Tak-Wai Wong, Hrsg., *Brecht and East Asian Theatre* (Hong Kong: Hong Kong University-Press, 1982), S. 119-129. Vergleiche zugleich Tatsuji Iwabuchi, "Brecht-Rezeption in Japan aus der Perspektive der Theaterpraxis," in Elisabeth Gossmann und Günter Zobel, Hrsg., *Das Gold in Wachs: Festschrift für Thomas Immoos* (München: Iudicium Verlag, München, 1988), S. 249-264. Vergleiche auch Michiko Tanigawa, "Politik der Kulturen—Rezeption des deutschen Theaters im Hinblick auf die Modernisierung Japans," in Eiichiro Hirata und Hans-Thies Lehmann, Hrsg., *Theater in Japan* (Berlin: Theater der Zeit, 2009), S. 186-197. Vergleiche insbesondere Tadashi Uchino, "Political Displacements: Towards Historicizing Brecht in Japan, 1932-98," S. 29-52, in *Crucible Bodies: Postwar Japanese Performance from Brecht to the New Millennium* (London and Calcutta: Seagull Books, 2009).
3   Hirokazu Akiba, "Brecht-Rezeption in Japan: Am Beispiel von Hisashi Inoue," *Dreigroschenheft* 4 (2010): S. 18-22.
4   Hisashi Inoue, "Nachrede zu 'Vater Mockinpott wieder' (auf Japanisch), in Hisashi Inoue *Vater Mockinpott wieder (Mockinpott shi,hutatabi),* (Tokyo: Kodansha Verlag, 1985), S. 248.
5   Die japanische Bewegung des Untergrund-Theaters beginnt erst jetzt als wissenschaftlicher Gegenstand untersucht zu werden. Im Herbst 2008 fand an der Waseda Universität (als GCOE-Programm) eine dreitägige internationale Konferenz zum Thema "Reconsidering the Unterground Theatre of the 1960s" statt. Gleichzeitig fand eine Ausstellung von Postern des Untergrundtheaters statt.

6   Koreya Senda, "Brecht-engeki to watashi (Brechts Theater und ich)," in Koreya Senda, *Dramaturgie von Senda Koreya*, Bd. 6 (Tokyo: Miraisha Verlag, 1982), S. 287.
7   David G. Goodman, jetzt Professor für Japanische Literatur an der University of Illinois, war einer der Mitbegründer des BTT und Herausgeber der ersten englischen Theaterzeitschrift in Japan, *Concerned Theatre Japan*, die aktiv versuchte, neues japanisches Drama und Theater außerhalb Japans bekannt zu machen. Goodman arbeitet zur Zeit an einer Geschichte des modernen japanischen Dramas.
8   Interview mit Makoto Sato (auf Japanisch) in *Hyogikai-Tushin* (*Neuigkeiten vom BTT*) 21 (September 1981): S. 13.
9   Interview mit Makoto Sato (auf Japanisch) in Ebd. 56 (November 1984): S. 8.
10   Damals konnte man solche Slogans häufig auf den Postern oder Flugblättern des BTT lesen.
11   Dabei wurde auch mein Buch berücksichtigt: Michiko Tanigawa, *Seibo to Shofu wo koete –Brecht to Onnatati no Kyousei (Frauenbilder jenseits von Hure und Heiliger. Brechts Symbiose mit den Frauen)* (Tokyo: Kadensya Verlag, 1988). Vergleiche Michiko Tanigawa, "Der Apfel Brechts und seiner Frauen. Reise auf der Suche ihrer Spuren im Exil," in Rainer Noltenius, Hrsg., *Bertolt Brecht und Hans Tombrock – Eine Künstlerfreundschaft im skandinavischen Exil* (Essen: Klartext Verlag, 2004), S. 17-25.
12   Tawadas japanische Texte: Yoko Tawada, (auf Japanisch:) "< Bre. Brecht> no Si yori ("Gedichte aus ‚Bre. Brecht'"), in *Subaru* 12 (2003): S. 72-83. Vergleiche auch Michiko Tanigawa, "Performative Über-setzungen/über-setzende Performance. Zur Topologie der Sprache von Yoko Tawada," in Christine Ivanovic, Hrsg., *Yoko Tawada. Poetik der Transformation. Beiträge zum Gesamtwerk* (Tübingen: Stauffenburg Verlag, 2010), S. 351-368.
13   Port B: 30. September 2010: <http://www.portb.net/eng/arch_frame.html?brecht/bre_home.html>.

Jan-Jan-Opera and Osaka Rap
Part I:
Echoes of Brecht in the Theater *Ishinha*

Joachim Lucchesi

The theater group *Ishinha* was founded in 1970 by Yukichi Matsumoto in Osaka and belongs to the most significant avantgarde theaters in Japan. The Jan-Jan-Opera, developed by Matsumoto from 1991 on, derives from the Jan-Jan-dialect of the region of Kansai. It is used for a form of musicalized speaking called "Osaka Rap." It is a polyrhythmic, choric-syllabic and five- or seven-bar form of *Sprechgesang*, an onomatopoeic music exploring the sound of words.

Matsumoto's productions recall theatrical experiments by Brecht, they unite rhythm, movement, choral singsong, music and choreographed mass movement in a collective of arts. Both use gestus as an essential element of their theater. At the same time they produce tension in their texts by emphasizing the uniqueness of a thought or an image through the rhythmically accentuated placing of a syllable, word, or group of words.

1970 gründete Yukichi Matsumoto in Osaka die Theatergruppe *Ishinha*, die seitdem zu den bedeutendsten Avantgarde-Theatern Japans gehört. Matsumotos ab 1991 entwickelte Jan-Jan-Oper leitet sich vom Jan-Jan-Dialekt der Kansai-Region her, er wird benutzt für ein musikalisiertes Sprechen, "Osaka Rap" genannt. Es ist ein polyrhythmischer, chorisch-syllabischer und fünf- oder siebentaktiger Sprechgesang, eine lautmalerische Wortklang-Musik.

Matsumotos Produktionen erinnern an Experimente des Theaters von Brecht, sie vereinen Rhythmus, Bewegung, chorischen Singsang, Musik und choreographierte Massenbewegung zu einem Kollektiv der Künste. Beide benutzen den Gestus als wesentliches Element ihres Theaters. Zugleich stellen sie jeweils eine Spannung in ihren Texten her, indem sie durch das rhythmisch akzentuierte Platzieren einer Silbe, eines Worts oder einer Wortgruppe das Besondere eines Gedankens oder eines Bildes hervorheben.

Jan-Jan-Oper und Osaka Rap
Teil 1
Brecht-Nachklänge im Theater *Ishinha*

Joachim Lucchesi

Die Theatergruppe *Ishinha*, 1970 von Yukichi Matsumoto in der Hafenstadt Osaka gegründet und inzwischen mit renommierten Preisen ausgezeichnet, ist heute eines der bedeutendsten Avantgarde-Theater Japans. Ihre außergewöhnlichen Produktionen erregen dort, aber auch in anderen Teilen der Welt, großes Aufsehen. Das von der Gruppe Mitte der 1980er Jahre entwickelte Outdoor-Theater bricht mit seiner Bevorzugung spektakulärer Auftrittsorte tradierte Muster internationaler Theater-Verortung: so werden gigantische Rangierbahnhöfe Tokios zu industriellen Open-Air Panoramen (*Shonen-gai/Stadt der Jungen*, 1991), Hafendocks in Osaka dienen als soziale Metaphern (*Romance/Romanze*, 1996) oder ein großer See wird in den Spielort mit einbezogen (*Kokyu Kikai/Atemmaschine*, 2008). Diese und andere Spielwelten—oft aufwändige Theaterarchitekturen—vermitteln symbolhaft einen Querschnitt durch Lebenswelten im 20. und 21. Jahrhundert. Matsumotos weitgehender Verzicht auf den institutionalisierten und "verorteten" Theaterbetrieb, sein Experimentieren mit Formen des sich stets neu bildenden und verschwindenden Outdoor-Theaters, sein Aufbau einer auf Kollektivität der Lebens- und Kunstbereiche basierenden Theatergruppe—also Leben und Kunst an einem Ort—deutet bereits auf ein ästhetisches Konzept, das in den Produktionen zur vollen Entfaltung gelangt.

Seit 1991, rund zwanzig Jahre nach Gründung von *Ishinha*, inszeniert der 1946 in Kumamoto auf der Insel Kyushu geborene Matsumoto die von ihm entwickelte Jan-Jan-Oper. Die Bezeichnung leitet sich von einer sehr lebendigen, urbanen Arbeiterwohngegend in Osaka her, wo der vom Hochjapanischen abweichende Jan-Jan-Dialekt der Kansai-Region gesprochen wird; dort ist auch die Gruppe *Ishinha* beheimatet. Doch entspricht die Jan-Jan-Oper, die Ähnlichkeiten zum balinesischen Sprechgesang des Kecak aufweist, nicht einem europäisch geprägten Operntypus mit Solisten, Arien, Duetten, Ensembles, Chören und so weiter. Sie bezieht sich auch nicht auf andere asiatische Formen wie die Peking-Oper (Jingju). Vielmehr benutzt sie den Osaka-Dialekt für ein musikalisiertes Sprechen, das auch "Osaka Rap" genannt wird. Es ist ein polyrhythmischer, chorisch-syllabischer und fünf- oder siebentaktiger Sprechgesang, in dem der vibrierende Puls der Straße hörbar wird, eine lautmalerische Wortklang-Musik. Die sprachliche Kommunikation zwischen den Akteuren auf der Bühne besteht zumeist aus Abfolgen einzelner, semantisch unverbundener Worte, die rhythmisch repetiert werden. Die Kraft der Worte, von denen Matsumoto die metallisch hart klingenden bevorzugt, entwickelt sich aus ihrer beschwörenden Wiederholung, aus dem Gestus ihres beharrlichen Aufrufens:

> I have been influenced by his [that is Kenji Miyazawa's[1]] forms of expression, as if there is spirit inside a lump of mineral. The fact that the lines in my scripts are often strings of metallic and material nouns may be because I learned about the mineral quality of expression from Kenji Miyazawa. I have never staged a Miyazawa play but I probably have been influenced by his worldview. But for me, Kenji Miyazawa is a literary giant, so I don't try to talk about his work like an authority.[2]

Jan-Jan-Oper kann verstanden werden als ein Dialog ohne Konversation, als Musik ohne Gesang, als Tanz ohne das Tänzerische. Die traditionellen, klassischen Kunstformen des Theaters wie Sprache, Gesang und Tanz werden bei *Ishinha* zugleich aufgerufen und verweigert. Doch keineswegs entsteht daraus ein Anti- oder Verweigerungstheater, im Gegenteil: die Produktionen sind von einer hohen Sinnlichkeit und Expressivität, einem Unterhaltungswert im besten Brechtschen Sinn. Die Akteure fühlen sich gegenüber ihrem Publikum als Entertainer verpflichtet, als Lieferanten eines höchst unterhaltsam zu gestaltenden Theaterabends—dieses Dienstleistungsbewusstsein gegenüber dem Publikum, dem Kunden, dem Mandanten und so weiter ist ein prägender Charakterzug der im Kansai-Gebiet lebenden Menschen. Er sei sich nicht ganz sicher, äußert Matsumoto, ob ihr Theaterstil etwas mit Osaka zu tun habe. Aber er vermute, dass ihr Theater, falls es in Tokyo beheimatet wäre, dort einen traditionellen Standard pflegen würde. Obwohl die Bezeichnung Jan-Jan-Oper ihre Verortung im Opernhaus assoziieren lässt, ist ihre Präsentation eher mit einem großdimensionierten Zirkus vergleichbar, einer Sportarena oder einem zeitgenössischen Themenpark der Unterhaltungsindustrie. Dass *Ishinha* vor allem bei Gastspielen immer wieder in die Situation gerät, auf herkömmlichen Theaterbühnen auftreten zu müssen, widerspricht dem nicht.

Im Laufe der Jahre entwickelte Matsumoto seine Idee von einem Gesamtkunstwerk, die zwar zu Richard Wagner oder Brecht Affinitäten aufweist, im Ganzen jedoch einmalig ist. Das Ineinandergreifen von chorischen Arrangements, blitzschnellen Positionswechseln, von Musik, polyrhythmisch anspruchsvollem Sprechgesang und artistischen Präzisionsgesten der Darsteller entwickelt einen bildmächtigen Ausdruckssog, der den Zuschauer in seinen Bann zieht: er wird emotional stark berührt, ohne dabei seine intellektuelle Wachheit zu verlieren. Ein Idealzustand, eine Zuschaukunst ist das, die sich Brecht für sein Publikum immer erhofft hatte: mit Rauschzuständen zwar, doch ohne die Klarheit des Denkens trübende Vergiftungserscheinungen durch Drogen. Bildet das europäische Theater der Gegenwart im Allgemeinen—aber auch zu

Brechts Zeiten und davor—Orte der Intimität und der Konzentration auf das sich dar- und ausstellende Subjekt, auf den Einzeldarsteller, so zeigt Matsumoto ein nahezu entindividualisiertes, körperhaft-physisches Massentheater, wo subjektiver Entfaltung und detailreicher Typisierung nur wenig Raum gegeben wird.

Matsumotos Produktionen, die gewollt oder ungewollt an Experimente des deutschen und russischen Avantgarde-Theaters eines Brecht, Erwin Piscator, Alexander Tairow oder Wsewolod Meyerhold erinnern, vereinen Rhythmus, Bewegung, chorischen Singsang, Musik und choreographierte Massenbewegung zu einem Kollektiv der Künste. Hier entfalten sich Aktionsräume eines nichtillusionistischen Antiheldentheaters, welches das subjektiv-individualistisch geprägte westeuropäische Theater heute kaum noch kennt. Matsumotos Menschen- und Architekturbilder sind virtuos gestaltet, ja ritualisiert und von Zitaten des internationalen Films, der Fotografie, der Architektur, des Dadaismus und der surrealistischen Malerei beeinflusst. Er setzt in eine manchmal schwer zu enträtselnde, auf Überwältigung zielende Bilderwelt präzis choreographierte Darstellermassen, einem menschlichen Maschinentheater ähnlich, das auch von Fritz Langs Film *Metropolis* oder heutigen Video-Clips geprägt sein könnte.

Die sorgfältig komponierte Performance mit ihrer raffinierten Lichtregie weist epische und parabelhafte Elemente auf, die an Kafka oder Brecht erinnern. Sie ist mit einer repetierenden, minimalistischen Musik durchsetzt und fordert von der Gruppe neben sportiver Höchstleistung eine Künstlichkeit in der musikalisierten Darstellung und Bewegung, die jedoch soziale Bezüge zur "offenen" Welt nicht ausschließt. Jeweils über einige Monate hinweg arbeitet Matsumoto an einer neuen Inszenierung zusammen mit den Akteuren—seinen von ihm so genannten "urban kids" —obschon sie durchschnittlich etwa 25 Jahre alt sind. In diesem Zeitraum lebt er mit ihnen zusammen, der Spielort Theater wird zum Lebens- und Erfahrungsort erweitert. Aus diesem komplexen Gravitationszentrum heraus entwickelt er das künstlerische Konzept seines Theaters:

> The thing that I am most concerned about is how today's young people have lost a sense of home. They have no hometown in their hearts. I tell the young people in our company to create a hometown in their hearts, even if they have to go out and find one deliberately. A person without a nostalgic hometown is not really a full person. That hometown doesn't have to be one with a traditional Japanese style wooden house. It could be the South harbor section of Osaka where Ishinha does its outdoor productions, or it could be an apartment building. I tell them to find a hometown and create lots of legends around it. Because I believe you can find nostalgia almost anyplace. I think the

> novelist Haruki Murakami has tried to create something like the nostalgia of an apartment complex. I think everyone should find or create their own hometown.³

Immer wieder bilden Vergangenheit und Zukunft großer Städte mit ihrer "Masse Mensch" (dominanter Fokus auch bei Brecht) ein Thema von *Ishinha*. So behandelt Matsumoto in seinem Projekt *Nostalgia* die inzwischen vergessenen japanischen Emigrationsströme Richtung Brasilien zu Beginn des 20. Jahrhunderts; er zeigt die Entwurzelung der auf Verdienst und Wohlergehen hoffenden Aussiedler, ihre allmähliche Verwandlung zu Nippon-Brasileiros, ihre Ausbeutung, Enttäuschung, ihr über Generationen schwindendes Heimweh sowie den damit einhergehenden Verlust ihrer kulturellen und sprachlichen Identität. Matsumoto breitet ein sozialgeschichtliches Panorama aus, das nicht nur Zeitgeschichte Japans und Brasiliens zum Vorschein bringt, sondern auch Modell ist für all die gewaltigen Aus- und Einwanderungsbewegungen, Kriege und Katastrophen, welche die Welt des 20. Jahrhunderts nachhaltig geprägt haben.

Obdach- und Heimatlosigkeit, Entwurzelung, Entfremdung und Flucht quer über Kontinente und Ozeane sind Erfahrungen, die auch Brecht—"öfter als die Schuhe die Länder wechselnd"⁴—machen musste und die er eindringlich zur Sprache gebracht hat. Im übertragenen Sinn ist Matsumotos Biographie gleichfalls vom Transitären, Instabilen geprägt; es stellt Bezüge zur eigenen Theaterarbeit her, die sich mit den Outdoor-Produktionen immer wieder verflüchtigt. Assoziationen zu Wanderbühnen und Thespiskarren drängen sich auf, letzterer verwandelt sich auf der Bühne in den geschäftig-rollenden Planwagen der Mutter Courage.

Drei zentrale Elemente prägen das Theater *Ishinha*: die Körperarbeit, die damit verbundene Musik sowie das Bühnenbild. Bereits vor der Fixierung und Niederschrift des Stücks beginnt Matsumoto mit der Körperarbeit. Der Regisseur und Stückeschreiber, der sein Theater auch als Komposition körperlicher Ausdrucksfolgen, als ein In-sich-Hineinversenken in eigene Körperlichkeit begreift, verweist auf sein Konzept einer gewollt "unnatürlichen Bewegung," auf Verweigerung eines physiologisch natürlichen Bewegungsablaufs. Diese Austreibung natürlich gegebener Körperbewegungen erfordert eine mühevoll einstudierte Technik, wenn beispielsweise ein Siebenachtel-Beat für Beinbewegungen und ein Dreiachtel-Beat für die Arme erforderlich sind. Hinzu kommt die gesamte Ensemblechoreographie sowie chorischer Sprechgesang in unregelmäßigen Rhythmen: jeder Darsteller hat also mit seinem Körper und seiner Stimme eine Vielzahl komplizierter, oft gegenläufiger Prozesse zu koordinieren. Eine hochartistische Angelegenheit ist dies, welche die Gattungsgrenzen zwischen Gymnastik, modernem Ballett, Dancefloor und Stimmlichem aufbricht, um etwas Neues zu formen. Matsumoto betont, dass die musikalisch begleitete Bewegung auf der Bühne auch kein Jazz Dance sei, dafür hätten die Akteure keine geeigneten Körper. Doch das, was sie zeigten, entspräche ihrer individuellen Körperlichkeit. Erstaunlich ist hierbei, dass *Ishinha* keinen Choreographen beschäftigt, denn die Akteure entwickeln ihre Bewegungsabläufe in kollektiver Probenarbeit.

Obwohl die Musik ein wesentliches Element ist, wird sie, wie beim Film, meist erst gegen Schluss der Probenarbeit konzipiert und komponiert; vor ihrer Fertigstellung benutzen die Akteure eine Rhythmusmaschine zur Fixierung der Bewegungsabläufe. Musikalischer Leiter und Komponist seit über 15 Jahren ist der 1959 in Osaka geborene Avantgarde-Gitarrist Uchihashi Kazuhisa, der in seiner Heimat, aber auch weltweit, als einer der begabtesten seines Faches gilt. Er ist in der freien, avancierten Musikszene zu Hause und beherrscht ganz unterschiedliche Musikstile, die er der Opernmusik, der Jazzmusik, der experimentellen improvisierten Musik und dem Post-Rock entnimmt. Für *Ishinha* komponiert er Musik mit minimalistischem Gestus, die an die Minimal Music eines Philip Glass, Terry Riley oder Steve Reich erinnert, oder er stattet sie mit frei improvisierten Jazzeinlagen aus.

Im Bereich der Outdoor-Produktionen ist es nicht angebracht, von Bühnenbildern im traditionellen Sinn zu sprechen. Der Bühnenort wird so gewählt, dass er in einer riesigen Fabrikhalle, auf einem Rangierbahnhof, im Hafen von Osaka oder an einem See steht, wobei die Umgebung das Bühnenbild mitbestimmt. Kalkulierte Blickentfaltungen sorgen dafür, dass der den Theaterort umschließende nahe und ferne Raum als "Akteur" mitspielt—in der japanischen Gartenkunst verwendet man dafür den bildhaften Ausdruck der "geborgten Landschaft." Die Zuschauer erhalten einen dreidimensionalen Blick aus der Vogelperspektive auf die oft nach hinten ansteigende Bühne mit ihren vielfältigen Architektursymbolen. Der kunstvolle Bühnenbau hat zusammen mit einer ausgeklügelten Lichtregie immer wieder hohes Lob bekommen, nicht nur von Theaterspezialisten, sondern zum Beispiel auch von Architekten. In diese Bühnenbilder mit Industrie-, Großstadt- und Naturlandschaften werden Großleinwände für Bild- und Filmprojektionen gesetzt, den Theaterort durchziehen echte Wasserkanäle oder spektakuläre Wasserfälle:

> People whose training is in theater tend to think in terms of simplification or symbolist methodology. They say for example, "You can't use water on a stage, so let's use paper," and they think in terms of abstraction. That becomes their theory. "Theater" itself is an abstract thing. The film people I know...tend to want to use the real thing, and they dislike things that are artificial or synthetic. So they choose the real thing whenever they can. Even

> though movies are an art form where reality is converted into images on film, they are more inclined to insist on the real thing. When we are working to create outdoor productions, that kind of approach used by movie people often provides us with good examples.[5]

Matsumoto verweigert sich also der konventionellen Abstraktion des Theaters und bevorzugt es, mit echten Requisiten, echten Gegenständen zu arbeiten. Er bekennt, dass er stark vom Film und dem dort bevorzugten Umgang mit "realem" Material beeinflusst sei, und dass er von Regisseuren wie Federico Fellini, Bernardo Bertolucci oder Akira Kurosawa gelernt habe, die für ihre sorgfältig komponierten Bilder berühmt sind. Dass Matsumoto von medialen Bildwelten und von der Verwendung "echter" Requisiten inspiriert wird, ist eine Arbeitsweise, die ihn auch in die Nähe Brechts rücken lässt:

> There are interesting films that come along from time to time, like *Blade Runner* and *Bagdad Cafe* and *Bad Blood (Mauvais Sang)*, and the Japanese director Katsuhiro Otomo's *Memories*, and the list goes on and on. And, when it's a Fellini or Bertolucci film I can't resist watching to the end. Among the Japanese directors I like Kaneto Shindo. I think his *Hadaka no Shima* is a masterpiece. I like the gritty humaneness of it. There is also the movie *Hadaka no Jukyu-sai* based on the story of the 19-year old Norio Nagayama who was given the death sentence. I like movies that follow the traditional theories. I love Kurosawa. He was a true artist, very skillful at layouts, maybe even more so than Picasso, I think. He was very good at drawing, and he planned and filmed his shots very carefully. For example, if an actor is standing here in one shot, he has to be over here in the next shot.[6]

Vor einigen Jahren hat Matsumoto das ehrgeizige Theaterprojekt *Trilogie des 20. Jahrhunderts* begonnen und 2010 fertiggestellt, eröffnet hatte er es mit der Performance *Nostalgia* aus dem Jahr 2007. Zur Vorgeschichte: Bei einem Gastspiel in der brasilianischen Hafenstadt Santos 2005 entdeckte Matsumoto bei einer Busfahrt halbverfallene Häuser, die zu Beginn des 20. Jahrhunderts von japanischen Immigranten errichtet wurden. Sie waren Vertreter einer ersten großen Einwanderungswelle – vorwiegend aus der armen Landbevölkerung – die 1908 in Brasilien ihr Glück suchten. Dort bemühten sie sich, ihre japanische Kultur zu bewahren, und lehrten die Kinder Japanisch. Aber im Laufe der Generationen verlor sich diese Tradition, verloren sich die heimatlichen Verwurzelungen immer mehr. Zwar sprechen deren Nachfahren, die Nippon-Brasilieros, heute noch Japanisch, doch ist es längst nicht mehr das ursprüngliche und für heutige Japaner nur schwer zu verstehen.

Nostalgia (2007)
Regie: Yukichi Matsumoto
Bühnenbild: Takeshi Kuroda
©Foto: Kôji Fukunaga

Die Performance *Nostalgia* thematisiert im Gedenken an den 100. Jahrestag der ersten japanischen Immigration den Lebensweg des jungen Mannes Noichi, der mit dem Schiff nach Santos kommt. Er erfährt dort die Schikanen der Einwanderungsbehörde, lernt die junge Portugiesin Ann kennen und lieben. Als sie auf einer Farm von einem Landbesitzer vergewaltigt wird, erschießt Noichi ihn, und zusammen mit Ann muss er fliehen. Bei ihrer Reise über den südamerikanischen Kontinent schließt sich ihnen ein Junge, der Eingeborene Chikino, an. Sie arbeiten hart in verschiedenen Jobs und erleben den Umbruch der Zeiten: Gewalt und Ausländerhass gegen die Japaner, 1941 Pearl Harbor, den Kriegsbeginn zwischen Japan und den USA, den Zusammenbruch des faschistischen Deutschlands. Szenisch eingerahmt wird das Stück durch den Riesen He, der sinnstiftend einen britischen Bowler Hat trägt. Dieser scheinbar traurige und heimatlose Riese symbolisiert vieles, er kann für das Gewissen, für die Geschichtserfahrung der Menschheit stehen und wandert ruhelos durch die Zeiten, Erdteile und Katastrophen von Matsumotos *Trilogie des 20. Jahrhunderts*.

Der zweite Teil der Trilogie trägt den Titel *Kokyu-Kikai/Atemmaschine*. 2008 uraufgeführt, wurde die Performance am und im See Biwa bei Kyoto gezeigt, aus dem in der Schlussszene Wasser auf die Bühne strömt. Das Stück erzählt von drei Brüdern Abel, Kain und Isaak – osteuropäischen Kriegswaisen während und nach dem zweiten Weltkrieg –, die zusammen mit dem Mädchen Olga und anderen obdachlosen Jungen überleben und sich in den stalinistischen Verhältnissen des Polens der Nachkriegszeit wiederfinden. Auch hier thematisiert Matsumoto Gewalt, Vertreibung, Krieg und Nachkriegszeit im 20. Jahrhundert, nunmehr in Osteuropa. Wenn er den Attentatsversuch auf einen polnischen KP-Funktionär zeigt, dann ist es ein versteckter Fingerzeig auf Andrzej Wajdas berühmte, 1958 entstandene Verfilmung von Jerzy Andrzejewskis Roman *Asche und Diamant*.

Kokyu-Kikai (*Atemmaschine*, 2008)
Regie: Yukichi Matsumoto
Bühnenbild: Takahiro Shibata
©Foto: Kôji Fukunaga

Was, so wäre zu fragen, könnten Impulse oder Einflüsse Brechts sein, die bei *Ishinha* nachhallen? Zunächst: ein eindeutiger Bezug Matsumotos auf Brecht, ein Bekenntnis zu ihm und seinem Theater sind in den dem Verfasser zugänglichen Quellen nicht nachzuweisen. Trotz einer möglichen Distanz des japanischen Regisseurs gegenüber international etablierten Theaterformen, zu denen Brechts Theater zählt, können jedoch einige direkt oder indirekt wirkende Bezugspunkte vermutet werden:

1. Brechts Interesse am Sport sowie seine Nutzbarmachung für ein neues Theater lässt Vergleiche zum Theater *Ishinha* zu. Brecht kritisiert (zum Beispiel in *Mehr guten Sport*[7]), dass das Publikum der Sportarenen und im Zirkus jenen Spaß an den Vorgängen habe, der ihm im Kunsttempel Theater ausgetrieben würde. Eine Möglichkeit, wie das Theater zu erneuern sei, stellte für Brecht der Sport dar: anstelle des Schauspielhauses der Sportpalast. Brechts Kritik zielt auf das westeuropäische Theater der 1920er Jahre, trotzdem rückt Matsumotos entschiedene Bevorzugung des Sportiven, des Körperhaften in die Nähe von Brechts Denkansatz.

2. Das episches Theater Brechts beinhaltet eine Absage an alle Formen von bloßer Abbildung und Reproduktion der Wirklichkeit. Auch Matsumotos episches Theater entbehrt der Illusion Realitäten abzubilden, es liefert Irritationspunkte und Überraschungen, um die künstlichen Bildwelten bedeutungsvoll aufzuladen. Wie Brecht verweigert er sich einer Vereinnahmung durch den traditionellen Theaterbetrieb und erprobt neue Spielorte und Darbietungsweisen. Da beider Theater jeweils eine künstliche Spielwelt sein soll, ergibt sich die Notwendigkeit, konsequent alle ästhetischen Mittel einzusetzen, um das Spiel im Spiel zu zeigen.

3. Schon in seinen frühen Balladen verwendet Brecht ganz unterschiedliche Rhythmisierungen, die zu einem aufmerksamen Lesen und Zuhören anregen sollen. Diese Arbeitstechnik schöpfte Brecht aus zwei Beobachtungen, die ihn "bei der Bildung unregelmäßiger Rhythmen beeinflußten:" zum einen die "kurzen, improvisierten Sprechchöre bei Arbeiterdemonstrationen," zum anderen die Ausrufe eines Berliner Straßenhändlers, welcher zum Kauf von Rundfunktextbüchern aufforderte.[8] Neben diesen Beispielen aus dem öffentlichen Raum der Straße verweist Brecht auf generelle Veränderungen der akustischen Umwelt, die zu einer Änderung unserer physiologischen Wahrnehmung über das Gehör führen. Als Beispiel führt er eine Szene aus dem Film *Shall We Dance?* von 1937 an, "wo der Tänzer Astaire zu den Geräuschen einer Maschinenhalle steppte."[9] Im Maschinenraum eines Schiffes imitiert Astaire zur Gershwin-Nummer "Slap That Bass" Bewegungen und Geräusche der Maschinen, tanzend begleitet von schwarzen Mechanikern als modernes Maschinen-Ballett. Der chorisch-syllabische Sprechgesang in Matsumotos Theater lässt einen engen Bezug zu Brechts Positionen im Aufsatz "Über reimlose Lyrik mit unregelmäßigen Rhythmen" vermuten. Klar unterschieden ist dagegen ein anderer Bereich: während Brecht mit syntaktisch kompletter, gedichteter Sprache operiert, dekonstruiert Matsumoto sie in einzelne Bestandteile, in Substantive, Zahlwörter, Ausrufe, Silben oder Vokale. Gesellschaftlich verbindliche Kommunikation mittels Sprache wird bei ihm in andere theatrale Ausdrucksformen verlagert.

4. Rhythmisches und Visuelles gehören sowohl bei Brecht als auch bei Matsumoto eng zusammen, sind sinnstiftende Elemente, welche Haltung und Bedeutung auf der Bühne zusammenbringen. *Ishinha* stellt verblüffende Bezüge zu einem Gedicht Brechts her:

> Das Operieren mit bestimmten Gesten/Kann deinen Charakter verändern/Ändere ihn./Wenn die Füße höher liegen als das Gesäß/Ist die Rede eine andere und die Art der Rede/Ändert den Gedanken./Eine gewisse heftige/Bewegung der Hand mit dem Rücken nach unten bei/Einem Oberarm, der am Körper bleibt, überzeugt/Nicht nur andere, sondern auch dich, der sie macht.[10]

5. Brecht und Matsumoto benutzen den Gestus als wesentliches Element ihres Theaters; sie verwenden "eine Sprachweise, die zugleich stilisiert und natürlich" ist.[11] Dies erreichen sie, indem sie auf Haltungen achten, die den Sätzen und Worten eingeschrieben sind: das ist eine gestische Sprache, weil sie Ausdruck für die Gesten der Menschen ist.[12] Zugleich stellen sie jeweils eine synkopierende Spannung in ihren Texten her, indem sie durch das rhythmisch akzentuierte Platzieren einer Silbe, eines Worts oder einer Wortgruppe das Besondere, Überraschende eines Gedankens oder eines Bildes hervorheben.

6. Ebenso greifen beide auf Formen und Bilder des Massentheaters der 1920er Jahre in Deutschland und der Sowjetunion zurück—man denke an Brechts *Maßnahme*, an das Theater Meyerholds, oder an Matsumotos *Mizumachi/Stadt am Wasser* aus dem Jahr 2000.

Die japanische Theatergruppe *Ishinha* entwickelt in ihren Produktionen eine ästhetische Eigenständigkeit im komplexen Spiel mit der nichterfüllten Konvention: sie zeigt Dialoge, die nicht gesprochen werden, Songs, die nicht gesungen werden und Tanz, der nicht getanzt wird. Vielleicht ist die Verweigerung jener theatralen Konventionen Matsumotos ein entscheidender Schritt mit Brecht und über Brecht hinaus.

Anmerkungen

1   Japanischer Dichter, 1896-1933.
2   Jun Kobori, "Leaders of Japan's avant-garde theater. The World of Yukichi Matsumoto and Ishinha," *Performing Arts Network Japan*, Artist Interview, Jun Kobori interviewer and ed., 28 November 2005, <http://www.performingarts.jp/E/art_interview/0511/4.html>
3   Ebd.
4   Bertolt Brecht, *Werke. Große kommentierte Berliner und Frankfurter Ausgabe*, Bd. 12, Werner Hecht, Jan Knopf, Werner Mittenzwei und Klaus-Detlef Müller, Hrsg. (Frankfurt/Main: Suhrkamp Verlag, 1988), S. 87 (im folgenden abgekürzt als BFA).
5   Kobori, "Leaders of Japan's avant-garde theater."
6   Ebd.
7   BFA 21, S. 119-122.
8   BFA 22, S. 361.
9   Ebd., S. 363.
10 BFA 14, S. 187.
11 BFA 18, S. 78.
12 Ebd., S. 78-79.

Jan-Jan-Opera and Osaka Rap
Part 2:
Yukichi Matsumoto's *Mizumachi* and *Keaton*

Akira Ichikawa

Matsumoto's *Mizumachi*, which his theater group Ishinha performed at Osaka's South Harbor in 1999, is about immigrants, like many other plays by Matsumoto. His archetypical image is a landscape close to the water; river and ocean indicate the only escape route. By reflecting the perspective of drifters and strangers, his plays aim to alienate from the outset, on a structural level. In *Keaton* (2004), Matsumoto compares the indoor theater to the modern sound film — in contrast to the outdoor theater which is more reminiscent of the silent film. Different from Brecht, Matsumoto includes Keaton rather than Chaplin in his play. His main character is often a young boy with a white face, a white shirt, and black pants: His appearance suggests a monochromatic world. Matsumoto's characters have in common that they swim against the tide. "Does man help his fellow man?" Matsumoto presents a new kind of *Lehrstück*.

In Matsumotos *Mizumachi*, das seine Theatergruppe Ishinha 1999 am Südhafen von Osaka aufführte, geht es, wie in anderen Stücken Matsumotos, um Einwanderer. Sein Urbild ist die Landschaft am Wasser, als Fluchtweg sieht man den Fluss und das Meer. Dadurch, dass seine Stücke den Blick der Dahintreibenden und Fremden reflektieren, sollen sie von vornherein, also schon struktuell, verfremden. In *Keaton* (2004) vergleicht Matsumoto das Indoor-Theater mit einem modernen Tonfilm — im Gegensatz zum Spiel im Freien, das eher an einen Stummfilm erinnert. Anders als Brecht nimmt Matsumoto nicht Chaplin, sondern Keaton in sein Stück auf. Bei ihm tritt in der Hauptrolle oft ein Junge mit einem weißen Gesicht, einem weißen Hemd und einer schwarzen Hose auf: Seine Erscheinung deutet auf eine monochrome Welt hin. Gemeinsam ist Matsumotos Figuren, dass sie gegen den Strom schwimmen. "Ob der Mensch dem Menschen hilft?" Matsumoto entwirft eine neue Art von Lehrstück.

Jan-Jan-Oper und Osaka Rap
Teil 2
Yukichi Matsumotos *Mizumachi* und *Keaton*

Akira Ichikawa

1. Outdoor-Theater

Die 1970 von Yukichi Matsumoto in Osaka gegründete Theatertruppe *Ishinha* ist durch ihre aufwendigen Bühnenbilder und Massenperformances mit Wort, Musik und Tanz im Freien bekannt. *Ishin* bedeutet eigentlich "Reformation" und *ha* ist eine Schule, eine Gruppe. Matsumoto versucht, das herrschende Theater umzuwälzen und ist dabei auf der Suche nach einem neuen, einmaligen Theater. Er baut nicht nur ein Theater im leeren Raum, sondern umgibt dieses Theater zugleich mit einer ganzen "Stadt," in der es viele Stände gibt und in der man essen und trinken kann. Das Theater steht im Mittelpunkt des Spektakels.

Matsumoto hat in einem Interview gesagt: "Ich fühle mich nicht so wohl im (Indoor) Theater, das nur ein ausgeliehener Kasten ist. Im Freien spielen heißt nicht nur ein Theater draußen aufbauen, sondern auch am Rand stehen,"[1] das heißt er möchte nicht Bestandteil des etablierten Systems werden, sondern ein marginaler Mensch, ein dahintreibender Außenseiter bleiben. Die Bühne von *Ishinha* kommt wie der Wind auf und verschwindet mit dem Wind. Die einmalige Performance im einmaligen Theater wird von ihm immer wieder betont.

Brecht versuchte Ende der 1920er Jahre jenseits des herkömmlichen Theaters, das durch den Zwang, Abendunterhaltung zu verkaufen, allzu unbewegliche Grenzen hatte, einen neuen Typus theatralischer Veranstaltungen zu entwickeln.[2] Seine Lehrstücke sind ein Versuch, eine andere Art von Performance in einer anderen Art von Theater zu zeigen.

2. *Mizumachi* (水街 *Stadt am Wasser*, 1999)

Matsumoto inszenierte 1999 *Mizumachi*. *Ishinha* spielte es am Südhafen von Osaka und ließ die Stadt hinter einem von einem großen Schwimmbecken dominierten Bühnenbild in Erscheinung treten. In dem Stück geht es um die Einwanderer, die Anfang des 20. Jahrhunderts nach Osaka gekommen sind. 1903 fand die fünfte nationale Industrieausstellung in Osaka statt, und in der Folgezeit entwickelte sich die Stadt zu einem bedeutenden Industriezentrum.

維新派 ［水街］南港野外特設劇場［大阪］1999   photograph: Fukunaga Kohji

Mizumachi (Stadt am Wasser, 1999)
Regie: Yukichi Matsumoto
Kôji Fukunaga ©

2.1. Matsumoto, Fritz Lang, Brecht — Arbeiterszenen

Matsumoto stammt von der kleinen Insel Amakusa im Süden Japans. Die Eltern ließen sich scheiden, und die Mutter zog mit dem zweijährigen Sohn nach Osaka. Matsumoto ist selbst einer der Einwanderer, die in seinen Stücken oft auftreten. Im Stadtviertel Taisho in Osaka wohnen auch heute noch viele Einwanderer aus Okinawa, das nach dem Zweiten Weltkrieg lange zu Amerika gehörte. Man brauchte sie als billige Arbeitskräfte, und sie wurden gezwungen, harte Arbeit zu verrichten. Trotzdem verdienten sie sehr wenig und wohnten in Baracken am Wasser oder in Booten. Es gab eine eindeutige Diskriminierung der sogenannten *uchinan-chu*, das heißt der Menschen aus Okinawa, von Seiten der *yamaton-chu*, das heißt von Bewohnern der japanischen Hauptinsel Honshu.

Die Arbeiterszenen in *Mizumachi* erinnern an Szenen aus Fritz Langs Science-Fiction-Stummfilm *Metropolis*, der 1927 uraufgeführt wurde, und dessen Wolkenkratzer-Ästhetik vermutlich von New York inspiriert war. In der gigantischen Metropolis leben zwei gegensätzliche Gesellschaften: im oberen Teil der Stadt lebt eine Oberschicht in absolutem Luxus, während unten die Arbeiterklasse an riesigen Maschinen für den Gewinn der Reichen schuftet. Zweierlei Uhren signalisieren: Ausbeutung. In *Mizumachi* hingegen tritt kein Kapitalist auf. Hier weist nur eine gigantische Maschine auf Ausbeutung hin, und ein roter Sonnenuntergang deutet die Erschöpfung der Arbeiter an — ein Szenenbild, das von Robert Wilson stammen könnte.

Eine ähnliche Szene gibt es auch in Brechts *Gutem Menschen von Sezuan*. Der Flieger Yan Sun ist zum Vorarbeiter in einer Tabakfabrik avanciert. Er macht sich sogar das "Lied vom achten Elefanten" für die Steigerung der Produktivität zunutze, indem er die an Charlie Chaplins *Modern Times* erinnernden Fabrikarbeiter dazu bewegt, das Lied mitzusingen. Praktiken kapitalistischer Ausbeutung spiegeln sich hier.[3] Bei Matsumoto agieren die Fabrikarbeiter mit nicht gesprochenem Wort, mit nicht getanztem Tanz. Sie rufen staccato sinnlose und sinnvolle Wörter im Osaka-Akzent und bewegen sich dazu im Viereck wie Marionetten. Der "Osaka Rap" in *Mizumachi* klingt dabei wie der balinesische Sprechgesang Kecak.

2.2. Dahintreibende, Einwanderer/Auswanderer

In Matsumotos Inszenierungen geht es oft um Dahintreibende, Einwanderer/Auswanderer. In *Mizumachi* zum Beispiel trifft Takeru das Mädchen Nao, eine Einwanderin aus Okinawa. Der Name Takeru kommt von Yamato-Takeru no Mikoto, dem Helden einer alten japanischen Legende, das heißt er ist ein echter Japaner. Er hat Naos kleiner Schwester geholfen, die ins Wasser gefallen ist. Diese Begegnung ist der von Freder und Maria in *Metropolis* ähnlich, obwohl Takeru eigentlich auch einer der Dahintreibenden ist. Er schließt mit anderen Leuten (überwiegend Kindern und Jugendlichen) Freundschaft. Dann macht er eine Reise zum Atlantischen Ozean, und Nao entscheidet sich, nach Brasilien auszuwandern, wo ihr Onkel wohnt, um ein besseres Leben zu suchen. Die Reise der Dahintreibenden reicht bis in das letzte Segment der *Trilogie des 20. Jahrhunderts* auf einer Insel bei Okayama im Juli 2010. Matsumotos Stücke reflektieren den Blick der Heimatlosen, der Dahintreibenden und der Fremden. So soll das Stück von vornherein, also schon strukturell, die Situation verfremden.

2.3. Das Urbild Matsumotos: Eine Landschaft am Wasser

Das Matsumotos Inszenierungen zugrundeliegende Urbild ist die Landschaft am Wasser: die Landschaft seiner Heimat Amakusa, aber auch die Stadtlandschaft Osakas, einer Stadt sowohl des Rauches als auch des Wassers. Als Fluchtweg sieht man den Fluss und das Meer. Flucht hat aber bei Matsumoto eine ganz andere Funktion als beispielsweise bei Kafka. Während der Fluchtweg bei Kafka als irrationale Verwandlung ins Tier figuriert und damit in Selbstentfremdung mündet, bieten bei Matsumoto Fluss und Meer die reale Möglichkeit der Auswanderung mit dem Schiff. Die Überwindung einer ausweglosen Situation wird bei Matsumoto also im Gegensatz zu Kafka sehr realitätsnah gestaltet. Fluss und Meer sind nicht nur Synonyme für Flucht, sondern auch für Aufbruch zu neuen Ufern gerade ohne Notwendigkeit der Selbstentfremdung. In diesem Sinne ist die Verortung des Südhafens in *Mizumachi* sehr effektvoll, weil das Publikum während der Vorstellung die Hafenlandschaft als geborgten Bühnenhintergrund sieht und zum Beispiel ein Schiffshorn hört.

Keaton (2004)
Regie: Yukichi Matsumoto
Bühnenbild: Takeshi Kuroda
Kôji Fukunaga ©

Brecht wohnte während seines Exils in Dänemark in einem Haus mit Strohdach am Svendborger Sund. Der Dichter schrieb Gedichte, den Kampf der Freunde in Deutschland verfolgend, und schickte sie ihnen. Und zwar nicht als "Emigrant, der aus freiem Entschluss auswanderte, sondern als Vertriebener."[4] Er schreibt in "Schlechte Zeit für Lyrik:" "Die grünen Boote und die lustigen Segel des Sundes/Sehe ich nicht. Von allem/Sehe ich nur der Fischer rissiges Garnnetz."[5] Die Landschaft am Wasser blieb ihm, der sich sicher als ewiger Emigrant fühlte, eine typische Exillandschaft. Brecht wohnte gerne am Wasser, zunächst Ende der 1920er Jahre in Utting am Ammersee, dann in Berlin am Weißen See, und zuletzt in Buckow am Buckower See. Am Wasser entstanden ausgezeichnete Gedichtsammlungen wie zum Beispiel die *Svendborger Gedichte* und *Buckower Elegien*.

3. *Keaton* (2004)

Ein anderes Stück von *Ishinha* soll nun betrachtet werden: *Keaton* (2004). Der Titel verweist auf den weltberühmten Komiker Buster Keaton (1895-1966). Wie *Mizumachi* wurde *Keaton* am Südhafen von Osaka aufgeführt.

Die Geschichte ist folgende: Es regnet. Da ist ein altes Kino, das schon eine Ruine ist. Wataru, ein Waisenkind, kommt ins Kino hinein, wo einige obdachlose Kinder wohnen. Plötzlich dreht sich der große, rostige Projektor und sie sehen einen Film, der zeigt, wie Arbeiter in eine Fabrik gehen. Die Kinder treten in die Welt des Films ein, das heißt sie wechseln plötzlich von der Realität des Zuschauerraums in einen Film, der eine Industriestadt der 1920er Jahre zeigt und in dem dann Wataru "Onkel

Keaton" trifft. Die episch lockere Folge relativ selbständiger Nummern erinnert an Brechts Dramaturgie.

3.1. Nicht Chaplin, sondern Keaton

Keaton zählte neben Chaplin zu den erfolgreichsten Komikern der Stummfilmzeit. Wegen seines bewusst ernsten, stoischen Gesichtsausdrucks wurde er "the Great Stoneface" und "der Mann, der niemals lachte" genannt. Als Kind wusste er schon: "Wenn ich lache, lacht das Publikum nicht."[6] Ein weiteres Markenzeichen war sein runder, flacher Filzhut. Bei Matsumoto tritt Keaton als Wanderer mit zwei großen Koffern und seinem Hut auf.

Matsumoto vergleicht das Indoor-Theater mit einem *Tôki*, das heißt einem modernen Tonfilm, wohingegen das Spiel im Freien eher wie ein Stummfilm sei.[7] Anders als Brecht nimmt er aber nicht Chaplin, sondern Keaton in sein Stück auf. Daran kann man sehen, dass er den Verfremdungseffekt weiter als Brecht treibt.

Brecht versuchte, zwei Elemente, nämlich Humor und Komik, mit seinem epischen Theater zu verbinden. Der schwierige Terminus "Verfremdung" ist als Antithese zu dem der "Einfühlung" im "Aristotelischen Theater" gedacht, das uns zu einer Art Illusion verführt. Er ist vom "großen Charlie" sehr beeinflusst worden. Brecht war vor allem von der Spielweise fasziniert: "Chaplin, der frühere Clown, hatte nicht die Tradition des Theaters und ging neu an die Gestaltung menschlichen Verhaltens heran."[8]

Matsumoto meint aber, dass Chaplin zu kunstvoll und sentimental spiele, während Keatons Welt mineralisch und hart sei: "Bei Chaplin weint man und der Mund wird wässerig, aber bei Keaton fließt kein Blut, auch wenn man ihn sticht. Den Eindruck habe ich."[9] Matsumoto meint, man könne das Universum aus Keatons Perspektive betrachten. Er sieht zwar bei beiden den Gegensatz von Einfühlung und Verfremdung, aber er findet mehr komische Distanzierung bei Keaton. Die Entscheidung für Keaton und nicht für Chaplin führt dazu, dass unter rein schauspielerischen Gesichpunkten die Verfremdungseffekte bei Matsumoto diejenigen bei Brecht übertreffen.

3.2. Der Junge und die alleinstehende Mutter

Bei Matsumoto tritt in der Hauptrolle oft ein Junge auf, mit einem weißen Gesicht, einem weißen Hemd, einem Hut und einer schwarzen Hose. Seine Erscheinung deutet auf eine monochrome Welt hin. Anders als die Erwachsenen hat der Junge die Fähigkeit, die Welt zu durchschauen. Er ist ein Obdachloser, ein Dahintreibender, und heißt oft Wataru. *Wataru* heißt "überqueren," "über etwas (zum Beispiel einen Fluss oder das Meer) gehen." Der Name symbolisiert das Thema seiner Stücke, nämlich von einer Welt in eine andere zu gehen.

Im Vergleich zur Titelgestalt in Michael Endes Märchen-Roman *Momo* (1973) ist Wataru eher eine Verliererfigur. Momo, die als Obdachlose in einem Amphitheater lebt, kämpft in ihrer Phantasie-Welt gegen die übermächtig erscheinenden grauen Herren und schafft es, den Menschen die gestohlene Zeit zurückzubringen. Wataru sieht keine Möglichkeit, in seiner Welt gegen die Armut zu kämpfen, sondern flieht. Wie zuvor erwähnt, bedeutet seine Flucht aber zugleich einen Aufbruch zu neuen Ufern. Seine Zukunft erscheint daher nicht völlig hoffnungslos. Vor die Wahl "Flüchten oder Standhalten"[10] gestellt, entscheidet sich Matsumoto hier für die Flucht und deren positiven Aspekt des Aufbruchs.

Viele wichtige Frauenfiguren Brechts sind alleinstehend: Mutter Courage, Pelagea Wlassowa in *Die Mutter,* Shen Te in *Der gute Mensch von Sezuan* und so weiter. Und auch Grusche in *Der Kaukasische Kreidekreis* ist fast eine alleinerziehende Mutter. Der Junge bei Matsumoto und die alleinstehende Mutter bei Brecht: gemeinsam ist diesen Figuren, dass sie gegen den Strom schwimmen.

3.3. Ruine und Gasse als Orte der Gemeinschaft

Die Spielorte Matsumotos sind häufig Ruinen und Gassen. Er selbst hat sich dazu folgendermaßen geäußert:

> Ruinen und Gassen sind Wohnungen des Windes. Wenn man Bonsai-Pflanzentöpfe auf die Veranda stellt, gehören sie dem Eigentümer. Aber auf der Gasse wirken sie, als stünden sie in einem Verkaufsstand auf der abendlichen Straße. Vorbeigehende sehen sie und können sie leicht stehlen. Es gibt keine Grenze zwischen den anderen und mir, im Sinne des Besitzens.[11]

Die Gemeinschaft spielt in Brechts Lehrstücken eine zentrale Rolle. Gemeinschaft bei Brecht bedeutet Kommunismus. Bei Matsumoto bilden Einwanderer, die in Ruinen und in Gassen hausen, eine primitive Gemeinschaft, die noch nicht als kommunistisch dargestellt wird, aber jedenfalls zu einem neuen Lehrstück führt.

3.4. Ob der Mensch dem Menschen hilft? – eine neue Art Lehrstück

Mit der Aufführung der *Dreigroschenoper* (1928) war Brecht schlagartig weltberühmt geworden. Aber es war ihm bald verhasst, als Verfasser dieses Stückes angesprochen zu werden. Es wurde Brecht rasch bewusst, dass die Gesellschaftssatire der *Dreigroschenoper* mühelos von der Unterhaltungsindustrie vereinnahmt und dabei ihr provokativer Effekt entschärft worden war. Durch die enorme Arbeitslosigkeit in Deutschland und die Weltwirtschaftskrise änderten sich die politschen und wirtschaftlichen Verhältnisse so stark, dass das Stück die Aktualität der Zeitereignisse nicht einholen konnte.

Brecht versuchte indes, seine Theaterpraxis direkt im Inneren der Arbeiterkulturbewegung und in Schulen weiterzuführen, und zwar mit einem neuen Genre, den Lehrstücken. Sie hätten eigentlich von vornherein besser "Lernstücke"("learning plays") heißen sollen, denn es ging um wechselseitiges Lehren und Lernen von Menschen, die eine Textvorgabe nach ihren eigenen Erfahrungen und Ideen interpretieren und auf diese Weise das Stück zusammen konstruieren.

Das 1930 uraufgeführte und in Zusammenarbeit mit dem Komponisten Paul Hindemith entstandene *Badener Lehrstück vom Einverständnis* ist für Männer- und Frauenchöre geschrieben und verwendet sowohl Film- als auch Clownszenen. Im *Badener Lehrstück* geht es um die Frage, ob der Mensch dem Menschen hilft.

Am Ende der achten Szene von *Keaton* ertönt donnernder Klang und, von Blitz begleitet, fliegt weißes Magnesiumpulver herum. Und dann wird es plötzlich dunkel. Ob eine Kernexplosion stattgefunden hat? Oder ob der Dritte Weltkrieg ausgebrochen ist? All das weiß man nicht. Danach beginnt die neunte Szene, also M9[12] "Thomason Zirkus." Wataru ist ohnmächtig auf die schräge Bühne gefallen, das heißt der Filmprojektor dreht sich nicht mehr und Keaton ist verschwunden. Keatons Leben ist von Watarus Leben abhängig. Ob der Mensch dem Menschen hilft?

Die von Wataru abgespaltenen und nur im Bühnentext, nicht aber auf der Bühne entsprechend nummerierten Doppelgänger 1, 5, 6, 7, 8, 9, 12, 15 und 16 (alle wahrscheinlich ebenfalls obdachlos) suchen Wataru mit Taschenlampen und rufen: "Ohoooi, Ohoooi." Sie finden den gefallenen Wataru und fangen an, große Zahnräder zu drehen, statt ihm aufzuhelfen: "Hei, ei, ei, e, hei, ei, ei, e," "hei, ya, hei, ya" singen sie im Chor, wie in der griechischen Tragödie, im No-Drama, oder in Brechts Lehrstücken. Erst dreht sich ein Zahnrad, und dann drehen sich auch die anderen Zahnräder, eines nach dem anderen. Keaton steht auf und hilft Wataru auf. Keatons Kopien 13, 14, 17, 18, 20, 21, 22, 23 und 24 treten auf und bewegen sich lebhaft.

"Brechts Lehrstück organisiert aufführend ein positives Kollektiv, das durch die Zusammenarbeit der einzelnen Spieler gekennzeichnet ist, in der sich jeder Spieler als ein dialektisch denkendes, das heißt als ein das Verhältnis von ihm und der Gesellschaft mitdenkendes Subjekt qualifiziert."[13] In diesem Sinne steht Matsumotos *Keaton* Brechts

Lehrstücken sehr nah. Wie bei Brecht ist die Trennung von Denken und Handeln aufgehoben. Brechts Lehre ist sehr einfach und eindeutig: In der Klassengesellschaft, in der Zeit der Gewalt hilft der Mensch dem Menschen nicht, darum sollen die Menschen die Menschheit und die Welt verbessern. "Ändernd die Welt, verändert euch!"[14]

Auch Matsumoto erteilt uns eine dialektische Lehre: die "abgespaltenen" Personen können dem "Original" helfen (man kann das auch so interpretieren, dass die Arbeiterklasse ihren Mitgliedern hilft); das heißt dass der Mensch, gerade weil er in seinem Sein von anderen abhängig ist, wiederum den anderen hilft. Wataru und Keaton sind als Lebenspartner aneinander gebunden. Matsumoto stellt uns hiermit eine neue Art von Lehrstück vor, in dem eine Dialektik im Mittelpunkt steht, die Stärke aus Abhängigkeit entstehen lässt.

3.5. Jan-Jan-Oper

Matsumotos Stücke sind durchweg Opern. Der moderne Komponist Uchihashi Kazuhisa hat sie im Zusammenarbeit mit Matsumoto vertont. Die Schauspieler singen die Texte im Chor wie einen Rap-Song, der als Sprechgesang in einem fünf- oder siebentaktigen Rhythmus geschrieben ist. Die Texte enthalten musikalische Instruktionen: die Schauspieler sprechen singend, singen sprechend. Sie beginnen die Proben mit Körperarbeit und bemühen sich dabei um unnatürliche Bewegungen; sie bewegen ihre Beine in einem siebentaktigen Rhythmus und bewegen ihre Arme dreitaktig dazu. Mit verfremdendem Gestus wird singend getanzt, tanzend gesungen, vergleichbar fast einer sozialistischen Revue.

Matsumoto hat Malerei an der Pädagogischen Hochschule Osakas studiert. Er entwirft seine Bühnenbilder selbst und benutzt dabei Motive von Giorgio de Chirico, Marcel Duchamp und M. C. Escher. Das Pissoirbecken auf dem Rücken Keatons zum Beispiel geht auf Duchamps berühmtes *ready-made* zurück. Insgesamt verwirklicht Matsumoto in den Aufführungen von *Ishinha* Richard Wagners Begriff des Gesamtkunstwerkes. In seiner Performance sind verschiedene Künste wie Bühnengestaltung, Musik, Malerei, Tanz/Choreografie, Schauspielkunst und Rap-Texte äquivalent vereint und überschreiten ihre jeweiligen Grenzen. Das ist auch Brechts Ideal. In diesem Sinne haben Wagner, Brecht und Matsumoto etwas gemein.

Anmerkungen

1 Yukichi Matsumoto, "Long Interview 1: Expressive Conception," *Ishinha Taizen* (Osaka: Matsumoto-Kobo Verlag, 1998), S. 28.
2 Bertolt Brecht, "Das Deutsche Drama vor Hitler," *Werke. Große kommentierte Berliner und Frankfurter Ausgabe*, Band 22, Werner Hecht, Jan Knopf, Werner Mittenzwei und Klaus-Detlef Müller, Hrsg. (Frankfurt/Main: Suhrkamp Verlag, 1989), S. 167. (Im folgenden abgekürzt als BFA.)
3 Vgl. Akira Ichikawa, "Brechts *Guter Mensch von Sezuan* als Komödie inszeniert," *Befremdendes Lachen*, Hans-Peter Bayerdörfer und Stanca Scholz-Cionca, Hrsg. (München: IUDIZIUM Verlag, 2005), S. 295-304.
4 Brecht, "Über die Bezeichnung Emigranten," BFA 12, S. 81.
5 Brecht, "Schlechte Zeit für Lyrik," BFA 14, S. 432.
6 Thomas A. Dardis, *Keaton, the Man Who Wouldn't Lie Down*, Übers. Takahiko Iimura (Tokio: Libroport Verlag, 1987), S. 25.
7 Yukichi Matsumoto. "Long Interview for *Romance*," *Ishinha Taizen* (Osaka: Matsumoto-Kobo Verlag, 1998), S. 60.
8 BFA 22, S. 166.
9 Ebd., S. 61.
10 Horst-Eberhard Richter, *Flüchten oder Standhalten* (Gießen: Psychosozial-Verlag, 2001).
11 Yukichi Matsumoto, "Long Interview for *Romance*," a.a.O., S. 15.
12 Matsumoto nennt seine Szenen "M." "M" steht für "Musik," weil er seine Inszenierungen als Opern betrachtet.
13 Taekwan Kim, *Das Lehrstück Bertolt Brechts* (Frankfurt/Main: Peter Lang, 2000), S. 56.
14 BFA 3, S. 46.

Der Versuch einer taoistischen Lesart des Lehrstücks *Die Horatier und die Kuriatier*

Andreas Aurin

Bertolt Brechts philosophische Prägungen bezüglich der Dialektik sind weitgehend bekannt—Hegel, Marx, Engels und Lenin. Eher unbekannt ist jedoch, dass Brecht bereits sechs Jahre bevor er sich 1926 mit Marx zu beschäftigen begann, mit einer Form der Dialektik fernöstlichen Ursprungs in Berührung gekommen war, nämlich der Philosophie des Taoismus und dem Buch *Dàodéjīng* des Laotse. Dieser Artikel untersucht den Einfluss des Taoismus auf das *Lehrstück*, ein sowohl musikalisches als auch didaktisches Genre, das versucht, dialektisches Denken zu lehren. Eine vergleichende Textanalyse zwischen dem *Dàodéjīng* und dem letzten Lehrstück *Die Horatier und die Kuriatier* arbeitet nicht nur inhaltliche Ähnlichkeiten heraus, sondern demonstriert auch sprachliche Übereinstimmungen. Während taoistische Gedanken die Motivation und den Verlauf der Fabel beeinflussen, kollidieren sie unweigerlich mit Ideen marxistischen Hintergrunds. Ihrer scheinbaren Unvereinbarkeit zum Trotz, werden beide Philosophien als miteinander kompatibel dargestellt.

The philosophical influences on Brecht's understanding of dialectics are well known — Hegel, Marx, Engels, and Lenin. What is less well known is that Brecht, six years before studying Marx in 1926, had already encountered a notion of dialectic from the Far East, i.e. the philosophy of Taoism and Laozi's book *Dàodéjīng*. This article explores the Taoist influence on the *Lehrstück*, a musical as well as didactic genre fostering dialectical thinking. A comparative textual analysis between the *Dàodéjīng* and the last *Lehrstück*, The Horatians and the Curiatians, will not only demonstrate affinities with regard to content but also illuminate linguistic similarities. By stressing the motivation and outcome of the fable, Taoist thought subsequently collides with ideas that are ascribed to Marxism. Hence, two seemingly incompatible philosophies will be shown to be compatible.

Towards a Taoist Reading of the *Lehrstück The Horatians and the Curiatians*

Andreas Aurin

As is well known, the notion of dialectics is central to the works of Bertolt Brecht, with the *Lehrstücke*[1] allowing him to stage dialectical processes as he understood them from his reading of Hegel, Lenin, Engels, and Marx, with the latter being indisputably the most striking influence on him. Shortly after his first encounter with Marx's *Capital* and his study of other Marxist literature in 1926, Brecht made contact with the *Neue Musik* movement and its proponents such as Paul Hindemith, Kurt Weill, Hanns Eisler, and Paul Dessau. Both Brecht's encounter of dialectical materialism and his involvement in the *Neue Musik* movement led to the development of the first two *Lehrstücke* within the festival of *Deutsche Kammermusik Baden-Baden* in 1929: *Der Lindberghflug,* a collaborative work between Brecht, Hindemith and Weill, and *Lehrstück*,[2] a collaborative work between Brecht and Hindemith. Thus, and as shown in recent studies,[3] the *Lehrstück* constitutes a musical genre that teaches dialectical thinking as such by utilizing Marxism and its theory of dialectic as one attempt to investigate processes within society, an ever-evolving construct of interacting elements. By being in contradiction to each other, these elements pull "the social whole in different directions, pushing towards different outcomes…and it is this [dialectic] which determines the shape of society and all its component parts, determines *history*."[4] However, it is important to note that the notion of dialectical materialism stresses the development of history as a product of human labor. Thus, as understood by Brecht, dialectical thinking describes a method that enables us to operate with contradictory units apparent in all parts of society in order to provoke change. Dialectical contrast or contradiction is here understood as the core feature not only of the *Lehrstück* but also of Brechtian epic theater. Yet, "so wird im folgenden die Rede von 'Dialektik' sein müssen, ohne dass erklärt wird, was dies ist;…ihre Kenntnis [wird] boshafterweise vorausgesetzt."[5] Hence, during his lifelong engagement with the dialectic method, Brecht did not, however, propose a coherent theory or conceptualization.

What is less well known, and arguably less evident, is that even before studying Marxist philosophy Brecht encountered a concept of dialectics from the Far East. According to Brecht's *Tagebuch*, journalist Frank Warschauer showed him Laozi's *Dàodéjīng* in September 1920: "Aber er zeigte mir Lao-tse, und der stimmt mit mir so sehr überein, dass er immerfort staunt."[6] Brecht's *Tagebuch* does not explore either his first encounter with the *Dàodéjīng* or the reason for Warschauer's astonishment in any more detail. Perhaps Brecht's affinity for the Chinese Philosopher stems from the methodological way of argumentation used in the *Dàodéjīng*.

The following remarks will propose an alternative reading of Brecht's last *Lehrstück* titled *The Horatians and the Curiatians*, a reading that is based on Taoist thought and aims to provide a broader understanding of the dialectics within this *Lehrstück*. Justified by the subtitle given by Brecht himself, the "*Lehrstück* about Dialectics for Children" reveals dialectics as its explicit object[7] and thus aims to teach dialectical thinking to children. The following pages will demonstrate the conceptual and stylistic affinities between the *Dàodéjīng* and Brecht's *The Horatians and the Curiatians* by not only showing the similarities between Brecht's statements and Taoist thought but also by unveiling points of contact between Taoist and Marxist philosophies. However, first some brief remarks regarding the genesis, subject matter, and argumentational method of the book *Dàodéjīng*.[8]

The *Dàodéjīng* is one of the two most important pre-Qin texts, most likely compiled over an extended time period prior to 221 BC. Although the book is not directly associated with a particular school or doctrine, its authorship is conventionally ascribed to Laozi, who is considered the founder of Taoism. Like other Taoist texts, the *Dàodéjīng* is characterized by a tendency to reassess and reveal the shortcomings of previous philosophies—especially Confucianism—by comparing them with ideas, practices, and values of the present day.

The word *dào* refers to a Taoist understanding of reality and signifies a material source of all things as well as a universal principle inherent in all things. *Dào* in this second and more opaque meaning refers to the real and eternal *dào*, a metaphysical condition of a dynamic and constantly transforming whole. Although the concept of *dào* cannot be adequately rendered into a foreign language it is usually translated into English as "path" or "way." The *Dàodéjīng* examines how this universal principle is present in many areas of human life such as health, government, metaphysics and ethics, revealing the transformation and movement of *dào* within the world. This examination is characterized by a dialectical approach to existing dichotomies, which are in a constant state of change. The notion of change as well as the linguistic simplicity used in the *Dàodéjīng* might have been the decisive factor for Brecht's interest in the book. In particular the Taoist concept of "the flux of things," an "image of social political process," caught Brecht's attention because, according to Antony Tatlow, "it adds the concept of process [to] the prediction of a social transformation."[9]

Brecht's utilization of Taoist philosophy will be elaborated through a textual comparison of the *Dàodéjīng* and *The Horatians and the Curiatians*, particularly by focusing on the marked linguistic as well as conceptual similarities between both texts. To ensure an accurate analysis, Richard Wilhelm's German translation of the *Dàodéjīng* from 1911[10] – the translation used by Brecht[11] – provides the textual foundation.

The Horatians and the Curiatians is based on material in Titus Livius' history of Rome *Ab urbe condita* (book I, 22-26) which describes events that took place around 670-640 BC during the reign of Tullus Hostilius. Brecht's first draft dates back to 1934, when he was living in exile in Denmark. However, his main engagement with the *Lehrstück*-text, written in collaboration with Margarete Steffin, spans the period between August and October 1935. During this time Hanns Eisler was expected to stay in Svendborg to discuss the "main musical problems"[12] with Brecht. However, due to Eisler's involvement with the International Society of New Music in Prague, where he was called in at short notice, their work was interrupted, leading to a time conflict that ended their collaboration on this piece. *The Horatians and the Curiatians* was published in Moscow in 1936 in the journal *Internationale Literatur*. However, it was never performed until after Brecht's collaboration with the East German composer Kurt Schwaen, who set the *Lehrstück* to music in 1955/56.[13]

In Livy's story, the Roman Horatians and the Albanian Curiatians are engaged in a battle for dominance over southern Italy, with each contender being equal in strength and material resources. Prior to the development of the *Lehrstück*, Brecht reflected on the question of victory and defeat in order to motivate the fable's structure. Unlike Livy, Brecht decided to make the two forces unequal by presenting the Curiatians as materially superior. However, his *Lehrstück* draws on ideas about the unexpected outcome of such an opposition, ideas that are to be found in the *Dàodéjīng*:

> Sind die Waffen stark, so siegen sie nicht.[14]

And:

> Dass Schwaches das Starke besiegt,
> weiß jedermann auf Erden,
> aber niemand vermag danach zu handeln.[15]

The passage from which the former quotation is taken presents the dialectical metaphor of soft water that is powerful, hard and insuperable when flowing, which is the core concept of Taoist philosophy.[16] The soft/hard opposition, the most significant example of the many binary oppositions given in the course of the *Dàodéjīng*, accentuates contrast yet implies a certain interplay. Presented as a reversed hierarchical system, each side of the binary is presented as not only distinct but also dependent on its opposite with which it is entangled in a constant process of development.[17]

In addition to the inequality of the two forces, the other significant alteration Brecht made to Livy's story was to change the Horatians' motives for becoming involved in warfare. Unlike Livy's Horatians and Curiatians, who are both equally aggressive and supportive of a state of war, Brecht's Horatians go to war in order to defend their goods and chattels and to protect their country from harm and danger. One reason for this alteration was Brecht's interest in the Taoist idea about warfare, particularly its prohibition of a material action motivated by aggression and its concept of *wúwèi*, a term often translated as meaning "no action." The prohibition is expressed in the following way in the *Dàodéjīng*:

> Die Waffen sind Geräte des Unheils,
> ...
> Nur wenn er nicht umhin kann, gebraucht er sie.[18]

or:

> Wenn man Liebe hat im Kampf,
> so siegt man.
> Wenn man sie hat bei der Verteidigung,
> so ist man unüberwindlich.[19]

Fighting with the deep affection of love relates to the concept of wisdom in the *Dàodéjīng*, personified in the figure of the sage, to whom are ascribed virtuous attributes such as friendliness, courteousness, and placidity. The decision of the Horatian fighters to defend themselves does not transgress the Taoist prohibition because it is motivated by love for community and a deep reluctance to engage in warfare. The *Dàodéjīng* states:

> Wo zwei Armeen kämpfend aufeinanderstoßen,
> da siegt der, der es schweren Herzens tut.[20]

However, in Brecht's *Lehrstück* it takes three individual battles to achieve the ability to act in agreement with "the flux of things."

1. The Battle of the Archers

The first section of Brecht and Steffin's *Lehrstück*, titled "The Battle of the Archers," demonstrates "the flux of things" as inherent in nature. The Taoist understanding of "the flux of things" expresses dialectics as inherent in nature and conceives of nature as being in a constant state of change. However, the Taoist metaphor of flux describes neither a linear nor a teleological movement. Rather the phrase refers to a cycle of continuation. To act in agreement with the cycle is essential to achieve the best outcome of a situation. However, the cyclic behavior of "the flux of things" subsequently turns an advantageous situation into a disadvantage. In the *Lehrstück*, the author's depiction of the movement of the sun during one day of the battle can be read as a demonstration of the cycle of continuation in nature. Brecht clarifies that movement in a sketch he made in order to illustrate three different phases of the position of the sun that are significant for the first day of the battle. The three phases demand the adaptability of both fighters so that they can successfully defeat their opponents.

In the first phase, the Horatian deliberately places the Curiatian in the disadvantageous position with the sun glaring in his face. Yet the Horatian fails to successfully launch his arrow. Meanwhile the sun changes its altitude so that in the second phase both fighters are dazzled and fail to defeat their opponent. Being aware of the sun's movement the Horatian Chorus encourages their man to immediately start fighting with his fists before the sun has changed to its second phase: "A good position/ Does not stay good for ever…Irrevocably/Morning becomes midday."[21] However, the Horatian is slow to change to the fistfight mode, and as the sun moves towards the third phase of evening, he alone must deal with the sun in his eyes, leading to his ultimate defeat. Hence, in the course of a day the disadvantage of the Curiatian has become an advantage that enables him to defeat his opponent.

The inflexibility of the Horatian causes his defeat as it is at odds with the cycle of continuation and, most notably, his own collective. The Chorus of Horatians concludes: "It [our army] clung to one position/It clung to one weapon/And it clung/To one plan. But inevitably/The sun travelled across the heavens."[22] The *Dàodéjīng* presents a remarkably similar position on the importance of adapting to "the flux of things:"

> Wer festhält, verliert es.
> Also auch der Berufene:
> …
> Er hält nicht fest, so verliert er nicht.[23]

According to the *dào,* "the flux of things," the unceasing development and change of events and processes through time cannot be disrupted by retaining a particular situation. Hence, by not acting in accordance with the *dào* one loses one's place within it.

2. The Battle of the Spearmen

The point of convergence between Taoist and Marxist philosophies becomes apparent in the course of the second part of the fight, "The Battle of the Spearmen," and is even more evident in the third part. Aware of the material superiority of the Curiatian spearman, the Horatian decides on a long march towards the edge of a cliff to ambush the Curiatian who is at the cliff's base in the valley. The Horatian plans to defeat the Curiatian by "crush(ing) him beneath rock fragments"[24] located at the cliff's edge. The Horatian's march, however, bears unexpected difficulties. In using his spear in seven different ways—as, for example, a "third foot," a "measuring stick," or a "balancing pole"—he already demonstrates that he is beginning to understand "the flux of all things" as shown to him in the first battle. Thus, he is able to progress to the cliff's edge. A textual comparison of this part of the *Lehrstück* with the *Dàodéjīng* reveals significant linguistic similarities, which cannot be attributed only to Brecht's understanding of flux as a cyclic process of change, but also to his attraction to the naivety of the language used in the *Dàodéjīng*. Before using the spear in six different ways, the first conversion of the Horatian's tool closes the cycle of "the flux of things" by using the wood of the spear in its original sense:

> Meine Lanze, die einmal
> Ast einer Eiche war, soll wieder ein Ast sein.
> ...
> Viele Ding sind in einem Ding.[25]

The cyclic return of things to their origin can be directly related to the *Dàodéjīng*:

> Die Dinge in all ihrer Menge,
> ein jedes kehrt zurück zu seiner Wurzel.[26]

While the "Seven Conversions of a Spear" demonstrates Brecht's awareness of the cycle of continuation, a core feature of Taoist philosophy, it includes another aspect that diverges from the *Dàodéjīng*. The Horatian's ability to interrupt and change the cycle of continuation has to be understood within a Marxist context and demonstrates a major point of divergence between the two philosophies. Taoism argues that transitoriness is already inherent in all things and cannot be manipulated by humans. Marxism, by contrast, proposes that processes can, and in certain circumstances must, be changed by human intervention so as to obtain social benefit. Thus, the Horatian has to actively engage in the process in order to change the utilization of his tool. Brecht clarifies this action-based notion of change through the use of the first person: "Wieder/sehe *ich* auf meine Lanze./ *Ich* sage, sie soll mein Sprungbrett sein."[27] The Horatian understands that he is able to put his thoughts, a product of human labor, into action by changing his tool in seven different ways.

At the end of the march and exhausted by his efforts, the Horatian fighter is unable to overcome his tiredness and falls asleep, consequently missing the opportunity to defeat his opponent passing by the cliff. As demanded by his chorus, "worse than a lost battle/Is wasted effort,"[28] he decides to return the same way, overcoming the same difficulties in order to confront the Curiatian once again. By demanding the Horatian's retreat, the chorus anticipates the key moment of the last battle: "Fighting your way back steadily/Is a part/Of the new advance."[29]

Before addressing the third part of the *Lehrstück*, it is important to evaluate "The Ride on the Flood," the second part of "The Battle of the Spearmen," as it conveys the most striking reference to contradiction in Taoist philosophy. As mentioned previously, this is the metaphorical picture of the water, an image of natural process, which is described in the *Dàodéjīng* as follows:

> Auf der ganzen Welt
> gibt es nichts Weicheres und Schwächeres als das Wasser.
> Und doch, in der Art, wie es dem Harten zusetzt,
> kommt nichts ihm gleich.
> Es kann durch nichts verändert werden.[30]

According to Tatlow, the image of the flowing water conveys different meanings within Brecht's poems. When discussing the early poems, Tatlow elucidates the way they present the idea that trying to resist the water is senseless, hence "one must give oneself to the water."[31] By contrast, while the use of flowing water imagery in the later poems does "convey a sense of inevitable process,"[32] it also suggests that the strength of the water's destructive forces "is temporary and they can be mastered, [allowing us to] take confidence in the beneficence of water."[33] In "The Ride on the Flood" Brecht uses the image of flowing water to signify both agency, that is mastery of the flood, and then acquiescence, a falling into the water and dying. In this section the Horatian is depicted as having to deal with an impassable river. In order to meet with his opponent the Horatian decides to ride the torrent. Through adding the full force of the impassable river to his own human power, the Horatian is able to wound his opponent. However, by trying to master and thus provoking the immutable state of the water he disagrees with the *dào* and subsequently dies:

> Wer Mut zeigt in Waghalsigkeiten,
> der kommt um.
> Wer Mut zeigt, ohne waghalsig zu sein,
> der bleibt am Leben.[34]

In order to defeat the Curiatian, the third Horatian fighter, taught by the previous battles, acts in accordance with the *dào*.

3. **The Battle of the Swordsmen**

Concurrent to the development of this *Lehrstück*, Brecht commenced his work on *Buch der Wendungen*, a work influenced by various Asian philosophies including Taoist thought. In fact, one of the sheets from the *Horatian and the Curiatian*-folder of materials in the Bertolt Brecht Archive contains the following story,[35] titled *Die Mittel wechseln*:

> Meti erzählte: Drei Leute von *Su* sah man mit drei Leuten von *Ga* kämpfen. Nach langem Kampf waren zwei der Leute von *Su* getötet; von den Leuten von *Ga* war einer schwer und ein andrer leicht verwundet. Da ergriff der einzig überlebende Mann von *Su* die Flucht. Die Niederlage von *Su* schien vollständig. Aber dann sah man plötzlich, dass die Flucht des Mannes von *Su* alles geändert hatte. Sein Gegner von *Ga* verfolgte ihn, allein, da seine Landsleute verwundet waren. Er wurde, allein, von dem Mann aus *Su* getötet. Und ohne Verweilen ging der Mann aus *Su* zurück und tötete mühelos die beiden verwundeten Gegner. Er hatte begriffen, dass Flucht nicht nur ein Zeichen der Niederlage, sondern auch ein Mittel zum Sieg sein kann. Noch etwas fügte *Meti* hinzu: Man muss auch deshalb den Mann von *Su* einen Dialektiker nennen, weil er den Feind als einen in einer ganz bestimmten Hinsicht uneinheitlichen Feind erkannte. Alle drei konnten noch kämpfen, aber nur einer konnte noch laufen… Diese Erkenntnis ermöglichte die Trennung.[36]

This passage from the *Buch der Wendungen* provides a short summary of the last and decisive battle between the Horatians and Curiatians. As a strategy of war, the flight of the Horatian echoes the *Dàodéjīng*, which suggests:

> Bei den Soldaten gibt es ein Wort:
> …
> Ich wage nicht, einen Zoll vorzurücken,
> sondern ziehe mich lieber einen Fuß zurück.[37]

The decision to retreat by moving one foot backwards paradoxically creates a new attack, which is an example of changing the means of warfare in accordance with "the flux of things." By not only identifying the defects of his opponent, but also adapting his own reaction to the changing circumstances, the Horatian manages to transform the strength of the three Curiatians into weakness. Through underestimating the Horatian's ability to pursue in correspondence with the *dào*, the Curiatians are subsequently defeated:

> Es gibt kein größeres Unglück,
> als den Feind zu unterschätzen.
> Wenn ich den Feind unterschätze,
> stehe ich in Gefahr, meine Schätze zu verlieren.[38]

This comparison of *The Horatians and the Curiatians* with the *Dàodéjīng* suggests marked points of linguistic and conceptual overlap between the two texts. Most significantly, the Taoist concept of "the flux of things" shapes not only the structure but also the course of the *Lehrstück*. Moreover, understanding this conceptualization of flux facilitates a more thorough understanding of the dialectical thought embodied within the play. According to Brecht's essay "Fünf Schwierigkeiten beim Schreiben der Wahrheit," dialectics is "die Lehre vom Fluss der Dinge... eine Betrachtungsweise, die das Vergängliche besonders hervorhebt."[39] By employing an approach to "the flux of things" informed by Taoist thought Brecht demonstrates how the victory of the materially "weak" over "the strong" can occur. As addressed by Tatlow in his discussion of Brecht's early poems, the dialectical quality of the Taoist message that "predicts victory from the moment of apparent defeat"[40] can therefore also be encountered in the last *Lehrstück*.

Investigating the Taoist approach to dialectics leads to the question of compatibility between Taoist and Marxist philosophies. With regard to the issues of goal-orientated action and human agency the two philosophies appear incompatible. However, by changing the depicted war into one that arises from the Horatians' will to defend themselves, a reaction that is tolerated by both Taoism and Marxism, Brecht enables a compatibility between these philosophies. Consequently, and most notably apparent in the second and third battle, Brecht then demonstrates the points of convergence and divergence of both philosophies. In doing so, the *Dàodéjīng* provides a methodological approach for establishing a dialectical strategy as well as awareness of how to work with cyclical movement, multiplicity, change, difference, and retreat. However, the social aim and its derivation have to be understood within a Marxist context.

In opposing the non-action feature of *wúwèi* with an action-based Marxist approach to "the flux of things" and by demonstrating their compatibility, not only the Horatian—like the last fighters of *Su* in the *Buch der Wendungen*—but also the playwright himself have to be called dialecticians.

Endnotes

1   The understanding of the *Lehrstück* as a musical genre is based on recent studies by Klaus-Dieter Krabiel, *Brechts Lehrstücke. Entstehung und Entwicklung eines Spieltyps* (Stuttgart and Weimar: Metzler, 1993); Andrzej Wirth, "The Lehrstück as Performance," *The Drama Review* 43.4 (1999): pp. 113-121; and Joy H. Calico, *Brecht at the Opera* (Los Angeles: University of California Press, 2008), pp. 16-34. All three studies elaborate on

the *Lehrstück* within the context of 1920s' music culture, commencing their investigation with the *Neue Musik* movement and the festivals of *Neue Musik* in Baden-Baden (1929) and Berlin (1930), where the *Lehrstück* was first developed by Hindemith, Weill and Brecht. Following Krabiel's reassertion of "the primacy of music in the Lehrstück," (Calico, p. 17) Calico takes this even further by claiming the *Lehrstück* as an independent musical genre, describing it as "anti-opera musical theater" (ibid.) and thus as Brecht's greatest critique of opera (ibid., p. 6). The genre's origin indicates that music constitutes the most important feature within the *Lehrstück* with its function being "dialectical music" involving a method of analyzing socio-economic processes or behavioral patterns by revealing their inherent contradictions. As a constituent part of *Neue Musik*, the *Lehrstück*-genre utilizes and generates new musical styles that are characteristic to the aesthetics of the 1920s. Hence, reclaiming the primacy of music in the *Lehrstück* opposes most previous research that, by taking a litero-centric approach, "has overlooked that the Lehrstucke [sic] are libretti and can be interpreted only in relation to the vocal, musical, and choreographic performance" (Wirth, p. 113).

2   Also known as *Das Badener Lehrstück vom Einverständnis*.
3   See Krabiel, *Brechts Lehrstücke*; and Calico, pp. 16-34; see also endnote 1.
4   Colin Counsell, *Signs of Performance: An Introduction to Twentieth-Century Theater* (London and New York: Routledge, 1996), p. 80.
5   Bertolt Brecht, "Die dialektische Dramatik," circa 1930, in *Große kommentierte Berliner und Frankfurter Ausgabe* (BFA), ed. Werner Hecht, Jan Knopf, Werner Mittenzwei, Klaus-Detlef Müller (Berlin, Weimar, Frankfurt/Main: Aufbau, Suhrkamp, 1988-2000), vol. 21, pp. 431-443, here p. 432 (henceforth *BFA* volume, page number); see also Brecht's own footnote: "Quellen: Also etwa ...," ibid.
6   Bertolt Brecht, "Tagebuch September 1920; Donnerstag, 16. - Dienstag, 21.," in *BFA* 26, p. 168.
7   Krabiel, p. 259.
8   See for next three paragraphs: Karyn L. Lai, *An Introduction to Chinese Philosophy* (New York: Cambridge University Press, 2008), pp. 81-92.
9   Antony Tatlow, *The Mask of Evil* (Berne: Peter Lang, 1977), p. 457.
10 Laotse, *Tao te king. Das Buch vom Sinn und Leben*, 4th ed., trans. Richard Wilhelm (Munich: Deutscher Taschenbuchverlag, 2005).
11 Heinrich Detering, *Bertolt Brecht und Laotse* (Göttingen: Wallstein, 2008), p. 13.
12 Bertolt Brecht, "An Hanns Eisler, Svendborg, 29. August 1935," in *BFA* 28, pp. 518-520, here pp. 518-519. Translation in Bertolt Brecht, *Letters*, trans. Ralph Manheim (London: Methuen, 1990), pp. 211-212.
13 Although it was recorded by Herbert Kegel and the *Leipziger Rundfunkchor* in April 1956, *The Horatians and the Curiatians* premiered only after Brecht's death at the University of Halle in 1958, where it was directed by Dr. Hella Brock.
14 Laotse, "Chapter 76," p. 89.
15 Ibid., "Chapter 13," p. 21.
16 See Detering, p. 15.
17 See Lai, pp. 81-84.
18 Laotse, "Chapter 31," p. 39.
19 Ibid., "Chapter 67," p. 80.
20 Ibid., "Chapter 69," p. 82.
21 Bertolt Brecht, *Collected Plays: Three*, ed. John Willett (London: Methuen, 1997), p. 185.
22 Ibid., p. 187.
23 Laotse, "Chapter 64," p. 76.
24 Brecht, *Collected Plays*, p. 190.
25 Bertolt Brecht, "Die Horatier und die Kuriatier," in *BFA* 4, p. 291.
26 Laotse, "Chapter 16," p. 24.
27 Brecht, "Die Horatier und die Kuriatier," in *BFA* 4, p. 291, emphasis by the author.
28 Brecht, *Collected Plays*, p. 190.

29 Ibid., p. 192.
30 Laotse, "Chapter 78," p. 91.
31 Tatlow, p. 455.
32 Ibid.
33 Ibid., p. 456.
34 Laotse, "Chapter 73," p. 86.
35 Editorial notes to *Buch der Wendungen*, in *BFA* 18, p. 487.
36 Bertolt Brecht, "Die Mittel wechseln—Buch der Wendungen," in *BFA* 18, pp. 54-55.
37 Laotse, "Chapter 69," p. 82.
38 Ibid.
39 Bertolt Brecht, "Fünf Schwierigkeiten beim Schreiben der Wahrheit," circa 1935, in *BFA* 22.1, p. 87.
40 Tatlow, p. 459.

Die Tapferkeit im Nicht-Tun: Die taoistische Überlebensstrategie in Bertolt Brechts *Schweyk* und Anna Seghers' *Transit*

Weijia Li

In beiden Werken geht es um *Wu-wei*, eine Überlebensstrategie im chinesischen taoistischen Sinne. Schweyk versucht, durch seine scheinbare Gehorsamkeit gegenüber den Nazis sowie durch seine List und Tricks zu überleben. Seidler, der Protagonist in *Transit*, will der Verfolgung und Lebensbedrohung ohne große Anstrengungen entgehen. In beiden Fällen ist das Überleben jedoch nicht nur das endgültige Ziel in einer lebensbedrohlichen Situation. Das Überleben selbst ist zugleich eine Art von Widerstand und schafft damit die Basis für Widerstand gegen die Nazi-Besatzung. Schweyks Sabotage in der Kriegszeit und Seidlers Schlussentscheidung zu bleiben und zu kämpfen anstatt zu flüchten sind gerade Hoffnungszeichen für jeglichen Widerstand gegen das Nazi-Regime und dessen verbrecherischen Krieg. Sowohl Brecht als auch Seghers verleihen der taoistischen *Wu-wei-Lehre* eine neue Dimension und Anwendbarkeit.

Both works deal with *wu-wei*, a Chinese Taoist strategy of survival. Schweyk tries to survive by his feigned obedience to the Nazis as well as by his tricks and cunning. Seidler, the protagonist of *Transit*, wants to escape from danger and persecution without much apparent effort. However, in both cases survival is not just the final goal in a life-threatening situation. Survival in itself is a form of resistance and therefore establishes the basis for resistance against the Nazi occupation. Schweyk's sabotage during the war and Seidler's final decision to stay and fight instead of to escape are precisely symbols of hope for any resistance against the Nazi regime and its war crimes. Both Brecht and Seghers thus give the Taoist *wu-wei* a new dimension and applicability.

Braveness in Non-Action:
The Taoist Strategy of Survival in Bertolt Brecht's *Schweyk* and Anna Seghers' *Transit*

Weijia Li

Brecht's intensive engagement with Chinese Taoism led him to adapt various aspects of Taoist philosophy in his work. One of his contemporaries, Anna Seghers (1900-1983), who studied Chinese language and philosophy at the University of Heidelberg from 1920 to 1924, also embedded Taoist elements in her writings. Even so, the research on Brecht's encounter with China has not yet compared Brecht's and Seghers' respective receptions of Taoism despite the similar political beliefs and personal experiences of these two authors as German writers in exile. This article, therefore, provides the first comparative analysis of Taoist elements in the works of Brecht and Seghers by focusing on Brecht's play *Schweyk in the Second World War* (in the following abbreviated as *Schweyk*) and Seghers's novel *Transit*, both written in 1943/44.[1]

Brecht's *Schweyk* is a satirical drama about a common man, Schweyk, who is forced into WWII and manages to survive. Schweyk overcomes various dangerous situations at Gestapo Headquarters, a military prison, and a "voluntary" labor service. His strategy of survival in this play resonates pervasively with a fundamental theme in Taoism: *Wu-wei* (Non-action).[2] Despite extensive research on Taoist elements in Brecht's work since the early 1970s, however, there has been very little discussion of the presence of Taoist thought in this particular play. To this day, Tatlow's masterful monograph *Mask of Evil: Brecht's Response to the Poetry, Theatre and Thought of China and Japan* (1977) is the only study that explicitly approaches the play's theme of survival from a Taoist perspective. Tatlow argues that *Schweyk* exemplifies the teaching of the *Tao Te Ching* that an inflexible strategy will not triumph,[3] and that the play's protagonist is "a symbol of indestructibility."[4] Yet Tatlow believes that Schweyk's attitude towards Nazism and war should not be misunderstood as passivity or yielding. Tatlow considers the "Moldaulied" in the play as a metaphor for the power of water to move stones. He argues that Schweyk's survival strategy exemplifies the symbolic meaning of water described in chapter 78 of the *Tao Te Ching*: "Nothing in the world is as yielding and receptive as water; yet in attacking the firm and inflexible, nothing triumphs so well."[5] Tatlow further highlights this observation about Schweyk by quoting from Brecht's *Arbeitsjournal*, where Brecht defines Schweyk as follows: "seine unzerstörbarkeit macht ihn zum unerschöpflichen objekt des missbrauches und zugleich zum nährboden der befreiung."[6] But what Tatlow fails to discuss is the connection between Schweyk's strategy of survival and one of the essential thoughts in the *Tao Te Ching*, namely *wu-*

wei (non-action). This particular Taoist element is also largely reflected in Anna Seghers' *Transit,* a novel that shares many similarities with *Schweyk.* A comparison between the two works will illustrate varying approaches towards the Chinese *wu-wei* within a German literary context.

As mentioned earlier, Schweyk's survival strategy can also be understood as an example of *wu-wei* as interpreted by Brecht. A dialectical interpretation of *wu-wei* can be found in chapter 73 of the *Tao Te Ching*: "Those bold in daring will die; those whose braveness lies in not daring will survive."[7] In other words: *Wu-wei* means "to dare not to dare." Schweyk's survival strategy is to abandon direct and potentially self-destructive actions and to pursue an indirect way of resistance instead. One should not underestimate the effects of this form of "indirect" resistance, however. Some scholars have criticized *Schweyk* as "weak" and even "disorienting."[8] Such criticism often results from the expectation of a tragic and glorious hero who, of course, never appears in Brecht's work. Brecht instead presents a dialectical relationship between weakness and indestructibility. *Wu-wei*, or non-action, means the abandonment of ("heroic") self-destruction in a life-threatening situation and the choice of ("cowardly") survival as a basis for resistance. Acting without self-destroying actions is not only Schweyk's survival strategy but also the art of sustainable resistance. Critical works on the play often overlook the power and effects of Schweyk's indirect resistance. Schweyk's pretense, for example, causes a train loaded with food and weapons, desperately needed by the German soldiers, to be sent to the wrong place. His business of selling dogs leads to clashes between the Gestapo, the SS, and a local collaborator with the Nazis. On the Eastern Front, he protects a Russian family and teaches the German soldiers how to surrender to the Russians. All of his activities indicate that his "non-actions," in fact, pose a threat to Hitler's war.

In *Transit,* which is partly based on her own experiences, Seghers describes the life of German refugees in the years of 1940 and 1941 in Marseille. As the German army invaded France, many German refugees tried to go overseas by ship. For the trip, they not only needed a ticket but also the required paperwork: a visa to enter a country of their destination along with a transit visa allowing them to access this country via other countries.[9]

Seidler, the protagonist and narrator of the novel, is a young German antifascist who, after fleeing from Germany, has just arrived in Marseille. In the novel, all other refugees fight desperately and with all means for the visas and ship tickets, mostly in vain. Seidler, by contrast, obtains all the necessary papers for traveling to Mexico (even though that was not his original plan), and he gets them almost without any effort. Note the dialectical concept of "effects without action" versus "action without effects" here, which studies of Seghers' work so far have only described as a paradox: "So wenig der Held seine Abfahrt betreibt, um so reibungsloser klappt es mit der schrittweisen Anbahnung und Erledigung seiner Formalitäten für ein schutzgewährendes Asyl in Mexiko."[10] Indeed, the novel shows Seidler's attitude as *wu-wei*: In his case, non-action means distancing himself from the hectic and purpose-driven actions of the other refugees. Yet he manages to achieve his goals without effort. While all the other immigrants are tormented by their obsession of getting the transit visas, Seidler just wants to stay in Marseille.[11] He goes to the Mexican consulate not to apply for a visa but to return the visa of another person named Weidel, who got this visa but then committed suicide in a hotel in Paris. While all the other applicants vigorously push to the front of the line at the consulate, Seidler himself behaves quite differently, with the characteristic Taoist peace: "I waited, half amused, half bored. When my name was called, I entered the consular official's office without any particular feeling or definite purpose—still half amused, half bored."[12] Because of a bureaucratic mix-up, however, the impatient consulate secretary erroneously takes Seidler for Weidel and therefore provides him with the visa and the paid ship ticket originally reserved for the latter.[13]

Other episodes in the novel further support the *Tao Te Ching*'s warning against *wei*, action: "He who acts, harms…Whereas the people of the world, at their tasks, constantly spoil things when within an ace of completing them."[14] A German doctor, for example, is afraid that he won't be able to depart.[15] After obtaining a visa, a transit visa, and a ticket, he abandons his lover and rushes to the port to secure his own departure. However, it turns out that his selfish, hectic action is all in vain: Moments before his scheduled departure, he finds out that he is not able to board the ship because the military commission has confiscated all cabins for their officers. Another example is the story of a conductor who needs to get an overseas employment contract in order to attain a visa, with which he could then apply for the transit visa. In addition to these two visas, he will have to obtain the permission to leave France, the so-called *visa de sortie*, before the transit visa expires. But the processing of this *visa de sortie* lasts so long that his transit visa expires. Therefore, he has to renew the employment contract so that the visa and transit visa can be extended.[16] When Seidler meets the conductor again after a long time, the conductor tells him that his second *visa de sortie* has been issued "just half a week too late" after his regular visa expires.[17] This visa will be extended only if he can renew the contract of employment again. And if he cannot get it renewed within a month, his *visa de sortie* will also expire. At last, the conductor collapses in the Mexican consulate when finding out that he miscounted the passport photos he was supposed to submit in order to get the visa.

Transit incorporates another aspect of *wu-wei*: *Jing* (quietness, silence, or harmony). According to the *Tao Te Ching*, quietness provides an insight into the true nature of things: "Return to the root is called Quietness;/Quietness is called submission to Fate;/What has submitted to Fate has become part of the always-so/To know the always-so is to be Illumined."[18] In the novel, Seidler fully demonstrates this *wu-wei* attitude: When the German soldiers come to the French village where he has found refuge, he suddenly becomes less and less afraid as he falls into a meditation-like quietness:

> As for myself, I grew suddenly quite calm. Here I am, I thought, and the Germans are going past me, occupying France. But France has often been occupied, and every invader has been hurled out of the country again. France has often been sold and betrayed before, and you too, my fine gray-green young fellows, have often been sold and betrayed. My fear had vanished completely; the swastika was only a shadow. I saw the most powerful army in the world draw up beyond my hedge and march off, I saw the boldest empires crumble and young and daring nations arise, I saw the masters of the world rise to the top and drop into oblivion. I alone had an illimitable span of time in which to live.[19]

Doing what is most simple is precisely the desired attitude toward life in Taoism. Facing the ever-changing world, Seidler behaves like an observer resting in an eternal quietness. The flowing nature of things—in this case history and the war—is one of the major themes in Taoist thought.

In *Transit*, *wu-wei* means neither passivity nor resignation, and by no means the rejection of resistance. Non-action is reflected in Seidler's distancing himself from self-destructive behavior and selfish expediency as well as in his decision to stay and fight instead of fleeing. In the end, Seidler has the option to go overseas, but he ultimately decides to stay in France: "I now want to share with these people good and evil, refuge and persecution. When the time comes for resistance…I will grab up a gun."[20] For the other refugees, the long-awaited trip overseas promises no final rescue because the ship, according to rumors, might have run over a mine and sunk.

Both Schweyk and Seidler face oppressive situations caused by the German occupation and/or military aggression. They survive because of the ways in which they engage with the oppressive orders surrounding them. One should note that how to deal with the order (or disorder) of a jeopardized society is a central theme in the *Tao Te Ching*. Schweyk's wisdom and survival strategy are to first submit to the oppressive order without reservation and in an exaggerated manner, and then to destroy this order with a small manipulation at the right moment. Seidler ignores the order when it comes to the paperwork for travel. He stands aside and waits until the order destroys itself by letting the bureaucracy run its course. Both Schweyk's wisdom and Seidler's attitude reflect the *wu-wei* in chapter 36 of the *Tao Te Ching*: "In order to deplete it, it must be thoroughly extended. In order to weaken it, it must be thoroughly strengthened. In order to reject it, it must be thoroughly promoted."[21]

In both works, the protagonists' strategy of survival mirrors the idea of *wu-wei*, namely the abandonment of self-destruction in a precarious situation. Furthermore, in both works the abandonment of direct, potentially self-destructive (but "heroic") actions establishes the opportunity and basis for sustainable resistance. Survival is no longer the ultimate goal of *wu-wei*. Schweyk's sabotage, which he may bring about unconsciously, and Seidler's final decision to stay and fight instead of fleeing are symbols of hope for any resistance against the Nazi regime. Brecht and Seghers thus lend a new dimension and specifically German context to *wu-wei*, a central Chinese Taoist notion.

Obviously, *Schweyk* and *Transit* do not have any explicit Chinese themes. Scholars are often more comfortable writing on Taoist elements in the widely acknowledged "China-works" of German writers, for example, *Die drei Sprünge des Wang Lun* by Alfred Döblin and *Der gute Mensch von Sezuan* by Brecht. One could easily be skeptical of the major argument of this essay since both *Schweyk* and *Transit* are "non-China" works, and since neither one of the texts explicitly engages with the Chinese Tao. However, previous research has provided sufficient evidence for both writers' intensive encounter with Chinese Taoism. It is undeniable that the fascination with China, especially the Tao-fascination of many German intellectuals, is a cultural historical phenomenon that has not gained enough attention among scholars. Brecht's encounter with China should not be investigated as an isolated case. Further research on this topic will require more intertextual, intercultural, and interdisciplinary investigation. In conclusion, I quote a statement by psychologist Carl Gustav Jung. In 1930, Jung wrote in a memorial address in tribute to Richard Wilhelm, the German translator of many Chinese philosophical classics, including the *Tao Te Ching*:

> The spirit of the East is really at our gates. Therefore it seems to me that the translation of meaning into life, the search for the Tao, has already become a collective phenomenon among us, and that to a far greater extent than is generally realized.[22]

Endnotes

1   I discuss the Taoist elements of Anna Seghers' *Transit* at length in Weijia Li, *China und China-Erfahrungen in Leben und Werk von Anna Seghers* (Berne: Peter Lang, 2010), pp. 131-142.
2   *Wu wei* can also be translated as "without action" or "effortless doing."
3   *Tao Te Ching*, chapter 76, in R. L. Wing, ed., *The Tao of Power* (Garden City: Doubleday, 1986), p. 76.
4   Antony Tatlow, *The Mask of Evil: Brecht's Response to the Poetry, Theatre and Thought of China and Japan. A Comparative and Critical Evaluation* (Berne: Peter Lang, 1977), p. 462.
5   Tatlow, p. 465.
6   Bertolt Brecht, *Arbeitsjournal*, 27 May 1943. In Werner Hecht, ed., *Bertolt Brecht Arbeitsjournal* (Frankfurt/Main.: Suhrkamp, 1973), p. 569.
7   Wing, p. 76.
8   See Jan Knopf, ed., *Brecht Handbuch*, Vol. 1 (Stuttgart: Metzler, 2001), p. 490.
9   Anna Seghers, *Werkausgabe. Das erzählerische Werk* I/5 (Berlin: Aufbau-Verlag, 2001), p. 47.
10 Sigrid Thielking, "Warten — Erzählen — Überleben. Vom Exil aller Zeiten in Anna Seghers' Roman *Transit*," *Argonautenschiff* 4 (1995), pp. 127-138.
11 Seghers, *Werkausgabe* I/5, p. 50.
12 Anna Seghers, *Transit*, trans. James Austin Galston (Boston: Little, Brown and Company, 1944), p. 56. The original German text: "Ich hatte halb belustigt gewartet, halb gelangweilt. Und ohne Gefühl und ohne Absicht betrat ich das Zimmer des Konsulatskanzlers, als man mich aufrief, halb belustigt, halb gelangweilt." Seghers, *Werkausgabe* I/5, p. 54.
13 Seghers, *Werkausgabe* I/5, p. 103.
14 *Tao Te Ching*, chapter 64, in Arthur Waley, ed., *The Way And Its Power* (London, George Allen & Unwin, 1934), p. 221.
15 Anna Seghers, *Werkausgabe* I/5, p. 91.
16 Ibid., p. 46.
17 Ibid., p. 70.
18 *Tao Te Ching*, chapter 16, in Arthur Waley, p. 162.
19 Seghers, *Transit*, p. 10-11. The original German text: "Ich aber wurde plötzlich ganz ruhig. Da sitze ich nun, dachte ich, und die Deutschen ziehen an mir vorbei und besetzen Frankreich. Aber Frankreich war schon oft besetzt — alle haben wieder abziehen müssen...Meine Angst war völlig verflogen, das Hakenkreuz war mir ein Spuk, ich sah die mächtigsten Heere der Welt hinter meinem Gartenzaun aufmarschieren und abziehen, ich sah die frechsten Reiche zerfallen und junge und kühne sich aufrichten, ich sah die Herren der Welt hochkommen und verwesen, nur ich hatte unermesslich viel Zeit zu leben." Seghers, *Werkausgabe* I/5, p. 12.
20 Seghers, *Transit*, p. 311. The original German text: "Ich will jetzt Gutes und Böses hier mit meinen Leuten teilen, Zuflucht und Verfolgung. Ich werde, sobald es zum Widerstand kommt...meine Knarre nehmen." Seghers, *Werkausgabe*, p. 279.
21 Wing, p. 36.
22 Carl Gustav Jung, "In Memory of Richard Wilhelm," in Richard Wilhelm, ed., *The Secret of The Golden Flower* (London: Routledge & Kegan Paul, 1931), p. 146. The original German text: "Der Geist des Ostens ist wirklich ante portas. Darum scheint es mir, dass die Verwirklichung des Sinnes, das Suchen des Tao, bei uns in weit stärkerem Maße bereits kollektive Erscheinung geworden ist, als man allgemein denkt." In Richard Wilhelm, ed., *Das Geheimnis der goldenen Blüte* (Jena: Diederich, 1929), p. XV.

Brechts *Guter Mensch* und die traditionelle humanistische chinesische Philosophie: Annäherung an ein ethisches Subjekt

Zheng Jie

Dieser Aufsatz versucht, das inkonsistente Verständnis des menschlichen Subjekts zu erklären, wie man es in Brechts Werk findet, angefangen bei seinen frühen Stücken, den Lehrstücken, bis zu den großangelegten epischen Dramen. Meine These ist, dass seine späteren Werke eine Neubestätigung des Humanismus zeigen (beeinflußt von der klassischen chinesischen Philosophie) — ein Zug, der ein Abweichen von seinen früheren Werken und dem Theater der Lehrstücke markiert. Ich werde hauptsächlich *Den guten Menschen von Sezuan* als Beispiel gebrauchen, um zu untersuchen, wie chinesisches Denken (insbesondere Konfuzianismus und Taoismus) Brecht einen Weg bieten, die Dualismen herauszufordern, die die westliche Vorstellung von Subjektivität festlegen (Selbst/Anderer, Subjekt/Objekt, schlecht/gut und so weiter). Des weiteren werde ich analysieren, auf welche Weise Brechts "neuer Mensch," der, wenn auch in einem materialistischen Rahmen, dem Prinzip des Tao folgt, einer ethischen Erwiderung fähig ist und vielfältige Perspektiven und dialektische Praktiken versteht.

This paper attempts to explain the inconsistent understanding of the human subject as it can be found in Brecht's work, from his early plays, the *Lehrstücke*, to the large-scaled epic dramas. I suggest that his later works demonstrate a reassertion of humanism (informed by Chinese classical philosophy) — a trait that marks a point of departure from his early works and *Lehrstücke* theater. I shall mainly use *The Good Person of Szechwan* as an example to investigate how Chinese thought (in particular, Confucianism and Taoism) offers Brecht a means to challenge those dualisms that define Western notions of human subjectivity (self/other, subject/object, good/bad, etcetera). Furthermore, I will analyze in what ways Brecht's "new type of man," following the principle of *tao*, albeit within a materialist framework, is capable of ethical response and understands multiple perspectives and dialectical practices.

Brecht's *Good Person* and Traditional Humanistic Chinese Philosophy: Towards an Ethical Subject[1]

Zheng Jie

For those critics who hold the view that the thematic concerns of Brecht's work could be categorized into the youthful nihilism and mature communism of the *Lehrstücke*, his later works present a problem. And while many critics, having noticed an explicit rupture between his earlier works and later works, share the view that ethical problems become the main concern in his later works,[2] it is quite clear that Brecht concerned himself with ethical problems throughout his life. Moreover, attempts to reread Brecht's early plays and his *Lehrstücke* have predominantly focused on his portrayal of the destabilization of the individual.[3] In fact, before Brecht left Germany in the year of 1933, he had already begun to question the conventional concepts of ethics. For instance, when Brecht talked about unemployment in Germany, he concluded that

> the ethical needs of these social strata need not be satisfied ethically. the satisfaction of their material needs is ethical enough…without satisfaction of material needs no ethics, and that is acceptable. but: ethics for the satisfaction of these needs is not acceptable. material needs as ethical, ethical ones as material, this is not grasped. all sorts of material for the book of change.[4]

This passage from Brecht's journal provides a key to one of the themes of the Brechtian theory of ethics. Here Brecht, though unintentionally, expounds the poignant lyric—"Food is the first thing. Morals follow on." in *The Threepenny Opera* (1928)—a formulation that bears close affinity with the Confucian saying "Food before morals."

We should be wary of forming a stable and monolithic discourse of Brecht's understanding on his new type of man, especially considering the fact that his ideas were constantly changing and developing. The plays Brecht wrote in the early and mid-1920s are characterized by his rejection of the concept of the individual as integral to bourgeois ethics.[5] His use of a Marxist configuration of subjectivity (particularly in his *Lehrstücke*) is typically misunderstood as signifying his belief, in such a case, of class over ethical issues.[6] Louis Althusser, however, justifies this perspective with his analysis of the ideological consciousness, which serves as the root of totalitarian enslavement:

> If we carry our analysis of this condition a little further we can easily find in it Marx's fundamental principle that it is impossible

> for any form of ideological consciousness to contain in itself, through its own internal dialectic, an escape from itself, that, *strictly speaking, there is no dialectic consciousness*: no dialectic of consciousness which could reach reality itself by virtue of its own contradiction; in short, there can be no "phenomenology" in the Hegelian sense: for consciousness does not accede to the real through its own internal development, but by the radical discovery of what is *other than itself*. [7]

Althusser's implication is that a consciousness of the self is, firstly, an image of ideological consciousness and, secondly, a false consciousness that includes pretensions to "exhaustive self-recovery and self-representation in the form of a consciousness of self."[8] Althusser's Marxist reading of Brecht is engaged with a critique of the consciousness of Brecht's characters as subject to the economic mode of production. However, it will become clear, when we speak of the dynamic of Brecht's later plays, that Althusser's presumption is one-sided, as he makes no differentiation between the various stages of Brecht's work.

Brecht is decidedly vague in his reestablishment of ethics. As a Marxist, he accuses capitalism of neglecting the full development of human beings, saying that "thus we also find the crippled, one-sided, empty human beings," and going on to assert that we should fight for "a fulfilled human world" which "develops humanity in those individuals engaged in the fight."[9] Elsewhere he writes: "Capitalism does not only dehumanize, it also creates humanness, namely in the active struggle against dehumanization. Even today human beings are not machines, they do not function as simply a part of machinery."[10] This reveals Brecht's emphasis on the autonomy of the individual and suggests his suspicion of the economic basis of human nature. The passage may not be sufficient to prove that Brecht has departed from a Marxist view of subjectivity and humanity in many important ways. However, it has become apparent that a sole reliance on Marxist moral philosophy fails to explain Brecht's moral picture.

There is a clear development in Brecht's configuration of subjectivity, individuality, and ethics in his later works. His first plays are in this respect entirely destructive: his heroes are either, like Baal and Shlink, completely asocial, dismissive of bourgeois ethics and at the mercy of their "instincts and vitality;"[11] or they are, like Galy Gay, ready to surrender to the changing constellation of pressures and social relationships; or they are the young comrades in *The Measures Taken*, subjecting the self to the collective and refusing moral autonomy. Frederic Ewen notices that in Brecht's later plays "the human and humane element becomes dominant:" *Mother Courage*, for example, "is now modified by a profound sympathy."[12] He calls this change of Brecht's attitude "Marxist humanism."[13] While Ewen's observation is shared by many other critics, his explanation is a subject of some dispute. Martin Esslin, taking an opposing view, claims that Brecht's later plays are more an expression of his instincts and thus a demonstration of his failure to completely follow the discipline of Communism, which "provided a technique of self-control, discipline, and rational thought."[14] John Willett, however, emphasizing Brecht's humanist attitude (which is associated with romanticism), comes to the conclusion that it is "his natural sympathy" that gives "a new warmth" to his character and his later plays.[15] Addressing this long disputed ambivalence concerning Brecht's later plays, this paper, while not attempting to minimize the influences as stressed by the above critics, focuses on the place of Chinese influence in Brecht's reconfiguration of the human subject and ethics—a subject that is yet little understood.

It should be noted that although, as Sean Carney suggests, Brecht is not a proper Marxist who firmly shares the orthodox class analysis that "class and class-consciousness define the effective determinant of the subject,"[16] he never discarded his earlier assumption that human beings have to be seen as "the sum of all social circumstances."[17] Brecht, in his plays, constantly deals with the problem of how the autonomy of individuality is threatened within capitalist production relations. Yet we find that a concern with ethical problems and their relation to human subjectivity continues to mark the plays he wrote in his later years, in particular, *Galileo, Mother Courage, The Good Person of Szechwan, The Caucasian Chalk Circle*, and *Mr. Puntila and His Man Matti*. Furthermore, a closer examination of these works suggests a number of elements within Brecht's reflections on the very nature of ethics issues (such as "goodness") and their constitutional function for one's subjectivity bear a close parallel to humanistic ideas from Chinese philosophy (chiefly Confucianism and Taoism). It is in this context that the relationship of Brecht's *Good Person* to Chinese classical philosophy becomes crucial to a better understanding of Brecht's reconfiguration of the idea of the human subject. To this end, his consideration of such issues in his later works is perhaps best seen as a product of an ongoing dialogue (both affirmative and disruptive) between Western intellectual traditions and the philosophy of humanism within the Chinese tradition. In "negotiation" with Marxism, Confucianism and Taoism, though not unifying in themselves, operate on different levels in Brecht's thinking. For while it may be an exaggeration to claim that Chinese influence plays a dominant role in Brecht's reflection on ethics and subjectivity (indeed, such an assumption would be just as misleading as negating the relation of Chinese thought to Brecht's work), my contention is that what Chinese thought offers is a clear means of challenging the dualisms that define traditional notions of human subjectivity (self/other, subject/object, good/bad, etcetera), and, thus, plays a crucial role in helping Brecht formulate his views. As we shall see, Brecht's "new type of man," following the principle of *tao*, albeit within a materialistic framework, is capable of ethical response and understands multiple perspectives and dialectical practices.

Goodness and Friendliness

In his notes to *The Caucasian Chalk Circle*, Brecht identifies the primary contradiction of the play: "The more Grusha does to save the child's life, the more she endangers her own; her productivity tends to her own destruction."[18] It turns out that this is a theme best summarized in Shen Teh's desperate confession to the gods in the *Good Person*: "goodness to others and to myself could not both be achieved."[19]

The Good Person of Szechwan (1943) tells the story of a prostitute named Shen Teh, who is rewarded with a gift of money for her kindness by three gods who have come to earth in search for a "good person"—something that turns out to be very scarce. What is particularly striking about the play is that Shen Teh shows a natural tendency to be good. As Peter Ruppert observes,

> Her goodness is a natural unfolding of herself; she shares her possessions freely, loves spontaneously, and reveals a genuine desire to help others. The significant values that emerge from her actions are friendliness, cooperation, peace, equality. These values flow effortlessly, without conscious deliberation.[20]

Similar virtues can also be found in several other of Brecht's characters, for example, Grusha, who sacrifices her own security and happiness for an unrelated child, and Azdak, who, in the disguise of shrewdness and carelessness, judges in favor of the poor and the oppressed. Renata Berg-Pan suggests a close affinity between Brecht's views of human nature and those of Mencius, a follower of Confucius.[21] Unlike Confucius, who asserts that goodness is an ideal quality to be attained with life-long strenuous efforts, Mencius regards goodness as a quality innate in all men. In one of his essays, Mencius relates the famous "the-child-in-the-well" example:

> When a child falls down a well, witnesses to the event will immediately feel alarm and distress, not to gain friendship with the child's parents, nor to seek the praise of their neighbors and friends, nor because they dislike the reputation [of lack of humanity if they did not rescue the child]…The feeling of commiseration is the beginning of humanity; the feeling of shame and dislike is the beginning of righteousness; the feeling of deference and compliance is the beginning of propriety; and the feeling of right and wrong is the beginning of wisdom.[22]

Berg-Pan suggests that Brecht very likely knew this passage, since it reminds us of the inner activities going on in Grusha when she decides to save the child and later gradually develops love for him.[23]

The manifestation of true human nature is, in Mencius' metaphor, like the growth of a tree. Only when it is forced to grow by outer forces does it lose its potential to grow naturally. Likewise, the natural goodness in human nature cannot develop fully as a result of external influences. The metaphor of the tree reminds us of the conflicting identities of Shen Teh and Shui Ta resulting from the opposition between "goodness to oneself" and "goodness to others," as illustrated by Wang's story.

> In Sung there is a place known as Thorn Hedge. There catalpas, cypresses and mulberries flourish. Now those trees which are nine or ten inches in circumference are chopped down by the people who need stakes for their dog kennels. Those which are three or four feet in circumference are chopped down by rich and respectable families who want planks for their coffins. Those which are seven or eight feet in circumference are chopped down by persons seeking beams for their luxurious villas. And so none reaches its full quota of years, but is brought down prematurely by saw or by axe. That is the price of utility. [24]

Wang is probably the only one who shows genuine concern for Shen Teh. His story is taken from *Zhuangzi*, an anthology of early Taoist writings. The message is that the least useful is the most fortunate. Wang, however, concludes by saying that the least good is most fortunate. Wang's modifications of the implication of the story echoes Mencius' claim about how, like the growth of a tree, human's innate tendency towards virtue is always threatened by outside destructive forces.

It is this natural virtue that is discernible in Brecht's later characters. When they are not exposed to negative circumstances, they cannot bear to see the sufferings of others. Besides the two mentioned good women, Grusha and Shen Teh, even the various negative characters in Brecht's plays still demonstrate innate goodness. For example, Mother Courage displays the loving traits of a mother to her own children despite the fact that she is a war profiteer who also sacrifices them to her commercial instinct; or Mr. Puntila, when drunk, overflows with kindness, although he reverts to a different type when he is sober. It is in Puntila's drunkenness, the state in which he is least restrained by societal chains, that he is seen to manifest his innate virtue. In attempting to explain this characterization in Brecht, both Antony Tatlow and Berg-Pan suggest that Chinese philosophy offers observations about individual behavior and conduct which, to quote Tatlow, "amount to modification of what is reconcilable with dogmatic Marxist theory and political practice."[25] Their view is echoed by Fredric

Jameson, "...Chinese 'wisdom' is there to compensate for this lack [if not this incapacity] in Marxism, and to close the gap."[26] Such a reading is reasonable for two obvious reasons: first, that classical Marxism (with its assumption that social class "is the only determining factor in the shaping of the subject")[27] does not explicitly discuss the complex ethical dimension of human nature, second, that it rejects any appeal to universal and normative moral principles in a class society. However, it is also true that Marxism contains similar visions of how class society has separated/alienated humans from their "nature" as a species-being.

All the characters (even though it is difficult to decide at this point whether they are good or evil) show that their innate goodness only deteriorates when they are forced into violent competition by a desire for money—a major negative cultivating influence on the characters. Brecht's optimism regarding human nature coincides with that of Mencius, both of whom believe that goodness is the natural condition of mankind. Here we should note the extent to which Mencius' view of moral deterioration is in tune with the Marxist view that it is external constraints that prevent a man from developing all his potentialities. Brecht, swiftly linking Marx with Chinese thinkers, suggests that it is the capitalist system that makes men evil, and insinuates the possibility that their innate human nature will fully manifest itself once they are governed in a classless society: Brecht seems to leave the issue open in the end of the *Good Person* with a strong hint that "the world should be changed" "to help good people to a happy end."[28]

Another quality, friendliness, is stressed in Brecht's poem "Legend of the Origin of the Book *Tao-te-ching* on Lao-Tzu's Road into Exile." The poem opens with a bleak picture of the old man and his last journey: infirm and despondent over the presence of "wickedness," Lao Zi was leaving his country forever. This is a society in which "goodness had been weakening a little."[29] The teachings of Lao Zi are, rather, a direct consequence of turmoil in society. Brecht is well aware of the similarity between the corrupt society, in which Lao Zi and Confucius lived, and modern Germany. The poem offers an occasion to discuss the role that friendliness plays in a society where human relationships are abused.

There are different versions of the original legend of how Lao Zi puts down his thoughts on paper at the request of the customs official. According to one of the versions, Lao Zi has to compose a book to bribe the "keeper of the pass" in order to pass the border. The most popular version is that this customs official is well educated and recognizes him as soon as he arrives. Realizing what a great loss it will be if Lao Zi were to leave the country forever without leaving behind any work, he asks him to write down his thoughts. The modification that Brecht makes to this poem concerns the interaction between Lao Zi and the customs man. In Brecht's poem the customs man does not know the name of Lao Zi and is obviously an impoverished government man; as the poem puts it, "surely not of the race of conquerors."[30] The customs official simply becomes interested in Lao Zi's remarks about water. Brecht points out the theme of this poem in the last stanza,

> But the honor should not be restricted
> To the sage whose name is clearly writ.
> For a wise man's wisdom needs to be extracted.
> So the customs man deserves his bit.
> It was he who called for it.[31]

Brecht concludes that we should praise the customs man as well. In Walter Benjamin's reading, the poem preaches something that Brecht values very highly in Chinese culture: friendliness, a quality that emphasizes the caring quality in human relationships. For without the quality of friendliness, even with the wisdom of Lao Zi and the customs man's desire for knowledge, it would not be possible for him to elicit the wisdom of Lao Zi. Friendliness comes from both sides: from the official who kindly provides food and accommodation and from Lao Zi, who responds to the request of the customs official. According to Benjamin, Brecht values friendliness as fundamental to human relationships.

> "The classics," an old Chinese philosopher has said, "lived in the darkest and bloodiest times and were the friendliest and most cheerful people that have ever been seen." The Lao Tzu of this legend seems to spread cheerfulness wherever he goes. His ox, undeterred by the old man's weight on his back, is glad of all the green grass it can find. His boy is cheerful when, in order to explain Lao Tzu's poverty, he puts in dryly: "A teacher, you see." The customs official by his toll-gate is in a cheerful mood, and it is this cheerfulness that inspires him with the happy idea of asking for the results of Lao Tzu's research. Finally, how could the sage not be cheerful himself? At the first turning of the road he put out of his mind the valley, which only a moment before had made him glad. What would his wisdom be worth if he could not also forget his anxiety about the future almost as soon as he felt it? [32]

It is undoubtedly this quality of friendliness and goodness in Chinese society that ignites Brecht's interest in Chinese thought. In Brecht's characters goodness and friendliness are interlocked, and their meaning lies in the fact of acknowledging each other's needs by responding to them. Nevertheless, this perspective is inadequate to explain how the characters (such as Galileo, Mother Courage, Lucullus, Shen Teh, Grusha, Mr. Puntila, and Schweyk) are constructed as a combination of complex and even contradictory qualities, which runs like a motif through his works succeeding the *Lehrstücke* period, during which moral standards were often questioned and even suspended. The following discussion will make a distinction between Confucian goodness and Taoist goodness to demonstrate how Brecht reworked conflicting Chinese philosophical traditions with Western thinking (particularly Marxism) in the formulation of his own ideas.

Redefining Goodness

Characters like Shen Teh and Azdak are often considered by Brecht scholars to be the type of split characters. Anne Herrmann, for example, gives a Marxist reading of the *Good Person* and stresses how the unification of the contrasting qualities is non-negotiable: "Here the split subject embodies neither a mimetic doubling nor a division which can be restored; rather, it represents divisiveness as the symptom of a capitalist system in which moral goodness and economic survival are mutually exclusive."[33] Other critics argue for the unity of Brecht's characters. Shlomo Biderman describes the succession of contradictory roles Azdak takes—"accused, convict, judge, oppressor, oppressed, freedom fighter and collaborator,"[34] and arrives at the conclusion that Azdak is portrayed as a characterless man and that "being characterless ensures that he is a thinking man."[35] The unity in Azdak, according to Biderman, is based on the annulation of individual identity. Willett, on the contrary, argues that "the unity of the figure is constructed by the way in which its individual properties and characteristics contradict each other."[36] Willett's confirmation of this unity provides a starting point for this discussion of Shen Teh's subjectivity and its relation to ethics, yet the study will take a different path by emphasizing how the Taoist concept of the "unity of opposites" illuminates Brecht in his understanding of morality and identity. Clearly, this identification of the relations of opposites in the constitution of the subject will require us to adopt a different kind of perspective to observe the character on stage, namely, a Taoist notion that the natural human condition is one of flux and is paradoxical.

Within western culture the legitimacy of the words good and evil has often been questioned (one needs only mention Nietzsche, Foucault, de Man, and Lacan). Nietzsche, for example, argues that Christianity provides a set of moral rules for self-justification. To illustrate his rejection of Christianity as a slave morality which categorizes things rigidly as good and bad, Nietzsche quotes sarcastically in his essay "On the Genealogy of Morals," "Let us be unlike those evil ones. Let us be good. And the good shall be he who does not do violence, does not attack nor retaliate, who leaves vengeance to God, who, like us, the patient, the humble, the just ones."[37] Nietzsche's critique of moral values is based on his belief that "the value of these values themselves must be called into question."[38] Brecht shares with Nietzsche a critique of the blind acceptance of Christian premises in his consideration of morality and a reevaluation of moral values, but it is more in the spirit of Lao Zi that the Brechtian characters go beyond the "good/evil" or "good/bad" distinction while at the same time showing an innate "goodness."

Lao Zi, like Mencius, believes that human nature tends towards the good. However, Lao Zi does not prescribe the specific conduct associated with the quality of goodness as Confucius does. As regards the title of his book *Tao Te Ching*, the word *tao* means "the way," a term that is also used by Confucius and Mencius, but that, within the context of Taoism, implies the essential process and natural order of the universe as characterized by the harmony of opposites. Moreover, *te* means "virtue" and the compound word *tao te* means "ethics." Thus, the literary translation of the book's title is "The Canon of the Way and the Virtue." The movement of *tao* is expressed in two aspects: the interdependence of opposites (that is, there would be no good without evil, no love without hate, no male without female) and the alternation of opposites. However, the paradoxes are best understood as correlatives that are not mutually exclusive but, rather, represent the natural flow of the forces of reality.[39] (Note the analogy between the Taoist paradox and Marxist dialectics.) It is in this sense that Lao Zi associates authentic and ethical action with the movement of *tao*. In contrast to the Confucianists' argument for innate goodness as a justification for their advocated traditional virtues, Lao Zi suggests that goodness and friendliness issue from a spontaneous source and simply should not be reified into, in Eric Sean Nelson's words, "arbitrary rules, static hierarchical relations of subordination, and unresponsive rituals."[40] Here we notice how Lao Zi's standpoint is echoed by a similar line of thought in the Marxist critique of objectivism in ethics, defined by E. Kamenka as "the presented impartiality and universality of moral injunctions and codes."[41]

From this perspective, while goodness and friendliness remain deeply instinctive, this does not mean that they must correspond to specific moral principles. Apparently, the gods in the *Good Person* would think otherwise. "When we do find people who are halfway good, they are not living a decent human existence,"[42] says one of the gods, when they fail to find one more good person besides Shen Teh. "Terrible is the temptation to do good,"[43] says the singer in *The Caucasian Chalk Circle*, and this line summarizes the difficulty of being good in a wicked society while retaining one's coherent identity. "Your original order to be good while yet surviving," says Shen Teh to the gods in the *Good Person*, "Split me like lightning into two people. I/Cannot tell what occurred: goodness to others/And to myself could not both be achieved."[44] Shen Teh's remarks are often cited as evidence for the two dominant readings of the fate of Shen Teh. As Willett would have it, "in a competitive society goodness is often suicidal."[45] On the other hand, Ruppert finds it symptomatic of the "dialectical opposition between self and society, between personal happiness and collective well-being."[46] Both views, however, ignore one important moral narrated by Shen Teh, that is, that "The load of commandments forced me into the sludge."[47] Here again arises the question of the nature of ethics (a question posed in all plays by Brecht, from *Baal* to *The Measures Taken*, and most persistently in the *Good Person*); that is, on what foundation are our moral principles built?

It is notable that the legitimacy of moral values as prescribed by the commandments is not questioned in the beginning of the *Good Person*. When Shen Teh first meets the gods, she admits that she does not obey the commandments and thus fails to be a good person. The gods dismiss her excuses as the doubts of an essentially good person. According to the logic of the play's opening, the commandments by the gods are supposed to be the ideal moral standard for the people to follow. At this point in the play goodness is assumed to be an abstract quality that is in strict opposition to evil. The moment when the gods acknowledge Shen Teh as a good person, ironically she ceases to function as an ethical subject. Now she is Shen Teh with the attribute of "goodness"—a moral object that is class-bound and constrained by bourgeois ethics. From the beginning, Shen Teh is uncertain whether she could be as good a person as the gods request: "How can I be good when everything is so expensive"?[48]

In her pursuit of goodness, Shen Teh eventually has to invent Shui Ta. When Shen Teh plays the role of Shui Ta, she carries a mask implying that Shui Ta is not part of good Shen Teh. Realizing that "the good have no means of helping themselves and the gods are powerless," she states that "the good cannot remain good for long in our country."[49] At this point she questions the legitimacy of the commandments: "the divine commandments are not much use against hunger."[50] In fact, she directs her attack upon the whole moral system as endorsed by the gods: "So why can't the gods make a simple decision/That goodness must conquer in spite of its weakness?—/Then back up the good with an armored division/Command it to: 'fire!' and not tolerate meekness?"[51] Even Wang realizes how ridiculous the commandments are since Shen Teh "failed in her love because she obeyed the commandment to love her neighbors."[52] Near the end of the play, when the gods finish their search disheartened, even they begin to question their own commandments: "... our commandments seem to be fatal! I fear that all the moral principles we have evolved will have to be cancelled."[53]

It would appear that a closer investigation of the gods' commandments as narrated by Shen Teh is required:

> Of course I should like to obey the commandments: to honor my parents and respect the truth. Not to covet my neighbor's house

would be a joy to me, and to love, honor and cherish a husband would be very pleasant. Nor do I wish to exploit other men or to rob the defenseless. But how can it be done? Even by breaking one or two of the commandments I can barely manage.[54]

The commandments remind us both of the ten commandments of Moses—which serve as the foundation of morality and law in Western society—and of specific norms regarding personal behaviors prescribed by Confucius. The difference is that ethical ideals and methods are conveyed more indirectly in Confucius' texts. Moreover, it should be remembered that Brecht has been critical of Confucian moral teachings. Later the first god suggests that business is a hindrance to moral integrity: "Were the Seven Good Kings in business? Did Kung the Just sell fish? What has business to do with an upright and honorable life?"[55] Seven good kings and Kung (Confucius) are all considered to represent the ideal of *Junzi* ("gentlemen") who through learning and self-cultivation achieves moral nobility. According to Confucius' teachings, the profits from commerce are acknowledged to be in opposition to the cultivation of morality and humanity in *Junzi*. As Confucius says in *The Analects*, "A gentleman takes as much trouble to discover what is right as lesser men take to discover what will pay."[56] As such, it becomes interestingly apparent that Brecht refuses to fully endorse either bourgeois ethics (the gods) or Confucian ethics. By radically recasting "moral principles"—something that is an essential element of "knowing yourself" (Foucault's term)—Brecht untangles the relations between the subject and ethics.

We find that Brecht's critique of Christian and Confucian ethics has its roots in Marxism and Taoism. Both have situated authentic ethics in a realm beyond the bounds of rules and principles. Consider the following passage from the *Tao Te Ching*,

> That is why it is said: "After Tao was lost, there came the 'power';
> After the 'power' was lost, then came human kindness."
> After human kindness was lost, then came morality,
> After morality was lost, then came ritual.
> Now ritual is the mere husk of loyalty and promise-keeping
> And is indeed the first step towards brawling.[57]

This indicates clearly the four yardsticks guiding human life including human ethics and activity, with the *tao* as the highest standard to be fulfilled, and ritual as the lowest, maintaining the organization of authority-driven social relationships—an indication of the decay of the spirit of the *tao*. For Lao Zi, such a celebration of ethics codified in rules, norms, and conventions not only organizes hierarchical social relations but also reflects the degradation of *tao* into man-made hierarchical relations.[58]

Like Lao Zi, Marx also rejects the concept of ethics as prescribing a set of general moral principles and, further, critiques the instrumentalization of the ethical. As Marx wrote in the *German Ideology*, "The Communists do not preach morality at all."[59] The difference is that whereas in Taoism it is "the natural" (*tao*) that is favored over "the artificial" (morality), in Marxism it is Marx's "free man" who serves as the basis of ethics, philosophy and all human activity.[60] Thus, while the Taoists say that Taoist virtue aligns with natural processes such as the flow of water, Marx's materialistic critique of morality is accompanied by a prophecy: only when man is liberated from the "contradictions" of capitalism into Communism can he recognize himself as a social being and thus achieve true freedom, realize his potentialities and, ultimately, become an ethical subject.

The example of Shen Teh reveals how morality fails, yet Brecht appears to share with Chinese philosophers an optimism for humanity. Shen Teh's question regarding the validity of the Commandments invites a skeptical reconsideration of such an assault, as well as the question: what is goodness? Such specification is difficult, however, as it becomes clear that Brecht is coming to terms with a perception of goodness that is closer to Lao Zi's idea. Shen Teh describes the good people she came across:

> There are still friendly people, for all our wretchedness. When I was little once I was carrying a bundle of sticks and fell. An old man helped me up and even gave me a penny. I have often thought of it. Those who have least to eat give most gladly. I suppose people just like showing what they are good at; and how can they do it better than by being friendly? Crossness is just a way of being inefficient. Whenever someone is singing a song or building a machine or planting rice it is really friendliness. You are friendly too.[61]

As discussed earlier, friendliness (or benevolence) and goodness are two fundamental qualities that, in most cases, would be interchangeable in a Chinese context. In contrast to the gods' displeasure that there is only one good person in this world, Shen Teh finds that the world is not in want of friendly people. One could simply say that Brecht sings the song of class solidarity (with Shen Teh as his mouthpiece), except that this would diminish our impression of Shen Teh's capacity for analyzing the complex issues related to humanity in a ruthless world. In fact, Shen Teh not only gives due recognition of the integrity of other ethical subjects ("an old man" and "you"), but also implies "ethical responsiveness" in Taoism — clarified by Nelson as "worldly attunement and responsiveness to the non-hierarchical and reversible relationality that prediscursively and pre-cognitively constitutes ethical immediacy"[62] — as a means of establishing a relationship both within oneself and between oneself and others. Consider Grusha who, unlike Shen Teh, does not think of disciplining herself with codified morality (from the moment she "steals" the child). She does things in the most natural way and thus produces motherhood within herself. Both Shen Teh and Grusha embrace an attitude that emphasizes the ethical experience very much in tune with the Taoist attitude towards ethics.

The Relativity of Good and Bad

The gist of the social message underlying the *Good Person* depends on an a priori acceptance of the very existence of two opposing personas within one person, each demonstrating qualities that would be exclusive from each other. Such a distinction would automatically require that Shen Teh acquire qualities opposed to those of Shui Ta. But is Shui Ta the very opposite of Shen Teh? To our surprise, Shui Ta is also capable of feeling pity and sorrow for the poor, but he simply does not take action to show his compassion. Instead, he quotes a poem on the miserable conditions of people living and laments that "nothing has changed…" since the eleventh century: "That so many of the poor should suffer from cold what can we do to prevent?/To bring warmth to a single body is not much use./I wish I had a big rug ten thousand feet long,/Which at one time could cover up every inch of the city."[63] Does the gods' declaration that Shen Teh is a good person automatically define all the others as bad people? Wang says that Shui Ta was not a wicked man and does not believe that he could kill Shen Teh. Wang, the water-seller, turns out to be cheating in his business, but he shows genuine concern for Shen Teh, insisting that he will find out Shen Teh's whereabouts. Even Shui Fu, who exploits the poor people and breaks Wang's arm, confesses that he is attracted by the goodness of Shen Teh's heart and is willing to help her feed people by providing shelter in his building for Shen Teh's dependents driven out by Shui Ta. Despite the fact that Shu Fu wants to win her heart, the fact that he makes her out a blank check and demands nothing in return manifests something of his goodness. Shu Fu stands up to the audience and asks them what they think of him. He asks the audience: "Could one be more unselfish?"[64]

As the gods complain about their search for the good people, the third god says, "Our search is not progressing well. Now and again we come across a good start, admirable intentions, a lot of high principles, but it hardly adds up to a good person. When we do find people who are halfway good, they are not living a decent human existence."[65] The gods' complaint points to the fact that no one is good in their strict sense of the term. Brecht's own comments on good and evil from when he was drafting the play help to clarify his thinking: "…the main danger was of being over-schematic. li gung had to be a person if she was to become a good person. as a result her goodness is not of a conventional kind; she is not wholly and invariably good, not even when she is being li gung. nor is lao go conventionally bad, etc."[66] The names of Shen Teh (li gung) and Shui Ta (lao go) are spelt differently in his working journal. The idea of relativity of good and bad expressed by Brecht echoes Lao Zi's teachings:

> It is because every one under Heaven recognizes beauty as beauty, that the idea of ugliness exists.
> And equally if every one recognized virtue as virtue, this would merely create fresh conceptions of wickedness.
> For truly "Being and Not-being grow out of one another;
> Difficult and easy complete one another.
> Long and short test one another;
> High and low determine one another.
> Pitch and mode give harmony to one another.
> Front and back give sequence to one another."[67]

Here we see how Brecht shares Lao Zi's criticism of the definitions of good and bad (or rather the distinction between good and bad) as absolute truth claims. Recognizing the relativity of good and bad, Lao Zi argues for the complementary nature of the opposites, that is, that the act of defining something good immediately indicates something else is bad. In the *Tao Te Ching* Lao Zi frequently points out that only in a badly governed country are virtues necessary. We see, for example, that in *Mother Courage* this idea is vividly explored, as Mother Courage sarcastically reflects on virtue: "All virtues which a well-regulated country with a good king or a good general wouldn't need. In a good country virtues wouldn't be necessary."[68] In the case of Azdak, evil actions are undertaken because of good intentions. However, it turns out that Azdak's career as a judge is glorified as "an age of justice." Brecht explains why Azdak appears to be a mixture of good and bad:

> I knew I couldn't just show that the law as it exists has to be bent if justice is to be done, but realized I had to show how, with a truly careless, ignorant, downright bad judge, things can turn out all right for those who are actually in need of justice. That is why Azdak had to have those selfish, amoral, parasitic features, and be the lowest and most decrepit of judges.[69]

Azdak's decisions are usually right morally: he protects the rights of the oppressed and the poor. But in professional terms, he is a "bad" judge since he disregards the laws (which are associated with authority). Azdak is a "good" "bad" judge, who "twists" the laws while valuing the basic principle of "ethical responsiveness" in human relationships. The example of Azdak not only implies Brecht's faith in our moral command of ourselves, but requires us to adopt a dialectic conception of moral categories to view his characters.

Recognition of the relativity of good and bad does not justify the ethical confusion in a corrupted society. As we can see in characters such as Shen Teh, Azdak, and Grusha, Brecht insists that some form of humanism is necessary for the preservation of human rights, although he does not specify what that humanism consists of. His articulation of the Taoist ethics—and their integration with certain of his Marxist beliefs (such as the materialistic concept of history)—becomes, then, the central aim of these works.

Reconfiguring Subjectivity

The story of Shen Teh raises the question as to the character's personal identity. In the Epilogue one of the actors appears before the curtain with the provocative remarks: "…consider as you go/what sort of measures you would recommend/To help those good people to a happy end."[70] Thus the audience is confronted with this question left out in the play: how to change society in order that it should be possible for man to live a happy life? Perhaps, above all, Brecht suggests a demand for a new subjectivity, which has to come after the socialist revolution. However, here lies the dilemma: how can the subject, despite all its illusions, make himself the measure of all things when he is in fact the expression of outer forces? "The demand [*exigence*] for an identity," Foucault insisted, "and the injunction to break that identity, both feel, in the same way, abusive."[71] Such a demand for deconstruction and transgression is "abusive" because it assumes in advance what one must do when social forces are changed, but Brecht evades specifying this new concept of subjectivity for a changed society.

Brecht's rejection of a unified, unchanging identity does not suggest his belief in ontological destruction. Taking Shen Teh as an example, the only tool that can assure her of her continued existence is the mask, which she uses to disguise her identity as Shen Teh; however, the mask is itself a paradox.

> The etymology of the mask is disputed, but located between ways of enmeshing on the one hand, and masquerading on the other. The mask is a means to deprive the character of individuality, in order to enable an objectification or universalization; and yet the mask is far from concealing the person; rather, it becomes the person in the very moment of adoptive stillness…as an instance of depersonalized impersonation, the mask remains an oxymoron and serves as the visualization of a lasting paradox…[72]

The paradox of the mask is that, according to Martina Kolb, it cannot completely fulfill its task of "blotting out" subjectivity and individuality: on the contrary, it only functions when Shen Teh, in disguise, takes necessary measures to ensure her survival through all hardships and, furthermore, makes her spontaneous actions of human kindness and compassion practicable. As the paradox of the mask demonstrates, the seemingly battered subject and negation of subjectivity only imply a reassertion of a unified being. Kolb's claims provide a starting point for us to pursue what is left out in her discussion: the connection between this paradox of subjectivity and ethical issues.

Shen Teh's confusion of identity emerges acutely out of her struggle with the moral problem. Caught between two images of herself—kind and innocent Shen Teh, and tough and ruthless Shui Ta—she exemplifies the dilemma of how to think about the individual in the fabric of human relationships. This rejection of the rigid categories of moral judgment indicates a dialectical view of human existence and, moreover, implies a new perspective for anchoring images of the self.

Tatlow observes that "Belief in a stable ontology is, of course, only 'traditional' within Western culture," and he further points out how East Asia, especially philosophical Buddhism, views ontology differently.[73] We should add that in Taoism "there exists no ontologically fixed self" (to borrow Tatlow's words of philosophical Buddhism) that would result from the interaction of seeming opposites. The famous story of Zhuang Zi's dream of being a butterfly elucidates this ontological instability:

> Once Chuang Chou [Zhuangzi] dreamt he was a butterfly, a butterfly flitting and fluttering around, happy with himself and doing as he pleased. He didn't know he was Chuang Chou. Suddenly he woke up and there he was, solid and unmistakable Chuang Chou. But he didn't know if he was Chuang Chou who had dreamt he was a butterfly, or a butterfly dreaming he was Chuang Chou. Between Chuang Chou and a butterfly there must be *some* distinction! This is called the Transformation of Things.[74]

Indeed, there exists no such conception as ontology in ancient China; it is therefore hard to arrive at the conclusion that the autonomy of the self is determined. Similarly, Brecht's characters take subject positions confronted with moral dilemmas in various situations, a fact which explains why it is that on more than one occasion Brecht manages to disturb the opposition between these two points of view. In the beginning Shen Teh consciously makes a differentiation between Shen Teh and Shui Ta, as she emphasizes to Sun "if you like me, you can't like him."[75] "It is impossible for him to be where I am."[76] Soon, however, Shen Teh finds she is unsure of her identity given by the gods. Near the end of the play Shen Teh admits that "Shui Ta and Shen Teh, I am both of them."[77] She continues saying, "…I could feel how gradually altered and/My lips grew tight and hard. Bitter as ashes/The kind word felt in my mouth."[78] Her degree of self-knowledge, or awareness of agency varies, and her identity is constantly constructed and manipulated by the gods. Shen Teh finally has to settle on the fact that she does not have the same type of relationship to herself when she constitutes herself as a moral subject. The attitude is not to replace one identity with another but to embrace a dialectic view of the conditions where things including identity are not seen as fixed and unchangeable, and thus to readily accept oneself as existing in a state of flux. In Taoism there is no a priori theory of the subject or a rigid standard of moral behaviors. This self-reflection needs to acknowledge the relation of subject positions (or different forms of the subject) to ethical choices. Undoubtedly there are conflicts between these different positions of the subject. Confronted with various ethical choices, a person, in each different case, establishes a different relationship to oneself. In this formulation, we see Brecht engage in a re-examination of morality, of the relationship between ethics and subjectivity, and of the knowing subject.

It should be emphasized that Brecht does not appeal to some archaic mode of morality or ethical practice but to make visible a Chinese conceptualization of ethics that might illuminate contemporary humanist issues in Germany. Ancient Chinese society during the Warring States Period (403-221BC) was characterized by disorder and chaos. Yet it is within this very context that Confucianism and Taoism emerged with their shared aim to restore not only the order of society but also of humanity. Brecht wishes to vindicate a moderate humanism, a view that attributes significant but not absolute autonomy and self-knowledge to human subjects, a view that supplies flexible relationships between ethical choices and subject positions. It is not his desire to suggest a preference of Chinese "wisdom" over Western thought but, rather, to contribute to a mode of thinking informed by Chinese philosophy.

Endnotes

1   The author would like to thank Daniel Jernigan, who never failed to give valuable criticisms and suggestions throughout the writing of this paper, and Andrew Kimbrough for his encouragement and support. She is deeply indebted to Friedemann Weidauer and Markus Wessendorf for their editorial assistance.
2   See Introduction to Bertolt Brecht, *The Good Person of Szechwan* (London: Methuen Drama, 2002), p. iv.
3   See Elizabeth Wright, *Postmodern Brecht: A Re-Presentation* (London: Routledge, 1989); Astrid Oesmann, "The Theatrical Destruction of Subjectivity and History: Brecht's *Tommeln in der Nacht*," *The German Quarterly* 10.2 (1997): pp. 136-50; and Rainer Friedrich, "The Deconstructed Self in Artaud and Brecht," *Forum for Modern Language Studies* XXVI.3 (1990): pp. 282-97.

4   Bertolt Brecht, *Journals 1934-1955* (London: Methuen, 1993), p. 30.
5   For a detailed discussion of Brecht's rejection of the traditional concept of the individual in his early plays, see Erich Speidel, "The Individual and Society," in *Brecht in Perspective* (Harlow: Longman House, 1982), pp. 45-63.
6   For example, David J. Grossvogel writes in his introductory chapter on Brecht, "*The Expedient* conveyed a political message that was easy to read—the need for self-effacement and commitment to an ideological discipline" (David J. Grossvogel, *Four Playwrights and a Postscript* (New York, Cornell University Press, 1962), p. 9.
7   Louis Althusser, *For Marx* (London: Verso, 1986), p. 143.
8   Ibid.
9   Michelle Mattson, "Brecht and the Status of the Political Subject," in *Brecht Unbound* (Newark: University of Delaware Press, 1992), pp. 29-40; here p. 39.
10 Ibid., p. 33.
11 Speidel, p. 60.
12 Frederic Ewen, *Bertolt Brecht: His Life, His Art and His Times* (London: Calder & Boyars, 1970), p. 325.
13 Ibid.
14 Martin Esslin, *Brecht: A Choice of Evils* (London: Methuen, 2002), p. 225.
15 John Willett, *The Theatre of Bertolt Brecht* (London: Methuen, 1977), p. 86.
16 Sean Carney, *Brecht and Critical Theory* (London: Routledge, 2005), p. 6.
17 Bertolt Brecht, *Brecht on Theatre* (London: Methuen, 1964), p. 46.
18 Bertolt Brecht, *The Caucasian Chalk Circle* (New York: Arcade, 1994), p. 104.
19 Brecht, *The Good Person of Szechwan*, p. 105.
20 Peter Ruppert, "Brecht's 'Der Gute Mensch Von Sezuan'," *South Atlantic Bulletin* 41 (1976): pp. 36-43, here p. 38-9.
21 According to Berg-Pan, Brecht owned a copy of Mencius' work translated by Wilhelm, but the book contained no markings. Nevertheless, Brecht most probably has read his works since he was somewhat familiar with Mencius' view of human nature.
22 *The Mencius* 2A: 6 in Wing-tsit chan, *A Source Book in Chinese Philosophy* (Princeton: Princeton University Press, 1963), p. 65.
23 Renata Berg-Pan, *Bertolt Brecht and China* (Bonn: Bouvier Verlag Herbert), p. 88.
24 Brecht, *The Good Person of Szechwan*, pp. 69-70.
25 Antony Tatlow, *Mask of* Evil (Berne: Peter Lang, 1977), p. 443.
26 Fredric Jameson, *Brecht and Method* (London: Verso, 1998), p. 35.
27 Carney, p. 23.
28 Brecht, *The Good Person of Szechwan*, p. 109.
29 Walter Benjamin, *Understanding Brecht* (London and New York: Verso, 1998), p. 70.
30 Ibid., p. 70.
31 Ibid., p. 72.
32 Ibid., p. 73.
33 Anne Herrmann, "Travesty and Transgression: Transvestism in Shakespeare, Brecht and Churchill," *Theater Journal* 41.2 (1989): pp. 133-54, here p. 143.
34 Shlomo Biderman, "What Kafka Lost and Brecht Rediscovered," in *Bertolt Brecht: Performance and Philosophy* (Tel Aviv: Assaph Books, 2005), pp. 131-45, here p. 135.
35 Ibid.
36 Willett. p. 196.
37 Friedrich Nietzsche, *The Birth of Tragedy* and *The Genealogy of Morals* (New York: Anchor Books, 1956), p. 179.
38 Ibid., p. 153.
39 As Jeaneane D. Fowler and Merv Fowler explain: "contrary to most western thought it is not the triumph of good over evil, of light over darkness, of the divine over the demonic that is the Chinese goal, but the perfect balance between *yin* and *yang* polarities that enables the self to transcend them in activity. Evil is but temporary disharmony, just as night is the temporary suspension of day" (Jeaneane D. Fowler and

Merv Fowler, *Chinese Religions: Beliefs and Practices* [Brinton: Sussex Academy Press, 2008], p. 52).
40 Eric Sean Nelson, "Responding with *Dao*: Early Daoist Ethics and the Environment," *Philosophy East & West* 53.3 (2009): pp: 294-316, here p. 304.
41 E. Kamenka, *Marxism and Ethics* (London: St Martin's Press, 1969), p. 4.
42 Brecht, *The Good Person of Szechwan*, p. 70.
43 Brecht, *The Caucasian Chalk Circle*, p. 25.
44 Brecht, *The Good Person of Szechwan*, p. 105.
45 Willett, p. 84.
46 Ruppert, p. 36.
47 Brecht, *The Good Person of Szechwan*, p. 104.
48 Ibid., p. 11.
49 Ibid., p. 48.
50 Ibid.
51 Ibid., p. 49.
52 Ibid., p. 70.
53 Ibid., pp. 98-9.
54 Ibid., p. 10.
55 Ibid., p. 40.
56 Confucius, *The Analects* (Beijing: Foreign Language Teaching and Research Press, 1998), p. 45.
57 Lao Zi, *Tao Te Ching* (Beijing: Foreign Language Teaching and Research, 1998), p. 79.
58 Nelson, p. 304.
59 Karl Marx and Friedrich Engels, *The German Ideology* (Moscow, Progress Publisher, 1964), p. 267.
60 For a full discussion of this claim concerning Marxism and ethics, see Kamenka, p. 11.
61 Brecht, *The Good Person of Szechwan*, p. 36.
62 Nelson interprets the essential feature of the spirit of the *tao* manifest in human society as ethical responsiveness. See Nelson, pp. 303-4.
63 Brecht, *The Good Person of Szechwan*, pp. 28-4.
64 Ibid., p. 57.
65 Ibid., p. 71.
66 Brecht, *Journals*, p. 128.
67 Lao Zi, p. 123.
68 Brecht, *Mother Courage and Her Children* (New York: Grove Press, 1991), p. 39.
69 Brecht, *Journals,* p. 311.
70 Brecht, *The Good Person of Szechwan*, p. 109.
71 Michel Foucault, *Ethics: Subjectivity and Truth* (New York: New Press, 1997), Introduction XVIII.
72 Martina Kolb, "The Mask as Interface: Brecht, Weigel and the Sounding of Silence," *Communications from the International Brecht Society* 34 (June 2005): pp. 80-93, here p. 87.
73 Antony Tatlow, *Shakespeare, Brecht and the Intercultural Sign* (Durham and London: Duke University Press, 2001), p. 23.
74 Zhuang Zi, *The Complete Works of Chuang Tzu* (New York: Columbia University Press, 1968), p. 49.
75 Brecht, *The Good Person of Szechwan*, p. 63.
76 Ibid., p. 65.
77 Ibid., p. 105.
78 Ibid., p. 106.

Of Brecht's Chinese Peripeties:
The Practice of Transcultural Flexions

Günther Heeg

Metis, Zeus's first lover and the mistress of wise counsel, is the goddess of those who can turn the stories that they find themselves subjected to, unexpectedly towards a serendipitous ending. Brecht's *Me-ti/Book of Turns* does not refer to the Greek goddess but rather to the Chinese social ethicist Mo Di or Mê Ti. Nevertheless, the Greek Metis and Brecht's "Mê-Ti" both have a lot to say about the twists and turns of life in a foreign land, the vicissitudes of exile, and the possible cultural appropriations of the Other. In *Me-ti* Brecht develops a materialistic "Art of Action" that is also transideological and transcultural. In my paper I use Brecht's *Me-ti* as a model and starting point for a theory of the practice of transcultural flexions. Moreover, it will interrelate Brecht's appropriation of foreign cultures and contemporary critical approaches to shed new light on both endeavours.

Metis, erste Geliebte des Zeus und Meisterin des klugen Rats, ist nach Michel de Certeau die Göttin all jener, die den Geschichten, denen sie unterworfen und in die sie verstrickt sind, eine unverhoffte glückliche Wendung zu geben vermögen. Brechts *Meti/Buch der Wendungen* bezieht sich nicht auf die griechische Göttin, sondern auf den chinesischen Sozialethiker Mo Di oder Mê Ti. Gleichwohl haben die griechische Metis und Brechts "Mê-ti" gemeinsam viel zu sagen zu den Wendungen eines Lebens in Fremdheit, zu den Wechselfällen des Exils und den möglichen kulturellen Aneignungen des Fremden, Anderen. Brecht arbeitet in *Me-ti/Buch der Wendungen* an einer transideologischen und transkulturellen materialistischen "Kunst des Handelns." In meinem Beitrag soll Brechts Text zum Modell und Ausgangspunkt eines Konzepts der Praxis transkultureller Flexionen werden. Der Austausch zwischen Brechts Technik der Aneignung fremder Kulturen und gegenwärtigen Ansätzen soll sich für beide Unternehmen als fruchtbar erweisen.

Brechts chinesische Wendungen:
Me-ti und die Praxis kultureller Flexionen

Günther Heeg

Brechts *Me-ti* ist ein unvollendetes Werk, eine kaum geordnete Sammlung von Anekdoten, Aphorismen, Geschichten und Kommentaren in sieben Mappen, weitgehend ohne Reihenfolge und ersichtlichen Aufbauplan, unveröffentlicht zu Brechts Lebzeiten. Nicht einmal der Titel steht fest. Gleichwohl oder deshalb: Die Sammlung gehört zu den wichtigen Schriften Brechts. Sie stellt Brechts Textproduktion in den dreißiger Jahren vor, auf der Flucht durch die Länder ohne dauerhaft sicheren Ort. "(D)as in chinesischem Stil geschriebene Büchlein mit Verhaltenslehren,"[1] wie Brecht den *Me-ti* in einem Brief an Karl Korsch 1936 nennt, begleitet ihn durchs Exil in einer Zeit, in der nicht nur der Nationalsozialismus von einem Triumph zum nächsten eilt, sondern auch der Aufbau des Sozialismus in den Moskauer Prozessen in sich zusammenstürzt. Das Schreiben Brechts verzeichnet diese Schläge, die den Emigranten treffen, das heißt es schlägt aus wie der Zeiger eines Seismographen, der die Stöße des Erdbebens registriert. Die Zacken der Ausschläge, um im Bild zu bleiben, sind die extremen Bewegungen des Schreibens zwischen Erschütterung und Absicherung, Vertreibung und Landgewinnung, der Erfahrung von Fremdsein und der Verfremdung der Fremdheitserfahrung. Sie haben sich als Schichten im fertigen Text sedimentiert. Wenn dieses "Büchlein," das Brecht am Herzen liegt, der Selbstverständigung des Flüchtlings dient, dann nicht in dem Sinne, dass es Privates festhält, sondern dass es das Leben in der Fremde und im Fremden als selbstverständliche Voraussetzung der Existenz und das Oszillieren zwischen dem Eigenen und dem Fremden als Grundzug des Schreibens ansieht. Wir wollen uns den Wendungen dieses Schreibens zuwenden, indem wir die Schichten des Werks und ihr Verhältnis zueinander freilegen.

I

Die deutschen Entdecker des *Me-ti* in den sechziger und siebziger Jahren haben wenig Gespür für das seismographische Schreiben Brechts. Die aus der Studentenbewegung aufgebrochen sind, den Kontinent Brecht zu erobern, suchen einen Guru als politischen Lehrmeister, der jederzeit Herr der Lage ist und für jede Situation einen Rat weiß. Die Erfahrung des Fremden, die durch die Texte geht, berührt sie so wenig wie der sprichwörtliche Sack Reis, der in China umfällt. Vor allem gehe es in *Me-ti* darum, "die wichtigsten politischen Vorgänge der Zeit marxistisch in chinesischem Gewand zu analysieren,"[2] so der Herausgeber Klaus Völker im Nachwort der Suhrkamp-Ausgabe von 1967. China, das ist hier "nur" Maske und Verkleidung, Verfremdung als überlegener poetischer Kniff.

Nicht des Nachdenkens wert scheint die Frage, warum es denn die Maskierung braucht, was Maske und Verkleidung zu sein vorgeben und was sie verbergen. Und nahezu tabu ist der Gedanke, die Technik der Verfremdung könne in Fremdheit selbst wurzeln, der angeblich souveräne literarische Trick sei aus der Not dessen geboren, der dem/im Fremden ausgesetzt ist. So ausgestattet mit Denkverboten gehen die Interpreten der siebziger Jahre der unterschätzten chinesischen Maske und Verkleidung auf den Leim. Die Formel "Me-ti sagte" erhält alle Weihen der Autorität. Als einen "Grundkurs in Dialektik"[3] sieht Jan Knopf das Werk an. Me-ti lehrt Dialektik, das ist die für den Klassenkampf "nützliche Lehre,"[4] die man aus dem *Buch der Wendungen* zieht. Allenfalls streitet man sich im Kalten Krieg zwischen Ost und West, Bundesrepublik und DDR noch darüber, welche Art von Dialektik denn zum Zuge komme, die "offene" von Karl Korsch[5] oder doch die "klassische" von Lenin.[6]

Gleichgültig welche: Schwer erträglich aus heutiger Sicht sind die Demonstrationen dieser Dialektik am Beispiel der leninistischen Bündnispolitik oder der Kollektivierung der Landwirtschaft in der Sowjetunion, in denen, wie im Text "Das Seine tun und die Natur das Ihre tun lassen," Dialektik als historischer Lernprozess erscheint, durch den die Bauern nach der bürgerlichen Bodenreform von 1917 gleichsam von selbst einsehen, dass die Bearbeitung der kleinen Flächen unwirtschaftlich und ihre Zusammenlegung in Kolchosen die einzig vernünftige Lösung ist. Heute, da uns nicht mehr Blindheit und falsch verstandene Rücksichtnahme im Kampf der politischen Lager von der Einsicht abhalten, dass diese Art von Dialektik, gewaltsam umgesetzt, Millionen von Menschen das Leben gekostet hat, erkennen wir die Bedeutung von Hegels Satz "Abstraktionen in der Wirklichkeit geltend machen, heißt Wirklichkeit zerstören."[7] Deshalb ist es ruhig geworden um den *Me-ti* in den letzten Jahren, hat sich Schweigen über ihn gebreitet wie eine Maske der Scham. Was sie verbirgt und enthüllt zugleich, ist die Verkehrung von Ohnmacht in Macht, Auslieferung in Überlieferung, Leere in Lehre. Diese Verkehrung macht eine wesentliche Schicht der Rezeption und mit Sicherheit auch eine nicht unbedeutende Schicht des Werks aus. Aber sie ist nur eine von mehreren seiner Schichten, die, über die einzelnen Texte hinweg und durch sie hindurch, untereinander korrespondieren. Der angesprochene Text jedenfalls, wie apologetisch er auch vom Autor intendiert gewesen sein mag, hält unbestechlich fest, dass der "natürliche" Lernprozess, den er vordergründig feiert, nichts anderes als die "Verwirklichung" des "Programms" von Ni-en-leh, das ist Lenin, war und sät so erste Zweifel an der gelungenen Synthese zwischen der Weisheit des politischen Führers und den Leiden der Bevölkerung.

Das Leid wird nicht angesprochen in dieser unerbittlichen Exposition der unerbittlichen Lehrstunde der Dialektik. Aber es steht im Zentrum gleich des ersten Textes "Auf einen Hauptpunkt hinweisen,"[8] der als Ergänzung und Konterkarierung zur genannten Geschichte der Dialektik verstanden werden kann.

> Meister Meti unterhielt sich mit Kindern. Ein Junge ging plötzlich hinaus. Als Meti nach einiger Zeit ebenfalls hinausging, sah er im Garten den Jungen hinter einem Strauch stehen und weinen. Im Vorbeigehen sagte Meti zu ihm gleichgültig: man kann dich nicht hören, der Wind ist zu stark. Als er zurückkehrte, bemerkte er, dass der Junge aufgehört hatte zu weinen. Der Junge hatte den Grund, den ihm Meister Meti für sein Weinen genannt hatte, nämlich: gehört zu werden, als einen Hauptpunkt erkannt.[9]

Die Geschichte, eine Übermalung der Szene mit dem weinenden Knaben, dem ein Groschen gestohlen wurde, aus dem Lehrstück *Der böse Baal der asoziale*, wendet sich gegen den bloßen emotionalen Ausdruck des Leidens, der schamhaft vor den anderen versteckt wird, und plädiert dafür, ihm angemessen, das heißt wirksam, Gehör zu verschaffen. Wie und in welcher Sprache das geschehen soll, sagt die Geschichte nicht. Nur so viel verrät sie, dass der Junge dafür "aufgehört hatte zu weinen." Aus der Abwesenheit der Tränen auf die Beendigung des Leids zu schließen, das sich im Selbstmitleid nicht erschöpft, wäre mit Sicherheit verkehrt. Im Gegenteil: Es sollte uns Ansporn sein, in der dem Affektiven vordergründig fern stehenden Sprache der nachfolgenden Texte, in ihrer Rhetorik und ihren argumentativen Wendungen, die Spur der Tränen und des Leids wiederzuentdecken, die sich, notgedrungen, in einer anderen Sprache Gehör verschaffen müssen und die der Grund für Brechts seismographisches Schreiben, sein Oszillieren zwischen Eigenem und Fremdem sind.

II

Edward Said hat den Orientalismus als Projektion des Westens beschrieben, durch welche sich dieser des Orients bemächtigt, indem er ihn auf das Supplement und Gegenbild des Okzidents reduziert.[10] Der Ursprung des Orientalismus ist, so Said, in der Angst vor der fremden Welt des Ostens zu suchen. Im Orientalismus wird das Bild des Orients projektiv domestiziert. Dieser domestizierte Orient erscheint nun als begehrtes, fetischisiertes Objekt, das einen Ausgleich schaffen soll für das Ungenügen an der eigenen Lebensform. Die China-Adaptionen von Wissenschaftlern und Künstlern in den ersten Jahrzehnten des vergangenen Jahrhunderts stehen im Horizont des Orientalismus und verhalten sich auf unterschiedliche Weise zu ihm. Ganz in seinem Bann steht Klabund, der in seinem Nachwort zur Übersetzung des *Tao Te Ching* 1921 schreibt:

> Der östliche Mensch schafft die Welt, der westliche definiert sie. Der westliche ist der Wissenschaftler. Der östliche Mensch ist

> der Weise, der Helle, der Heilige, der Wesentliche. Zu werden wie er, zu sein wie er: ruft er uns zu; denn wir sind müde des funktionellen, des mechanischen, des rationellen Da-seins und Dort-denkens. Der Relativismen des Willens und der Wissenschaft. Der unfruchtbaren Dialektik. Des geistigen Krieges aller gegen alle. Die Sehnsucht nach einem wahren Frieden der Seele, dem absoluten Sinn in sich und an sich ist deine tiefste Sehnsucht, Mensch![11]

Klabunds Hinwendung zu China, von der er sich Heilung vom Leiden an der Welt des Westens verspricht, bleibt Chinoiserie: Bemächtigung und Einverleibung des Fremden, die den Abstand zwischen ihm und dem Eigenen auslöscht und das Fremde um seine Fremdheit bringt.

Ungleich differenzierter ist Brechts Haltung zu China. Er, der auf seine Kenntnisse der chinesischen Philosophie stolz war, ist sich des Abstands dazu stets bewusst. Das zeigt sich schon daran, dass er dort, wo er "China" als bloße Verfremdungstechnik der Geschichte der Weimarer Republik und des Nationalsozialismus instrumentalisiert, von "Chima" spricht. Diese rein poetische Verfremdung—Chima für Deutschland—macht die zweite Schicht des *Buchs der Wendungen* aus. Dass die chinesische Verkleidung aber einen tieferen Grund hat und nicht zuletzt einem Zwang zur Camouflage dessen entspringt, der unfreiwillig unterwegs ist, dafür spricht eine nicht publizierte Notiz, die hervorhebt, dass das Buch geschrieben sei, als stamme es von einem alten chinesischen Historiker, um seinen Autor zu verbergen.

Vorsicht war nicht nur angesichts des nationalsozialistischen Feindes, sondern mindestens ebenso sehr gegenüber den sowjetischen Freunden angebracht. Denn bei aller offiziellen Parteinahme für Lenin und auch Stalin, die in die Texte eingestreut ist—"Me-ti hielt sich an der Seite Ni-ens,"[12] das heißt Stalins—ist nicht zu übersehen, wie sehr Brechts Vertrauen in den Aufbau des Sozialismus in einem Land im *Buch der Wendungen* erschüttert ist. Davon zeugen die immer wiederkehrende Beschäftigung mit dem stalinistischen Personenkult und den Schauprozessen sowie der zunehmende Zweifel an der generellen Strategie des Kommunismus, gipfelnd in der unbeschönigten Beschreibung des Niedergangs der Komintern ("Aufbau und Verfall unter Ni-En"[13]) und einer kommentarlos lapidaren Darstellung der "Theorie des To-Tsi,"[14] das ist Trotzki, die die bisherige Entwicklung in der Sowjetunion in Frage stellt. Das *Buch der Wendungen* dokumentiert Brechts Anstrengungen, mit der Widerlegung der politischen Ideen, Orientierungsmuster und Voraussagen zurechtzukommen, die ihm bislang Halt zu geben schienen. So lesen sich manche Texte als der verzweifelte Versuch, an den bereits erschütterten weltanschaulichen Strukturen festzuhalten, indem sie ihnen einen kleinen kontrafaktischen Dreh der Auslegung geben, der gerade noch als Übereinstimmung mit der leninistischen Doktrin durchgehen kann, aber im Grunde Brechts Lenin ist, mit dem er allein auf weiter Flur steht. Diese Kompromissbildungen bilden eine weitere, dritte Schicht des Texts. Oft aber wendet sich dieser Dreh, wie der Blick auf ein Vexierbild, am Ende gegen Doktrin und Wirklichkeit, etwa wenn es in dem offiziell apologetischen Text "Me-ti für Ni-en" am Ende heißt: "Der Aufbau in einem Land war ebenso eine Bedingung des Aufbaus in anderen Ländern als dieser eine Bedingung für die Fertigstellung des Aufbaus in einem Land."[15]

Hier—vierte Schicht des Buchs—, in der Umwendung der Formel vom Aufbau des Sozialismus in einem Land, die auf keinen Sprecher zurückzugehen und von keinem Ort auszugehen scheint, ist weniger Me-ti als Metis, die erste Geliebte des Zeus und Meisterin des klugen Rats, am Werk. Sie ist nach Michel de Certeau die Göttin all jener, die den Geschichten, denen sie unterworfen und in die sie verstrickt sind, eine unverhoffte glückliche Wendung zu geben vermögen.[16] Es ist Metis, der Göttin Geschick, die das *Buch der Wendungen* befreit aus der Zwickmühle der totalitären Systeme, in die Brecht eingeklemmt ist, und es hinaustreibt ins Offene einer "Kunst des Handelns," die über keine Ordnung verfügt, die ihr Rückhalt und eine sichere Ausgangsposition für das Handeln geben würde, sondern eine Kunst, die die Verstelltheit des eigenen Orts und der eigenen Zeit für eine gezielte Verstellung der ganzen Geschichte zu nutzen weiß. Damit dies gelingt, braucht das *Buch der Wendungen* den Weg in eine andere Fremde als die eigene, braucht es den Umweg über China.

III

Es muss Metis, die Göttin, gewesen sein, die Brecht das Buch *Mê Ti, des Sozialethikers und seiner Schüler philosophische Werke*[17] in die Hände gespielt hat. Es handelt sich dabei um eine Übersetzung der Schriften des chinesischen Philosophen Mo Di oder Mê Ti (circa 470-400 vor Christus) und dessen Schule des Mehismus oder Mohismus, besorgt und eingeleitet von Alfred Forke, eine wissenschaftliche Ausgabe, die den im Vergleich mit Konfutse und Laotse unbekannten Philosophen 1922 erstmals nach Deutschland gebracht hat. Es muss die Göttin des klugen Rats gewesen sein, denn dieses Buch, das sich Brecht in Svendborg in Leder einbinden ließ und fortan durchs Exil geschleppt hat, ermöglicht ihm, die eigene politische und kulturelle Fremdheitserfahrung zu verfremden, das heißt zeitlich und räumlich zu versetzen. Der Zweck der Verfremdung und Versetzung, mit der Brecht auf die zunehmende Entfremdung und Enteignung des eigenen politisch-kulturellen Umfelds reagiert, ist ein mehrfacher: Entkommen, Abstand gewinnen und Aneignung des Fremden. Weil die Letztere im Fremdwerden des Eigenen wurzelt, nimmt sie nicht die Gestalt der Bemächtigung an. Die

Aneignung des Fremden meint zunächst die Annahme von Fremdheit als Grundannahme der eigenen Existenz. Sie ist die Voraussetzung des gelingenden Umgangs unter Fremden in einem transkulturellen Zwischen-Raum. Die Bewegungen, die von der Erschütterung der eigenen kulturellen Orientierungsmuster und Handlungskonventionen zur Aneignung des Fremden im transkulturellen Raum des Dazwischen führen, nenne ich "kulturelle Flexionen." Sie resultieren aus einer Praxis, die für das Zusammenleben zwischen den Kulturen und durch die Kulturen hindurch lebensnotwendig, überlebensnotwendig ist. Das *Buch der Wendungen* ist ein Experimentierfeld der Praxis kultureller Flexionen und des Dazwischen.

Was hat Brecht an Mê-Tis, des Chinesen, Schriften angezogen? Hauptsächlich wohl dessen pragmatische Fundierung des Denkens, die Verbindung von Ideen und ethischen Grundsätzen mit praktischem, veränderndem Handeln. Brecht ist angezogen davon, dass Mê-Ti das zerfallende Feudalsystem zum Beginn der Periode der "Kämpfenden Staaten" (403-222 vor Christus) nicht wie Konfuzius, als dessen Herausforderer er auftrat, durch Tugendideale retten wollte, sondern eine Reform der Gesellschaft durch pragmatisches ethisches Handeln anstrebte. Mê-Ti gründete, so Forke, seine ethische Pragmatik "nicht auf ein unwandelbares Sittengesetz, einen Kategorischen Imperativ, sondern utilitaristisch auf Nützlichkeits- und Zweckmäßigkeitsrücksichten und fragt daher stets nach den Wirkungen der sittlichen Vorschriften auf die menschliche Gesellschaft und das Staatsleben."[18]

Ausgehend von der Vorstellung einer "allumfassenden Liebe," die die Gleichheit aller ins Auge fasst, entwickeln die Schriften Mê-Tis und der Mehisten die Lehren von der "Bevorzugung der Tüchtigen" (anstelle des Geburtsrechts des Adels), der "Geltendmachung der Gleichmäßigkeit," der "Verdammung des Eroberungskriegs," der "Verdammung des Fatalismus" und andere mehr. Kaum eine Passage von Mê-Ti ist in Brechts *Buch der Wendungen* auch nur indirekt eingegangen, aber die Bezüge sind — vor allem in der Sammlung von Maximen und Aphorismen unter dem Titel "Verurteilung der Ethiken"[19] — nicht zu übersehen. "Ganz allgemein sollte gelten, dass jedes Land, in dem besondere Sittlichkeit nötig ist, schlecht verwaltet wird,"[20] heißt es im Aphorismus "Es sollte in einem Land keine besondere Sittlichkeit brauchen."[21] Immer aber nehmen sie eine eigene, dem chinesischen Philosophen gegenüber fremde Gestalt an, auch wenn sie seine Haltung als Geste zitieren: "FREIHEIT, GÜTE, GERECHTIGKEIT, Geschmack und Großzügigkeit sind Produktionsfragen, sagte Me-ti zuversichtlich."[22]

Das lockere Verhältnis zwischen Brechts Me-ti und dem chinesischen Mê-Ti zeigt: Dieser ist nicht der Hausphilosoph des *Buchs der Wendungen*. Zu Recht hat man auf den Einfluss des Laotse und des *Tao Te Ching* aufmerksam gemacht, die sich in den Figuren des *wu wie*, des Nicht-Handelns beziehungsweise des Handelns im Einverständnis mit dem Fluss der Dinge und in der Lehre von der Stärke des Schwachen zeigt. Die Bezugnahmen auf Elemente der chinesischen Philosophie machen die fünfte wesentliche Schicht des *Buchs der Wendungen* aus. Aber die chinesische Philosophie geht nicht als Lehre, als philosophische Doktrin in das *Buch der Wendungen* ein. Brecht überformt, ergänzt oder ersetzt nicht die marxistisch-leninistische Dialektik durch chinesische Philosopheme. Selbst dort, wo es der Titel wie im Text über die Kollektivierung der Landwirtschaft nahelegt—"Das Seine tun und die Natur das Ihre tun lassen"—handelt es sich nicht um ein Amalgam, sondern um ein Fremdmachen von beidem, der leninistischen Dogmatik sowie der taoistischen Lehre vom Nichthandeln und dem Fluss der Dinge. Der Grund dafür liegt in einer doppelten Operation Brechts: 1. Der in der Fremde unterwegs ist, reißt alles, Eigenes und Fremdes, aus dem Zusammenhang. 2. Er eignet sich das Zusammenhanglose an, nicht, indem er es verschmilzt und sich einverleibt, sondern indem er der Zusammenhanglosigkeit selbst Raum gibt, um das Zusammenhanglose in Konstellationen zu bringen.

Wenn Brecht die Dinge aus dem Zusammenhang reißt, handelt er nicht anders als die Wirklichkeit selbst, in der der Zusammenhang und die Geschlossenheit von Kulturen in den Schüben der Globalisierung seit dem Beginn der Neuzeit durch immer neue kulturelle Hybridisierungen auseinandergerissen wird. Längst ist das Eigene vom Fremden durchsetzt, wenn es denn je in jener Reinheit existiert hat, die von Fundamentalisten jeder Couleur behauptet wird. Dass wir dennoch in der Begegnung mit Anderen stets von der Fremdheitserfahrung und der Entgegensetzung von Eigenem und Fremden ausgehen, ist nach Bernhard Waldenfels[23] unserer besonderen, nicht hintergehbaren Weise der Welterfahrung geschuldet, ein Rest Ungleichzeitigkeit des Gleichzeitigen selbst. National- und Regionalkulturen ebenso wie politische und religiöse Weltanschauungskulturen, die mit ihren imaginären Identitätsangeboten Halt versprechen, verpflichten uns kontrafaktisch auf kulturelle Praktiken der Entgegensetzung und Abgrenzung, die jenen "clash of civilizations" herbeizuführen drohen, den Konservative prophezeien beziehungsweise diagnostizieren zu können glauben.[24] Brecht verzeichnet im *Buch der Wendungen* die Erschütterung der eigenen politischen Bezugskultur, des Kommunismus, und präsentiert ihre Bruchstücke. Um sie als solche kenntlich zu machen, aber auch um jeden kulturellen Totalitätsanspruch zurückzuweisen und auf dessen Kontingenz zu insistieren, braucht es die Zusammenstellung mit den Bruchstücken fremder Kulturen. Und es braucht den Raum zwischen den Einzelteilen der Kulturen, die Ausstellung des fehlenden Zusammenhangs. Wie wichtig dieser für das Zusammenleben zwischen und innerhalb der Kulturen ist, hat Brecht in einem Text zu einem scheinbar anderen Thema, dem Text "Über die Malerei der Chinesen" hervorgehoben:

> Wie man weiß, verwenden die Chinesen nicht die Kunst der Perspektive, sie lieben es, nicht alles von einem einzigen Blickpunkt aus zu betrachten. Auf ihren Bildern sind mehrere Dinge einander nebengeordnet, sie verteilen sich auf ein Blatt, wie Einwohner ein und derselben Stadt sich auf diese Stadt verteilen, nicht etwa unabhängig voneinander, aber nicht in einer Abhängigkeit, welche die Existenz bedroht…Der chinesischen Komposition fehlt ein uns ganz und gar gewohntes Moment des Zwanges. Diese Ordnung kostet keine Gewalt. Die Blätter enthalten viel Freiheit…Die chinesischen Künstler haben… viel Platz auf ihrem Papier. Einige Teile der Fläche scheinen unbenutzt, diese Teile spielen aber eine große Rolle in der Komposition; sie scheinen ihrem Umfang und ihrer Form nach ebenso sorgfältig entworfen wie die Umrisse der Gegenstände. In diesen Lücken tritt das Papier selber oder die Leinwand als ein ganz bestimmter Wert hervor…Das bedeutet unter anderem einen lobenswerten Verzicht auf die völlige Unterwerfung des Zuschauers, dessen Illusion nicht ganz vervollständigt wird. Wie diese Bilder liebe ich die Gärten, in denen die Natur von ihren Gärtnern nicht ganz verarbeitet ist; die Platz haben; in denen die Dinge nebeneinanderliegen.[25]

Natürlich beansprucht Brechts Beschreibung nicht, das Wesen der chinesischen Malerei korrekt zu erfassen—wenn das überhaupt methodisch möglich ist. Was er vorführt, ist die Entdeckung einer Resonanz des Fremden, die eigene Vorstellungen anspricht, indem sie ihnen erst zur Sprache verhilft. Die Responsivität der chinesischen Malerei, die sich von der Projektion unterscheidet, weckt das Bild eines freien Nebeneinanders unterschiedlicher kultureller Muster und Praktiken, die dem Fremden buchstäblich Raum lässt.

Die Ausstellung von Fragmenten, die aus dem kulturellen Zusammenhang gefallen sind, öffnet bei Brecht nicht dem Relativismus und der Beliebigkeit Tür und Tor. Denn die Bruchstücke sind historisch aufgeladen, an ihnen haftet die Geschichte der Schichten, von denen die Rede war. Wir sprechen von den verschiedenen Schichten des Werks, weil sich Geschichte in ihnen abgelagert hat. Treten diese Bruchstücke in den Texten untereinander in Aktion, werden sie gestisch: Als Geste zitieren sie Geschichte und setzen sie in eine singuläre Beziehung zu allen anderen Gesten.

Es ist wohl der Anklang des Gestischen gewesen, der Brecht vor allen Inhalten der Lehre bei den chinesischen Philosophen angesprochen hat. Keine philosophischen Systeme hat er dort gefunden, nicht metaphysische Implikate haben ihn interessiert, sondern die praktische Ausrichtung dieser Philosophie als Verhaltenslehre. Attraktiv war sie für ihn als

Anleitung für eine Kunst des Handelns unter widrigen Umständen, das heißt als Kunst des Überlebens. "ME-TI SAGTE: denken ist etwas, das auf Schwierigkeiten folgt und dem Handeln vorausgeht."[26] Dass das Gestische dieses Denkens etwas mit der prekären Lage der Denkenden zu tun hat, liegt nicht so fern, wenn Brecht wiederholt auf die Rolle der Emigrationen in deren Leben aufmerksam macht: "Die chinesischen… Philosophen pflegten, wie ich höre, ins Exil zu gehen wie die unsern in die Akademie."[27] Das Leben in der Fremde treibt die Fremdheit der Gesten hervor, die in Brechts Schreiben korrespondieren. Abgeschnitten vom Ursprung ihrer Kultur nehmen die gestischen Emigranten den Leser mit auf die Suche nach Affinitäten und Resonanzen. Über die Zeiten und Räume hinweg bilden sie Konstellationen. Worauf verweisen sie? Was zeigt sich durch sie hindurch?

IV

Zuallererst zeigen die Gesten die Brüchigkeit des autoritativen Zeigens selbst. Es ist die Haltung des Hin-Weisens in der Figur des chinesischen Weisen—"Me-ti sagte"—, die in der Konstellation der textuellen Gesten nachdrücklich erschüttert wird. Sie wird erschüttert, aber sie wird nicht hinfällig. Adorno hat am "chinesischen Brecht" den "sprachlichen Gestus von Weisheit, die Fiktion des von epischer Erfahrung gesättigten alten Bauern als poetischen Subjekts" als "erschlichen" und als "Echo archaischer gesellschaftlicher Verhältnisse" in Frage gestellt.[28] Diese In-Fragestellung unternehmen die Texte Brechts aber bei genauer Lektüre bereits von sich aus. Unter den Themenfeldern des *Buchs der Wendungen* nehmen die Geschichten von Kin-jeh und Lai-tu, die von den Schwierigkeiten der Liebe von Ruth Berlau und Brecht handeln, einen besonderen Platz ein. Man wollte sie schon als Fremdkörper aus dem Ganzen entfernen, weil ihr vermeintlich privater Charakter nicht zu den großen politischen Anliegen wie der Kritik am "heroischen Pauperismus"[29] der Nazis oder der Verarbeitung des sozialistischen Debakels passt. Das ist ein Irrtum. Denn gerade diese Texte, in denen der Liebende, Kin-jeh, anstelle Me-tis die Haltung des "Lehrers" gegenüber seiner "Schülerin" und Geliebten Lai-tu einnimmt, zeigen die Anstrengung, die es kostet, aus der Position dessen, der der Liebe und der Geliebten ausgeliefert ist, in die des Lehrmeisters zu gelangen. "Wie soll ich Lai-tu noch schreiben? Fragte Kin-jeh. Sie schreibt mit dem Kaugummi im Mund, ich schreibe mit Zittern."[30]

Eine Zitterpartie ist diese Beziehung, in der es um Leben und Tod zu gehen scheint. "LEBEN UND STERBEN"[31] ist das letzte der Blätter des Buches überschrieben. Unter diesem Motto enthält es eine Stalin-Exegese und drei Bemerkungen über die Liebe. Die letzte geht so: "LAI TU SAGTE ZU KIN JEH: ich liebe Dich so, was wird aus mir werden? Kin Jeh antwortete: Was du aus Liebe machst, kann dich nicht entwürdigen."[32]

Erfahrung spricht aus diesem Satz, Erfahrung, die das Verhältnis zwischen Lehrer und Schülerin, Weisem und Ratsuchendem reversibel macht und in Fluss bringt. Weise am Weisen ist die Haltung der erschütterten Autorität, das heißt das Verhältnis, das er zu Unvermögen, Ohnmacht und Leidenschaft unterhält. "Die leidenschaftlichen Menschen," sagt Me-ti an anderer Stelle, "finden in der Ruhe keine Ruhe, sondern nur in der Bewegtheit."[33] Die Bewegtheit von Brechts Schreiben lässt Kin-jeh und Lai-tu die Plätze tauschen, vertreibt die Geste des Bescheid-Wissens von dem Ort, an dem sie sich auskennt und schickt sie auf die Reise. Das ist ihre Rettung und Chance: Die bewegte Geste, die die Geschichte ihrer Erschütterung zeigt, kann sich dem Fremden zuwenden, ohne Bedürfnis und Zwang, es einordnen und darüber verfügen zu müssen. Als Geste in Bewegung setzt sie sich in Beziehung zur eigenen Beziehungslosigkeit, das heißt der unmöglichen Beziehung auf ein unbestreitbares Eigenes, wie zu der begehrten Beziehung zum gefürchteten Fremden. Ohne sicheres Terrain hier wie dort übt sich die bewegte Geste/die Geste in Bewegung im In-Beziehung-Setzen des Beziehungslosen, sie wird zur Geste der reinen Vermittlung.

V

Damit wendet sich auch die Figur des Dritten, um die zentrale Texte des *Buchs der Wendungen* immer wieder kreisen. Sie fragen nach den Möglichkeiten der historischen Selbstbetrachtung und des Lebens in der dritten Person oder versuchen, das Menschen und Völker Verbindende der "Dritten Sache" plausibel zu machen. Dass die Versetzung des Einzelnen in die dritte Person und das "Sich selbst als historisch betrachten" heraushelfen sollen aus den Unwägbarkeiten der Zweierbeziehung ist den Texten ziemlich unverstellt zu entnehmen: "Das Leben, gelebt als Stoff einer Lebensbeschreibung, gewinnt eine gewisse Wichtigkeit und kann Geschichte machen;"[34] wenn jeder erst sein eigener Geschichtsschreiber ist, "wird er sorgfältiger und anspruchsvoller leben."[35] Aber die Identifikation mit dem Dritten der symbolischen Ordnung im Sinne Jacques Lacans, die hier so verlockend erscheint, ist nicht der Fluchtpunkt der Texte, sondern der Bezugspunkt, von dem sie ausgehen und den sie aufgeben. Das zeigt "DIE DRITTE SACHE:"

> Me-ti sagte, dass das Verhältnis zwischen zwei Menschen gut sei, wenn da eine dritte Sache vorliege, der das Interesse beider gelte. Mi-en-leh fügte hinzu, dies gelte auch für das Verhältnis beliebig großer Menschenmengen. Dadurch, dass sie gemeinsam einer äußeren Sache ergeben sind, ordnet sich alles unter ihnen viel leichter, eben nach dem Bedürfnis dieser Sache. Was Me-ti sich Gutes erwartete, wenn zwei Hände, etwa von Mann und Frau, sich bei einer gemeinsamen Arbeit, beim Eimertragen, berühren, das erwartete sich Mi-en-leh für ganze Völker, wenn sich ihre Hände beim Treiben des Rades der Geschichte berühren.[36]

Einfach und einleuchtend scheint zunächst, was die Vertreter der Dritten Sache hier zu deren Vorteil bildhaft vorbringen. Aber die Bilder, die die Distanz zwischen dem Allgemeinen der symbolischen Ordnung und dem Einzelnen überbrücken sollen, zeigen bei näherer Betrachtung eher den Abgrund zwischen beiden. Die Hände, die sich beim Wassertragen berühren, können die gemeinsame Arbeit durch das Begehren und die damit einhergehende Rivalität beflügeln wie (zer)stören – mehr noch als Brecht dürften das die Frauen gewusst haben, die mit ihm zusammenarbeiteten. Vom Wassertragen von Mann und Frau dann auf das Rad der Geschichte zu kommen, das die Völker gemeinsam antreiben, ist ein Sprung in den Kitsch des sozialistischen Realismus oder/und eine intertextuelle Reminiszenz an das Glücksrad der Fortuna, mehr noch: an Brechts eigene, kurz zuvor geschriebene "Ballade vom Wasserrad," in denen die, die das Rad treiben, bekanntlich immer unten bleiben. Und andererseits: Welches Versprechen liegt nicht in der Vorstellung einer "Politik der Berührung?" Und: Verspricht Berührung in all ihren Schattierungen nicht einen Ausweg aus der Fatalität des Begehrens? Ist Berührung nicht ein geeignetes Medium für den Umgang unter Fremden? Je näher man die Bilderwelten von "DIE DRITTEN SACHE" anblickt, umso fremder blicken sie zurück.

Der Text blättert die (Bilder-)Welten auf, die sich zwischen dem Anspruch der dritten Sache und dem Leben der Einzelnen auftun. Das mag die Herren der symbolischen Ordnung – Mi-en-leh und Me-ti, oder das autoritative Autoren-Ich – stören und vom Sockel stoßen, nicht aber den "dritten Mann," der unter der Oberfläche der Textordnung den Text umwälzt und umtreibt und uns schreibend den Reichtum an Möglichkeiten enthüllt, die der vermeintliche Abgrund zwischen den Bildern und Dingen, den Sprechenden und den Handelnden enthält. Möglichkeiten des Unterscheidens und Trennens wie des Verbindens und Kombinierens, Möglichkeiten der Erschütterung wie der Setzung, des Erfahrens wie des Tuns. Das ist "DIE GROSSE METHODE" des Schreibens, angetrieben von der Geste in Bewegung, deren Agent der dritte Mann, der Schreibende, ist: Ein Picaro oder Landstreicher, der zwischen den Welten, dem Krieg der Länder und dem Kampf der Parteien, nach Möglichkeiten des Überlebens sucht.

VI

Der Picaro oder Landstreicher als dritter Mann, der das *Buch der Wendungen* schreibt, misstraut jeder symbolischen Ordnung. Das macht ihn zum geeigneten Mann für den Umgang mit fremden Zeiten und Räumen, macht ihn zum Fachmann für kulturelle Flexionen, die die Bruchstücke und Segmente des vormals "Eigenen" und "Fremden" in einem dritten Raum[37] zueinander in Beziehung setzen. Der dritte Mann findet, erfindet dritte Räume, transkulturelle Räume. So wie in jener Geschichte im *Buch der Wendungen*, die ganz ohne Me-ti auskommen kann, der Erzählung "WEI UND YENS UNFÄHIGKEIT, ZUCHT ZU HALTEN:"[38]

> Der Winter, die schlechteste Jahreszeit, überraschte die Feinde in einem Land, fast entblößt von Lebensmitteln. Die Faulheit der Bauern, erzeugt durch die Grausamkeit der Gutsherrn, war schuld, dass wenig da war, und die Bauern waren immerhin selbstsüchtig genug, alle ihre eigenen Vorräte wegzuschaffen und zu verstecken. Das feindliche Heer bekam einen gewaltigen Hunger zu spüren.
>
> Rücksichtslos und gewissenlos, wie die Leute von Hao waren, die von klein auf zu allen Soldatentugenden erzogen worden waren, bemächtigten sie sich der Gutsherrn und machten die meisten nieder, da sie nichts herbeischaffen konnten. Dann aber löste sich ihr Heer in der furchtbaren Hungersnot auf und floh der Grenze zu. Die Hauptmasse der Leute von Hao ging in den Landesteilen an der Grenze zugrunde, die von ihnen verwüstet worden waren.
>
> Im Frühjahr krochen die Bauern aus ihren Hütten wieder hervor, und wie Yen es gehofft hatte, zeigte sich bei ihnen ihre alte Schwäche, die Selbstsucht, in einem erstaunlichen Ausmaß. Die Gutsbesitzer waren getötet vom Feind oder eingeschüchtert und wehrlos, und die Bauern, sicher, ihre Ernte selber einfahren zu können, stürzten sich wie Irre auf die Aussaat.
>
> Wei blühte auf.
>
> Als der gute Herrscher Yen starb, konnte man wahrheitsgemäß sagen, dass er ohne militärische Siege, nur durch die Feigheit seiner Untertanen einen großen Krieg gewonnen hatte und ohne viele Regierungsdekrete oder Ermahnungen das Land wie in einen Garten verwandelt hatte.[39]

Ohne Zweifel klingen in dieser Geschichte die taoistischen Lehren vom Nichthandeln und von der Stärke des Schwachen an. Die Erzählung kann in gewisser Weise als Gegenstück zur tödlichen Dialektik von Bodenreform und Kollektivierung der Landwirtschaft gelesen werden, auf die wir zu Beginn eingegangen sind. Doch wenn sie dieser Dialektik den Boden entzieht, heißt das nicht, dass sie auf dem Boden des Taoismus Land zu gewinnen versucht. Zur Demonstration der Lehren des *wu wei* und der Stärke des Schwachen eignet sich die Erzählung nicht. Wie Antony Tatlow bemerkt hat, trägt zum Sieg der Bauern die Selbstzerfleischung der eigenen und der fremden Herren nicht wenig bei.[40] Ebenso wenig schlägt in der Geschichte ein Herz für die maoistische Bauernrevolution. Mit diesen Bauern ist keine Revolution zu machen. Was also geschieht im Raum der Erzählung zwischen dem alten und neuen China, der Sowjetunion und dem skandinavischen Exil des Schreibenden? Nicht mehr als dass alle, die diesen (dritten) Raum betreten, die "Regierungsdekrete und Ermahnungen" ihrer kulturellen Landesherrn hinter sich gelassen haben. Die Geschichte zeigt vor, was jeder aus der Konkursmasse der Kulturen gerettet und mitgebracht hat. Die Weltbilder, seien sie marxistischer, taoistischer, mehistischer oder maoistischer Art, sind *perdu*. Übrig geblieben stehen die Gesten im Raum: Die lapidare Geste der Mitteilung von Krieg und täglicher Bedrückung. Die Gesten der Grausamkeit. Die Geste der Anmaßung, die der Soldatentugend innewohnt, und die sich tödlich gegen die Anmaßenden richtet. Die Gesten der Feigheit und des Selbsterhaltungstriebs der Bauern, die Schwäche der Selbstsucht, die Gesten der "Irre(n)," die "das Land in einen blühenden Garten verwandelt." Die Gesten verweisen auf Nichts, jedenfalls nichts Wegweisendes. Sie zeigen nichts als die Überreste ihrer Geschichte. Warum lesen wir sie mit Vergnügen?

Vielleicht: Weil das Nichts der Raum der reinen Vermittlung ist. Vielleicht: Weil in diesem Raum das In-Beziehung-Setzen des Beziehungslosen möglich wird — dank des "eingreifenden Denkens" aller dritten Männer und Frauen, Picaros und Landstreicherinnen, die die Gesten in Bewegung versetzen. Und nicht zuletzt vielleicht: Weil die bewegten Gesten Beziehungen unter Fremden stiften, die potentiell eine glückliche Wendung nehmen können. "Alle Gefühle hoffen auf einen guten Ausgang"[41] — das ist der "Empfindungsblock,"[42] den der dritte Raum von Brechts *Buchs der Wendungen* ausstrahlt. Wer da meint, da sei kein Ausgang, nirgendwo, dem sei mit Me-ti gesagt: "Umwälzungen finden in Sackgassen statt."[43]

Anmerkungen

1   Bertolt Brecht zitiert in Klaus-Detlef Müller, "Brechts Me-ti und die Auseinandersetzung mit dem Lehrer Karl Korsch," *Brecht-Jahrbuch* 7 (1977): S. 9-29; hier S. 9.
2   Klaus Völker, "Anmerkungen," in Bertolt Brecht, *Gesammelte Werke. Prosa 2*, Band 12, Herta Ramthun, Klaus Völker (Frankfurt/Main: Suhrkamp, 1967), S. 729-733; hier S. 729, Anmerkung 1.
3   Vergleiche Jan Knopf, "Kleiner Grundkurs Dialektik. Aphoristik in Brechts Me-ti," in Heinz-Dieter Weber und Robert Ulshöfer, Hrsg., *Der Deutschunterricht. Kleine literarische Gattungen I* (Stuttgart: Ernst Klett, 1978), S. 37-52.
4   Wolfgang Fritz Haug, "Nützliche Lehren aus Brechts ‚Buch der Wendungen,'" in Wolfgang Fritz Haug, Hrsg., *Bestimmte Negation. "Das umwerfende Einverständnis des braven Soldaten Schwejk" und andere Aufsätze* (Frankfurt/Main: Suhrkamp, 1973), S. 70-93; hier S. 70.
5   Vergleiche Müller, "Brechts Me-ti," S. 9-29.
6   Vergleiche Werner Mittenzwei, "Der Dialektiker Brecht oder Die Kunst, ‚Me-ti' zu lesen," in Wolfgang Fritz Haug, Hrsg., *Brechts Tui-Kritik. Aufsätze, Rezensionen, Geschichten* (Karlsruhe: Argument, 1976), S. 115-149.
7   Georg Wilhelm Friedrich Hegel, *Vorlesungen über die Geschichte der Philosophie III*, Band 20 (Frankfurt/Main: Suhrkamp, 1993), S. 331.

8   Bertolt Brecht, *Buch der Wendungen*, in derselbe, *Werke: Große kommentierte Berliner und Frankfurter Ausgabe*, Band 18, Werner Hecht, Jan Knopf, Werner Mittenzwei, Klaus-Detlev Müller und andere, Hrsg., (Berlin: Aufbau, und Frankfurt/Main: Suhrkamp, 1988-2000), Bd. 18, S. 47 (im Folgenden BFA).
9   Ebd..
10 Vergleiche Edward Said, *Orientalism* (London: Penguin Books, 2003).
11 Klabund, Nachwort zu *Mensch, werde wesentlich. Laotse Sprüche. Deutsch von Klabund* (Berlin-Zehlendorf: Heyder, 1921), S. 32.
12 BFA 18, S. 120.
13 Ebd., S. 168.
14 Ebd., S. 172.
15 Ebd., S. 120.
16 Vergleiche Michel de Certeau, "Die Zeit des Geschichten-Erzählens," in derselbe, *Die Kunst des Handelns* (Berlin: Merve, 1988), S. 155-178.
17 Alfred Forke, *Mê Ti: des Sozialethikers und seiner Schüler philosophische Werke* (Berlin: Kommissionsverlag der Vereinigung Wissenschaftlicher Verleger, 1922).
18 Ebd., S. 51.
19 BFA 18, S. 152.
20 Ebd., S. 55.
21 Ebd.
22 Ebd., S. 152.
23 Vergleiche Bernhard Waldenfels, "Zwischen den Kulturen," *Deutsch als Fremdsprache* 26 (2000): S. 245-261.
24 Samuel P. Huntington, *The Clash of Civilizations and the Remaking of World Order* (New York: Simon & Schuster, 1996).
25 Bertolt Brecht, "Über die Malerei der Chinesen," in BFA 22.1, S. 133.
26 BFA 18, S. 62.
27 BFA 28, S. 447.
28 Theodor W. Adorno, *Noten zur Literatur. Gesammelte Schriften*, Band 11, (Frankfurt/Main: Suhrkamp, 2003), S. 422.
29 Herbert Marcuse, *Kultur und Gesellschaft*, Band 1 (Frankfurt/Main: Suhrkamp, 1967), S. 53.
30 BFA 18, S. 175.
31 Ebd., S. 55.
32 Ebd., S. 193.
33 Ebd., S. 139.
34 Ebd., S. 188.
35 Ebd., S. 131.
36 Ebd., S. 173.
37 Vergleiche Homi K. Bhabha, *Die Verortung der Kultur* (Tübingen: Stauffenburg, 2007) und Edward W. Soja, *Thirdspace. Journeys to Los Angeles and Other Real-and-Imagined Places* (Malden: Blackwell, 2004).
38 BFA 18, S. 148.
39 Ebd., S. 148.
40 Antony Tatlow, "Peasant Dialectics: Reflections on Brecht's Sketch of Dilemma," in William Tay, Hrsg., *China and the West: Comparative Literature Studies* (Hong Kong: Chinese University Press, 1980), S. 277-285.
41 Angelika Wittlich, *Alle Gefühle glauben an einen glücklichen Ausgang*, TV-Dokumentation über den Regisseur Alexander Kluge, 3sat, Premiere am 18.02.2002.
42 Gilles Deleuze und Félix Guattari, "Perzept, Affekt und Begriff," in dieselben, *Was ist Philosophie?* (Frankfurt/Main: Suhrkamp, 2000), S. 191-237.
43 BFA 18, S. 127.

Under the Chinese Mask: Brecht's "Six Chinese Poems" Revisited

Yuan Tan

This paper compares Brecht's "Six Chinese Poems," which he wrote in exile, to the sources on which they are based, namely Arthur Waley's English translation of classical Chinese poems. The major focus is on Brecht's intentional deviations from Waley's translations and on the reflection of his exile experience in his own versions. In his first note on Bai Juyi's life, Brecht already emphasizes the critical inclination of the Chinese poet and portrays this expatriate and indomitable social critic almost as his own contemporary. Brecht's deviation from his source for the purpose of self-reflection can also be seen in his own versions of the poems. Through intentional adaptation and omission he turns classic Chinese poems into modern ones and characterizes Bai Juyi as an idealized social critic poet — as someone who never stopped protesting against the authorities despite frequent expatriation. Under the Chinese mask, what the reader finally discovers is Brecht's own idealized self-portrait.

Dieser Essay vergleicht Brechts "Sechs chinesische Gedichte" aus seiner Exilzeit mit Arthur Waleys englischen Übersetzungen klassischer chinesischer Gedichte, auf denen sie basieren. Der Essay konzentriert sich in erster Linie auf Brechts Abweichungen von Waleys Vorlage und auf die Reflexion seiner eigenen Exilerfahrungen in den Übertragungen. Bereits in der ersten Anmerkung zu Po Chü-yis Leben hebt Brecht die kritische Haltung des chinesischen Dichters hervor und stellt diesen Exilanten und unbeugsamen Sozialkritiker fast als seinen Zeitgenossen dar. Auch bei der Übersetzung der Gedichte weicht Brecht immer wieder zugunsten einer Selbstreflexion von Waley ab. Durch gezielte Abänderungen und Auslassungen formuliert er die alten chinesischen Gedichte in moderne Zeitgedichte um und macht Po zum idealen sozialkritischen Dichter, der trotz mehrmaliger Verbannungen auf seiner Kritik an den Herrschenden besteht. Unter der chinesischen Maske erkennt der Leser letztendlich Brechts idealisiertes Selbstporträt.

Unter der chinesischen Maske: Neue Studien zu Brechts "Sechs chinesischen Gedichten"

Yuan Tan

1938 veröffentlichte Brecht "Sechs chinesische Gedichte" in der Exilzeitschrift *Das Wort*. Für die Übersetzung benutzte er die Ausgabe *170 Chinese Poems* des englischen Sinologen Arthur Waley.[1] In seinen Anmerkungen schreibt Brecht: "Diese Gedichte sind ohne Zuhilfenahme der chinesischen Originale aus der englischen Nachdichtung Arthur Waleys übertragen, die von Sinologen sehr gerühmt wird."[2] Brechts Veröffentlichung enthält: "Die Freunde," "Der Politiker," "Die Decke," "Der Drache des schwarzen Pfuhls," "Ein Protest im sechsten Jahre des Chien Fu" und "Bei der Geburt seines Sohnes." Für diesen Zyklus spielt der Dichter Po Chü-yi (772-846) eine wichtige Rolle, da er die Hälfte der von Brecht übertragenen Gedichte geschrieben hat. Brechts Auswahl ist indirekt von Waley beeinflusst, da von den 170 Gedichten in der englischen Vorlage 60 von Po stammen. Waley versieht Pos Gedichte noch zusätzlich mit einer "Introduction," die bei den anderen Dichtern der Sammlung nicht zu finden ist. Brecht übernimmt die englische "Introduction" zum Teil in seine Anmerkungen, in denen er vor allem Pos Leben und die Hauptmerkmale seiner Gedichte vorstellt.

1. Von Waleys "Introduction" zu Brechts Anmerkungen

In *Brechts chinesische Gedichte* schreibt Antony Tatlow:

> Man sollte wohl eher sagen, dass Brecht sich deshalb von der chinesischen Lyrik oder vielmehr von diesen Gedichten angezogen fühlte, weil sie gewisse Eigenschaften seiner eigenen Lyrik teilen, nämlich erstens die Tradition der Sorge um die Gesellschaft, zweitens den vergleichsweise direkten, umgangssprachlichen Ton...und drittens die elliptische Präzision der Verse...[3]

Dass Brecht selbst diesbezügliche Affinitäten zwischen seinen Gedichten und der chinesischen Lyrik bemerkt hat, steht außer Frage. Allerdings sind Brechts "Chinesische Gedichte" doch auf keinen Fall wortgetreue Übersetzungen. Vergleicht man seine Texte mit den Originalen, fallen sowohl Abweichungen als auch Sinnverschiebungen auf. Die Differenzen verweisen darauf, dass die Affinitäten allein nicht alles gewesen sein können, was Brecht angezogen haben muss. Die Analyse dieser Differenzen bildet den Schlüssel zum Versuch einer neuen Interpretation der "Sechs chinesischen Gedichte."

Brechts Anmerkungen zu Po fangen so an: "Die drei Gedichte 'Der Politiker,' 'Die Decke' und 'Der Drache des schwarzen Pfuhls' sind von Po Chü-i, einem der größten Meister der chinesischen Lyrik. Er stammte aus einer armen Bauernfamilie und wurde selbst Beamter."[4] Bereits am Anfang lässt sich eine bedeutende Änderung erkennen: Es stimmt, wie Brecht schreibt, dass Pos Familie arm gewesen sei. Aber Brecht verschärft die Lage der Familie. In der englischen Vorlage hat Waley eigentlich Pos Herkunft und Kindheit so beschrieben: "Po Chü-yi was born at Ta-yüan in Shansi…His father was a second-class Assistant Department Magistrate. He tells us that his family was poor and often in difficulties."[5] Pos Vater, der eigentlich ein Beamter war, wird bei Brecht zu einem armen Bauern stilisiert, was den chinesischen Dichter zum Angehörigen der unterdrückten Klasse macht. Aber Po selbst — seine Geburt, Kindheit und seine Freundschaft mit anderen Dichtern (vor allem mit dem politisch aktiven Yüan Chen, der mit Po mehrere Gedichte ausgetauscht hat), oder auch seine Karriere in "the political capital of the empire"[6] — ist für Brecht nicht von Interesse. Er schreibt nur einfach: "Er…wurde selbst Beamter." Offensichtlich möchte Brecht gar nicht erwähnen, dass Po einst politisch aktiv war und auch Karriere am Kaiserhof machte. Trotz seines Desinteresses an Pos Karriere zeigt Brecht hingegen großes Interesse an den Eigenschaften von Pos Lyrik, die er ausführlich beschreibt:

> "Wie Konfuzius betrachtet er die Kunst als eine Methode, Belehrung zu vermitteln" (Waley)…Von sich sagte er: "Wenn die Tyrannen und Günstlinge meine Lieder hörten, sahen sie einander an und verzogen die Gesichter." Seine Lieder waren "im Mund von Bauern und Pferdeknechten," sie standen geschrieben "auf den Wänden von Dorfschulen, Tempeln und Schiffskabinen."[7]

In seiner "Introduction" hat Waley die Besonderheiten von Pos Gedichten so kommentiert:

> Like Confucius, he regarded art solely as a method of conveying instruction…He accordingly valued his didactic poems far above his other work, but it is obvious that much of his best poetry conveys no moral whatever…The didactic poems or "satires" belong to the period before his first banishment. "When the tyrants and favourites heard my Songs of Ch'in, they looked at one another and changed countenance," he boasts…[B]ut Po's satires are as lacking in true wit as they are unquestionably full of true poetry. We must regard them simply as moral tales in verse…His poems were "on the mouths of kings, princes, concubines, ladies, plough-boys, and grooms." They were inscribed "on the walls of village-schools, temples, and ship-cabins."[8]

Brecht findet bei Waley die Aussage, Po sei an einer didaktischen Funktion der Literatur interessiert. Er betont, dass sowohl Po als auch Konfuzius dieses Interesse teilen, "vergisst" aber Waleys Kritik, dass Pos beste Gedichte gerade nicht didaktisch seien ("but it is obvious that much of his best poetry conveys no moral whatever"). Zugleich "vergisst" Brecht Waleys Hinweis, dass Pos satirische Gedichte nur vor seiner ersten Verbannung eine zentrale Stellung eingenommen hätten. Darüber hinaus deutet Waley noch mit der Formulierung "he boasts" an, dass Po die Wirkung seiner Satire übertrieben habe, und stellt fest, dass "Po's satires… [are] lacking in true wit," weshalb man sie "simply as moral tales in verse" betrachten solle. Brecht verheimlicht jedoch diese Kritik und hebt nur den sozialkritischen Charakter von Pos Lyrik hervor. Zugleich erweckt er den Eindruck, als seien Pos Gedichte gerade bei den Armen ("Bauern und Pferdeknechten") beliebt. Doch bei Waley liest man, dass sie ebenfalls bei "Königen, Prinzen, Konkubinen, Damen" ("kings, princes, concubines, ladies, plough-boys, and grooms") beliebt seien. Eigentlich hat Pos Popularität nach Waley nichts mit Klassenunterschieden zu tun, weshalb sie auch für Brechts rückblickende Überarbeitung keine Rolle hätten spielen müssen. Warum verschweigt also Brecht gerade Pos Beliebtheit bei den Königen, Prinzen, Konkubinen und Damen? Weil der Leser sonst den Widerspruch zwischen der Beliebtheit bei den Herrschenden und der "Kritik an den Herrschenden" bemerken würde. In seiner "Introduction" hat Waley diesen Widerspruch eigentlich schon erklärt: "Content, in short, he valued far above form: and it was part of his theory, though certainly not of his practice…"[9] Po habe also seine Theorie nicht durchgeführt, zumindest nicht konsequent ("The…'satires' belong to the period before his first banishment"). An diesen Abweichungen erkennen wir, wie sorgfältig Brecht versucht, das idealisierte Bild eines sozialkritischen Dichters zu vermitteln: Po stamme aus einer Bauernfamilie und kritisiere stets die Herrschenden und werde deswegen von der unterdrückten Klasse geliebt. Im Vergleich dazu ist Waleys Darstellung bei weitem objektiver.

Auch die Verbannung des chinesischen Dichters stößt auf großes Interesse bei Brecht. In diesem Kontext erwähnt Brecht bereits um 1934[10] seine verehrten chinesischen Vorgänger Li Po und Tu Fu im frühen Exilgedicht "Die Auswanderung der Dichter:"

> Li-Po und Tu-Fu irrten durch Bürgerkriege
> die 30 Millionen Menschen verschlangen
> …
> So Heine und so auch floh
> Brecht unter das dänische Strohdach.[11]

In "Das letzte Wort," das ebenfalls 1938 entstanden ist, verbindet Brecht seine eigenen Exilerfahrungen noch enger mit denen der chinesischen Dichter:

> Die älteste aller Lyriken, die noch besteht, die chinesische, erfuhr Beachtung von Seiten gewisser Fürsten, indem die besseren ihrer Lyriker individuell gezwungen wurden, mitunter die Provinzen zu verlassen, in denen ihre Gedichte zu sehr gefielen. Li Tai-po war zumindest einmal im Exil, Tu Fu zumindest zweimal, Po Chü-yi zumindest dreimal. Man sieht: Die Sesshaftigkeit war nicht das Hauptziel dieser Literatur, noch war diese Kunst lediglich eine Kunst, zu gefallen.[12]

Dieses Verständnis sieht man noch in Brechts Brief an Karin Michaelis vom März 1942, in dem er die Exilerfahrungen deutscher Schriftsteller mit denen chinesischer Lyriker und Philosophen vergleicht:

> Unsere Literaturgeschichte zählte nicht so viele exilierte Schriftsteller auf wie etwa die chinesische...Die chinesischen Lyriker und Philosophen pflegten, wie ich höre, ins Exil zu gehen wie die unsern in die Akademie. Es war üblich. Viele flohen mehrere Male, aber es scheint Ehrensache gewesen zu sein, so zu schreiben, dass man wenigstens *ein*mal den Staub seines Geburtslandes von den Füßen schütteln musste.[13]

Auch in seinen "Sechs chinesischen Gedichten" vermittelt uns Brecht am Beispiel Pos das Bild eines unnachgiebigen chinesischen Exilanten:

> Er wurde zweimal ins Exil geschickt. In zwei langen Denkschriften, betitelt "Über das Abstoppen des Kriegs," kritisiert er einen langen Feldzug gegen einen kleinen Tartarenstamm, und in einem Zyklus von Gedichten satirisierte er die Räubereien der Beamten und lenkte die Aufmerksamkeit auf die unerträglichen Leiden der Massen. Als der Kanzler von Revolutionären getötet wurde, kritisierte er ihn, weil er nichts getan hatte, die allgemeine Unzufriedenheit zu lindern, und wurde verbannt. Sein zweites Exil verdankt er seiner Kritik des Kaisers, dessen Missregierung er für die Umstände verantwortlich machte.[14]

Doch in der englischen Vorlage sieht Pos Exil etwas anders aus. Waley weist da eindeutig auf Pos Veränderung sowie Zurückgezogenheit am Verbannungsort hin.[15] Brecht behauptet zudem, dass Po stets auf seiner sozialkritischen Haltung beharre. Nach Waley richtet sich Pos Kritik an der Räuberei jedoch gar nicht gegen die ganze herrschende Klasse, sondern allein gegen die "niederen Beamten" ("minor officials").[16] Was den Kanzler betrifft, weicht Brecht ebenfalls von Waley ab. In der englischen Vorlage liest man zwar, dass Po Kritik an der Unfähigkeit des getöteten Kanzlers übe, seine Verbannung verdanke sich aber der Beschuldigung durch seine politischen Gegner, seine Machtbefugnisse überschritten und ungeachtet des Todes seiner Mutter weiter gedichtet zu haben. Auch "sein zweites Exil" bedeutet nicht dasselbe im Kontext der europäischen Exilgeschichte um 1938. In der Tat wird Po nur versetzt ("removed")[17] und nicht verbannt: Er wird Gouverneur einer der wichtigsten und zugleich schönsten südchinesischen Städte, Hangchow (Hangzhou). Brecht vermittelt den Eindruck, als sei Po allein wegen seiner Kritik an einem Herrscher und seines Mitleids mit den Armen verbannt worden. Gerade durch diese gezielten Änderungen ist die Kausalität zwischen Pos Sozialkritik und Exil vollständig hergestellt. Zugleich wird der chinesische Dichter für Brecht zum Vorbild: Das mehrfache Exil aufgrund der Kritik an den Herrschenden sollte nicht als Tragödie betrachtet, sondern als Kennzeichen erfolgreicher Sozialkritik und dichterischen Ansehens wahrgenommen werden. Pos Gedichte waren gerade dank seiner unnachgiebigen Stellung weit verbreitet und wirkungsvoll. Brecht sieht in Po eine geschichtliche Widerspiegelung seiner eigenen Erfahrung: sozialkritische Dichter wie Po und er selbst müssten mit einem langen Exil rechnen. Das idealisierte Bild des verbannten Dichters weist die gewünschten Parallelen mit der gegenwärtigen Situation Brechts auf. Denn Brecht sieht seine satirische "Legende vom toten Soldaten," in der er Kritik an der deutschen Kriegsführung während des ersten Weltkriegs übt, als unmittelbaren Grund für sein Exil,[18] und schreibt 1933 in seinem Gedicht "Als ich ins Exil gejagt wurde:"

> Als ich ins Exil gejagt wurde
> Stand in den Zeitungen des Anstreichers
> Das sei, weil ich in einem Gedicht
> Den Soldaten des Weltkriegs verhöhnt hätte.
> ...Jetzt
> Wo sie einen neuen Weltkrieg vorbereiteten;
> Entschlossen, die Untaten des letzten noch zu übertreffen,
> Brachten sie Leute wie mich zuzeiten um oder verjagten sie
> Als Verräter
> Ihrer Anschläge.[19]

Insgesamt zeichnet Brecht nicht nur ein perfektes Bild des ins Exil vertriebenen Dichters Po, sondern er konstruiert auch durch gezielte Auslassung und Abänderung eine ausgezeichnete geschichtliche Widerspiegelung seines eigenen Exils. In der Retuschierung spiegelt sich zugleich Brechts Hoffnung, den endgültigen Sinn des Exils zu finden. Er rekonfiguriert nicht nur einen chinesischen Dichter, sondern er vermittelt auch seine Stellungnahme zum Exil: Furchtlos sich den Widrigkeiten des Exils zu stellen und dabei an der sozialen Verantwortung des Dichters, der den "kleinen Leuten" gehört und von ihnen geliebt wird, festzuhalten. Insoweit dient das historische Beispiel aus der alten Dichtungswelt Chinas schließlich der Selbstreflexion Brechts.

2. Abweichungen und Hinzufügungen in den "Sechs chinesischen Gedichten"

Waleys *170 Chinese Poems* repräsentieren ein breites Spektrum an chinesischer Lyrik, aus dem Brecht aber nur sechs Gedichte auswählt. Brechts Interesse konzentriert sich vor allem auf zwei Themen: die Kritik an den Herrschenden und das Exilleben.[20] Brechts hauptsächliches Auswahlkriterium sind die Gemeinsamkeiten der deutschen und chinesischen Exilerfahrungen, die ihm den Rekurs auf den chinesischen Dichter ermöglichen.

Das erste Gedicht von Po, das Brecht aus dem Englischen übersetzt, ist "Der Politiker" über die Verbannung eines Staatsrats. Das lyrische Ich, ein Dorfbewohner, der zum Verkauf seiner Kräuter in die Hauptstadt geht, wird Zeuge der Verbannung eines Staatsrats:

> Das war ein Staatsrat. Einer von den größten.
> Zehntausend Käsch Diäten jährlich auf den Tisch. Der Kaiser
> Kam dreimal täglich in sein Haus. Erst gestern
> Aß er zur Nacht noch mit Heroen. Heute
> Ist er verbannt ins hinterste Yai-chou.
> So ist es immer mit den Räten der Könige.
> Gunst und Ungnade zwischen zwölf Uhr und Mittag.
> Grün, grün, das Gras der östlichen Vorstadt, durch das
> Die Strasse zu den Hügeln führt. Zuletzt
> Hat er den "Coup" gemacht, der nicht fehlgehn kann.[21]

Die ersten Zeilen hat Brecht relativ wortgetreu wiedergegeben. Nur die gefährliche Lage im Kaiserhof, wo "Favour and ruin changed between dawn und dusk,"[22] wird noch verschärft zu "Gunst und Ungnade zwischen zwölf Uhr und Mittag." Die wichtigste Änderung findet man in den letzten vier Zeilen des Gedichts. Das lyrische Ich in Waleys Fassung zeigt eine gewisse Zufriedenheit mit dem zurückgezogenen Leben und kämpft gegen die Widrigkeiten des Exils an. Deswegen wird in den letzten vier Zeilen von "hermit" und "resting in peace" gesprochen.[23] Brecht hingegen lässt sowohl das Wort "hermit" als auch die Zeile "Resting in peace among the white clouds" völlig verschwinden und gibt nur drei Zeilen wieder. Diese unübersehbare Änderung weist darauf hin, dass Brecht das Exil anders deuten möchte: Den politischen Umständen im Kaiserhof zu entfliehen ist eine kluge Entscheidung. Doch das Exil bedeutet keine Flucht oder Zurückgezogenheit. Der Exilant verliert zwar die Hauptstadt, aber er bekommt nun die "Vorstadt," das heißt die Welt der unterdrückten Klassen, als Spielraum. Unter die "kleinen Leute" zu gehen und mit ihnen zusammenzuarbeiten ist der richtige Weg, der "nicht fehlgehn kann."

In den "Sechs chinesischen Gedichten" empfindet man die Sympathie mit den Verarmten sowie die Kritik an den Herrschenden, vor allem in der Übertragung von Pos Gedicht "Die Decke" (später: "Die große Decke"), die später mit wenigen Änderungen ins Theaterstück *Der gute Mensch von Sezuan* einfließt. Auffällig ist, dass verschiedene Bedeutungsschichten desselben Gedichts in den verschiedenen literarischen Umsetzungen unterschiedlich akzentuiert werden. Schon Waleys Übertragung ist keine wortgetreue Übersetzung. Das Motiv der "großen Decke" taucht in zwei Gedichten von Po auf. Waleys Gedicht soll die Fassung mit vierzehn Zeilen als Vorlage benutzt haben.[24] Er hat die Zeilen 9, 10, 13 und 14 ausgewählt und zu einem Vierzeiler gemacht:

> THAT so many of the poor should suffer from cold what can we do to prevent?
> To bring warmth to a single body is not much use.
> I wish I had a big rug ten thousand feet long,
> Which at one time could cover up every inch of the City.[25]

An Waleys Übersetzung erkennt man noch Pos Beweggründe: Der Dichter bekleidete zu dieser Zeit ein hohes, aber nutzloses Amt in der zweiten Hauptstadt Luoyang.[26] Er beklagt sich im Gedicht darüber, im kalten Winter nur sich selbst und nicht auch die Armen mit dem neuen Mantel wärmen zu können. Daher wünscht er sich eine riesige Decke, mit der die ganze Stadt zugedeckt und erwärmt würde. Waley hat zwar nicht das vollständige Gedicht übersetzt, aber er hat Pos Sorge und Mitleid gut wiedergegeben.

Brechts Vierzeiler folgt der Übersetzung Waleys:

> Der Gouverneur, von mir gefragt
> Was, den Frierenden unserer Stadt zu helfen, nötig sei
> Antwortet: Eine zehntausend Fuß lange Decke
> Welche die ganzen Vorstädte einfach zudeckt.[27]

Brechts Bearbeitung besteht vor allem in dem neu hinzugefügten Satz am Anfang: "Der Gouverneur, von mir gefragt." Mit diesem Satz kehrt er die Verhältnisse innerhalb des chinesischen Gedichts um. Es wird jetzt zu einem Gespräch zwischen dem lyrischen Ich und einem Gouverneur. Und durch diese Änderung wird das Gedicht doppeldeutig. Es geht nicht mehr nur um die soziale Anteilnahme des lyrischen Ichs am Elend der Armen, sondern auch um Kritik an der Missregierung. Einerseits wird deutlich, dass niemand in der Lage ist, so vielen Armen zu helfen. Als "Die Decke" ins Theaterstück *Der gute Mensch von Sezuan* einfließt, wird das Gedicht von Shui Ta so kommentiert: "Das Unglück besteht darin, dass die Not in dieser Stadt zu groß ist, als dass ein einzelner Mensch ihr steuern könnte."[28] Andererseits bildet das Gedicht eine Karikatur des Gouverneurs: Auf die ernsthafte Frage hat der Herrscher nur die resignierte Antwort, dass man nichts tun könne als auf ein Wunder zu warten. Brecht hat weiterhin "the City" als "die ganzen Vorstädte" übersetzt, damit der implizierte soziale Gegensatz klarer ausgedrückt wird. Die Kritik an den Herrschenden ist somit viel schärfer als in der englischen Vorlage. Dort wünscht der zuständige Politiker zumindest noch, dass er die Armut in der Stadt mit einem Wunder beseitigen könne ("I wish I had a big rug"). In Brechts Übertragung ist nur die Resignation des Gouverneurs zu empfinden. Das Gedicht lässt sich auch noch anders deuten: Der Herrscher der Stadt will die Not überhaupt nicht zur Kenntnis nehmen. Er möchte das Elend der Vorstädte einfach überdecken und verschweigen, anstatt den Armen zu helfen. Damit wird das Gedicht zu einer politischen Satire und einer unverkennbaren Kritik an den Herrschenden, den Gouverneur eingeschlossen.

Ähnlich verhält es sich bei dem Gedicht "Der Drache des schwarzen Pfuhls," einer politischen Satire, in der Po die Räuberei der niederen Beamten thematisiert. Im Chinesischen trägt das Gedicht den Nebentitel: "Ji Tan Li Ye" ("Eine Satire auf die raubgierigen niederen Beamten"). Dazu schreibt Waley: "He had satirized the rapacity of minor officials and called attention to the intolerable suffering of the masses."[29] Doch die Kritik an den niederen Beamten allein entspricht Brechts Vorstellungen weniger. Es gelingt ihm einmal mehr, durch eine feine Umarbeitung das alte chinesische Gedicht grundsätzlicher und zugleich von seiner eigenen Zeit sprechen zu lassen, indem er die über tausend Jahre alte politische Satire in ein Gedicht mit Zeitbezug verwandelt.[30] In der englischen Fassung werden das Morgengebet und die Feierabendhymne in Pos Gedicht so übersetzt:

> When the dragon comes, ah!
> The wind stirs and sighs
> Paper money thrown, ah!
> Silk umbrellas waved.
> When the dragon goes, ah
> The wind also—still.
> Incense-fire dies, ah!
> The cups and vessels are cold.[31]

In Brechts Übersetzung steht hingegen:

> Gegrüßt seist du, Drache, voll der Gaben!
> Heil dir im Siegerkranz
> Retter des Vaterlands, du
> Bist erwählt unter den Drachen und erwählt ist
> Unter allem Wein der Opferwein.[32]

Waley hat die Hymne wortgetreu übersetzt. Dagegen weicht Brecht in dieser Passage weit von der Quelle ab.[33] Die erste Zeile bezieht sich auf das "Ave Maria," das katholische Gebet zur Lobpreisung der Gottesmutter: "Gegrüßt seist du Maria, voll der Gnade."[34] Die zweite und dritte Zeile spielen auf den Anfang der preußischen Königshymne an: "Heil dir im Siegerkranz, Herrscher des Vaterlands!" Brecht zitiert zwar aus der berühmten Hymne, aber er nimmt hier eine Sinnverschiebung vor: "Retter des Vaterlands" spielt ironischerweise auf das Selbstlob der Nazis an.

Auffällig sind zudem die Formulierungen, die einen deutlichen zeitgeschichtlichen Bezug aufweisen. Brecht redet den Drachen mit "Heil dir" an, so wie sich die Leute im Dritten Reich mit "Heil Hitler" begrüßten. Er scherzt, dass der Drache "im Siegerkranz" "Retter des Vaterlands" sei, so wie die Nazis und Militaristen jeden Tag vom Vaterland reden und Hitler als Retter feiern. Brecht ironisiert, dass der Drache "erwählt unter den Drachen" sei, so wie die Rassenideologie des Nationalsozialismus die Auserwähltheit der deutschen Nation für die Umgestaltung der Welt behauptet. Der Opferwein sei auch "erwählt unter allem Wein," während das erwählte Volk unter allen Völkern (5 Mose 7:6) zum Opfer des Hitler-Regiments wird. Mit diesen Formulierungen verleiht Brecht der alten chinesischen Satire einen neuen Bezug auf den grundsätzlichen politischen Diskurs seiner Zeit. Mit diesem Bezug ist der satirische Ton in Brechts Übertragung noch besser als in der Vorlage zu erkennen. In der englischen Vorlage heißt es:

> A dragon by itself remains a dragon, but men can make it a god. Prosperity and disaster, rain and drought, plagues and pestilences—
> By the village people were all regarded as the Sacred Dragon's doing.[35]

Brechts Übersetzung lautet:

> Ein Drache
> Bleibt vielleicht ein Drache, aber die Menschen
> Können aus ihm einen Gott machen. Die Dorfbewohner
> Betrachten gute Ernten und Misswachs
> Heuschreckenschwärme und kaiserliche Kommissionen
> Steuern und Seuchen als Schickungen des sehr heiligen Drachen.[36]

Bei Po sowie bei Waley betrachten die Dorfbewohner nur Naturkatastrophen als göttliche Fügung. Brechts Übersetzung spricht zusätzlich von der Missregierung (kaiserliche Kommissionen, Steuern), die ebenfalls als eine Schickung des Drachen angesehen wird. Nun wird nicht nur der Aberglaube kritisiert, sondern auch das Manöver der Herrschenden entlarvt: Sie machen aus dem Drachen einen Gott und überzeugen die Unterdrückten davon, dass die Unterdrückung göttliche Fügung sei. Somit wird nun nicht mehr der Aberglaube der Dorfbewohner, sondern die Täuschungsmanöver der Nazis und die Vergöttlichung Hitlers satirisiert.

Den deutlichen Zeitbezug erkennt man auch an Brechts Übertragung des Gedichts "Ein Protest im sechsten Jahre des Chien Fu:"

> Die Hügel und Bäche der Ebene
> Macht ihr zu eurem Schlachtfeld
> ....
> Eines einzigen Generals Reputation
> Heißt: zehntausend Leichen.[37]

"Im sechsten Jahre" spielt auf die Gegenwart Brechts an. Die Übersetzung ist nämlich 1938, also im sechsten Jahr der nationalsozialistischen Herrschaft, entstanden.[38] Die Kritik an der Kriegsführung und den Generälen bei Po entspricht Brechts Kritik an den Nazis und ihrem Militarismus. Mehrere Typoskripte enthalten noch die Anmerkung: "Wie man aus der Zahl zehntausend sieht, war die Zivilisation zur Zeit, wo dieses Gedicht entstand, noch wenig entwickelt. Die Reputation der Generäle war damals noch verhältnismäßig billig."[39] Dadurch, dass Brecht den Zivilisationsstand seiner Zeit mit der Zahl der Kriegstoten in Verbindung bringt, hinterfragt er den Sinn der Zivilisation. So hat das Gedicht nach tausend Jahren an aktueller Bedeutung gewonnen.

3. Zusammenfassung: "Die List, die Wahrheit unter vielen zu verbreiten"

Aus der obigen vergleichenden Gedichtinterpretation geht hervor, dass Brecht sich nicht nur aufgrund der Affinitäten zwischen der alten chinesischen Lyrik und seiner eigenen von Pos Gedichten angezogen fühlt. Vielmehr legt er besonderen Wert auf den modernen Zeitbezug der alten Gedichte. Im Typoskript hinterlässt Brecht sogar unter einem chinesischen Gedicht den Vermerk: "Dieses Gedicht ist so aktuell wie an seinem ersten Tag."[40] Für Brecht besteht diese Aktualität vor allem in zweierlei Hinsicht. Einerseits findet Brecht in der Biographie Pos sein Ideal des verbannten sozialkritischen Dichters. Durch die Hervorhebung der Verbindung zwischen Pos sozialkritischem Standpunkt und seinen Exilerfahrungen zieht Brecht die bereits vor tausend Jahren hoch entwickelte chinesische Dichtkunst zur eigenen Selbstermutigung, Tröstung für erlittenes Unrecht und Bekräftigung der eigenen Zukunftsperspektive heran. Andererseits formuliert er durch gezielte Abänderung die alten chinesischen Gedichte in moderne Zeitgedichte um. Zu diesem Zweck stellt Brecht an mehreren Stellen den Bezug zu seiner Zeit, den er in ihnen nicht unmittelbar vorfindet, mit Hilfe großzügiger Änderungen, die sogar Sinnverschiebungen einschließen, her. Dieses geschickte Manöver erinnert an seine Beschreibung über "die List, die Wahrheit unter vielen zu verbreiten:"[41]

> Zu allen Zeiten wurde zur Verbreitung der Wahrheit, wenn sie unterdrückt und verhüllt wurde, List angewandt. *Konfutse* fälschte einen alten, patriotischen Geschichtskalender. Er veränderte nur gewisse Wörter. Wenn es hieß, "Der Herrscher von Kun ließ den Philosophen Wan töten, weil er das und das gesagt hatte," setzte Konfutse statt töten "ermorden." Hieß es, der Tyrann soundso sei durch ein Attentat umgekommen, setzte er "hingerichtet worden." Dadurch brach Konfutse einer neuen Beurteilung der Geschichte Bahn.[42]

Unverkennbar ist Brechts Anwendung derselben List bei der Übersetzung der "Sechs chinesischen Gedichte." So stilisiert seine Beschreibung von Pos Leben und Lyrik den chinesischen Dichter in ein aktuelles Vorbild für die deutschen Exilanten. Und seine Übertragung "Der Drache des schwarzen Pfuhls" richtet sich nicht mehr gegen die niederen Beamten, sondern gegen Hitler und Nazis. Und Pos Gedicht "Die Decke," in dem die soziale Anteilnahme des Dichters am Elend der Armen zum Ausdruck kommt, verwandelt sich in eine sozialkritische Satire auf die Indifferenz der Herrschenden gegenüber den Armen. Zusammenfassend lässt sich sagen: Durch die gezielten Hinzufügungen und Abweichungen von der Vorlage wandelt Brecht die alten chinesischen Gedichte zugunsten seiner Selbstreflexion mehr und mehr in moderne Zeitgedichte um.[43] Auf diese fast unspürbare Weise verbreitet er schließlich nicht nur seine Kritik am Nazi-Regime, sondern auch seine Gedanken zur zeitgenössischen Exilliteratur unter den deutschen Exilanten. Man könnte auch sagen: Wenn man den "Sechs Chinesischen Gedichten" ihre chinesische Maske entreißt, kommt darunter das siegesbewusste Lächeln Brechts zum Vorschein.

Anmerkungen

1   *Bertolt Brecht Werke: Große kommentierte Berliner und Frankfurter Ausgabe*, Bd. 11, Werner Hecht, Jan Knopf, Werner Mittenzwei und Klaus-Detlev Müller, Hrsg. (Berlin: Aufbau, und Frankfurt/Main: Suhrkamp, 1988-1997), S. 386. (Im Folgenden abgekürzt als BFA.)
2   Bertolt Brecht, "Sechs chinesische Gedichte," *Das Wort* 8 (1938): S. 87-89 und S. 157, hier S. 157.
3   Antony Tatlow, *Brechts chinesische Gedichte* (Frankfurt/Main: Suhrkamp, 1973), S. 24.
4   Brecht, *Sechs chinesische Gedichte*, S. 157. In der neueren Fassung von 1950

schreibt Brecht den Namen des Dichters als "Po Chü-yi," was auch der gängigen Buchstabierung entspricht: BFA 11, S. 388. Der Name des Dichters wird heute in China als "Bai Juyi" buchstabiert.
5   Arthur Waley, Übers., *170 Chinese Poems* (New York: A. A. Knopf, 1919), S. 105.
6   Ebd.
7   Brecht, "Sechs chinesische Gedichte," S. 157.
8   Waley, *170 Chinese Poems*, S. 110-112.
9   Ebd., S. 111.
10 Das Gedicht blieb zu Brechts Lebenszeit unveröffentlicht. Vergleiche BFA 14, S. 593.
11 Ebd., S. 256.
12 BFA 22, S. 455.
13 BFA 23, S. 9.
14 Brecht, "Sechs chinesische Gedichte," S. 157.
15 Po soll sich später von der Sozialkritik zurückgezogen haben. Im Exil dichtete er über "Indian rock," "many flowers and exotic trees," "which were a constant delight to its new Governor," und so weiter. Siehe Waley, *170 Chinese Poems*, S. 108.
16 Ebd., S. 107.
17 Ebd., S. 108.
18 Vergleiche Peter Paul Schwarz, *Lyrik und Zeitgeschichte. Brecht: Gedichte über das Exil und späte Lyrik* (Heidelberg: Stiehm, 1978), S. 19-21.
19 BFA 14, S. 185-186.
20 Vergleiche Jan Knopf, Hrsg., *Brecht-Handbuch. Gedichte* (Stuttgart und Weimar: Metzler, 2001), S. 219.
21 BFA 11, S. 257.
22 Waley, *170 Chinese Poems*, S. 138.
23 Ebd.
24 Tatlow, *Brechts chinesische Gedichte*, S. 41-42.
25 Waley, *170 Chinese Poems*, S. 157.
26 In der Tang-Zeit (618-907) war Luoyang neben der Hauptstadt Chang'an die größte Stadt Chinas, die schätzungsweise über eine Million Einwohner hatte. Als zweite Hauptstadt waren in Luoyang alle Behörden vertreten. Aber war der Kaiser nicht zugegen, fehlte den meisten Beamten die Arbeit. Vergleiche Shiyi Wang, *Bei Juyi* (Xi'an: Volksverlag, 1983), S. 273, 282.
27 BFA 11, S. 257.
28 In Bertolt Brecht, *Der gute Mensch von Sezuan*, in BFA 6 verteidigt Shui Ta mit diesem Gedicht seine Härte gegen die Armen, weil niemand in der Lage sei, so vielen Armen zu helfen. Im *Sezuan*-Stück wird die erste Zeile wie folgt abgeändert: "Gouvernör, befragt, was nötig wäre." BFA 6, S. 196.
29 Waley, *170 Chinese Poems*, S. 107.
30 Vergleiche Edgar Marsch, *Brecht-Kommentar zum lyrischen Werk* (München: Winkler, 1974), S. 261.
31 Waley, *170 Chinese Poems*, S. 122.
32 BFA 11, S. 258.
33 Diese Abweichung ist von der Brecht-Forschung noch nicht genau untersucht worden. Tatlow meint zum Beispiel: "Brecht has changed very little apart from the substituted passage, but he has transformed Waley's poem." Antony Tatlow, *The Mask of Evil. Brecht's Response to the Poetry, Theatre and Thought of China and Japan. A Comparative and Critical Evaluation* (Frankfurt/Main, Bern, Las Vegas: Peter Lang, 1977), S. 120-125.
34 Marsch, *Brecht-Kommentar*, S. 261.
35 Waley, *170 Chinese Poems*, S. 121.
36 BFA 11, S. 258.
37 BFA 11, S. 263-264.
38 Vergleiche Marsch, *Brecht-Kommentar*, S. 262.

39 BFA 11, S. 390.
40 Ebd.
41 BFA 2, S. 81.
42 Ebd.
43 Renate Berg-Pan, *Bertolt Brecht and China* (Bonn: Bouvier, 1979), S. 33-34.
Vergleiche dazu Marsch, *Brecht-Kommentar*, S. 257.

Grandma, Pietism, and the Missionaries: Origins of Bertolt Brecht's Interest in China

Eberhard Fritz

During his youth Bertolt Brecht was strongly influenced by his maternal grandmother Friederike Brezing nee Gamerdinger (1838-1916), who was a pietist. Brecht owed his literary expressiveness and profound bible knowledge to her influence. One of the fundamental activities of the Pietist movement in Wuerttemberg, with which Friederike Brezing was deeply involved, was mission work among the "heathens." The Basel Mission, which was also very well established in the Kingdom of Wuerttemberg, had been active in China since 1850. The magazine of the mission regularly published articles on various regions of China. Comparisons between articles in the mission magazine and Brecht's "Chinese" works suggest that Brecht's interest in China could have been aroused by his reading of the magazines during his youth. This is strongly indicated by his extraordinary interest in the Chinese philosopher Confucius. It will be an important task for future Brecht studies to further investigate those influences in order to verify the argument of this article.

In seiner Jugend wurde Bertolt Brecht grundlegend von seiner Großmutter mütterlicherseits, der pietistisch eingestellten Friederike Brezing geb. Gamerdinger (1838-1916) beeinflusst. Ihr verdankte er seine sprachliche Ausdrucksfähigkeit und seine profunde Bibelkenntnis. Zieht man die Eigenarten des württembergischen Pietismus, in dessen Tradition die Großmutter verhaftet war, in Betracht, dann rückt das pietistische Grundanliegen der Mission in das Blickfeld. Die Basler Mission verfügte im Königreich Württemberg über einen starken Rückhalt und war auch in China aktiv. In ihrer Missionszeitschrift wurden zahlreiche Berichte aus allen Regionen Chinas veröffentlicht. Inhaltliche Vergleiche legen nahe, dass Brechts Interesse an China durch die Lektüre von Missionszeitschriften in seiner Jugend erweckt worden sein könnte. Besonders sein ungewöhnliches Interesse am chinesischen Philosophen Konfuzius ist dafür ein starkes Indiz. Es wird eine wichtige Aufgabe der künftigen Brecht-Forschung sein, diese Einflüsse weiter zu erforschen und zu verifizieren.

Die Großmutter, der Pietismus und die Missionare:
Neue biografische Erklärungsansätze in Bezug auf Brechts "chinesisches Werk"

Eberhard Fritz

Die Forscherin Renata Berg-Pan schreibt in ihrem grundlegenden Werk über Bertolt Brecht und China:

> Brought up in a household where he found little to nourish his intellect and taught by teachers whose 'worthless educational materials' did not offer him very much either, Brecht discovered his literary tastes and their satisfactions on his own. This includes his discovery, if we may call it that, of things Chinese and oriental. Brecht provides an interesting contrast to Hermann Hesse whose appreciation of oriental culture, especially Indian and Chinese, was fostered by his parents and grandparents who had been missionaries in the orient. Brecht seems to have relied primarily on sheer accident and good luck at first...[1]

Berg-Pan fährt fort:

> Brecht's knowledge of things Chinese was sporadic in his early years and, unlike Hesse, he received no inspiration and stimulation from home. He had to rely on accident.[2]

Diese Feststellungen Berg-Pans sind in der Brecht-Forschung bislang unwidersprochen geblieben. Geradezu idealtypisch scheinen mit Brecht und Hermann Hesse zwei der bekanntesten Literaten vertreten zu sein, deren geistige Einflüsse unterschiedlicher nicht sein könnten.[3] Während Hesse sozusagen die "große weite Welt" schon in die Wiege gelegt worden war, fand Brecht offenbar durch Zufall einen Zugang zur chinesischen Kultur. Obwohl in der Brecht-Forschung die von der fernöstlichen Kultur beeinflussten Werke eine breite Beachtung gefunden haben,[4] blieb bisher die Frage völlig unbeantwortet, welche Einflüsse ihn dazu führten, sich mit diesem Kulturkreis zu beschäftigen. Nun ist es zweifelsohne nicht einfach, einen schlüssigen Ansatz zur Beantwortung dieser Frage zu finden, denn es gibt keine kausale Beweiskette. Allerdings dürfte das völlige Fehlen jeglicher Hinweise damit zusammenhängen, dass der Familiengeschichte Brechts in der mütterlichen Linie bislang nicht die gebührende Aufmerksamkeit geschenkt wurde.[5] Zu unbedeutend erschien die Frage nach den Einflüssen, als dass sie weiter verfolgt worden wäre. Antony Tatlow hat zum Beispiel festgestellt: "Here we need to understand why Brecht used what he used and how he used it. Where he first encountered it does not very much matter."⁶ Die Forschung ließ sich womöglich von Brecht selbst in die Irre führen, der nicht nur literarisch seine Motive verfremdete, sondern auch das geistig-religiöse Umfeld seiner Herkunftsfamilie eher zu marginalisieren schien: "There are few hints and reminiscences regarding his home life in Brecht's work."⁷ Da Brecht selbst offenbar seine Jugendzeit in Augsburg nicht als besonders wichtig erachtete, sah man wohl keinen Grund, sich näher damit zu beschäftigen.

Geht man allerdings den eher zufälligen Bemerkungen über die frühen Jahre nach, so erweisen sie sich plötzlich als nicht mehr ganz so unwichtig, wie es auf den ersten Blick erscheinen mag. Brecht selbst führte sein sprachliches Ausdrucksvermögen und seine profunde Bibelkenntnis auf seine Großmutter Friederike Brezing zurück.⁸ Beide Fähigkeiten bildeten eine Grundlage für sein literarisches Werk. Diesem Hinweis ging Hansjörg Kammerer in einem von der Brecht-Forschung weithin unbeachteten Aufsatz nach.⁹ Kammerer wies erstmals dezidiert auf die Einflüsse des württembergischen Pietismus hin, dem die Großmutter anhing.¹⁰ Da der Aufsatz aber in den *Blättern für Württembergische Kirchengeschichte* und damit in einer kirchengeschichtlichen Zeitschrift erschien, wurde er in der Literaturwissenschaft nicht rezipiert. Allerdings muss konstatiert werden, dass auch Kammerer noch Forschungsbedarf anmeldet, weil ihm einige Lücken bewusst sind.¹¹ Insofern bildet seine Studie eine Grundlage, um in Verbindung mit der Literatur und einschlägigen Quellen zu weiterführenden Ergebnissen zu kommen.

Die Großeltern Brezing

Als Brecht am 10. Februar 1898 in Augsburg als Sohn eines katholischen Vaters und einer protestantischen Mutter geboren wurde, kamen die Eltern überein, das Kind protestantisch taufen zu lassen. Dies dürfte die religiöse Einstellung der Eheleute Brecht widerspiegeln,¹² denn während der als Geschäftsführer der Papierfabrik Haindl¹³ tätige Vater Berthold Friedrich Brecht als Kasual-Kirchgänger beschrieben wird,¹⁴ war die Mutter Sophie geborene Brezing sehr stark pietistisch geprägt. Brecht bezeichnete sie einmal als "[einen] Eindringling, sie ist die rebellierende Protestantin in der Familie"¹⁵ und bringt damit zum Ausdruck, dass in der Familie Brezing Religiosität nicht nur habituell gelebt wurde. Vielmehr durchdrang sie alle Lebensbereiche; man meint in der Äußerung Brechts auch ein Element der Widerständigkeit gegen die kirchlichen Autoritäten und Lehren wahrzunehmen.¹⁶ Dieser dezidiert protestantischen Lebensauffassung war es geschuldet, dass sich die Eltern hatten protestantisch trauen lassen. Eine katholische Taufe ihrer Kinder wäre danach nicht mehr in Frage gekommen.

Stammbaum der mütterlichen Ahnen von Bertolt Brecht

Georg Friedrich Brezing (*1756 Haiterbach) ∞ II 1795 Katharina Barbara Zürn, Balingen	Johannes Brezing, Kübler ∞ Anna Maria Manz (*Walddorf bei Altensteig)	Johann Georg Gamerdinger, Schuhmacher, Leiter der Pregizerianer (1775-1845) ∞ 1811 Anna Katharina Heimerdinger (1774-1838) Weil im Schönbuch	Johannes Böpple, Metzger und Gemeindepfleger (1786-1864) ∞ Elisabeth Wörn (1777-1845) Weil im Schönbuch
Christian Gottlob Brezing, Strumpfweber ∞ 1852 Christiane Gottliebin Brezing (*1806 Haiterbach) Neubulach			Johannes Gamerdinger, Schuster (1809-1844) ∞ Elisabeth Böpple (1814-1867) Weil im Schönbuch
Joseph Friedrich Brezing, Stationsvorsteher (1842 Neubulach – 1922 Augsburg) ∞ 1866 Friederike Gamerdinger (1838 Weil im Schönbuch – 1916 Augsburg)			
Berthold Brecht (1869 Achern - 1939), Geschäftsführer bei der Papierfabrik Haindl ∞ 1897 Sofie Brezing (1871 Roßberg – 1920) Augsburg			
Bertolt Brecht, Schriftsteller (1898-1956)			

Dieses Element einer überzeugten und lebendigen Religiosität verstärkte sich, als die Großeltern Brezing im Herbst 1900 nach Augsburg kamen und in unmittelbarer Nähe der Familie Brecht eine Wohnung bezogen.[17] Nun gehörten regelmäßige Besuche bei den Großeltern zum Lebensalltag. Vor allem nach dem sonntäglichen Gottesdienst schaute man regelmäßig bei ihnen vorbei. In den wenigen Schilderungen und Erwähnungen der Großeltern wird deutlich erkennbar, dass die Großmutter in der ehelichen Beziehung eine dominierende Rolle einnahm. Sie war belesen und gebildet, obwohl sie nie eine höhere Schule besucht hatte. Dem jungen Eugen Berthold Brecht und seinem Bruder Walter erzählte sie in spannender Weise biblische Geschichten.[18] Andeutungen der Brüder Brecht lassen darauf schließen, dass die Religiosität der Großmutter von einer starken Nüchternheit, aber auch von fundamentalistischen Auffassungen geprägt war. Denn einerseits kam es ihr, Walter Brecht zufolge, "nicht so sehr darauf an, uns den christlichen-religiösen Inhalt nahe zu bringen, als darauf, ohne Langeweile erzieherisch zu wirken,"[19] andererseits konnte sie sich bei starkem Regen fragen, ob es je wieder aufhören würde zu regnen, wenn es doch bei der Sintflut auch nicht mehr aufgehört hatte.[20] Immerhin regte sie die Kinder zu Fragen an und ärgerte sich über dumme Fragen, wollte also durchaus zu ihrer Bildung beitragen.[21] An den wenigen Bemerkungen über Friederike Brezing in den Lebenserinnerungen von Walter Brecht wird erkennbar, dass sie fest in der Kultur des protestantischen Württemberg verhaftet war. Nicht nur der schwäbische Dialekt fiel dem Jungen auf, sondern auch eine damit verbundene Denkweise, die sich sehr von der großbürgerlichen

Mentalität der wohlhabenderen Schicht in Augsburg, welcher die Familie Brecht angehörte, unterschied. Wiewohl dieses Denken religiös durchdrungen war, wurzelte es auch im Kleinbürgertum, in den sozialen Rahmenbedingungen einer Gesellschaftsschicht mit knappen Ressourcen.

All diese Hinweise erschließen sich erst, wenn man den Lebenslauf des Ehepaars Brezing näher untersucht. Man kann davon ausgehen, dass beide Eheleute pietistisch eingestellt waren. Im protestantischen Württemberg hatte der Pietismus als Frömmigkeitsbewegung eine breite Anhängerschaft gefunden und wesentlichen Einfluss auf die Kirche erlangt.[22] Allerdings muss vor einer Überschätzung der Bewegung gewarnt werden, denn gerade im Leben der ländlich geprägten Gegenden vermischten sich religiöse Motive mit den Erfordernissen einer vom Mangel geprägten Gesellschaft. Wenn zum Beispiel der Arbeitseifer, die Sparsamkeit oder eine rigide Sexualmoral religiös legitimiert wurden, so ermöglichten diese Ideale auch ein äußerst einfaches Leben, wie es viele Menschen führen mussten. In Württemberg war die Realteilung üblich, bei der alle Kinder, gleich welchen Geschlechts, den gleichen Anteil am Nachlass ihrer Eltern erbten. Dies führte zu einer Zerstückelung der Güter und einer Aufsplitterung der Vermögen. Gleichzeitig aber entstand neben der dünnen vermögenden Oberschicht und der im Prekariat lebenden Unterschicht eine relativ breite bürgerliche Mittelschicht, welche sich in Bescheidenheit üben musste, um mit den vorhandenen Mitteln auszukommen. Der Bruder Brechts, Walter, beschrieb den Großvater Brezing als "vermögenslosen Beamten," also als Angehörigen der knapp über der Subsistenz lebenden Mittelschicht.[23] Insbesondere der Pietismusforscher Joachim Trautwein hat einen engen Zusammenhang zwischen der Sitte der Realteilung und der Entwicklung des württembergischen Pietismus hergestellt.[24] Die Validität dieser These ist in der historischen Forschung indessen kritisch diskutiert worden.[25] Vielleicht reflektiert Brecht bewusst oder unbewusst die Herkunft seiner Mutter, wenn er sich in einem frühen Gedicht mit den "geringen Leuten" solidarisiert.[26] Denn obwohl Sophie Brecht nicht der bäuerlich-handwerklichen Schicht entstammte, sondern als Tochter eines Beamten bereits mit einer anderen Lebenswelt in Berührung gekommen war, hatte die Eheschließung mit einem aufstrebenden Angestellten in einer Fabrik für sie einen bedeutenden sozialen Aufstieg mit sich gebracht.[27] Die Familie gehörte nun zur wohlhabenden bürgerlichen Schicht und konnte sich sogar eine Hausangestellte leisten—ein Komfort, der für Friederike Brezing nicht vorstellbar gewesen war. Wiewohl Sophie Brecht sich sowohl geografisch als auch in sozialer Hinsicht von ihren familiären Wurzeln entfernt hatte, war sie sicherlich von einer Jugend in einfachen Verhältnissen geprägt.[28]

Kennzeichnend für den Pietismus waren Versammlungen außerhalb des Gottesdienstes, in denen neben Gebeten und Liedern die Betrachtung biblischer Texte im Mittelpunkt stand.[29] Entweder las man zum jeweiligen Bibeltext Betrachtungen aus Erbauungsbüchern oder bat die anwesenden Männer um eine persönliche Stellungnahme. Die Rolle der Frauen war auf das Zuhören beschränkt; sie ergriffen kaum je das Wort. Innerhalb des württembergischen Pietismus gab es verschiedene Strömungen. Die Mehrzahl der Pietisten gehörte den Versammlungen an, die sich schließlich 1857 im Altpietistischen Gemeinschaftsverband organisierten. Diese Hauptrichtung des Pietismus war eng mit der protestantischen Kirche verbunden, indem ihre Mitglieder Funktionen innerhalb der Gemeinde übernahmen. Allerdings prägte der Pietismus auch seine eigene Kultur aus mit einem florierenden Büchermarkt, lokaler oder regionaler pietistischer Prominenz sowie neuen sozialen Formen wie Frauengruppen oder Jugendarbeit. Daneben zählten seit dem frühen 19. Jahrhundert die Bibelverbreitung, die Innere Mission—beispielsweise die Gründung von Rettungshäusern und Anstalten—sowie die Äußere Mission zu seinen Anliegen.[30]

Neben dieser Hauptrichtung bestanden noch zwei kleinere Gruppierungen. Die Anhänger des aus der bäuerlichen Schicht stammenden Theosophen Michael Hahn (1758-1819) hatten sich in einem eigenen Verband organisiert.[31] Hier wurden der Heiligungsernst, die schlussendliche Allversöhnung und die Ehelosigkeit als besondere Form christlichen Ernstes betont. Im Gegensatz dazu berief sich die kleinste Gruppe innerhalb des Pietismus auf den Haiterbacher Stadtpfarrer Christian Gottlob Pregizer (1751-1824).[32] Nach ihrer Auffassung war der Mensch nach der Bekehrung endgültig erlöst und konnte danach keine Sünde mehr begehen. Dies gab Anlass zu einer Religiosität, in der die Freude des erlösten Christen im Mittelpunkt stand. Schwungvolle, fröhliche Lieder und hoffnungsvolle Betrachtungen prägten die Versammlungen der "Pregizerianer." Sie wurden deshalb vielfach als "Galopp"- oder "Juchhe-Christen" verspottet.[33]

Allen pietistischen Gruppen ist gemein, dass sie die Lebenswelt und die Mentalität ihrer Mitglieder grundlegend prägten; freilich konnte eine strenge religiöse Erziehung auch dazu führen, dass sich der oder die Betroffene als Erwachsene völlig von der Kirche abwandten.[34] Durch die ständige Meditation von religiösen Texten und die dauernde Anwendung auf das alltägliche Leben bildeten sich konkrete Handlungsanweisungen heraus, die im christlichen Sinne als "verbindlich" angesehen wurden.[35] Die Memorierung und ständige Wiederholung von Liedern, Gedichten und biblischen Texten führte zur Verinnerlichung religiöser Normen. Pietisten begriffen diese Texte als unmittelbare Handlungsrichtlinien für ihr Leben. Manche Wendungen wurden Bestandteil der Alltagssprache und brachten moralische Urteile über sich selbst und über andere zum Ausdruck. Wenn also beispielsweise jemand äußerte "Darauf liegt kein Segen," dann handelte es sich um ein vernichtendes Urteil über eine

Handlungsweise. Nicht selten wurde die Dramatik gesteigert, indem man in der "Sprache Canaan" sprach und damit in einer "ausgeprägten Eigensprachlichkeit" kommunizierte.[36] Dabei konnten "fromme," in einem sanften oder gar süßlichen Tonfall vorgetragene Äußerungen— beispielsweise "Was unser Herr Jesus wohl dazu sagen würde?" — wesentlich mehr Schuldgefühle hervorrufen als aggressive moralische Vorwürfe. Auch wenn sich eine Person später vom Christentum lossagte, blieb diese tiefe innere Matrix erhalten.

In seiner Studie verortet Kammerer die Religiosität der Familie Brezing in der Hahn'schen Gemeinschaft. Entsprechend zieht er Parallelen zwischen Werken Brechts und den religiösen Grundsätzen Hahns.[37] Aber bereits die Stadt Haiterbach im Schwarzwald als Herkunftsort des Brecht-Großvaters Joseph Friedrich Brezing hätte in eine andere Richtung weisen müssen. Tatsächlich lässt sich die Familie Brezing im Umkreis der Pregizerianer verorten. Die Großmutter Friederike Brezing war die Tochter des Schusters Johannes Gamerdinger (1809-1844) und seiner Frau Elisabeth Eberhardina geb. Böpple (1814-1867) aus Weil im Schönbuch. Johannes Gamerdingers gleichnamiger Vater (1775-1845), der ebenfalls Schuhmacher war, nahm in der Region um seinen Heimatort bei den Pregizerianern eine führende Stellung ein.[38] Bis an sein Lebensende leitete der ältere Gamerdinger die örtliche Versammlung der Pregizerianer in Weil im Schönbuch.[39] Der jüngere Gamerdinger starb 1844, als seine Tochter Friederike fünf Jahre alt war, aber auch er und seine Frau Elisabeth dürften in der Pregizer-Gemeinschaft sozialisiert worden sein. Da sowohl in Haiterbach als auch in Weil im Schönbuch aktive Gruppen der Pregizerianer bestanden, lernten sich Joseph Friedrich Brezing und Friederike Gamerdinger höchstwahrscheinlich als junge Leute in den Kreisen der Pregizerianer kennen. Sie wurden 1866 in Weil im Schönbuch getraut. Mehrmals in seinem Leben musste das Ehepaar umziehen, weil der Mann bei der Württembergischen Eisenbahn beschäftigt war und immer wieder versetzt wurde.[40] Deshalb kam die Tochter Sophie 1871 im oberschwäbischen Ort Rossberg bei Bad Waldsee zur Welt. Immerhin brachte es Joseph Friedrich Brezing bis zum "Königlich Württembergischen Stationsvorstand"[41] eines kleinen Bahnhofs, stieg also aus der Handwerkerschicht in die untere Beamtenhierarchie auf. Als uniformierter Staatsangestellter stellte er auch äußerlich eine Autorität dar, und die "knurrenden Befehle," die er im Alter seiner Frau erteilte,[42] rührten sicherlich von seiner beruflichen Position her.

Wenn auch die Familie Gamerdinger innerhalb der Gruppe der Pregizerianer eine prominente Stellung inne hatte, so nahm die Tochter Friederike an den weiteren Entwicklungen des württembergischen Pietismus Anteil. Sie löste sich zumindest teilweise von den Pregizerianern ab, wahrscheinlich teils bedingt durch Entwicklungen innerhalb der Gemeinschaft, teils auch durch die Berufslaufbahn ihres Ehemannes. Wie die Gemeinde Hahns gerieten auch die Anhänger Pregizers nach dem Tod ihres Anregers 1824 in eine Krise. Bei beiden Gemeinschaften, welche ohnehin nicht von den namensgebenden Personen begründet worden waren,[43] fanden sich keine dominanten Führungspersönlichkeiten zur Fortsetzung der Arbeit. Deshalb drohte den Gruppen aufgrund der fehlenden Aktualisierung ihrer religiösen Ausdrucksformen die Erstarrung. Der Pfarrer von Weil im Schönbuch schrieb 1842, dass die Pregizerianer

> selbst seit dem Absterben ihrer früheren Redner, zum Beispiel der persönlichen Bekannten des Pregizers, nicht mehr wissen, worin sie sich unterscheiden mögen...Bey ihnen ist es auch erkennbar, daß sich die überspannten Pregizerschen Begriffe von der Gerechtigkeit des Glaubens und dessen Freudigkeit verwischt haben.[44]

Zu den alten Männern, die den Pfarrer Pregizer noch persönlich gekannt hatten, zählte auch der inzwischen siebenundsiebzigjährige ältere Gamerdinger, der drei Jahre nach der Abfassung dieses Berichtes verstarb. Einige der Pregizer-Versammlungen tendierten dazu, sich den kirchenloyalen pietistischen Gruppierungen anzuschließen. Damit ging ihnen freilich in erheblichem Maß ihre spezifische Religiosität und Überzeugungskraft verloren. In diese Lücke stieß zumindest im Stuttgarter Raum der Vikar Gustav Werner (1809-1887) aus dem nicht weit von Weil im Schönbuch gelegenen Ort Walddorf. Nach seinem Amtsantritt 1834 nahm er verarmte Kinder bei sich auf und gründete für sie eine Rettungsanstalt.[45] Rasch gewann er eine bedeutende Schar von Anhängern vor allem unter den jungen Mädchen, so auch in Weil im Schönbuch. Diese förderten sein Werk mit Geld- und Sachspenden, so dass Werner im Jahr 1840 ein Haus in Reutlingen erwerben und seine Arbeit dort in erweiterter Form fortführen konnte. Schon von Anfang an hatten einige Frauen und Männer aus Weil im Schönbuch Werner unterstützt und ihn in Walddorf und dann in Reutlingen besucht. Seit dem Herbst 1841 bildete sich ein kleiner Freundeskreis, welcher weiterhin durch Besuche in Reutlingen den Kontakt zu Werner hielt.[46] Acht Jahre später wurde eine regelmäßige Versammlung von Werner-Anhängern begründet. Obwohl solche Versammlungen verboten waren, da Werners Religiosität am Rand der württembergischen Landeskirche verortet werden musste, blieb dem örtlichen Kirchenkonvent als kirchenleitendem Gremium nichts anderes übrig, als diese Versammlung zu gestatten. Zu groß war das Interesse an diesem Prediger, als dass die Obrigkeit es hätte unterdrücken können. Auch die etwa alle sechs Wochen stattfindenden Vorträge Werners in der häufig überfüllten Schulstube von Weil musste der Kirchenkonvent tolerieren. Gegen die Genehmigung der Versammlung schritt jedoch die Kirchenleitung ein, weil sich der Kirchenkonvent über einen generellen Beschluss aller württembergischen Kirchenkonvente, die Versammlungen

Werners nicht zu dulden, hinweg gesetzt hatte. Allerdings genoss Werner gerade in den pietistischen Kreisen eine so große Popularität, dass man ihm nur schwer beikam. Mit seinem Beispiel tätiger Nächstenliebe bot er den frommen Kreisen eine Aufgabe und eine Orientierung.[47]

Zur Finanzierung des Kinderhauses und weiterer sozialer Einrichtungen für behinderte Menschen wollte Werner eine christliche Fabrik gründen. Deshalb kaufte er in Reutlingen eine Papiermühle und versuchte sich als Unternehmer. Das Werk wuchs rasch an, indem Werner zahlreiche Zweigeinrichtungen gründete. Allerdings übernahm er sich wirtschaftlich und geriet in eine ökonomische Krise, so dass seine Einrichtungen nur mit Mühe gerettet werden konnten. Zu den Anhängerinnen Werners gehörte auch die junge Friederike Gamerdinger.[48] Das ist insofern bemerkenswert, als sie sich damit zwar von der theologischen Linie der Pregizerianer abwandte, welche weder die Äußere noch die Innere Mission befürworteten — ein bereits erlöster Mensch bedurfte der Mission nicht mehr —, sich aber wiederum einem kirchlich sanktionierten, charismatisch auftretenden christlichen Sozialreformer anschloss. Werner stand in der Tradition des elsässischen Pfarrers und Sozialreformers Johann Friedrich Oberlin[49] und war von dessen Nachfolger Kaspar Weigelin während eines längeren Aufenthalts stark beeinflusst worden.[50] Auch er hatte radikalpietistisches Gedankengut aufgenommen, nicht nur von dem schwedischen Theosophen Emanuel Swedenborg,[51] sondern auch aus der "klassischen" radikalpietistischen Literatur.[52] Vielleicht trug dieser gemeinsame Erfahrungshintergrund dazu bei, dass sich Friederike Gamerdinger den Werner'schen Anstalten in Reutlingen eng verbunden fühlte. Anlässlich der Trauung des Ehepaars Brezing-Gamerdinger in Weil im Schönbuch schenkte Werner der Braut eine ihr gewidmete Bibel.[53]

Es ist davon auszugehen, dass die Familie Brezing auch an ihren verschiedenen Wohnorten nach Möglichkeit pietistische Versammlungen besuchte. Allerdings gab es nirgends eine Gemeinschaft von Pregizerianern, so dass sich die Eheleute wohl der pietistischen Gruppe anschlossen. Ein regelmäßiger Besuch des Gottesdienstes dürfte ebenso selbstverständlich gewesen sein wie zumindest für Friederike Brezing die Lektüre erbaulicher Literatur. Die Tochter Sophie Brezing wuchs in Höfen, Altbach und Pfullingen auf. Zweifelsohne wurde ihr geistiges und kulturelles Interesse durch die Versammlungen stimuliert, denn woher hätte eine junge Frau aus einer minder vermögenden Familie sich sonst weitergehende Kenntnisse aneignen können? In den Jahren 1883 bis 1892 wohnte die Familie Brezing in dem kleinen Dorf Altbach bei Esslingen. Während dieser Zeit ist dort eine kleine pietistische Versammlung und eine Gruppe der Hahn'schen Gemeinschaft belegt. Ob auch die Familie Brezing eine der Versammlungen besuchte, ist allerdings unbekannt, da bei den als informell betrachteten pietistischen Versammlungen in aller Regel keine Mitgliederlisten geführt wurden. Ausdrücklich bemerkte der

Pfarrer von Zell, dass die Aktivitäten in Altbach für die Bibelverbreitung, die Mission und das für die Unterstützung der protestantischen Diasporagemeinden gegründete Gustav-Adolf-Werk nicht sehr rege seien.[54]

Eine völlig andere Situation fand die Familie in Pfullingen vor, wo Joseph Friedrich Brezing im Jahr 1892 die Stelle des Bahnhofsvorstehers antrat. Da der Bahnhof nicht an einer Hauptlinie lag, sondern an der Echazbahn, einer Bahnverbindung auf die Schwäbische Alb, war diese berufliche Position nicht mit einem bedeutenden Einkommen verbunden.[55] Immerhin konnte Brezing als Beamter für seine Kinder auf einen beruflichen Aufstieg hoffen, insbesondere durch günstige Heiratsverbindungen. Im Gegensatz zu den Dörfern, in denen die Familie bislang gelebt hatte, bot Pfullingen—auch unter dem Einfluss der nahen Stadt Reutlingen, wo Werner seine diakonischen Anstalten aufgebaut hatte—ein städtisches Ambiente. Freilich machten sich innerhalb des Ortes sehr starke soziale Unterschiede bemerkbar. Pfullingen lag vor den Toren der bedeutenden Gewerbestadt Reutlingen und bot mit einigen großen Fabriken zahlreiche Arbeitsplätze. Nach den Angaben der Pfarrer in den regelmäßigen Berichten an die Kirchenleitung fehlte eine bürgerlichen Mittelschicht völlig, so dass "der kleinere Kreis der Großindustriellen den niederen Klassen unvermittelt" gegenüberstand.[56] Die Kinder aus der ärmeren Bevölkerungsschicht arbeiteten in den großen Fabriken in Pfullingen und Reutlingen, sobald sie die Schule verließen. Dadurch verdienten sie von Anfang an Geld und konnten sich Dinge leisten, die den Kindern aus Bauern- oder Handwerkerfamilien meist verwehrt blieben.[57] Dieser zahlenmäßig starken Einwohnerschicht der Fabrikarbeiter standen wenige sehr vermögende Familien gegenüber, darunter die großen Fabrikbesitzer. Dabei galt der Inhaber der Papierfabrik Laiblin als sozial sehr engagiert. Er gewährte nicht nur seinen Arbeitern einige Vergünstigungen, sondern stiftete auch zahlreiche soziale Einrichtungen in der Gemeinde.[58]

Insgesamt herrschte in der Stadt ein reges religiöses Leben. Von den 4794 Einwohnern im Jahr 1882 waren 96,5% protestantisch. In der Kirchengemeinde bestand eine große pietistische Versammlung mit etwa 150 Mitgliedern, die sich einen eigenen Betsaal hatte erbauen lassen. Hauptsächlich Frauen besuchten die Versammlungen, denen nur 25 bis 30 Männer angehörten. Zu den "Bibelstunden" und Betstunden, die den Winter über im Saal der pietistischen Gemeinschaft gehalten wurden, erschienen 200 bis 300 Personen.[59] Im Gegensatz zu Altbach engagierte man sich in den pietistischen Kreisen Pfullingens auch stark für die Innere und Äußere Mission:

> Das Interesse für christliche Bestrebungen zeigt sich durch das Lesen von vielen christlichen Blättern und eine reiche

Opferwilligkeit für Gustav-Adolf-Verein, Juden- und Heidenmission und allerlei Anstalten. Viele Fabrikmädchen sammeln unter sich für Mission und andere gute Zwecke.[60]

Diese religiös eingestellten jungen Fabrikarbeiterinnen bildeten einen "Missionsverein," indem sie sich an einem Werktag abends im Saal der pietistischen Gemeinschaft trafen. Ein Lehrer oder Geistlicher las ihnen vor, wahrscheinlich vor allem Berichte über die und aus der Mission. Der "Missionsverein" war ein Pendant zum 1885 gegründeten "Jünglingsverein," in dem sich die pietistisch gesinnten jungen Männer versammelten. Auch in der Höhe der Spenden zeigte sich das überaus starke Interesse an der Äußeren Mission: alleine die "Halbbatzenkollekte" zu Gunsten der Basler Mission erbrachte jährlich 600 Mark.[61] Es ist kaum vorstellbar, dass sich die Familie Brezing diesen pietistischen Anliegen verschloss. Ob die junge Sophie Brezing ebenfalls dem Missionsverein angehörte und die Vorleseabende im "Stundenhaus" besuchte, lässt sich nicht feststellen. Aber sie hatte durchaus die pietistische Gesinnung ihrer Eltern übernommen, kannte sich in der Bibel aus und las später den beiden Söhnen daraus vor.[62] Man kann davon ausgehen, dass sie — wie ihre Mutter Friederike — auch sehr viele Choräle aus dem württembergischen Gesangbuch von 1841 und womöglich noch weitere Lieder aus pietistischen Liederbüchern auswendig konnte.[63]

So lernte der aufstrebende katholische Kaufmann Berthold Brecht in Augsburg durch ihre Schwester eine junge Frau aus einer sehr pietistisch eingestellten Familie kennen.[64] Obwohl er nicht so religiös eingestellt war wie seine Frau, tolerierte er ihre pietistisch gefärbte Frömmigkeit. Jedoch war auch in Augsburg das Alltagsleben noch ganz und gar von der Religion bestimmt. In der Schule, wo das Fach Religion eine große Bedeutung hatte, gehörte das Memorieren von Bibeltexten und Kirchenliedern zum Grundkanon des Religionsunterrichts. Durch den regelmäßigen Kirchenbesuch prägten sich die Texte noch mehr ein. Wenn Brecht später im Stil der Kirchenchoräle Adolf Hitler auf ironische Weise lächerlich machte, konnte er nicht nur auf das in seinem Religionsunterricht Gelernte zurückgreifen, sondern auch auf das reichhaltige, lebendig vermittelte religiöse Wissen seiner Familie. So dürfte es kein Zufall sein, dass seine ersten Texte intensiv von religiösen Themen und Begriffen durchdrungen sind.[65]

Pietismus und Mission

Diese Zusammenhänge bilden den Hintergrund für eine These bezüglich Brechts Erwerb von Kenntnissen im Kindes- und Jugendalter, die sich zwar nicht endgültig verifizieren lässt, aber doch sehr plausibel erscheint. Seit dem frühen 19. Jahrhundert gehörte die Äußere Mission zu den Grundanliegen des württembergischen Pietismus.[66] Im Jahr 1815 war in Basel ein Missionshaus gegründet worden, welches auf wesentliche Initiativen württembergischer Pietisten zurückging und sehr viele Kandidaten aus Württemberg aufnahm.[67] Rasch wuchs das Missionshaus dank hoher Spenden aus den "frommen Kreisen" an und dehnte seine Aktivitäten aus. Sein großer Erfolg war vor allem einer ausgedehnten, hervorragend organisierten Öffentlichkeitsarbeit zu verdanken.[68] Die von ihm herausgegebenen *Missionsblätter* waren in den pietistischen Versammlungen weit verbreitet und wurden dort häufig vorgelesen.[69] Spezielle regelmäßige Kollekten erbrachten die notwendigen Spendengelder zur Fortführung der Arbeit. Darüber hinaus veranstalteten die pietistischen Kreise immer wieder "Missionskonferenzen," bei denen ausführlich über die Arbeit der Basler Mission berichtet wurde. Wenn sich Missionare auf Heimaturlaub befanden, erwartete die Missionsleitung von ihnen, dass sie Gemeinden und Versammlungen besuchten. Dadurch kamen die einfachen Leute und potenziellen Spender in direkten Kontakt mit den auf den Missionsfeldern tätigen Personen.[70] Seit 1850 war die Basler Mission in China aktiv und wirkte vor allem in der Provinz Kanton.

In der Forschung begriff man Mission lange als kulturelle Einbahnstraße mit dem Ziel, fremde Völker zu "zivilisieren" und ihnen die Werte und Normen des westeuropäischen oder nationalen Christentums überzustülpen.[71] Wenn dieser Aspekt auch weiterhin im Blick bleiben muss, so hat die jüngere Forschung jedoch gezeigt, dass er den Sachverhalt nur verengt darstellt.[72] Ebenso wäre es verkürzt, die Mission nur im Zusammenhang mit der Kolonialisierung zu sehen, da ihre Anfänge lange vor dem Einsetzen der kolonialistischen Bestrebungen des Deutschen Reiches liegen.

In den fremden Ländern wurden die Missionare mit der jeweiligen Kultur konfrontiert.[73] Jeder Versuch, die Kultur ihres Heimatlandes direkt auf die Menschen im Missionsland zu übertragen, musste schon deshalb problematisch erscheinen, weil die Missionare eine verschwindende Minderheit bildeten. Nicht zuletzt deshalb setzten sich viele Missionare mit der Kultur ihres Missionslandes auseinander. Sie studierten Sprache, Kultur und Gewohnheiten der Bewohner und schrieben darüber Artikel in den Missionsblättern.[74] Damit eröffneten die Zeitschriften ihren Leserinnen und Lesern Einblicke in fremde Länder und Kulturkreise, freilich aus dem religiösen Blickwinkel der Missionare. Bedenkt man, dass sich die meisten Anhänger des württembergischen Pietismus in der Schicht der einfachen Bauern und Handwerker fanden, so erahnt man die Bedeutung der Missionszeitschriften in diesen Kreisen für die Volksbildung.[75]

Im Jungfrauenverein des Gustav Werner wurden Berichte aus der Mission vorgelesen.[76] Dort waren also die jungen Frauen mit der

Äußeren Mission konfrontiert. Auch wenn eine schwere wirtschaftliche Krise die Einrichtungen in ihrem Bestand gefährdete und sicher alle Kräfte auf deren Erhaltung konzentrierte, stand Werner der Äußeren Mission nicht ablehnend gegenüber. Nach dem überstandenen Konkurs der Werner'schen Anstalten im Jahr 1860 konsolidierte sich das Werk und etablierte sich als solide soziale Einrichtung innerhalb der württembergischen Landeskirche. Die Verbindung der Familie Brecht zu den diakonischen Einrichtungen Werners blieb bestehen, weil der Cousin Brechts, Max Brecht, aufgrund einer Behinderung im Bruderhaus Reutlingen lebte und der Vater Berthold Brecht die Pflegschaft für den Neffen übernommen hatte. Wiewohl man nach den Erinnerungen von Walter Brecht in der Familie selten über den Cousin sprach, blieben die Werner'schen Anstalten im Bewusstsein der Familie.

Im deutschen Kaiserreich gewann der Protestantismus nach 1871 insgesamt an Selbstbewusstsein. Durch den Kulturkampf wurde er zur beherrschenden Ideologie des Kaiserreiches. In diesem Zusammenhang kam es nicht nur zur Integration der Werner'schen Anstalten in die evangelische Landeskirche in Württemberg, sondern auch die Äußere Mission erhielt neue Impulse. Durch das Interesse des Deutschen Reiches an eigenen Kolonien richtete sich das Interesse der Öffentlichkeit verstärkt auf andere Weltgegenden. Die Mission unter den "Heiden" wurde als wichtige kulturelle Leistung des Protestantismus verstanden.

Missionszeitschriften als kulturgeschichtliche Quellen

In den pietistischen Kreisen waren Zeitschriften wichtige Medien zur Vermittlung religiösen Wissens.[77] Sie schufen in den pietistischen Gruppen eine gemeinsame Identität und Sprache. Dabei nahmen Missionszeitschriften auf Grund ihrer Multifunktionalität eine Sonderrolle ein. Mit ihnen warben die Missionsgesellschaften für eine gute Sache und zugleich für die praktische Verwirklichung des christlichen Glaubens auf den Missionsfeldern in aller Welt. In den Artikeln der Missionare konnte man aus erster Hand detaillierte Berichte aus fernen Ländern lesen, wie man sie sonst nirgends fand. Denn die Missionare schrieben über viele Themen, für die sich die akademisch gebildete Welt nicht interessierte.[78] Die Berichte der Missionare waren allerdings ideologisch gefärbt, weil sie die Zustände in den Missionsländern aus protestantischer Sicht schilderten und selbstverständlich von einer Überlegenheit und Universalgültigkeit des christlichen Glaubens ausgingen. Nichtsdestoweniger erweckten sie Neugierde auf die fremde Kultur. Besonders in Zeiten, in denen ein Land auch politisch in das Interesse der Öffentlichkeit rückte wie beispielsweise China während des Boxeraufstandes, konnte man in den Missionszeitschriften weitergehende Informationen über die Kultur und Geschichte erhalten.[79] Die persönlich gefärbten Erlebnisberichte lasen sich lebendiger als wissenschaftliche Abhandlungen, zu denen die bäuerlich-handwerklichen Schichten ohnehin kaum Zugang hatten. Deshalb kann der Beitrag der Missionszeitschriften und auch der entsprechenden Bücher[80] für die Bildung ihrer Leserschaft wohl kaum überschätzt werden. Allerdings boten die Zeitschriften den Vorteil, dass sich die Kosten auf einen größeren Zeitraum verteilten, sie also auch von weniger vermögenden Familien abonniert werden konnten.

Die am weitesten verbreitete Zeitschrift der Basler Mission, das *Evangelische Missions-Magazin*, erreichte weite pietistische Kreise in Württemberg. In den Versammlungen wurde daraus vorgelesen oder auf der Grundlage einzelner Artikel erzählt oder zitiert. Deshalb ging der Einfluss der Zeitschrift über den unmittelbaren Abonnentenkreis hinaus. Eine besondere Bedeutung erlangte das *Missions-Magazin* auch deshalb, weil darin nicht nur Berichte der Basler Missionare publiziert wurden. Vielmehr berichtete man auch über die Aktivitäten anderer Missionsgesellschaften in China. Auf diese Weise erhielten die Leserinnen und Leser Informationen über chinesische Provinzen, in denen die Basler Mission nicht aktiv war. Beispielsweise wirkten einige tausend amerikanische Missionare in verschiedenen Gegenden des chinesischen Reiches.[81]

Da die Listen der regelmäßigen Bezieher nicht mehr erhalten sind, kann nicht ermittelt werden, ob Friederike Brezing das *Missions-Magazin* oder eine andere Missionszeitschrift[82] bezog. Eine inhaltliche Analyse des *Evangelischen Missions-Magazins* lässt es aber als wahrscheinlich erscheinen. In einer groß angelegten Untersuchung hat Julia Mack die kulturgeschichtliche Bedeutung des Magazins herausgestellt. In den Ausgaben 1898 bis 1916, also von der Geburt Brechts bis zum Tod der Großmutter Friederike Brezing, erschienen 284 Artikel über China. Zwar war die Basler Mission nicht in der Provinz Sichuan aktiv; trotzdem wird die Provinz zwar nicht häufig, aber doch immerhin vier Mal erwähnt.[83] Bezüglich des Brecht'schen Werkes verdienen vor allem die Bezüge zwischen der Provinz Setschuan und den Begriffen "Aufstand" und "Konfuzianismus" Beachtung,[84] denn diese Konnotation weist einen Zusammenhang zu seinem bekannten Werk *Der gute Mensch von Sezuan* auf, wie auch die Schreibweise der Provinz in den Ausgaben des Missionsmagazins von 1913 und 1916 am ehesten seiner Schreibweise ähnelt.[85] Hier lässt sich die Aussage von Han-Soon Yim exemplifizieren, dass Brechts "Interesse über den literarischen Materialwert von Person und Lehre des Philosophen [Konfuzius] hinaus auch in die sozialhistorischen Aspekte des alten China eindringt."[86] Allerdings könnte die Lektüre der Missionszeitschrift auch eine Erklärung dafür liefern, warum Brecht sich im Gegensatz zu anderen Schriftstellern und zum allgemeinen Trend "intensiv um ein Verständnis des Konfuzius bemüht hat."[87] Überblickt man das *Evangelische Missions-Magazin*, dann springen folgende

Aufsatztitel ins Auge: "Konfuzius, der Heilige Chinas" (1903), "Der Konfuzianismus in China, einst und jetzt" (1913) und—im selben Heft, in dem wiederum "Setschuan" erwähnt ist—"Die Wiedereinführung des Konfuzianismus als Staatsreligion. Von einem deutschen Missionar in China" (1916). In einer intensiven Untersuchung sämtlicher Artikel des *Missions-Magazins* und eventuell weiterer Missionsblätter und anderer Missionspublikationen in Bezug auf Brechts Werk müsste geklärt werden, ob sich weitere Bezüge herstellen lassen.

Bei einer genaueren Betrachtung des Aufsatzes "Konfuzius, der Heilige Chinas"[88] von Charles Piton (1835-1905) springen zunächst einige vom Verfasser zitierte Aussagen des Konfuzius ins Auge, die an biblische Formulierungen anknüpfen. "So lange der Himmel die Wahrheit nicht untergehen lassen will, was können mir Menschen tun?" (Konfuzius)[89] deckt sich inhaltlich mit dem Psalmwort "Gott ist mit mir, darum fürchte ich mich nicht; was können mir Menschen tun?" (Psalm 118, 6). Auch die Aussprüche des Konfuzius "Und der weise Mann verdorret gleich dem Gras" oder "Wenn der große Berg einstürzt, zu wem soll ich aufsehen?"[90] weisen eine hohe Affinität auf zu den Psalmworten "Du lässest sie dahinfahren wie einen Strom, und sind wie ein Schlaf, gleichwie ein Gras, das doch bald welk wird, das da frühe blühet und bald welk wird und des Abends abgehauen wird und verdorret" (Psalm 90, 5-6) und "Ich hebe meine Augen auf zu den Bergen. Woher kommt mir Hilfe? Meine Hilfe kommt vom Herrn, der Himmel und Erde gemacht hat" (Psalm 121, 1-2).[91] Wenn sich Konfuzius über die geringe Anerkennung durch die Zeitgenossen mit dem Bewusstsein "Der Himmel kennt mich" tröstete, fühlte sich der bibelkundige Leser an den Bibelvers "Freuet euch aber, dass eure Namen im Himmel geschrieben sind" (2. Mose/Exodus 32, 32) erinnert. Der Verfasser Piton erkennt gewisse Parallelen zwischen dem Leben des Konfuzius und bestimmten Aussagen der Bibel,[92] wiewohl er keinen Zweifel daran lässt, dass Konfuzius nicht mit Jesus Christus gleichzusetzen sei. So kritisiert Piton heftig die kalte, diesseitsorientierte Religiosität des Konfuzius,[93] dessen Ahnenkult, bei dem die "Ahnen wie Götter verehrt werden,"[94] seinen Aufruf zur Rache von Vergehen, mit der "er die Lehre, Böses mit Gutem zu vergelten, verwirft."[95] Er schreibt auch, dass Konfuzius mehrfach Unwahrhaftigkeit vorgeworfen wurde, und schildert den "Heiligen Chinas" trotz aller ihm zugeschriebenen guten Eigenschaften doch als "heidnisches" Gegenbild von Jesus Christus. Unter Bezugnahme auf den kurz zuvor beendeten Boxeraufstand, welcher wohl den Artikel motivierte, beendet Piton seinen Aufsatz mit einem flammenden Aufruf zur Missionierung Chinas:

> Ereignisse wie die, welche im Jahr 1900 das Reich bis in seine Grundfesten erschüttert haben, sind am besten dazu angetan, die Chinesen an der Solidität des darauf errichteten Staatsgebäudes zweifeln zu machen. Sie müssen lernen, ihre Blicke nicht nach

dem grauen Altertum zu richten, um Heilung von den Schäden zu suchen, an denen sie leiden...Das Heil für sie liegt lediglich zu den Füßen dessen, der gesagt hat "Welche der Sohn frei macht, die sind recht frei."[96]

Wiewohl dieser Aufsatz mit seiner Tendenz zur Schwarz-Weiß-Malerei als typisch für eine Missionszeitschrift angesehen werden kann, so verfehlte die Beschäftigung mit fernen Ländern sicher nicht ihre Wirkung auf Menschen, deren sonstiger Zugang zu solchen Themen eher begrenzt war. Auch für Brecht kann man die Lektüre solcher Zeitschriften wahrscheinlich machen. Ausgehend von seinem Werk lassen jedenfalls Indizien darauf schließen, dass ihm das Thema Mission vertraut war.[97] In seinen Entwürfen und veröffentlichten Arbeiten des Jahres 1920 — also im kurz nach dem Tod der Großmutter entstandenen Frühwerk — verwendet er mehrere Male die religiös implizierten Begriffe "Mission" und "Missionar" in einem verfremdeten Zusammenhang. Möglicherweise werfen die Sätze "Sie kämpfen nicht wie ein Boxer. Sie kämpfen wie ein Missionar. Wie ein Missionar, der ein Atheist ist" aus *Im Dickicht*[98] das bezeichnendste Licht auf die Einstellung Brechts zur Religion. In diesen schlagwortartigen Sätzen hat Brecht wohl am prägnantesten seine Persönlichkeit und seine "Lebensmission" umrissen. Würde man zu einer weitgehenden Interpretation neigen, dann könnte man hier ein Erbe der außerkirchlichen Religiosität sehen, wie sie in der Sozialisation der Großmutter Friederike Brezing angelegt war. Die Pregizerianer blieben gerade noch in der Kirche, bewegten sich aber innerhalb der Württembergischen Landeskirche am Rande des religiösen Spektrums. Auch Gustav Werner wurde in den ersten Jahrzehnten seiner Wirksamkeit von der Amtskirche ausgeschlossen und sanktioniert.

Bereits in seinen jungen Jahren beschäftigte sich Brecht intensiv mit China, wobei von ihm selbst kaum Äußerungen über die Ursprungsimpulse vorliegen. Zwar könnte man die Beschäftigung mit Laotse auf Anregungen von Frank Warschauer zurückführen, der ihm im September 1920 anlässlich eines Besuchs in Baden-Baden wohl eine Ausgabe der Werke des chinesischen Philosophen zeigte.[99] Ob indessen das Interesse an diesem Buch auf einem Vorwissen Brechts beruhte oder er dadurch tatsächlich das erste Mal in Berührung mit den Lehren Laotses brachte, muss offen bleiben. Die Artikel in den Missionszeitschriften und -büchern waren sicher nicht dazu geeignet, umfassend in die Lehren der chinesischen Philosophen einzudringen. Sie könnten jedoch durchaus einen Anstoß zur weiteren Beschäftigung mit dem chinesischen und im weiteren Sinne mit dem asiatischen Kulturkreis gegeben haben. Aus diesem Ursprungsimpuls heraus beschäftigte sich Brecht dann näher mit den entsprechenden Themen.

Besonders signifikant erscheint unter den Werken des Jahres 1920 der Titel eines Gedichts "Interimsberichte an die Missionen."[100] Im Frühjahr des Jahres hatte Brecht sogar ein "Missionsbuch" in Angriff genommen, in dem zwar von der protestantischen "Religion" nicht die Rede ist, sondern von der "allein wahren katholischen und der allein wahren atheistischen Religion."[101] Aber auch hier ist wieder der Verfremdungseffekt zu berücksichtigen, wobei Brecht auf die konventionelle katholische Konfession des Vaters und nicht auf die "rebellischen" Glaubensüberzeugungen der Mutter und der Großmutter reflektiert. In extremer Intensität setzte sich Brecht um diese Zeit mit der Religion auseinander, indem er die religiös aufgeladene Sprache seiner Jugend mit der inzwischen gewonnenen atheistischen Einstellung kontrastierte. Für sein gesamtes dichterisches Werk blieben indessen die Bibel und die protestantischen Choräle die wichtigsten Impulse.[102] Daneben aber nutzte er chinesische Philosophie und Kultur als verfremdende Effekte, wobei er sich fast ausschließlich mit vermittelten Stoffen wie Übersetzungen von Gedichten und Sekundärliteratur beschäftigte. Das reale alltägliche Leben der Chinesen dagegen interessierte Brecht überhaupt nicht, obwohl er während seines Exils in den Vereinigten Staaten im chinesischen Viertel von Santa Monica ohne Probleme das Leben chinesischer Einwanderer hätte erkunden und so zumindest einen mittelbaren Zugang zur chinesischen Kultur hätte suchen können.[103] Am Beispiel des Stückes *Der gute Mensch von Sezuan* hat Tatlow sehr schön gezeigt, wie sich bei Brecht Europäisches mit Chinesischem mischt. Dabei war sich Brecht durchaus der Gefahr bewusst, anstelle authentischer Milieus das Stück als "Folklore" und "Chinoiserie" zu konzipieren.[104] Allerdings scheute er sich nicht, biblische Begriffe in einen chinesischen Kontext einzufügen.[105] Andererseits erinnert der Name der Hauptperson Shen Te an den chinesischen Begriff "Schin-tao," "Geist-Straße," der in dieser Schreibweise im Aufsatz von Piton über Konfuzius erscheint.[106] Die "historische Unverbindlichkeit" im chinesisch beeinflussten Werk Brechts, wie sie Han-Soon Yim konstatiert,[107] die teilweise "ziemlich oberflächliche und dürftige Information,"[108] auf welche er seine Texte aufbaute, könnte auf das von vornherein indirekt vermittelte Bild von China hindeuten.[109] Nach Erkenntnissen der jüngeren Forschung gibt es Parallelen zu Hermann Hesse. Dieser lässt zwar seinen Roman *Siddhartha* in Indien spielen, das er viele Jahre vor der Veröffentlichung selbst besucht hatte. Aber auch er benutzte die fremdartige Umgebung vorwiegend als Kulisse für einen Stoff, der nach Ansicht des Hesse-Forschers Barry Stephenson auf Württemberg zielt, und in dem sich der Dichter im Grunde mit seiner pietistischen Sozialisation auseinandersetzt.[110]

Abschließend muss noch einmal betont werden, dass die Beschäftigung mit den Missionsblättern dokumentarisch nicht fassbar ist. Doch bildete das Interesse an der christlichen Mission einen zentralen Punkt im pietistischen Selbstverständnis. So ist es auch ohne Quellenbelege kaum vorstellbar, wie Friederike Brezing gerade diesen Bereich hätte ausblenden sollen. Weitere Studien werden möglicherweise noch mehr Hinweise zutage fördern, aus denen sich weitere Verbindungen zwischen der Sozialisation Brechts im Zusammenhang mit seiner Prägung durch den württembergischen Pietismus und seiner Beschäftigung mit "exotischen" Stoffen erschließen lassen. Darin liegt zweifelsohne eine wichtige Aufgabe für die zukünftige Brecht-Forschung.

Anmerkungen

1   Renata Berg-Pan, *Brecht and China* (Bonn: Bouvier, 1979), S. 29.
2   Ebd., S. 31.
3   Zum Einfluss des Pietismus auf Hesse vgl. Barry Stephenson, *Veneration and Revolt. Hermann Hesse and Swabian Pietism* (Waterloo/Canada: Wilfrid Laurier University, Press 2009).
4   Berg-Pan, *Brecht and China*; Antony Tatlow, *Brechts chinesische Gedichte* (Frankfurt/Main: Suhrkamp, 1973); derselbe, *The Mask of Evil: Brecht's Response to the Poetry, Theatre and Thought of China and Japan. A Comparative and Critical Evaluation* (Bern, Frankfurt, Las Vegas: Peter Lang, 1977), S. 81-152; Jan Knopf, *Brecht-Handbuch. Lyrik, Prosa, Schriften. Eine Ästhetik der Widersprüche* (Stuttgart: J. B. Metzler, 1984), S. 102-105 (chinesische Gedichte); Han-Soon Yim, *Bertolt Brecht und sein Verhältnis zur chinesischen Philosophie* (Bonn: Institut für Koreaforschung, 1984); Ulrich von Felbert, *China und Japan als Impuls und Exempel. Fernöstliche Ideen und Motive bei Alfred Döblin, Bertolt Brecht und Egon Erwin Kisch* (Frankfurt/Main: Peter Lang, 1986); Yuan Tan, *Der Chinese in der deutschen Literatur. Unter besonderer Berücksichtigung chinesischer Figuren in den Werken von Schiller, Döblin und Brecht* (Göttingen: Cuvillier, 2007), S. 148-247; Heinrich Detering, *Bertolt Brecht und Laotse* (Göttingen: Wallstein, 2008).
5   Hans Mayer, *Bertolt Brecht und die Tradition* (Pfullingen: Neske, 1961); Jan Knopf, *Bertolt Brecht* (Stuttgart: J.B. Metzler, 2000). Nur über die Großmutter väterlicherseits ist eine Studie erschienen: Robert Minder, "La grand'mère retrouvée ou les origines souabes de Bert Brecht," *Etudes Germaniques* (avril-juin 1965): S. 275-289; derselbe, "Brecht und die wiedergefundene Großmutter," in derselbe *"Hölderlin unter den Deutschen" und andere Aufsätze zur deutschen Literatur* (Frankfurt/Main: Suhrkamp, 1968). Hansjörg Kammerer, "Bertolt Brechts Prägung durch schwäbische Frömmigkeit. Ein bisher verdrängter Sachverhalt," *Blätter für Württembergische Kirchengeschichte* 98 (1998): S. 199, weist auf die Verwechslung der Großmütter im Aufsatz Minders hin, denn Karoline Brecht stammte nicht aus dem schwäbischen, sondern aus dem badischen Raum.
6   Tatlow, *The Mask of Evil*, S. 4.
7   Berg-Pan, *Brecht and China*, S. 26.
8   Werner Frisch und Kurt Walter Obermeier, *Brecht in Augsburg* (Berlin und Weimar: Aufbau, 1986), S. 159.
9   Kammerer, *Bertolt Brechts Prägung*, S. 191-201.
10 Ebd., S. 201.
11 Ebd.
12 Werner Hecht, *Brecht-Chronik* (Frankfurt/Main: Suhrkamp, 1997); derselbe, *Brecht-Chronik. Ergänzungen* (Frankfurt/Main: Suhrkamp, 2007).
13 Jürgen Schmid, *Brecht und Haindl* (Augsburg: Wißner, 1999).
14 Walter Brecht, *Unser Leben in Augsburg, damals. Erinnerungen* (Frankfurt/Main: Suhrkamp, 1984), S. 156.

15 Frisch und Obermeier, *Brecht in Augsburg*, S. 159.
16 Die religiöse Einstellung wird bei Reinhold Jaretzky, *Bertolt Brecht* (Reinbek bei Hamburg: Rowohlt, 2006), fast vollständig ignoriert.
17 Kammerer, *Bertolt Brechts Prägung*, S. 192.
18 Brecht, *Unser Leben*, S. 196.
19 Brecht, *Unser Leben*, S. 196, 229.
20 Hecht, *Brecht-Chronik*, S. 28.
21 Kammerer, *Bertolt Brechts Prägung*, S. 191.
22 Hartmut Lehmann, *Pietismus und weltliche Ordnung in Württemberg vom 17. bis zum 20. Jahrhundert* (Stuttgart: Kohlhammer, 1969).
23 Brecht, *Unser Leben*, S. 192; vergleiche S. 194-195.
24 Joachim Trautwein, *Religiosität und Sozialstruktur* (Stuttgart: Calwer, 1972).
25 Hartmut Lehmann, "Probleme einer Sozialgeschichte des württembergischen Pietismus," *Blätter für Württembergische Kirchengeschichte* 75 (1975): S. 166-181.
26 Brecht, *Unser Leben*, S. 263-264.
27 Vergleiche auch Jürgen Hillesheim, *Augsburger Brecht-Lexikon. Personen – Institutionen – Schauplätze* (Würzburg: Königshausen & Neumann, 2000), S. 51-52.
28 Vergleiche die Bemerkungen von Walter Brecht über die Sparsamkeit der Mutter in Brecht, *Unser Leben*, S. 195.
29 Vergleiche zur Lebenswelt des Pietismus Manfred Jakubowski-Tiessen, "Eigenkultur und Traditionsbildung," in Hartmut Lehmann und andere, Hrsg., *Glaubenswelt und Lebenswelten. Geschichte des Pietismus*, Band 4, (Göttingen: Vandenhoeck & Ruprecht, 2004), S. 195-210.
30 Eberhard Fritz, "Die Konsolidierung des württembergischen Pietismus im frühen 19. Jahrhundert. Eine Befragung von 1821 als Dokument einer Übergangszeit," *Blätter für Württembergische Kirchengeschichte* 108/109 (2008/2009): S. 363-392.
31 Joachim Trautwein, *Die Theosophie Michael Hahns und ihre Quellen. Quellen und Forschungen zur württembergischen Kirchengeschichte*, Band 2 (Stuttgart: Calwer, 1969).
32 Gotthold Müller, *Christian Gottlob Pregizer (1751-1824). Biographie und Nachlass* (Stuttgart: Kohlhammer, 1962); Eberhard Fritz, "Christian Gottlob Pregizer und die 'Pregizerianer.' Zur Genese einer pietistischen Gruppierung im frühen 19. Jahrhundert," in Norbert Haag, Siegfried Hermle, Sabine Holtz, Jörg Thierfelder, Hrsg., *Tradition und Fortschritt. Württembergische Kirchengeschichte im Wandel. Festschrift für Hermann Ehmer* (Epfendorf: bibliotheca academica, 2008), S. 239-268.
33 Joachim Trautwein, "Freiheitsrechte und Gemeinschaftsordnungen um 1800. Pietismus und Separatismus in Württemberg," in Württembergisches Landesmuseum Stuttgart, Hrsg., *Baden und Württemberg im Zeitalter Napoleons*, Band 2 (Stuttgart: Dr. Cantz'sche Druckerei 1987), S. 333.
34 Vergleiche Andreas Gestrich, "Alltag im pietistischen Dorf. Bürgerliche Religiosität in ländlicher Lebenswelt," *Die alte Stadt* 20 (1993): S. 47-59; derselbe, "Pietistische Dörfer in Württemberg. Lokal- und regionalgeschichtliche Zugänge zur Sozialgeschichte der Religion," *Protokoll der Sitzung des Arbeitskreises für Landes- und Ortsgeschichte* 87 (1996): S. 11-31; Ulrich Herrmann und Karin Priem, Hrsg., *Konfession als Lebenskonflikt. Studien zum württembergischen Pietismus im 19. Jahrhundert und die Familientragödie des Johannes Benedikt Stanger* (Weinheim/München: Juventa, 2001).
35 Aus einer sehr kritischen Perspektive heraus werden die Grundsätze pietistischer Erziehung einseitig, aber treffend und prägnant behandelt bei Martin Scharfe, *Die Religion des Volkes. Kleine Kultur- und Sozialgeschichte des Pietismus* (Gütersloh: Gütersloher Verlagshaus, 1980), S. 48-72.
36 Hans-Jürgen Schrader, "Die Sprache Canaan. Pietistische Sonderterminologie und Spezialsemantik als Auftrag der Forschung," in Hartmut Lehmann und andere, Hrsg., *Glaubenswelt und Lebenswelten. Geschichte des Pietismus*, Band 4 (Göttingen: Vandenhoeck & Ruprecht, 2004), S. 404-427.
37 Kammerer, *Bertolt Brechts Prägung*, S. 193-194.
38 Fritz, *Christian Gottlob Pregizer*, S. 262.

39 Landeskirchliches Archiv Stuttgart A 29 Bü 5062 (Pfarrbericht Weil im Schönbuch, 1842).
40 Kammerer, *Bertolt Brechts Prägung*, S. 192, Anmerkung 5.
41 Brecht, *Unser Leben*, S. 192.
42 Brecht, *Unser Leben*, S. 196.
43 Weder Michael Hahn noch Christian Gottlob Pregizer begründeten eine Gemeinschaft; ihre Anhänger schlossen sich zusammen und benannten sich nach ihnen. Deshalb werden die Anhänger Hahns auch in den Quellen zunächst "Michaelianer" genannt, später "Hahner" oder "Hahnische;" die Anhänger Pregizers nannte man seit dem frühen 19. Jahrhundert "Pregizerianer."
44 Landeskirchliches Archiv Stuttgart A 29 Bü 5062 (Pfarrbericht Weil im Schönbuch, 1842). Hier bezieht sich die Äußerung auf Christian Gottlob Pregizer.
45 Karl-Heinz Bartel, *Gustav Werner. Eine Biographie* (Stuttgart: Quell, 1990); Gerhard K. Schäfer, Hrsg., *Dem Reich Gottes Bahn brechen. Gustav Werner (1809-1887). Briefe, Predigten, Schriften in Auswahl* (Stuttgart: Kohlhammer, 1999).
46 Landeskirchliches Archiv Stuttgart A 29 Bü 5062 (Pfarrbericht Weil im Schönbuch, 1842).
47 Vergleiche Walter Göggelmann, *Dem Reich Gottes Raum schaffen. Königsherrschaft Christi, Eschatologie und Diakonie im Wirken von Gustav Werner (1809-1887)*. (Heidelberg: Diakoniewissenschaftliches Institut, 2007).
48 Möglicherweise deutet Friederike Gamerdingers Wechsel der Denomination von den Pregizerianern zu Gustav Werner auf einen Generationenkonflikt hin; vergleiche dazu Andreas Gestrich, "Pietismus und ländliche Frömmigkeit in Württemberg im 18. und 19. Jahrhundert," in Norbert Haag, Sabine Holtz und Wolfgang Zimmermann, Hrsg., *Ländliche Frömmigkeit. Konfessionskulturen und Lebenswelten 1500-1800* (Stuttgart: Thorbecke, 2002), S. 355-356.
49 Loïc Chalmel, *Le pasteur Oberlin* (Paris: Puf 1999); Chalmel hebt auf S. 41 bis 42 besonders die mystischen Einflüsse als entscheidende Antriebe für die sozialen Aktivitäten Oberlins hervor.
50 Schäfer, *Gustav Werner*, S. 519-520. Weigelin schenkte ihm Bücher der in radikalpietistischen Kreisen viel gelesenen mystischen Schriftstellerinnen Antoinette de Bourignon und Madame Guyon. Auch Johann Friedrich Oberlin hatte diese Schriften intensiv gelesen. Vergleiche Eberhard Fritz, "Johann Friedrich Oberlin und die pietistische Bewegung in Straßburg. Zum Einfluss des radikalen Pietismus auf den elsässischen Pfarrer und Sozialreformer," *Pietismus und Neuzeit* 34 (2008): S. 167-188.
51 Eberhard Zwink, *Gustav Werner und die Neue Kirche. Die Auseinandersetzung mit dem Swedenborgianer Johann Gottlieb Mittnacht* (Reutlingen: Gustav Werner Stiftung zum Bruderhaus, 1989).
52 Schäfer, *Gustav Werner*, S. 248, wo sich Gustav Werner auf Johann Jakob Rambach und die "Berleburger Bibel"—die allgemein in den radikalpietistischen Kreisen gebrauchte Bibelausgabe mit mystisch-spiritualistischen Kommentaren—beruft.
53 Kammerer, *Bertolt Brechts Prägung*, S. 195; Erdmut Wizisla, Bearbeitung, *Die Bibliothek Bertolt Brechts. Ein kommentiertes Verzeichnis* (Frankfurt/Main: Suhrkamp, 2007).
54 Landeskirchliches Archiv Stuttgart A 29 Bü 5375 (Pfarrbericht Pfarrei Zell, 1884). In diesem Jahr zählte das Dorf Altbach 594 Einwohner.
55 Vergleiche Gerhard Prinz, "Württembergs Eisenbahnpersonal um 1900," *Schwäbische Heimat* 4 (1992): S. 384-391.
56 Landeskirchliches Archiv Stuttgart A 29 Bü 3631 (Pfarrbericht Pfullingen, 1894).
57 Landeskirchliches Archiv Stuttgart A 29 Bü 3631 (Pfarrbericht Pfullingen, 1882).
58 Landeskirchliches Archiv Stuttgart A 29 Bü 3631 (Pfarrbericht Pfullingen, 1892). Die Frage, ob Sophie Brezing in der Papierfabrik Laiblin, möglicherweise im Büro, beschäftigt war, lässt sich nicht klären. Nach Auskunft des Stadtarchivs Pfullingen sind die Akten der Fabrik nicht mehr erhalten, und der Eintrag im Ehebuch Pfullingen über die Eheschließung des Paares Brecht-Brezing enthält keine Berufsangabe

der Braut. Es ist jedoch auffällig, dass beide Schwestern Brezing Männer aus der Papierindustrie heirateten.

59   Landeskirchliches Archiv Stuttgart A 29 Bü 3631 (Pfarrbericht Pfullingen, 1894).

60   Landeskirchliches Archiv Stuttgart A 29 Bü 3631 (Gleich lautende Formulierung in den Pfarrberichten Pfullingen 1892 und 1894).

61   Landeskirchliches Archiv Stuttgart A 29 Bü 3631 (Gleich lautende Formulierung in den Pfarrberichten Pfullingen 1894 und 1898).

62   Brecht, *Unser Leben*, S. 229.

63   Das Lieblingslied von Sophie Brezing "So nimm denn meine Hände" (Brecht, Unser Leben, S. 197) könnte ein Indiz dafür sein, dass die Familie Brezing sich aus einer sehr engen pietistischen Gesinnung hin zu einer altpietistisch-kirchlichen Religiosität entwickelt hatte. Vergleiche auch Jürgen Hillesheim, "Zwischen 'Frühlingserwachen,' Melancholie und kleinbürgerlicher Enge: Ein Notizbuch Sophie Brechts, der Mutter des 'Stückeschreibers,'" *The Brecht Yearbook* 35 (2010): S. 241-265.

64   Über eine Berufstätigkeit Sophie Brezings ist nichts bekannt. Im Heiratsregister erscheint kein Beruf, so dass nicht klar ist, ob die junge Frau vor ihrer Eheschließung berufstätig war oder nicht. Auf jeden Fall bedeutete die Eheschließung einen sozialen Aufstieg, der in der Forschung immer mitbedacht werden sollte.

65   Klaus Völker, Bearbeitung, *Brecht-Chronik. Daten zu Leben und Werk* (München: Deutscher Taschenbuch Verlag, 1997), S. 8-11; Bertolt Brecht, *Gedichte und Gedichtfragmente* 1913-1927 (Berlin und Weimar: Aufbau Verlag, 1993), S. 7, 9. Jedoch ist zu berücksichtigen, dass Brecht als Pubertierender wohl eine schwere Glaubenskrise durchmachte. Vergleiche Frank Thomsen, Hans-Harald Müller und Tom Kindt, *Ungeheuer Brecht. Eine Biographie seines Werks* (Göttingen: Vandenhoeck & Ruprecht, 2006), S. 11-15.

66   Lixin Sun, *Das Chinabild der deutschen protestantischen Missionare des 19. Jahrhunderts. Eine Fallstudie zum Problem interkultureller Begegnung und Wahrnehmung* (Marburg: Tectum, 2002), S. 322, 85-93.

67   Paul Steiner, *Hundert Jahre Missionsarbeit. Zur Erinnerung an das hundertjährige Bestehen der Basler Mission 1815-1915* (Basel: Basler Missionsbuchhandlung, 1915); Wilhelm Schlatter, *Geschichte der Basler Mission 1815-1915. Mit besonderer Berücksichtigung der ungedruckten Quellen*, 3 Bände (Basel: Basler Missionsbuchhandlung, 1916); Band 1: *Die Heimatgeschichte der Basler Mission*, Band 2: *Die Geschichte der Basler Mission in Indien und China.*

68   Andrea Kittel, "Erbaulich und ergötzlich. Missionswerbung in der Heimat," *Der ferne Nächste. Bilder der Mission – Mission der Bilder 1860-1920*. Ausstellungskatalog. Ludwigsburg 1996, S. 165-174.

69   Eberhard Gutekunst, "'Noch lebt des Wortes Kraft.' Missionszeitschriften und Missionstraktate," *Der ferne Nächste*, S. 151-164.

70   Thorsten Altena, *"Ein Häuflein Christen mitten in der Heidenwelt des dunklen Erdteils." Zum Selbst- und Fremdverständnis protestantischer Missionare im kolonialen Afrika 1884-1914* (Münster: Waxmann, 2003), S. 82-84.

71   Thoralf Klein, "Wozu untersucht man Missionsgesellschaften? Eine Antwort am Beispiel der Basler Mission in China," *Jahrbuch für Europäische Überseegeschichte* 5 (2005): S. 73-99; vergleiche auch Hermann Wellenreuther, "Pietismus und Mission," in Hartmut Lehmann und andere, Hrsg., *Glaubenswelt und Lebenswelten. Geschichte des Pietismus*, Band 4 (Göttingen: Vandenhoeck und Ruprecht, 2004), S. 182-185.

72   Sun, *Das Chinabild*, S. 322.

73   Ebd., S. 171-314.

74   Vergleiche zum Konflikt zwischen der Missionsgesellschaft in Europa und den Missionaren in China Thoralf Klein, *Die Basler Mission in der Provinz Guangdong (Südchina), 1859-1931. Akkulturationsprozesse und kulturelle Grenzziehungen zwischen Missionaren, chinesischen Christen und lokaler Gesellschaft* (München: Iudicium 2002); derselbe, "Die Basler Mission in China als transkulturelle Organisation: Der Konflikt zwischen autoritärer Führung 'von oben' und synodaler Partizipation 'von unten' im

Prozess der kirchlichen Indigenisierung, 1860-1930," in Artur Bogner, Bernd Holtwick und Hartmann Tyrell, Hrsg., *Weltmission und religiöse Organisationen. Protestantische Missionsgesellschaften im 19. und 20. Jahrhundert* (Würzburg: Ergon, 2004), S. 639-663.

75 Damit soll die Bedeutung der säkularen Reiseliteratur (zum Beispiel Unterhaltungsblättern wie "Gartenlaube," Zeitschriften wie "Daheim," "Über Land und Meer," "Westermanns Monatshefte" oder auch Büchern) nicht verkannt werden. In kirchlich-pietistischen Kreisen bevorzugte man jedoch eindeutig die Missionszeitschriften wegen ihres moralisch-belehrenden Charakters.

76 Schäfer, *Gustav Werner*, S. 235.

77 Altena, *Ein Häuflein Christen*, S. 23-24.

78 Sun, *Das Chinabild*, S. 322.

79 Vergleiche Willy Rüegg, *Die chinesische Revolution in der Berichterstattung der Basler Mission*, Dissertation, Universität Zürich 1988.

80 Evident ist der Einfluss der Mission auf Hermann Hesse, der aus einer protestantischen Missionarsfamilie stammte. Sein Großvater Hermann Gundert war einer der bedeutenden Publizisten auf diesem Gebiet gewesen. Weit verbreitet in protestantischen Kreisen war sein Buch Hermann Gundert, *Die Evangelische Mission, ihre Länder, Völker und Arbeiten* (Calw und Stuttgart: Calwer, 1894).

81 Vergleiche Luise Oehler, *Das neue China. Nach dem engl. Original von A. H. Smith. Mit einigen Abbildungen, zwei Karten und einer Statistik der protestantischen Missionen in China* (Basel: Basler Missionsbuchhandlung, 1909); Wilhelm Oehler, *China und die christliche Mission in Geschichte und Gegenwart* (Basel: Basler Missionsbuchhandlung, 1925).

82 Gutekunst, *Noch lebt des Wortes Kraft*, S. 151-164.

83 N.N.: Der Aufruhr in der chinesischen Provinz Sztschuen, *Evangelisches Missions-Magazin, Neue Folge* 39 (1895): S. 431-434; Otto Lohß, "Der Konfuzianismus in China, einst und jetzt" (mit Erwähnung von "Szetschuan"), *Evangelisches Missions-Magazin, Neue Folge* 57 (1913): S. 261-264, 301-304, 363–368; F. Raeder, "Die Mottschen Konferenzen auf den evangelischen Missionsfeldern Asiens" (mit Erwähnung von "Szetschuen"), *Evangelisches Missions-Magazin*, S. 529-532; N.N.: "Rundschau. China" (mit Erwähnung von "Setschuen"), *Evangelisches Missions-Magazin, Neue Folge* 60 (1916): S. 279. Für die Zusammenstellung danke ich Julia Mack, Basel.

84 Zu Brechts Beschäftigung mit dem Konfuzianismus vergleiche Yim, *Bertolt Brecht*.

85 Jan Knopf, Hrsg., *Brechts "Guter Mensch von Sezuan"* (Frankfurt/Main: Suhrkamp, 1982); Wolf-Egmar Schneidewind und Bernhard Sowinski, *Bertolt Brecht: Der gute Mensch von Sezuan. Interpretation* (München: Oldenbourg, 1992); Peter Paintner, *Erläuterungen zu Bertolt Brecht: "Der gute Mensch von Sezuan"* (Hollfeld: Bange, 1997); Franz-Josef Payrhuber, *Bertolt Brecht: Der gute Mensch von Sezuan* (Stuttgart: Reclam, 2006).

86 Yim, *Bertolt Brecht*, S. 6.

87 Yim, *Bertolt Brecht*, S. 66.

88 Charles Piton, "Konfuzius, der Heilige Chinas," *Evangelisches Missions-Magazin, Neue Folge* 47 (1903): S. 1-22, 59-79.

89 Ebd., S. 12.

90 Ebd., S. 14.

91 Die Bibelzitate wurden nach der Luther-Übersetzung wiedergegeben, die Bertolt Brecht vertraut war. Vergleiche Gotthard Lerchner, "Traditionsbezug zur Lutherbibel im Werk Brechts," in Gotthard Lerchner, Irmhild Barz Ulla Fix und Marianne Schröder, Hrsg., *Gotthard Lerchner – Schriften zum Stil* (Leipzig: Leipziger Universitätsverlag, 2002), S. 146-165.

92 Piton, *Konfuzius*, S. 17.

93 Ebd., S. 22.

94 Ebd., S. 62, 65.

95 Ebd., S. 66.

96 Ebd., S. 79.

97 Für Hinweise und Material bedanke ich mich bei Erdmut Wizisla, Berlin.
98 Bertolt Brecht, *Werke: Große kommentierte Berliner und Frankfurter Ausgabe*, Band. 1, Werner Hecht, Jan Knopf, Werner Mittenzwei und Klaus-Detlev Müller, Hrsg. (Berlin: Aufbau, und Frankfurt/Main: Suhrkamp, 1988-2000), S. 423 (im folgenden abgekürzt als BFA).
99 Yim, *Bertolt Brecht*, S. 27.
100 BFA 13, S. 183.
101 BFA 19, S. 585, Anmerkung zu S. 45, Zeile 37.
102 Eberhard Rohse, *Der frühe Brecht und die Bibel. Studien zum Augsburger Religionsunterricht und zu den literarischen Versuchen des Gymnasiasten* (Göttingen: Vandenhoeck & Ruprecht, 1983). Thomas Naumann, "Brecht und die Bibel," in Therese Hörnigk und Sebastian Kleinschmidt,Hrsg., *Brechts Glaube: Religionskritik. Wissenschaftsfrömmigkeit. Politische Theologie* (Berlin: Verlag Theater der Zeit, 2002), S. 159-203.
103 Yim, *Bertolt Brecht*, S. 22.
104 Antony Tatlow, "China oder Chima?," *Brecht heute/Brecht Today. Jahrbuch der Internationalen Brecht-Gesellschaft* 1 (1971): S. 44-45.
105 Ebd., S. 37.
106 Piton, *Konfuzius*, S. 75.
107 Yim, *Bertolt Brecht*, S. 7.
108 Ebd., S. 164.
109 Vergleiche die Bemerkungen von Ingrid Schuster, *China und Japan in der deutschen Literatur 1890-1925* (Bern und München: Francke, 1973), S. 166, über das Bild von "neuen Menschen" im chinesischen Gewand.
110 Stephenson, *Veneration and Revolt*, S. 132-133.

Brechts (Streifzug in den) Maoismus

Friedemann Weidauer

Dieser Aufsatz untersucht die wenigen Texte, die Brecht mit Mao verbinden. Es soll gezeigt werden, dass Brecht Maos "Bekräftigung des ständigen Wandels " (Tatlow) aufgrund seiner eigenen Denkstrukturen attraktiv gefunden haben muss, während ihm Maos "Rückkehr zu revolutionärer Authentizität" (Jameson) in der erstickenden Atmosphäre der DDR der 1950er Jahre etwas Erleichterung verschafft haben muss. Was Brecht bei Mao fand, unterstützte seine eigenen Überzeugungen, dass das Proletariat einerseits reif für eine führende Rolle in der Revolution sei und andererseits auch reif genug für revolutionäre Kunst, eine Meinung, die die Parteifunktionäre sicher nicht mit ihm teilten.

The paper investigates the scant textual evidence that links Brecht to Mao. As I would like to show, Mao's "affirmation of perpetual change" (Tatlow) attracted Brecht on the basis of the structural similarity to his own way of thinking, while the promise of a "return to revolutionary authenticity" (Jameson) in Maoism provided Brecht some relief from the stifling atmosphere of East Germany in the 1950s. What Brecht found in Mao's writings supported his own conviction that the proletariat is ready to lead the revolution and also ready for revolutionary art, quite in opposition to what the East German party functionaries believed.

Brecht's (Brush with) Maoism

Friedemann Weidauer

Being Bertolt Brecht in the GDR of the 1950s must have been difficult. Now that everything was supposed to change for the better after the "große Veränderung," things were instead going downhill. The constant harassment by the state bureaucracy on his commute to and from Buckow[1] and in other aspects of daily life, the almost daily trouble with Berlau, but above all a government that did not share his assessment of the political situation, much less his view of the role of theater in this new state, to Brecht must have made him feel as if he had gone *vom Regen in die Traufe*: a confluence of misery was dampening the euphoria about "die große Veränderung" that had already put less robust personalities in a suicidal mood: "Trübe Stunden. Erlöschende Kraft. Die Gräue des Alterns. Freudlosigkeit an der Arbeit. Keine Perspektive. Erschlaffung aller Fähigkeiten. Gleichgültigkeit…Wie soll das anders enden, als mit einem allgemeinen Zusammenbruch?"[2] is Hanns Eisler's assessment of his own situation. But a new sun was rising in the East: "Aber die Völker erheben sich zu einem besseren Dasein. Und wie jämmerlich ist meine völlige Energielosigkeit. Wenn ich an China denke, wenn ich an die frische Kraft der endlich befreiten Arbeiter und Bauern denke. Es ist entsetzlich, ihrem Vorbild nicht nachfolgen zu können."[3] That, however, is exactly what Brecht had in mind, to follow the example of China, not in the sense of political action, but for the practice of his theater. In the context of the cultural politics of the GDR this is the problem that presented itself to Brecht: 1. If you believe that the masses are ready for a theater that presupposes a fairly advanced political consciousness while the state believes that they first have to be educated by the example of the classics of the cultural heritage, you have to assert that the masses are ready for your type of theater. 2. If you believe that the class the state sees as its ally, the bourgeoisie in East Germany's *Bündnispolitik*, is the real culprit in Hitler's rise to power, you have to show that the class struggle with the bourgeoisie has yet to happen *in* the theater. This is in short at the center of Brecht's efforts during the early years of the GDR. While they helped him to avoid sinking into the same melancholy as his friend Eisler, they did not help him out of the isolation that the early consolidation of East Germany's *Kulturpolitik* had caused him and like-minded artists.

Political Philology

The translation of one of the texts by Mao Zedong is in itself an example of the cultural politics of these years. This text also serves as one of the main pieces of evidence in the case for "Brecht's Maoism." As the following brief history of the fate of the poem in the hand of various translators will show, here, as elsewhere, we can draw a clear line between those who believed that the dialectic lives on after the establishment of a regime with the semblance of socialism, and those who, under the pretense of defending what had just been achieved, postulated a consolidation of power in the hands of those who had gained the upper hand. We will see a turn towards advocating a permanent party bureaucracy as the one that had been established in the GDR after 1945 at a similar moment in Chinese history once Mao had made significant advances in establishing himself as the new ruler of China.

The poem "Gedanken bei einem Flug über die große Mauer" was given to Brecht by Eisler (BFA 11, p. 390). Non-sinologists looking at the various translations of it must be amazed how little certainty the original text seems to offer the translator. The sinologists themselves have spent considerable effort to defend the broad bandwidth of meanings that the translations have given the poem. However, what seems to have been at work here is a politically influenced practice of translation that shifted the meaning of the poem according to political exigencies, that is, whether one advocated a kind of "permanent revolution" or favored a consolidation of the political gains the party in power had made. Fritz Jensen appears to have been the main perpetrator by producing two very different translations that served as the basis of further elaborations according to the political point of view of the respective scholar.

The endlessly quoted poem in its first three stanzas lists the "vielen Freier" China has had over the centuries and comes to the conclusion in its last stanza: "Alle verdarben./ Aber auch heute/ Seht euch die großen Herren an: immer noch/ Voll der alten schlimmen Begehrlichkeit."[4] This is Brecht's version based on Fritz Jensen's first version from 1936: "Sie alle verdarben – und siehe,/ auch heute/ All die großen, glänzenden Herren,/ immer noch/ So voll der alten Begehrlichkeit."[5] So far no problems, the changes seem to be within a range of possible interpretations of the original Chinese. But the next version should raise some eyebrows: "Alle dahin!/ Zählst du auf frei gesonnene Menschen,/ wende den Blick zum Heute."[6] This version by Joachim Schickel in turn is based on Jensen's 1955 translation: "Sie alle verdarben. So findet/ weithin/ übers Vergangene schweifend,/ das Aug/ die wahren Helden erst heute."[7] Tatlow calls the first version "irreführend" and regrets that Brecht based his version on it since as he claims: "die Pointe zum Beispiel geht verloren."[8] According to him the point of the less misleading version then would be that Mao Zedong as the first one will do it differently, will not fail, will not succumb to the old sinful desires. If you want to glorify Mao Zedong rather than point out the dialectic moment at this point in history, the contradiction between a new beginning and the possibility that old mistakes might be made again – and we can be fairly sure that this is what Schickel wanted to do – the tamed second version is the one to go by. However if you want to stress "die alten Laster" that stick to the new leaders as well, as Brecht was fond of pointing out, one should stick to the earlier version. The reasons for Jensen's 180 degree philological turn are fairly obvious: He had returned to Austria in 1948 after spending the years of German-Austrian fascism in China. In 1953 he returned to China to work as a correspondent for the Austrian *Volksstimme*, the newspaper of the Austrian communist party, as well as for *Neues Deutschland*. Working in China where Mao Zedong was consolidating his power for an East German State firmly under Stalinist control,[9] it seemed like a wise choice for Jensen not to remind readers that the new rulers in either country might be susceptible to the "alten Begehrlichkeiten" since this is exactly what they were. Or, to put it in more neutral words, this later version stands for those who believe there should be no experiments at the moment, that what has been gained should be defended and consolidated.

Similarly, Schickel's use of the undialectic and sycophantic later version can also be explained in the context of the ideologic trench wars of the 1960s in West Germany when one needed virtuous figureheads to promote one's version of Marxism in the battle against all others. The "alten Begehrlichkeiten" would have put Mao on the same level as the "revisionist" Stalinists.

Brecht of course immediately latched onto the dialectic moment in the earlier version, he probably would have been very suspicious of the purified later one, because it contains exactly that aspect in Maoism that he needed to survive the calcifying GDR, that the dialectic lives on, that new answers create new contradictions, that ultimately the class struggle in the GDR had yet to take place in the theaters since the revolution had come in the form of a present from the Red Army. Mao Zedong himself most likely associated the "alten Begehrlichkeiten" with those he was competing against over the control of China, but also probably did not exclude himself from being at risk since he clearly saw the danger of repeating Stalinist mistakes, in the sense of giving in to the tendency of establishing a caste of professional party bureaucrats. At least initially Mao believed that the practice of the revolution had to be kept so transparent that the farmer or housewife would be able to perform its work. The call for professionals and specialists meant giving up on making processes transparent. "To establish and build the Communist Party is in fact to prepare the conditions for the elimination of the Communist Party and all political parties."[10] To give up on this idea is one of the "old sinful ways." "Me-Ti sagte: Man soll keinen auf einem öffentlichen Posten halten, weil er 'Erfahrung' in gerade dieser Angelegenheit hat. Er soll lernen, seine Erfahrung weiterzugeben, statt sie als Besitz zu verwerten" (BFA 18, p. 189).

Thus the word at the heart of the philological differences in the various translations of the poem is also the word that lays bare the biggest sin of

Stalinism, as Brecht put it in this quote from the *Buch der Wendungen*, the sin Mao himself was to commit once he had become the Great Helmsman. It is the word *fengliu*. Since the lexicographers of the People's Republic of China assumed that Mao Zedong was referring to himself by this word, they saw the need to define a new, purged meaning of this word with its use by the Great Helmsman in this poem as the only reference for establishing this new meaning.[11] The new meaning of *fengliu* was now "eine Person, die sowohl grosse Verdienste als auch literarisches Talent hat," a meaning that according to the philologist quoted here exists nowhere outside the People's Republic.[12] All other meanings were henceforth deemed outdated, as for example the one with the connotations: "frei, ungezwungen; hemmungslos; sittlich verwahrlost, verkommen" or "zur alten Gesellschaft gehörig."[13] It seems safe to assume that the word, no matter what philological spin it was given later on, at the point in time when Mao Zedong was using it had the meaning "great men with a certain amount of licentiousness dating back to former social formations." Thus, by a bit of luck, Brecht used a translation that hit the nail on its head and incidentally also best conveyed the meaning Brecht wanted it to have. In the meantime, modern day usage seems to have gone back to the pre-Mao Zedong connotations, you find words like "outstanding, free-spirited," but also "promiscuous, licentious" as well as meanings in combinations with other words such as "merry widow, affair, one-night stand."[14] The work of the party philologists had been in vain.

Assessing the political situation after 1945

The other much stressed link of Brecht to Maoism is his praise of Mao Zedong's text "On Contradiction." The translation of the poem and Brecht's reception of Mao's text "On Contradiction" prompts Terry Eagleton to talk of "Brecht's Maoism" dating to the year 1949 when Brecht actually translated the poem.[15] Indeed, Brecht writes in February 1955: "Die Lektüre, die im vergangenen Jahr den stärksten Eindruck auf mich gemacht hat, ist Mao Tse-Tungs Schrift 'Über den Widerspruch'" (BFA 23, p. 339). He also recommends the book to the members of the Berlin Ensemble (BFA 23, p. 585). That doesn't really say much because the man liked a lot of books and recommended a lot of books. Around the same time Brecht wrote: "Ich halte ein Studium der theoretischen Schriften Schillers für sehr nützlich. Wir können aus ihnen ebensoviel gewinnen—wenn wir sie kritisch verwerten—als aus einigen seiner Stücke" (BFA 23, p. 308). I don't think anyone has called Brecht a typical German idealist because of this, though the textual support is as strong as that for his "Maoism."

One might as well talk about Brecht's Trotskyism since the assessment of the political situation in Germany resembles a Trotskyite analysis of the division of Germany after 1945. As so often, Brecht's view is contained in a single line that contains much more than appears on first sight: "O Deutschland, wie bist du zerrissen…/Tätst du dir selber vertrauen/Wär alles ein Kinderspiel" ("Deutschland 1952," BFA 15, p. 260). While this refers to the specific situation right before the 17th of June 1953 and is supported by Brecht's very differentiated view of the German masses, it also echoes what Brecht finds so attractive and refreshing about Mao. In the last year of his life and after the death of Stalin he dreams of "die Liquidierung des Stalinismus durch gigantische Mobilisierung der Weisheit der Massen durch die Partei" (BFA 23, pp. 417-418.). Brecht trusts the masses when it comes to political action as well as to knowing what is good theater, and hence he is in direct opposition to the East German party in its political strategy and its cultural politics. It is, however, not blind trust. First of all, the petite bourgeoisie must be mistrusted as they are the ones who brought Hitler to power; for the SED however, they were meant to be *Bündnispartner*, not because they didn't perceive of the petit bourgeoisie in the same way, but because of economic necessity they had to find a form of appeasement with it. This of course simultaneously led to the second point of conflict between Brecht and the party that centered around the party's dubious and uncritical use of the *kulturelles Erbe*:

> Indem wir uns bemühen, die Gegenwart zu meistern und in die Zukunft vorzudringen, müssen wir zugleich in den Zeiten zurückgehen, müssen anfangen, das Erbe der Vergangenheit an uns zu reissen, bis wir, höher steigend, auch die Gipfel jener Erbgebirge zu erblicken vermögen, die, bisher im Nebel verhüllt, unsichtbar vor uns lagen. Wir wissen: dieses gewaltige Erbmassiv muss von uns bezwungen werden, diese Parmire des geistigen Erbes müssen von uns erobert werden.[16]

The alpine imagery is magnificent, but still these words by Becher must have hurt Brecht's ears. What about not being intimidated by the classics? What about bringing the classics up to the new stage of social developments rather than "going back in time?" Because this is what must have hurt the most: that the classics are supposedly still far ahead of us, their true achievements still "shrouded in mist." *Undialektisch* would be one of the more polite words Brecht would have used in this context. While the party didn't want to scare away the audiences that had grown fond of their Lessings, Goethes and Schillers and hoped to pull the proletarian masses up to their supposed heights, these were the audiences that Brecht saw as the battle ground for a belated class warfare as the theater had to make up for what in reality had not happened: a proletarian revolution on German soil. The dialectic needs to keep moving: "Türangeln werden nicht wurmstichig."[17] Bad news for the party functionaries: how the maggots attack when you stand still, we can read in Monika Maron's *Stille Zeile Sechs* (1991).

In fact, Brecht saw then more than ever before the need for dialectic theater for the GDR audiences: "Die Konflikte werden in unseren Stücken noch geraume Zeit in der Hauptsache Klassenkonflikte sein—anders als in der USSR. Ein grosser Teil unseres Publikums...hat so wenig gelernt wie die Courage" (BFA 23, p. 304). The choice of Courage of course also indicates which class in Brecht's eyes still needed to be brought up to the current state of affairs in the history of class struggles, namely the petite bourgeoisie.

Unfortunately, in Brecht's opinion, the younger generations of any class could not be trusted either. As late as 1954 Brecht remarked about some younger people with whom he was in fact working on a theater production: "Vor 10 Jahren...hätten alle drei, was immer sie von mir gelesen hätten, mich...schnurstracks der Gestapo übergeben" (BFA 27, p. 350). And this verdict doesn't just apply to a few individuals, it applies to all young people: "Kurz, unsere Jugend ist eine Hitlerjugend...Sie vereinen das Denkvermögen von Kindern mit der Unbelehrbarkeit von Greisen." (BFA 23, pp. 130- 131). Yet, having been seduced by the Nazis is just another sign that in fact they yearn for some sort of socialism: "Die [deutsche] Jugend war bis ins Proletariat hinein, wie es scheint, gefangen durch jene sozialistischen Züge, welche bei Unternehmungen wie dem Krieg allein durch das allgemeine Ziel, den Wegfall der ökonomischen 'Freiheit' usw., mächtig in die Phantasie eingreifen" (BFA 27, p. 258). The urge to join the Nazis thus represents a misguided desire for socialism. So what is to be done with these senile minds in youthful bodies? Give them enough dialectic theater so that they learn to learn again:

> Vernunft kann nicht einfach produziert werden; sie muss produziert werden in dem großen Produktionsprozess der Gesellschaft...[M]an sollte die bequeme Hoffnung aufgeben, diese jungen Leute hätten viel gelernt von ihren Erlebnissen katastrophaler Art. Die Erlebnisse lehren nur den, der lernen will und gelernt hat zu lernen (BFA 23, p. 131).

The fortunate coincidence that the state of mind of the young audiences, as Brecht sees it, calls for exactly the type of theater he has to offer can cause one to pause for a moment and wonder if he was putting the cart before the horse. And even though in this respect he shares the mistrust of the party officials of the masses, or at least of their younger representatives, he does not draw the same conclusions. While Brecht thinks the theater is the place where you learn to see and to learn as Andrea does in *Galileo*, the official line of cultural politics advocated a much slower path that first sought to instill the values of bourgeois humanism in the younger generations by way of plays like *Nathan the Wise* and the rest of the cultural heritage.

It becomes apparent in all aspects discussed so far that Brecht's political analysis of the post-War situation calls for exactly that type of theater that he wishes to practice, and one wonders whether Brecht turned things around so that the problem at hand would fit the solution he could offer. But the fact that other non-dogmatic Marxist thinkers, whether Maoist or Trotskyite, came to similar conclusions helps to diffuse this suspicion. Of course it also explains the enthusiasm Brecht showed when he found out that it was simply the calcified ideological environment of the Stalinist dominated sphere that had made him an outcast. "Durch alle diese Wochen halte ich im Hinterkopf den Sieg der chinesischen Kommunisten, der das Gesicht der Welt vollständig verändert. Dies ist mir ständig gegenwärtig und beschäftigt mich alle paar Stunden" (BFA 27, pp. 298 – 299) is what he wrote in his *Journal* two days before he started working on "Gedanken beim Überfliegen der Großen Mauer." Why, without knowing Chinese, he says he "translated" ("übersetzte") the poem is somewhat of a mystery. But to translate for Brecht doesn't just mean to go from one language to the other, it also means to find the right new wording of a text for a new context, to "carry over" a text from one context to another.[18]

But if you have to count the petite bourgeoisie as well as the youth of all classes out, who can carry forth the revolutionary impulse emanating from China? It is clear that for Brecht the mostly agrarian revolution in China could not serve as a blueprint for Germany in which the proletariat had already achieved a certain level of class consciousness: "Und die Moabiter Proleten sehe ich noch nicht ganz als Hirten" (BFA 27, p. 228). What Brecht had hoped for was, as Jameson put it, "the return to revolutionary authenticity."[19] And it is the proletariat of the older generations that have struggled against Hitler on whom Brecht puts his hopes. It had, in his view, only been defeated by the inability of the leaders of the left parties to form a common front against Hitler. In tune with a Trotskyite analysis of the failure of left resistance against Hitler and of the Potsdam agreement, he saw the German workers as having been betrayed twice, a "nahezu beispiellose Doppelniederlage" (BFA 23, p. 104). Going back to the years of exile this is also how Brecht's view of the Nazi era differs from Thomas Mann's: The Germans were Hitler's first victims.[20] While the rhetoric of the SED functionaries in spite of their deep-seated suspicion of the working class tried to construct it as the victorious class, thereby confusing their own survival in exile as a pars pro toto victory of the workers, they treated the supposed victors like children in both cultural and everyday politics. The suspicions about the working class were not so much based on the assumption that Hitler had succeeded in ideologically undermining the consciousness of the proletariat but rather on its traditional tendency to refuse to fall into lockstep with the directives from Moscow, and this exactly justifies Brecht's hope in this class, but also puts him at odds with those in power in yet another important respect. Even more, he envisioned a unified Germany beyond capitalism and Stalinism: "Wenn Deutschland einmal vereint sein wird, jeder weiss, das wird kommen, niemand weiss, wann—wird es nicht sein durch Krieg" (BFA 23, p. 416). Since he saw the West as a *Kriegstreiber* and since on the other hand the *Kriegstreiber* would also not acquiesce to a Stalinist expansion westward, the inner logic of this statement suggests that unification would have to start independently from within Germany once, as has been quoted above, Germany would have learned to believe in itself. As further evidence of the assumption of a second *Niederlage*, the GDR at this point (1956) was already not discussing the option of a unified Germany in concrete form anymore, reunification was, just as in the West, relegated to the rhetoric realm of national anthems and holidays. To keep this option as a *reale Perspektive* in play yet again put Brecht at odds with those in power.

Similarly, Brecht insisted that the valiant efforts of the proletariat to defeat the Hitler regime only failed because of the insurmountable odds against them. This, in turn, created constant frictions with a regime that claimed the proletariat first had to be brought up to the level of humanism represented by the classic cultural heritage, that it was not ready for artistic experiments and that it had to be kept in the tight grip of the party. So as to emphasize the role of the proletarian resistance he downplays the importance of any other strikes against Hitler: "Aber der 14. Juli!…Die einzige Möglichkeit, den Krieg mit einiger Aussicht auf Erfolg fortzuführen…Die Fortführung des Nazistreichs zu Beginn des Krieges. Ein Plagiat!" (BFA 23, p. 103) On the other hand Brecht finds: "Ich kenne die Ziffern der im Dritten Reich ermordeten Widerstandskämpfer. Sie sind riesig" (BFA 23, pp. 100-101). He cites the strength of the SS as proof of the strength of the workers since only their strength could have justified diverting so much manpower away from the war effort (BFA 23, p. 102). And in a letter to General Clay in the summer of 1948 he asserts "Mindestens 30 Divisionen ziviler Kämpfer sind gegen Hitler gefallen. Der überwältigend größere Teil davon teilte keineswegs Ihre sozialen Ansichten" (BFA 29, p. 462). All this is of course a huge embarrassment to the party elite that would like to present itself as the only legitimate resistance against Hitler even though their main achievement had been to survive the murderous atmosphere in Moscow. Even more, according to Brecht the war efforts of the Western allies had been partially aimed at decimating the proletariat, yet another Trotskyite position: "Die Verzögerung der zweiten Front erlaubte ihr (der deutschen Bourgeoisie), Westrussland gründlich zu zerstören und das deutsche Proletariat tiefer zur Ader zu lassen als Thiers 1871 das Pariser" (BFA 27, p. 270).

It is obvious that all aspects of Brecht's analysis of the situation after 1945 hints in the direction of a *Kulturpolitik* in direct opposition to the one implemented by the party. What Brecht found so fascinating when he started to discover Mao was that at the opposite end of the landmass dominated by Stalin someone had come up with ideas that supported his own convictions. While Brecht certainly would have been disgusted by what the Cultural Revolution looked like when it was put into practice, perhaps more by its undialectical iconoclasm than by the cruel way in which it was implemented, Mao's ideas, at this point not yet formulated as a program for action, certainly appealed to him. It must have been an enormous relief to hear that not all Marxist inspired regimes were going down the same wrong road, and perhaps he hoped that a victorious Mao Zedong might bring the party he had to deal with to reconsider its cultural politics. But it isn't exactly anything new that Brecht found in Mao Zedong. "Über den Widerspruch" reaffirmed Brecht's trust in the dialectic[21] and allowed him to get a theoretical grip on what was happening in the Stalinist party apparatus: "Die Befreiung von den Lastern braucht mehr Zeit als die Revolution. Sie wird beim zweiten Mal etwas leichter sein" (BFA 23, p. 417). This is also the lesson learned from the poem and its mention of the *fengliu*: New contradictions arise when the formerly suppressed class comes to power and repeats the mistakes of the old class in power, but being aware of this tendency, as Mao Zedong was, will help prevent these same mistakes. The biggest one of these mistakes was indeed to force the dialectic to come to a standstill: "Eine der schlimmsten Folgen des Stalinismus ist die Verkümmerung der Dialektik" (Ibid.). Directly tied up with this is of course a cultural practice that would resemble Mao Zedong's (yet to happen) cultural revolution more than the formalist approach to the cultural heritage practiced by the GDR. This in turn would be a partial putting into practice of Mao Zedong's idea that democracy and dictatorship can exist alongside each other: "Democracy for the people, dictatorship over the reactionaries."[22] Since the party in East Germany mistook the people for the reactionaries, the result was predictable. In contrast, Brecht saw in Mao Zedong's thinking how "democracy for the People" and "trust in the masses" necessarily lead to a notion of cultural politics that would resemble the "blossoming of a hundred flowers and the contending of a hundred schools of thought."[23] Even in dark times the creativity of the masses must not be underestimated as Brecht states about his childhood memories of Augsburg:

> Die Arbeiterinnen der nahen Papierfabrik erinnerten sich nicht immer aller Verse eines Liedes und improvisierten Übergänge, wovon vieles zu lernen war. Ihre Haltung gegenüber den Liedern war ebenfalls lehrreich. Sie gaben sich ihnen keineswegs naiv hin…Allzuweit waren sie nicht von jenen hochgebildeten Kompilatoren der Homerischen Epen entfernt, die von Naivität angetan waren, ohne selber naiv zu sein" (BFA 23, p. 268).

Brecht admired Chinese culture and saw its early roots develop fully under Mao Zedong.[24] In contrast, the GDR seemed engaged in ignoring its cultural roots or treating them as relics.

By the same logic, ignoring the "wisdom of the masses" might in fact lead to a situation where the cultural superstructure starts to impede the transformation of society.[25] It is fairly obvious that in Brecht's view the formalist implementation of socialist realism on all forms of art would constitute such an impediment. It is probably no coincidence that this problem is being addressed in the revision of *Turandot* of 1953. This revision falls into the same time period as Brecht's first exposures to Mao Zedong as well as the events surrounding the 17th of June that according to Brecht laid bare many of the mistakes of the regime. The play is about the power of the superstructure and how it can slow down change. It is also a play about how new contradictions evolve as older ones are overcome. At first the "Bund der Kleidermacher" works with the "Bund der Kleiderlosen" against the emperor, but as things develop, the "Bund der Kleidermacher" insists on "discipline" while the "Bund der Kleiderlosen" voices Luxemburgian positions: "Nur in völliger Freiheit kann die Freiheit errungen werden" (BFA 9, p. 140). The two sides then proceed to hit each other over the heads with the works of Marx ("Ka-Me"). To engage the contradictions is, as Brecht believes, almost an anthropologic constant, to suppress this urge goes against human nature: "Es ist ein Vergnügen des Menschen, sich zu verändern…In der materialistischen Dialektik sind Art und Gründe dieser Veränderungen gespiegelt" (BFA 23, p. 297).

At best, Brecht's encounter with Mao provided him some breathing room in the increasingly stifling atmosphere of the GDR, but the initial enthusiasm turned into bitter cynicism towards the end of his life. When Eisler, his *Leidensgenosse*, handed him the *Ode des Mao Tse-tung* in 1948, he euphorically notes: "Mein rechnen mit einer Renaissance der Künste, ausgelöst von der Erhebung des Fernen Ostens, scheint sich früher zu lohnen, als man hätte denken sollen" (BFA 27, p. 293). But in 1956 he predicts the *Endsieg* of formulaic socialist realism:

> Durch die Tätigkeit des I.f.Sch.v.B. (Instituts für Schreibung von Büchern) war nun fast die ganze Bevölkerung imstande, Romane zu schreiben. Es fielen nur etwa 9% der Bevölkerung aus, die dem A.f.L. (Amt für Literatur) angehörten, das dafür zu sorgen hatte, dass alle Romane einander genau glichen…Etwa 98% der Bevölkerung war endlich imstande, sich dem eigentlichen Lebenswerk zu widmen, dem Ausstellen von Formularen (BFA 20, pp. 210 - 211).

Brecht predicted this for the 1990s, and had the GDR survived that long it would have certainly achieved this. To end on a less gloomy note, let's for a moment revive Maoist zeal "im O-Ton der 1960er Jahre:" "Die Wandlung der Widersprüche, ein Fatum für Dogmatiker; der Umschlag der Widersprüche, ein Schrecken für Revisionisten;…die Besonderheit der Widersprüche, eine Provokation derjenigen, die alles und jedes, bloss nicht Kultur revolutionieren wollen."[26] Today socialist realism and the GDR are dead, and hardly anyone would still understand this quote today.

Endnotes

1   See Bertolt Brecht, *Werke, Grosse Berliner und Frankfurter Ausgabe*, Vol. 30, eds. Werner Hecht, Jan Knopf, Werner Mittenzwei und Klaus-Detlef Müller (Frankfurt/Main and Berlin: Suhrkamp and Aufbau Verlag, 1988-2000), pp. 39-140. In what follows this edition will be quoted as BFA by volume and page number.
2   Hanns Eisler, *Gesammelte Werke, Serie III, Band II: Musik und Politik—Schriften 1948—1962* (Leipzig: VEB Deutscher Verlag für Musik, 1968), p. 307.
3   Ibid.
4   Antony Tatlow, *Brechts chinesische Gedichte* (Frankfurt/Main: Suhrkamp, 1973), p. 141.
5   Ibid., p. 142.
6   Ibid., p. 147.
7   Ibid., p. 149.
8   Ibid.
9   See the biography by Eva Barilich, *Fritz Jensen. Arzt an vielen Fronten* (Wien: Globus, 1991).
10 Mao Zedong, "On Contradiction," in *Selected Works of Mao Tse-tung*, Vol. I (Foreign Languages Press: Peking, 1967), pp. 317-47, here p. 339.
11 Friedhelm Denninghaus, "Wie Bertolt Brecht und wie man in Peking Mao Zedong übersetzte," *Hefte für ostasiatische Literatur* 2 (1984): pp. 79-93, here pp. 87 - 89.
12 Denninghaus, p. 87.
13 Ibid.
14 *NCIKU Online Chinese* Dictionary, 2007, 21 Apr. 2010, <http://www.nciku.com/>.
15 Fredric Jameson, *Brecht and Method* (London and New York: Verso, 1998), p. 138 and BFA 27, p. 299.
16 Johannes R. Becher as quoted in Karl-Otto Maue, *Hanns Eislers 'Johann Faustus' und das Problem des Erbes--Göppinger Akademische Beiträge*, Nr. 113 (Göppingen: Kümmerle Verlag, 1981), p. 11.
17 Mao Zedong quoted in Joachim Schickel, *Grosse Mauer, grosse Methode--Annäherungen an China* (Stuttgart: Klett, 1968), p. 300.
18 See Kristopher Imbrigotta, "Brecht's 'Fischweiber': Crossroads of Criticism and Transformation," *Brecht Yearbook* 34 (2009): pp. 227-242 and Tatlow pp. 8 - 9.
19 Jameson, p. 138.
20 See Ehrhard Bahr, *Weimar on the Pacific: German Exile Culture in Los Angeles and the Crisis of Modernism* (Berkeley: University of California Press, 2007), pp. 226 - 227.
21 Jameson, p. 154.
22 Mao Zedong, "On the People's Democratic Dictatorship," in *Selected Works of Mao Tse-tung*, Vol. IV (Foreign Languages Press: Peking, 1969), pp. 411-24, here p. 417.
23 Mao Zedong, "Be Activists in Promoting the Revolution," in *Selected Works of Mao Tse-tung*, Vol. V (Foreign Languages Press: Peking, 1977), pp. 483-97, here p. 495.
24 See Jameson, p. 138.
25 See Schickel, pp. 202 - 203.
26 Ibid., p. 199.

Brecht-Aufführungen in Bangladesch: das Unvertraute vertraut machen

Farzana Akhter

Es gibt keinen Zweifel daran, dass Brecht der wirksamste, maßgebendste und radikalste Theatermann seiner Epoche war, und es gibt kaum ein Land, in dem Brechts Stücke nicht inszeniert worden sind. Seine Ästhetik hat politische Dramatiker und Theateraktivisten auf der ganzen Welt beeinflusst, insbesondere in Ländern der Dritten Welt wie Indien und Bangladesch. Seit Beginn der modernen bengalischen Theaterbewegung in den frühen 1970er Jahren ist Brecht ein häufig gespielter Dramatiker in Bangladesch. Die soziopolitischen Bedingungen nach dem Unabhängigkeitskrieg von 1971 machten Brecht besonders relevant für das bengalische Publikum. Dieser Aufsatz beschreibt, wie zwei seiner Stücke – *Der gute Mensch von Sezuan* und *Die Dreigroschenoper* – für den bengalischen Kontext adaptiert worden sind, um das Unvertraute vertraut zu machen, und versucht die Bedeutung aufzuzeigen, die die Themen und Botschaften dieser Stücke nach wie vor für die Bevölkerung von Bangladesch haben.

There is no doubt that Brecht is the strongest, most influential and most radical theater man of his era, and there is hardly any country where Brecht's plays have not been staged. His aesthetics have affected political playwrights and theater activists throughout the world, especially in Third World countries like India and Bangladesh. Brecht has been a popular playwright in Bangladesh ever since the beginnings of a modern theater movement in the country in the early 1970s. The socio-political conditions after the Liberation War of 1971 also made Brecht eminently relevant for Bengali audiences. This paper will discuss how two of his plays – *The Good Person of Szechwan* and *The Threepenny Opera* – have been adapted into a Bengali context to make the unfamiliar familiar, and show how the themes and messages of these plays resonate in Bangladesh.

Performing Brecht in Bangladesh: Making the Unfamiliar Familiar

Farzana Akhter

Peter Brook in his book *The Empty Space* wrote, "Brecht is the key figure of our time, and all theater work today at some point starts or returns to his statements and achievement."[1] Indeed, Brecht is the strongest, most influential and most radical theater man of the era and there is hardly any country where Brecht's plays have not been staged. Brecht's plays have been performed in almost every part of the earth and have been adapted into almost any medium: theater, film, and the novel. From Moscow and Berlin to New York, Kalkota and Dhaka, his plays have passed the test of time and have influenced many.

It is quite amazing that in spite of coming from a different cultural, religious and socio-political context Brecht's plays have had a tremendous influence on Bangladeshi theater activists and audiences. Until now fourteen of Brecht's plays have been performed in Bangladesh in either translated or adapted versions. This is not a small number, considering the fact that the history of an active Bangladeshi theater is only about four decades long. No other playwright has succeeded in creating such an impact on our audience. Even the enthusiam for Shakespeare could not match the enthusiasm for Brecht, although Shakespeare has his own appeal and audience here. This essay will analyze how two of Brecht's plays—*The Good Person of Szechwan (Shot Manusher Khoje)* and *The Threepenny Opera (Janatar Rangasha)*[2]—have been adapted into our cultural context to make the unfamiliar familiar, and show the relevance of the themes and messages of these plays for our country.

To understand the relevance of a theater tradition or even an individual play to the socio-political and cultural context of a society requires unearthing the reasons behind its acceptance in that society. Various factors—the expectations of the audience and the historical moment in which a work appears, among others—have a role to play in the success of that work. The socio-political climate of Bangladesh from the mid-1970s to the late 1990s and the development of a strong theater movement in the country made Brecht eminently suitable and accessible to radical theater groups. Brecht's dramatic theory, political philosophy, and his preoccupation with marginalized people also made his work relevant in Bangladesh. Furthermore, Brecht's theory of the theater as a process of social change readily appealed to our theater activists. After the Liberation War of 1971, when Bangladesh declared itself free from Pakistan's control, there was widespread reformation in every sphere of governance and social life. Politics was toddling towards democracy, the demand for the formation of a stable society was felt, but the country as a whole was going through dire straits. There was great pressure for massive reconstruction and rehabilitation of the war-ravaged country. Although the state apparatus was weak, it had to tackle massive problems: establishing law and order, disarming civilian freedom fighters, rehabilitating refugees, reconstructing infrastructure, managing industries left by non-Bengali owners, negotiating with the international community for recognition and assistance, and so on. It was felt, however, that without fundamental shifts in political and social thinking these gigantic tasks would be impossible to tackle. People's participation in nation-building was seen as a must, and the capitalist economic system failed to generate any enthusiasm. A lot of people felt that only socialism could bring the people together and ensure widespread participation in nation-building. However, the government's efforts were flawed, and no sustained attempts to apply socialist principles were observed. Amid such chaotic conditions our theater activists sought for a theater that would awaken the critical mind of the audience and galvanize them into social and political awareness and action. Brecht's epic theory offered them an effective method for jolting people out of passivity and engaging them in creating a socially and politically stable country. Though the plays belong to a different era and are set in an entirely different national context the theme and the subject matter of both plays seem to address our major socio-political issues—the greed and corruption of society and government, and the proletariat's desire for equality.

It was thus that Brecht was introduced to the audience of Bangladesh in 1975 through his famous play *The Good Person of Szechwan*. The play was performed in Dhaka in Bangladesh Mahila Shamity (Ladies Association Auditorium) in December that year by the theater group Nagarik Nattyasampraday. As Bangladesh had no standard theater stages the theater group had to improvise with whatever was available. The small size of the stage posed an impediment to the performance. The acting area was only 22 feet by 20 feet large, and because of such space constraints and lack of technical support the group had to make certain changes in the script. One such change was the way the gods in the play exit. While in the original play the gods leave the stage floating on a pink cloud, the gods in the Bangla version made their exit simply by dancing to the beat of percussion drums. Moreover, next to the two wings of the stage there were two walls which created a great obstacle for the actors. Nevertheless, surmounting all the difficulties the theater group succeedeed in enthralling 400 plus spectators with their performance. In fact the play was such a great success that it was produced almost 100 times at different times in different places all over the country. *The Good Person of Szechwan* was adapted as *Shot Manusher Khoje* (meaning "in search of a good person") by Aly Zaker, an eminent actor of our country. Zaker made several changes in the translation to make the play culturally familiar and acceptable to the Bangali audience. In fact, he dismantled and reconstructed the play according to our social and cultural context. He changed the setting to a small town in Bangladesh. Shen Te became Fuli and Shui Ta, Ful Mohammed. Furthermore, Yang Sun was no longer an unemployed pilot but became an unemployed taxi driver. Another change that he made to accommodate the cultural and religious sentiments of Bangali audiences was to get Fuli (Shen Te) married to Nawab (Yang Sun) before she conceived. This was because in a Muslim country like Bangladesh conceiving a baby out of wedlock is quite unacceptable.

The Good Person of Szechwan underscores the message that it is impossible to retain one's good qualities in a capitalist society. Poverty and need drive away the humane qualities of people and turn them into self-centered individuals. This applies to Bangladesh almost more than to any other country. The play *Shot Manusher Khoje* was performed in a crucial period when Bangladesh was going through great economic and political turmoil. The nation had come out of a war only four years before and it was a time of reconstruction. Unfortunately, like any other war-torn country, Bangladesh had become politically and economically unstable. The nation-wide famine of 1973 and 1974 aggravated problems. Moreover, there were considerable moral problems after the 1971 war. While most of the rich were already corrupt, the impoverished strata of Bangladeshi society were losing their moral scruples, too. When it comes to survival people often do not think about right or wrong. The only thing that matters then is satiating hunger. On an empty stomach one cannot think of being a good person with morals and ethics. As Mackie says in *The Threepenny Opera*: "Food is the first thing, Morals follow on."[3] This is exactly what happened with many Bangladeshi people. Being compelled by hunger and poverty, many people had to sacrifice their humanity and choose a life of degradation. The picture painted in the play — the poor taking advantage of Fuli's goodness and exploiting her mercilessly without giving a thought to her needs — is indeed a true reflection of Bangladeshi society at that time.

The position of women in society, especially in Third World countries, has always been neglected. They have to overcome the hurdles of patriarchy to establish their own identity. With every step they have to wage war against the norms set by men as a means of subjugating the women. Brecht's Shen Te is the quintessence of every woman of Bangladesh, and her predicaments are the predicaments that every woman in our country faces. In order to protect herself and her business Shen Te has to take on the false identity of a man who has the necessary ruthlessness to bring her affairs in order. This is the story of our country's women who have to have a male counterpart to survive in a capitalist and male-dominated society. In order to save herself from being abused and trodden upon, Fuli invents an alter ego: a male cousin named Ful Mohammed, who is cold and stern and has the capability of bringing things under control.

In spite of possessing these qualities herself, Fuli has to project them on to her alter ego, because the patriarchal society she is a part of would never acknowledge a woman as the possessor of such qualities denoting social superiority. Fuli breaks the age-old notion that women are weak and hence incapable of surviving in society without the assistance of their male counterparts. Even today it is quite difficult in our society for a woman to establish a business on her own and to lead a "good" life. A woman entrepreneur in Bangladesh needs the support of a male, who is often her husband, father, brother, or trusted relative, and some amount of supervision to succeed in the business world. For educated and well off women, however, this is not required anymore.

The second play by Brecht that became quite popular among Bangali audiences is *The Threepenny Opera,* translated into Bangla as *Janatar Rangashala.* An earlier Bangla version of the play, however, was performed in 1983 as *Tiin Paisar Pala,* but this was an adaptation done by the Indian theater person, Rudraprashad Sengupta. Later, in 1996, the theater Nagarik Natyaangan staged Bangladeshi actor Mujibur Rahman's adaptation *Janatar Rangashala.* The play has proved to be a perennial favorite and is staged even today. Keeping the Brechtian form intact, Rahman has resituated the play in a Bangladeshi context. Peachum becomes Salim Sheik, Mackie is changed to Kalu and Polly to Sokina, while Jenny becomes Jorina and Brown is Bagha Salam. Even the behavior of the beggars, especially the nagging of the lady beggars and their style of speech and mannerisms, are beautifully transformed to reflect our country's situation. In fact, one can draw a distinct parallel between the social conditions of Brecht's era and our age. Now, as then, the misuse of money and the belief that money can buy everything and remove all sorrows have divided society into "Haves" and "Have-Nots." Class distinctions are set up based on financial rather than meritorious conditions.

The use of various regional dialects is another important change that was brought in by the translator in order to strike a tone of familiarity and to reflect the diversity of our cultural heritage. The use of regional dialect is in fact widespread in our culture. Though the official language is Bangla, a majority of the people speak their own dialects. In the play Salim Sheikh speaks in the Noakhali dialect. His wife from Kolkata speaks in Kolkata Bangla, while the beggars use different regional dialects. Only Sokina, Kalu, and Salam speak standard Bangla. Indeed, what we have here can be compared to Mikhail Bakhtin's concept of the dialogic, or, as he puts it in his essay "Discourse in the Novel," "a diversity of social speech types."[4] Even in the songs the translator has taken special care to reflect the cultural codes of our country. A close analysis of one of the songs sung by Sokina (Polly) will show how the songs are infused with our socio-cultural elements. In the song Sokina says,

> O Mother when I was a little kid
> I used to saunter around the house and the yard
> And sometimes in a corner of a room
> I sat alone with toy pots and pans
> To play at cooking and cleaning.
> From the fair Father used to bring
> Small glass bangles
> And red ribbons, along with
> Red saree.
> Decked with the saree and the glass bangles
> I arranged my doll's wedding.

She further says that when she was growing up she had to obey her parents' instructions of behaving like a decent girl and not to mix with boys, and to be careful of not falling for anyone's seduction. All these are indeed specific cultural reflections of our society. A feminist would point out how from earliest childhood on our parents instill the seeds of discrimination in a girl. In a patriarchal society, parents begin to discriminate against a girl from an early age, inculcating in her a sense of what are supposedly desirable qualities in a girl. The girls are supposed to play with dolls and kitchenware, and when they are growing up it is their sole duty to protect themselves from being seduced by a boy.

In the Bangla version, the hypocrisy of the so-called businessmen of our country is revealed through the character Kalu (Mackie). In reality Kalu is a thief and a crook, there is no crime that he has not committed, and yet all his misdeeds are concealed behind the veneer of being an entrepreneur. Similar to Kalu, many criminals, people of high-class society, and even some of the political leaders of Bangladesh pretend to be business leaders, but in reality they are criminals like Kalu who are involved in smuggling, terrorism and other anti-social activities. These people easily succeed in acquiring a respectable position in society. In *The Threepenny Opera* Mackie tells Polly that in a few weeks he will switch to banking because it is safer and more profitable. In our country, too, business ventures such as opening a bank, a private university, or a private TV channel are often merely scams through which many rich and powerful people carry on their illegal activities. Again, Mac's final speech brings to light the truth about the business world:

> We bourgeois artisans, who work with honest jemmies on the cash boxes of small shopkeepers, are being swallowed up by large concerns backed by the banks. What is a picklock to a bank share? What is the burgling of a bank to the founding of a bank? What is the murder of a man to the employment of a man?[5]

Mackie accuses big business of doing exactly what he does himself, namely stealing. The only difference is that the big companies do it legally and with more money. These allegations are also valid for our society. Kalu says:

> We are mere petty businessmen...Compared to the big multi-national corporations we are small thieves. What is the breaking of a trivial cash box to the plundering of the share market? How can you compare one or two murders with the wholesale trafficking of thousands of people to foreign markets?

In the Bangla version, the attention has shifted to contemporary market scandals and malpractices. Multi-nationals are looked at with suspicion as agents of disempowerment and poverty, while big players in the share market are considered enemies of the people. The Bangla version centralizes these players in place of big companies and banks as the references are closer to the audiences' everyday experience.

For an adaptation to succeed, it needs to achieve an almost complete correlation to the social, political and cultural codes of the society into which it is adapted. With great dexterity Mujibur Rahman incorporates a satirical attack on the government while retaining the original theme of political corruption. We get a glimpse of Bangladesh's political situation in the 1980s through Kalu's speech. During that time the country was under military law, with the military dictator, Hussain Mohammad Ershad, having very cleverly taken over the country in the name of disciplining it, utilizing autocratic means by enforcing martial law. As a result, a single-party system representing military interests became the norm, with the leader wielding almost absolute power. Indeed from 1975 to 1990 — the period which saw direct and indirect military rule — the norm was for the rulers to float their own parties. These parties got all the votes since the state machinery was employed to ensure their victory. Ershad founded Bangladesh Jatyo Party, while his predessor General Ziaur Rahman formed Bangladesh National Party. It was not until 1990 that multi-party democracy returned. The period until 1990 was indeed, an era of sheer lawlessness, the political leaders seemed to have lost any sense of patriotism, and whoever got the opportunity plundered the country without the slightest prick of conscience. The entire country became dysfunctional. Again, the Queen's pardoning and ennobling of Mac replicate our corrupt society. A criminal like Kalu escaped trial merely by bribing the ruling party and becoming a member of the government party. One did not really need any qualification to become a member of a political party; the only thing that one needed was money. Money opened every possible door to the corridors of power and wealth. This is exactly what happened in Bangladesh then. Criminals and outlaws like Kalu roamed openly and fearlessly in Bangladesh only because they belonged to the powerful political party. Again, in Act III of *The Threepenny Opera*, when Brown comes to arrest Peachum, we hear Peachum uttering the bitter truth, "Our judges are totally unbribable: no amount of money can bribe them to dispense justice."[6] The situation that prevailed at that time was very similar to the lawless condition of our country. Corruption and anarchy had gnawed the country hollow. The lower courts of our country were corrupt, money or political power could swing a judgment in favor of a criminal. Alas, the situation has not changed much, though the dictator was forced out of power in 1991.

The most corrupt place in Bangladesh even today is the police department. The scenario is no different from what Brecht portrayed in *The Threepenny Opera*. At one point in the play Mac says:

> seldom have I undertaken the smallest job without giving my friend Brown a share of the proceeds (a considerable share, Brown) as a token and a proof of my unswerving loyalty to him. And seldom has the all-powerful Sheriff—...organized a raid without previously giving a little tip-off to me, the friend of his youth.[7]

Criminals befriend or buy the police to get away with their crimes. Kalu and Salam's relationship is in fact the mirror image of the relationship between criminals and many police officers in Bangladesh. Many criminals here have a good rapport with the police department whom they bribe to ensure continued protection. Additionally, before raids the police often inform the criminals so that they can escape arrest. Kalu says that he has always shared his spoils with his friend Salam, and Salam, on the other hand, has tried his best to reciprocate Kalu's generosity. When Salam comes to meet Kalu and his new bride, Sokina, he brings a gift for her. The gift is one of the sarees which he got as bribe for dispatching the smuggled sarees they had seized that day. Kalu, too, continues committing crimes nonchalantly because he knows he would never be caught by his "friend"—the Sheriff. For the all-powerful Sheriff, one just has to read "the Police" and one gets a picture that faithfully reflects the corrupt elements in that department. The criminals always seem to be out of reach of the law, and even if they are caught after much effort they are always set free the same or the next day. This cat-and-mouse game of law enforcers arresting the criminals only to let them go again after having lined their pockets is a common phenomenon in our country.

There is no doubt that theater, in a country where working-class people are oppressed daily by the state machinery and the monied classes, plays an important role in changing entrenched notions about class, ethnicity and gender, and thus contributes to reforming the social structure. Thus in Bangladesh, where a large number of people live in abject poverty and struggle hard to rise above a subhuman level of existence, Brecht's plays became popular as they are infused with social problems and invite social protest and challenge. From 1975 to 2002, that is for 27 years, Brecht's plays dominated the Bangladeshi stage. Brecht was performed with immense zeal not only in the capital city Dhaka but also in various other cities of the country. Yet from the mid-1990s on productions of Brecht's plays began to dwindle in number as the focus gradually shifted to folk and indigenous drama. Nevertheless, Brecht has not totally disappeared from our stage but is performed even today. Plays such as *The Threepenny Opera* and *Roundheads and Peakheads* are still being staged because the issues raised by them are as evident in today's strife-torn society as they were when Brecht wrote them.

A close analysis of Brecht's plays will prove that they are more relevant for the Third World societies of today than for those in the developed world. Though the Marxist ideal, one which a majority of people believed in in their search for a revolutionary ethics, may not be the obvious answer anymore, class struggle and economic disparities still exist in large measure throughout the world. Brecht's plays strongly appeal to those working towards social change, particularly in countries like Bangladesh. If we contemplate on Brecht's plays we can see that they have lost none of their impact since the social problems they deal with press on us now as ever. Often declared dead, Brecht continues to live on our stage in his plays. For many theater people, Brecht's call to "change the world" through theater is still a valid guideline. And in Bangladesh, where political stability is yet to come, where the gap between the rich and poor is increasing day by day and the proletariat is being pushed to the periphery, Brecht's call for social change is very much pertinent. Though the same scenario prevails in the industrialized countries, too, in Bangladesh, as in many developing countries, the pursuit of human rights, and the rights of the marginalized and underprivileged has an accompanying vision that Brecht often articulates in his plays. What Brecht stood for is what conscientious people everywhere stand for. His works, therefore, easily resonate in every society where inequality rules and the rights of the poor are neglected. And in the theater world, in spite of the revival of folk theater and the fusion of genres, there will ultimately always be a place for Brecht. As long as there is exploitation, war and dictatorship, there will be Brecht and his creative and ingenious dramaturgy.

Endnotes

1   Peter Brook, *The Empty Space* (London: MacGibbon and Kee, 1968), p. 72.
2   The titles in brackets refer to the Bangla versions.
3   Bertolt Brecht, *The Threepenny Opera*, in Desmond I. Vesey and Eric Bentley trans., *Three German Plays* (London: Penguin Books, 1963), p. 142.
4   Mikhail Bakhtin, "Discourse in the Novel," in Julie Rivkin and Michael Ryan, eds., *Literary Theory: An Anthology* (Oxford: Blackwell Publishers, 1998), p. 32.
5   Brecht, *The Threepenny Opera*, p. 222.
6   Ibid., p. 206.
7   Ibid.

Brechtsches Theater trifft buddhistische Ästhetik: Kamron Gunatilakas *The Revolutionist*

Parichat Jungwiwattanaporn

Ein links-humanistisches Theaterensemble, die *Crescent Moon Theater Group*, die in den späten 1960er Jahren gegründet worden war, gehört zu den Pionieren des zeitgenössischen thailändischen Theaters, das moderne westliche Theatertechniken und –theorien angewandt hat. Dieser Aufsatz untersucht eine von Brecht beeinflusste thailändische Produktion, *The Revolutionist*, die unter Kamron Gunatilaka entwickelt und unter seiner Regie aufgeführt wurde. Seit seiner ersten Aufführung 1987 sehen Kritiker *The Revolutionist* als eines der wichtigsten thailändischen Stücke des zwanzigsten Jahrhunderts an. *The Revolutionist* stellt den Führer der thailändischen Revolution von 1932 Pridi Banomyong dar, einen fortschrittlichen Intellektuellen, der später politischen Intrigen reaktionärer Kräfte zum Opfer fiel. Der Aufsatz stellt einen Kontext zwischen thailändischer Nationalgeschichte, der Definition des "Thailändischen" und der Demokratie thailändischen Stils her. Er analysiert nicht nur die Brecht'schen Aspekte des *Revolutionist*, sondern zeigt auch die Gebiete auf, auf denen Brechts Verfremdungseffekt mit der buddhistischen Vorstellung von *chit-wang* ("entleerter Geist") überlappt. Der bestimmende Stil des *Revolutionist* könnte am besten als eine einzigartige buddhistisch-brechtsche Ästhetik beschrieben werden.

A leftist-humanist theater ensemble, The Crescent Moon Theater Group, founded in the late 1960s, was among the pioneers of contemporary Thai theater employing modern Western theater techniques and theories. This paper explores an original Brecht-influenced Thai production, *The Revolutionist*, which was developed and directed by Kamron Gunatilaka. Since its first performance in 1987, critics consider *The Revolutionist* one of the most important Thai plays of the 20th century. *The Revolutionist* depicts the story of the leader of the 1932 Thai revolution, Pridi Banomyong, a progressive intellectual who later fell victim to the political intrigues of reactionary forces. This paper provides a background on Thai nation, Thai-ness, and Thai-style democracy. It not only analyzes the Brechtian aspects of *The Revolutionists*, but also demonstrates areas of overlap between Brecht's *Verfremdungseffekt* and the Buddhist notion of *chit-wang* ("emptied mind"). The overall style of *The Revolutionist* might best be described as a unique Buddhist-Brechtian aesthetics.

Brechtian Theater Meets Buddhist Aesthetics: Kamron Gunatilaka's *The Revolutionist*

Parichat Jungwiwattanaporn

Bertolt Brecht in Thailand

Brecht's plays were first introduced to Thailand in an academic setting, namely in Western literature courses at Chulalongkorn University in the late 1960s and at Thammasat University in the early 1970s.[1] The first directors to use Brechtian theater techniques in Thai productions were all from the West: the American Gary Carkin and the Germans Norbert Mayer and Wolfram Mehring. Mayer, for example, was invited by the Goethe Institute in Bangkok in 1976 to teach an acting workshop and to direct the first production of a Brecht play in Thailand, *The Exception and the Rule*. Mayer's staging of this *Lehrstück* opened on June 29, 1976 under the Thai title *Nee Lae Lok* (*This is the World*) at the Silp Bhirasri auditorium before touring to Chiang Mai University and Silapakorn University.[2] The performers were all members of the Crescent Moon Theater Group (CMTG), which had been co-founded by the director Kamron Gunatilaka in 1973. Over the following years, major universities as well as independent theater groups would translate and produce a number of other plays by Brecht, including *The Good Person of Szechwan* (dir. Sodsai Phantumkomol, Chulalongkorn University, 1979), *The Threepenny Opera* (dir. Matani Ruttanin, Thammasat University, 1984), *The Life of Galileo* (dir. Rassamee Paoluengthong, Theatre 28, 1985), *Mother Courage and Her Children* (dir. Noppamas Sirigaya, Chulalongkorn University, 1986), and *Antigone* (dir. Sineenadh Kietprapai, Crescent Moon Theatre Group, 2006). The one major monograph on Brecht produced in Thailand to date, *Dramatic Literature by Bertolt Brecht: A Critical Study*, was published in 1983 by the respected scholar Chetana Nagavajara.[3] In 2000, the Goethe Institute of Bangkok organized a series of film screenings and exhibitions as well as a theater production of *Man Equals Man* directed by Chonprakun Junrueng to commemorate Brecht's life and work. Brecht's influence can be discerned in a wide range of modern Thai theater, from mostly experimental and presentational productions by small theater groups in the late 1960s to the political theater work of the CMTG in the 1970s to performances by independent groups in the decades since.[4] As regards Thai theater overall, however, the engagement with Brecht's ideas and aesthetics has been most consistent in Kamron's productions with the CMTG over the last three decades.

Kamron Gunatilaka and the Crescent Moon Theater Group

1966 saw the founding of the leftist-humanist Crescent Moon Literary Group (*Gloom Wannasil Phrachan Siew*), which produced and published original plays, poetry, and social criticism as well as translations. In the early 1970s, during the student-led political movement in Thailand, the group transformed into the CMTG. As a new theater ensemble of mostly inexperienced actors who desired to improve their craft within a short period of time, the CMTG participated intensely in training workshops that were mostly conducted by Western theater practitioners from a script-based tradition, even though they also taught the theater theories and performance techniques of Brecht, Antonin Artaud, and Jerzy Grotowski. The CMTG devised their early theater productions (*The Rural I, The Rural II, The Rural III, The Obnoxious Sammie, The Mother, Before Dawn*) more or less via trial and error. Over time, however, the CMTG grew from a group of experimenting students into a professional theater company that shook the foundations of elite theater in Thailand. The CMTG members not only participated in a Brecht workshop with Mayer, they also convinced the German director to add Thai folk theater (*likay*) elements to his production of *The Exception and the Rule* with the group. Three months after this collaboration, university students started another political protest movement that immediately came under attack by the reactionary military faction, the ruling class, the government media, and various right-wing groups. On October 6, 1976, the left-right political polarization finally escalated in armed attacks on student protestors and members of the general public during a large demonstration at Thammasat University, which also featured the performance of a short

A Thai Children's Game (*Ree-Ree-Khao-Sarn*) representing the endless transfer of power among right-wing military leaders. Photo courtesy of Crescent Moon Theatre/Sineenadh Keitprapai.

dramatic skit by members of the CMTG. The skit alluded to the recent return of exiled dictator General Thanom Kittikhachon to Thailand, which had also prompted this major protest. Along with more than three thousand students, several of the CMTG members were arrested. Kamron, the director of the group, was not present at Thammasat University and escaped the arrest. He went to France and joined Mehring's Théâtre de la Mandragore in Paris as an apprentice. The incident led to the dissolution of both the student movement and the CMTG.

From its inception to its first disbanding in 1976, the CMTG maintained its position as an independent theater group that used theater to express the predicament of Thai society and to evoke in the audience a desire for political and social change. Highly skilled in improvisational theater, the CMTG developed a new way of creating original theater and, in the process, signaled a rebellion against the centralized power structures through its Brechtian and Grotowskian artistic sensibility. When Kamron returned to Thailand in 1986, he quickly wrote and directed *The Revolutionist*, a play inspired by Pridi Banomyong (1900-1983), a former Prime Minister of Thailand and one of the prominent leaders in the 1932 revolution that changed Thailand to a constitutional monarchy. *The Revolutionist* is perhaps the most frequently revived contemporary play in Thailand. Between 1987 and 2010, *The Revolutionist* was produced on six occasions (1987, 1995, 1997, 1999, 2000, and 2010).[5] After the success of *The Revolutionist* in 1987, Kamron struggled for almost a decade to train a new generation of the CMTG. The years 1995 and 1996 marked the most productive time in his career as a director since he could finally not only collaborate with a host venue (the Saeng Arun Arts Center) but also establish the new CMTG with a group of young actors. During this period, the CMTG produced six major productions, three of which were directed by Kamron.[6] Unfortunately, the Asian financial crisis of 1997 forced the venue to close down. The new CMTG members dispersed once again. With only a few remaining members, the new CMTG, led by Kamron's disciples Sineenadh Ketprapai and Teerawat Moonvilai, have finally found a new space at Pridi Banomyong Institute in Bangkok, where they have held workshops and performances regularly since 2002.

Thai Nation, Thai-ness, and Thai-style Democracy

By paying homage to Pridi's life and political heritage, Kamron's *The Revolutionist* undermines the hegemonic narrative of modern "Thai-style democracy." Although the governing system of Thailand changed from an absolute monarchy to a constitutional monarchy after the revolution of 1932, Thai history textbooks remain elusive about that political transformation and continue to portray the monarchy as the most important force in the making of the Thai nation and of Thai identity while downplaying constitutional rights under the rule of democracy.

Nevertheless, since the 1990s, Thai as well as international scholars from various disciplines have come to disagree with the prevalent metanarrative of Thailand's recent political history. These scholars argue that the ideas of Thailand as a nation-state and of Thai-ness as a unique identity are actually products of modernization initiated by various kings less than two hundred years ago.[7] When Siamese hegemony was threatened by Western imperialism in the early 20th century, King Vajiravudh—or Rama VI (reigned 1910-1925)—countered the influence of Western powers by creating and promoting a specific Thai nationalism and ideology characterized by the concept of the "Three Pillars." The king declared that it was the duty of all Thais to love, be loyal to, and defend the three most important foundations of Siam, namely the nation (*chat*), religion (*satsana*, i.e. state-sanctioned Buddhism), and the king (*phra mahagasat*). King Rama VI successfully disseminated his Three Pillars ideology through his own songs, poems, and theatrical productions. This ideology was further implanted into Thai consciousness during a series of pro-capitalist, military-led governments between the late 1940s and the 1980s. To this day, "consensual" respect for the Three Pillars (in a Gramscian, hegemonic sense) can be easily observed in the daily life of Thais.[8] Another oppressive aspect of Thai society is the notion of Thai-ness, which presupposes that citizens not only know and accept their place within the social hierarchy but also exhibit behaviors appropriate for their respective gender, class, and economic status—in school and at work, in government offices and at private institutions. Individuals of lower social status are expected not only to use a coded language befitting their status but also to show complete submission to others of higher social standing. Thais have learned to determine how to interact with and treat each other according to a cultural quantification of everyone's social value. The exploitation of this class-based system is colloquially referred to as *sakdina*, i.e. superiority of the privileged over the underprivileged.[9] The most visible form of this attitude can be found in the exploitation of the *lèse majesté* law created in 1908.[10] This law, as specified in Thai Criminal Law, was written to protect the monarchy from the most egregious cases of insult, but in the modern political history of Thailand it has often been used by law enforcement officers, royalist civilians and politicians to suppress even respectful criticism in a most draconian fashion. During the current monarchy, hundreds of political activists have been charged, convicted, and in many cases imprisoned for offenses against the *lèse majesté* law. After decades of hegemonic reinforcement, the *sakdina* culture has undermined a genuine democratization of Thai society by compelling the Thai people to accept double standards as the social norm.

The bloodless *coup d'état* of September 19, 2006, which overthrew the elected civilian government of Prime Minister Thaksin Shinawatra (known as Thaksin) and abrogated the Constitution of 1997, has divided public opinion and fractured Thai society even further. After a series of civil upheavals and military crackdowns in April and May 2010, Thailand continues to be under a military-backed government. The usurpation of power backed by the military is nothing new in Thai-style Democracy, which, for the past seventy years, has been controlled by the ruling elite (right-wing royalists and autocratic bureaucrats), the military (who often claim power in order to "protect the monarchy"), capitalists, as well as liberal socialists.[11] The military coup as the mode of "power negotiation" most typical of Thai-style Democracy suggests that this democracy is almost entirely dominated by the right-wing ruling class. Considering seventeen military *coups d'état* and a succession of unstable governments over the past seventy years, the notion of "democratization" has been used in the public realm to accommodate a desire for the modernization of Thai society while at the same time concealing the fact that the *sakdina*-based hegemony has remained unchanged.

Pridi Banomyong and *The Revolutionist*

Despite his significant contributions to modern Thai society, the textbook histories of Thailand barely mention Pridi Banomyong. In his 17 years of service to his country, from the 1932 revolution to the beginning of his political exile in 1949, Pridi greatly modernized various aspects of Thai legislation, economy, politics, education and social welfare, all of which served as a catalyst for the subsequent progress of Thai society over the next five decades. During WWII, as a regent to the then very young King Rama VIII, Pridi was the leader of the underground *seri-Thai* (Free Thai) movement, which fought against the Japanese military occupation of Thailand. The Free Thai movement allowed Thailand to be considered a

Pridi Banomyong (Nimit Pipithkul). Photo courtesy of Crescent Moon Theatre/Sineenadh Keitprapai.

sovereign state instead of a defeated nation after WWII. Later in his life, Pridi was recognized by King Rama VIII as a "Senior Statesman" for his immense efforts in serving his country. Regardless of his contributions, Pridi's political enemies managed to tarnish him with the most severe accusation, namely that of having participated in the regicide of King Rama VIII. Although this charge was later proved to be groundless in court, Pridi's reputation was severely damaged and his People's Party destroyed as a consequence. After going into exile in 1949, Pridi never returned to Thailand. When he passed away on May 2, 1983 in Paris, the right-wing government then in power neither recognized nor honored his achievements. Until today, the Thai public has been led to believe that the First Constitution from 1932 was not the outcome of a revolution by the Thai people that subverted the absolute monarchy but a concession made voluntarily by King Rama VII. Kamron's play *The Revolutionist* is a counter-hegemonic attempt to reclaim the buried historical memory of Pridi's political reforms.

Brechtian Influences in *The Revolutionist*

The Revolutionist opens with a chorus lamenting how the history of the people's struggle has been forgotten. This is followed by an actress's solemn delivery of a soliloquy about a Promethean orphan boy who, left alone in a world filled with perpetual darkness, flies to the sun, the moon, and the stars only to discover that they are illusions. The boy then returns to earth and realizes that it is covered with garbage and filth. In Kamron's play, the boy's tale (adapted from Georg Büchner's *Woyzeck*) serves as an allegory of the political life of Pridi, i.e. of a commoner who dared to question and to change Thai *sakdina* culture. After this opening, the play continues with twenty-five scenes that chronologically portray key incidents in Pridi's career. This episodic structure is periodically interrupted by seemingly unrelated short skits and dramatic scenes drawn from popular novels, songs, children's games, poems, and historical accounts familiar to Thai audiences.

In contrast to other modern plays staged in Thailand, the text of *The Revolutionist*, which has been published in both Thai and English, rejects conventional dramatic form in favor of a montage of third-person journalistic narration, songs, dramatic scenes, and monologues reminiscent of Erwin Piscator's productions from the 1920s and Brecht's epic theater.[12] Kamron explores a wide linguistic range in his script, depending on the respective theme and setting of each skit. A documentary/journalistic style, for example, is used for the narration; the formal diction of Thai elites of the 1950s is employed for upper-class characters; whereas word-choices neutral with regard to gender and class characterize the revolutionary side. In addition, *The Revolutionist* uses many other presentational theater elements[13] to create a Brechtian *Verfremdungseffekt* (estrangement effect):[14] soliloquies in the middle of a scene, the constant transformation of the actors into different characters, as well as the use of socially coded gestures (Gestus) and symbolic movements.

During the scene in which Pridi defends the national economic plan that he co-drafted in parliament, the chorus members change from narrators into farmers by miming the ritualistic rice-planting movement in slow motion. The surrealistic juxtaposition of two unrelated actions creates a surprising effect of estrangement. The mimed farmers represent what is in the back of Pridi's mind—the poor farmers and the exploited masses. Despite Pridi's defense, the Permanent Constitution turns out to be a result of negotiations between the monarch and the constitutional assembly, making the audience realize that Pridi's efforts to provide equal rights and more opportunities to the lower classes through the means of political, economic, and legislative reform cannot overcome the "old powers."

What makes *The Revolutionist* an exceptional example of Thai political theater is the fact that it invites the audience to question the legitimacy of the enforced metanarrative of Thai political history. In the scene following a character's announcement of the revolution's success, for example, all actors suddenly break through the "fourth wall" and walk right into the audience to distribute copies of the Declaration of the Revolution from 1932, which is also read over the loudspeaker system:

> Fellow citizens, when the present King ascended the throne most citizens had hoped that he would reign benevolently and judiciously. Subsequent events have proven that such hope is illusory and groundless. The King still esteems himself above the law and still indulges in nepotism, appointing his kindred and lackeys to assume important positions. Furthermore, the King has failed to heed his citizens' cry for justice, allowing government officials to continue to abuse their power, to exploit, to engage in illegal and corrupt practice. The King and his cronies have completely neglected the wellbeing of the masses as witnessed by the dire economic state the country is now in.[15]

Chetana Nagavajara has pointed out that the distribution of the Declaration to the audience is "another masterful device to reify the message of the play in a much more concrete manner than Brecht himself"[16] did. The distributed copies of the Declaration, with its revolutionary content, momentarily render the hegemonic *sakdina* culture of Thai society strange for an audience not used to ever hearing any criticism of the monarchy. Although this historical document is available to the public, it has never been allowed to appear in official school textbooks.

As a Brechtian production with minimal technical equipment, all of the 25 scenes of *The Revolutionist* are mounted on a mobile set consisting of three slanted platforms placed on a dark bare stage. Simple costumes with few accessories neutralize the social class and gender of the characters. Actors use *tableaux vivants* to end each scene, and they also use suggestive movements and gestures to demonstrate the Brechtian Gestus of their characters.[17] Within a span of one hour and twenty minutes, the play depicts Pridi's life from the year of the revolution in 1932 until his death in 1986 through an anti-realistic representation of key moments in his political career.

Beyond Brecht: The Buddhist Dialectics of *The Revolutionist*

The Revolutionist is not only influenced by Brecht but also by Buddhist philosophy, and substitutes compassion for the usual violent aspects of revolution. Pridi, who was a Buddhist in real life, is portrayed as a selfless revolutionary motivated more by empathy for the people rather than a desire for power. In the scene following the distribution of the declaration, for example, the Pridi character delivers following soliloquy:

> There are still many people who loathe and fear changes like they dread evil phantoms or spirits. In other words, the horrendous threats they perceive—and hence the fear they have—are merely a figment of their imagination. They have spread fanciful and malicious lies that the blue blood of aristocrats will carpet the streets of every city and town…The main objective of this revolution is to correct the widespread socioeconomic inequalities, to overthrow the yoke of oppression. I have no desire to shift the concentration of power from a single person to a single group. Remember I am a lawyer. All I ever wanted is to eliminate or minimize inequalities in their various disguises. The hideous thought of slaughtering human lives has never crossed my mind.[18]

The play, however, not only emphasizes Pridi's appreciation of human life but also demonstrates the aristocrats' apprehensions of the new democratic age in a scene titled "Mae Ploy" ("Madame Ploy") and adapted from Kukrit Pramoj's royalist novel *The Four Reigns*.[19] Madame Ploy sees the revolution as being "harsh, cruel, and heartless" and considers the revolutionaries traitors to the monarchy.[20] The revolutionaries, on the other hand, see themselves through Pridi's eyes as those who want to "eliminate or minimize inequalities in their various disguises." For Pridi, "the hideous thought of slaughtering human lives" was never an intention of the revolution since it is against main Buddhist principles to take life.[21] Pridi's Buddhist attitude is consistent throughout the script, especially when he discusses the impermanence of all things and the inevitability of change.

Mae Ploy (Sineenadh Keitprapai), an aristocratic lady who cannot imagine a Thailand without an Absolute Monarchy. Photo courtesy of Crescent Moon Theatre/Sineenadh Keitprapai.

Buddhist-Brechtian Aesthetics

As regards his production aesthetics, Kamron does not totally deny emotional effects. At the same time, however, he hopes that the presentational aspects of his staging may compel the audience to use more of their cognitive faculties to question the portrayed social and political aspects of Thai history rather than to fall into the trap of *catharsis*.[22] In order to arrive at this result, Kamron employs not only estrangement effects through his presentational style but also the Buddhist aesthetics of *chit-wang* (emptied mind). *Chit-wang* as a Buddhist concept was introduced by the revolutionary Thai monk Buddhadasa, who combined the notions of *suññata* (voidness) and *anattā* (no-self, no-ego) in order to make both abstract concepts more attainable. Buddhadasa explained *chit-wang* in the following statement:[23]

> *Chit-wang*—Mental emptiness is the state in which all the objects of the physical world are present (and being perceived) as usual but none of them is being grasped or clung to as "mine"...Thus *chit-wang* is not a vacuous mental state. It is not "void" of content. All objects are there as usual and the thinking process is going on as usual, but they are not going the way of grasping and clinging with the idea of "I" and "mine."[24]

From the above statement, it is clear that Buddhadasa's notion of *chit-wang* has less to do with the ontological "emptiness" of Western philosophy rather than with one's psychological as well as mental condition. What is "voided" in the mind is the self-centered psychological and intellectual attitude of "I" or "ego" (*attā*), and the result is *anattā*, or non-attachment to the ego. While *chit-wang* has been used as a specific term dealing with the psychological aspect of non-atttachment, the Buddhist concept of *suññata* (emptiness or openness) has been used in a much larger sense. For a serious Buddhist practitioner, the mind needs to be in a state of *anattā* first before it can grasp the super-reality of *suññata* (emptiness or openness).[25] The *mise en scène* and performance style of *The Revolutionist* clearly aim at leading the spectator to such a state of *suññata*.

For his production, Kamron designed a minimalist but multi-purpose set consisting of three movable and slanted platforms, painted in grey and placed on a dark bare stage. These three platforms served many functions from elevating the actors' bodies to creating different visual arrangements. The set, together with the movements of the actors, was also used to indicate different locations such as a parliament house, a street, a battlefield, and a part of a house. The lighting consisted of plain Fresnel lights without any additional color. The main musical instrument was one big traditional Thai drum (*klong tad*) to accentuate scene changes. All actors (except for the Pridi performer), regardless of gender, were dressed in simple black shirts and pants. Although the costume color and design varied in later productions, all the designs remained minimalistic with one simple shade of color. In a few scenes, minimal accessories, costume pieces, and props were used to indicate characters. The actors also served as running crew, helping to move the platforms as needed. Using choreographed patterns of movement and a presentational style of acting, each of the twelve actors played a variety of roles, ranging from anonymous narrators and historical figures to characters from Thai leftist as well as royalist novels. The bare stage of the production may have seemed dull and unremarkable at first sight, but once the actors appeared on stage, there was a sense of "a creation out of nothing." It was the minimalist and transient aspect of the production, its three-dimensional emptiness and simplicity that suggested a visual and auditory state of *suññata*. To the Thai sensibility, all actions are fleeting: they appear momentarily only to be gone again the next moment, leaving the empty stage behind.

The written script of *The Revolutionist* indicates the characters' non-attachment to their egos and suggests an actor-audience relationship based on the notion of *chit-wang*. In this type of performance, the audience is like an observer, or similar to the bystanders in Brecht's "Street Scene," while the actors are comparable to the demonstrators acting out the story.[26] In performances of *The Revolutionist*, the actors always seem to merely indicate rather than fully embody their characters. Sineenadh Keitprapai, one of the cast members, recalls that, for at least six months in Kamron's system of actor training, we have to learn how to be neutral or devoid of ego (*attā*) without being attached to a certain way of expression. Then we had to learn how to act out the story as though we were the storyteller, not the characters themselves.[27]

Although Kamron never theorizes the acting style in his version of Brechtian theater, he emphasizes that he would like his actors to be able to completely detach themselves from their characters and to execute the characters' actions with an attitude of *anattā*.[28] The ability to act in a state of *anattā* produces a kind of *chit-wang* effect that very much coincides with Brecht's own vision of dialectic acting:

> The actor does not allow himself to become completely transformed on the stage into the character he is portraying… Once the idea of total transformation is abandoned the actor speaks his part not as if he were improvising it himself but like a quotation.[29]

The acting style in *The Revolutionist* has a quotational quality, and Brecht himself has made a statement that is analogous to the concept of *anattā*: "Using the third person and the past tense allows the actor to adopt the right attitude of detachment."[30] The concept of *anattā* can be visually detected in *The Revolutionist* in the way the actors move and use their bodies, i.e. in the non-verbal Gestus, which can switch quickly from one social code to another, or from one character to another — including non-human entities (e.g. an actor might use movement and sound to mime the transformation into a chorus member, army tank, boat, ocean, wind, etc.). Throughout the performance, actors use their bodies as though they were neutral vehicles, ready to be transformed into anything. Kamron has thus taken Brecht's Gestus to another level by combining it with Buddhist *anattā*. His Buddhist-Brechtian aesthetic therefore simultaneously produces a Buddhist *chit-wang* effect and Brecht's *Verfremdungseffekt*.

Conclusion

If, in dialectical terms, the metanarrative of the royalists is the thesis of the political history of Thailand, then Kamron's play operates rather like an antithesis to this hegemonic history. Although the play tries to follow a dialectical structure by moving back and forth between the viewpoints of the ruling royalists and the revolutionaries, the play primarily focuses on Pridi's life as a Buddhist-Marxist visionary, whose ideals were far too progressive for his contemporaries. As a production, *The Revolutionist* manages to combine Brechtian and Buddhist elements to depict metaphorically the power struggle between both political factions as well as the repressed narrative of Pridi's achievements, challenging the audience to take action to reclaim the long-lost democracy.

Endnotes

1   At Chulalongkorn University, Sodsai Phantumkomol started to offer courses in Western drama at the Department of Literature in 1964 and founded the Drama Department in 1966. At Thammasat University, Mattani Mojdara Rutnin began to offer courses on Western Theater at the English Department in 1971.
2   With regard to foreign plays, it is common practice among theater practitioners in Thailand to replace the original titles with ones that seem to have a stronger appeal for Thai audiences.
3   This research was published under the Thai title *Wannakam Lakhon Khong Brecht: Karn Suksa Chueng Wicharn* (Bangkok: Thai Wattanapanit, 1983).
4   Independent Thai theater groups influenced by Brecht include MAYA, Makhampom, B-Floor, and MANTA.
5   The 1999-2000 productions were directed by Nimit Pipithkul. The 2010 production was directed by Sineenadh Keitprapai. Both directors maintained the core directorial concept of the original production.
6   *My Name is Phan* (*Goo Chue Phaya Phan*), *A Mid Winter's Dream* (*Kwam Fan Glang Duen Nao*), and *Madam Mao's Memories* (*Madam Mao*), a solo performance.
7   Starting with the reign of King Rama IV (reigned 1851-1868), who applied modern Western cartography and geography to claim hegemony over local lordships and chiefs, the subsequent kings and the ruling class continued to lay the foundation for the modern Thai nation-state (formerly known as Siam) by adopting many western ideas of law, government, commerce, healthcare, education, science, and technology. Since the late 19th century, Siamese kings have used military force and governmental policies to create both territorial and cultural hegemonies over regional ethnic groups, thus making them internal colonial subjects of Siam. See Michael Kelly Conners, *Democracy and National Identity in Thailand* (London: Routledge Curzon, 2003); Neil A. Englehart, "Democracy and the Thai Middle Class: Globalization, Modernization, and Constitutional Change," *Asian Survey* 43.2 (2003), pp. 253-279; Pasuk Phongpaichit and Chris Baker, *Thailand's Crisis* (Chiang Mai: Silkworm Books, 2000); *Jumpon Nimpanitch, Phattana Karnmueng Thai: Ammattayathippatai Thanathippatai rue Prachathippatai* (Thai Political Development: Bureaucratic Polity, Plutocracy, or Democracy) (Bangkok: Chulalongkorn University Press, 1995); Thongchai Winichkul, *Siam Mapped* (Honolulu: University of Hawaii Press, 1994).
8   All Thais, for example, are expected to stand still when hearing the national or royal anthem, and Buddhist holidays are major national holidays. The laws still severely punish anyone who does not demonstrate respectful behavior towards the Three Pillars.
9   The word *sakdina* has its root in the economic system that the Siamese kings established five hundred years ago. The historical conjecture of the *sakdina*-based policies of coercion imposed by the Siamese ruling class used to be based on "bonds of personal objection," e.g. slave to master, commoner to conscription chief, tributary lord to king, etc. (Baker and Phongpaichit 2000, p. 24).
10 Article 112 states: "Whoever defames, insults or expresses any action of discontent against the King, the Queen, the Heir-apparent or the Regent, shall be punished with imprisonment of three to fifteen years."
11 See Pasuk Phongpaichit and Chris Baker, "Thailand: Fighting over Democracy," *Economic & Political Weekly*, 13 December 2008, pp. 18-21; Patrick Joy, "Problems in Contemporary Thai Nationalist Historiography," 20 March 2003, <http://kyotoreview.cseas.kyoto-u.ac.jp/issue/issue2/article_251.html>; Wiwat Catithammanit, *Kabot Santi Phap (The Peace Rebel)* (Bangkok: Kobfai, 1996); Charnvit Kasetsiri, *Prawat Karnmueang Thai 2475-2500 (Political History of Thailand 1932-1957)* (Bangkok: Social Sciences and Humanities Textbooks Foundation, 2006)
12 See Kamron Gunatilaka, คำรณ คุณะดิลก. *คือผู้อภิวัฒน์* 2475 (*Kue Phu Apiwat*, literal trans. *The Revolutionist of 1932*, abbreviated in the following as *The Revolutionist*)

(Bangkok: Pridi Banomyong Institute and the Committee on the Project for the National Celebration on the Occasion of the Centennial Anniversary of Pridi Banomyong, B.E. 2542).

13 As Brecht stated, "The essential of the epic theater is perhaps that it appeals less to feelings than to the spectator's reason. At the same time, it could be quite wrong to try and deny emotion to this kind of theater." (Qtd. in John Willett, ed., *Brecht on Theatre: The Development of an Aesthetic*, New York: Hill and Wang, 1964, p. 23).

14 In his writings, Brecht gives many examples of how the third-person narration could be more effective and powerful than the "old fashioned" first-person narration. His examples include "witnesses addressing the court" and "actors paraphrasing the verse's content in vulgar prose in a rehearsal" (Willett, pp. 138–139).

15 *The Revolutionist*, pp. 40-41.

16 See Chetana Nagavajara, "The Brechtian Connection: Innovations on the Contemporary Thai Stage," *Fervently Mediating: Criticism from a Thai Perspective (Collected Articles 1982 – 2004)* (Bangkok: Chomanad Press, 2004), p. 243.

17 Ibid.

18 *The Revolutionist*, p. 43.

19 Kukrit Pramoj, คึกฤทธิ ปราโมช. *สี่แผ่นดิน* (*The Four Reigns*) (Phranakorn: Prae Pittaya, 1962).

20 *The Revolutionist*, pp. 46-47.

21 Ibid, p.44.

22 Personal Interview with Kamron Gunatilaka from 6 October 2006.

23 Buddhadasa (1906-1993), a well-known Thai monk/philosopher, who established an unorthodox temple known as Suanmokkh (Garden of Liberation) in a southern province in 1932 after vigorously studying the Buddhist sutras and practicing meditation in the surrounding forest for over a decade. Based on his belief that Buddha's teachings are about a spiritual liberation effected by the actualization of the laws of nature, he spent his whole life articulating a new understanding of what he called "pristine Buddhism." He produced a great number of publications and sermons that remain significant for Thai society today. Buddhadasa was the first reformist who went against the state-sanctioned Buddhist doctrine and who proposed the idea of a "dhammic socialism," which related socialist ideology to Buddhism.

24 Quoted in Peter A. Jackson, *Buddhadasa: A Buddhist Thinker for the Modern World* (Bangkok: Siam Society, 1988). Jackson notes that he would normally disagree with the translation of *wang* as "empty" or "emptiness" because this misleadingly implies that *chit-wang* is a state of mental activity. However, where others have used the term "empty" in translating Buddhadasa's work, he retained the term for the sake of faithfulness to the cited text (Jackson, p. 334).

25 According to the Buddhist master teacher Tenzin Palmo, in her book *Reflections on a Mountain Lake* (Ithaca: Snow Lion Publications, 2002), p. 253, *suññata* is considered the ultimate nature of reality because there is no inherent permanent existence of a subjective self or of objective phenomena. While the words *anattā* and *suññata* are often used interchangeably since they share a similar quality of the realization of void-ness, *chit-wang* refers to an emptiness related more to *anattā* than *suññata*. However, in Thailand, the term *anattā* is mostly used to refer to "detachment from self" rather than "non-existence."

26 Willett, pp. 121-125.

27 Personal Interview with Sineenadh Keitprapai from 4 December 2005.

28 Personal Interview with Kamron Gunatilaka from 29 July 2007.

29 Willett, p. 138.

30 Ibid.

Der Gute Mensch von Korea: Lee Jarams *Sacheon-ga* als Dialog zwischen Brecht und *Pansori*

Jan Creutzenberg

Nach Jahrzehnten der anti-kommunistischen Zensur wurden Brechts Theaterstücke erst gegen Ende der 1980er Jahre für eine breitere koreanische Öffentlichkeit aufgeführt. Griff man bei der Inszenierung zunächst größtenteils auf westliche Vorbilder zurück, so begannen kreative Theatermacher bald damit, einzelne Elemente aus "traditionellen" Aufführungskünsten aufzugreifen und lokale Bezüge zu integrieren, um Brechts Theater einem zeitgenössischen Publikum näherzubringen. Mit *Sacheon-ga* (2007), einer Adaption des *Guten Menschen von Sezuan* mit den Mitteln des koreanischen Musiktheaters *pansori*, treibt LEE Jaram, selbst ausgebildete *pansori*-Sängerin, diesen "interkulturellen" Ansatz auf die Spitze. Begünstigt durch strukturelle Ähnlichkeiten zwischen Brechts Konzept des epischen Theaters und den Konventionen von *pansori*, verlegt dieses "Lied von Sichuan" nicht nur die Parabel ins heutige Seoul, sondern konfrontiert Brechts Theater auch mit dem für *pansori* charakteristischen narrativen Solo-Gesang. Das Resultat dieses theatralen Dialoges ist einerseits ein verfremdender Blick auf Brechts *Guten Menschen*, andererseits eine politische Aktualisierung der tradierten *pansori*-Praxis.

Subject to anti-communist censorship for decades, the first productions of Brecht's plays in Korea emerged in the late 1980s. Initially following Western models, theater practitioners soon started to integrate elements from "traditional" performing arts as well as local references in order to address contemporary Korean audiences. With her recent production *Sacheon-ga* (2007), singer-songwriter LEE Jaram radicalizes this "intercultural" approach by adapting Brecht's *The Good Person of Szechwan* in the style of *pansori*, a peculiar form of Korean music theater. Nurtured by structural similarities between the conventions of *pansori* and Brecht's *epic theater*, this "Song of Sichuan" not only relocates the plot of Brecht's parable to modern-day Seoul but confronts Brechtian drama with the solo singing-storytelling specific to *pansori*, enabling a theatrical dialogue. The result of this theatrical dialogue is both an alienating take on Brecht's *Good Person* and a political re-actualization of *pansori* practice.

The Good Person of Korea: Lee Jaram's *Sacheon-ga* as a Dialogue between Brecht and *Pansori*

Jan Creutzenberg

Introduction

Both as playwright and theater theorist, Bertolt Brecht can be considered one of the greatest appropriators of world theater culture. From his essay on "Alienation Effects in Chinese Acting" to *The Judith of Shimoda*, East Asian themes, texts, and techniques have been constant reference points throughout his work. In turn, Brecht's creative output spawned new approaches towards theater around the globe, also inspiring ways of re-functioning the theatrical heritage in parts of Asia.[1]

The recent Korean production *Sacheon-ga*, a lose adaptation of Brecht's *Good Person of Szechwan*,[2] allows a closer listening to the "dynamic, ongoing echoes of this mutual relationship."[3] Singer-songwriter LEE Jaram has not only modified the Brechtian setting to address current Korean realities, the whole plot has been re-created in the style of *pansori*, a "traditional" form of music theater that centers around a solo singer-storyteller and is considered one of Korea's most representative performing arts.[4] At the same time, *Sacheon-ga* deviates from the orthodox minimalism of contemporary mainstream *pansori* practice—maintained by the need to conserve a cultural asset[5]—and freely employs additional actors and musicians to support, sometimes even replace, the single drummer who, in a "traditional" setting, serves as the only back-up musician.

The deliberate melange of Brechtian drama and *pansori* "tradition" that characterizes *Sacheon-ga* is already indicated by this rather odd title whose literal translation ("The Song of Sichuan") does not serve justice to its implicit meaning.[6] It is composed of two words: "Sacheon," the Korean rendering of the Chinese characters that designate the province of Sichuan in Southwestern China, home of the eponymous *Good Person*, is followed by "ga," a syllable that generally annotates "song," as in *gasa* ("lyrics") or *gasu* ("singer"). In the case of *Sacheon-ga*, however, the suffix connotates a specific kind of song: a song of *pansori*.[7] As a matter of fact, the titles of all five songs of the canonical *pansori* repertoire, like *Chunhyang-ga* ("The Song of the Girl Chunhyang") or *Sugung-ga* ("The Song of the Underwater Palace"), end in this syllable.

In a nutshell, the title "Sacheon-ga" intertwines a localized reference to Brecht's drama with an allusion to the conventions of *pansori*. In the same vein, the production *Sacheon-ga* presents a dialogue between Brecht and *pansori*—live on stage. In the following, I will discuss in what kind of context, based on which conditions, and to what ends this happens. After providing a brief history of Brecht's reception in Korea, I will highlight several structural similarities between Brecht's concept of epic theater and the conventions of *pansori* that make a performative dialogue possible. Then I will analyze several scenes from *Sacheon-ga*, arguing that both Brecht's *Good Person* and the practice of *pansori* are transformed in the process of performance.

1. Brecht in Korea: "Brand New and Rather Old at the Same Time"

The history of Brecht's theatrical reception in South Korea is a rather short one.[8] It was as late as 1988 that the performance of a Brechtian play, *The Threepenny Opera*, for the first time grasped the attention of a larger public. The delayed reception of Brecht's plays was the result of a strict policy of anti-communism, the ideological base of the authoritarian regimes that had ruled the country with only short interruptions since the end of World War II. While censorship could not completely prevent access to Brecht's works, non-commercial performances at the Goethe Institute were rare and attracted only small numbers of germanophile Koreans and expatriots, which probably accounts for the fact that they could be staged in the first place.[9] Certainly not by chance, the relaxation of governmental intervention in the performing arts that made Brecht's official Korean debut possible occured in the wake of the 1988 Seoul Olympics, which retrospectively marked an important turning point in a slow process of democratization.[10]

By contrast, Brecht's theoretical writings had already been in circulation among Korean intellectuals since the 1970s, despite the official ban. On the one hand, scholars of German language and literature had access to his texts by reading the German original. Won-Yang RHIE, himself one of the protagonists of the fruitful academic discourse on Brecht in Korea (which produced an astonishing output of thirty MA-theses on Brecht in the 1980s alone), calls this a reception "under the counter."[11] On the other hand, Korean playwrights and stage directors got in touch with Brecht's concept of theater mainly via English translations and analyses of Brecht's works, as many of these practitioners studied in the United States.[12] "Through the backdoor" (Rhie) Brecht became a "role model for writers in the fight against the established social system."[13] On an aesthetic level, Brecht's theatrical theories furthermore provided an alternative to the prevailing "primitive realism" that progressive directors like LEE Youn-taek tried to overcome.[14]

What is specific to the reception of Brecht in Korea is not so much the "integration of certain Brechtian ideas and techniques into original, local dramatic creations," which Michael Bodden identifies as a major trend in productions of Brecht in Asia,¹⁵ but rather the appropriation of his theories in the absence of productions of his plays and, as a result, the division between theoretical and practical Brechtians. Commenting on the situation in the late 1980s when Brecht's plays finally became available for staging, Seok-Hee Choi poignantly characterizes Brecht in Korea as "brand new and rather old at the same time."¹⁶

The divided reception of Brecht's theories led to a likewise divided encounter with his plays. The academics, who often also acted as translators, were generally guardians of *Werktreue*, preferring truthfulness to the original text and more conventional ways of staging them. Borrowing a term used by James Brandon to categorize productions of Shakespeare in Asia, this can be called a "canonical" approach towards Brecht: one that tries to replicate a supposed original.¹⁷ For example, Eun-soo JANG stresses that the 1988 production of *Threepenny Opera* mentioned above¹⁸ "tried to stick as much as possible to the original text. With only a few exceptions all parts were reproduced in Korean. Weill's music, too, was played by the orchestra without much divergence."¹⁹

Most practitioners, however, skipped this phase of supposedly "necessary replication" and proceeded in "developing the potential of these dynamic encounters" between Brecht and Korean culture.²⁰ Using his plays as material, apt for deconstruction and re-contextualization, they engaged in an experimental process of "productive destruction."²¹ Since the 1990s, "intercultural" productions have prevailed, for example, OH Tae-suk's *Threepenny Opera* (1996, Mokhwa Repertory Company), a comment on recent post-dictatorial politics in Korea,²² or LEE Youn-taek's *Mother Courage* (2006, Street Theatre Troupe), a relocated "chronicle of the Korean War" (thus the slightly altered subheading) staged on the occasion of the 50th anniversary of Brecht's death.

While numerous Korean productions of Brecht include diverse methods, motives, or material borrowed from different kinds of Korean performing arts to evoke a sense of locality,²³ Lee Jaram's approach is of a more holistic sort, taking the mutual entanglement a step further: *Sacheon-ga* is, as far as I know, the first attempt to create an overall adaptation of a Brechtian play with the means offered by a single form of "traditional" Korean theater, in this case *pansori*.²⁴ By writing, staging, and performing a new song of *pansori* based on Brecht's *Good Person*, she enables a theatrical dialogue between the two theatrical "traditions."²⁵

2. Epic Theater and the Conventions of *Pansori*: Similar Means for Different Reasons

It was only a matter of time before a *pansori* singer would turn to Brecht. Although inspired by performing arts of Chinese and Japanese origin,

Brecht's concept of epic theater shares several structural similarities with "traditional" *pansori* practice.

First, *pansori* is epic storytelling, not representational drama. The story a *pansori*-performer recites does not follow a well-crafted plot. Based on constellations "borrowed from the pervasive library of folk literature,"[26] the songs of *pansori* combine material from very different sources, including fragments of local legends, popular folk tales, Shamanist narrative songs, Buddhist allegories, and classical Confucian literature. The characteristical succession of spoken and sung passages integrates songs of religious as well as mundane origin. Some of these interpolated songs, "well-formed structures with their own internal integrity"[27] such as the "Love Song" from *Chunhyang-ga*, have become stand-alone hits outside the context of a full-length *pansori* performance, not unlike the Brecht/Weill compositions "Mack the Knife" or "Alabama Song." The result is an eclectic, highly heterogeneous series of episodes.

Although this principle of montage may cause stylistic irregularities as well as problems on a narrative level, from simple plot holes to fundamental contradictions in character development,[28] "[t]he spectators are not bothered by these inconsistencies, because their attention is directed to the development of particular episodes."[29] Thus, as Brecht demands, "each scene [stands] for itself." Likewise, the "eyes [lie] on the course" of action, not so much on the outcome, as the general plotlines are usually well known among the informed audience.[30]

Second, *pansori* is non-illusionistic show-and-tell rather than naturalistic acting. The *pansori* performer is always caught between two stools: At one time, he is the narrator of a story, told in the third person and in past tense. Then he momentarily steps into the shoes of one character he just talked about, sometimes even entering into a dialogue with himself. For example, when presenting the grief of an old man over his recently deceased wife in a performance of *Simcheong-ga* ("The Song of the Girl Simcheong"), *pansori* performer CHOI Yeong-gil juxtaposes several perspectives on the man's mourning in a single scene that lasts only a few minutes.[31]

By repeatedly switching between re-enacting the characters' behaviour and describing their actions, the performer creates a tension, "for the narrator never quite eliminates himself and the character is never fully realized."[32] This "mediating role" (Pihl) is in line with Brecht's demands of a "New Technique of Acting," as the *pansori* performer "does not allow himself to become completely transformed...into the character he is [only temporarily] portraying."[33] As an epic "singer of tales," he rather "make[s] himself observed standing between the spectator and the event."[34] Fluctuating between recounting and displaying, he engages the audience with "a definite gest of showing"[35] that continuously draws the individual spectator's focus from the character portrayed to the actor portraying and vice versa.³⁶

Third, there is no fourth wall in *pansori*. In addition to his roles as narrator and part-time actor, the *pansori* performer also acts as a host to his audience. He regularly engages in short comments, sometimes even directly addressing individual spectators, on topics that are in no way related to the storyline, for example, when he talks about his physical exhaustion after two hours of continuous performance. This apparent role conflict stresses the social situation constituted by the performance, which goes well beyond the story delivered.³⁷ In sum: The *pansori* singer "is neither a narrator nor a character but a disclaiming performer engaged in personable and often humorous rapport with the audience."³⁸

In return, the listeners interact with the performer by calling out stylized calls of encouragement, participating in the rhythm of the performance and, by demonstrating their acquaintance with the "rules of the game," constituting themselves as an interacting "audience of experts."³⁹ By retaining the control over his own contributions, however, the individual listener does not become "a passive (suffering) part of the total work of art," which Brecht rejects.⁴⁰ He rather remains an active participant and co-creator of the theatrical event he takes part in. Although a *pansori* performance actualizes the "negotiation of multiple voices"⁴¹ inherent in the underlying tradition, the singularity of the singer's voice, through its various transformations from narrator to actor to host, results in a vocal authority that is not contested but rather confirmed by the audience's affirmative participation.

It has to be made clear, however, that *pansori* is not epic theater per se.⁴² The conventions used in traditional *pansori* practice today, as well as the canonical songs performed, are basically a product of the socio-political situation in the 19th century, the heyday of *pansori*. According to Marshall R. Pihl, *pansori* originated in the commercially motivated practices of itinerant entertainers and "developed...in response to the demands of audiences."⁴³ For example, the eclectic texts mentioned are the result of the heterogeneous audiences *pansori* singers had to cater to.⁴⁴

Historically speaking, the structural similarities between epic theater and the conventions of *pansori* are thus based on completely different intended effects: While *pansori* performers tried to evoke a joyful community among their specific audience,⁴⁵ Brecht's aim was to make the spectators individually "come to grips with things."⁴⁶ Despite these different intentions, however, it is the similarities between their practical approaches that make *pansori* a plausible and, as I will discuss in the following section, also a productive means for staging Brecht.

3. *Sacheon-ga* on Stage: Relocalization and "Pansorization"

Sacheon-ga follows more or less the episodic pattern provided by Brecht's original play, from the arrival of the gods to the final trial, including scenes in the Good Person's shop, the romantic encounter with her suicidal husband-to-be, and an arranged wedding that goes terribly wrong. However, both content and form of the *Good Person* have been significantly changed.

First, the setting has been relocated from Brecht's allegorical China to modern-day Korea. Besides the "Koreanization" of the characters' names, numerous details have been changed to relate to Korean realities. For example, using the money she received from the gods, Sun-deok (the Korean Shen Te) opens a *bunsikjip*, one of the cheap snack restaurants that can be found at virtually every corner in Seoul; she falls in love with Gyeon-sik (Yang Sun), a melancholy but charming wanna-be sommelier without money, when he is trying to drown himself in the Han river; after noticing her pregnancy, she continuously takes the disguise of her older cousin Jae-su (Shui Ta) and turns the small restaurant into a food factory that eventually becomes involved in politics, alluding to state-like conglomerates like Hyundai or Samsung as well as the economic activities of real-life politicians.

Second, the whole play has been reshaped in accordance with the conventions of *pansori*. Instead of being enacted by multiple actors, the story is mainly presented by a solo singer. Lee Jaram, a trained *pansori* performer, switches with ease between locations, characters, and situations using only the power of her voice and gestures. On a textual level stylistic elements like the frequent use of metaphoric language, allusions to literature, onomatopoeia, parodies of well-known *pansori*-songs as well as Korean pop music, and the integration of extensive epic catalogues of, for example, the various kinds of food offered in the restaurant further stress this *pansorization* of Brecht's play.

At the same time, *pansori* conventions have been modified to fit the demands of Brecht's play, most notably by the introduction of extra actors in certain scenes and several musicians that back up the single drummer. Furthermore, unlike in most *pansori* performances, Lee Jaram does not wear a colorful *hanbok* — quite literally the "national dress" of Korea — but a wine-red skirt and a black jacket, leaving her long wooden hair pins and the fan as the only references to the typical outfit of a *pansori* singer performing in a more "traditional" frame. In the following, I will try to clarify the characteristics and the effects of this two-fold transformation by focusing on the various depictions of the three gods.[47]

In the very first scene of *Sacheon-ga*, three actors (dressed in black pants and white shirts) who have been sitting among the audience, successively rise up, enter the stage, walk on perpendicular paths and, straight-faced, without saying a word, repeatedly stop to perform a series of mechanical movements: kneeling down, putting the hands on the ground, and jumping in the air with their feet. At this point it is not clear who these actors represent—or if they represent anything at all, for that matter. It is much later that they return in the roles of the three gods. Only in retrospect does it become clear that this opening scene establishes the recurring motive of monotonous repetition on part of the gods and at the same time, by presenting a warped gesture of submission, visualizes the formulaic principles on which the gods' idea of goodness is based.

The pantomime lasts only a few minutes. The lights turn off and on again. Then Lee Jaram enters the stage which she will not leave during the two-hour performance. She begins with a short song, designed to set the mood for the performance and to allow her to warm up her voice. She then introduces herself by singing the first line of "My Name is Yesora!," a pop song that gained her fame as a child star in the early 1980s and that still rings a bell with Korean audiences. Without interruption, she turns to the time and place that her version of Brecht's *Good Person* is set in, changing step by step from dry description ("in the Republic of Korea... during a hot summer...in a city called Sacheon") to more fancy imagery, combining current sayings with newly made-up colloquialisms ("in times of hunger-nurturing neoconservatism...times of discord and distrust... when closing one's eyes, one's nose will be cut off...taxi drivers turn into thieves, policemen into rapists...").[48]

Interwoven with this classical exposition,[49] Lee Jaram mentions "three nameless, suspicious fellows"—the three gods, of course—who, in search of a good person, walk from house to house. First, they arrive at the "Tower Palace," a luxurious high-rise apartment building boasting glass pillars and a carp pond in the entrance hall. After some struggles with the door bell, a hearty "Open, Sesame!" summons the tenant who asks the strangers to identify themselves.[50]

The gods' responses—all delivered by Lee Jaram—mark them distinctively as representatives of Christianity, Buddhism, and Confucianism, the three main religious cultures in contemporary South Korea: first a hymn-like melody ("To point out the corruption in this world, we have come here ourselves"); then, in a snarling voice, an incantation ("You must have accumulated a lot of wealth in your former lives, as you are living in abundance..."); and finally, more along the line of classical *pansori* singing, a take on the alleged virtues of Confucian patriarchism ("Honor the elders to cleanse yourself! If you serve us, there shall be only sons in this home for many generations!"). Despite their best efforts, the gods earn only laughter, both on part of the rich tenant and the audience.

Reduced to their slogans and stereotypical ways of chanting and praying, a Korean audience will certainly be familiar with these allusions, as the audible laughter indicates. The comical effect of the scene is maximized by the fact that Lee Jaram switches roles with virtuosity, a characteristic feature of *pansori* solo singing. The *pansori*-style presentation of the "Koreanized" gods from Brecht's play provides the laughing audience with a sense of collective self-affirmation, which is based not so much on "the communal heritage shared between performer and audience," as in "traditional" *pansori*,[51] but on a shared critical perception of contemporary realities in Korea.[52]

In the course of the performance, the "gods" also appear as characters on stage, depicted by the three actors, now wearing long white robes and props that identify them pars pro toto as the Christian-Buddhist-Confucian triumvirate described and enacted by Lee Jaram earlier.[53] Twice they return to the stage to make short (and rather uninspired) statements on being good and the bitter realities of love (for example, "If everyone were good, how great that would be," "Love is a sea of tears," "Love requires sacrifice," etcetera) while dancing and chanting to the music provided by an electric bass and a variety of percussion. Lee Jaram remains calm during these interludes that resemble mantra-like religious chants, sometimes also evoking triumphant Gospel songs. Detached from the world *Sacheon-ga* is set in, the world of people at the margins of society, these gods are both in different spheres and on a different stage.

It is only in the finale, the trial scene, that the three actors-as-gods and the *pansori* singer interact with each other for the first time. After various witnesses have testified in favor of Jae-su (Shui Ta) and the severe regime he imposes, the three actors appear on stage, asking for Sun-deok (Shen Te) to come out. Lee Jaram, who up until now has performed the whole trial scene by switching constantly between the narrator, the culprit Jae-su, and the different witnesses, appears at first more or less speechless. While the three gods make guesses about Sun-deok's fate, Lee Jaram (still in the role of Jae-su) seems to struggle with herself, finally breaking the news: "She went on a journey. She will be back shortly."

Quite relieved, the gods start singing their respective catchphrases ("Hallelujah!," "Holy Buddha!," "Long Live the Sons!"), then repeat "Do like good Sun-deok does" over and over again. In-between their chorus appearances, Lee Jaram, now representing the employees of Jae-su's factory or, more generally, the "voice of the people," brings up the material situation the gods ignore: "What about our wages? Our rightful claims?...Our unfair treatment? The injustice?" But in vain: The gods just keep repeating themselves.

More striking than what Lee Jaram sings about, however, is the fact that she *does* sing at all. By objecting, albeit in rhythm with the gods' chorus, she has broken one of the fundamental characteristics of *pansori*: the singularity of the singer's voice that is traditionally assured by the fact that there is no more than one person singing on stage. Brecht's trial scene, however, which implicates a separation between prosecutor and culprit, allows Lee Jaram to raise her voice, not only in a metaphorical but also in a material sense, against the gods and the "abstract concept of goodness" they represent and proclaim by mere repetition.[54]

This attempt of a dialogue is destined to fail, though: Finally, by crying out her disenchantment with the divine experiment, "There is nothing more I can do," Lee Jaram, once again in the role of the Good Person, regains the initiative and leads the play to the Brechtian open end.

In contrast, the dialogue between Brecht and *pansori* practice proves fruitful: On the one hand, the role-switching of the *pansori* singer brings out the contradictions inherent in the Brechtian characters quite effectively without retreating to over-acting. On the other hand, the confrontational finale of Brecht's *Good Person* forces the singer to take a stand. Lee's silence after more than an hour of almost continuous singing and acting, broken by a gesture of re-empowerment would not have been as drastic if performed without an active (though not re-active) counterpart. In other words: The singer's vocal authority needs to be broken first in order to be regained, which is impossible in "traditional" one-person *pansori*. The additional actors thus enhance the means of expressing resistance within a *pansori* context.

Conclusion: Between Communal Unity and Individual Alienation

In the early 1990s, as a result of the delayed reception of Brecht's plays on Korean stages, Seok-Hee Choi diagnosed a "superficial familiarity" with Brecht's works. She suggested that "Brecht should be 'alienated' to make a fruitful reception possible."[55] More recently, PARK Chan E. wondered whether *pansori*, "suppressed by its 'public' mission as a 'national tradition,'" could be "resuscitated to depict modern life beyond victimization and mourning, to tell stories of the people, places, and affairs of this world with humor as well as pathos."[56] The theatrical dialogue of *Sacheon-ga* is an answer to both of them: In an act of productive reception, it exploits the theatrical means of *pansori* to present new perspectives on *The Good Person of Szechwan* and, at the same time, actualizes the "traditional" repertoire with this contemporary "Song of Sezuan."[57]

What kind of possibilities does the productive reception of Brecht's *Good Person* in the framework of experimental *pansori* offer to prospective audiences? On the one hand, *Sacheon-ga* addresses issues that many Korean spectators can obviously relate to. Besides hypocrisy in the name of religion, these include political corruption, real-estate management, and popular discourses on female beauty, to name just a few. By relating directly to the audience, Lee Jaram creates moments of awareness that are emotionally intensified by the shared laughter of the spectators. In other scenes, whether of solitary lament or confrontational self-empowerment, the affective vocal style of the *pansori* singer appears to grasp the audience's attention even beyond the social critique implied in the lyrics.

In contrast to these situations of temporary unity, *Sacheon-ga* also confronts audiences of diverse aesthetic tastes and backgrounds with various unexpected experiences: For example, Brechtians might be irritated by the free adaptation of the original play, focusing on the changes that draw connections to the social realities in Korea. For well-versed *pansori* aficionados, the mere fact that a story from outside the canon is being told should provoke a different style of watching, listening, and participating. Theatergoers more accustomed to the catchy melodies of musicals will probably find the hoarse, sometimes breathtaking *pansori* voice most unfamiliar. By challenging established patterns of perception time and time again, *Sacheon-ga* puts the focus on the individual spectator's relation to Brecht as well as *pansori*.[58]

The interplay of communal experiences and moments of alienation, shared emotions and disappointed expectations puts not only contemporary Korean society, Brecht's anti-capitalist parable, and the means of "traditional" theater on trial but also the circumstances that determine each spectator's perceptions and reactions. In this sense *Sacheon-ga* remains true to Brecht's ultimate claim about the function of theater: "The human being is the object of the *inquiry*."[59]

Endnotes

1   Compare Michael Bodden, "Brecht in Asia: New Agendas, National Traditions, and Critical Consciousness," in Siegfried Mews, ed., *A Bertolt Brecht Reference Companion* (Westport/CT and London: Greenwood, 1997), pp. 379-397.
2   Performance, text and composition Lee Jaram, dir. Nam In-woo, dramaturgy Choe Ye-jeong, stage design Won Yeo-jeong, costume design Gang Jeong-hwa, Chongdong Theater, Seoul, 30 Nov. 2007. While *Sacheon-ga* has been subsequently shown in different venues, my analysis is based on a video recording of the 2007 version and a working script provided by Lee Jaram. When, for the sake of simplicity, I refer to the production as "Lee Jaram's *Sacheon-ga*," this is meant to underline Lee's fundamental engagement, not to degrade the contributions of the other people involved. With the exception of proper names with established transcriptions or translations, I render all Korean terms using the Revised Romanization. Korean names are given in the usual order, that is, family name followed by given name, with the exception of scholars adopting a different order when publishing abroad. To avoid confusion, I mark Korean family names with capitals on the first mention and in bibliographical references.
3   Quote from the call for papers of "Brecht in/and Asia," 13th Symposium of the

International Brecht Society, University of Hawai'i at Mānoa, May 2010. This essay is an expanded version of my presentation "The Good Person of Korea: Crosscultural Synergies and Challenges in Lee Jaram's *Sacheon-ga*."

4   Acknowledged as a "National Intangible Cultural Property" since 1964, *pansori* has been declared a "Masterpiece of the Oral and Intangible Heritage of Humanity" by the UNESCO in 2003. Compare Keith Howard, *Preserving Korean Music: Intangible Cultural Properties as Icons of Identity* (Aldershot and Burlington: Ashgate, 2006), pp. 60-67. I put "tradition" in quotation marks to stress the fact that, though based on inherited conventions, the respective performances are inevitably subject to transformative impulses, whether intended or not, of the new context they take place in. In this sense, performed "tradition" is always a re-creation. More specifically, the usual Korean term for "traditional Korean music," *gugak* (literally "national music"), not only carries political implications but its application to contemporary practices called "traditional" is also heavily disputed. Compare Hilary Finchum-Sung, "Performing the 'Traditional' in the South Korean Musical World," *Folklore Forum* 38.1 (2008): pp. 55-81.

5   Chan E. PARK, proponent of a creative actualization of *pansori* practice, notes that official *pansori* "indeed thrives much less on improvisation or new composition than on collective tradition and confirmation of its past." Chan E. Park, *Voices from the Straw Mat: Toward an Ethnography of Korean Story Singing* (Honolulu: University of Hawai'i Press, 2003), p. 15.

6   Korean translations or performances of Brecht's *Guter Mensch von Sezuan* usually feature the title *Sacheon-ui Seonin* ("The Virtuous Person of Sichuan," as in the first published translation by IM Han-sun, in Bertolt Brecht, *Huigokseon* [Selected Plays], [Seoul: Hanmadang, 1987]) or *Sechuang-ui Chak-han Yeoja* ("The Good-Hearted Woman of Sichuan," as in the translation by BAK Jun-yong published as a single volume [Seoul: Podowon, 1992]).

7   Not to be mistaken for a short musical stance, a song of *pansori* lasts for several hours and includes spoken passages as well as individual shorter songs.

8   In the following, the term "Korea" refers exclusively to the Republic of Korea (South Korea) because as far as I know there have been no productions of Brecht in the "communist" Democratic People's Republic (North Korea). In this paragraph, I draw mainly from three papers by Korean scholars of German language and literature: Won-Yang RHIE, "Bertolt Brecht in Korea. Einige Aspekte der Brecht-Rezeption in Zusammenhang mit der Entwicklung des koreanischen Theaters," *Beureohiteu-wa Hyeondae Yeongeuk* 5 (1998): pp. 127-152; Eun-Soo JANG, "Brecht heute auf der koreanischen Bühne," *Beureohiteu-wa Hyeondae Yeongeuk* 5 (1998): pp. 153-165 (*Beureohiteu-wa Hyeondae Yeongeuk* ["Brecht and Contemporary Theatre"] is the *Jahrbuch* of the Korean Brecht Society, the referenced papers can be downloaded at <brecht.german.or.kr/jungbo.net/Hwizard/contents/jahrbuecher/band5.htm>, 27 Sept. 2010); Seok-Hee CHOI, "Wie fremd ist Brecht in Korea?," in Yoshinori Shichiji, ed., *Begegnungen mit dem "Fremden." Grenzen–Traditionen–Vergleiche* (Akten des VIII. Internationalen Germanisten-Kongresses, Tokyo 1990), Vol. 6 (München: iudicium, 1991), pp. 375-381. Translations of German quotes are mine.

9   Rhie mentions student productions, supposedly in German, of *Der Gute Mensch von Sezuan* and *Die Kleinbürgerhochzeit* in the 1970s by the group Freie Bühne (compare Rhie, "Brecht in Korea," p. 132). According to Choi, these performances "did not receive any attention by the Korean public" (Choi, p. 376). The Goethe Institute promotes German language and literature abroad and, in the case of its Seoul branch, "offered its guests in times of deprivation an intellectual oasis where free discussions were possible and the writings of officially prohibited authors like Brecht could be read." (Won-Yang RHIE, "Über den Wandel der Rolle des Goethe-Instituts Korea. Einige Gedanken zum 40jährigen Bestehen," lecture held in 2008, available at <www.goethe.de/mmo/priv/4843612-STANDARD.pdf>, 27 Sept. 2010.)

10   "Demonstrations and other opposition resulted in the abolition of the Censorship Law of the Performance Ethics Committee. All dramatists and theatre companies

were freed from the threats and restrictions of the Committee, and relieved of the psychological anxiety and self-censorship they had gone through prior to a Committee review." Sang-cheol HAN, "The Korean Theatre of the 1980s: The Predominance of Socio-Political Drama," in Hyung-Ki KIM and Seon-Ok LIM, eds., *Sketching in Contemporary Korean Theatre* (Seoul: Korean Association of Theatre Critics, 2006), pp. 20-31, here p. 25.
11   Compare Rhie, "Brecht in Korea," pp. 131-132.
12   Compare ibid.
13   Yun-Cheol KIM, "The Influence of Western Drama on Contemporary Korean Theatre," in Hyung-Ki KIM and Seon-Ok LIM, eds., *Sketching in Contemporary Korean Theatre* (Seoul: Korean Association of Theatre Critics, 2006), pp. 41-49, here p. 48.
14   "Brecht and Korean Theatre," Lecture held at the Symposium of the Korean Society of German Studies, May 1998, quoted in RHIE, "Brecht in Korea," p. 146.
15   Bodden, p. 380.
16   Choi, p. 377.
17   Compare James R. Brandon, "Some Shakespeare(s) in Some Asia(s)," *Asian Studies Review* 20.3 (April 1997): pp. 1-27.
18   Ensemble Minjung, dir. JEONG Jin-su, Hoam Art Hall, Seoul. 10 Dec. 1988. After one week of performances, the production was revived the following spring.
19   Jang, "Brecht heute auf der koreanischen Bühne," p. 157.
20   Antony Tatlow, "The Context of Change in East Asian Theatre," in *The Brecht Yearbook* 14, John Fuegi et al., eds. (Hong Kong: International Brecht Society, 1989), pp. 9-10, here p. 10.
21   Jang, "Brecht heute auf der koreanischen Bühne," p. 162.
22   Compare ibid., pp. 157-156.
23   For example, KIM Suk-Man's *Story of the White Circle* (1999, Hakchon Ensemble), an adaptation of Brecht's *Caucasian Chalk Circle*, features a variety of "traditional" arts such as painting, fashion, and music: "Because the Koreans prefer 'Korean beef,' the play was given a Korean look." (Ibid., p. 159.)
24   For a discussion of other "new" *pansori* songs that deal, among others, with recent Korean history or the life of Jesus, compare Hae-kyung UM, "New P'ansori in Twenty-first-century Korea: Creative Dialectics of Tradition and Modernity," *Asian Theatre Journal* 25.1 (2008): pp. 24-57.
25   In this sense, *Sacheon-ga* fits Brandon's definition of "intercultural" productions (unlike many other productions regularly described as intercultural) in that "[l]ocal and foreign sources of authority coexist in performance, with neither authority subsuming, or erasing, the other." (Brandon, p. 18.)
26   Marshall R. Pihl, *The Korean Singer of Tales* (Cambridge: Harvard University Press, 1994), p. 69.
27   Pihl, p. 86.
28   Compare ibid., p. 85.
29   Woo Ok KIM, *P'ansori: An Indigenous Theater of Korea* (Dissertation New York University, 1980), p. 141.
30   Bertolt Brecht, "The Modern Theatre is the Epic Theatre (Notes to the opera *Aufstieg und Fall der Stadt Mahagonny)*" [1930], in John Willett, ed. and trans., *Brecht on Theatre: The Development of an Aesthetic* (London: Methuen, 1964), pp. 33-42, here p. 37.
31   He begins with a sorrowful outcry ("My wife Gwak-ssi has died..."), followed by a recount of the widower's actitivities ("Padding through the room...") illustrated with onomatopoeia ("deodeum, deodeum"), finally adding some reflecting comments by an external narrative instance ("Is this true? Is this a joke? Or is it real? What has happened?"). After describing the set up of the funeral ("A flag...as well as ornaments... are carried along, on both sides of the bier"), he shoulders his fan, evoking a coffin bearer carrying the dead body away. (Performance at the National Theater of Korea, 29 Sept. 2008, video recording provided by the National Theater.)
32   Pihl, p. 10.

33 Bertolt Brecht, "Short Description of a New Technique of Acting which Produces an Alienation Effect" [1951], in John Willett, ed. and trans., *Brecht on Theatre: The Development of an Aesthetic* (London: Methuen, 1964), pp. 136-147, here p. 137.
34 Bertolt Brecht, "Indirect Impact of the Epic Theatre (Extracts from Notes to *Die Mutter*)" [1933], in John Willett, ed. and trans., *Brecht on Theatre: The Development of an Aesthetic* (London: Methuen, 1964), pp. 57-62, here p. 58.
35 Brecht, "New Technique of Acting," p. 136.
36 In Erika Fischer-Lichte's terms, this technique provokes frequent perceptive shifts between the semiotic and the phenomenal body, leading to "a state of betwixt and between" on part of the audience, too. Compare Erika Fischer-Lichte, *The Transformative Power of Performance: A New Aesthetics*, Saskya Iris Jain, trans. (New York: Routledge, 2008), pp. 88-89.
37 Compare Fischer-Lichte, *The Transformative Power of Performance*, p. 170. For a musicologist's perspective on the social aspects of concerts, compare Christopher Small, *Musicking: The Meanings of Performing and Listening* (Middletown, Connecticut: Wesleyan University Press, 1998).
38 Park, p. 3.
39 I analyse these transformative processes in which both the performers and the audience establish a performative discourse on their own virtuosity in Jan Creutzenberg, "P'ansori als Performance: Stimmlichkeit, Interaktion und Zeitwahrnehmung in einer Aufführung von *Simch'ŏng-ga*," unpublished M.A. Thesis, Free University Berlin, 2010. On audience participation compare Yeonok JANG, "P'ansori Performance Style: Audience Responses and Singers' Perspectives," *British Journal of Ethnomusicology* 10.2 (2001): pp. 99-121.
40 Brecht, "The Modern Theatre is the Epic Theatre," p. 38.
41 Park, p. 21.
42 Compare Daihyun KIM, *P'ansori als Aufführungskunst* (Trier: Wissenschaftlicher Verlag, 1997; Dissertation University Bochum, 1995). I agree with Frank Episale who criticizes the "misguided attempt[s] to 'legitimize' the study of an unfamiliar form [of theater by recurring to Brecht]" in his presentation "Brecht (Not) in Asia: On the Mis-Application of Brechtian Ideas to Ta'ziyeh and other 'Traditional' Theatres," 13th International Brecht Society Symposium (see endnote 3).
43 Pihl, pp. 4-5.
44 "P'ansori was sung to any audience that would pay: fishermen or farmers in the markets, rich men at their banquets, or successful state examination candidates celebrating their good fortune. The kwangdae [= *pansori*-singer] had to be ready to satisfy many demands: they reflected the viewpoints of the lower classes, but they also had to be responsive to aristocratic tastes." (Pihl, p. 5.)
45 "[P]'ansori was born and developed as a musico-narrative entertainment in the free spirit of storytelling that allowed creative and flexible exchange between performer and audience." (Park, p. 235.)
46 Bertolt Brecht, "The Epic Theatre and its Difficulties" [1927], in John Willett, ed. and trans., *Brecht on Theatre: The Development of an Aesthetic* (London: Methuen, 1964), pp. 22-24, here p. 23. Of course Brecht was not against theatrical entertainment in general (thanks for this remark to Joerg Esleben), it had to be subordinate, however, to his political program. Furthermore, Brecht's aim "to divide rather than unify its audience" (Peter Brooker, "Key words in Brecht's theory and practice of theatre," in Peter Thomson and Glendyr Sacks, eds., *The Cambridge Companion to Brecht*, 2nd edition [New York: Cambridge University Press, 2006], pp. 209-224, here p. 213) is in sharp contrast to the efforts of pre-modern *pansori* singers to evoke a "communal spirit." (Park, p. 245.)
47 As my analysis is based on a video recording, my inferences to transformative processes in the perception of individual spectators have to remain speculative. They should be considered potential reactions rather than inevitable effects.
48 From a working script of the 2009 version of *Sacheon-ga*, kindly provided by Lee

Jaram. The quoted passages do not diverge from the 2007 version. All translations from Korean are mine.

49 The succession of warm-up song, self-introduction, description of place and time of the story mimicks the typical beginning of a "traditional" *pansori* performance.

50 The building's name is a clear reference to the Samsung Tower Palace, a luxury residential complex in Southern Seoul, famous for its automated service and security facilities. The Korean term used in *Sacheon-ga*, "Tapgol Paelliseu," combines the Sino-Korean word for "pagoda" or "tower" with an English loanword for "palace," paralleling the perceived juxtaposition of Western capitalism and Eastern tradition in contemporary Korea.

51 Park, p. 243.

52 Of course, laughter does not necessarily indicate mutual agreement. On the dynamics of laughter in theater performances, compare Jens Roselt, "Chips und Schiller. Über Lachgemeinschaften im zeitgenössischen Theater und ihre historischen Voraussetzungen," in Werner Röcke and Hans Rudolf Velten, eds., *Lachgemeinschaften. Kulturelle Inszenierungen und soziale Wirkungen von Gelächter im Mittelalter und in der Frühen Neuzeit* (Berlin: De Gruyter, 2005), pp. 225–244.

53 These props include a crucifix, a Buddhist bell and a *gat*, a horse-hair head reminiscent of neo-Confucian society in the pre-modern Choseon-era.

54 Christopher McCullough, "The Good Person of Szechwan," in Peter Thomson and Glendyr Sacks, eds., *The Cambridge Companion to Brecht*, 2nd edition (New York: Cambridge University Press, 2006), pp. 118-131, here p. 122.

55 Choi, p. 381.

56 Park, p. 275-276.

57 On the productive reception of Brechtian theater within the context of "traditional" theater compare Erika Fischer-Lichte *The Show and the Gaze of Theatre: A European Perspective*, Jo Riley, trans. (Iowa City: University of Iowa Press, 1997), pp. 150-157. Whether *Sacheon-ga* has the power to alter the vocabulary and repertoire of *pansori* on a larger scale or, on the other hand, will inspire new takes on Brecht that stress multi-perspective storytelling over, for example, prop-based anti-realism, remains to be seen.

58 How audiences abroad will react to this *Good Person from Korea*, and if Lee Jaram's "Brecht-Pansori" can give new impulses to the rampant *Brecht-Müdigkeit*, remains to be seen: After a guest performance at the International Theatre Festival "Kontakt" in Toruń, Poland (May 2010), where Lee received the "Best Actress Award," *Sacheon-ga* is scheduled to be shown in Los Angeles, Chicago, Washington D.C., and Paris.

59 Brecht, "The Modern Theatre is the Epic Theatre," p. 37.

Ein postkolonialer Brecht?

Marc Silberman

Gilt Brecht nach der postkolonialen Wende lediglich als ein weiterer "toter, weißer, männlicher Europäer," dessen Ruf in den epistemologischen Interessen der Ost/West- und Nord/Süd-Dichotomien verankert ist? Sind Brechts räumlich nach Asien versetzte Fantasien, nicht zu sprechen von den ethnisch gefärbten Fantasien eines Chicago oder Mahagonny, nichts anderes als postkolonialer Exotismus, eine nützliche Projektionsfläche, um die reduzierten Subjekte (und Subjektivitäten) der westlichen Macht zu verhandeln? Die kurze Antwort ist nein, aber ihre offensichtliche Eindeutigkeit verdeckt die Art und Weise, wie postkoloniale Theorie und Kritik die Perspektive verschieben und die kritischen und performativen Praktiken Brecht gegenüber komplizieren können. Eine "postkoloniale Annäherung" kann hilfreich sein, um folgende vier Fragestellungen zu klären und zu untersuchen: den biografischen Kontext von Brechts Exil-Erfahrung; Nachklänge kolonialer Fantasien in Brechts frühem Werk, in dem Figuren-Stimmen (durch Bauchrednerei) und -Gesichter (durch ethnische Verkleidung/Maskierung) kulturelle Stereotypen nachahmen; die Überlagerung von Epischem Theater und volkstümlichen Spielformen "marginalisierter" oder "peripherer" Gesellschaften in Ost-Asien und Afrika; und Brechts eingreifende Ästhetik als zukunftsorientierter Beitrag zur postkolonialen Moderne.

Has the postcolonial turn rendered Brecht as just another "dead, white, male European writer" whose reputation is anchored in the epistemological interests of the East/West and North/South divides? Are Brecht's imagined displacements to Asia, not to speak of his ethnically tinged fantasies of Chicago and Mahagonny, simply postcolonial exoticism, a convenient projection screen for negotiating the diminished subject(ivities) of Western power? The short answer is no, but its seeming transparency conceals the way that postcolonial theory and criticism can shift perspectives and complicate critical and performance practices vis-à-vis Brecht. A "postcolonial approach" will help clarify and test four issues: the biographical context of Brecht's forced diasporic experience; resonances of colonial fantasies in Brecht's early works where characters' voices (ventriloquism) and faces (ethnic drag) mimic cultural stereotypes; the overlap between Epic theater and popular presentational modes of "marginalized" or "peripheral" societies in East Asia and Africa; and Brecht's interventionist aesthetics as an ongoing contribution to postcolonial modernisms.

A Postcolonial Brecht?

Marc Silberman

Why the question mark in my title? The rise in intonation is not so much intended to express skepticism about whether there is such a thing as a postcolonial Brecht as to query the gains that another postal-theory can bring to those interested in Brechtian theater and thinking. I say "another postal-theory" because I have engaged in a similar inquiry in a not dissimilar context. Almost two decades ago, at the 8th International Brecht Society Symposium held in December 1991 in Augsburg, Germany, my presentation was called: "A Postmodernized Brecht?" There the paper title's final question mark was a response to the momentous changes and soaring expectations after the fall of the Berlin Wall and the implosion of communism: "A new world order, a new Brecht," so I began my paper then and continued:

> If Marx was right that being determines consciousness (and granted, many today would deny him all credibility), then could we not expect with the end of the Cold War a different Brecht waiting to be discovered behind traditional scholarship and theatre practice? Does an other Brecht exist beyond the ideological encrustations of the past? Who needs this other Brecht in a postindustrial, postmodern epoch with new social relations unencumbered by class struggle and hegemony?[1]

Notwithstanding the tongue-in-cheek naiveté conveyed by these questions, I did proceed to consider how Brecht might fit into a postmodern theoretical framework, concluding that – as a strategy of reading (or re-reading) – it opened up some new and challenging questions.

Here I will employ a similar approach, focusing not on Brecht's oeuvre, on his plays, novels, stories, poems, or even essays, but rather on our reading practices and how postcolonial theory might engage or clarify larger issues about Brechtian dramaturgy and thought in response to accelerating globalization. Thus, I will ask whether the postcolonial turn has rendered Brecht as just another "dead, white, male European writer," whose very reputation as a major representative of high modernism is anchored in the epistemological interests of the binary divides between East and West or North and South that postcolonial studies interrogate. Furthermore, I will raise the question whether postcolonial theory reveals that Brecht's imagined displacements to China, Japan, and India, not to speak of his ethnically tinged fantasies of migration to Chicago, Alabama, Alaska, and Mahagonny, are simply Eurocentric exoticism, where the body of the Other offers a convenient projection screen for negotiating the diminished subject(ivities) of Western power? The short and emphatic answer to these questions is no, but the answer's seeming transparency conceals the way that postcolonial theory can shift perspectives and potentially open up new questions to complicate both critical and performance practices vis-à-vis Brecht. Since the "postcolonial" signifies a position against imperialism and undoes Western hegemony by recognizing minority cultures as the global majority, it seems to overlap in important ways with issues of class and social violence that preoccupied Brecht. I will focus here on a "postcolonial approach" with the goal of testing issues generated by its critical potential: where does Brecht fit into colonial discourse? Did his own exile experience generate a diasporic consciousness? Why have Brechtian techniques been adapted by some (post)colonial or subaltern writers for "writing back?" And finally, can a Brechtian hermeneutics or dramaturgy serve the postcolonial goal of social and political change?

To begin with a few clarifications: postcolonial studies focus generally on the interactions between European nations and the societies they colonized in the modern period. The European empire is estimated to have controlled as much as 85 percent of the globe by the time of the First World War, having consolidated its control over several centuries.[2] Some have claimed that Germany's historically late entrance into colonial domination in the late nineteenth century and its quick exit after signing the Versailles Treaty in 1919 exempted it from the "postcolonial condition," but there is ample evidence from historical chronicles as well as from sources in the realm of scientific exploration, travel literature, and philosophical speculation that Germany indeed participated in Europe's violent imperial reach.[3] Postcolonialism was a critical concept first employed in the 1960s and 1970s to designate a period of decolonizations following the Second World War, and thus seemingly exempting Germany, but in the meantime it has accrued a much wider meaning that references interdisciplinary political, theoretical, and historical investigations grounded in the context of colonialism as well as contemporary globalization. Because decolonization entailed more than just a political transfer of power, postcolonial studies have addressed it as a multilayered process, including political imagination, modernization, the formation of new elites, and cultural transformation. In short, a postcolonial approach aims to introduce a new perspective that shifts the focus in the twentieth century from the impact of two world wars to the process of global decolonization.

Brecht is rarely mentioned in the context of postcolonial writers, and one could legitimately ask why he should be? In its originary meaning postcolonial writers were identified as those who wrote out of resistance to colonial regimes or in the context of colonial discourses that continued to shape cultures where revolutions had overthrown formal ties to colonial rulers. Nonetheless, Brecht's works – poems, plays, and prose

– are saturated with references to East Asia, the Middle East, India, American expansionism, Niggers and Negroes, the yellow peril, the brown-skinned, etcetera. While scholars have traced these references to the colonial fantasies of Rudyard Kipling and Karl May or to the drastic portrayals of capitalist practices in novels by Upton Sinclair and Frank Norris, they belong as well to larger metaphors of modernity and the urban jungle in which the Other often stands in for the complexity of capitalist society. Here Brecht intersects with postcolonial writing that explores the dynamics of power and hegemony. He recognized early on how knowledge about the world is generated under specific relations between the powerful and the powerless and then circulated repetitively to legitimate imperial interests. Set in colonial India, his play *Mann ist Mann* (A Man's a Man), written in various stages between 1918 and 1931, deconstructs mechanisms of control and subjugation by creating characters with voices and faces that mimic cultural stereotypes, using techniques that postcolonial criticism has codified as ventriloquism, mimicry, and ethnic drag.[4] Similarly, the play *Puntila und sein Knecht Matti* (Puntila and His Man Matti) is a comic send-up of the Hegelian master-slave dialectic, presenting a parable of subjugation under capitalist conditions that shows how categories assumed to be natural and immutable are in fact reversible. The learning play *Die Ausnahme und die Regel* (The Exception and the Rule), which became a favored Brecht play in the 1950s in decolonizing countries, also thematizes the master-slave constellation but stages demonstrably the possible answers to the question: Whose side are you on? These are among the very issues and concepts that postcolonial studies analyze and contest.

While Edward Said's 1978 book *Orientalism*, a founding text in postcolonial studies, treated primarily fantasies about the Middle East, its major contribution lies in the more general argument that an archive of Western knowledges and languages acquired the capacity to shape external realities as well as the subjectivities of those subjected to colonial discourses and colonial rule.[5] It is relevant to ask, therefore, whether Brecht's use of the exotic Other contributes to the material-discursive construct that shapes real and imagined existences or whether his "othering" – be it of race, class, or gender – engages and contests universalizing discourses, power structures, and social hierarchies. From the perspective of intellectual history Brecht emerged from the volatile context of the First World War and political revolution when modernization and secularization energized many European artists to seek alternatives to the mediocrity and social atomization they saw around them. The visions of renewal that characterized the historical avant-gardes found them turning to non-European sources for inspiration: to African "primitivism," or Asian "passivity," or Arab "sensuality." Yet Brecht distinguishes himself from German writers such as Hermann Hesse, Stefan Zweig, and Alfred Döblin, who also employ colonial tropes, by developing aesthetic forms and dramaturgical strategies that invoke a "postcolonial potential." Specifically he introduces figures like Galy Gay in *Mann ist Mann*, Kragler with his African trauma in *Trommeln in der Nacht* (Drums in the Night), Garga in *Dickicht der Städte* (The Jungle of the Cities), Shen Te in *Der gute Mensch von Sezuan* (The Good Person of Sezuan), Azdak in *Der kaukasische Kreidekreis* (The Caucasian Chalk Circle), just to mention the most obvious, all of them dramatic characters from the margins who sabotage hierarchies and complicate binaries. In this respect Brecht's plays offer a level of reflection about cultural difference and the reproduction of conventional discourse that is part and parcel of postcolonial critique. His overdrawn parodies aim at colonialism and capitalism as world systems; his irony undermines the widespread romantic images of the colonial Other; and it is no coincidence that Brecht's alter ego, Herr Keuner, who became a tool of self-reflection in anecdotes, stories, and journal notes throughout his life, has a subversive potential that Brecht considered to be the source of Asian wisdom.

Brecht was compelled to leave Germany by the rise of the Nazis: his journey began in 1933, taking him briefly to Prague, Vienna, Zurich, and Paris before he settled in Denmark to wait out the threat. But the Nazi threat came closer and lasted longer than he expected, forcing him to flee to Sweden for a year in 1939, and then Finland for another year, until he and his family were able to enter the United States via the Soviet Union, settling in Los Angeles for the next six years. Not until 1949 did he resettle in East Berlin after a hiatus in Switzerland for eighteen months. The anxiety of fleeing from the Nazis inflected Brecht's textual engagements with power structures and social hierarchies. The fifteen year migrancy put everything in his life into flux, providing an existential encounter that became his own personal "alienation effect," so to speak, and bringing him into proximity with the diasporic writing of postcolonial subjects. Adaptation to changes and dislocations guided his productivity during these exile years. The shifting political, social, and personal conditions of survival confirmed and extended techniques of the Epic theater he had been developing prior to 1933 but also engendered new strategies to construct different forms of knowledge and ways of seeing the world. In the exile writings I pinpoint in particular a transformation in the relationship between the playwright and the audience, between the writer and the reader in his prose, between the speaker and the addressee of his poems. In the pre-exilic writings Brecht assumed an emphatically modernist position aimed against the preservation of tradition and cultural legacy. Both sides of the writer-recipient relationship were assumed to be quintessential anonymous city dwellers, wearing the mask of the alienated subject in the crowd who must learn to exist in a faceless collective. Brecht's irony and humor gave way to anger and injunctions in the diasporic experience of personal migrancy and political defeat. In other words, geographical distance and uncertainty changed the relation to the audience, reader, addressee, and the faceless collective became the affirming community of solidarity against his enemies.

As instructive as these contextual moments and biographical experiences may be, Brecht's most significant contribution to postcolonial studies is to be sought in his dramaturgy and hermeneutics, yet here the dynamics of mutual exchange should not be ignored. Brecht took global popular forms and transformed them not only into staging techniques but also into a *Weltanschauung* committed to undermining oppressive social structures. We find him borrowing the gestural quality of Chinese opera and the abstract structure of Japanese Nôh theater or adapting story-telling elements and forms of clownery from peasant cultures. No wonder, then, that from the perspective of audience spectatorship scholars and playwrights have identified common traits shared by Brecht's Epic theater and the popular theater of "marginalized" or "peripheral" societies in East Asia, South Asia, and Africa.[6] These traits include a presentational approach to acting, the presence of a narrator, the integration of song and music, the use of masks, and most striking, the interaction between stage and audience like that at a sports event. For some this compatibility with indigenous cultures has been considered Brechtianism *avant la lettre*, for others it offers a transformative model of "talking back" or "writing oneself into history," where colonial subjects and subalterns are integrated into the theatrical event as reasoning, thinking agents who can effect social change.

From another perspective Brecht's anti-Aristotelian, non-mimetic theater offers a counter model to hegemonic European forms of psychological realism and emotional identification. Especially his non-naturalistic plays with their elements of farce, satire, and agitprop can combine well with indigenous performance traditions or rituals, offering a more explicit engagement with the audience than conventional "elite" European theater. Of course, Brecht is not the sole influence to be mentioned here; one thinks of Antonin Artaud and Jerzy Grotowski on the one hand, who experimented with different anti-illusionist techniques of engaging the audience through shock and emotional stress, or on the other hand of a mediator of Brecht like Augusto Boal who developed a theater of pedagogy for impoverished communities to rehearse social change. In any case it is important to keep in mind that the transfers back and forth have not been seamless. Brecht's borrowings occurred through his own contemporary lens and for his own needs, while his commitment to "complex seeing" was a reaction to the historical context of European modernist theater and is not always adaptable to other vernacular or postcolonial modernisms. Moreover, the arena for postcolonial literatures and critiques is often situated ironically in urban theaters and universities, mediated by a class of well-educated people who themselves are implicated in the postcolonial structures of power. This is a conundrum that Brecht knew all too well at the end of his life.

Finally, postcolonial theory launched a vigorous epistemological critique of Western knowledge as Eurocentric and universalizing, that is, as a mode of rationalist thinking that excludes other traditions and ways of knowing. This is a reasonable position vis-à-vis the nineteenth-century tradition of hermeneutics that consistently conflates foreignness or otherness with error, uncertainty, or absence of understanding and thus regards it as a problem to be solved or a deviation to be disciplined. But while knowledge and reason may be forms of domination, they are not always complicit in Western hegemony; they can also critique and lead to changes in hegemonic relations by developing strategies of resistance and narratives of emancipation. Indeed Brecht was less interested in understanding or examining the Other than in transforming and measuring what it does to us as readers and spectators. This is the foundation of his interventionist aesthetics, which is both a collective experience and a cognitive *process*. His texts open up spaces to imagine self or group identity from a marginal perspective, that of the oppressed and the "kleine Leute" fleeing their impossible circumstances. The empirical evidence for the global adaptation of Brecht's plays, theater practices, and model of thinking politically about culture suggests that he continues to be a central player wherever new, postcolonial modernisms are forming.

Is this, then, the titular postcolonial Brecht, defining a space where epistemology, ethics, and politics come together in the service of emancipation? Maybe, but what have we gained from this brief excursion into postcolonial theory? First, decolonizing Brecht, or better, decolonizing scholarship on Brecht means analyzing anew from *our* contemporary time the historical context in which he generated his practices and critical thinking. He lived in the belly of the dragon but also developed modes of representing and performing the hierarchical power relations between the center and the periphery. Second, postcolonial studies recognize and hone in on the mutually constitutive process of "othering" and its essentially binary structure, dovetailing with Brecht's dynamic, dialectical presentation of difference, insisting that relationships of inequality cannot be reduced to binary antagonisms. Third and finally, postcolonialism, like postmodernism, does not mark a temporal end but rather is the sign of an emancipatory project; that is, it announces a goal yet to be achieved, the dismantling of imperial and Eurocentric domination in a globalizing world. In fact, I myself am not convinced that we are advancing fast enough in this project. From my perch in the USA, it looks as if the show is largely still being run by the same old players. A postcolonial Brecht can sharpen our understanding of how knowledge was produced and disseminated in the past and thereby help focus attention on the emerging world where new (post)colonies are being formed with new forms of expression.

Endnotes

1 "A Postmodernized Brecht?" *Theatre Journal* 45.1 (March 1993): pp. 1-19.
2 There is an enormous literature on postcolonial studies; a critical overview can be found in Ania Loomba, *Colonialism/Postcolonialism* (London and New York: Routledge, 1998); also Neil Lazarus, ed., *Cambridge Companion to Postcolonial Literary Studies* (New York: Cambridge University Press, 2004), offers diverse points of entry.
3 On the German colonialist discourse, see Sara Friedrichsmeyer, Sara Lennox, and Susanne Zantop, eds., *The Imperialist Imagination: German Colonialism and Its Legacy* (Ann Arbor: University of Michigan Press, 1998), as well as the more recent and critical study by Monika Albrecht, *"Europa ist nicht die Welt:" (Post)Kolonialismus in Literatur und Geschichte der westdeutschen Nachkriegszeit* (Bielefeld: Aisthesis, 2008), especially chapter 2 on "(Post-) Koloniale Amnesie? Zur deutschen Kolonialismusdiskussion," pp. 34-138.
4 Katrin Sieg discusses oppositional strategies developed by Brecht that underpin postcolonial, feminist, anti-racist theater in Katrin Sieg, *Ethnic Drag: Performing Race, Nation, Sexuality in West Germany* (Ann Arbor: University of Michigan Press, 2002), pp. 14-15.
5 Edward Said, *Orientalism* (New York: Vintage, 1978).
6 On Indian theater, see Virginie Magnat, "Girish Karnad's *Hayavadana*: A Postcolonial Reading," *genre* 22 (2001): pp. 169-77 (discussing Karnad's rediscovery through a Brechtian lens of nonrealistic forms in traditional Indian Yakshagana), and Aparna Dharwadker, "John Gay, Bertolt Brecht, and Postcolonial Antinationalisms," *Modern Drama* 38.1 (Spring 1995): pp. 4-21; on East Asian theater, see Antony Tatlow, *Shakespeare, Brecht, and the Intercultural Sign* (Durham: Duke University Press, 2001), especially chapter 2 on "Intercultural Signs: Textual Anthropology," pp. 31-79, for a discussion of the construction of the subject and gestural acting; on African theater, see Amine Khalid and Marvin A. Carlson, "Al-halqa in Arabic Theatre: An Emerging Site of Hybridity," *Theatre Journal* 60.1 (March 2008): pp. 71-85 (discussing Brecht as spiritual father for the story-telling techniques and epic structure in plays by several North African dramatists), and Brian Crow, "African Brecht," *Research in African Literatures* 40.2 (Summer 2009): pp. 190-207.

Imperialer Brecht? Bertolt Brechts komplexe Darstellung des Imperialen in *Mann ist Mann*

Melissa Dinsman

Dieser Aufsatz analysiert die in Bertolt Brechts *Mann ist Mann* zentrale Interaktion mit dem asiatischen "Anderen." Es besteht innerhalb des Stücks eine im Marxismus verwurzelte Dichotomie zwischen Humanismus und dem, was Samir Amin als "Eurozentrismus" beschreibt. Während es jedoch Brechts Absicht in *Mann ist Mann* ist, den ökonomisch ungerechten status quo des Imperialismus herauszufordern, schleicht sich trotzdem eine andere Hierarchie in sein Werk ein, nämlich die des Okzidents gegenüber dem Orient. Dieser Aufsatz bietet eine genaue Textanalyse der kolonialen Situation in *Mann ist Mann* mit besonderem Augenmerk auf die asiatisch/irische Beziehung. Meine Absicht ist es, einen Dialog zwischen den Werken Edward Saids, Amins und Brechts herzustellen mit dem Zweck zu zeigen, dass das Stück unbewusst die imperiale Haltung bestätigt, und zwar gerade beim Versuch, ihr entgegenzutreten.

This essay analyzes the central interaction with the Asian "Other" as found in Bertolt Brecht's *Mann ist Mann*. Within this play there exists a dichotomy rooted in Marxist thought between humanism and what Samir Amin describes as "Eurocentrism." Yet while Brecht's intention in *Mann ist Mann* is to challenge the inequitable economic status quo found in imperialism, another hierarchy nevertheless creeps into his work: Occident versus Orient. This essay provides a close reading of the colonial situation as presented in *Mann ist Mann*, paying particular attention to the Asian/Irish relationship. My intent in this essay is to create a dialogue between the works of Edward Said, Amin and Brecht, with the purpose of showing how this play unknowingly reconfirms the imperial position, even in its attempt to counter it.

Imperial Brecht? Bertolt Brecht's Complex Portrayal of Empire in *Mann ist Mann*

Melissa Dinsman

> "They cannot represent themselves; they must be represented."
> —Karl Marx[1]

In *Mann ist Mann*, Bertolt Brecht's 1926 work set in India, Brecht attempts to represent and give power to the "Other," namely the Irish porter Galy Gay. Yet while doing so, Brecht also simultaneously slips into the language, and at times action, of the patriarchal West, thereby usurping the very power he is attempting to give. This, according to Edward Said, is understandable, for the individual is no match against his cultural upbringing. As he states in *Orientalism*:

> For if it is true that no production of knowledge in the human sciences can ever ignore or disclaim its author's involvement as a human subject in his own circumstances, then it must also be true that for a European or American studying the Orient there can be no disclaiming the main circumstances of *his* actuality: that he comes up against the Orient as a European or American first, as an individual second.[2]

My objective in this essay is not to deny or minimize the power and success of Brecht's work. Nor is it to suggest that Brecht's position on Empire and colonized peoples is simplistic. Instead, it is my intent to create a dialogue between the core works of Said and Samir Amin on the one hand and Brecht's *Mann ist Mann* on the other, thereby highlighting the means by which this play unknowingly reconfirms the imperial position, even in its attempt to counter it. Before we can continue with a discussion of Brecht's texts, however, it is necessary to have an understanding of Orientalism and Eurocentrism and how these theories relate to Marxism. It is also imperative that we gain an understanding of Marx's—and to a certain extent Friedrich Engels'—position on imperialism and its complicated relationship to the proletarian revolution.

I. Understanding the "Isms:" Orientalism, Eurocentrism and Marxism

According to Said's seminal work *Orientalism*, the Orient is to a large extent a place of the European imagination, "a place of romance, exotic beings, haunting memories and landscapes, remarkable experiences."[3] From this, "Orientalism" develops as the academic discipline "by which the Orient was (and is) approached systematically, as a topic of learning, discovery, and practice;" however, Said also uses the term "to designate the collection of dreams, images, and vocabularies available to anyone who has tried to talk about what lies east of the dividing line."[4] From this definition it is already possible to understand how any Western writer, including Brecht, even in an attempt to counter an imperial capitalist power, would become "Orientalist," for the vocabulary available to him is the result of centuries of studies and imaginings of the East done by the West. It is not, however, Said's objective to claim that Orientalism is, in its entirety, a Western invention. Nor is it his intention to claim that "Orientalism is evil, or sloppy, or uniformly the same in the work of each Orientalist."[5] What Said wants us to understand is that Orientalism carries with it the weight of imperialism, as the height of this nineteenth-century discipline corresponds to the height of imperial power; for Said is correct when he states, "The Orient is not only adjacent to Europe; it is also the place of Europe's greatest and richest and oldest colonies, the source of its civilizations and languages, its cultural contestant, and one of its deepest and most recurring images of the Other."[6] Yet, one may ask how it is that I can take *Orientalism*, a text that focuses upon British, French and American Orientalisms, and transfer it to Brecht, a German writer. In *Orientalism*, Said draws attention to the fact that Germany, along with numerous other European countries, partakes in Orientalism. In fact he mentions the work of Goethe and Schlegel as being particularly Orientalist. This is a position that Todd Kontje takes up in his work *German Orientalisms*. In this critical text, Kontje traces German participation in Orientalism back to the First Crusade and questions Said's exclusive link between Orientalism and empire. Kontje challenges Said's suggestion that Orientalism in Germany was performed to a lesser degree than in Britain and France due to the country's lack of colonial power until the late 1800s. Instead, he argues,

> By participating in the intellectual project of Orientalism, Germans sought to overcome their sense of cultural and political subordination to other European powers, suggesting that although they had neither nation nor empire, they nevertheless belonged to modern European civilization.[7]

Yet claiming its Europeanness was not the sole goal of German Orientalism. As Kontje states, "German writers oscillated between identifying their country with the rest of Europe against the Orient and allying themselves with selected parts of the East against the West," in which "the absence of empire becomes a source of moral strength and national pride."[8] This oscillation is key in understanding Germany's complicated literary history when it comes to Orientalism. For as Kontje posits, it is this vacillation, "between a compensatory Eurocentrism and an anti-Western, anti-Semitic Indo-Germanicism" that makes the Germans, as he calls it, "doubly damned:"

> in the first instance they turn belatedness into an excuse for self-righteousness even as they participate in the intellectual project of

European Orientalism and look forward to a day when they, too, can claim their place in the sun; the second lays the groundwork for a theory of Germanic racial superiority that led to Hitler and the Holocaust.[9]

It is thus by way of Kontje that we come to our second "-ism." Through a specific "Othering" of the Orient, an essentialist claim to Europeanness emerges. Europe becomes that to which the Orient is compared; it becomes the center of religion and morality (Christianity) and culture (Greek ancestry). Eurocentrism, as Amin states, "present[s] itself as universalist, for it claims that imitation of the Western model by all people is the only solution to the challenges of our time."[10]

The question thus becomes, is Marxism, with its endeavor to counter the West's capitalist hegemony and its attempt to provide representation for the Other, Eurocentric? For Amin and Said, Marxism is a peculiar case, one that is filled with contradiction. As Amin notes,

> Marxism is constituted as part of a contradictory movement that is at once the continuation of the philosophy of the Enlightenment and a break with this philosophy. To its credit, it successfully demystifies the fundamental economism of the dominant ideology, to such an extent that after Marx it is no longer possible to think the way people did before him. But Marxism encounters limits that it always finds difficult to surmount: It inherits a certain evolutionist perspective that prevents it from tearing down the Eurocentric veil of the bourgeois evolutionism against which it revolts.[11]

It is the latter part of this statement that is significant for our purposes, for it displays Marxism's evolutionary base (in which socialism is the stage following capitalism) that keeps it from breaking free of its Eurocentrism. For Marx, the Asiatic mode of production needed to be overcome; it was an economic path resulting in a dead end.[12] Instead, Marx's historical materialism privileged the European means of production, with the understanding that capitalism was the means by which socialism would be reached. This Eurocentric position, however, is not surprising. As Amin rightly states, the circumstances of the nineteenth century created a social movement that yielded Marxism. Thus it is understandable that Marxism (along with other nineteenth century movements) did not call "into question the capitalist and European content that it transmitted. Europe was the model for everything, and the idea of calling into question its civilizing mission could only seem preposterous."[13] For Said, the contradiction emerges in the contrast between Marx's privileging of the western economic system and his humanitarian concern for the East:

> Karl Marx identified the notion of an Asiatic economic system in his 1853 analyses of British rule in India, and then put beside that immediately the human depredation introduced into this system by English colonial interference, rapacity, and outright cruelty. In article after article he returned with increasing conviction to the idea that even in destroying Asia, Britain was making possible there a real social revolution. Marx's style pushes us right up against the difficulty of reconciling our natural repugnance as fellow creatures to the sufferings of Orientals while their society is being violently transformed with the historical necessity of these transformations.[14]

The above complication added by Marx to Eurocentric and Orientalist thought can be found both throughout the articles he wrote as a journalist for the *New York Daily Tribune* (*NYDT*) during his time in London and in the letters he exchanged with Engels. It is by way of these articles and letters, specifically the ones concerning India and Ireland, that we can gain an understanding of just how Marx could simultaneously decry imperialism as western brutality and praise it as necessary for an egalitarian future (this will be especially relevant for the upcoming discussion of *Mann ist Mann*).

In "The British Rule in India," written June 10, 1853 for the *NYDT*, the juxtaposition of humanism and Eurocentrism is apparent.[15] Here Marx seems to be sympathizing with the plight of the colonized Indians when he states, "There cannot, however, remain any doubt but that the misery inflicted by the British on Hindostan is of an essentially different and infinitely more intensive kind than all Hindostan had to suffer before." Yet the source of this sympathy quickly becomes evident, as the suspected humanism is substituted for economic frustration:

> All the civil wars, invasions, revolutions, conquests, famines, strangely complex, rapid, and destructive as the successive action in Hindostan may appear, did not go deeper than its surface. England has broken down the entire framework of Indian society, without any symptoms of reconstitution yet appearing.[16]

Therefore, if Marx has an issue with British rule in India it is not that it inflicts suffering upon the native inhabitants but, rather, that it stifles economic growth. Without "reconstitution" of economic stability via capitalism, India cannot move on to the next economic stage. Thus Marx later states, in the very same essay,

> England, it is true, in causing a social revolution in Hindostan, was actuated only by the vilest interests, and was stupid in her manner of enforcing them. But that is not the question. The

question is, can mankind fulfil its destiny without a fundamental revolution in the social state of Asia?[17]

Here, we are again faced with a striking contradiction in Marx's thinking. England is depicted both as the oppressor who uses "vile" and "stupid" means to obtain her selfish imperial desires, but she is also the catalyst for "revolutionizing" the Asian state. Marx's humanity and his Orientalism are thus simultaneously employed.

This duality in Marx returns again in "The Future Results of British Rule in India:"

> What we call [India's] history, is but the history of the successive intruders who founded their empires on the passive basis of that unresisting and unchanging society. The question, therefore, is not whether the English had a right to conquer India, but whether we are to prefer India conquered by the Turk, by the Persian, by the Russian, to India conquered by the Briton.[18]

Here India becomes not only a *tabula rasa* that requires colonization to mold it into a progressive shape, but Britain is positioned as the best possible colonizer. For Marx, England alone had the ability to both destroy the old Asiatic mode of production and provide the foundation for a Western society in India; yet the language he uses to privilege Britain is filled with Eurocentric discourse. As he states, "The British were the first conquerors *superior*, and therefore, *inaccessible* to Hindoo civilization."[19]

Marx, however, was not alone in his contradictory position on India. In a letter sent September 12, 1882, Engels states: "Once Europe is reorganised, and North America, that will furnish such colossal power and such an example that the *semi-civilised* countries will follow in their wake of their own accord. Economic needs alone will be responsible for this."[20] Thus even when writing in support of India as a nation with the ability to change or "progress" economically, she remains child-like; India is only "semi-civilised" in comparison to Europe and North America. All of this is not to say that Marx and Engels were staunch supporters of empire; rather, the intention here is to point out that Marx and company had a troubling position on imperialism due to their economic focus. Moreover, this position was firmly rooted in Eurocentric thought. Even critics of Said's reading of Marx, such as Pranav Jani, who finds that Marx — in the wake of the Indian Revolt of 1857 — had changed his position on British imperialism and saw instead the "colonized Indians as agents in their own history, who, as in the classic model of the bourgeois-proletarian relation, needed to struggle *against* the colonizers to win their liberation,"[21] still do not find fault in the Eurocentrism of Marxism in and of itself. For it is the unrecognized and inherent European (or Western) focus of Marxist thought, one that relies on an Orientalist understanding of the East, that provides Marxism with its complexity and contradiction with regards to empire.

Yet India was not the only imperial concern for Marx and Engels. In a telling statement on the situation of India, Marx also makes a very poignant comparison:

> Hindostan is an Italy of Asiatic dimensions, the Himalayas for the Alps, the Plains of Bengal for the Plains of Lombardy, the Deccan for the Apennines, and the Isle of Ceylon for the Island of Sicily. The same rich variety in the products of the soil, and the same dismemberment in the political configuration...Yet, in a social point of view, Hindostan is not the Italy, but the Ireland of the East.[22]

Thus India is compared to Ireland, a nation whose colonial status, although still under some debate today, was considered settled by Marx and Engels. Strikingly, the same dichotomy between humanitarian concerns and Eurocentric stereotypes plagues these discussions as well.[23] It is therefore not surprising that in an 1856 letter to Marx, Engels, after his return from Ireland, writes:

> Gendarmes, priests, lawyers, bureaucrats, squires in pleasing profusion and a total absence of any and every industry, so that it would be difficult to understand what all these parasitic growths found to live on if the misery of the peasants did not supply the other half of the picture...Ireland may be regarded as the first English colony and as one which because of its proximity is still governed exactly in the old way, and here one can already observe that the so-called liberty of English citizens is based on the oppression of the colonies.[24]

Again, as we saw above in Marx's "The British Rule in India," it is the economic situation that is the true disappointment for Engels, for it was thought that the situation in Ireland would be a catalyst for a proletarian revolution in England.[25] It is also interesting to note the similarity in discourse used to describe the Irish; they, like the Indians, are depicted as child-like and irrational: "With the Irish, feeling and passion predominate; reason must bow before them. Their sinuous, excitable nature prevents reflection and quiet, preserving activity from reaching development—such a nation is utterly unfit for manufacture as now conducted."[26] Thus Ireland, like India, is not yet ready for the revolution; she too is "semi-civilised" and is reliant upon Europe and America for leadership. It would seem that even in his sympathy for the Irish and their plight, Engels emphasizes the supposed weaknesses of Irish culture, thereby marking them as Other. The connection that Marx and Engels suggest between India and Ireland, accentuated by the similar rhetoric used to describe both colonized nations, becomes extremely significant when turning to the work of Brecht, specifically *Mann ist Mann*. Set in India with an Irish porter, Galy Gay, as the main character, *Mann ist Mann* is entrenched in empire. Yet, with its main focus being the issue of identity in a capitalist world, questions of empire become simplified, and the Orientalist undercurrent that challenges Brecht's humanism is ignored. Thus the next section of this essay will discuss Brecht's complex and often troubling presentation of empire in *Mann ist Mann*, connecting issues of identity not only to capitalism but also to the very nature of being colonized.

II. Mann ist Mann and the "Stage Irishman"

Mann ist Mann is a text entrenched in the complications of the imperial system. With its exotic setting, the play proudly shows its Rudyard Kipling influences. According to James K. Lyon, numerous elements from the elephant and drinking soldiers to exotic names such as "Punjab," "Peschawur," "Rankerdan," and "Calcutta" are echoes of Kipling.[27] Even more specifically, however, Lyon connects segments of plot from *Mann ist Mann* to Kipling's "Soldiers Three" and "The Incarnation of Krishna Mulvaney."[28] Another scholar who draws a connection between Brecht and Kipling is Jack Dunman. During a talk given in November 1966, Dunman praises Kipling's ability to transcend "a good many prejudices and stock responses, because [he] was interested first in the humanity of his characters; colour, race, language and class were only secondary."[29] It is this humanism that Dunman also locates in Brecht. Other critics, however, are quick to mention Brecht's own Eurocentrism in pulling from Kipling and thereby adopting problematic aspects of the latter's work. As Lion Feuchtwanger states, in a very early review of *Mann ist Mann*, "The superficial circumstances of the plot are fantasy; the city of Kilkoa in which the action takes place is something invented in every respect by someone from Augsburg; the soldiers have been borrowed in a completely childlike way from Kipling."[30] Yet even Feuchtwanger's issue with the play concerns Brecht's own borrowings as inauthentic; nothing is said of Kipling's own portrayal. For Said, who spends a considerable amount of time discussing Kipling's *Kim* in his text *Culture and Imperialism*, the issue with Kipling is that he is "in a sense blinded by his own insights about India, confusing the realities that he saw with such color and ingenuity, with the notion that they were permanent and essential."[31] This critique of Kipling, however, is not meant to devalue the writings of the author. On the contrary, Said's goal is simply to point out the complexities of empire and its unconscious effects on our cultural awareness. It is important to remember that "*Kim* [like numerous other texts by Kipling] is a work of great aesthetic merit; it cannot be dismissed simply as the racist imaginings of one disturbed and ultra-reactionary imperialist."[32]

Thus even in his critical depictions of the British in India, Kipling is immersed in the language and images from an Orientalist discourse. With an understanding of Kipling's complicated position concerning empire, albeit a cursory one, it is easier to comprehend how these contradictions find their way into Brecht's work. Include Brecht's interest in Marx, and a Eurocentric depiction of the East seems almost inevitable. Even Brecht was aware of his own Orientalist leanings. After viewing the film *Gunga Din*, based on a short story by Kipling, Brecht comments on the inaccurate depiction of the Indians, and how he simultaneously noticed this discrepancy and ignored it:

> Ich selber war gerührt und beifällig gestimmt und lachte an den richtigen Stellen. Und das, obwohl ich die ganze Zeit wusste, dass da etwas nicht stimmte, dass die Inder keine primitiven, kulturlosen Menschen sind, sondern eine uralte, großartige Kultur haben, und dass dieser Gunga Din auch ganz anders beurteilt werden konnte, zum Beispiel als ein Verräter an seinem Volk. Ich war gerührt und belustigt, weil die ganz falsche Darstellung künstlerisch gelungen und mit einem großen Einsatz von Talent und Geschick unternommen war.[33]

It is the quality of the art that allows Brecht to look beyond the Eurocentrism of the West. It is this same quality that allows many readers to do the same with Brecht. While he is careful not to present the colonized Indians in *Mann ist Mann* as "primitive" or "uncultured," Brecht's portrayal of Galy Gay's moldable identity can be understood as Orientalist, especially when one considers Ireland's peculiar relationship to empire.

Mann ist Mann is the story of Galy Gay, an Irishman in India who leaves his home to buy a fish and is slowly coerced (or manipulated) into becoming a soldier in the British army. Of the soldiers we are introduced to, Galy Gay is the only one given a nationality; Uria Shelley, Jesse Mahoney, Polly Baker and Jeraiah Jip may suggest specific nationality by name, but they are characterized only as "Vier Soldaten einer Maschinengewehrabteilung der britischen Armee in Indien."[34] Thus before the play even begins we are presented with a complicated colonial process. We have British soldiers in India and we have an Irish porter, who coming from a colonized nation is co-opted into the army, a frequent occurrence historically. Galy Gay begins what can only be described as a journey towards identity, by expressing what one imagines as the typical sentiment of the colonized. He has no desire to partake in the military actions of the British, and states that the soldiers are "die schlimmsten Menschen auf der Welt."[35] Yet, within a few pages, this staunch declaration is forgotten, as the man who by his own right claims that he "kann...allerdings nicht nein sagen" forgets the purchase of the fish and starts his transformation into a soldier.[36]

As the play progresses, Galy Gay's lack of a fixed identity is quickly made evident. Known by the objects he possesses, Galy Gay moves through multiple identities, all of which are brought about by his inability to say "no." Thus the man looking for a fish becomes a soldier once he puts on a uniform, only to be transformed into an elephant owner when given one to sell. Following the reading of his own eulogy, Galy Gay becomes Jeraiah Jip, before he is ultimately identified as the successful soldier, "der die Bergfestung Sir el Dchowr gefällt hat."[37] Although it is possible to read these transformations in numerous ways central to Marxist thought, such as man's inability to maintain his own individuality in a capitalist society due to mass production, or man's dependence on materialism to provide identity, one can also read these transformations as central to the way in which a colonized subject is identified, for the colonized cannot afford an individual identity. (This is also found in the work of the Irish Revivalist playwright J. M. Synge, who has the deceased Michael in *Riders to the Sea* identified not by his body, but rather by the stitching in his stocking.[38]) However, it is not only that Galy Gay (the colonized subject) is identified *through* commodities, but also that he *becomes* a commodity himself: "Ja, ein Mann ist wie der andere. Mann ist Mann," so much so that Brecht suggests that man too can be constructed like an automobile: "ein Mensch wie ein Auto ummontiert."[39] This confusion between man and commodity certainly plays a part in empire, as was suggested in section I. For the imperial West, man (labor) was considered a commodity, just like the goods he or she produced.

Yet what the above confusion between man and commodity also suggests is the colonized subject's complacency with empire. At no point does Galy Gay struggle against the molding of his identity. In fact, at certain moments Galy Gay's character seems almost a stereotype of the easily duped colonized. Take for example the crafty plot set forth by the British soldiers to convince Galy Gay that he is Jeraiah Jip, and that the person who was Galy Gay has committed treason by selling an elephant belonging to the British army and was therefore justifiably shot. These soldiers' cunning is so acute that they are able to persuade Galy Gay to give his own eulogy.[40] Although an excellent moment of gestus in terms of Brecht's epic theater, this is also, to a certain extent, a stereotypical image of the "semi-civilised" stage-Irishman who needs the British for advancement. It is also a moment in the text when Galy Gay's commodity status reaches an all-time high, as he becomes purely "useable" by the British soldiers. Moreover, we return again to the idea that an individual identity is too dear for the colonized. It would seem that an identity (Galy Gay, the Irish porter who thinks soldiers "die schlimmsten Menschen auf der Welt") results only in death in the imperial realm. Thus towards the end of *Mann ist Mann*, Galy Gay is no longer interested in who he is, or even in his own name, for a name does not provide practical worth: "Ein Name ist etwas Unsicheres: darauf kannst du nicht bauen."[41] His name only gains significance in terms of the collective (that is, the British military). Once Galy Gay realizes that it is only through the collective that individuality can be obtained, that what is important is "Nicht, was *ein* Mann will, sondern was *alle* wollen," is he able to say that he knows the value of his name: "ich weiss, was ein Name wert ist."[42] Of course, his name now is no longer Galy Gay. Instead, he has become Jeraiah Jip, the man who forced Sir el Dchowr (the mountain fortress) to collapse and has cleared the way for the British troops to continue their colonizing march through India.

While this ending is certainly striking from a Marxist perspective, it achieves a new and troubling level of complexity when one considers the position Ireland held as a colony. While early postcolonial critics, as seen in *The Empire Writes Back*, were uncomfortable classifying Ireland as a colony, due to "their subsequent complicity in the British imperial enterprise,"[43] postcolonial criticism surrounding Ireland has since boomed. As shown above, Ireland was regarded by Engels as "the first English colony" and has even been associated by Kipling with the East: "By every test that I know, the Irish are Oriental."[44] Thus even those with questionable records on imperialism recognize the Irish as a subject of it.[45] Yet understanding Ireland as a colonized country does not remove the complications of its position within the Empire. Due to Ireland's close proximity to the "center" (that is, England) as well as to Europe, Ireland was given certain "benefits" not granted to other colonized countries.[46] Such benefits include some of the first nationalized schools and the ability to work as civil servants in other colonized countries. As Liam Kennedy states,

> members of the Irish gentry and middle classes participated willingly in the administration of the imperial system world-wide. Thousands of Irish officers and soldiers manned its defences. Ireland, in effect, was a junior partner in the vast exploitative enterprise known as the British Empire.[47]

Thus, Ireland, in many respects, can be considered England's "right-hand man" when it came to colonization. The Irish, in fact, served in the English army for many of its conquests in Africa and India.

Understanding this aspect of Ireland's colonial history, Galy Gay's usurpation into the British forces takes on an added layer of complexity. Galy Gay is no longer only the victim of imperialism, as seen through his manipulation into the British army; instead he becomes part of the means by which India is colonized. Read through the lens of Marx, as discussed in the first section, Galy Gay could be interpreted as the hero of the story, permitting the continued economic progress of India by allowing capitalism to flourish. It is Galy Gay that successfully penetrates and destroys the old Asiatic mode of production as represented by the mountain fortress; thus without the help of the Irish, the next phase of historical materialism could not be reached in India. It is significant that at no time in *Mann ist Mann* is the Indian way of life considered feasible for the future. Instead, it is depicted solely as something to be destroyed, an obstacle to overcome. This is certainly evident in the imagery associated with the fortress, but there is also a parallel moment in the beginning of the play, in which the four soldiers loot and somewhat destroy a Tibetan pagoda. It should be noted, however, that the temple's destruction is not complete, for it would seem that in order for historical materialism to progress, the help of the Irish Galy Gay is needed.

This Eurocentric undercurrent within the text does not diminish the value of the play that Brecht has put forth. On the contrary, it only makes *Mann ist Mann* more interesting, as it unconsciously discusses the relationship Marxism has to imperialism, displaying how this social and economic theory privileges Europeanness even when critiquing it. As readers and delighters of Brecht's work, we often look past the Orientalist and Eurocentric elements in his texts, just as Brecht looked beyond the Eurocentric depiction of the film *Gunga Din*. Yet these elements should not be overlooked, for they add a richness and complexity to Brecht's work that by no means takes away from his achievement. On the contrary, these complications when it comes to empire and the Other show how involved Brecht was with his time. I am certainly not suggesting that the undercurrent of Eurocentrism in Brecht's work should be celebrated, but rather that Brecht, like Marx and Kipling before him, is, as Said states with regards to *Kim*, "in a sense blinded by his own insights about India [and Ireland], confusing the realities that he saw with such color and ingenuity, with the notion that they were permanent and essential."[48]

As has been shown, the work of Brecht oscillates between challenging hierarchical relationships and reconfirming (some of) them as well. Yet it is important to note that Brecht's work, unlike that of Kipling's, has been largely celebrated by the developing world and its theater. According to Frederic Jameson, Brecht's dramas have had an impressive impact on the West and the East, on First as well as Third World countries:

For bourgeois publics, fasting on a diet of theatrical minimalism, there had to be something Shakespearian about the lavish costumes and settings, and the texts which ranged across the entire world repertory (from Noh to Molière, from Shakespeare himself to Beckett, if not the epics of Chinese romance and the Chicago gangster saga). It was not hard for him to become, for a time, "the greatest playwright in the world." For the Third World, finally, the peasant aspects of Brecht's theatre, which made plenty of room for Chaplinesque buffoonery, mime, dance, and all kinds of pre-realistic and pre-bourgeois stagecraft and performance, secured for

Brecht the historical position of a catalyst and an enabling model in the emergence of many "non-Western" theatres from Brazil to Turkey, from the Philippines to Africa.[49]

Thus, according to Jameson, it would appear that Brecht's performances contain within them elements to be appreciated by every type of audience, be it the Western enjoyment of the exotic settings or the interest of the colonized in the occasional slapstick routine, a reminder of the "pre-realistic and pre-bourgeois stagecraft."

As has been discussed throughout this paper, *Mann ist Mann* is a powerful play in terms of Marxist thought. It deals with the issues of identity as they emerged in the growing industrial world. Yet with the influence of Marx and Kipling hanging over him, Brecht also includes within his work elements of Eurocentrism and Orientalism associated with the very capitalist and bourgeois empire that he is critiquing. Identity's mutability, as seen in *Mann ist Mann*, is thus transformed from a non-essential element of humanity to a quality that is too dear for the colonized to afford. Additionally, while Brecht can be said to give a voice to the Other, by way of Galy Gay, he is also simultaneously usurping this voice, by way of the conniving British Army. Like Kipling's and Marx's leanings before him, Brecht's Western influences are not intentionally placed within his texts. Instead, the Eurocentrism found in the playwright's work very much results from the fact that he is so firmly rooted in twentieth-century European culture. All of this is not to suggest that the significance of Brecht's plays and their revolutionary elements are diminished by this strain of Eurocentrism, for this has already been disproved by Brecht's success in the formerly colonized world. Rather, the undercurrent of an Orientalist discourse and specifically European positioning, as found in *Mann ist Mann*, serves only to add complication to Brecht's already intricate works.

Endnotes

1 Karl Marx, "The Eighteenth Brumaire of Louis Bonaparte," in Robert C. Tucker, ed., *The Marx-Engels Reader*, 2nd ed. (New York and London: W.W. Norton, 1978), pp. 594-617, here p. 608.
2 Edward Said, *Orientalism* (New York: Vintage, 1979), p. 11.
3 Ibid., p. 1.
4 Ibid., p. 73.
5 Ibid., p. 341.
6 Ibid., p. 1.
7 Todd Kontje, *German Orientalisms* (Ann Arbor: University of Michigan Press, 2004), p. 5.
8 Ibid., pp. 3, 6.

9   Ibid., p. 8.
10 Samir Amin, *Eurocentrism*, Russel Moore, trans. (New York: Monthly Review, 1989), p. vii.
11 Ibid., p. 77.
12 The Asiatic mode of production was a term used by Marx and Engels to refer to a distinct form of social relations that characterized pre-capitalist Asian societies and differentiated them from the Occident. Marx and Engels were critical of this mode of production because of the large role of the central state, which led to a despotic regime, along with the lack of private property, which prevented the transformation to more "advanced" forms of social and economic relations. The various stages of economic development as understood by Marx can be located in a variety of notes found in Karl Marx, *Pre-Capitalist Economic Formations*, Jack Cohen, trans. (New York: International Publishers, 1989).
13 Amin, *Eurocentrism*, p.126.
14 Said, *Orientalism*, p. 153.
15 By 1853, Marx had already written ten articles on India for the *NYDT* and would write thirty-one more concerning the 1857 insurrection. See: Pranav Jani, "Karl Marx, Eurocentrism, and the 1857 Revolt in British India," in Crystal Bartolovich and Neil Lazarus, eds., *Marxism, Modernity and Postcolonial Studies* (Cambridge: Cambridge University Press, 2002), p. 82.
16 Karl Marx and Frederick Engels, *Collected Works*, Vol. 12 (New York: International Publishers, 1975), p. 126.
17 Ibid., p. 132.
18 Ibid., p.217.
19 Ibid., p. 218 (my emphasis). One reason for Marx's privileging of England was due to the fact that England was at the most advanced stage in the progression of historical materialism, as it was the first country to experience the industrial revolution.
20 Karl Marx and Frederick Engels, *Selected Correspondence 1846-1895*, Dona Torr, trans. (Westport: Greenwood Press, 1975), p. 399 (my emphasis).
21 Jani, "Karl Marx, Eurocentrism, and the 1857 Revolt in British India," pp. 81-97, here p. 83.
22 Marx and Engels, *Collected Works*, p. 125.
23 The further impact of this dichotomy with regards to the peculiarity of the Irish colonial situation will be discussed in the following section.
24 Marx and Engels, *Selected Correspondence*, p. 93.
25 According to Marx, the Irish question was of the utmost significance to the English worker, and what was needed in Ireland was a) self-government, b) an agrarian revolution, and c) protective tariffs against England, which the Union had removed. In a letter from Marx to Engels, sent November 30, 1867, Marx states with regards to the Irish situation: "The next question is, what shall *we* advise the *English* workers? In my opinion they must make the *repeal of the Union*...into an article of their *pronunziamento*. This is the only *legal* and therefore possible form of Irish emancipation which can be admitted in the programme of an *English* party." See: Marx and Engels, *Selected Correspondence*, p. 229.
26 Karl Marx and Frederick Engels, *Ireland and the Irish Question* (New York: International Publishers, 1972), p. 42.
27 James K. Lyon, "Kipling's 'Soldiers Three' and Brecht's *A Man's a Man*," in Siegfried Mews and Herbert Knust, eds., *Essays on Brecht: Theater and Politics* (Chapel Hill: University of North Carolina Press, 1974), pp. 99-113, here p. 108.
28 Lyon claims that Brecht started reading the works of Kipling extensively from 1916 onwards, and provides proof of Kipling's influence in both "Kipling's 'Soldiers Three' and Brecht's *A Man's a Man*" and James K. Lyon, *Bertolt Brecht and Rudyard Kipling: A Marxist's Imperialist Mentor* (The Hague: de Gruyter Mouton, 1975).
29 Jack Dunman, "Kipling and the Modern World," *The Kipling Journal* 170 (1969): pp. 5-10, here p. 8.

30 Lion Feuchtwanger, "Bertolt Brecht Presented to the British," in Anton Kaes, Martin Jay and Edward Dimendberg, eds., *The Weimar Republic Sourcebook* (Berkeley: University of California Press, 1994), pp. 540-541, here p. 541.
31 Edward Said, *Culture and Imperialism* (New York: Vintage, 1993), p. 162.
32 Ibid., p. 150.
33 Bertolt Brecht, *Bertolt Brecht Werke: Große kommentierte Berliner und Frankfurter Ausgabe*, Vol. 22.1, eds. Werner Hecht, Jan Knopf, Werner Mittenzwei and Klaus-Detlef Müller (Frankfurt/Main: Suhrkamp Verlag, 1993), p. 592.
34 Bertolt Brecht, *Mann ist Mann* (Frankfurt/Main: Suhrkamp Verlag, 1982), p. 160.
35 Ibid., p. 167.
36 Ibid., p. 169.
37 Ibid., p. 222.
38 An added connection between the work of Brecht and Synge can be seen in Brecht's 1937 adaptation of *Riders to the Sea*, entitled *Señora Carrar's Rifles*. See: J. M. Synge, *Riders to the Sea, The Complete Plays of John M. Synge* (New York: Vintage Books, 1935) and Bertolt Brecht, *Señora Carrar's Rifles, Brecht Collected Plays: Four* (London: Methuen World Classics, 2001).
39 Brecht, *Mann ist Mann*, pp. 187, 190.
40 Ibid., p. 210.
41 Ibid., p. 216.
42 Ibid., pp. 219, 221.
43 Bill Ashcroft, Gareth Griffiths and Helen Tiffin, *The Empire Writes Back: Theory and Practice in Post-colonial Literatures* (London and New York: Routledge, 1989), p. 33.
44 Quoted in: Deepika Bahri, *Native Intelligence: Aesthetics, Politics, and Postcolonial Literature* (Minneapolis: University of Minnesota Press, 2003), p. 61.
45 Kipling also plays with the complexities of the Irish situation in *Kim*, as pointed out by Said: "That Kim himself is both an Irish outcast boy and later an essential player in the British Secret Service Great Game suggests Kipling's uncanny understanding of the workings and managing control of societies." See: Said, *Culture and Imperialism*, p. 141. From this description, it is again possible to see the connection between the work of Kipling and that of Brecht.
46 I am using the term "benefit" in the loosest possible sense, for while the Irish were granted certain perks due to their skin color and proximity to England, they were still a colonized country. As Said states, "the imperial relationship is there in all cases. Irish people can never be English any more than Cambodians or Algerians can be French." A hierarchy exists "whether or not the latter [the colonized] is white." See: Said, *Culture and Imperialism*, p. 228.
47 Quoted in: Bahri, *Native Intelligence*, p. 64. It should be noted, however, that those Irish who participated in Empire were often part of the Anglo-Irish community and not the native Catholic community. Deepika Bahri gives a very balanced reading of the issues surrounding Irish post-coloniality in *Native Intelligence*.
48 Said, *Culture and Imperialism*, p. 162.
49 Frederic Jameson, *Brecht and Method* (London and New York: Verso, 1998), p. 18.

Der "Herr des Südmeers" und seine "Maori-Frau:" Die Rolle der Tahiti-Metapher in Brechts Frühwerk

Gudrun Tabbert-Jones

Die Südsee hatte seit langem die Phantasie zivilisationsmüder Europäer beflügelt. Tahiti war für viele zum Inbegriff eines "natürlichen," paradiesischen Lebens auf einer zivilisationsfernen Insel geworden, eine Alternative zur modernen Welt. Brechts Verwendung des Tahiti-Motivs in Briefen und Werken aus den frühen zwanziger Jahren muss im Kontext dieses Naturdiskurses betrachtet werden. Von besonderer Bedeutung ist das Tahiti-Motiv in *Im Dickicht der Städte*. Am Anfang des Stückes flüchtet sich Garga in den Traum von einem besseren Leben auf Tahiti, um die harte Realität vergessen zu können. Am Ende des Stückes verabschiedet er diesen Traum als lächerliches Hirngespinst. Im Laufe der Handlung hat eine Verwandlung stattgefunden. Aus dem Idealisten Garga ist ein Realist, ein harter Großstadtmensch geworden, ein Prozess, der sich anhand seiner von Episode zu Episode wandelnden Einstellung zu Tahiti verfolgen lässt. Spätere Äußerungen Brechts zum Thema Tahiti bestätigen seine Ablehnung exotischer Alternativen. Nicht Flucht nach Tahiti, in die Natur, sondern eine den modernen großstädtischen Lebensverhältnissen gemäße Haltung schlägt er vor. Der vorliegende Beitrag untersucht die Funktion des Tahiti-Motivs in dem Stück *Im Dickicht der Städte* unter Berücksichtigung von Briefen, Kommentaren, sowie des ersten Stückes *Baal*, in dem noch nicht Tahiti, sondern die Natur als Alternative zu zivilisiertem Leben kritisch hinterfragt wird.

The Southern Pacific had captured the imagination of many young Europeans for quite some time. Tahiti represented paradise to them, an alternative to Western civilization. Brecht's use of the Tahiti metaphor in his letters and works from that period has to be placed in the context of this discourse. In his play *In the Jungle of the Cities* the Tahiti motif plays an important role. At the beginning of the play, Garga, one of the central characters, dreams of a better life in Tahiti to help him forget reality. At the end he rejects that dream as a juvenile aberration. As the plot evolves, Garga undergoes a transformation from an idealist into a hardcore realist, a city dweller. The manner in which his opinion about Tahiti changes from episode to episode illustrates the different stages of his transformation. To get a sense of Brecht's own views of Tahiti and his view of man's relationship with nature in general it is helpful to take Brecht's notes, letters, the poem "Tahiti," as well as his first play *Baal* into account.

The "Lord of the South See" and His "Maori Woman:" The Function of the Tahiti Metaphor in Brecht's Early Works

Gudrun Tabbert-Jones

The South Sea has had a long appeal to the imagination of Europeans, and Brecht was no exception. "Der Herr des Südmeers an den Herrn des Nordmeers," this is how Brecht begins a letter to Arnold Bronnen, in 1922.[1] He calls Marianne Zoff his "Maori woman."[2] He refers to his attic room as his island, "meine Insel,"[3] his "Kral."[4] Tahiti in particular seemed to have captured his imagination. Reflecting on his troubled courtship with Marianne he writes: "Ich will vielleicht Tahiti nicht aufgeben,"[5] and after the birth of their daughter: "Der Vater ist ein Genie, das Kind liegt in frischer Wäsche, Tahiti ist eine schöne Gegend."[6] These and other references reflect what Brecht calls "meine Neigung zu exotischen Dingen."[7] Brecht's fascination with Tahiti is easily explained. He had read Paul Gauguin's letters and his autobiographical novel *Noa Noa*.[8] In a letter to Marianne Zoff he reflects on his own situation and compares it to that of Gauguin whose letters he just read:

> Ich habe mich wieder ganz in mein Augsburger Zimmer unter dem Dach verkrochen, komme nur wegen der Mahlzeiten herunter und arbeite doch nichts, obwohl es noch dazu regnet. Soviel ich kann, schlafe ich und oft denke ich darüber nach, dass es viel zu leicht ist zu leben — obwohl ich dieser Tage die Briefe Gauguins gelesen habe, die aus der Südsee (in der Wildnis, in der Natur scheint man nur von Geld zu träumen!!!).[9]

"Hidden away" in his island retreat, his attic room, frustrated and depressed about not being able to produce, Brecht draws comparisons between himself and Gauguin, who had moved to Tahiti and idealized the easy life on an island untouched by the ills of civilization. His colorful depictions of happy natives were on display in many European museums and were widely admired. Gauguin's Tahiti conjured up notions of paradise and captured the imagination of many young Europeans, and some of them actually left Europe in search of a better place to live. Tahiti became a magic word. Departure fever was in the air. The remote islands in the Pacific Ocean seemed to be an alternative to Western civilization. *Zivilisationsflucht* was considered a solution to *Zivilisationsmüdigkeit*. Brecht's interest in Tahiti has to be understood in that context. However, it was not the geographical place but the wide-spread notions about Tahiti that intrigued him. He used it as a metaphor to describe longing for inner distance: "Tahiti bedeutet für den jungen Brecht die (nicht genauer lokalisierte) Ferne, in die er sich sehnt."[10] But the Tahiti metaphor also describes a mental disposition, attitudes, and modes of behavior that fall outside the social norms, very much depending upon the context in which Brecht uses it. When he refers to himself as the "Herr der Südsee" he means it in a positive sense. When he refers to Marianne as his "Maori woman" he means her exotic looks as well as her eccentric life-style. Depending on the state of his rocky relationship with Marianne, the image may have positive or negative implications. In spite of his fascination with exotic things and Tahiti in particular, Brecht never mentions anywhere that he actually wanted to visit the islands. He had both feet firmly on the Swabian ground.

Brecht viewed Gauguin's writings as a resource. Another important source from which he drew was the poetry by Arthur Rimbaud, whose view of civilization was similar to that of Gauguin. He too had turned his back on civilized society and, in his poems, idealized the "natural" life, outside the social norms. Brecht frequently uses quotes from Rimbaud to describe anti-social forms of behavior and attitudes. Gauguin's Tahiti and Rimbaud's poetry had *Materialwert* for Brecht. The images he borrowed from these sources became part of his new metaphorical vocabulary. Brecht describes his new language as "thinking in pictures." In 1929, he writes: "Es gibt keine Sprache, die jeder versteht. Es gibt kein Geschoss, das ins Ziel trifft...[Ich] denke in Bildern."[11] Although fascinated by Gauguin and Rimbaud and the lives they had led, Brecht had no intention to follow their example. He had no desire to give up his sheltered existence, his "Augsburger Zimmer unter dem Dach," his island, to which he could retreat, a place that allowed him to isolate himself from the outside world and concentrate on his work, yet from which he could emerge at any time during the day and enjoy regular meals and "room service," a luxury few other artists had. Brecht never made it a secret that he needed a comfortable environment in order to be able to write. He needed a place that would make it possible for him to gain mental distance from the world outside, where he could take off for flights into fantasy. This was his island, the equivalent to Gauguin's Tahiti.

Tahiti was also a favorite topic among his close circle of friends. In a poem entitled "Tahiti" (1921) Brecht describes an enjoyable evening, drinking and smoking with friends, on a "Rosshaarkanapee" which seems to be moving. They imagine it to be a ship taking off with them to Tahiti:

> Der Schnaps ist in die Toiletten geflossen
> Die rosa Jalousien herab
> Der Tabak geraucht, das Leben genossen
> Wir segelten nach Tahiti ab.
>
> Wir fuhren auf einem Rosshaarkanapee[12]

In the following stanzas, Brecht describes a voyage through different time zones, across the equator, and on to Cape of "Good Horn," Java, and eventually into the wild blue yonder, toward the "Nordpassatwind." Strange things occur en route. Gedde, presumably a girlfriend, gives birth to a phantom, part human, part seagull, illustrating the absurdity of this fantasy. In an earlier version, the last line of the first verse read: "Wir segelten nach Alaska ab."[13] Alaska and Tahiti are interchangeable, they serve as metaphors to describe a longing for distance, but for Brecht that meant inner distance, a change of perspective, not a real trip to Tahiti.

Rather than traveling to exotic places, Brecht uses exotic places and images to experiment with ideas and topics that reflected the *Zeitgeist* of that period. Tahiti as an alternative to Western civilized life was the subject of many conversations among intellectuals and artists. Some of them traveled to exotic lands, others chose the bohemian way of life. Brecht experimented with these ideas, on paper and in the company of friends. Getting drunk in a comfortable setting and fantasizing about an imaginary voyage or roaming around in the "Lechwiesen" at night, singing songs that were considered "obscene," upsetting the upright citizens of Augsburg, was their version of a vagabond life, their way of revolting against bourgeois discipline and values.

In spite of these experiments with anti-bourgeois life-styles, Brecht was quite conventional in his work habits. He adhered to a strict work schedule and felt guilty and depressed when he looked at empty pages at night. In his diary and letters, he frequently mentions laziness and his efforts to overcome it: "Ich habe ein schlechtes Gewissen, dass ich so faul bin,"[14] and: "Gegen meine Faulheit und Schwäche will ich vorgehen."[15] He defines laziness as a resistance to change. Gauguin's Tahiti seemed to be the "ideal" place to succumb to one's "natural" tendencies of trying to feel comfortable and content. In that sense, the Tahiti metaphor was negatively charged. The idea that Tahiti and what it represented might hinder rather than foster creativity occurred to him early on. In 1921 he writes: "Darum wollen wir alles gut machen, dass wir, wenn wir in Tahiti sitzen, sagen können: Es war alles gut, aber Tahiti hindert uns, es gut zu machen, meine Lieben."[16] Tahiti—associated with eternal summer, sun, natural wilderness, and a total freedom of restrictions of any kind— symbolizes temptations that could lead away from the ambitious goals Brecht had set for himself. In a letter to Hans Otto Münsterer (1918), he complains about summer: "Arbeiten kann man wenig, wenn der Sommer so verflucht schön ist."[17] It is a continuous battle for him to keep those temptations at bay. In a letter to Marianne Zoff (1921), we read: "Ich habe also den Kampf gegen den Sommer aufgenommen, der ein elender Rest ist. Habe das Zimmer frisch tapeziert, Lektüre geholt, Schädelweh bekämpft…"[18] Taking on domestic chores, inside, not outside his room, is the best way of battling summer. Working in an enclosed space, in a room, is preferable to any space outside no matter how enticing it may be.

In a story entitled "Herr Keuner und die Natur," Herr Keuner is asked to step outside to enjoy nature: "Warum fahren Sie, wenn Sie Bäume sehen wollen, nicht einfach manchmal ins Freie?" He replies, "Ich habe gesagt, ich möchte sie sehen aus dem Hause tretend" and adds, "[o]hne Arbeit in der Natur weilend, gerät man leicht in einen krankhaften Zustand, etwas wie Fieber befällt einen."[19] Similarly, in a fictitious conversation entitled "Gespräch über die Südsee" (1930), an editor encourages a writer to sail to the "Südsee." At the end of their long conversation about all the advantages and disadvantages of such a voyage, the writer concludes that Tahiti would be far too boring and monotonous, and definitely not a place for him: "Die Südsee ist mir auf Jahre hinaus verleidet."[20]

These quotes document Brecht's position on *Zivilisationsflucht*. Not changing one's geographical location but changing one's attitude would be the right way to deal with reality. In his diary (1921) we find the following note: "Vergessen, dass Arbeit nicht gut ist. Weil jede Arbeit gleich gut ist!!!"[21] Work was his main focus and, in order to be able to work and adhere to a strict work schedule, he needed a "warm" room, a clean desk and orderly daily routines. Living in "natural" (that is, primitive) surroundings, exposed to the elements, the winds, the blistering sun, without a roof over his head seemed like a nightmare. Sunny California, one of the many stations during his exile years, was his Tahiti, and he strongly disliked it and its perceived artificiality. While young Brecht had no desire to live in "natural" environments, in the wilderness, or on a sunbathed island, he experimented with characters that exemplified that way of life in his plays.

Baal, the central character of his first play, escapes from society and its rules and embarks upon a life against social norms, following Rimbaud's example whose life gave rise to scandal in his time. Nature, not society seems to be a more suitable place for him. The first scene clarifies Baal's position towards society. He provokes his audience with boorish behavior, extreme arrogance, and songs that are "obscene" by bourgeois standards, demonstrating that he does not abide by the rules of social etiquette. He makes it clear that he does not wish to conform, no matter what it may cost him. At the end of that scene Baal escapes into the open, leaving his audience in a state of shock. In subsequent episodes we see him wandering about, a social outcast, associating with vagrants and tramps. He follows his "natural" drives and his animal instincts since this is what he understands as living by nature. Nature is his source of inspiration. He sings songs in which he idealizes nature in its many manifestations. In his songs, the man Baal identifies with "Baal," the ancient God of nature.

Not civilized society but nature sets the rules by which he lives. He treats other human beings as if he were the merciless God Baal who devours his creatures. The man Baal feeds on people and casts them aside once he has eaten his fill, a metaphor that particularly applies to his treatment of women. Living in nature, living by the rules of nature, has a dehumanizing effect. A man who no longer considers himself as part of the human race turns into a brute. Ultimately, Baal is faced with the consequences of his behavior. He discovers the hard way what it means to emigrate into nature. The man Baal, whose last hour is approaching, realizes that he is human after all. He cries out for his mother in despair and pleads with his younger companions not to abandon him: "Könnt ihr nicht noch etwas dableiben?" As if he suddenly remembered the rules of bourgeois etiquette, he shifts to formal address with his companions: "Sie werden nicht gern allein sterben, meine Herren."[22] What a surprising change for someone who mocked all social conventions, who mistreated and abused others who did not identify with the human race! Confronted with the specter of his own mortality, Baal reclaims his human identity: "Ich bin keine Ratte!"[23] Yet, his physical state proves him wrong. Unable to walk upright like a human being he is reduced to "crawling" on hands and knees like a lowly creature, reaching out to the stars in vain.[24] Baal's death disillusions us about man's relationship with nature. Seeking refuge from society in the wilderness, living in total freedom, may sound intriguing in poetry but not in real life.

With *Im Dickicht der Städte* Brecht begins to focus on the big cities, the new *Lebensraum* of man, but Tahiti is not far away. Neither escaping to Tahiti nor retreating into nature but changing one's attitudes and adapting to the new environment will solve the problem of *Zivilisationsmüdigkeit*. Brecht uses two central characters, Garga and Shlink, to debate different ideological positions. The debate follows the rules of a boxing match, a sport Brecht admired during that period, yet it is not a fight with fists here but with words and ideas: "Es handelt sich nicht um Ringkämpfe mit dem Bizeps. Es sind feinere Raufereien. Sie gehen mit Worten vor sich."[25] Brecht instructs his audience to observe the verbal action as if they were spectators of a sports event, and not to look for psychological or philosophical explanations. Each "fighter" targets his opponent's "soft" spots, figuratively speaking, trying to gain the upper hand and ultimately knocking him out. While it may be easy to observe a fight with fists, it is difficult to "observe" a "(boxing) match" with words. In his comments on *Im Dickicht der Städte,* Brecht explains:

> Als Kampfzonen werden bestimmte Vorstellungskomplexe verwendet, welche ein junger Mann von der Art des Georg Garga von der Familie, von der Ehe oder seiner Ehre hat. Diese Vorstellungskomplexe benutzt sein Gegner, um ihn zu schädigen. Außerdem erzeugt der eine Kämpfer im anderen gewisse

Gedanken, die ihn zerstören müssen, er schießt Gedanken in seinen Kopf wie Brandpfeile.[26]

But how can Brecht's theory be put into practice? Erwin Faber, who played in the first production in Munich, explains how difficult it was for the actors to "act" in a play that followed the logic of a boxing match.

> Right in the first scene, Garga is continually harpooned by Schlink...but I [Garga] react to it...Both he [Engel who played Schlink] and I realized that the audience would sit there and have no idea what was happening on stage, because Brecht had intended that Garga's and Schlink's conflict be completely non-physical and that we attack each other only with words... he (Brecht) wanted to produce an effect like that of reading a book...It happened that this one collided with the other but did not really collide. We were just fish in an aquarium.[27]

Faber does not mention the difficulties in deciphering the many metaphors that are used to describe a character. "Tahiti" represents Garga's *Vorstellungswelt*, jungle metaphors express Shlink's attitude. Tahiti is a point of contention between the two characters, particularly in the first scene where it is mentioned seven times.

This is what actually happens: Shlink, an elderly businessman, approaches Garga, a young clerk in a bookstore, with a strange proposition. He does not want to buy a book but his opinion about a book of travels—an offer the young man takes as a personal insult: "Ich verkaufe Ihnen das Neue Testament aber nicht meine Ansicht darüber."[28] What seems to be an absurd proposition is, in fact, a verbal "blow" to Garga's notions about honor and personal integrity. He obviously takes pride in his high ethical standards and is not willing to compromise, regardless of what it may cost him. Shlink promptly replies: "Dass Sie Ansichten haben, das kommt, weil Sie nichts vom Leben verstehen." This brief verbal exchange between the two main characters clearly shows where each of them "stands." Garga is the idealist, holding on to bourgeois notions about honor, family and love, yet at the same time he is dreaming of Tahiti and the unconventional lifestyle it represents. Shlink, on the other hand, knows about Garga's ideals, but particularly his habit of dreaming of Tahiti on his sofa, while the world around him is crumbling. He also knows about Garga's dire economic situation and uses that knowledge against him. Offering to buy Garga's opinion is a prelude to what Shlink will be "attacking" next: "Miss Jane Montpassier sagt, Sie wollten nach Tahiti!" Garga proudly replies: "Man wählt seine Unterhaltungen nach Geschmack. Man liebt Tahiti, wenn Sie nichts dagegen haben." Garga talks as if he were a gentleman who could afford such dreams. Shlink seems amused: "Sie sind gut unterrichtet. Das ist das einfache Leben. Man lebt wie eine Eidechse."[29] With his sarcastic remarks about Tahiti Shlink attempts to spoil Garga's dream world. The real Tahiti, as Shlink describes it, is far from what Garga imagines it to be. Cut off from civilization, in primitive surroundings, one is reduced to live like a lizard, a lowly creature, losing one's human face and identity. Life on Tahiti would be miserable. It is the last place on earth where any civilized person would wish to go. In spite of these disparaging remarks on island life, Shlink urges Garga: "Fahren Sie nach Tahiti. Man wäscht sich dort nicht."[30] Brecht would describe Shlink's way of attacking Garga as "shooting troubling thoughts like arrows into his brain," an attempt to undermine his ideological position. Tahiti also allows him to put Garga's sense of family into question. Garga had turned down the money that was offered to him because in his dream world life is easy and money is not needed, a thought that we also run across in Brecht's autobiographical notes. Dreaming of paradise, on a sofa, while those closest to him suffer, also explains Garga's contentment in spite of his untenable situation. Shlink reproaches him for being blind: "Sie kneifen einfach die Augen zu. Die Familienkatastrophe ist unaufhaltsam. Nur Sie verdienen, und Sie leisten sich Ansichten. Fahren Sie lieber gleich nach Tahiti."[31] As far as Shlink is concerned, only the losers and maladjusted would consider escaping, rather than accepting the challenges of modern life, allegations that are hard to ignore. While Shlink is caught up in the "(boxing) match," he acts as if he were a sports enthusiast, excited about the game he is watching: "Ich kann Sie beim Stehen besser sehen. Wir sprachen von Tahiti. Wissen Sie was darüber?"[32]

As it turns out, Garga knows nothing about Tahiti except for what he has read. Gauguin's *Noa Noa* seems to be his only source of information. He has blind faith in books. They are a substitute for reality. So it is only logical that books are being targeted next. One of Shlink's assistants pulls books from the shelves to "trash" them, literally: "Das sind also Bücher? Ein schmieriges Geschäft! Wozu gibt es das? Es gibt genug Lügen. 'Der Himmel war schwarz, nach Osten zogen Wolken.' Warum nicht nach Süden? Was dieses Volk alles in sich hineinfrisst!"[33] Garga responds by calling for arms, as if his life were at stake: "Man spießt die Literatur auf!...Holen Sie den Revolver!"[34] Obviously he is struggling to hold his "ground," a development Shlink notices with satisfaction. The last target in this "round" of the "match" is Garga's notion about love. Jane, his girlfriend who has "sold" herself to one of Shlink's men, is brought in. His response is surprising. He is not morally outraged as he was when Shlink offered to buy his opinion but rather seems to make the same adjustment to reality as Kragler in *Trommeln in der Nacht* made in a similar situation. The two names, Kragler and Garga, suggest similarities between the two characters. Rather than rejecting Jane, Garga asks her to go away with him to Frisco, and not to Tahiti, as we might have expected. Here it is helpful to compare the two versions, *Im Dickicht* and *Im Dickicht der Städte*. In the earlier version, Garga says: "Ich habe nach Tahiti wollen, ich schmeiße es dir vor die Füße. Ich habe eine Familie, meine Mutter ist katholisch."³⁵ In the later version Brecht omits references to Tahiti, to family and religion. Here Garga simply proposes: "Gehen wir fort! Zusammen! Nach Frisco. Wohin du willst. Ich weiß nicht, ob ein Mann allzeit lieben kann, aber pass auf, ich verspreche dir: ich bleibe bei dir." The last lines emphasize that Garga is making a promise which, shortly afterwards, he will break, demonstrating that he has changed. At the end of the first scene Garga rips off his clothes, offers Jane for sale, and asks for a ticket to the islands: "Hier meine Stiefel!…Hier mein Taschentuch. Ja, ich versteigere diese Frau! Ich werfe euch diese Papiere um die Ohren! Ich bitte um Virginiens Tabakfelder und um ein Billet nach den Inseln. Ich bitte, ich bitte um meine Freiheit."³⁶ In other words, Garga sheds his old identity like a growing snake sheds its skin. What could be more brutal than selling the woman to the highest bidder to whom he just promised loyalty and devotion? He has turned into the man "auf den man nicht bauen kann," to paraphrase a line from Brecht's poem "Vom armen B.B."³⁷ Shlink seems satisfied. One of his assistants remarks: "Endlich ist er aus der Haut gefahren. Nehmen wir sie mit."³⁸

In subsequent scenes, Tahiti is used as a weapon by Garga as well as by Shlink. Garga, the man who no longer can be trusted, does not leave for Tahiti but he makes Shlink believe he still wants to go there. Everything he does from now on is intended to "trick" Shlink, to outmaneuver him, to make him think he knows what he is thinking. In the second scene Garga has joined the ranks of social outcasts, vagrants and tramps, but he seems not to have given up old habits. He is still supporting his family with odd jobs, and Shlink believes he still dreams of Tahiti: "Sie trinken. Sie arbeiten für ihre Familie vier Wochen wie ein Pferd und kommen so leicht nach Tahiti…auf dem Sofa."³⁹ Garga responds by requesting money for the voyage: "Hinterlegen Sie das Geld in der Vereinigten Schiffahrtsgesellschaft für mich,"⁴⁰ and he promises: "Ich gehe nach Tahiti, ich danke für die Karte. Kommen Sie, Pavian! Schiffsbillette!"⁴¹ But again, he has no intentions to travel. Promising that he will go to Tahiti is part of his ploy to trick Shlink into believing that he has swallowed the bait. "Tricking" Shlink with false promises and assurances is his strategy for winning the game.

In the scene "Opferung der Familie" Garga tentatively asks his mother to go south with him but not to Tahiti: "Ich bitte Dich, mit mir nach dem Süden zu gehen. Ich arbeite dort, ich kann Bäume fällen. Wir machen ein Blockhaus und du kochst mir. Ich brauche dich notwendig." Garga seems to be toying with the idea of going into the wilderness, anticipating his mother's response. The earlier version provides more specific answers to the question whether or not the wilderness is a viable place to live: "Willst du, die ich liebe, wie Vieh umkommen lassen, das ins Hochwasser kommt?"⁴² From her perspective, the prospect of being stranded in the wilderness without the people she loves and die like an animal is terrifying. In the later version she does not explain why she does not want to live and die in the wilderness but focuses on the consequences of his behavior for those he is leaving behind: "Wohin sagst du das? In den Wind? Aber wenn du zurückkommst, dann kannst du hier nachsehen, wo wir gewesen sind in der letzten Zeit, die wir hatten."[43] In both versions Garga's mother takes a stance against *Zivilisationsflucht*.

In the scene "In den Kohlelagern" the fight between Shlink takes a new turn. Shlink tries to "hook" Garga with Tahiti again, but he is not longer interested: "Sie wissen, dass Tahiti ein nackter Stein ist, der das Maul öffnet, und dass ich es weiß."[44] Not Tahiti but the smokestacks of the factories, life in the big city, attract him now. The following lines illustrate to what extent Garga has changed: "und [ich] denke, wie es jetzt mit George Garga ist?! Was geschieht mit ihm? Sein Feind verzweifelt. Er schießt Gedanken in sein Hirn und jener denkt mit dem Magen weiter!"[45] The new Garga is no longer interested in Tahiti and dismisses such dreams as juvenile fantasies. While Shlink is dying with his eyes cast on the city, Garga is heading for the city, ready to fight for survival in this jungle, made by man and for man.

In conclusion, it can be said that Brecht never shared the enthusiasm of some of his contemporaries for a "natural" way of life in the woods or on Tahiti as an alternative to urban living. Baal, the main character in his first play, rejects civilized society only to die in the woods like an animal and shunned by his own kind. Baal's lonely death in the woods is certainly not a good prospect. In *Im Dickicht der Städte*, Brecht dispels the myth of finding paradise outside the civilized world. Tahiti, as Garga envisions it, is nothing but a figment of his imagination. Although posing as his opponent, Shlink has been preparing him for life in the city. He began by demolishing his ideals and dreams that made Garga oblivious of the world around him. Dreaming of Tahiti, resting comfortably on a sofa while his family was falling apart best illustrates Garga's failings. In his letters Brecht had repeatedly mentioned that Tahiti and everything it represented led to idleness and sloth, tendencies he thought needed to be fought. However, Brecht shows that attitudes such as those represented by Garga are not permanent. Under Shlink's "guidance" he turns into a fighter and acquires the qualities needed to survive in the big city jungle. The new Garga summarizes best what Brecht tried to convey: "Und das Geistige, das sehen Sie, das ist nichts. Es ist nicht wichtig der Stärkere zu sein, sondern der Lebendige."[46] This is the first play in which Brecht demonstrates that the individual is not a fixed entity but a construct that can be altered, a notion he will further develop in *Mann ist Mann*. The title *Im Dickicht der Städte* is Brecht's answer to the discourse on *Zivilisationsflucht*. Not Tahiti, not nature, but the city is man's true habitat.

Endnotes

1 Bertolt Brecht, *Werke: Große kommentierte Berliner und Frankfurter Ausgabe*, Vol. 28, eds. Werner Hecht, Jan Knopf, Werner Mittenzwei, and Klaus-Detlev Müller (Berlin: Aufbau, and Frankfurt/Main: Suhrkamp, 1992), p. 198, hereafter BFA. I would like to thank Marc Silberman for helpful suggestions and editorial advice, and Elena Danielson for proofreading.
2 BFA 28, p. 135.
3 BFA 28, pp. 135, 188.
4 BFA 28, p. 176.
5 BFA 26, p. 194.
6 BFA 26. p. 205.
7 BFA 21, p. 123.
8 Paul Guiguin, *Noa Noa*, Luise Wolf trans. (Berlin: Cassirer, 1920).
9 BFA 28, pp. 118-119.
10 BFA 13, p. 486.
11 BFA 26, p. 172.
12 BFA 13, p. 238.
13 BFA 13, p. 485.
14 BFA 28, p. 165.
15 BFA 28, p. 154.
16 BFA 26, p. 210.
17 BFA 28, p. 66.
18 BFA 28, p. 122.
19 BFA 18, p. 20.
20 BFA 19, p. 254.
21 BFA 26, p. 188.
22 BFA 1, p. 136.
23 BFA 1, p. 137.
24 Ibid.
25 BFA 21, p. 57.
26 BFA 24, p. 28.
27 Stuart McDowell, "Actors on Brecht: The Munich Years," in Carol Martin and Henry Bial, eds., *Brecht Sourcebook* (London, New York, Routledge 2000), p. 78.
28 BFA 1, p. 346.
29 BFA 1, p. 441.
30 Ibid.
31 BFA 1, p. 442.
32 BFA 1, p. 349.
33 BFA 1, p. 350.
34 BFA 1, p. 351.
35 BFA 1, p. 352.
36 BFA 1, p. 446.
37 BFA 11, p. 120.
38 BFA 1, p. 446.
39 BFA 1, p. 358.
40 BFA 1, p. 359.
41 BFA 1, p. 365.
42 BFA 1, p. 369.
43 BFA 1, p. 457.
44 BFA 1, p. 376.
45 BFA 1, p. 386.
46 BFA 1, p. 386.

Brechts Asien vs. Brechts Griechenland: Kulturelle Konstrukte und die Erklärungskraft einer binären Opposition

Martin Revermann

Dieser Aufsatz argumentiert, dass unser Verständnis von Brechts Verhältnis zu Asien erheblich davon profitiert, das antike Griechenland in die Analyse einzubeziehen. Ich untersuche die Art und Weise, in der Brecht zwei unterschiedliche Arten des Anderen konstruiert—eine positive, was Asien angeht, und eine überwiegend negative, was das antike Griechenland betrifft—mit dem Ziel, sein eigenes Projekt einer Erneuerung des Theaters schärfer zu definieren und besser zu propagieren. Brechts Asien und Brechts Griechenland konstituieren eine binäre Opposition von eigener Dynamik, die neues Licht auf Brecht und seine Methode utilitaristischer Aneignung wirft. Insbesondere argumentiere ich, dass Brecht Asien vorzog, weil es das bessere, d.h. nützlichere Andere darstellte. Das antike Griechenland hingegen war in mehrerer Hinsicht kompromittiert. Das zweite Hauptargument dieses Artikels ist, dass diese binäre Opposition instabil, zuweilen sogar paradox ist.

This paper argues that in order to improve our understanding of Brecht's relationship with Asia it is extremely helpful to insert his relationship with Greece into the picture. I examine the ways in which Brecht constructed and developed two notions of the Other, a positive one of Asia and a largely negative one of Greece, in order to refine and promote his own project of theatrical innovation. Brecht's Asia and Brecht's Greece constitute a binary with specific dynamics, which sheds new light on Brecht and his method of utilitarian appropriation. I argue in particular that when Brecht faced this choice, Asia prevailed by virtue of being the better, i.e. more useful, Other while Greece was in a number of ways compromised. The second major point being made is that this binary is unstable and at times even paradoxical in nature.

Brecht's Asia versus Brecht's Greece: Cultural Constructs and the Explanatory Power of a Binary

Martin Revermann

Setting up the Binary

The title chosen for this piece is in need of further clarification. This article will not be concerned with a comparative formal and structural synopsis of Asian and Greek theater in the Brechtian oeuvre. Such an analysis, which would have to pay particular attention to dramaturgical and theatrical equivalences between Brecht and the theatrical traditions of the Far East, is a useful exercise in its own right and has, in part, been attempted some time ago in the seminal monograph by Antony Tatlow.[1] Nor will this piece be concerned with the repercussions in Brecht's non-dramatic works (the poems and novels) of Asian cultural practice, especially philosophy, as has also been done by Tatlow and, more recently, in Heinrich Detering's stimulating pamphlet on Brecht and Laotse.[2] The approach adopted here, by contrast, is contextual and conceptual, since I am primarily interested in "Asia" and "Greece" as cultural constructs made by an eminent Western playwright, theater practitioner and theoretician. Such conceptualizations are in part informed by larger cultural discourses. There is, for one thing, the obsession of the *fin de siècle* with *chinoiserie* and *japonisme* (in the visual arts and crafts, in literature, in music and in architecture).[3] And there is — not least in the wake of Friedrich Nietzsche's *Birth of Tragedy* (first published in 1872, with initially hostile reactions) and the enthusiasm with which it, and Nietzsche's work in general, was starting to be received from the 1890s onwards[4] — the renewed interest of creative avant-garde minds in Greek tragedy since the turn of the century. For them Greek tragedy begins to serve as a vehicle expediting the escape from the artistic status quo by resurrecting this much-coveted art form as emphatically archaic and pre-modern, and as something that, in the perception of its re-creators, is pure, unspoiled, raw, ritualistic and sacred in a conveniently non-Christian sense of the word. Hugo von Hofmannsthal is perhaps the best-known representative of this kind of response, which is characterized by deep resentment towards the classicizing idealism of the Romantics and their illustrious predecessors of the Enlightenment.[5] Instead, the chronological distance and ideological otherness of Greek tragedy are heavily emphasized, especially through the use of costume and scenic space as well as the presentation of violence and acts of ritual. But all the distancing of Greek tragedy as a raw and atavistic artistic expression of humankind's remote mythical past serves, ultimately, the sole purpose of drawing it *closer* to the contemporary artist as the embodiment of, and platform for, a fresh start, a creative awakening and an energizing renewal: a catalyst for artistic modernity.

Yet, as formative as those broader cultural, artistic and theatrical trends may have been, in Brecht's case individual choices and very deliberate appropriation surely play an extraordinarily important role. It is crucial to remember that Brecht had a distinctly utilitarian approach to any kind of tradition: whatever its pedigree and cultural capital, any "classic" or artifact of old had *to do something for him* before Brecht would even consider spending any artistic and creative resources on it. This spirit of utilitarian appropriation, evident in his artistic practice throughout his life, is perhaps most clearly articulated, in print at any rate, in Brecht's preface to the *Antigone* model book of 1949:

> Selbst wenn man sich verpflichtet fühlte, für ein Werk wie die Antigone etwas zu tun, könnten wir das nur so tun, indem wir es etwas für uns tun lassen.[6]
> (Even if one felt obliged to do something for a work like the Antigone, we could only do this by letting the play do something for us.)

Even more blunt and revealing, perhaps, is an unpublished fragment entitled (by Brecht) "Über die japanische Schauspieltechnik" ("On Japanese Acting Technique").[7] It is dated, by the editors of the BFA (where it was printed for the first time in 1992), to circa 1930 which is the period when Elisabeth Hauptmann prepared for Brecht (German) translations of Arthur Waley's widely influential (English) translations of Noh-plays (published in 1921), a collaboration which resulted in *Der Jasager* and *Der Neinsager* (both based on the Noh-play *Taniko*). The fragment then predates the remarks from the *Antigonemodell* by almost two decades.

Brecht starts by announcing that he wishes to analyze "certain elements of a foreign art of acting" for their "usefulness" ("Verwendbarkeit")(!). This requires, Brecht continues, the view that in art there is such a thing as a technical standard which is something "transportable" ("etwas Transportables") that can be taken out of its original context and built, like a module, into another one. Brecht concludes the note:

> Die japanische Schauspieltechnik...kann natürlich für uns nur insoweit etwas bedeuten, als sie für unsere Probleme Bescheid weiß. Das Japanische an ihr, überhaupt ihr ganzer "Charakter," "Individualwert" usw. ist in dieser Untersuchung irrelevant.
>
> (The Japanese craft of acting...can, of course, only mean something to us insofar as it knows something of relevance to our problems. Its Japanese element, its whole "character" and "individual value" etc. is irrelevant in this inquiry.)

Asia, and Greece, and any other part of pre-Brechtian culture, then, had to be of use value for Brecht in order to merit his attention. Consequently, in Brecht's case there can be no such thing as "Asia" and "Greece:" there is only "Brecht's Asia" and "Brecht's Greece." And a promising way, I submit, to examine those two cultural constructs in Brecht's case is by looking at them as a binary, that is, as opposing concepts that, at least in part, help to define and explain each other by way of mutual opposition. Lumping together under the label "Asian theater" the very diverse theater traditions of the Far East seems legitimate, in this context at any rate, not least because Brecht himself (like other artists of his time) was not overly concerned with making painstaking differentiations between, say, Noh, Kabuki and the classical Chinese theater: they were all perceived to be equally Other, to such an extent that a nuanced acknowledgement of their respective differences had to appear irrelevant.

Even if Brecht never articulated this binary explicitly, there are, it will become clear, strong reasons to believe that for Brecht ancient Greece and its theatrical tradition (including, of course, Aristotle, its main surviving contemporary theoretician) stood in direct opposition to the various forms of Asian theater. This is not least because Greece, its drama and Aristotle are often treated by Brecht as a metonymy for pre-Brechtian Western theater *tout court*, a "depraved" and "parasitic" art informed by the aesthetics of a thoughtless and inefficient "cult of the beautiful" which has to be overcome by the novel "theater of the scientific age" — to paraphrase, with quotations, from the preface to the *Short Organon for the Theater* of 1948.[8] It would, I believe, not at all be misleading to argue that for Brecht the opposition between Asia and Greece is thoroughly dialectical in nature, with Brechtian drama itself emerging as a higher-level synthesis of the two opposites. And even though I will end this paper with exploring the limits, tensions and ruptures of this binary, its explanatory power, while perhaps slim for either Asian or ancient Greek theater, strikes me as quite considerable *for Brecht*—especially, in fact, at those very points where the binary breaks down or at least becomes destabilized.

Looking at Brecht's Asia via Greece

The triangulation between Brecht, Asia and Greece attempted here deserves attention on the following grounds. First, Brecht's relationship with Asia will arguably be understood better and more profoundly by inserting Greece into the picture. This is because Asia and Greece can justifiably be regarded as two alternative choices available to any artist of the historical avant-garde to achieve rather similar artistic goals. There is, to begin with, the strong desire for, and the perceived need for, emancipation (to the point of liberation) from the Western tradition, which was widely felt to be suffocating, constraining and sterile.[9] Secondly, both traditions could easily serve as means of de-familiarization that were sure to catch the attention of audiences, unsettle them and force them to re-conceptualize their theatrical experience, a principal concern of the period's avant-garde theater artists. But perhaps most importantly, both traditions were seen as vehicles, to use this concept once again, for re-invigorating Western (that is, European) theater, some kind of regenerative blood transfusion.[10]

The means of access to this Far Eastern source of new energy in the late 19th and early 20th century varied in general and were different for individual artists specifically.[11] One prime venue of contact is distinctly colonial in nature: this is the series of grand public (world) exhibitions which, set in the colonizers' countries, put on display the exotic cultural richness of the colonized Other, be it from China, Bali or Japan (which only very recently had opened itself to the West, and was first put "on exhibit" in 1867). Antonin Artaud, for instance, in 1931 watched those Balinese performers who would so memorably inscribe themselves into *The Theater and its Double* at the Colonial Exposition (!) in Paris where the Balinese suitably performed at their colonizers' habitat, the Dutch Pavilion.[12]

For Brecht, the points of contact varied from the philosophical and cerebral (writings by and about Chinese philosophers) through the literary (notably those Noh-translations by Hauptmann which were previously mentioned) to the performative. This last point of contact in particular cannot possibly be over-rated, since only through physical contact the appeal of the Asian traditions as "total theater" (to deploy a term from the sub-title of Pronko's 1967-book) could be experienced in full. Tatlow mentions that Brecht saw Kabuki actors in Berlin around 1930, though it must be noted that this is based on orally communicated recollections of Hauptmann and Herbert Ihering—actual documents illustrating when exactly and under precisely which circumstances all of this came about apparently do not exist.[13] Given Brecht's strong interest in Japanese theater, especially around 1930, it is certainly more than plausible that Brecht should have made the effort to see those actors perform (which was, after all, an extremely rare opportunity) while they were in Berlin. Well-attested and well-known, by contrast, is Brecht's performative encounter with Jingju (often, though misleadingly, referred to as "Beijing Opera"). It was occasioned in 1935 by the visit of the actor Mei Lanfang to Moscow, then (and now) commonly considered to be the unrivalled master-actor of Jingju. In March and April 1935 Brecht saw Mei Lanfang perform and participated in discussions with him and his fellow-actors.[14] These encounters proved formative and more or less instantly prompted two of Brecht's key theoretical texts, the "Bemerkungen über die chinesische Schauspielkunst" (published in the autumn of 1935) and "Verfremdungseffekte in der chinesischen Schauspielkunst" (published in late 1936).[15]

Asia and Greece, then, are two Others to choose from. This project required, as far as Asia was concerned, a respectful and at least incipiently de-colonized openness to the artistic richness and cultural value of the Far East which, at the turn of the century and in the early decades of the 20th century, was in the firm grip of the European colonial powers (including Germany, of course). On the other hand, the project required making Greece less Western and more primal than it had been previously, especially during German Romanticism and its Philhellenism which elevated the Greeks of old to early incarnations of the ideals of the Enlightenment, notably the ideal of an autonomous and self-governing subject (Goethe's *Iphigenie auf Tauris* is a case in point). This less Western and more primal Greece is, of course, central to Nietzsche's *Birth of Tragedy* and its idealization of tragedy as an art form which manages to integrate the polarities of Dionysiac and Apolline elements — that is before its destruction by Euripides and the spirit of Socratic Enlightenment. In Brecht's lifetime, this primal, de-Westernized Greece found one of its most acclaimed articulations in the work of Hugo von Hofmannsthal (his *Electra*, for instance).

It is the first of the two central points I wish to make in this paper that when Brecht, like many other avant-garde artists, faced this choice, Asia prevailed qua being the better, that is, the more useful, Other. The Asian traditions were more exotic and distanced as well as more performative and actor-centered. They also, perhaps surprisingly, struck at least some Western critics not as mature, complex and enigmatic but as primal, pure and, compared to Western theater, quite straightforward: "Urform des Theaters," as Ihering succinctly put it when summarizing his impressions of the Kabuki actors who supposedly visited Berlin in late 1930 and early 1931.[16] Moreover, Asian theater was conveniently under-theorized. Note, for instance, that the extensive and extremely important body of treatises on Noh and Noh acting by Zeami was only re-discovered in 1908, and subsequently made its way into the Western consciousness very slowly, by way of (not always particularly reliable) translations which gradually started appearing.[17] No mention is made of Zeami in any of the writings which constitute the standard Brecht edition (BFA), and it is unclear whether Brecht ever read any passages from Zeami as were available to him and Hauptmann in Waley's English translation of Noh plays from 1921 which they demonstrably used.[18] It is indeed a fascinating, if somewhat futile, exercise to speculate how Brecht would have responded to those treatises and some of their principal concerns: the ongoing formation of an actor, for instance, or the question of an actor's emotional control, or Zeami's frequent remarks on how Noh actors can succeed, or fail, in establishing a rapport with their audiences. Asia therefore came with an intriguing element of the unknown, an appealingly (and conveniently) uncharted territory into which Brecht could then handsomely project his own theoretical ideas about a new kind of acting which distances performer, character and audience from each other.

Last but certainly not least, Asia was politically much less compromised than Greece was. Asia was something for Brecht that Greece could never possibly have been: the clean slate. If anything, Asia was a part of the world that was victimized by European colonialism (an extreme form of capitalism) and in need of Marxist revolutionary redemption. There are indeed Brechtian texts which insinuate or even emphatically explore the notion of a victimized Asia. In *The Measures Taken* the disguised agitators from the U.S.S.R. experience an exploited China, which in turn is contrasted with the newly liberated Russia. And without wishing to push to an extreme the Chinese coloring of the *Good Person of Szechwan*, its prostitute-protagonist Shen Te is surely a victim of all kinds of exploitation (sexual and otherwise). At least in the new epilogue he wrote for this play in 1953 Brecht explicitly invoked the notion of an *allegorical* Szechwan, a city situated in an Asian country previously occupied by exploitative powers and a city now annihilated (!) by the advent of the (Maoist) Revolution:

> Zuschauer, wisse, die Hauptstadt von Sezuan
> In der man nicht zugleich gut sein und leben kann
> Besteht nicht mehr. Sie mußte untergehn.
> Doch gibt's noch viele, die ihr ähnlich sehn.[19]
> (Spectator, know, the capital of Szechwan in which you can't be good and live at the same time, it is no longer. It had to perish. But there are many still which share a resemblance with it.)

If Szechwan and Shen Te can be referred as allegories of a victimized Asia, the case is all the more compelling in Brecht's *The Judith of Shimoda*, an adaptation of a Japanese play by Yamamoto Yuzo written (in collaboration with Hella Wuolijoki) in Finland in 1940. The Brechtian play has a complicated textual history, and its reconstruction is controversial. It was not available in print until 1997, when it was published, very much as a fragment, in the BFA.[20] Hans Peter Neureuter's reconstruction of a full play script, using a complete Finnish version found in Wuolijoki's bequest and translating the missing scenes into German, was published in 2006.[21] But while these editorial difficulties are significant, none of the points I am about to make here are substantially affected by them.

Brecht's play tells the story of the geisha Okichi who, in 1856, agrees to serve the first American consul in Shimoda to prevent her home town from being attacked by the technologically superior Americans. Her "military service" ("Kriegsdienst"),[22] as the act of self-sacrifice through prostitution to the "dirty white devils" ("schmutzigen weißen Teufeln")[23] is euphemistically referred to, wins her heroic status in Japan. But the play does not end here. It jumps ahead 20 years, at which point Okichi is an alcoholic and an outcast in the society that once worshipped her while the *myth* of Okichi and her heroic deed continues to be glorified in communal memory as a self-serving traditional tale: it is others, and not the heroine herself, who have profited from Okichi's sacrifice. The victimization, again, takes on the form of prostitution and rape, and there are indications that at least for the play's closure Brecht envisaged a staging which unmistakably linked the rape of the Asian woman with the gradual triumph of colonialism and Europeanization: at the end of the play, Brecht notes, one can see "the fruit of Okichi's sacrifice and that of other sacrificial animals: high-rises and European costume (even if that may require a bit of poetic licence)."[24]

Greece, on the other hand, was a very different story altogether, especially in view of the strong links between the discipline of Classics — ever-present in schools, universities and 19th-/early 20th-century German culture at large — and the political right, in particular the national-conservative right and the Catholic right.[25] In this connection between the discipline of Classics and right-wing ideology, especially national-conservative and militarist ideology, there lies one reason — surely not the exclusive reason but an important one nonetheless — for Brecht's fierce anti-Aristotelianism in some of his key theoretical writings. Not only does Brecht, with his polemical polarizing mind, genuinely enjoy setting up as his scapegoat Aristotle, a major cultural icon of the Western tradition. The deeper reason is that Aristotle is entirely ineligible as a positive model from the very start, because he prominently embodies a cultural tradition that for Brecht is politically severely compromised by its strong intellectual and not least institutional ties with German national-conservative and militarist ideology. Aristotle comes "with baggage," of a kind detested by Brecht the politician and ideologue.

That the ancient Greeks and Romans came "with baggage" Brecht experienced early on. There was, of course, no way of escaping classical antiquity for a young educated German of Brecht's generation, and even if Brecht's upbringing in a mercantile upper-middle-class household in Augsburg saved him from the *humanistisches Gymnasium* with its relentless emphasis on Latin *and* Greek, Brecht nonetheless got his fair share of exposure to the former at the *Realgymnasium*. At this kind of school there would, characteristically, be no instruction in ancient Greek. But Brecht did receive intensive instruction in Latin, from the very start in 1908 (at age 10). Of the Roman poets Horace was covered extensively, and it is one of the most famous anecdotes in Brecht's biography that his cynical comments in a written assignment on Horace's ill-fated line *dulce et decorum est pro patria mori* (*Odes* 3.2.13) nearly got him expelled from school.[26] This incident, if anything, illustrates how pervasively ancient culture was being claimed and appropriated by the national-conservative ideology of the ruling elite, and how radically even the very young Brecht clashed with this ideology and their representatives (this incident, however, evidently did not stand in the way of Brecht's life-long affection for, and admiration of, Horace, which is quite well-documented).[27]

While ancient Greek theater, like classical antiquity in general, came "with baggage" (of all sorts), and while as a performance it was accessible only via a theatrical establishment which Brecht considered to be artistically ossified as well as politically naive at best, the Asian traditions were markedly different. They had a freshness, immediacy and sophisticated otherness—experienced by Brecht in few, brief and isolated but nonetheless formative theatrical encounters—that was bound to appeal to Brecht the politician as well as the artist.

Exploring a Destabilized Binary

It had been my central contention that the binary "Brecht's Asia" versus "Brecht's Greece" represented a choice between two different kinds of Other, and that for Brecht Asia with its theatrical and philosophical traditions was the "better," more useful, more eligible Other. Having said all this, I think it is fascinating, and highly illuminating, to watch how this binary becomes destabilized once we start looking into it in more depth to discover tensions, frictions and even outright paradoxes. This, the unstable and at times even paradoxical nature of the binary, is the second central point of my paper. I wish to start illustrating this point with Brecht's Greece, in particular Brecht's Aristotle. The anti-Aristotelianism in Brechtian theorizing about epic/dialectical theater is well-known and well-pronounced, given that the attacks are launched in such crucial theoretical writings as the "Notes on the Opera *Rise and Fall of the City of Mahagonny*" and the *Short Organon*. One is left to wonder, however, whether Brecht actually realized how much of Aristotle he in fact admitted into his theory, if only through the backdoor, as it were. Thus paragraph 65 of the *Short Organon* reads:

> Auf die "Fabel" kommt alles an, sie ist das Herzstück der theatralischen Veranstaltung. Denn von dem, was *zwischen* den Menschen vorgeht, bekommen sie ja alles, was diskutierbar, kritisierbar, änderbar sein kann. Auch wenn der besondere Mensch, den der Schauspieler vorführt, schließlich zu mehr passen muß als nur zu dem, was geschieht, so doch hauptsächlich deswegen, weil das Geschehnis um so auffälliger sein wird, wenn es sich an einem besonderen Menschen vollzieht. Das große Unternehmen des Theaters ist die "Fabel," die Gesamtkomposition aller gestischen Vorgänge, enthaltend die Mitteilungen und Impulse, die das Vergnügen des Publikums nunmehr ausmachen sollen.[28]

(Everything hangs on the 'story;' it is the heart of the theatrical performance. For it is what happens *between* people that provides them with all the material that can be discussed, criticized, altered. Even if the particular person represented by the actor has ultimately to fit into more than just what is happening, it is mainly because that which is happening will be all the more striking if it reaches fulfillment in a particular person. The 'story' is the theater's great enterprise, the complete fitting together of all the gestic operations, embracing the communications and impulses that now go to make up the audience's entertainment.)

This line of reasoning is entirely Aristotelian, to a point even that it could have been lifted straight out of Aristotle's *Poetics*: the emphasis on the pivotal importance of plot, and its superior place over character in the creation of dramaturgical and theatrical meaning, is at the very center of Aristotle's theory of tragedy. The resemblance between Aristotle and Brecht even becomes uncanny when their respective diction is taken into account. Brecht speaks of the plot as "the heart of the theatrical performance" ("das Herzstück der theatralischen Veranstaltung") — Aristotle called it "the first principle and the *soul*, so to speak, of tragedy"![29] And when Brecht uses the verb "sich vollziehen" ("to reach fulfillment"), it is hard not to connect Brecht's peculiar diction with Aristotle's notion of *telos* ("fulfillment," "goal," "completion"), a notion which is central not just to Aristotle's theory of dramatic poetry but his whole philosophy, especially his ethical and natural philosophy. It is largely irrelevant, for the present purpose at least, whether these resemblances are based on (direct or mediated) influence from Aristotle or whether they are equivalent notions which both thinkers arrived at independently. What matters here is that Brecht is significantly more Aristotelian than he would ever have imagined or wished.[30] This point, derived from a central theoretical piece by Brecht, could be substantiated more fully and interestingly by analyzing Brechtian theatrical practice: his emphasis on plot-driven and logically consistent dramaturgy from which there are only very few exceptions (I would count *In the Jungle of the Cities* as one of them); or the way in which some of Brecht's most acclaimed plays can fruitfully be analyzed using either Aristotelian theoretical tools or perspectives derived from the modern analysis of Greek drama. Brecht's Greece, by comparison with the Asian option, may have turned out to be the worse Other. But both theoretically and in his actual playwriting Brecht ended up (without, it would appear, ever realizing it) being much closer to Aristotle and the Greek camp than he was ever to the world of Noh, Kabuki and Jingju.

Tensions and paradoxes, however, are not confined to Brecht's relationship with Greece, but are at least equally evident, and profound, in Brecht's conception of Asia and the Asian theatrical traditions. As a result, the binary established in this paper on "Brecht's Greece vs. Brecht's Asia" becomes, again, destabilized. Brecht's attraction to Asia and its theatrical traditions is grounded in a very perceptive and, I am convinced, largely intuitive understanding of some of their key elements: their distinct approaches to the dichotomy between performer and character, and the strong appeal that both Jingju and Noh make on the imaginative power of their audiences, thus turning audiences not into passive consumers but active and engaged collaborators and co-creators of theatrical meaning. The notion of an alert, responsive and engaged audience is obviously critical to Brecht's thinking about theater and its potential for achieving social transformation. The total theater that the Asian traditions, despite their manifest individual differences, all seem to offer is more than welcome to the historical avant-garde with its need for a re-calibration of Western theater, and Brecht is by far not the only one to fall under their spell.

Despite all of this, Brecht never fully realized that there is an equally important element in the Asian theatrical traditions (especially in Noh but not exclusively there), which is not only at odds with the Brechtian project but in fact stands in direct opposition to it. This is the spiritual, metaphysical, introverted, anti-materialist and politically largely conformist nature of much of Asian theater: its extreme inwardness and interiority which privileges the journey towards the transformation of the self over ambitions to effect any transformation in and of the world we happen to live in physically and materially speaking—a world, one might add, which loses more and more of its relevance the further the meditating and self-reflexive subject progresses while moving along this path of inner transformation. This means, in social terms, largely an acceptance of, and conformism with, the social status quo, an acceptance which, from a Brechtian point of view, would have to be seen as despicably lethargical. This is particularly evident in many Noh plots, an art form which since the late 14th century had been under the personal patronage of the shogun and therefore was, and remained, in essence court theater. It consequently has the strongest of ties and interactions with the Japanese aristocracy and its value systems.[31] If anything, it is Kabuki, rather, which explores topics of social conflict and class-based tension, not exactly surprisingly given that Kabuki owes its existence and popularity to the rise of the merchant class (a feature, one would think, which might have interested Brecht, were it not for the fact that his familiarity with Kabuki never extended that far).[32]

Brecht's "Asia" and Brecht's "Greece" are, indeed, constructs: selective to the point of being grossly reductionist, judgmental, tendentious, and constructed for their use value as vehicles for Brecht the utilitarian appropriator. As constructs, they tell us fairly little about either Asia or Greece—but rather a lot about Brecht, as I hope to have demonstrated. Brecht did not want to *understand* Asia or Greece, which would have required considerable time and effort as well as a genuine openness to nuances, grey areas and incompatibilities of the cultural Other which, it seems, Brecht was never prepared to develop. He was intent on *using* Asia and Greece in order to foster, refine and sharpen the one and only project which mattered after all: his own. In this scheme, only one of those two Others, Asia, was eligible to serve officially as a positive foil to, and a catalyst for, the development of Brechtian theory and theatrical practice. The theater of Greece and its greatest theoretician, on the other hand, are set up as reactionary forces (both ideologically and artistically), even if in reality there is significantly more affinity than Brecht would have wished, or cared, to admit. The resulting tensions and frictions are worthy of our attention as one way of understanding fundamental aspects of Brecht's "dialectical theater" (a term he, towards the end of his life, started to prefer over "epic theater"), even if the dialectics that have been discussed here are quite different from those Brecht was referring to when he coined this term. The road from Brecht to Asia via Greece is circular in that it leads back to where it started, to Brecht. But it is one of those roads which are worth taking for the vistas it offers along the way, and because having travelled on it we will look with different eyes at our point of departure.[33]

Endnotes

1   Antony Tatlow, *The Mask of Evil. Brecht's Response to the Poetry, Theatre and Thought of China and Japan. A Comparative and Critical Evaluation* (Berne/Frankfurt/Las Vegas: Peter Lang, 1977). Because of the methodology adopted, mention should also be made of Mae J. Smethurst, *The Artistry of Aeschylus and Zeami: A Comparative Study of Greek Tragedy and No* (Princeton: Princeton University Press, 1989), an important comparative study of Noh and Greek tragedy which focuses on structural and dramaturgical equivalences.

2   Heinrich Detering, *Bertolt Brecht und Laotse* (Göttingen: Wallstein Verlag, 2008), a pithy contextualizing analysis of one of Brecht's most famous poems, the "Legende von der Entstehung des Buches Taoteking auf dem Weg des Laotse in die Emigration" (published in 1939 as part of the *Svendborger Gedichte*).

3   Nicola Savarese, *Teatro e spettacolo fra Oriente e Occidente* (Rome/Bari: Editori Laterza, 1992) provides an ambitious and wide-ranging narrative of Western artistic responses (mainly but not exclusively theatrical) to Far Eastern culture until the early 20th century. For these dynamics between theater traditions in the 20th century itself, Leonard Pronko, *Theater East and West: Perspectives Toward a Total Theater* (Berkeley/Los Angeles: University of California Press, 1967) is foundational, see also Tatlow, *The Mask of Evil*, pp. 92-131, pp. 163-177, as well as Antony Tatlow, "Gesamtkunstwerk," *Monatshefte* 70 (1978): pp. 171-176.

4   M. Silk and J. Stern, *Nietzsche on Tragedy* (Cambridge: Cambridge University Press, 1981), pp. 90-131 (especially pp. 125-131); Ernst Nolte, *Nietzsche und der Nietzscheanismus*, 2nd ed. (Berlin: Herbig Verlag, 2000), pp. 233-306; and Werner Frick, *Die mythische Methode. Komparatistische Studien zur Transformation der griechischen Tragödie im Drama der klassischen Moderne* (Tübingen: Max Niemeyer Verlag, 1998), pp. 43-58, who refers to Nietzsche's *Birth of Tragedy* as a "Gründungsdokument" ("foundational document") for the novel ways of responding to Greek tragedy.

5   The topic has been extensively discussed by Frick, pp. 58-212, with specific reference not just to Hofmannsthal (especially the *Electra* of 1903) but also Hans Henny Jahnn's *Medea* (1926) and the later work of Gerhart Hauptmann (in particular the *Atridentrilogie*, written between 1940 and 1945). Richard Strauss' opera *Electra* (1909, for

which Hofmannthal provided the libretto) and Igor Stravinsky's *Oedipus Rex* (1927), an opera-oratorio with a libretto in Latin, pursue similar archaizing strategies (which can still be detected as late as 1969, in Pier Paolo Pasolini's Medea-film with Maria Callas in the title role).
6   Bertolt Brecht, *Werke: Grosse kommentierte Berliner und Frankfurter Ausgabe*, 30 vols. (+ index volume), ed. by Werner Hecht, Jan Knopf, Werner Mittenzwei, Klaus-Detlef Müller (Berlin und Frankfurt/Main: Aufbau-Verlag/Suhrkamp Verlag, 1988-2000). In the following abbreviated as BFA. Here BFA 25, p. 75.
7   BFA 21, pp. 391f.
8   BFA 23, p. 65.
9   Erika Fischer-Lichte, "The Reception of Japanese Theatre by the European Avant-Garde (1900-1930)," in Stanca Scholz-Cionca and Samuel L. Leiter, eds., *Japanese Theatre and the International Stage* (Leiden: Brill, 2000), pp. 27-42.
10   I should add at this point that both Greek and Asian theatricality is heavily gendered in that only male performers are allowed (there are only few, and temporary, exceptions to this in Asian theater). It is interesting, and revealing, that none of the artists of the historical avant-garde (certainly not Brecht) appears to have exploited this aspect.
11   Pronko, pp. 1-33, 115-137.
12   Ibid., p. 8.
13   Tatlow, *The Mask of Evil*, pp. 172, 228f., see also Tatlow, "Gesamtkunstwerk," pp. 173f. The group of (non-professional) Kabuki players visited Berlin in October 1930 and January 1931, "and Elisabeth Hauptmann was convinced that he saw them" (Tatlow, *The Mask of Evil*, p. 228; Brecht was definitely in Berlin at the time). Tatlow informs me via e-mail: "Elisabeth Hauptmann told me Brecht saw them, as did Herbert Ihering." In view of the oral nature of the attestation, there is consequently no mention of such an event in Werner Hecht's monumental Werner Hecht, *Brecht Chronik* 1898-1956 (Frankfurt/Main: Suhrkamp Verlag, 1997) and Werner Hecht, *Brecht Chronik Ergänzungen* (Frankfurt/Main: Suhrkamp Verlag, 2007).
14   Hecht, *Brecht Chronik*, pp. 437f.
15   BFA 22, pp. 151-155, 200-210, 934f., 959f. (note, however, that Silvija Jestrovic, *Theatre of Estrangement: Theatre, Practice, Ideology* (Toronto: University of Toronto Press, 2006) emphasizes the importance not of Chinese theater but of Russian formalism on Brecht's developing notion of *Verfremdung*). More than once has it been insinuated to me that Brecht's perceptions of Chinese acting are superficial, naïve and misleading. But reading Riley's excellent account of classical Chinese acting, especially her chapter on identity (Jo Riley, *Chinese Theatre and the Actor in Performance* (Cambridge: Cambridge University Press, 1997), pp. 137-175), has made me inclined to believe that the exact opposite is the case. It should also be mentioned that Brecht subsequently saw Chinese performers in New York: "Bei keinem seiner New-York Aufenthalte ließ er das chinesische Theater aus" (Werner Mittenzwei, *Das Leben des Bertolt Brecht oder Der Umgang mit den Welträtseln*, 2 Vols. (Frankfurt/Main: Suhrkamp, 1987), Vol. 2, p. 81).
16   Quoted in Tatlow, *The Mask of Evil*, p. 229.
17   Thomas Hare, *Zeami: Performance Notes* (New York: Columbia University Press, 2008), pp. 451-459 provides a brief summary.
18   Tatlow, *The Mask of Evil*, p. 228 with footnote 246 considers this to be a serious possibility.
19   BFA 6, p. 440. A similar sentiment is expressed in Brecht's very brief introductory remarks to the published version of the play that came out in 1953 (BFA 6, p. 176).
20   BFA 10, pp. 832-877.
21   Bertolt Brecht, *Die Judith von Shimoda. Nach einem Stück von Yamamoto Yuzo*, in collaboration with Hella Wuolijoki, reconstruction of the play script by Hans Peter Neureuter (Frankfurt/Main: Suhrkamp, 2006). Neureuter's reconstructed play script has been translated into English by Markus Wessendorf and staged at Kennedy Theater/

Honolulu in April 2010 (dir. Paul Mitri). This production was then performed, to great acclaim, during the 13th IBS Symposium on "Brecht in/and Asia" at the University of Hawai'i in May 2010.
22 Brecht, *Die Judith von Shimoda*, p. 30.
23 Ibid., p. 25.
24 BFA 10, pp. 834.
25 The discipline's most prominent scholar of the time, Ulrich von Wilamowitz-Moellendorff, is a notorious embodiment of these inter-connections, see especially Canfora's piece in William Calder, Hellmut Flashar, and Theodor Lindken, eds., *Wilamowitz nach 50 Jahren* (Darmstadt: Wissenschaftliche Buchgesellschaft, 1985) and, more generally, Ingo Gildenhard and Martin Ruehl, eds., *Out of Arcadia: Classics and Politics in the Age of Burckhardt, Nietzsche and Wilamowitz* (London: Institute of Classical Studies, 2003).
26 Mittenzwei, Vol. 1, pp. 42-45.
27 The brief 1953-dialogue on empathy (BFA 23, pp. 412-413) is a good example.
28 BFA 23, p. 92.
29 Aristotle, *Poetics*, chapter 6, 1450a38-39.
30 It is gratifying to see this important point being made so vigorously in Lehmann's ground-breaking work on post-dramatic theater (Hans-Thies Lehmann, *Postdramatisches Theater* [Frankfurt/Main: Verlag der Autoren, 1999], pp. 48, 63; and Hans-Thies Lehmann, *Postdramatic Theater*, Karen Jürs-Munby trans. [London: Routledge, 2006], pp. 33, 41).
31 Stephen T. Brown, *Theatricalities of Power: The Cultural Politics of Noh* (Stanford: Stanford University Press, 2001), pp. 9-15 and *passim*; Patrick O'Neill, *Early No Drama and Its Background* (London: Lund Humphries, 1958), as well as Thomas Looser, *Visioning Eternity: Aesthetics, Politics and History in Early Modern Noh Theatre* (Ithaca: Cornell University East Asia Program, 2008), esp. pp. 16-18, 121-169 and 171-197.
32 Looser, pp. 75-119, examines the economics of both Noh and Kabuki, setting out their differences but also stressing their similarities.
33 I wish to thank Antje Budde, Markus Wessendorf, and especially Alysse Rich for helpful comments.

Approaching Interculturalism with Brecht: Fritz Bennewitz's Theater Work in Asia

Rolf Rohmer

Fritz Bennewitz regarded his first production in India—Brecht's *Threepenny Opera*, New Delhi 1971—as "a foreign product imported to the Indian stage and not developed from the tradition of the Indian theater culture." Convinced that the historical situation required new international cultural relationships, he started searching for adequate intercultural practices. With nearly 50 productions over a period of 25 years in India, Sri Lanka, the Philippines and Bangladesh he developed his own intercultural strategies based specifically on Brecht's works and theories but opposed to simultaneous efforts by Brook, Schechner, Barba, and others. This essay focuses on the principles of Bennewitz's concept, examines his adaptation and modification of Brecht in the process, and also critically discusses the prospects of his approach.

Fritz Bennewitz betrachtete seine erste Inszenierung in Indien—Brechts *Dreigroschenoper* in Neu Delhi, 1971—als "ein auf die indische Bühne importiertes Produkt und nicht aus der Tradition dieser Bühne entwickelt." Überzeugt von der Notwendigkeit neuer internationaler Beziehungen im kulturellen Bereich begann er nach angemessenen interkulturellen Praktiken zu forschen. Mit fast 50 Inszenierungen in Indien, Sri Lanka, den Philippinen und Bangladesch über einen Zeitraum von 25 Jahren hinweg entwickelte er seine eigenen interkulturellen Strategien, die ausdrücklich auf Brechts Werken und Theorien beruhten, aber den gleichzeitigen Bemühungen Brooks, Schechners, Barbas und anderer entgegengesetzt waren. Dieser Essay konzentriert sich auf die der Konzeption Bennewitz' zugrundeliegenden Prinzipien, untersucht seine Aneignungen und Abänderungen Brechts im Verlaufe seiner Theaterarbeit, und bespricht zudem kritisch die Zukunftsaussichten seines Ansatzes.

Annäherungen an den Interkulturalismus mit Brecht: Fritz Bennewitz' Theaterarbeit in Asien

Rolf Rohmer

Fritz Bennewitz kam zum ersten Mal 1970 nach Indien. An der National School of Drama inszenierte er mit Studenten Brechts *Dreigroschenoper*. Die Produktion war erfolgreich, doch nach kurzer Zeit erkannte er:

> Diese Aufführung...hat das Interesse an Brecht befördert und ist durch die Absolventen der Schule als Methodenvermittlung weit über Delhi hinaus wirksam geworden. Trotzdem erschien mir die Wirkung dieser Arbeit begrenzt, weil sie doch weitgehend eine aus unserer Theatertradition und unseren Spielgewohnheiten auf die indische Bühne übersetzte Aufführung geblieben war.

Die selbstkritische Erkenntnis dokumentiert einen entschiedenen Wandel in Bennewitz' Weltsicht und Kreativität. Seine Lebenspraxis und sein künstlerisches Schaffen waren von geschichtlichem Denken getragen und durchdrungen. Er folgte dabei im Grundsätzlichen immer dem marxistischen Konzept von der sozialistischen Perspektive aller menschlichen Gesellschaft; die Existenz sozialistischer Staaten (darunter der DDR) blieb ihm daher, unbeschadet von mancherlei kritischen Einwänden an der politischen Praxis, Garant für soziale Zukunftsgestaltung. Es waren aber nicht die seinerzeit aktuellen politischen Strategien und ideologischen Dogmen, die ihn antrieben, sondern die aus der Geschichte der deutschen Arbeiterbewegung gewonnene, etwa an Franz Mehring oder Clara Zetkin orientierte Anschauung der Kulturgeschichte und Kunsttheorie. Er sah sich und sein Schaffen in einem Geschichtsprozess verortet, der mit der Säkularisation in der Renaissance begonnen hatte und durch die politischen und sozialen Umwälzungen in den Jahrhunderten seither schließlich zu einer kulturvollen, humanistischen Gesellschaftsverfassung führen musste. Im Hinblick auf gesellschaftliche und künstlerische Praxis waren für ihn drei Faktoren die wesentlichen Orientierungsgrößen: ein aus der europäischen Kulturgeschichte gewonnenes Menschenideal mit deutlichen Implikationen aus der klassischen Überlieferung in Deutschland, ein starker aufklärerischer Impetus und schließlich die dem entsprechende Überzeugung, durch künstlerische Anstrengung und Kreativität gesellschaftsgestaltend wirken zu können. Shakespeare, deutsche Klassik und Brecht waren für ihn ästhetische Leitbilder, weil sie in großen Umbrüchen der Geschichte wirksam waren und mit ihrem Schaffen ideell und methodisch Richtwerte für ein dem gesellschaftlichen Fortschritt dienliches Engagement gegeben hatten. Dass dabei Brecht als zeitgenössischer und seiner eigenen Weltanschauung nahestehender Autor für Bennewitz das große Vorbild wurde und blieb, versteht sich fast von selbst.

Dabei hatte es in der Aneignung Brechts durch Bennewitz mehrere Wendungen gegeben. In den ersten Jahren seiner Regiearbeit, zwischen 1958 und 1960, hatte er am Theater Meiningen spektakuläre Erfolge mit drei Brecht-Inszenierungen, insbesondere mit der *Dreigroschenoper*, erzielt. Mit einem jungen, spielfreudigen Ensemble, dessen Mitglieder wie auch er selbst zumeist in der Stanislawski-Tradition ausgebildet waren, ging er unbedenklich und unbedarft an Brecht heran, weil dies, wie er gesprächsweise kundtat, im Zuge der Zeit lag. Jahre danach urteilte er selbstkritisch: "Die Meininger *Dreigroschenoper* wies eine scheinbare Geschlossenheit auf. Ich möchte sie gleichsetzen mit Oberflächenspannung."[2] 1960 kam er ans Deutsche Nationaltheater Weimar und sah sich dort Anforderungen ausgesetzt, die er so beschrieb:

> Zu dieser Zeit war die marxistische Interpretation der deutschen Klassik historisches Bedürfnis…Weimar als Klassikerstadt, Pflegestätte deutscher Klassik, hatte einfach die gesellschaftliche Verpflichtung, entsprechende Inszenierungen vorzustellen. Ich habe deutsche Klassik inszeniert…[und] nach Bezugspunkten gesucht, die einer marxistischen Interpretation der Klassiker zuarbeiten halfen. Ich fand sie bei Brecht und Shakespeare.[3]

Dementsprechend nahm er Brechtstücke in sein Repertoire auf und fand angesichts der neuen Herausforderungen auch ein neues Verhältnis zu Brecht:

> Man hat sich austrainiert und fängt neu an, weil man sich an der Wirklichkeit reibt und gegen sich polemisiert. Außerdem stellt Brecht ein immerwährendes Training dar, das man braucht, um konkret zu bleiben. Ich habe das über Jahre hinweg an mir selbst beobachtet…Erst [jetzt]…stieß ich auf die Modelle. Das waren Entdeckungen. Sie regten mich zu einer Überfülle von Details an…[D]as Pendel schlug nach der anderen Richtung aus.[4]

Und schließlich heißt es mit Bezug auf weitere Brecht-Inszenierungen in späteren Jahren:

> Und dann wurde Brecht für mich nicht denkbar ohne Shakespeare und umgekehrt…Vieles ist anders als am Modell. Ich probiere diese Methode auch bei anderen Inszenierungen von Brecht-Stücken. Es hat im Grunde ein Abschied von Brecht stattgefunden, um mich ihm zu nähern.[5]

Die erneute Näherung ergab sich durch seine Arbeit im Ausland. Sie führte ihn im Laufe der Jahrzehnte in 27 Länder der Erde, immer wieder vor allem nach Indien, Sri Lanka und auf die Philippinen.

Ausgehend von seinen DDR-Erfahrungen und seinen sozialistischen Überzeugungen war Bennewitz zunächst bestrebt, in Ländern der sogenannten "dritten Welt" vermittels Theater für eine Umgestaltung der Gesellschaft zu werben und zu wirken. Er hielt dafür, dass das Theater in diesen Ländern zu diesem Zweck methodisch ausgestaltet werden müsste. Wie stark er dabei in den Traditionen befangen war, aus denen er kam, belegt eine andere Version des eingangs zitierten selbstkritischen Urteils über die *Dreigroschenoper* in Delhi 1970, die er in einer Retrospektive noch 1980 gebrauchte:

> Der Aufführung ist in der Presse und beim Publikum ein Erfolg bescheinigt worden, *als Beitrag zum indischen Nationaltheater* ist sie unwesentlich geblieben, da sie doch weitgehend noch eine aus unserer Theatertradition und aus unseren Spielgewohnheiten auf die Bühne übersetzte Aufführung war – ein auf die indische Bühne importiertes Produkt und nicht aus der Tradition dieser Bühne entwickelt.[6]

Trotz Erfahrung der geokulturellen Unterschiede schlug immer noch einmal die Vorstellung durch, der kooperative Austausch der jeweils beteiligten Theaterkulturen müßte zwar nicht ästhetisch und methodisch, wohl aber kulturpolitisch eine übereinstimmende Wirkungsstrategie fördern. Interkulturalismus als Ingredienz und Stimulans eines weltumspannenden gesellschaftlichen Fortschritts bedurfte nach seiner Ansicht einer solchen Ausrichtung. *Als Zugang* zur Bündelung und sozialpolitischen Orientierung der kulturellen Kräfte in den geokulturellen Zonen, *nicht als Endstadium* galt ihm das Konzept des Nationaltheaters, wie es aus dem seit der Renaissance sich nationalstaatlich strukturierenden Geschichtsverlauf in Europa erwachsen war und nun dem Identitätsbestreben in den neuen Staaten der entkolonialisierten Welt zu entsprechen schien.

Für sein Anliegen hielt er die Vermittlung des Brechttheaters für unabdingbar. Nach seinen eigenen wechselnden Erfahrungen mit Brecht hatte er dabei aber weder die "Modellstrategie" noch die Übertragung eines "methodischen Systems" im Auge. Bei aller noch fortwirkenden Bindung an seine tradierten Denkmuster hatte er doch ein Gespür dafür, dass andere geokulturelle Bedingungen eine spezifische und auch selektive Anwendung brechtscher Vorgaben erforderten. Er bezog sich methodisch vor allem auf das Prinzip der "Verfremdung" und konzeptionell-wirkungsstrategisch auf das der "Veränderung:" im Sinne Brechts sollte vor allem "Verfremdung" ins Theaterspiel eingebracht werden, um den sozialen Hintergrund von Verhältnissen, Figuren und Handlungen zu entdecken und zu vermitteln; mit "Veränderung" zielte er auf die kritische Qualifizierung von Theatertraditionen, die er für eine solche Aufgabe noch nicht gerüstet glaubte.

Als er aus Indien zurückkam, zeigte er sich tief beeindruckt von seiner Erfahrung des sozialen und kulturellen Lebens auf dem Subkontinent, und er begann daran zu zweifeln, dass Brechts Konzept per se Standards der Theaterpraxis "in der ganzen Welt" repräsentierte. Es ist zu bedenken, dass Bennewitz bis 1970 zwar in verschiedenen europäischen Ländern gearbeitet und auf Gastspielreisen auch außereuropäische Länder bereist hatte, aber bei seinen Aufenthalten dort im wesentlichen doch immer auf den Verkehr in Berufskreisen beschränkt geblieben war, die in etwa seinen heimischen Verhältnissen entsprachen. In Indien war er nun in eine völlig andere Situation geraten. Er arbeitete jetzt in einem Umfeld ohne institutionalisiertes, kaum auf professioneller Basis operierendes Theater, das die Gesellschaft als Ganzes beeinflussen konnte oder wollte. Er fühlte sich weitaus stärker ins soziale Leben und seine Probleme verwickelt als in Theaterangelegenheiten. Er erfuhr sehr konkret, dass und wie eng Theater und jede Art von Darstellung mit den Realitäten des sozialen Leben verbunden ist. So selbstverständlich die fundamentale These des brechtschen Theaterkonzepts für seine Arbeit war, so kritisch gestand er sich ein, dass sie in Europa doch eher ein strategisches Bekenntnis, ein Bestreben war, die im Verlauf der europäischen Kulturgeschichte verlorene soziale Bindung und Verantwortung des Theaters wieder zu gewinnen, als tatsächliche Grundlage der Theaterpraxis. Er wurde sich der tieferen Bedeutung, ja einer Art neuer Herausforderung bewusst, die mit Brechts Kategorie der "Verfremdung" gegeben war. Es ging für ihn nun nicht mehr darum, eine bisher vorwiegend spieltechnisch verstandene Methode zur Entdeckung und kritischen Erhellung des sozialen Hintergrunds von Verhältnissen, Figuren und Handlungen einer anderen Theaterpraxis zu vermitteln. Es kam ihm nun vielmehr darauf an, zu erproben, wie sie sich in einer Theaterkultur entfalten kann, die durch die enge Wechselbeziehung von sozialen Verhältnissen, kulturellen Traditionen und *performing activities* geprägt ist—*performing activities* in deutlicher lebenspraktischer Differenz zur "Darstellung" auf der europäischen Bühne.

Um sich der Möglichkeiten dafür zu vergewissern, studierte er eingehend die Aneignung außereuropäischer Theaterpraktiken durch Brecht und suchte nach Berührungspunkten zwischen dessen Theaterästhetik und den Theaterkulturen, in deren Bereichen er selbst tätig war. Er fand sie vor allem in deren epischen Traditionen und dem epischen Theater Brechts. Auch hier spielten die Modifikationen, wie die jeweilige geokulturelle Struktur und die aktuelle Situation sie *objektiv* sowie seine eigene persönliche Wahrnehmung und Qualifizierung sie *subjektiv* erforderten, eine wesentliche Rolle. Aus der Fülle seiner Überlegungen und Erprobungen heben wir neben dem Prinzip der Verfremdung dasjenige des Gestischen hervor.

Bislang hatte er Gestus vornehmlich als eine Art des physischen und vokalen Ausdrucks in der künstlerischen Darstellung verstanden, die durch Überhöhung die soziale Statur oder/und Absichten der Figur beziehungsweise einer Aktion verdeutlichen sollte. In diesem Sinne verstand er auch Gestus als spieltechnisches Komplement von "Verfremdung," mit ihr verbunden, um den sozialen Kontext der Fabeln zu beleuchten sowie kritische Einsichten und Impulse zu vermitteln. Zu diesem Zweck konnte Gestus durch Beobachtung gewonnen, in der schauspielerischen Aktion nachgestaltet und vermittelt werden. Um dies zu erreichen, hielt er, wenn nötig, auch eine Formalisierung und demonstrative Verdeutlichung für angebracht. Kurz gesagt: Gestus wurde eher als ein ästhetisches Konstrukt denn als reale Erfahrung verstanden.

Bennewitz war tief beeindruckt davon, Gestus in Indien als soziale Realität zu erfahren, als alltäglichen Ausdruck sozialen Seins und Verhaltens in Übereinstimmung mit persönlicher Identität, als eine unter allen Umständen wirksame Fähigkeit zur Kommunikation und als eine immanente Veranlagung "to perform"—was mehr ist als europäische "Darstellung" oder Selbstdarstellung. Seine Briefe aus Indien enthalten eine Fülle von Beobachtungen und Beschreibungen dieser Art. In ihnen wird zugleich deutlich, dass er dabei nicht nur Tatbestände registrierte; er machte große Anstrengungen, sich selbst in die Kontexte und Bedingungen einzuarbeiten. Das wurde ihm nicht allein durch die Beobachtung des sozialen und öffentlichen Lebens im Allgemeinen möglich, sondern vor allem durch die Zusammenarbeit mit Schauspielern und Amateuren aus nicht-städtischen und unterschiedlichen ethnischen Zonen. Immer wieder drückte er seine Bewunderung über diese Partner und ihre gewissermaßen "natürlichen" gestischen Potentiale aus; er sah sie "der realen Gestaltung und Entwicklung des sozialen Lebens" unmittelbar nahestehend. Er schätzte vor allem ihre "natürliche Fähigkeit," nicht nur sich selbst in ihrer sozialen Identität zu geben, sondern zugleich eine darüber hinausgehende menschliche Kraft, gewissermaßen eine grundsätzliche Humanität, zu verkörpern und auszustrahlen. Für Bennewitz gewann Gestus dadurch eine neue Bedeutung und Funktion. Er dokumentierte dies nicht durch wissenschaftliche Definition, sondern durch Umschreibung in seinem sehr persönlichen Stil: "Ihre Gesten sind *nicht angeschafft*" —in Bezug auf seine eigene bisherige Praxis das entscheidende Wort—"sondern von unten, aus ihrer Lebenserfahrung gewachsen."[7]

Dergestalt begriff er sehr schnell, dass weder sein anfängliches Sendungsbewusstsein noch sein ursprüngliches Produktionskonzept den Verhältnissen in den betreffenden Ländern und ihren Theaterkulturen angemessen war. Er begab sich auf die Suche nach einer eigenen Strategie.

Fritz Bennewitz erkannte die Veränderung und Erneuerung internationaler Kultur- und Theaterbeziehungen in der Welt von damals (und heute) nun als *die* geschichtliche Herausforderung und Chance. Dafür erschienen ihm die ästhetisch-provokative Innovationswut im westeuropäischen Theater wenig hilfreich, die Gestaltungskraft des Theaters im Osten zu wenig weltoffen; er verwarf den damals noch üblichen Export von Theaterprogrammen, die fremden Kulturen als Muster übertragen oder aufgedrückt oder infiltriert wurden, ebenso wie programmatische Versuche eines übergreifenden "Welttheaters" zum Beispiel à la Peter Brook.

Im Unterschied zu seinen Zeitgenossen gelangte er bei seinen doch so umfangreichen und intensiven praktischen Bemühungen nicht zu einem eigenen ausgearbeiteten oder ausgereiften interkulturellen Konzept. Die Gründe dafür sind vielfältig. An theoretischem Vermögen, seine eigenen Anstrengungen konzeptionell zu verallgemeinern und ins Verhältnis zum zeitgeschichtlichen Diskurs zu setzen, hat es wahrlich nicht gemangelt. Vielmehr waren die biographischen Bindungen seiner gesellschafts- und kulturpolitischen Herkunft, aus denen herauszutreten er sich in den internationalen Begegnungen zunehmend gedrängt sah, dafür maßgebend. Seine Hauptanstrengung sah er nicht darin, neue Modelle zu entwerfen und als bestimmt definierte interkulturelle Leistung zum Beispiel in Indien zu realisieren, sondern *sich selbst* in der sich verändernden Welt zu orientieren, *sich selbst* im Hinblick auf die Erfordernisse, die er erkannte, umzubauen.

Aus dieser Perspektive sah er durchaus Anlass, auf Distanz zum Beispiel zu den Konzepten Richard Schechners und Eugenio Barbas zu gehen, die Geltung als international wirksame Schulen erlangt hatten. Es war vor allem der Grundgedanke einer Theateranthropologie, der Bennewitz' Kritik herausforderte. "Theateranthropologie" fragt nach *allgemeinen* performativen Grundformen und Qualitäten und nach *allgemeinen* Ursprüngen theatraler Kreativität; sie sucht Konstanten und Überlieferungen dieses Potentials in den heutigen Kulturen auf und ist bestrebt, sie als Grundlage der interkulturellen Wechselwirkungen auf dem Gebiet des Theaters produktiv zu machen. Die Verdienste der Theateranthropologie vor allem hinsichtlich der Qualifizierung der schauspielerisch-performativen Darstellungsmittel und der Interaktion sind unbestritten — und manches davon ist, wenn auch ihm selbst offenbar unbewusst, in Bennewitz' Praxis eingegangen. Aber er fürchtete, dass die interkulturellen Implikationen dieser Konzepte letztlich doch einer europäisch-westlichen Sicht der Kulturgeschichte und Weltverhältnisse verpflichtet blieben, und stimmte darin mit Kollegen aus der "dritten

Welt" wie dem indischen Kritiker und Regisseur Rustom Bharucha oder dem nigerianischen Dramatiker und Nobelpreisträger Wole Soyinka überein. Der kultur*anthropologische* Ansatz jener Theorien und Praktiken mochte sich nicht zu Unrecht als historische Überwindung der Dogmen europäisch-westlicher Kultur- und Kunstkonzepte einschließlich aller Spielarten der Moderne verstehen. Bennewitz sah aber eine Gefahr darin, dass die Orientierung aufs Anthropologische und geschichtlich Ursprüngliche die je spezifische Geschichte der Nationen, Völker und Ethnien und damit auch deren eigenständige politische und kulturelle Gestaltung in der Gegenwart unterlaufen könnte. Für ihn lag der Verdacht eines neuerlichen internationalistischen, ja neokolonialistischen Konzepts europäischer Konvenienz und Dominanz nahe; er sah ihn bis zu seinem Lebensende in der zunehmend von Wirtschaftsinteressen geprägten globalisierten Welt nicht ausgeräumt.

Im Unterschied dazu erfuhr Bennewitz im Prozess der Selbstfindung nicht nur die Entgrenzung seiner gesellschafts- und kulturpolitischen Bindungen, sondern vor allem ein entschiedenes *Auftauchen aus der europäischen Geschichte* in eine im Umbruch befindliche Welt—wobei der Umbruch allerdings anders ausfiel als erwartet. Er stellte sich dieser Herausforderung vermittels Anstrengung seines historischen Bewusstseins. Bennewitz war bemüht, die historische Position der Partner, Völker und Regionen draußen, ihre geschichtlich gewachsenen kulturellen Strukturen und ihre künftigen Chancen zu begreifen und seine eigene Geschichte einzubringen in die Kooperation, wozu nicht Selbstaufgabe, aber ein historisch modifiziertes Selbstverständnis erforderlich wurde. Auch für seine internationale Arbeit blieb es bei der Orientierung an Shakespeare und Brecht, die aus historischen Umbrüchen der europäischen Gesellschaft heraus zu Weltautoren geworden waren und in deren Stücken beziehungsweise Theatermethoden er eine dialektische Einheit von Historischem und Allgemein-Menschlichem realisiert sah. Hinsichtlich seiner Arbeit mit Brecht (und Shakespeare) ordnete sich alles dem Grundanliegen des "Historisierens" zu: im kritischen Aufspüren der sozialen Hintergründe menschlichen Handelns und gesellschaftlicher Prozesse geschichtliche Perspektiven einsehbar zu machen und humanistische Werte zur Geltung zu bringen. Und er war sich klar darüber, dass dies ein langwieriger Prozess der Orientierung, der gegenseitigen Annäherung und der praktischen Experimente sein würde. Brechts *Kaukasischer Kreidekreis* schien ihm das geeignete Beispiel gleich für eine ganze Reihe von szenischen Experimenten. Er inszenierte ihn elfmal (!)—in Weimar, in New York, in verschiedenen Regionen Indiens und in Manila, darunter dreimal für Kinder und als Szenenstudium in der Schauspielerausbildung.

In diesem Sinne war er nicht auf die Ausarbeitung neuer Programme aus. Seine interkulturellen Bemühungen vollzogen sich über 27 Jahre vielmehr als ständige Wiederholung und Variation von praktischen Aktivitäten in Form von Inszenierungen, Seminaren und Dialogen in vielen Ländern. Dabei zeichneten sich im Verlauf der Zeit nun doch bestimmte Arbeitsprinzipien in seinem interkulturellen Engagement ab. Zentrales Anliegen war ihm die "Integration" dramatischer Angebote der einen Kultur in die jeweils andere, eine Einbettung in den fremden Kontext auf der Basis von "Äquivalenten," die jeweils herauszufinden und wofür Modifizierungen beiderseits zu realisieren waren. Er war bestrebt, die Programmatik der theatralen Modelle, Methoden und Stoffe, von denen er ausging und die er in den internationalen Austausch einbrachte, aufzubrechen, damit sie neuer, zeitgemäßer Übermittlung und Aneignung zugeführt werden konnten. So hat er zum Beispiel nie wie andere daran gedacht, Brechts Werke als modellhafte Theaterästhetik und -programmatik seinen ausländischen Partnern zu überantworten. Im Zusammenhang mit seinen Brechtinszenierungen draußen sprach er immer davon, dass er nicht "die Stücke" auf die Bretter gestellt, sondern "das Strukturprinzip der Stücke" ins indische Theater (beziehungsweise das der jeweiligen Region) eingebracht habe. Zu diesem Zwecke widmete er sich intensiv der Zusammenarbeit mit den Übersetzern, um Übertragungen der Werke in die Sprach- und Vorstellungswelt der verschiedenen Kulturkreise zu erreichen. Der jeweiligen Sprachen nicht mächtig, entwickelte er gleichwohl ein gestisches, stilistisches und akustisches Gespür für die je zutreffenden Ausdrucks- und Verhaltensweisen. Dies ermöglichte ihm, die Darsteller in seinen Inszenierungen zu leiten und gegebenenfalls zu korrigieren oder auch im Produktionsprozess eine Qualifikation der Übersetzung zu veranlassen. Seine Mitarbeiter in allen Ländern bestätigten übereinstimmend diese seine Fähigkeit und folgten seinen Weisungen und seiner Kritik ebenso erstaunt wie einsichtig. In diesem Sinne wurde "Integration" zum strategischen Hauptbegriff seiner interkulturellen Bemühungen. Dies wollte er leisten—und er erhoffte sich für die Zukunft, dies würde wechselseitig geschehen.

Ein Aspekt, der mit seinem Geschichts- und Theaterverständnis zusammenhing, blieb dabei für ihn von besonderer Bedeutung. Er schätzte (mit Brecht) das sozial begründete gestische Potential besonders asiatischer Theatertraditionen hoch ein. Zugleich aber bemerkte er, dass zufolge anderer geschichtlicher Erfahrungen entwicklungsgeschichtliches Denken und Gestalten in jenen Kulturen unterrepräsentiert waren. In der performativen Praxis zeigte sich dies nach seiner Beobachtung an der Unterschätzung oder Vernachlässigung der dramatischen Texte, in denen geschichtliche Assoziationen ja vornehmlich gebunden sind. Angesichts der aktuellen weltpolitischen Situation hielt er die Akzentuierung dieser Dimension für unverzichtbar. Daher drang er unermüdlich darauf, der Textstruktur und dem Wort in jenen kulturellen Traditionen und im schauspielerischen Agieren mehr Gewicht zu verleihen. Überzeugt davon, dass nicht jeder beliebige Text geeignet sei, den Weg in den Interkulturalismus zu ebnen, wählte er, übereinstimmend mit seinen Partnern, solche Stücke aus, die seine Intentionen am ehesten zu realisieren erlaubten. Das waren vornehmlich Werke Brechts und Shakespeares, einige Male auch Goethes *Faust*.

Auf Fritz Bennewitz' Weg durch die Länder und Kulturen waren nun auch Irrtümer nicht ausgeschlossen. In seinem interkulturellen Bestreben lehnte er Richard Schechners Theorie und Praxis vehement ab. Untersuchungen seiner *Faust*-Inszenierungen am La Mama Theater New York, in Manila und Bombay durch David John[8] belegen hingegen die Nähe seiner Inszenierungspraxis zu bestimmten konzeptionellen und methodischen Prinzipien Schechners. Oder: Bennewitz' "Integrationsstrategie" wirkte auf dem multikulturellen indischen Subkontinent nicht als interkulturelle Anstrengung, wie er selbst das verstand. Für die Partner dort fand er Beachtung als Produzent, der sich nicht wie andere als Sendbote oder Programmatiker des Brechttheaters (oder wessen Theater auch immer) betätigte und diese seine "antikoloniale" Einstellung mit einem hohen Arbeitsethos, ausgerichtet auf die regionalen sozialen und kulturellen Gegebenheiten, verband. Seine Freunde dort haben wohl darin recht, dass er zu einer bündigen interkulturellen Strategie oder einem interkulturellen Konzept nicht gelangte; aber beispielhaft an seiner Arbeit bleibt der historisch wesentliche Erkenntnisprozess, dass die kulturellen Beziehungen in der Welt von morgen andere sein müssen als die zu seiner Zeit dominierenden Strategien des Internationalismus.

Bennewitz selbst begann die Grenzen seines interkulturellen Engagements zu spüren. Das geschah, als Leben und Schaffen von Fritz Bennewitz im Kontext der gesellschaftlichen und politischen Prozesse in den achtziger und neunziger Jahren des vorigen Jahrhunderts sich problematisierten. Mit zunehmender Resignation beobachtete er die neuerlichen Spannungen in den internationalen Beziehungen, die aufbrechenden politischen und sozialen Widersprüche in den Ländern der "dritten Welt" und deren terroristische Zuspitzung sowie die Verflüchtigung von Zukunftsidealen. Seine Inszenierungen gerieten wiederholt in den Strudel politischer Auseinandersetzungen, und seine Arbeit draußen wurde mehr und mehr zur Mühsal angesichts hemmender Einflüsse der neuen Kulturindustrie, die sich überall ausbreitete. So tauchten nun auch immer häufiger Fragen nach dem eigenen Standort in Geschichte und gegenwärtiger Welt, nach der eigenen Identität auf. Im Verlaufe der Zeit stellte sich heraus, dass seine Erfahrungen draußen ihn den heimischen Verhältnissen eher entfremdeten als dass sie ihn deren kritischer Bewältigung näher brachten—Produktionsprobleme daheim nahmen zu.

Zugleich ahnte er, dass die Arbeit in der Fremde über die vorausgegangenen Erfolge hinaus neue Initiativen erforderte. Bei aller Variabilität war er doch einer kulturpolitischen Grundlinie gefolgt: der Vermittlung von Dramatik und damit der Bindung an literarische Traditionen. Alternativen dazu, wie sie in der heutigen interkulturellen Experimentierpraxis erprobt werden, blieben außerhalb seines Gesichtskreises. Ein halbes Jahr vor seinem Tode beschrieb er daher im Interview seine Erfahrung, dass "der Interkulturalismus sich erschöpft" habe, dass er "in der *globalen Welt'* nicht aufrecht zu erhalten" sei und dass "die Welten kulturell auseinander triften." Er spürte, dass seine Integrationsstrategie nicht mehr trug, und war mehr ahnungsvoll als gewiss, dass unter den veränderten weltpolitischen Bedingungen neue interkulturelle Anstrengungen notwendig und möglich seien. Aber er selbst fand nicht mehr die Kraft, dergleichen in seine Inszenierungen draußen einzubringen – Produktionsprobleme gab es nun auch dort.

Fritz Bennewitz starb niedergerungen durch eine jahrelang zehrende Krebserkrankung am 12. September 1995. Er erlitt das Schicksal eines Künstlers, der auf dem Weg ins globale Zeitalter die Heimat verloren hatte, aber in der Welt, die er ersehnte, noch nicht ankommen konnte.

Anmerkungen

1   Fritz Bennewitz, "Ajab Nyaya Vartulacha" [das ist: Beschreibung interkultureller Arbeitsprinzipien am Beispiel der Inszenierung des *Kaukasischen Kreideikreises* in Kooperation von Fritz Bennewitz und Vijaya Mehta, Bombay 1973], Typoskript mit handschriftlichen Einträgen von Fritz Bennewitz (Fritz-Bennewitz-Archiv, Leipzig [im Folgenden FBA], Dokumentengruppe AO-G 07: Texte von Fritz Bennewitz/1973-xx-xx.01), S. 1 – Publikation des vermutlichen Interviewtextes nicht nachgewiesen.
2   In: "Werkstattgespräch mit Fritz Bennewitz – aufgezeichnet von Ingeborg Pietzsch," zitiert nach dem ursprünglichen Text des Gesprächs in zwei Fassungen, Typoskript mit handschriftlichen Einzeichnungen von Fritz Bennewitz, (FBA, Dokumentengruppe AO-G 07: Texte von Fritz Bennewitz/1975-xx-xx.01), S. 5 der zweiten Fassung des Textes = S. 12 des Archivdokuments.
3   Ebd., S. 1 der zweiten Fassung des Textes = S. 9 des Archivdokuments.
4   Ebd., S. 4 der zweiten Fassung des Textes = S. 12 des Archivdokuments.
5   Ebd., S. 5-6 der zweiten Fassung des Textes = S. 13-14 des Archivdokuments.
6   In Werner Hecht, Karl-Claus Hahn und Elifius Paffrath, Hrsg., *Brecht 80 – Brecht in Afrika, Asien und Lateinamerika – Dokumentation* (Henschelverlag Kunst und Gesellschaft, Berlin 1980), [Abschnitt] "Theaterarbeit (Dialog)" [d.i. Protokoll einer Diskussion von Konferenzteilnehmern], S. 143-166, Bennewitz-Zitat S. 149. (Hervorhebung durch den Verfasser.)
7   Fritz Bennewitz, Brief an Ingeborg Pietzsch vom 10.08.1982 [als Antwort auf Fragen zu interkulturellen Arbeitserfahrungen], Typoskript mit handschriftlichen Einzeichnungen von Fritz Bennewitz, (FBA, Dokumentengruppe AO-G 07: Texte von Fritz Bennewitz/1982-08-10), S. 1-15. (Hervorhebung durch den Verfasser.)
8   Vergleiche David G. John, *Bennewitz. Goethe. Faust. German and Intercultural Stagings* (University of Toronto Press, 2011).

Vom didaktischen zum dialektischen interkulturellen Theater: Fritz Bennewitz und seine Inszenierung des *Kaukasischen Kreidekreises* in Mumbai

Joerg Esleben

Der Artikel versucht das Wesen und den interkulturellen Erfolg der Inszenierung von Brechts *Kaukasischem Kreidekreis* unter der Co-Regie von Fritz Bennewitz (Nationaltheater Weimar) und der marathisprachigen Regisseurin Vijaya Mehta in Mumbai (Indien) im Jahre 1973 zu bestimmen. Auf der Grundlage einer Analyse von Theaterkritiken und von Bennewitzs eigenen Schriften vertrete ich die These, dass die Arbeit an der Inszenierung für Bennewitz zu einem Lernprozess wurde und zur Teilhabe an einem theatralischen Austausch führte, welcher weitestgehend universalistische, essentialistische und neoimperialistische Tendenzen vermied. Seine dialektische Denk- und Arbeitsweise, die sehr wahrscheinlich in seiner DDR-Sozialisierung wurzelte, die er aber auf sehr individuelle, nuancierte und offene Weise anwendete, leistete einen bedeutenden Beitrag zur Schaffung von interkulturellem Theater, das eine nachhaltige Herausforderung an besser bekannte westliche interkulturelle Theaterprojekte darstellt.

The article attempts to determine the nature and degree of success as an intercultural theatrical experiment of the 1973 production of Brecht's *Caucasian Chalk Circle* in Mumbai (India) co-directed by Fritz Bennewitz of the Weimar National Theater and Marathi director Vijaya Mehta. Based on an analysis of reviews as well as of Bennewitz's own writings, I argue that for Bennewitz work on the production became a learning process that led him to participate in a theatrical exchange largely avoiding universalist, essentialist, and neo-imperialist pitfalls. His dialectical way of thinking and working, likely rooted in his GDR socialization yet applied in a highly individual, nuanced and open manner, contributed significantly to the creation of an intercultural theater that poses sustained challenges to its better-known Western counterparts.

From Didactic to Dialectic Intercultural Theater: Fritz Bennewitz and the 1973 Production of the *Caucasian Chalk Circle* in Mumbai

Joerg Esleben

The large body of intercultural theater work by Fritz Bennewitz, Brecht expert and artistic director of the *National Theater* in Weimar from 1960 to 1989, has received very little scholarly attention, though it presents an important contrast and challenge to the dominant forms of Western intercultural theater that have developed since the 1970s. This article focuses on an important starting point of Bennewitz's intercultural trajectory, the 1973 production of Brecht's *Caucasian Chalk Circle* in a Marathi adaptation that he co-directed with the prominent Marathi director Vijaya Mehta in Mumbai. By nearly all accounts, this production was highly successful, from the perspectives of Bennewitz, Mehta, and their cast as well as for audiences and critics in India, Germany, and Switzerland. It was also a milestone in Bennewitz's development of an intercultural theatrical aesthetics and politics, which he tested and reworked in many subsequent projects in India and other parts of Asia and the world.

The collaborative production came about as the result of a felicitous overlap in the objectives of the two co-directors: with the experiences and self-critical evaluation of his 1970 production of *The Threepenny Opera* in New Delhi in mind, Bennewitz was determined to achieve a more effective blending of Brechtian and Indian theater with his next project in India, and to find an Indian directing partner to this end.[1] He found such a partner in Vijaya Mehta, who has played a significant role among Indian theater artists utilizing Brecht to integrate urban and folk forms and to connect them to contemporary political concerns.[2] Bennewitz met Mehta at the First Asian Theater Conference in Mumbai in November 1972.[3] They discovered significant points of contact between their respective aesthetic and political goals, agreed on a co-directed production of the *Caucasian Chalk Circle*, and won the support of the literary and cultural association Mumbai Marathi Sahitya Sangh. The prominent Marathi poet and playwright C. T. Khanolkar created a Marathi adaptation of the play entitled *Ajab Nyaya Vartulacha*. Bennewitz translated this title as "the remarkable verdict with the circle" and interpreted "ajab" as also carrying the connotations of "strange," "wonderful," "beautiful," and "good."[4]

In the summer of 1973, Mehta came to Berlin so that she and Bennewitz could check Khanolkar's version against Brecht's original text (apparently by recourse to a re-translation from Marathi into German as well as to the English translation used by Khanolkar) and discuss their concept for the production.⁵ From the start, this concept seems to have been based on an agreement not simply to produce Brecht's play in translation but to transpose it fundamentally into Indian cultural, social, historical, and theatrical contexts, including the employment of a number of folk theater forms such as *tamasha*, *dashavtar*, and others. Bennewitz then came to Mumbai in October 1973, where he and Mehta worked on the production with semi-professional actors in an extremely narrow time frame and under working conditions that Bennewitz found very challenging, even though he adapted to them quickly. The production premiered in Mumbai in November 1973 and also played in New Delhi in December, in both cases to great critical acclaim. The production then came to Europe in 1974 for guest performances at the *Berliner Festtage*, at Bennewitz's home institution in Weimar, and in several other cities in the GDR as well as in Zürich. These guest performances met with great enthusiasm from German and Swiss audiences and critics.

Bennewitz formulated his impressions of and reflections on the production in personal letters, as he did with most of his other productions abroad, as well as in some program notes and a few brief articles.⁶ Based on the evidence provided by Bennewitz's writings and by reviews of the production's performances in India, Germany, and Switzerland, the present article attempts to determine the nature and degree of success of the *Chalk Circle* production as an intercultural theatrical experiment. For Bennewitz, work on the production became a learning process, which led him to participate in a theatrical exchange largely avoiding universalist, essentialist, and neo-imperialist pitfalls. His dialectical way of thinking and working, likely rooted in his GDR socialization yet applied in a highly individual, nuanced and open manner, contributed significantly to the creation of an intercultural theater that poses strong challenges to its better-known Western counterparts.

A first indication of Bennewitz's learning process can be found in his changing characterization of the working relationship he had with Mehta. As Bennewitz tells the story, a division of tasks evolved whereby Bennewitz organized the basic arrangement of scenes, Mehta then followed up with detailed work on acting and choreography integrating elements from *tamasha* and other folk theatrical forms, with Bennewitz finally coming back to fine-tune the acting and to impart to the cast his perspective on the meanings of the Brechtian text and on the appropriate acting methods for conveying them. In a letter from the early phase of the production, Bennewitz compares his role to that of a director at a large German theater and Mehta's to that of an assistant temporarily taking over from the master, who then "returns and corrects and does the fine-tuning or redoes everything."⁷ But if this comparison was ever truly representative of Bennewitz's attitude, this attitude must have changed over the course of the work. Two weeks later he plays on the double meaning of the German word *Mitarbeiter* as co-worker and subordinate employee when he writes that "Vijaya is an ideal co-worker — or rather, it is me who is actually the co-worker."⁸ In a long summative letter of November 1973, Bennewitz describes his role neutrally as "a combination of dramaturge, artistic consultant, commentator, plot organizer, guardian of turning points, and mediator of acting methods,"⁹ and he includes the following assessment (different versions of which appear in each of his published accounts of the production): "The success and lasting significance lie in the nature of such an international cooperation itself, in which partners unite their experience and knowledge to mutual advantage for a shared task, while respecting and admiring each other's traditions and achievements."¹⁰ There is evidence, then, of Bennewitz's growing sense of the importance not only of equality in the power relations between the collaborators but also of equal representation of respective elements from both cultural contexts in the intercultural blend.¹¹ Such evidence for growth in Bennewitz's awareness and acceptance of the principle of equal exchange can also be gleaned from his reflections on the relations between Brechtian aesthetics and politics and Indian folk theater, between story and history, and between textual and performative meanings.

Bennewitz, similarly to some of his Indian colleagues, argues in his letters that the integration of Brecht's plays in India must occur through folk theater rather than classical Sanskrit traditions since Brechtian theater is folk theater on a higher level of naïvité.¹² However, he perceives political deficits in the open, satirical folk form of *tamasha*, seeing a "loss...of ideological orientation, by which the fun degraded itself to mere entertainment, where once surely the unity of entertainment and enlightenment, which perfects itself in Brechtian theater, was vaguely present, definitely as an ideal possibility."¹³ This formulation creates a clear hierarchy between Brechtian theater as the most advanced expression of (European) reason and the Indian folk form as corrupted by excessive irrationality. But Bennewitz also increasingly saw the benefits of the Indian folk form. With regard to what he called the "dialectical twistedness of Brecht sentences [dialektischen Vertracktheit von Brecht-Sätzen]," he lauded the possibilities of folk forms with their open, improvisational qualities to solve textual problems with ad-libbed commentary and more direct illustration.¹⁴ The two traditions are treated as equal (though not as the same) in Bennewitz's comparative comment that "what in Germany we wanted to and, perhaps, did achieve with masks — the differentiation between worlds, between above and below — that is done here through the various theatrical styles and the use of various traditions of folk theater."¹⁵ In his published accounts, too, he emphasizes the advantage of Marathi folk theater for transposing the play successfully.¹⁶ Additionally, the initial hierarchy between folk theatrical elements and established Brechtian techniques is even reversed to some degree when he acknowledges that

Indian folk forms use music and the chorus in ways that allow theater "to integrate narrator and music in wholly different ways than has been achieved or is even possible for us at home."[17] Thus even if Bennewitz entered the project with a fairly clear hierarchical conception of the relation between Brechtian theater and Indian folk theater, he seems to have revised this conception into a more equitable and dialectical one.

One of the greatest challenges Bennewitz saw in the mediation between Brecht's text and Indian culture lay in achieving a proper relation between story and history, that is, in getting Indian actors and audiences to make the intended connections between the play's fable on the one hand and historical and social problems on the other hand. In his letter of November 1973, Bennewitz describes two essential steps in the adaptation of the text: the more straightforward, outward adaptation to Indian culture, and the more difficult task of making the play's messages comprehensible for an audience lacking not only a highly developed historical and dialectical consciousness but also a stock of historical occurences and constellations that could serve for comparison. Bennewitz argues that the historical and political context of India today has to be taken into account, and provides the example that the emancipatory story of the robber Irakli could be misunderstood as support for either the radical right Hindu nationalist party Shiv Sena or the radical left Naxalites: "and neither interpretation is congenial to Brecht's intentions, to mine, or to history."[18] In the same letter, he summarizes his misgivings about Indians' understanding of the play:

> Of course, there remain difficulties in the reception of the play and certainly also in the deeper understanding by all actors: the juxtaposition of GOOD and EVIL is still static like RAMA and RAWANA, not dynamic, dialectical, just as historical consciousness is static, not dynamic and dialectical.[19]

While these statements could give rise to the impression that Bennewitz was driven by a Eurocentric socialist missionary zeal, they should rather be seen as temporary way stations in the process of negotiating between Bennewitz's background and the Indian context in which he found himself. His description of the same challenge in his published account strikes a different note:

> The adaptation of the play became a living collective process shared by all who participated in the work. It is not limited to giving the characters Indian names and costumes, or to taking manners and customs into account—rather, the adaptation needs to integrate the play both as a story into the history there and into the theater and performance traditions of the country. Add to that the consideration of the particularities of the audience's faculty of historical association and comparison.[20]

The focus here lies on differences rather than deficits, and on the equal partnership in mediating between theses differences. In a review of the production, Joachim Fiebach discusses the adapted prologue, which rather than the original text's negotiation between two Caucasian agricultural collectives over a valley pits rural Indian landowning and landworking castes against each other in a struggle over water issues. Fiebach views the adapted prologue as a more adequate introduction to the play's themes for an Indian audience with its different historical, social, and aesthetic background. He argues that the adaptation thereby fulfills a necessary condition for the revolutionary effectiveness of the play and could thus serve as a practical model for the kind of Brecht reception that anti-imperialist theater artists in developing countries have theorized for some time.[21] Here, as in Bennewitz's final analysis, the focus is on mediating between European and non-European theater to achieve a common political goal, in a spirit of equality. Fiebach, however, also voices some doubts about the political efficacy of the project:

> Can this production fully achieve the intellectual excitation, the stimulation of critical and productive thinking about fundamental social contradictions, and thus the general tendency of Brecht's work?...Even though the staging clearly highlights the opposition between common people and feudal elite, i.e. exploiters – do the... familiar performance aspects not lead to an all too ingratiating representation of the events overall, rendering them – perhaps – "folkloristic," and thereby making it difficult for the audience to develop a critical, dialectical attitude?[22]

Fiebach thus sees the danger that the political edge of the Brechtian play may be lost in the transition to such different theatrical aesthetics as the performance registers of Indian folk theater. But it is precisely in this question of the relations between Brechtian text and Indian performative elements that Bennewitz seems to have undergone a profound learning process and contributed to a genuinely intercultural blend based on mutual and critical respect. One of his first reflections on this blend, after seeing a *tamasha* performance, is marked by some scepticism: "We would benefit from the immediacy of contact with the audience – they from some more meaning; it is as yet quite doubtful whether we can achieve this with the *Chalk Circle*. It would be a great chance for theater here, a kind of model case."[23] Despite the acknowledgement of the possible benefits that an Indian performative element could have for European theater, the emphasis here is still on the didactic mission of bringing meaning to Indian theater via Brecht. However, later in the same letter, when Bennewitz is weighing the open, improvisational performance style of *tamasha* against the need to guide the actors towards meaningful art, he writes: "Entirely new aspects and effects could be gained from the play if the experiment of transposing it into this form of folk theater succeeds."[24]

A balance of mutual benefits for Indian theater and for the understanding of the Brecht play begins to take shape here, a balance that is reinforced by Bennewitz's report from a later phase:

> Azdak and Schauwa are two extraordinarily experienced *tamasha* players, whose talent for improvisation reveals entirely new aspects of the play—I just have to watch out fiendishly (since a large portion of the text is totally changed) that the tendency towards farce, which is characteristic of *tamasha*, always curves back again towards depth of character and situation.[25]

The Brechtian text is here certainly not a sacrosanct repository of meaning but rather a basis for negotiation. Bennewitz's writings reveal how he became more and more knowledgeable about, and fascinated with, the performative aspects of *tamasha* and other folk theater, counting among these an open, unruly form focused on performance rather than text, the integration of gesture, music, and dance, the direct communication with the audience, and the granting of creative freedom to both actors and audience.[26] It is precisely in these performative elements that Bennewitz saw both a means to introduce established meanings of Brecht's text to the Indian stage and to illuminate new and significant aspects of this text. He argued that "the detour via Indian folk theater had turned out to be very useful for the discussion about Brecht and his interpretation today."[27] Many of the reviewers of the German and Swiss guest performances echoed this dialectical view. Kedar Nath and Elfriede Steyer emphasized the importance of the performative elements for communicating meaning across linguistic and cultural differences: "If the pantomimic element was one strong impression making understanding possible, the rhythmic element was another; both complemented each other."[28] The production of *Chalk Circle* and Bennewitz's reflections about it to some extent anticipate and confirm a current theoretical and practical emphasis in the area of intercultural theater on performative aspects as a critical corrective to the privileging of textual meaning.[29]

Interestingly, such emphasis on the text is prevalent in the Indian critical reception of the production. Many Indian reviewers focused on the adaptation of the play by C. T. Khanolkar and credited him, sometimes exclusively, with the successful mediation between Brechtian text and Indian culture and theater.[30] This holds true even for the only thoroughly negative review of the production by Lalita Bapat in the *Free Press Bulletin*. About Bennewitz's participation Bapat merely notes: "One could hardly find here any evidence of some definite contribution or guidance from the celebrated German director."[31] Instead, Bapat sees Khanolkar's adaptation as key to the production, but in a negative (and quite polemical) light: "During these efforts, he could not overcome several imbroglios and in the end appeared to have been desperate to infuse novelty more by the wanton use of obnoxious and dirty phraseology than anything else, perhaps on the realization that course was the only one left open." Of course, this focus on Khanolkar among the Indian reviewers could simply be read as an expression of the desire to underscore the Indian contribution to the production, in contrast to the heavy focus on Bennewitz among the German reviewers. However, the fixation on Khanolkar's text, this time in contrast to the highlighting of Indian performative elements in many German reviews, also suggests the need for more differentiated and complicated readings of the encounter between textual and performative cultures in intercultural theater.

Bennewitz most certainly made a significant contribution in the Mumbai *Chalk Circle* production to the successful mediation between textual and performative traditions, between the play's fable and Indian historical contexts, and between the aesthetics of Brecht and of Maharashtrian folk theater. Two longer quotes from Bennewitz's summative letter about the production will serve as jumping-off points for a conclusion:

> The highest priority was: the play, its story, its content, and its intention must reach and interest the masses. Thus it was clear that this could only happen through an adaptation by which the play would be integrated and assimilated into the theater here, not to be devoured by it but rather to enrich it through a catalytic effect and by offering new ideas.[32]
>
> It is most astonishing how the result is not at all a hodgepodge of expressive means and acting styles but rather an exciting and lively combination of the various elements, precisely because they maintain their mutual distinctiveness—this is probably, even surely, so because all these diverse elements have a common denominator: they are all folk theater styles. Consequently, there is no unity in the sense of a stylistic uniform, but rather the dialectical (ideal-democratic) unity of independent diversity.[33]

These two statements by Bennewitz with their emphasis on mutual, dialectic enrichment capture some of the key elements of his practical conceptualization of intercultural theater. The analysis of Bennewitz's writings and of theater reviews shows that the *Caucasian Chalk Circle* production was indeed a successful intercultural experiment, if the measures for such success are defined as equitableness, mutuality, exchange, and critical respect. Bennewitz's dominant attitude changed from that of a didactic mission to one of cooperation based on mutual respect and the dialectical combination of "East-German-Brechtian" and Indian folk theater styles. This approach, likely influenced by Bennewitz's grounding in Marxist dialectics but tempered by the encounter with wholly different theatrical aesthetics and politics, helped him avoid some of the pitfalls of Western interculturalism, such as universalist and essentialist attitudes, the tendency to decontextualize ritual or folk forms, the assumption of authority over the expressive means of a non-Western culture, and the disparaging of that culture's current contexts.[34] Bennewitz's encounter and critical engagement with the performative aspects of Indian theater contributed crucially to the success of this project. On the basis of these findings, it can be argued that the production demonstrates that the concept of "intercultural theater" should not be discarded with reference to a particular Western kind of interculturalism, but should be contested and critically adapted for each individual case.

Endnotes

1   Fritz Bennewitz, "Ein indischer *Kreidekreis*," *Theater der Zeit* 29 (1974): pp. 44-47, here p. 44.
2   Vasudha Dalmia, *Poetics, Plays, and Performances: The Politics of Modern Indian Theatre* (New Delhi: Oxford University Press, 2006), pp. 178-179.
3   Bennewitz, "Ein indischer *Kreidekreis*," p. 44.
4   Fritz Bennewitz, "*Ajab Nyaya Vartulacha*," Program Notes in the Fritz-Bennewitz-Archive, Leipzig; Fritz Bennewitz, "*Ajab Nyaya Vartulacha*," Magazine Article in the Fritz-Bennewitz-Archive, Leipzig, no publication data available; Bennewitz, "Ein indischer *Kreidekreis*," p. 44.
5   Bennewitz, "*Ajab Nyaya Vartulacha*," Magazine Article; Fritz Bennewitz, Program Notes for a performance of *Ajab Nyaya Vartulacha* at the Film & TV Institute of India, Poona, 29 August 1974; Fritz Bennewitz, "*Kreidekreis* im Marathi-Stil," *Der Morgen* 26 January 1974.
6   All references to Bennewitz's letters refer to the collection housed at the Fritz-Bennewitz-Archive in Leipzig under the directorship of Prof. Dr. Rolf Rohmer, to whom the author would like to express his gratitude. At the time of writing, an international collaborative research project with the aim of commentating and publishing selections from Bennewitz's writings in English translation is underway.
7   Bennewitz, Letter of 14 October 1973: "Ich hab das Stück durchorganisiert und es vorübergehend Vijaya in die Hand gegeben (eine Arbeitsweise nicht unähnlich der, wie Regisseure an großen Theatern oft arbeiten, wenn sie vorübergehend ihren Assistenten die Aufführung d.h. die Proben überlassen und nach einiger Zeit wiederkommen und korrigieren und die Feinarbeit machen oder alles umschmeissen)."
8   Bennewitz, Letter of 25 October 1973: "...Vijaya eine ideale Mitarbeiterin ist—d.h. der Mitarbeiter bin eigentlich ich."
9   Bennewitz, Letter of November 1973: "Meine Funktion ist eine Kombination von Dramaturg, künstlerischem Berater, Kommentator, Fabelorganisierer, Drehpunktüberwacher und Schauspielmethodenvermittler."
10 Bennewitz, "Ein indischer *Kreidekreis*," p. 47: "Der bleibende Erfolg und die nachwirkende Bedeutung liegen im Wesen einer solchen internationalen Kooperation selber, zu der Partner ihre Erfahrungen und Kenntnisse zu wechselseitigem Vorteil für eine gemeinsame Aufgabe vereinigen in der Achtung und Bewunderung für die jeweiligen Traditionen und Leistungen des anderen."
11 It is important to note that a very different representation of the work distribution between the co-directors exists. The anonymous author of the Program Notes for a performance of *Ajab Nyaya Vartulacha* at the Film & TV Institute of India, Poona, 29

August 1974, describes the process as follows: "Mrs. Mehta and Mr. Bennewitz divided the directorial responsibility and started treating separate scenes simultaneously. Soon a problem arose. Mr. Bennewitz could not communicate with the artistes except a few leading ones. The problem was not the difficulty of language alone, but one of understanding and perception. The two directors therefore adopted another method of rehearsals. Mrs. Mehta first explained to Mr. Bennewitz her concept of the entire play, the general treatment, entries and exits, the usage of improvised material, and the total absence of sets. Mr. Bennewitz was thrilled. Then every day for about two hours she discussed with Mr. Bennewitz in order to grasp the contents of each scene in terms of contradictions and the dialectics as also the movement pattern that he had in mind. After that, she would conduct the rehearsals and explain these contents to the artistes in her own way as she knew the capacities of each actor. After initial rehearsals, she would call upon Mr. Bennewitz to watch them. Not even once did Mr. Bennewitz object to what Mrs. Mehta had conceived and realised in the rehearsals. It was always a happy O.K. and a pat on the back." Though Bennewitz is here represented as far more passive, this version of events also stresses his intercultural learning process.

12 Bennewitz, Letter of November 1973.
13 Ibid.: "Verlust (oder vielleicht hat es das im von mir gemeinten Sinn nie so recht gegeben) an ideologischer Orientierung, durch den der Spaß sich zur bloßen Unterhaltung herunterdegradierte, wo sicher einmal die sich im Brecht-Theater vollendende Einheit von Unterhaltung und Aufklärung im Ungefähren, ganz sicher als ideale Möglichkeit vorhanden war."
14 Ibid.
15 Ibid.: "was bei uns mit den Masken erreicht werden sollte und vielleicht auch wurde: die Abgrenzung der Welten, das Oben und das Unten — das geschieht hier durch die verschiedenen theatralischen Gangarten und die Verwendung unterschiedlicher Traditionen des Volkstheaters."
16 Bennewitz, "Ein indischer *Kreidekreis*," pp. 45-46.
17 Bennewitz, Letter of November 1973: "den Erzähler und die Musik überhaupt ganz anders in das Stück hineinzunehmen, als uns das zu Haus gelungen ist oder überhaupt gelingen kann."
18 Bennewitz, Letter of November 1973: "und beides ist nicht im Sinne von Brecht, nicht im Sinne der Geschichte und in meinem."
19 Ibid.: "Es bleiben natürlich Schwierigkeiten in der Rezeption des Stückes zurück und sicher auch im tieferen Begreifen durch alle Schauspieler: die Gegenüberstellung von GUT und BÖSE ist noch statisch wie RAMA und RAWANA, nicht dynamisch, dialektisch, wie auch das Geschichtsbewußtsein statisch, nicht dynamisch, dialektisch ist." [Emphasis in the original]
20 Bennewitz, "Ein indischer *Kreidekreis*," p. 45: "Die Adaption des Stücks ist ein lebendiger kollektiver Prozeß aller an der Arbeit Beteiligten geworden. Sie beschränkt sich nicht darauf, den Personen indische Namen und Gewänder zu geben, Sitten und Gebräuche zu berücksichtigen — Adaption muß das Stück gleichermaßen als eine Geschichte in die Geschichte dort und in die Theatertraditionen und Spielgewohnheiten des Landes integrieren. Dazu kommen die Rücksichten auf Besonderheiten des historischen Assoziations- und Vergleichsvermögens des Publikums."
21 Joachim Fiebach, "Theatergruppe Bombay: *Ajab Nyaya Vartulacha* (*Der Kaukasische Kreidekreis*) von Bertolt Brecht," *Theater der Zeit* 12 (1974): pp. 14-15, here p. 14.
22 Ibid., p. 15: "Kann diese Inszenierung die geistige Beunruhigung, die Anregung kritisch-produktiven Denkens über grundlegende soziale Widersprüche, eben die allgemeine Tendenz des Brechtschen Werkes, voll erreichen?...Auch wenn von den Arrangements die Gegensätze zwischen Volk und Feudalen, sprich Ausbeutern klar aufgezeigt werden, schmeicheln die...vertrauten Darbietungsweisen das Gesamtgeschehen nicht zu sehr an, machen es — vielleicht — 'folkloristisch' und erschweren so kritische, dialektische Haltungsansätze der Zuschauer?"
23 Bennewitz, Letter of 14 October 1973: "Uns würde freilich ein bisschen von der

Unmittelbarkeit im Spielkontakt mit dem Publikum gut tun—ihnen ein bisschen mehr Sinn; ob wir das mit dem *Kreidekreis* schaffen, bleibt noch recht zweifelhaft. Es wäre eine große Chance für das hiesige Theater, eine Art Modellfall."

24 Ibid.: "Dem Stück können ganz neue Seiten und Wirkungen abgewonnen werden, wenn das Experiment der Übertragung in diese Form des Volkstheaters gelingt."

25 Bennewitz, Letter of 25 October 1973: "Azdak und Schauwa sind zwei außerordentlich erfahrene Tamasha-Spieler, deren Talent zur Improvisation dem Stück ganz neue Seiten abgewinnt—ich muss nur höllisch aufpassen (da ein großer Teil der Texte völlig verändert ist), dass die Tendenz zur Farce, die dem Tamasha-Stil eigen ist, immer wieder die Kurve in den Tiefgang der Figuren und Situationen kriegt."

26 See Bennewitz, Letter of November 1973.

27 Uwe Gerig, "*Kreidekreis* mit Weihrauchduft," *Neue Berliner Illustrierte* 49 (December 1974): pp. 24-25: "Brechts Auseinandersetzung mit dem Begriff 'Naivität,' seine Forderung nach Rückgewinnung der Einfachheit auf der Bühne, könne durch diese Zusammenarbeit nur gefördert werden, meint Fritz Bennewitz. Der Umweg über das indische Volkstheater habe sich als sehr nützlich für die Diskussion über Brecht und seine Interpretation heute erwiesen."

28 Kedar Nath and Elfriede Steyer, "Ein indischer *Kreidekreis*," *Wochenpost* 43 (1974): "War das Pantomimische der eine starke Eindruck, der Verstehen möglich machte, so war ein anderer das Rhythmische. Beides ergänzte einander."

29 See Christine Regus, *Interkulturelles Theater zu Beginn des 21. Jahrhunderts: Ästhetik-Politik-Postkolonialismus* (Bielefeld: Transcript Verlag, 2008), pp. 100-101.

30 See for example, the reviews in *Times of India* on 20 November 1973, in *Navshakti* on 22 November 1973, and on 24 November 1973 in a journal cited as *Blitz* in German program notes.

31 Lalita Bapat, "Adaptation of Brecht's play unimpressive," *Free Press Bulletin* 23 (November 1973).

32 Bennewitz, Letter of November 1973: "Das oberste Gesetz: das Stück, seine Geschichte, sein Inhalt, seine Absicht müssen die Massen erreichen und interessieren. Damit war klar, dass das nur durch eine Adaption (also Bearbeitung) des Stückes geschehen kann, durch die das Stück vom hiesigen Theater integriert und assimiliert werden kann, ohne von ihm aufgefressen zu werden, sondern eher in katalytischer Wirkung das hiesige Theater zu bereichern, ihm neue Angebote zu machen."

33 Ibid.: "Es ist höchst erstaunlich, wie sich überhaupt kein Mischmasch der Ausdrucksmittel und Spielweisen ergibt, sondern sich eine erregend lebendige Verbindung der verschiedenen Elemente herstellt, gerade dadurch, dass sie ihre gegenseitige Unverwechselbarkeit behalten—das ist wahrscheinlich und ganz sicher so, weil alle verschiedenen Elemente einen gemeinsamen Nenner haben: alles sind Spielweisen aus dem Volkstheater. Es gibt also nicht die Einheit einer stilistischen Uniform, sondern die dialektische (ideal-demokratische) Einheit des vielfältig Selbständigen."

34 See Dalmia, *Poetics*, p. 295.

Fritz Bennewitz' islamischer *Kaukasischer Kreidekreis* auf den Philippinen

David G. John

Dieser Aufsatz befasst sich zunächst mit der internationalen Theatertätigkeit des DDR-Theaterregisseurs Fritz Bennewitz (1926-95). Hauptzentren für seine Beschäftigung waren Indien und die Philippinen, die er beide häufig besuchte und wo er viele Stücke inszenierte, hauptsächlich Brecht und Shakespeare, für ihn die zwei Pole seiner sozialistischen Geschichtsauffassung. Seine Zusammenarbeit mit PETA, der *Philippine Educational Theater Association*, war in dieser Hinsicht besonders wichtig. Der Aufsatz analysiert dann Bennewitz' Inszenierung von Brechts *Kaukasischem Kreidekreis* auf Tagalog (*Ang Hatol na Bilog na Guhit*) in Manila 1977, die mit dem Preis der philippinischen Kritiker als beste des Jahres ausgezeichnet wurde. Drei Gründe für diesen Erfolg werden hier vorgeschlagen: Bennewitz' Gebrauch der Nationalsprache Tagalog, seine Anwendung traditioneller philippinischer Theaterkonventionen, und seine thematische Auseinandersetzung mit einem dringenden sozialpolitischen Problem, der Enteignung der islamischen Minderheit im Süden des Landes.

This essay first surveys former GDR director Fritz Bennewitz's (1926-95) international theater activity. Outstanding among his destinations were India and the Philippines, each of which he visited repeatedly and where he directed many works, primarily Brecht and Shakespeare, anchors of his socialist concept of history. It is argued that he found in the end a new home in the Philippines, especially through collaboration with the Philippine Educational Theater Association (PETA). The essay then focuses on his 1977 production of Brecht's *Caucasian Chalk Circle,* in Tagalog (*Ang Hatol na Bilog na Guhit*), staged in Manila. It was judged by Philippine critics to be the country's best production of the year, and the essay shows why it was so successful, the reasons being threefold: his use of the national language Tagalog, his use of Philippine theater traditions and conventions, and his addressing of a burning socio-political issue, the disenfranchisement of the Muslim minority in the south.

Fritz Bennewitz's Islamic *Chalk Circle* in the Philippines

David G. John

The late East German theater director Fritz Bennewitz made a unique contribution to intercultural theater, but his work has not received much attention. Born in East German Chemnitz in 1926, he was among the first to commit wholeheartedly to the GDR's socialist platform in the late 1940s, remaining doggedly loyal to its principles until his death in 1995, if not to the form in which they were implemented in the last decades of that regime. By the mid-seventies, Bennewitz sought a way to cultivate and propagate these socialist ideals, especially as they related to humanistic principles, without the stifling restrictions of the government censors in his homeland, namely by directing abroad. In the next quarter century he visited twenty-eight countries around the world and directed in twelve of them. The following essay will analyze one of his most important productions, set it within the context of his entire range of activities outside the GDR, and assess its significance as an example of the director's contribution to intercultural theater.

Bennewitz's activities outside the GDR may well be unparalleled among theater practitioners internationally, and are at least comparable to those widely known.[1] He began his professional directing career in 1955 at the Landestheater in Meiningen, famous for its leading role in the development of naturalistic theater in the late nineteenth century under the leadership of Duke George II of Saxe-Meiningen (1826-1914). He left in 1960 to assume a position as director, and soon thereafter director-in-chief at the Deutsches Nationaltheater in Weimar, in political terms the leading conservative voice of the GDR stage. Bennewitz remained there until 1990 when, as part of the general political house-cleaning of German reunification, he was dismissed abruptly. The growing dissatisfaction amongst a broad range of GDR citizens with the practical implementation of socialist ideals, which became increasingly apparent in the seventies and came to a climax in 1989, was shared but never voiced publicly by Bennewitz, although his private correspondence shows this.[2] Rather, he expressed it in what was for that time a unique way, by removing himself lawfully for extended periods from that environment and propagating the ideals of socialist humanism abroad through the medium of theater, even after the reunification and until his death. To do so he obtained permission from the Ministry of Culture, largely because of the personal support of influential and politically enlightened government officials, such as Irene Gysi (1912-2007), to attend international theater conferences, give lectures, lead theater workshops, and direct plays abroad. This included both socialist and non-socialist countries. He regularly sent home to his ministry the obligatory accounts of his activities, couched dutifully in Marxist and party terminology, many of which survive in the FBA. Naturally the question arises in readers' minds as to his possible role as a GDR functionary, which could be a plausible reason for the liberal granting of permission to travel. It is the author's conviction, however, that this was not the case. Recent personal interviews about Bennewitz with close friends and colleagues, including the prominent GDR theater critic Erika Stephan, Dieter Görne, Bennewitz's dramaturge for many important productions and *after* reunification for many years longtime artistic director of the Staatsschauspiel Dresden, and senior Berlin journalist Christoph Funke, described Bennewitz uniformly as a committed socialist who was not particularly interested in party politics and not involved in subversive work in his homeland.[3]

Bennewitz's authorization to travel, live, and work abroad for extensive periods was also facilitated by his membership in the International Theater Institute (ITI), a situation similar to that of his academic colleague Rolf Rohmer, Professor of Theater in Leipzig, and for a time Director of the Deutsches Theater in Berlin. The ITI is an international organization under the umbrella of UNESCO, whose mandate is to promote the international exchange of knowledge and practice in theater arts in order to consolidate peace and friendship among peoples.[4] It holds regular meetings internationally, many of which Bennewitz, often with Rohmer, attended. He also became a core member of the ITI's Third World Committee, which focused on countries where humanitarian economic development was most lacking. As a committed socialist, Bennewitz was well-versed in the canonical writings of Marx and Engels. His own commentaries are filled with quotations and paraphrases from these, as well as references to Hegel's dialectics. When interviewed by the GDR press about his productions abroad, he peppered his replies with Hegelian and Marxist references, but while abroad he just as noticeably did not. A political chameleon like so many of his countrymen, he knew when to talk the talk, but walking the walk always remained to him more important.

Bennewitz's lecturing and directing abroad focused overwhelmingly on Brecht and Shakespeare, for him the two pillars of modern theater's development. He saw Shakespeare's works as the forerunner of modern theater, showing the great sweep of history, Brecht's as the model for contemporary socio-political circumstances, exemplifying how the Marxist dialectic is now playing itself out.[5] Among all the countries he visited, it is obvious that he preferred to visit, and felt himself most productive, in India and the Philippines, where he directed eighteen and eleven times, respectively, a far greater volume of activity than in any other country. In both places Bennewitz associated himself with influential theater organizations and institutions which helped him integrate into the local scene, in India principally the National School of Drama (NSD) in Delhi and the National Center for Performing Arts (NCPA) in Bombay, now Mumbai, and in the Philippines PETA, the Philippine Educational Theater Association. Given his reputation in the GDR, he was quickly welcomed in both countries, and because of his extraordinary dedication to his craft, especially to the training of young actors, he soon became respected, revered, and even loved by many associated with these organizations.

In late 1977 and early 1978, with the support of PETA, Bennewitz directed a Muslim adaptation of Brecht's *Caucasian Chalk Circle*, in Tagalog. This is a hybrid language based on Spanish and belonging to the Australasian group, and is the basis for Filipino, the country's national language.[6] It is spoken by most Filipinos and is also the official language of many Philippine regions, including the city of Manila. Translated and adapted by Lito Tiongson and Franklin Osorio, the adaptation was described, oddly enough, as a musical dance-drama, elsewhere as a "musical-dance-comedy-drama," previewing from December 2-4, 1977 in Manila, and opening in January 1978.[7] In an interview after the run, Bennewitz described the process of his being

> invited by PETA...to preside over a seminar in Manila whose object was to discuss an adaptation of the *Chalk Circle* for the Philippine national theater movement, to examine the feasibility of integrating surviving and newly discovered elements of the national minorities' pre-colonialist folk theater into Brecht's play.

He saw this as a continuation of his experiments to use "artistic methods of conveying the play's social message under widely varying historical, cultural, ethnic, and other conditions."[8] Bennewitz had first visited the Philippines six years earlier as a guest of the First World Theater Conference, initiated and organized by PETA in cooperation with the ITI. The Third World Committee of the Institute was founded during this conference and Bennewitz became a consulting member from the start.[9] The timing of the production coincided intentionally with PETA's tenth anniversary, and the co-ordination of the official premiere in January 1978 with Brecht's eightieth birthday signalled the status of the German playwright's work. Partly because of Bennewitz's influence, by the eighties Brecht held an exemplary position in PETA's concept of world theater.

Islam at that time, and still today, is the second-largest religion in the Philippines, nearing about 10% of the population, far behind Christianity with about 90%.[10] While Brecht's *Kreidekreis* is largely secular in nature, with slight references to Christian practices, by emphasizing the religious and cultural sensitivities of the Philippines and their contemporary political consequences, especially with regard to the minority Muslim population, the choice of this play presented an opportunity to engage audiences on personal terms with the central themes of familial and cultural identity, civil rights, and the associated physical territory. This suited PETA's mandate well. By this time in Bennewitz's career, the *Chalk Circle* had also become something of an intercultural test case for the director. He had directed it in Germany in the early sixties, and in 1972 at theater festivals in Romania and Syria, in 1973 in Bombay, and just before the Philippine production in New York at Ellen Stewart's fabled LaMaMa Educational Theater Club (ETC). This last production was adapted as an educational experience for children, and the interracial socially-active mandate of that theater, like PETA's, had made it relevant for the intracultural relations of that city and country as well.[11] So in that sense, with his Manila *Chalk Circle* of 1977/78, Bennewitz was in principle not doing anything new. What made it different was the unique set of cultural parameters in which he was operating. This production was to be in fact just the next link in the chain, and not the end, for he planned further productions of the play in Latin America and Africa, though this goal was never met.

Bennewitz's Muslim *Chalk Circle* was a resounding success, and that in the opinion not only of the ideologically slanted reviewers back home in the GDR, but also of its Filippino audiences, the Filippino press, and his PETA associates. It was awarded the Kalinangan prize as the outstanding presentation of 1977 in a ceremony which at the same time lavished praise on the First Lady of Manila, Imelda Romualdez Marcos, for her unstinting support of the development and promotion of Filipino arts and culture.[12] It succeeded for three reasons. First, as almost all of his works directed abroad, Bennewitz produced it in the local language with the title changing to *Ang Hatol na Bilog na Guhit* (*The Judgment of the Chalk*); second, as a musical-dance-comedy-drama he adapted it to popular Philippine theatrical forms; third, by casting it as a Muslim play he addressed a burning indigenous issue of the Philippine people.[13]

PETA has not systematically archived its many productions, and the Philippine National Library's holdings on them are scant. However, the FBA has done so for many Bennewitz stagings, the director himself being an almost fanatical preserver. It holds the typed pages of Bennewitz's notes on the production and a text of *Ang Hatol na Bilog na Guhit* in Tagalog, as well as the extensive, printed program booklet, with one short exception also completely in Tagalog.[14] This booklet contains a plot summary and information on many aspects of the production, including notes on the selection of the play, the directorial approach (by Bennewitz himself, in English), the stage design, music, songs, and sound, as well as a full list of cast members and technicians, major actors' professional biographies, and the text of four of the songs, all of which closely parallel the original. These materials, supplemented by further documentation in the Brecht Archive in Berlin, give us a detailed picture of the production.

In the documentation, a terse comment on the plot reads, "Almost the same as the original play except the prologue;" a later one comments,

> My problem. Still don't know what situation in the near past will take in relation or the problem presented by the story proper. All I seem to know is, there's a rebel group operating in Basilan and thus Basilan is one of the strongholds. By the way, Basilan is headlined in today's newspaper.[15]

Basilan is an island province of the Philippines located for the most part within the autonomous territory in Muslim Mindanao (ATMM) on the southern Philippine Suli peninsula, one of the strategic regions in the Spanish colonists' plan in the sixteenth century to conquer the Sulu Muslims, and still a hotbed of religious and cultural rebellion against the Philippine government and the Roman Catholic Church. The producers of the show obviously wanted the action to incorporate the history of colonial occupation of their country, but also the immediacy of this conflict for the present. Co-adaptor Tiongson wrote that they wished to incorporate both the Spanish colonization and its effect on the religious and cultural minorities, and the Moro Wars, referring to the Moro Rebellion of 1899–1913, an armed military conflict between the United States military and Muslim Filipino revolutionary groups ("Moro" refers to the Muslims of the Southern Philippines). Despite the historical victories of the colonists, the Islamic Sultanate's power continued in the south, and in the end was even endorsed by the Spaniards who then focused their authority in the north. The play's action was to be located in Basilan, the main characters were all to be Islamic: Gruscha became Surma, the governor Datu, the prince the Raja, the Grand Duke the Sultan, the highest ruler in Islamic Basilan, and Azdak became Malik. The PETA notes further indicate that the Azdak figure "must be familiar with Muslim law," that the sets and costumes should all reflect the Muslim culture of the 1840s, and that the production should include Muslim songs on war, love and courage, Muslim dances and a wedding ceremony, and Muslim props such as swords and daggers. The program begins with an image of Gruscha fleeing with her child and the following synopsis (translated from the original Tagalog):

> During the celebration of Mohammed's birthday, the chieftain (datu) voiced opposition to the governor of Basilan. A conflict resulted and he was beheaded. His wife and servant managed to escape, as well as his son, who left with Surma, the housekeeper, who hid him from the soldiers and from Asim, the ruler. She sheltered the child and raised him in the northern mountains. After several years of searching for the child, who was still the governor's heir, he was found and both mothers claimed and fought for his custody. The play has two parts, the stories of Surma, the housekeeper, and of the judge, Malik.[16]

The plotline is much the same as in Brecht, with only the locale changed to Basilan and the beginning to Mohammed's birthday (February 26). Further program information sharpens the Muslim focus, outlining first the "Muslim War," when the Spaniards attempted to occupy the Philippines but failed in the Muslim region of Mindanao because of strong resistance, then the occupation of other parts of the Sulu peninsula by French, British, Dutch, and German colonists, with the Spanish (and their Catholicism) dominating from 1840 on. The program recounts how the island's governor joined forces with the Spanish, who made him king, and how the two remained in conflict thereafter, with the Muslims led by their chieftain, the Datu character in the adaptation. The program goes on to describe the set as a poor Islamic neighborhood with provisional structures made of wood and kerosene cans.[17] The music is said to derive from Muslim folk and Filipino national songs, accompanied by traditional Filipino instruments made in part of bamboo sticks and coconut shells, and including bongo and other drums and guitars. Finally, after biographical information on the actors and other participants, and director Bennewitz, the program concludes with the texts of the four songs, "The Flight to the Northern Mountains," "The Song of the Northern Mountains," "The Judgment," and "The Song of Surma." The Tagalog translations show no significant variance from Brecht's originals.

There is, however, a substantial difference between Brecht's prologue to the play and its Tagalog adaptation, as seen here:[18]

> Women and men folk occupy the stage, watching a house in an Islamic neighbourhood being demolished, as if hit by a typhoon. It's our turn next week, says one...what about my job...what will become of my source of income?...
> "Why do you speak of digging in the garbage?" asks another. "In our province it's better. We dig in the soil, not the garbage."
> "Yes, it's a farm, but it's not ours," is the reply. "We are the ones who planted. We are the ones who harvest. We are the ones who prepare and cook. But once it is cooked, they are the ones who eat the food." "Why is it like that?" the first asks.
> "And what about me?" asks another. "I am the one who makes the shoes, but look at *my* shoes, they're worn out."
> "I work in the factory where we make underwear and bras," says another. "Do you wear them," she's asked? "No!" "Then who wears them?" "They're for export," she replies.
> Storyteller: "Whether you live in Manila or in the province, whether you work in a factory or on a farm, are we not the ones who work and create?...Why is it so? What is left to us, why are we rejected?" There are cries of "Why, why, why?" from the people. "Let me explain it to you," replies the narrator. It's like the story in the Bible about King Solomon and the two mothers which was told to me by my grandmother.[19]

And so the action of the *Chalk Circle* begins, now re-set in an immigrant workers' slum in Manila. The scene depicted contemporary Manila and, sadly, despite the more than thirty years since, a side of Manila that is still much the same today. It brings together the city proletariat and the poor southern island Muslim migrants who were a feature of the city in 1978, having been dispossessed of their land in the Sulu region, reduced to poverty, and now become an obvious underclass of the working poor, with their bare feet and ragged appearance on the streets and in the factories of the capital.[20] Pitiful irony lies in the one speaker's reference to shoes if we recall that the production was awarded the Kalinangan prize at an event celebrating Imelda Marcos's contribution to the Arts, a person who was said to own three *thousand* pairs of shoes. This is a production not only about colonial oppression, but also domestic economic subjugation and exploitation, which in the director's view called for the oppressed to rise up no longer against colonial powers but rather their own countrymen and women.[21] The adaptation ended with Azdak's famous lines "I now lay down my judge's robe, because things are getting too hot. I'm not cut out to be a hero," hence abrogating any responsibility for correcting the injustice, as in the original.[22] Bennewitz insisted that Azdak's stance here "was intended to bring out the need for collective decision-making: the oppressed cannot delegate responsibility for their liberation to anyone else but themselves."[23]

Before the rehearsals began, Bennewitz called the cast together at the Raja Suleiman outdoor theater in the ruins of historical Fort Santiago where it would be staged, a venue of substantial historical significance. He was aware, as evident from his correspondence, that this stone fort, constructed first of wood by Sultan Suleiman, recalled the Spanish occupation in the sixteenth and ensuing four centuries of colonial domination. At this place, even *before* the translation and adaptation were finished, Bennewitz "began the rehearsal phase with a 'demonstration-interpretation' of the entire play in a series of scenes (Stationen), a process of lecturing and describing which continued without interruption for three to four hours."[24]

While he at first knew little about the Islamic context of the production, he was confident in being solely responsible for the Brechtian approach he would take. That was set in stone from the start, and the point should be made that despite his modest and generous willingness to learn about, adapt, and indeed bow to the cultural mores and practices of his host country, as in all the others where he directed, he was rigid in his convictions about Brechtian theory and stage practice. The Filipinos soon learned to love him, but they recognized too his hard-line core. The following observation by one Philippine theater critic ten years later, by which time Bennewitz had become a fixture there, describes the dichotomy:

> Most Filipino artists who have worked with the German director Fritz Bennewitz say he is a terror. But this is one terror who is loved, adored and respected by Filipino artists who have come to know him. Although he may direct with an "iron hand," many Filipino artists would still seize the opportunity to work with him even if it means doing a minor role.[25]

Bennewitz didn't come to Manila to learn a directing style. He brought that from Germany — his colonizing contribution, so to say. He *did* come to Manila to learn how to apply it to a new cultural setting and use it to address social issues for the benefit of the downtrodden. The Spanish brought Catholicism. Bennewitz brought Brecht.

In his correspondence during the weeks preparing the production there was much discussion of the play's Islamic focus. Bennewitz wrote of observing demonstration dances, costumes, and rituals by Sulu performers; of using the local people to advise staging the procession of the Sultan and his entourage to the mosque; and of listening to lectures on Islam's place in the history of the Philippines. It was not easy. Repeatedly he wrote of the difficulty he had penetrating this culture and religion, where, as opposed to his experience in India, he "had to strain to understand any of the language,…its logic, structure, gestural possibilities, its semiotics and signals, and the social, cultural, and ethnic sophistication which it contains."[26] He complained repeatedly about not having the intercultural support of an ally like Vijaya Mehta in India who served as ongoing liaison between the Indian actors, texts, and cultural context. At this point in Manila he seems to have had no such personal ally, despite the warm welcome PETA afforded him, a lacuna which gradually disappeared in the course of the next twenty years when he gained the friendship and confidence of many respected and indeed beloved colleagues, allies and friends there. After his last visit to the Philippines in 1995, he wrote to PETA stalwart Rody Vera, the translator and co-director of his final Philippine production, Goethe's *Faust I*,

> I don't know whether you can imagine what it means to me. My life has come full circle with that PETA-Faust — the most moving and meaningful celebration and documentation of 25 years of international co-operation with PETA as the one and only REAL home throughout so many years of almost three generations.[27]

In the end, his affinity to the Philippines seemed even greater than to India.

There was also much frustration with organizational matters. The entire rehearsal period was a mere four and a half weeks. The Malik-Azdak actor had to be replaced just a week before the opening when he was called away to a film contract for which he would actually be paid.[28] The other Philippine participants always remained a source of delight, but their competence was problematic:

> I am working with a group of people, 90% of whom are unbelievably kind, well-meaning, and willing, but at the same time with little ability in the sense of mature or methodologically grounded theater training. So to stage the play within just three weeks and at the same time workshop it, teach, demonstrate, explain, test, explore variations, rehearse to ensure comprehension of the individuality of a character…

seemed well nigh to impossible.[29] Bennewitz wrote of his frustration with the work ethic and devotion of the young actors, their concept of time as opposed to his own, and their blissful ignorance of the strict deadlines that faced them; yet he praised them highly when remembering that they were all unpaid amateurs who came to long late afternoon and evening rehearsals *after* their full shifts of daily work.[30] They belonged to PETA's "Kalinangan" acting ensemble, the same word used to describe the critics' annual prize, which means the "laborious task of cultivating rough terrain," an adept metaphor both for PETA's mandate and the agrarian themes of the play. Bennewitz also described his frustration working with the translators and adaptors to advance step by step from German to English to Tagalog to create the performance text, as follows:

> Then around 10 a.m. a few PETA people came with the latest section of the adaptation and translation into Tagalog, to be translated back into English so that I could check it over. That was my first great shock here a few days ago. It was a totally impossible and unusable translation and adaptation. So I quickly ordered a couple more to their number and tried to explain to them the principles of translating Brecht and how one adapts the historical and ethnic circumstances to his work; that translation and adaptation are a social process; and that even talent in the translator can lead both to true and distorted results if the talent lies in the hands of someone who comes from a wealthy house and has never felt the pangs of hunger.[31]

He was asking them in fact to do more than just translate, they should *feel* the translation and *feel* the problems of the work in their hearts and stomachs. Despite this frustration, Bennewitz's character always pulled him through, like a chameleon, infinitely adaptable to the changing practical and cultural circumstances around him, always embracing and accepting them, working toward a successful production. Even as a diehard atheist he was able to write with good humor: "I am also learning to cry out to 'Allah,' even if it sticks in my craw when I hear it all the time."[32] Soon he had gained the admiration of the entire PETA organization. He even gained an ally in the socially progressive branch of the Philippine Catholic Church. A priest involved in the production said of him, "Surprising how human the communists are, aren't they?" on which Bennewitz commented, with typical good humor, "You see how I'm jumping through the moral hoops of enlightenment to ingratiate our side!"[33] Speaking of Catholicism, what seemed to fascinate him most about this visit to the Philippines was the Philippine version of Roman Catholicism and its extravagant public rituals. In early November he marvelled at the intricate graveyard ceremonies and magnificent parades of All Souls' Day which introduced a week of celebration that consumed the entire city like an extended folk festival.[34] This clearly appealed to what he would later acknowledge as his allegiance to theater as an anthropological phenomenon, before turning away from this concept as a theoretical foundation, remaining loyal to his socialist model.

Philippine and East German theater critics were uniform in their praise of the production. The Manila press tied its significance closely to PETA's tenth anniversary and mandate to pursue social justice, a crescendo of praise which climaxed in the awarding of the Kalinangan prize.[35] There were numerous GDR reviews, based primarily on Bennewitz's own reports, and while they may well be suspected of political self-interest, their detail, at least, remains informative after the intervening thirty years. The best, and still internationally respected GDR theater journal *Theater der Zeit* published a capsule report of the production including Bennewitz's assessment of its function and importance. He reported "a storm of applause" after the premiere and stated the production's primary function to contribute to the creation of an independent national theater in the Philippines, which had also been the principle goal of PETA since its founding in 1967.[36] The numerous other East German reviews were rather reports that cited or slightly re-formulated the thematic thrust of the adaptation. Paraphrasing Bennewitz they described how he saw the adaptation as an exploration into the Philippines' identity, particularly the inclusion of ethnic minorities as exemplified by the Muslims of the Sulu archipelago. The relevant point for the GDR's socialist agenda was, however, that the farmers of that region had been dispossessed of their land, and forced into migration and poverty. Readers naturally linked this with one of the central doctrines of their own state, the GDR land reform (*Bodenreform*) instituted immediately after the war (1945-49) which seized land from the capitalist Junker class and returned it to the farmers, allowing it to blossom through co-operatives to provide a self-reliant substructure to the country's agricultural system which was to become one of the essential features of a "successful" economy. There was, finally, a report in *Der Morgen* (Berlin) about a plan to perform the production on a number of other Philippine islands, and while there is no evidence that this was ever realized, we do know that Bennewitz continued to adapt the play in similar fashion in several other countries, even in a version specifically for children, staged in New York, Sri Lanka, and numerous locations in India.[37]

In conclusion, let us look at the significance of the production in terms of broader intercultural relations. The Indian director and cultural critic Rustom Bharucha dedicated *The Politics of Cultural Practice* to his friends and, specifically, "Fritz Bennewitz, an intercultural seeker and one-eyed director, who saw the world differently."[38] He marked 1977 as the beginning of his own course toward a critique of interculturalism and intercultural theory, thus at exactly the same time as this production.[39] Bharucha was then a student at Yale University and had been struck by the monocultural social fabric and attitudes of that celebrated institution. His experience would probably have been similar had he attended most American or other universities at the time throughout the world. It was this realization that drove him to focus his theoretical writing and practical theater work in India and abroad on the concept of interculturalism. One of the arguments for which Bharucha has become known is the importance of *secularism* in intercultural politics and the arts. In *The Question of Faith* (1993) he defended the notion of the division of state and religion in politics, yet he insisted that even in the secular state it is necessary "for non-believers to enter the world of believers to understand how they experience that world and relate to it."[40] He argued thus for a place for religion in public life while at the same time for the clear separation of religion and state. He opposed what he called "communalism," political mobilization on the basis of religious identity of a community by an elite and the elite's own interest, and most strongly he condemned fundamentalism, which he defined as extremist religious ideology through which religious organizations assert their God over other religions. His 1994 essay "Somebody's Other. Disorientations in the Cultural Politics of our Times" describes the destructive consequences of communalism in its most drastic form.[41] Seven years later, in *The Politics of Cultural Practice*, Bharucha was ready to launch a public attack on the leading theorists and practitioners of intercultural theater, Peter Brook, Richard Schechner, and others. He formulated the need for a sharp differentiation between intercultural dynamics between different nation states and cultures, and "*intracultural* dynamics between and across specific communities and regions *within* the boundaries of the nation-state," and an awareness that "at a conceptual level of cultural practice, the 'intra' denotes the possible relationships between different cultures at *regional* levels."[42] Only in this sense can "multiculturalism" which many modern nations flaunt, be truly realized. Looking back, Bharucha has often said that the German director was a pioneer in interculturalism in the most positive sense. His activity in the Philippines is evidence of this. In fact, it can be argued that there is no better example of Bennewitz's pioneering intercultural and intracultural work than his *Chalk Circle* there, for it represents a rare attempt to bridge opposing and traditionally confrontational regional and religious cultures of that country, and in the estimation of the citizens of that country themselves, with great success.

Endnotes

1   Some of the biographical facts that follow have appeared in a handful of published accounts of Bennewitz's life and work, all of which, however, are scant. See, for example, Bernd C. Sucher, *Theaterlexikon. Autoren, Regisseure, Schauspieler, Dramaturgen, Bühnenbildner, Kritiker,* 2nd ed. (München: Deutscher Taschenbuch Verlag, 1999). The author's forthcoming book, David G. John, *Bennewitz. Goethe. Faust. German and Intercultural Stagings* (Toronto: University of Toronto Press, 2011) contains a detailed personal and artistic biography. The many details which follow in this article are based on primary sources in the Fritz-Bennewitz-Archiv (hereafter FBA), a private archive curated by Dr. Rolf Rohmer, owned by the Fritz-Bennewitz-Gesellschaft eingetragener Verein, and located at Sebastian-Bach-Straße 27, 04109 Leipzig, Germany. Materials in the archive have been organized but not yet catalogued.
2   Bennewitz's private statements about his disappointment with GDR socialism can be found in his correspondence in the FBA, for example in his letter from Delhi to a friend in Germany on 20 January 1990, p. 4.
3   The full texts of the interviews will appear in the author's forthcoming book, John, *Bennewitz. Goethe. Faust.*
4   See <http://www.iti-worldwide.org/aboutiti.html>, 27 September 2010.
5   Fritz Bennewitz, "Werkstattgespräch," Typescript with annotations, 26 pp., here p. 7, FBA.
6   See <http://en.wikipedia.org/wiki/Filipino_language>, 27 September 2010.
7   "PETA marks 10th year with 'Ang Hatol,'" *Philippine Panorama,* (22 November 1977): p. 21.
8   Fritz Bennewitz, "*The Chalk Circle* in Tagalog," pp. 25-27, here 26, photocopy FBA.
9   Ofelia R. Rondina, "Theater's lovable terror," *The Manila Chronicle,* 8 February 1987, unpaginated, FBA.
10 See <http://en.wikipedia.org/wiki/Religion_in_the_Philippines>, 27 September 2010.
11 See <http://www.lamama.org>, 27 September 2010.
12 "The Year's Best," *20 WB.* 19 January 1978, 2 pp., photocopy, FBA.
13 See descriptions of the forms by Nicamor G. Tiongson, *The World Encyclopedia of Contemporary Theatre. Asia/Pacific* Vol. 5, ed. Don Rubin (London and New York: Routledge), 1998, pp. 377-94.
14 *Ang hatol ng guhit na bilog* [The Judgment of the Chalk], program booklet, 16 pp., unpaginated, FBA.
15 "Ang Hatol," Production notes to the *Caucasian Chalk Circle* production of 1977/78. 3 pp., typescript, FBA.
16 The author wishes to express his sincere thanks to Plulippine native and Tagalog speaker Marimar McCauley, née diaz Espinosa, who assisted with this research project. All translations and interpretations of the original Tagalog materials were made possible by her.
17 The FBA houses a small selection of black and white scene photos which confirm this and further descriptions of the visual elements.
18 Bertolt Brecht, *Bertolt Brecht Werke: Große kommentierte Berliner und Frankfurter Ausgabe,* Vol. 8, eds. Werner Hecht, Klaus-Detlev Müller et al. (Berlin: Aufbau, and Frankfurt/Main: Suhrkamp, 1992), pp. 9-14, 186-91, hereafter BFA.

19 "Ang Hatol," p. 3, original in Tagalog.
20 Fritz Bennewitz, "Notauftrag," report to GDR officials about his activities abroad in 1978, typescript pp. 7, p. 5, FBA.
21 Bennewitz, "Notauftrag," p. 6.
22 BFA 8, p. 184.
23 Bennewitz, "*The Chalk Circle*," p. 27.
24 Bennewitz, Letters from Manila to partner Waltraut Mertes and others, in part on the *Chalk Circle* production, 1977, 23 single-spaced typescript pp.: 1) 1 November 1977, 14 pp.; 2) 14 November 1977, 4 pp.; 3) 17 November 1977, 3 pp.; 4) 18 Nov. 1977, 2 pp. FBA. Citations from Bennewitz's writings are the author's translations from the original German. References will be made to individual letters, here, Letter 1), p. 14.
25 Rondina, "Theater's lovable terror."
26 Bennewitz, Letter 1), pp. 2, 14.
27 Bennewitz, Letter to Rody Vera, 29 January 1995, FBA.
28 "Ein Azdak mit Klassenkampf-Erfahrungen. Oder: Widerlegung der These vom 'Klassiker' Brecht. TLZ-Gespräch mit Fritz Bennewitz über seine Arbeit in Manila," *Thüringische Landeszeitung* [Weimarer-Ausgabe]. *TLZ-Treffpunkt*, 11 Feburary 1978, p. 3.
29 Bennewitz, Letter 1), p. 4.
30 Bennewitz, "Kreidekreis."
31 Bennewitz, Letter 1), p. 2.
32 Ibid., p. 5.
33 Bennewitz, Letter 4), p. 2.
34 Bennewitz, Letter 1), pp. 10-11.
35 "The Cultural Scene" *20 WB*, 12 December 1977, unpaginated;"German director here for PETA play," *Philippine Panorama,* (18 November 1977); "HodgePodge. Show Bits" *Philippine Panorama.* (27 November 1977): p. 37; "PETA marks 10th year with 'Ang Hatol,'" *Philippine Panorama,* (22 November 1977): p. 21. Photocopies of all sources in the FBA.
36 Bennewitz, "'Kreidekreis' in Manila" *Theater der Zeit* 1 (1978): p. 69.
37 "Ein Azdak mit Klassenkampf-Erfahrung," p. 3.; Georg Mench[en], "Brechts 'Kreidekreis' auf Tagalog in Manila, Kulturbrief von den Philippinen," *Neues Deutschland* [Berliner-Ausgabe], 31 January 1978; Heiner Klinge, "Vom Brecht-Dialog bis zum Schlagerfestival," *Volksstimme* [Magdeburger-Ausgabe], 3 January 1978.; "'Kreidekreis in Manila.' Brechts Werk in philippinischer Fassung," *Der Morgen* [Berliner-Ausgabe], 7 December 1977; Heiner Klinge, "Brecht-Stück nun auf den Philippinen. Fritz Bennewitz inszenierte 'Kaukasischen Kreidekreis,'" *Sächsische Zeitung* [Dresdner-Ausgabe], 6 January 1978; "'Kreidekreis' in philippinischer Fassung. DDR-Regisseur Fritz Bennewitz inszenierte in Manila," *Mitteldeutsche Neueste Nachrichten* [Leipziger-Ausgabe], 2 December 1977; H[einer] K[linge?], "Brecht in Tagalog. Bennewitz inszenierte 'Kreidekreis' in Manila," *Sächsische Neueste Nachrichten* [Dresden], 7 Dec. 1977; photograph of one scene with details about the play's title and place of production, *Freie Erde* [Neustrelitz], 17 Dec. 1977. Photocopies of all sources in the FBA.
38 Rustom Bharucha, *The Politics of Cultural Practice* (New Delhi: Oxford University Press, 2001), p. v. Bennewitz had lost an eye in an auto accident in 1976.
39 Bharucha, *The Politics*, pp. 7-8.
40 Rustom Bharucha, "Editor's preface" in *The Question of Faith, Tracts for the Times*, Vol. 3 (London: Sangam, 1993), p. vii.
41 Rustom Bharucha, "Somebody's Other: Disorientation in the Cultural Politics of our Times," *Economic and Political Weekly* 29.3 (January 1994): pp. 105-110.
42 Bharucha, *The Politics*, pp. 2, 5, 8 and 11.

Wuolijoki, Brecht, "gute" Dramaturgie und *Die Judith von Shimoda*

Dennis Carroll

Die Judith von Shimoda war Teil eines Trios von Kollektivarbeiten, die Wuolijoki, Brecht und sein Anhang in schneller Folge in Finnland zwischen August und September 1940 in Angriff nahmen. Sie fingen mit *Herr Puntila und sein Knecht Matti* an, fuhren mit einer Umarbeitung der *Judith von Shimoda* fort und schlossen mit einer kollektiven Übersetzung von Wuolijokis Stück *Niskavuoren nuori emäntä* (*Die junge Geliebte des Niskavuori*) ins Deutsche ab. Obwohl Brecht Wuolijokis Dramaturgie als naturalistisch ablehnte, kann man seine kritischen Vorbehalte anfechten, und die Parallelen zwischen den Hauptfiguren Loviisa und Okichi in der *Judith von Shimoda* erweisen sich als überzeugend. Die Hauptmerkmale der Umarbeitung der Übersetzung von Glenn Shaw schliessen die Kürzung von vielen langatmigen Reden der Art ein, die Brecht für "psychologisch ausgerichtet" hielt. Die größte Änderung betrifft die hinzugefügte Rahmenhandlung, in der die Freunde des Zeitungsmagnaten die private Aufführung kommentieren, und die im Druck auffälliger als in der Aufführung zum Tragen kommt und die Umarbeitung mehr aristotelisch als episch erscheinen lässt.

The Judith of Shimoda was part of a trio of collaborative works embarked on in short order by Wuolijoki and Brecht and his entourage in Finland in August to September 1940. They began with *Mr. Puntila and His Man Matti*, continued with the adaptation of *The Judith of Shimoda* and concluded with the co-translation into German of Wuolijoki's play *Niskavuoren nuori emäntä* (*The Young Mistress of Niskavuori*). Though Brecht dismissed Wuolijoki's dramaturgy as naturalistic, his critical reservations can be challenged, and parallels between the main character, Loviisa, and Okichi in *The Judith of Shimoda* are strong. The major features of the adaptation of the Glenn Shaw translation include the trimming of many lengthy speeches of the kind Brecht thought "psychologically oriented." The biggest change is the addition of the "framing story" where the newspaper mogul's friends comment on the private performance, which is more obtrusive on page than on the stage, leaving the adaptation predominantly Aristotelian rather than Epic.

Wuolijoki, Brecht, "Well Made" Dramaturgy, and *The Judith of Shimoda*

Dennis Carroll

At the beginning of his draft translation of the Neureuter reconstruction of the Brecht/Wuolijoki adaptation *The Judith of Shimoda*, Markus Wessendorf refers to the translation/adaptation history of Yamamoto Yūzō's play *The Sad Tale of a Woman, the Story of Chink Okichi* as "palimpsest-like."[1] The play falls into two sections: the first focuses on the geisha Okichi saving her city from bombardment by reluctantly agreeing to serve the American consul; the second charts the ruination of her subsequent life. This essay also falls into two sections: I will note first some possible aesthetic imprints of the work of the Finnish writer and playwright Hella Wuolijoki as part of the collaboration and the palimpsest, and then go on to consider the Brecht/Wuolijoki changes and additions to their source, the 1935 English translation of Yūzō's play by Glenn Shaw.[2]

1

Wuolijoki, born in Estonia, earned her Master's degree in Helsinki, married a Finnish politician, made a fortune in timber after WW I, became known for her Marxist sympathies, was condemned to death for high treason during WW II and, after the commutation of her sentence in 1944, became a broadcast executive.[3] Altogether she wrote 20 full-length plays and ten short plays.[4] She was a woman of many paradoxes: mild feminist but leftist in politics, capitalist magnate and Marxist political theorist, a fluent speaker of German but with powerful Russian friends, and a radical who still recorded with much empathy the life of the prosperous Finnish peasantry, like the owners of Niskavuori farm estate in her most popular series of plays.[5]

Though part of the national drama canon in Finland, she is internationally still chiefly known for her championing of, and collaboration with, Bertolt Brecht when he with his family and entourage came to Finland from Sweden in 1940, fleeing the Nazis. The intense period of collaboration between Brecht and Wuolijoki occurred between July and December 1940. Wuolijoki offered her hospitality to the Brecht *ménage,* first at Wuolijoki's farming estate at Marlbäck from July to October, then in Helsinki from October until the following May, when Brecht and company left Finland for Vladivostock and, ultimately, Los Angeles.[6]

Brecht and Wuolijoki met at a time when Wuolijoki's popularity as a playwright in Finland was at its zenith. The Red/White political enmity dating from the atrocities of the Civil War (1917-18) was temporarily resolved by the unifying national emergency in late 1939, when the

Soviets attacked and attempted to invade Finland in the Winter War. After this war, the leading Finnish mainstream theaters finally considered her plays earlier relegated to smaller Leftist and community theaters.[7] This was particularly true of the three plays set in the countryside dealing with several decades in the fortunes of the Niskavuori farming dynasty on their estate in the province of Häme. During the year that Brecht was Wuolijoki's guest, *Niskavuoren nuori emäntä* (*The Young Mistress of Niskavuori*) was staged not only in the National Theatre but also in eleven other theaters.[8]

A trio of dramatic collaborative works emerged in short order between the Brecht entourage and Wuolijoki. First, there was *Mr. Puntila and His Man Matti*, from August 27th to about mid-October 1940, adapted from earlier play and film-treatment drafts by Wuolijoki, set in Finland, with the leading character a schizophrenic alcoholic landowner. The second project was the Glenn Shaw translation of *Chink Okichi* which Wuolijoki gave to Brecht on September 25th, a play she had bought the rights to, with the leading character a schizophrenic alcoholic geisha. The draft of *Puntila* was translated into German by Margarete Steffin, Brecht's secretary, and Wuolijoki herself read a free translation to Brecht.[9] Brecht took over and transformed the four-act play, a fairly habitual paradigm in Wuolijoki's plays, into a ten-scene play, with his work including the need to "dismantle the psychologically orientated conversations."[10] By October 3rd, Wuolijoki was won over by Brecht's version and was translating it into Finnish,[11] but from about September 25th to October 7th, when Wuolijoki's selling of her Marlbäck farm was complete, both were also working simultaneously on versions of *Chink Okichi* in German and Finnish. Brecht wrote in his *Journals*, "I quickly sketch a framing action and a few stage moves on the basis of the (bad) English translation" (September 25).[12] According to John Fuegi, Steffin also did a German translation of the Shaw version.[13] Wuolijoki's Finnish version included some of Brecht's "framing action" and its Interludes.[14] But at about this time Brecht ceased working on the Okichi project.[15] And finally, thirdly, there was another play which went into collaborative translation: Wuolijoki and Steffin's co-translation into German of Wuolijoki's *Niskavuoren nuori emäntä*.[16]

However, Brecht in his *Journals* rather put down his chosen collaborator because of what he thought was the misleading naturalism of Wuolijoki's dramatic method in the Niskavuori plays. His journal entries show he knew of the local reviews of the National Theatre production of *Niskavuoren nuori emäntä* and he stated:

> The trilogy demonstrates how the farm is not there for the people, but the people for the farm; how the property shapes the family and destroys all individual relationships. The newspapers fail to see any of this. Reason: the work is written in the naturalist

manner, so all of this is really background, it all just happens, it does not come to the fore. The climaxes in the drama don't coincide with the climaxes or pressure points in the subject. In [George Bernard] SHAW, the heart of the matter is either a subject of conversation or is dealt with in the preface.[17]

But Wuolijoki's playwriting is more like Brecht's than Brecht himself was willing to admit. In *Sahanpuruprinsessa* (*The Sawdust Princess*), the earlier version of *Puntila,* Wuolijoki had tried out a more theatricalist style.[18] Also, it is arguable that in all three plays of the trilogy, including *Niskavuoren naiset* (*The Women of Niskavuori*) and *Niskavuoren leipä* (*Niskavuori Bread*), the climaxes in the "drama" and the "subject" do coincide. *Niskavuoren naiset*, for instance, begins with a scene in which the notables of the parish meet at Niskavuori for a *kahvikutsut* (coffee party) in which coffee, bread and juice are served in carefully designated and status quo-cementing order, presided over by the mistress of Niskavuori, a gestic ritual ultimately subverted by the hero's smashing of one symbolic coffee cup. In *Niskavuoren nuori emäntä*, the fate of the farm and the fortunes of the Niskavuori family are also demonstrated and crystallized in the final act of the play. Juhani, the errant young husband, has been elected as a parliamentary representative and acts for local officials who are fighting against the continued hegemony of Swedish culture and language in Finland, and challenges those Finns who speak pidgin Swedish instead of Finnish and extol everything Swedish in their alliances with cultural elites. Wuolijoki's dramaturgy here is gestic—the cultural pretenders are presented in cameos of sharp and amusing satire. In this final act, the Niskavuori farm is exemplary of Finnish *sisu* (steadfastness) set against both Swedish and Russian domination.

The larger political subject is also centered throughout in the title character, the young mistress of Niskavuori, Loviisa. This of course is exactly the same position Okichi finds herself in at the outset of *The Judith of Shimoda*. Okichi is weakened by her own uncertainties and her greater public trial, whereas Loviisa finds the strength to reconcile herself to her designated social role as the new young mistress of Niskavuori and prevail, but at a price. The dichotomy between public service and personal fulfillment, faced by both Okichi and Loviisa, is held in graphic suspension in the tableau at the end of *Niskavuoren nuori emäntä*. Called outside by acclamation of a crowd of her husband's supporters, but facing the lack of his love, she almost collapses at the doorway, but then suddenly straightens up as the curtain falls.[19]

2

Wuolijoki was surely attracted to Yūzō's play, in Glenn Shaw's translation, for its subject and emphasis—that of a woman suddenly challenged to rise to the assumption of a social duty and, in Okichi's case, to resolve a national crisis; a woman involved with a man (Tsurumatsu, like Juhani, is unfaithful), the whole crisis encased in a plot and dramatic structure which is basically that of a well-made play rather than epic, and with sociopolitical issues dramatized mostly within the bounds of representationalism.

In describing and analyzing the differences between Glenn Shaw's published translation of the *Chink Okichi* play and the reconstruction of the Brecht/Wuolijoki version, the findings can fall into two natural sections. Firstly, there is the matter of the condensation of almost all the original Shaw-scenes, largely through the removal of many "psychologically orientated" conversations, but also including one significant transposition and one significant new scene. These changes don't compromise the basic realism of the original. Secondly, there is the more dubious addition of what Brecht called the "framing action" of the original scenes. This consists of considerable additional material, of a Prologue, Epilogue and ten Interludes in which Akimura, the mogul host, treats his guests in his *palais* to fully rehearsed excerpts of the play, apparently with the actors specially commissioned to present the work. The elaborate revolving-stage scenery specified in the Shaw translation is replaced by a few simple screens in this suggestive and stripped-down version. Akimura wants to prove to his guests that patriotism is not merely the preserve of the aristocratic class. His guests are Ray, an American journalist, Clive, a British Orientalist, and Kito, a Japanese poet. The Director of the production introduces the scenes of the play very briefly, and the scenes are rarely more than half a page and sometimes only a couple of lines long.

To deal with the changes to the original scenes first, it is true that all of the scenes have cuts, mostly of psychologically orientated conversations and material filling out the characters' backstories and sometimes their emotional reactions, with little or no social or gestic significance. However, there are some obvious changes. When Okichi and her lover Tsurumatsu reunite in Yokohama years after the events of Scenes 1-4 by chance, the scene is not representationally enacted by Okichi and Tsurumatsu, as in Shaw, but here merely narrated by the Director.[20] In Paul Mitri's production, Okichi and Tsurumatsu simultaneously and parodically mimed it. And a short, Expressionist Okichi nightmare scene with her trapped inside a palanquin is replaced by a scene in which the "mythicization" of Okichi is shown through a narrative folk ballad of her "heroic sacrifice" for the nation, sung by a street balladist to an appreciative crowd, which is heckled by the actual, drunken Okichi denigrating and even physically disrupting the performance and its sentimental falsities.[21]

Other cuts and changes of emphasis within the play itself (as opposed to the "framing" material) include a significant one early on. In Shaw's translation, the crucial "persuasion" scene in which the aristocratic Lord Isa convinces Okichi to take on the assignment precedes, and does not follow, the introduction of the scene between Okichi and Tsurumatsu. Brecht and Wuolijoki have moved it to a position immediately following the Lord Isa scene—Okichi has already decided what she will do. This allows us to calibrate the stages of Tsurumatsu's arguing that Okichi should go, and "alienates" more effectively his reasons for it, and her strategies of concealing that she has reached her own decision. So the scene is laden with irony and divested of sentimental pathos, and reminds us of similarly terse and contained scenes in *Puntila* and *Niskavuoren nuori emäntä*.[22]

Another significant change from the Shaw translation has to do with the sources for Okichi's weakness for sake. In Shaw it seems more "natural" and involuntary, a genetic proclivity out of the control of the drinker. More emphasis is placed on it, while in Brecht/Wuolijoki it does seem more voluntary and also more tied to specific challenges and stress points that give a rational reason for it, which makes it more translateable into social gestuses whenever it occurs.[23]

There are several examples of the condensation of the original text, a technique which shapes more clearly the gestic relationships between characters. In Shaw, for example, the relationship between Okichi and Prince Isa is complicated by the backstory that, in the past, he has used her services professionally.[24] In the Brecht/Wuolijoki version, he is more remote and formal, and has not met her before, and so the gestic relationship between them is uncomplicated by any "personal" factors.[25] His advice, and persuasion, is strictly based on the brand of sociopolitical morality he espouses. Similarly with Consul Harris—his interactions with Okichi are shredded of some purely erotic elements in that a somewhat cloying petting scene with Okichi after she has brought back the milk has been excised by Brecht/Wuolijoki. But a telling addition in this same scene, with strong gestic implications, occurs when Okichi bows down in deference in front of Harris and pleads for him not to leave until the following day, so she will not lose face in front of the City Council.[26] In the Brecht/Wuolijoki version, our eyes and minds are kept more constantly on the hegemony of social relationships, and the desire of some of the characters to defy them and go beyond them.

This brings us to a consideration of the "framing action." This is, of course, the most obviously Brechtian alteration to the original. The topics discussed by the vaguely assorted guests of Akimura fit rather perfunctorily with the characters of Ms. Ray and Mr. Clive, and the poet Kito. Also, the issues successively raised by each nodal point in the story—patriotism and its motives and who benefits from it; heroic action and how that is defined; the uses and consequences of celebrity; the dilemmas of mythologizing—are all given expectedly bald and didactic treatment in the Interludes. However, the Interludes, and specifically the lodestone character of Akimura, do alienate the bifurcated structure of the play, where with the first two acts (Scene 1-4 in Brecht/Wuolijoki) we are presented with the "public" and "heroic" action of Okichi and its national manifestations, and in Scenes 5-11, we get the "biographical" part of the play which settles back into a more conventional and expectable "well-made" shape and function. Ms. Ray, in asking for the additional scenes, expects a Hollywood-style biopic, and that is what she gets. In this case, it is the personal and private consequences of the heroic action and the way that it has wrecked Okichi's personal life and destroyed her. This structural bifurcation is alienated by the Interludes, which also alienate the separate scenes of the original as episodes in a more "epic" structure than originally existed. On the page the Interludes seem, and mean to seem, crudely interrupting and jack-knifed into the play scenes. In the theater, since the mogul and guests may be seen as "audience" throughout, and the Director of the play can act as an agent of segue from Interludes to Scenes (as happened in Paul Mitri's production), there is quite a bit of theatrical overlap and variety in the possibilities of interaction between the actors in the Shimoda play, Akimura, and his "guests."

In short, Brecht and Wuolijoki's additions and changes to the Shaw translation have respected the spirit of the original while gestically sharpening its situations. And Brecht, perhaps influenced not only by the idyllic Finnish countryside and its white nights of summer but also by the dramaturgical practices and folksy ebullience of Wuolijoki, trusted both in *Puntila* and in *The Judith of Shimoda* the use of a more constant representationalism, and also modified the hortatory presentationalism of the phase of his work immediately preceding this one. The sum total of the Brecht/Wuolijoki *Judith of Shimoda* is a [G. B.] Shavian/Wuolijokian "well-made" play, with the nodal points of its bifurcated structure and its thematic implications neatly highlighted by the inimitable additions.

Endnotes

1   Bertolt Brecht, *The Judith of Shimoda*, pre-production draft of English translation by Markus Wessendorf, August 25, 2008, title page. This is a translation of Bertolt Brecht, *Die Judith von Shimoda. Nach einem Stück von Yamamoto Yuzo*, in collaboration with Hella Wuolijoki, play script reconstructed by Hans Peter Neureuter (Suhrkamp: Frankfurt/Main, 2006). Even though Wessendorf's translation of Neureuter's reconstructed script hasn't been published in book form yet, it has already received a full stage production at Kennedy Theatre Honolulu in April/May 2010 (Dir. Paul Mitri) in conjunction with the

13th International Brecht Society Symposium on "Brecht in/and Asia" at the University of Hawai'i at Mānoa.
2   Yamamoto Yūzō, "The Story of Chink Okichi," in Yamamoto Yūzō, *Three Plays,* Glenn W. Shaw, trans. (Tokyo: Hokuseido Press, 1935), pp. 83-247.
3   S. E. Wilmer and Pirkko Koski, *The Dynamic World of Finnish Theatre: An Introduction to Its History, Structure and Aesthetics* (Helsinki: Like, 2006), pp. 96-98.
4   Raoul Palmgren, "Hella Wuolijoki ja Niskavuorelaiset" (Hella Wuolijoki and the Niskavuorians), Foreword to Hella Wuolijoki, *Niskavuoren tarina (Tale of Niskavuori)* (Helsinki: Love Kirjat, 1979), p. 8.
5   Pirkko Koski, "Introduction" to Hella Wuolijoki, "Law and Order," in S. E. Wilmer, ed., *Portraits of Courage. Plays by Finnish Women* (Helsinki: Helsinki University Press, 1997), p. 225.
6   Ralph Manheim and John Willett, "Introduction" in Bertolt Brecht, *Collected Plays 6,* Ralph Manheim and John Willet, eds. (New York: Vintage Books, 1976), pp. ix-xiii.
7   Wilmer and Koski, pp. 100-101.
8   Ibid., p. 99.
9   Ralph Manheim and John Willett, eds.,"Editorial Note," in Bertolt Brecht, *Collected Plays* 6 (New York: Vintage Books, 1976), p. 424; Erkki Tuomioja, *Häivähdys punaista. Hella Wuolijoki ja hänen sisarensa Salme Pekkala vallankumouksen palveluksessa (A Hint of Red. Hella Wuolijoki and Her Sister Salme Pekkala at the Service of the Revolution),* 10th ed. (Tammi: Hämeenlinna, 2008), p. 274.
10 Quoted in Manheim and Willett, "Editorial Note," p. 424.
11 Manheim and Willett, "Introduction," p. xiv.
12 Bertolt Brecht, *Journals 1934-1955,* ed., John Willett, Hugh Rorrison, trans. (New York: Routledge, 1993), p. 102.
13 John Fuegi, *Brecht and Company. Sex, Politics and the Making of the Modern Drama* (New York: Grove Press, 1994), p. 392.
14 Hans Peter Neureuter, *Brecht in Finnland: Studien zu Leben und Werk, 1940-1941* (Frankfurt/Main: Suhrkamp, 2007), p. 150.
15 Manheim and Willett, "Introduction," p. xv.
16 Fuegi, p. 392.
17 Brecht, *Journals,* p. 113.
18 Pirkko Koski, *Kaikessa mukana. Hella Wuolijoki ja hänen näytelmänsä (Finger in Every Pie. Hella Wuolijoki and Her Plays)* (Keuruu: Otava, 2000), p. 181.
19 Hella Wuolijoki, *Niskavuoren nuori emäntä,* in *Niskavuoren tarina,* p. 79.
20 Compare Yūzō, pp. 165-167, and Wessendorf, p. 40.
21 Compare Yūzō, pp. 234-236, and Wessendorf, pp. 73-76.
22 See Wessendorf, pp. 19-22.
23 Compare the emphasis on Okichi's involuntary partiality for sake in Yūzō, p. 115, and pp. 117-18, and especially pp. 204-205. The drink does not figure prominently in her persuasion by Lord Isa in Wessendorf, and her drinking of sake is more clearly motivated by her treatment (see Wessendorf, p. 34, pp. 47-48). However, classic excuses for involuntary alcoholism are still present in Wessendorf, p. 57.
24 Yūzō, pp. 117-118.
25 Wessendorf, pp. 14-15.
26 Compare Yūzō, pp. 141-142 and Wessendorf, p. 30.

"Furcht und Elend" nach dem 11. September: Mark Ravenhills *Shoot/Get Treasure/Repeat*

Markus Wessendorf

Dieser Essay untersucht die brechtschen Aspekte eines neueren britischen Stückes, das sich mit dem "Krieg gegen den Terror" auseinandersetzt: Mark Ravenhills *Shoot/Get Treasure/Repeat* von 2008. Ravenhills Stück suggeriert zahlreiche strukturelle, intertextuelle und thematische Parallelen zu Brechts *Furcht und Elend des Dritten Reiches*: nicht nur trägt *Shoot/Get Treasure/Repeat* den Untertitel "Ein epischer Zyklus kurzer Stücke," sondern zwei der 16 Szenen heißen "Furcht und Elend" und "Die Mutter." Während Brecht jedoch den Faschismus ins Visier nimmt, greift Ravenhill vor allem die Verlogenheiten eines Liberalismus an, die es dem Westen erlauben, die angeblich intolerante Kultur des Feindes "intolerant" zu behandeln und dabei trotzdem moralische Überlegenheit für sich in Anspruch zu nehmen. Der Essay bezieht Ravenhills Dramaturgie dabei auf eine Kritik am Liberalismus, wie sie von Wendy Brown, Talal Asad, Michel Foucault, Gilles Deleuze und Samuel Weber artikuliert worden ist.

This essay focuses on the Brechtian aspects of a recent play dealing with the "War on Terror": *Shoot/Get Treasure/Repeat* (2008) by British playwright Mark Ravenhill. Ravenhill's play suggests various structural, intertextual and thematic parallels to Brecht's *Fear and Misery of the Third Reich*: not only is *Shoot/Get Treasure/Repeat* subtitled "An Epic Cycle of Short Plays" but two of the 16 scenes are called "Fear and Misery" and "The Mother." Whereas Brecht targets fascism, however, Ravenhill attacks the hypocrisies of a liberalism that allows the West to treat a supposedly non-tolerant enemy culture "intolerantly" while still claiming the moral high ground. The essay links Ravenhill's dramaturgy to critiques of liberalism by Wendy Brown, Talal Asad, Michel Foucault, Gilles Deleuze, and Samuel Weber.

"Fear and Misery" Post-9/11: Mark Ravenhill's *Shoot/Get Treasure/Repeat*

Markus Wessendorf

The following essay touches upon the title of this volume only indirectly by analyzing the Brechtian aspects of a contemporary British play, Mark Ravenhill's *Shoot/Get Treasure/Repeat* from 2008.[1] Ravenhill's play addresses the West's response to Islamic Asia in the wake of the attacks of September 11, 2001 by focusing on the internal social, cultural, and psychological responses of Western liberal society to the "War on Terror" rather than on the foreign-policy dimension of the recent conflicts in Iraq, Afghanistan, and other parts of the Near and Middle East.

Even though a Brechtian legacy in contemporary British drama is widely acknowledged, Ravenhill, with few exceptions, is usually not associated with that lineage.[2] This may not only have to do with the sensationalist response to Ravenhill's first play *Shopping and Fucking* in 1996 but also with a critical reception that has mostly treated his theater work as another example of "In-Yer-Face-Theatre" (Aleks Sierz). Yet it is easy to demonstrate that Ravenhill aims for more than mere sensationalism and shock effects. His dramatic universe is ruled by "commodity fetishism;" alienation pervades social interaction and communication; bodies and sex are commodities; desire and even the experience of pain are fetishized. The Brechtian aspects of Ravenhill's work may have been overlooked because of the author's queer politics, his depiction of extreme bodily practices, his references to the British club scene of the 1990s, and a representation of fetishism that is often ambiguously caught up in what it describes. Yet exactly these characteristics link Ravenhill's work to Brecht's early plays (*Baal*, *In the Jungle of Cities*, *The Rise and Fall of the City of Mahagonny*, and the *Fatzer* fragment). Some of Ravenhill's more recent theater texts openly embrace a Brechtian dramaturgy, for example, his 2001 libretto for *Mother Clap's Molly House* (with music by Matthew Scott), which is modeled after *The Threepenny Opera*. Ravenhill has also frequently admitted his fascination for Brecht in articles and interviews. As a columnist for *The Guardian*, he reviewed a production of *The Good Soul of Szechuan* at the Young Vic in May 2008 under the title, "Don't Bash Brecht." Parts of this review read like a passionate defense of Brecht's work against unnamed critics:

> His play *The Mother* shows a working-class woman struggling to reconcile individual needs with the demands of a political cause. It's a beautiful, moving piece, painfully ignorant of the horrors of Stalinism that were to follow…If we can reconcile ourselves to Richard Strauss and—alarmingly—Leni Riefenstahl, surely it's time the Brecht-bashing came to an end.[3]

In an interview from December 2006 Ravenhill admitted to the journalist Mike Higgins:

> The other stuff I reread is Brecht: the letters, the diaries, the poems, the plays, the theory. I normally have some Brecht by my bed. It's a bit like the Forth Bridge, once I finish them I just start again.[4]

The most obvious example of Ravenhill's engagement with Brecht to date is his play *Shoot/Get Treasure/Repeat*. Its subheading, "An Epic Cycle of Short Plays," as well as the titles of two of the short plays clearly allude to Brecht's work: "The Mother" and "Fear and Misery." Some of Brecht's "Short Description[s] of a New Technique of Acting which Produces an Alienation Effect"[5] are directly applied in *Shoot/Get Treasure/ Repeat*—for example, the transposition of the dramatic dialog "into the third person."[6] In addition, there are striking structural similarities and thematic resonances between Ravenhill's 16-scene play and the 24 (or 27, depending on the edition) scenes of Brecht's *Fear and Misery of the Third Reich*. Whereas Brecht's play provides a panoramic x-ray of German society during the first five years of the Third Reich by portraying a wide range of mostly non-Nazi characters in their feeble and often opportunistic responses to the fascist regime, the vignettes of Ravenhill's cycle aim to capture the fear and misery of post-9/11 Western society. In her review of the first production of *Shoot/Get Treasure/Repeat* at the Edinburgh Fringe Festival in August 2007, critic Jenny Spencer pointed out the following parallel:

> With its combination of emotionally involving scenarios, barely suppressed anger, and cool political critique, Ravenhill's *Shoot/ Get Treasure/Repeat* bears striking resemblance in structure and theme to Brecht's *Fear and Misery of the Third Reich*...with everyday encounters between family, friends, and soldiers updated to address the current war on terror.[7]

Even so, Spencer also made clear that not the fascism of the Nazi regime but recent political tendencies within contemporary Western societies are the ideological target of Ravenhill's "Epic Cycle:"

> Yet the world sketched before us is not the Germany of World War II, but the equally terrifying world we now inhabit as members of a Western democracy intent on imposing its "freedoms" on the rest of the world. Although each play is different, the underlying questions are similar: how do rape, torture, starvation, suicide bombing, surveillance, trauma, evil, and war's collateral damage become a normalized part of our everyday lives? Perhaps more to the point, how are the lives we lead already implicated in the

war on terror? How far have we gone, and how do things get this far?⁸

Every single scene of *Shoot/Get Treasure/Repeat* evokes the same question: to what extent can Western democracies compromise their core values in their defense against major external threats without forfeiting those very values?

If the scenes of *Fear and Misery of the Third Reich* are often considered the most conventionally realistic scenes that Brecht ever wrote (despite the montage character of the sequence as a whole), *Shoot/Get Treasure/Repeat* moves back and forth between different aesthetic styles: some scenes are realistic (and comparable to those of *Fear of Misery of the Third Reich*), some employ a Brechtian transposition of dialog into the third-person, while others mostly feature lines spoken by a chorus of anonymous speakers suggestive of Brecht's *Lehrstücke*. Nonetheless, the overall tone of the Ravenhill text—a mocking treatment of his characters, their behaviors and obsessions—contrasts sharply with Brecht's more detached representation in *Fear and Misery of the Third Reich*. Also different from Brecht, the scenes of *Shoot/Get Treasure/Repeat* lack a chronological thread and hint at specific geographic locations only vaguely (some scenes are set in a Western nation suggestive of the United States or Great Britain, others in a country under Western military occupation such as Iraq or Afghanistan, others again evoke both settings). Several leitmotifs recur throughout Ravenhill's scenes: a woman with a broken wing, a bench bought at a garden center, a soldier with a blown-off head. The titles of the individual plays, furthermore, refer to a wide range of modern cultural production: *War and Peace, Birth of a Nation, Intolerance, The Mikado, War of the Worlds*, the Hollywood blockbuster *Armageddon*, and the Meat Loaf-song "I'd Do Anything for Love (But I won't do That)." The relationship between Ravenhill's short plays and the works to which their titles allude, however, is a mostly ironic one. (The second play of the cycle, "Intolerance," for example, explores less the cultural or sociological significance of its title, as D. W. Griffith's 1916-film did, rather than its dietary connotation, even though the caffeine intolerance of Ravenhill's monologizing suburban housewife can also be interpreted as a psychosomatic symptom of societal fears.) The most important difference between Brecht and Ravenhill may be the lack of political alternatives or positive role models in *Shoot/Get Treasure/Repeat*. Whereas a few isolated characters in Brecht's play (the workers in "The Chalk Cross," "Worker's Playtime" and "Consulting the People;" the wife in "Job Creation") represent at least the impulse of resistance against the Third Reich and the hope for an alternative political system, Ravenhill refuses to suggest any way out of the inherent contradictions and injustices of contemporary liberal Western society. None of the four groups of characters in *Shoot/Get Treasure/Repeat* justify any hope for future social change: neither the citizenry of a society threatened by terrorism nor the soldiers and security forces protecting this society; neither the declared enemies of liberalism (terrorists, suicide bombers, dictators, etc.) nor the enemy civilians now under military occupation by a Western nation.

Ravenhill has never specifically discussed *Shoot/Get Treasure/Repeat* as a critique of liberalism, but he has stated in an interview with Peter Billingham that,

> the vast majority of the theatregoing audience tends to be the liberal intelligentsia. In a kind of a post-ideological era they have tended to fudge any kinds of questions about morality without any kinds of political guidelines as to what morality might be or mean.[9]

> ...liberalism has its own taboos and "no-nos"—any form of racism or sexism or homophobia so it's kind of...it's not liberal about illiberal things—there's a kind of intrinsic contradiction there.[10]

The following analysis will focus on four interrelated aspects of contemporary liberalism that the short plays of *Shoot/Get Treasure/Repeat* render problematic: liberalism's notion of goodness, its claim to tolerance, its politics of protection, and its "just war" theory to justify draconian measures against enemies of liberalism. It may appear strange, particularly from an American perspective, that a play would address the shortcomings of Western liberalism by focusing on a "War on Terror" declared by a conservative and often liberal-bashing President. But, as Wendy Brown has pointed out in her essay on "Subjects of Tolerance: Why We Are Civilized and They Are the Barbarians," the logic of liberalism that legitimizes aggression towards "regimes deemed intolerable" while allowing "for the disavowal of the cultural imperialism that such aggression entails" (because of the supposed universality of the "inviolability of rights and choice") "was succinctly expressed by George W. Bush during the initiation of the U.S. war on Afghanistan in 2002..."[11]

Five of the short plays in *Shoot/Get Treasure/Repeat* are choric scenes, that is, scenes in which most of the characters are unnamed members of a chorus and most of the lines not assigned to any specific speakers. The chorus in these scenes addresses the audience directly as a stand-in for the enemy population. The scenes usually include one or two characters set apart from the chorus and identified by their generic features: boy, man, soldier, dictator, blind woman, etcetera. In the first of these scenes, "Women of Troy," a chorus of women in a hospital pleads with the audience to tell them the reasons for the ongoing campaign of suicide bombings. The chorus members cannot understand why they are under attack, since they perceive their own society as exemplary for humankind.

> …why do you bomb us?…We are the good people…It's a good community. All of our neighbors are good people…I only eat good food. Ethical food. Because I believe that good choices should be made when you're shopping…I work for the good of our society. Every day I deal with the homeless and the addicted and the mad and the lost…How good freedom and democracy truly is.[12]

The characters representing liberal Western society in *Shoot/Get Treasure/Repeat* not only emphasize the goodness of their lives, lifestyles, characters, friends, families, communities, consumerist choices etcetera but also identify the virtues of their own society with those of humanity at large. Even though the fundamental goodness of all humanity is a key notion of classical liberalism, Ravenhill's characters claim to be the sole embodiment of this notion.[13] In another choric scene, "The Odyssey," a chorus of soldiers is preparing to leave the country of the former enemy to which they have been deployed to spread freedom and democracy. The soldiers can barely wait to fly home, but in their evocation of familiar places, ordinary routines, friends, and family members they emphasize the perceived superiority of their own culture over the one they will leave behind.

> - Maybe you can't imagine this, but there is no shelling and bombing in our cities. Our cities are beautiful places. Beautiful shops. Leisure facilities. People who move about in freedom, every day making the democratic choices that shape their future.[14]

> - But our core values are everything because they are humanity's core values.[15]

The various scenes of *Shoot/Get Treasure/Repeat* imply, however, that the claim to represent humanity's core values does not prevent members of Western society from treating nonmembers of this society inhumanely. In "Twilight of the Gods," Jane, an administrator working for the occupation forces, interviews the former university teacher Susan. Susan is on the brink of starvation since her neighborhood, "Zone Eight,"[16] has received no food shipments in weeks. Jane has called Susan in to interview her for a report:

> me—I and my colleagues—we want to find out how you think we're doing, okay? Since we intervened, since the dictator's statue toppled, how do you feel things are going? We want to listen. Listen and get a picture. Alright?[17]

Susan only agreed to the interview because she was promised a meal, and makes several attempts to grab Jane's breakfast roll and coffee because she is so hungry. When she finally succeeds, Jane tries to stop Susan from eating—for humanitarian reasons.

> Well, if you'll help me with the report, you're going to get a supervised breakfast afterwards. A specially prepared purée, eaten under medical supervision. So that we don't risk killing you. We have learnt. We have progressed.[18]

Jane asks a number of questions that are irrelevant to Susan in her current situation, for example about her bus ride to the interview or the behavior of the checkpoint guards: "It's important that we keep a record of sexual harassment cases."[19] When Susan finally grabs the rest of the bread roll, gulps it down, collapses on the floor, and starts to choke, Jane becomes irate:

> I brought you your freedom. We fought our way through the desert to bring you our core values and now you can't even, you can't even—you grab like you've never seen—oh fuck.[20]

While Susan is dying in her arms, Jane confesses to her that her humanitarian engagement is primarily motivated by a sense of lack regarding her own life.

> Listen, Susan, I don't have a partner, I don't have a child. Susan, I have the most appalling taste in men…Susan, I think about having a child, but that moment's going now…[21]

The final scene of the play, "Birth of a Nation," makes a similar point and in equally stark terms. Here the chorus consists of artist-facilitators who want to "Heal through Art"[22] by bringing painting, dancing, writing, and performance installations to the formerly suppressed population of the enemy state. At the end of the scene a blind woman who was mutilated and lost her entire family in the wake of the invasion is brought forward. The chorus cheers her on as "Our first artist"[23] and pushes pen and brush into her hands.

> *The* **Blind Woman** *screams, throws pen and brush away.*
> - That's it, be brave. Express. Create. Be bold.
> - *The* **Blind Woman** *screams.*
> - It's happening, it's happening, it's happening.
> - *The* **Blind Woman** *convulses, her body in spasms.*
> - Oh yes dance dance dance.
> *The* **Blind Woman** *spasms, the* **Chorus** *applaud, lights fade to black.*[24]

The humanitarian facilitators working for the occupation forces in *Shoot/Get Treasure/Repeat* are not primarily motivated by a concern for the invaded country's suffering population but by a desire for self-affirmation and social recognition as Good Samaritans. They are insensitive to the plight of the people they are purported to help, and even get enraged if their supposed acts of selflessness are not appreciated or recognized as such.

Shoot/Get Treasure/Repeat also takes aim at liberalism's understanding of tolerance. In the already-mentioned scene, "Women of Troy," the female chorus considers the practice of tolerance a trait that renders their own "civilisation, a world of good people"[25] superior to other societies.

> - We know your culture's very different.
> - And that's okay. We accept that.
> - We tolerate, we accept, we celebrate —
> - We celebrate — exactly — we celebrate difference.
> - It's all part of being a good people.
> - It's what makes us the good people that we are.[26]

Wendy Brown, in the aforementioned essay, analyzes, with recourse to Sigmund Freud's and Raymond Williams's theories, some assumptions underlying liberalism's concept of tolerance. According to Williams, liberalism imagines nonliberal people to be ruled and determined by an authoritative and monolithic culture, in opposition to liberal people who are imagined not to be defined by but to have culture(s). Whereas culture, religion and ethnic identity are understood to be constitutive of the subject in nonliberal societies, they are treated as extrinsic to the subject in liberal societies.

> For liberal subjects, culture becomes food, dress, music, lifestyle, and contingent values. Culture *as* power and especially as rule is replaced by culture as merely a way of life...[27]

The characters representing Western liberalism in Ravenhill's play repeatedly refer to their consumerist notion of culture as superior to the culture of the subjected civilian population of the enemy state.

> - ...We have so much choice. Who will provide my electricity? Who will deliver my groceries? Which cinema shall I go to? There is a choice at home. I long to be back.
> - You haven't known that yet but you will one day.[28]

Brown emphasizes that the liberal notion of tolerance is linked to this culture of choice, as a value that is "available only to the self-regulating individual" (and, by extension, to secular states promoting such individualism), whereas "those captive to organicism and organicist practices are presumed neither to value tolerance, to be capable of tolerance, nor to be entitled to tolerance."[29] Several scenes in *Shoot/Get Treasure/Repeat* not only dramatize how the liberal notion of tolerance enables the most brutal treatment of the supposedly nonliberal "other" but also link this notion to liberalism's security concerns and politics of self-protection.

In "Paradise Lost," the flight attendant Liz drops by her downstairs neighbor Ruth in the early morning hours to ask her to stop screaming every night because it prevents her from falling asleep. Liz first suspects Ruth of being in a sadomasochistic relationship but then realizes that something else must be going on after spotting burn marks on her neighbor's skin. Despite this realization, Liz tells Ruth that she doesn't "want to get involved in [her] life."[30] When Liz tries to leave, Ruth clings to her desperately. Two men, Gary and Brian, arrive with a tool bag, and it becomes clear that they come every night to torture Liz into revealing information about her terrorist connections. Ruth first tries to protect Liz against her tormentors, but after Gary and Brian have convinced her that Ruth has trained suicide bombers and is indeed responsible for a recent bomb attack on a hospital in which friends of Liz died, she accepts Brian's offer of a hammer and bashes Ruth with it once before returning to her own apartment.

> **Brian** You go to bed, Liz. Put the waves on and get into bed.
> **Liz** I will—thank you.
> **Brian** And we'll try to keep the noise down.
> **Liz** Would you? I'd be really grateful. Thank you.[31]

In Ravenhill's pessimistic assessment of liberalism, tolerance always loses out to the impulse of self-protection. In scene after scene Ravenhill emphasizes the dependency of liberal society on illiberal security and military forces that sustain and at the same time undermine it. This is particularly apparent in "Love (But I Won't Do That)," in which a soldier blackmails Marion, a marketing executive, into having denigrating sex with him by threatening to withdraw from her house with his weapons and mines and to leave her and her kids to the mercy of insurgents.

> All you can hope for is a good clean bomb to carry you off straight away, nothing too messy— [32]

In exchange for security and protection, Marion eventually agrees to let the soldier ejaculate onto her face later that night while taking a picture of her.

> But tonight please start slowly. You can humiliate me later.[33]

Marion's eventual acquiescence to her own rape by the soldier in charge of protecting her household renders her humanist and liberal values irrelevant. The powerlessness of these values is already apparent at the outset of the scene, which starts with the soldier's opening line "I'm aching for a fuck."[34] Marion ignores this statement and tries to steer the conversation towards the topic of Fair Trade.

> Would you like more coffee?...This is Fairtrade, which is important, isn't it?...Even drinking a cup of coffee you can liberate or exploit —...We must make sure we only deal with the coffee farms where the labourers are treated with dignity...[35]

The soldier, however, ignores her indirect plea to be treated with dignity herself, and continues to harass her. He also reveals that he already touched her sexually last night, but she pretends not to have noticed that in her sleep. In Ravenhill's universe, Brecht's "wa(h)re Liebe" (real love = love as goods) functions less as a commodity in the capitalist economy of exploitative social relations than as the dues payment for continued protection by security forces.

Michel Foucault already pointed out in a lecture series in 1979 that liberal "governmentality" produces as well as organizes freedoms, along with security strategies of control and surveillance geared to prevent the dangers inherent to the production of freedom.

> Liberalism is not acceptance of freedom; it proposes to manufacture it constantly, to arouse it and produce it, with, of course, [the system] of constraints and the problems of cost raised by this production. What, then, will be the principle of calculation for this cost of manufacturing freedom? The principle of calculation is what is called security...The problems of what I shall call the economy of power peculiar to liberalism are internally sustained, as it were, by this interplay of freedom and security.[36]

A statement by Gilles Deleuze from 1976 provides perhaps the best if prescient link between Brecht's attack on the Third Reich and Ravenhill's critique of post-9/11 liberalism by describing the rise of the security state as a new form of fascism.

> The new fascism is not the politics and the economy of war. It is global agreement on security, on the maintenance of a "peace" just as terrifying as war. All our petty fears will be organized in concert, all our petty anxieties will be harnessed to make microfascists of us; we will be called upon to stifle every little thing, every suspicious face, every dissonant voice, in our streets, in our neighborhoods, in our local theaters.[37]

Samuel Weber, in a recent interview with Frank-M. Raddatz, suggests a link between Brecht's plays and liberalism's obsession with security:

> Our era, like Brecht's, is dominated not only by a politics of fear, but beyond that by a politics of protection: a protection against the unknown, the unfamiliar, and the unforeseeable — and in the name of the self at that. Politics as self-protection. The critical engagement with this politics and the attitudes and settings that this politics operates with, constitute a basic Brechtian figure: his plays try to depict what this notion of security is all about. Ever since Hobbes this exchange of freedom against security and protection has constituted the foundation of a liberal politics and political theory.[38]

The fourth scene of *Shoot/Get Treasure/Repeat*, "Fear and Misery," can be interpreted as a transposition of this "basic Brechtian figure" to the post-9/11 era. The short play unfolds as a dinner conversation between the married couple Harry and Olivia, while they are listening to the breathing sounds of their son Alex on a baby monitor. The obsession with surveillance and protection in Ravenhill's "Fear and Misery" is portrayed as a response to a heightened sense of insecurity not only triggered by the frightening outside world but also by an unstable domestic sphere, spousal distrust, fear of sexuality and the (female) body, etcetera. Apart from the baby monitor, which is mentioned repeatedly throughout the short play, the characters also refer to a smoke alarm in need of repair[39] and a car alarm going off outside.[40] When Olivia proclaims, "Security is the most important thing in this life," Harry immediately agrees, "It is."[41] Their fear of the outside world is so extreme and their desire to protect their child from the violence of that world so great that Harry and Olivia dissect their most intimate interactions. The scene starts with Harry obsessing about the moment of Alex's conception. When he presses Olivia to tell him that Alex "was conceived in calm,"[42] Olivia cannot comply but has to admit that there were "moments in the past when I've felt for a blink there's a blink of…rape and then it's back to love again."[43] Harry gets enraged about this confession, but Olivia calms him down not only by insisting that she loves him but also by thanking him for his protection.

> You're keeping us safe here. I know that. I really — I appreciate — my love…You work so hard to keep us out of harm's way and I thank you for that.[44]

The "blink of rape," the violent impulse and misogyny underlying Harry's lovemaking is confirmed, however, when Olivia asks him "What scares you about me?"[45] and he responds:

> That you won't wash your vagina. That you'll fuck a black man. That you'll have a breast removed.[46]

Similar to the relationship between Marion and the soldier in "Love (But I Won't Do That)," the marriage contract between Olivia and Harry is based on a tradeoff: she sleeps with him in return for his protection. Harry repeatedly asks the reluctant Olivia if she will sleep with him that night, but she only yields to his desire after he has told her of his plans to move their nuclear family to a gated community. The world that Olivia and Harry want to leave behind them and outside their gates is peopled by social rejects and marked by constant warfare. The war, however, has already intruded into their home: Alex has nightmares of a soldier whose head was blown off, and the next scene in the cycle, "War and Peace," plays out as a dialog between Alex and the soldier, who comes to visit him in his bedroom. *Shoot/Get Treasure/Repeat* demonstrates that the obsession with security has the unintended effect of negating two constitutive traits of liberalism: the autonomy of the individual and the openness of a society based on consensual civic and political liberties. Towards the end of "Fear and Misery," Harry shouts:

> WE NEED GATES. WE NEED TO, TO, TO…DRAW UP THE DRAWBRIDGE AND CLOSE THE GATES AND SECURITY, SECURITY, SECURITY, SECURITY. I CAN'T FIGHT THIS WAR EVERY DAY. WAR WITH THE SCUM…I'M NORMAL…I WANT TO FEEL SAFE BEHIND THESE GATES. THIS IS THE ONLY WAY I WILL FEEL SAFE. BEHIND THESE GATES. SO DON'T YOU—COMMUNITY, THAT'S A LIE. THERE'S NO COMMUNITY.[47]

Ravenhill's "Fear and Misery" invites comparison to "The Spy," one of the best-known scenes of *Fear and Misery of the Third Reich*. "The Spy" also features a nuclear family terrorized by the world outside and trying to feel safe within their own four walls. When the son Klaus-Heinrich suddenly disappears, the parents become increasingly paranoid about a comment the father made earlier, implying a critique of the Hitler regime. Both parents fear that their son, who is a member of the Hitler Youth, has run to the authorities to denounce his father, and both parents start to rehearse various arguments in their defense, in case they will be arrested and interrogated. When the son finally reappears with the chocolates that he has bought around the corner, the relief is only momentary—the scene has demonstrated the degree to which the Nazi regime has undermined any trusting interpersonal and interfamilial relationships. The parents in Ravenhill's play do not fear the government but, on the contrary, the lack of governmental protection from anyone not as "NORMAL" as themselves. They desire the security state provided by the Nazi regime in "The Spy" but, of course, as Brecht's play as well as other scenes in Ravenhill's own cycle amply illustrate, the realization of a "politics of self-protection" (Weber) may not lead to an improved sense of personal security but rather to the intrusion of the security apparatus into one's own private life. The families in both scenes fail to "DRAW UP THE DRAWBRIDGE AND CLOSE THE GATES" — against the ubiquitous *Polizeistaat* of the Nazi regime in "The Spy" and against an outside world of terror in "Fear and Misery" (represented by the headless soldier who has already intruded into Olivia and Harry's living quarters). What links both worlds, in Deleuze's words, are the petty fears and anxieties that "will be organized in concert" and "harnessed to make micro-fascists" of the protagonists.

In *Shoot/Get Treasure/Repeat* only a small step separates the politics of self-protection from the notion of a just war against the enemies of liberalism. Isolated suicide attacks are answered by a mobilization for total war. Ravenhill repeatedly insists on the apocalyptic theologico-political dimension of this mobilization, as opposed to the secular rationale of spreading freedom and democracy by which this mobilization is usually justified publicly. At the end of "Women of Troy," a Man with a backpack steps forward, introduces himself as a suicide bomber, and blows himself up after the chorus has greeted their death with several "Hallelujahs" and the motto "A good death for a good people."[48] A Soldier with a sword, "*half-man, half-angel,*"[49] steps out of the blinding light caused by the blast and announces, "Freedom and democracy and truth and light — the fight is never done. There are always enemies. We must fight." He lifts his sword high, upon which "*a great army fills the stage*," and declares, "Kill the bombers. Slaughter our enemies. In the name of the good people — begin."[50] Since the war against the enemies of freedom and democracy is conducted in the name of higher principles and the "good people," its legitimacy is also taken for granted. Ravenhill's critique of this "blind spot" of liberalism coincides with Talal Asad's analysis in his book *On Suicide Bombing* (2007) of the fallacies of the "just war" theory of the American philosopher Michael Walzer. (Like fellow "liberal hawks" Christopher Hitchens, Peter Beinart, Paul Berman, and Michael Ignatieff, among others, Walzer sided with the Bush and Blair administrations and provided ideological justification for the War on Terror and the invasion of Iraq.) According to Walzer, liberal democracies are justified in supreme emergencies to use organized violence to defend themselves against a collective enemy, even if this use of violence involves the momentary suspension of core liberal and humanitarian principles. Since terrorism deliberately risks civilian lives, Walzer condemns it in essence, different from war, which he only criticizes for its ephemeral transgressions. Violent excesses within the domain of war, furthermore, are ethically justifiable only if accompanied by moral scruple, a sense of remorse that will hopefully prevent this exceptional violence from being repeated in the future. Asad questions Walzer's moral distinction between war and terrorism by pointing out that, "If the moral scruple...must never be strong enough to inhibit successfully the use of evil means when necessary, is there any need for it to be present at all?"[51] According to

Asad, this contradiction has become even more twisted in recent times, ever since domestic public opinion in liberal democracies has criticized excessive war casualties in their own ranks. Liberal society's humanitarian concern for the lives of its own soldiers, argues Asad, has destabilized the traditional proportionality of war casualties on both sides. The result of this humanitarianism is the excessive civilian suffering on the enemy side.

> ...in deference to humanitarian law, the military of a liberal state—unlike the terrorist—does not normally target civilians, *unless it is compelled to do so*, but overriding concern for its own military casualties (again, partly in response to humanitarian sensitivities) means it must choose a strategy in which more enemy civilians die.[52]

The following conclusion by Asad succinctly articulates the moral scandal of post-9/11 liberalism, which is also the main theme of *Shoot/Get Treasure/Repeat*: "But what is especially intriguing is the ingenuity of liberal discourse in rendering inhuman acts humane. This is certainly something that savage discourse cannot achieve."[53]

In a 2006 review the renowned British theater critic Michael Billington compared Ravenhill unfavorably to Brecht: "But, at a time when state power is increasing in specific, well-charted ways, Ravenhill's play offers us symbolic generalities. What one craves is a modern Brecht who deals with living, correctable injustices."[54] Even though Billington referred to a production of Ravenhill's play *The Cut*, a similar response to *Shoot/Get Treasure/Repeat* would not be inconceivable. *Shoot/Get Treasure/Repeat* never provides any indication how the "living injustices" of post-9/11 liberalism might be corrected, or by which alternative political system liberalism might be replaced, but the same point could be made about some of Brecht's earlier works. Similar to *The Rise and Fall of the City of Mahagonny*, Ravenhill's play expects the spectator, through an effort of negative dialectical reasoning and imagination, to envision a better society radically negating the one depicted in the play. Brecht, of course, falsely assumed that the audience of *Mahagonny* would inevitably identify communism as the desired antithesis of his "city of nets." No such certitude characterizes the politico-dramatic analysis of post-9/11 liberalism in *Shoot/Get Treasure/Repeat*.

One could also criticize *Shoot/Get Treasure/Repeat* for being too unspecific about its ideological target, since the play conflates two conflicting schools of political liberalism: the militarist and imperialist neo-liberalism of the Bush and Blair administrations and the humanitarian liberalism more concerned with individual rights. But this irritating conflation (which seems even more real under the Obama administration) proves thought-provoking and efficacious in Ravenhill's play. As Talal Asad has argued, all citizens of Western society are implicated in this conflict, including a contemporary theater audience mostly constituted of the liberal intelligentsia:

> All constitutional states rest on a space of violence that they call legitimate. In a liberal democracy, all citizens and the government that represents them are bound together by mutual obligations, and the actions of the duly elected government are the actions of all its citizens. When the government acts against suspected terrorists and inferior military opponents, everyone is (rightly or wrongly) involved in the space of violence.[55]

Endnotes

1 Mark Ravenhill, *Shoot/Get Treasure/Repeat: An Epic Cycle of Short Plays* (London: Methuen Drama, 2008). Abbreviated in the following as *SGR*.
2 Janelle Reinelt, in her book, *After Brecht: British Epic Theatre* (Ann Arbor: University of Michigan Press, 1994), specifically discusses the playwrights Howard Brenton, Edward Bond, Caryl Churchill, David Hare, Trevor Griffiths, and John McGrath. Many other British dramatists could be added to this list, including John Arden and David Edgar. See also Margaret Eddershaw, *Performing Brecht: Forty Years of Performance* (London: Routledge, 1996). Peter Billingham is one of the first scholars to emphasize Ravenhill's "post-Brechtian stylistics." See Peter Billingham, *At the Sharp End: Uncovering the Work of Five Leading Dramatists* (London: Methuen, 2007), p. 124.
3 Mark Ravenhill, "Don't Bash Brecht," *The Guardian*, 26 May 2008.
4 Mike Higgins, "This Cultural Life: Mark Ravenhill," *The Independent*, 17 December 2006.
5 Bertolt Brecht, *Brecht on Theatre: The Development of an Aesthetic*, John Willett, ed. and trans. (New York: Hill and Wang, 1964), pp. 136-147.
6 Ibid., p. 138.
7 Jenny Spencer, Review of *Shoot/Get Treasure/Repeat* (at Traverse Theatre, Edinburgh, 7-26 August 2007), *Theatre Journal* 60:2 (May 2008): pp. 285-288; p. 286.
8 Ibid., p. 286.
9 Billingham, *At the Sharp End*, p. 126.
10 Ibid., p. 131.
11 Wendy Brown, "Subjects of Tolerance: Why We Are Civilized and They are the Barbarians," in Hent de Vries and Lawrence E. Sullivan, eds., *Political Theologies: Public Religions in a Post-Secular World* (New York: Fordham University Press, 2006), pp. 298-317; p. 314.
12 *SGR*, pp. 7-8.
13 The *Merriam Webster's Collegiate Dictionary* (11th edition, Springfield/Massachusetts: Merriam Webster, Inc., 2004) defines liberalism as a "political philosophy based on belief in progress, the essential goodness of the human race, and the autonomy of the individual and standing for the protection of political and civil liberties" (p. 716). The *American Heritage Dictionary* similarly defines liberalism as a "political theory founded on the natural goodness of humans and the autonomy of the individual and favoring civil and political liberties, government by law with the consent of the governed, and protection from arbitrary authority" (last looked up at <http://www.wordnik.com/words/liberalism> 28 July 2010).

14 *SGR*, pp. 179-180.
15 Ibid., p. 180.
16 Ibid., p. 157.
17 Ibid., p. 163.
18 Ibid., p. 162.
19 Ibid., p. 164.
20 Ibid., p. 165.
21 Ibid., p. 166.
22 Ibid., p. 194.
23 Ibid., p. 198.
24 Ibid., p. 199.
25 Ibid., p. 9.
26 Ibid., p. 10.
27 Brown, p. 301.
28 *SGR*, p. 180.
29 Brown, p. 315.
30 *SGR*, p. 169.
31 Ibid., p. 178.
32 Ibid., p. 104.
33 Ibid.
34 *SGR*, p. 95.
35 Ibid.
36 Michel Foucault, *The Birth of Biopolitics. Lectures at the Collège de France 1978-1979*, ed. Michel Senellart, trans. Graham Burchell (New York: Picador, 2008), p. 65.
37 Gilles Deleuze, "The Rich Jew," in David Lapoujade, ed., *Two Regimes of Madness: Texts and Interviews 1975-1995*, Ames Hodges and Mike Taormina, trans. (New York and Los Angeles: Semiotext(e), 2006), pp. 135-138; p. 138. Originally published in *Le Monde* (February 18, 1976, p. 26), the text is a review of Daniel Schmid's film *Schatten der Engel* (*Shadow of Angels*), which was based on Rainer Werner Fassbinder's controversial play *Der Müll, die Stadt und der Tod* (*Garbage, the City, and Death*) from 1975. I would like to thank Michael Shapiro for pointing me to this quote.
38 Frank-M. Raddatz, "Eine Welt ist kein Globus – Brecht und das Globalisierungstheater. Samuel Weber über das Spiel der Wiederholungen, Benjamin, Derrida und den Kampf der Bilder," *Brecht frißt* [sic] *Brecht* (Berlin: Henschel, 2007), pp. 252-271, here p. 262. (Trans. MW.)
39 See *SGR*, pp. 41, 45.
40 Ibid., p. 45.
41 Ibid.
42 *SGR*, p. 39.
43 Ibid., p. 40.
44 Ibid., p. 41.
45 Ibid., p. 44.
46 Ibid.
47 *SGR*, pp. 48-49.
48 Ibid., p. 15.
49 Ibid., p. 16.
50 Ibid., p. 17.
51 Talal Asad, *On Suicide Bombing* (New York: Columbia University Press, 2007), p. 18.
52 Ibid., p. 36.
53 Ibid., p. 38.
54 Michael Billington, "The Cut," *The Guardian*, 1 March 2006, p. 36.
55 Asad, p. 29.

Brechts Ostasien: Ein Überblick

Antony Tatlow

Diese Zusammenschau will sowohl feststellen, welche Perspektiven uns zu einem besseren Verständnis des unterschiedlich gedeuteten brechtschen Erbes verhelfen, warum es oft vereinfacht und missverstanden wurde, wie dieses Werk heute zu lesen sei, als auch die Berührungspunkte zur ostasiatischen Kultur erneut im Kontext ihres Potentials zur kritischen Beleuchtung dieses Werks festhalten.

This conspectus seeks to identify what is important for understanding Brecht's legacy, how his work can be re-read today, why it has been frequently simplified and misjudged, and to review the points of contact with East Asian culture while connecting them with a critical potential for reassessing that work.

Brecht's East Asia: A Conspectus

Antony Tatlow

A wrap-up is supposed to draw everything together.[1] In my experience, that usually misfires. Anyone left out is offended, everyone mentioned feels misunderstood. I will try something different, more like unpacking: topics not explored, misunderstandings not clarified, futures not addressed. I will stay with Brecht's East Asia, with discussions I had and the pre-postdramatic stress disorder productions I saw by people I knew.

But first, to an event outside our remit: the 2008 King's College Cambridge *Festival of Nine Lessons & Carols*. Brecht was part of it, not one of the lessons, but in Dominic Muldowney's setting of his poem "Maria" (1922).[2] In Asia he is almost exclusively a dramatist, so listen to this Christmas Carol text:

> The night when she first gave birth
> Had been cold. But in later years
> She quite forgot
> The frost in the dingy beams and the smoking stove
> And the spasms of the afterbirth towards morning.
> But above all she forgot the bitter shame
> Common among the poor
> Of having no privacy.
> That was the main reason
> Why in later years it became a holiday for all
> To take part in.
> The shepherds' coarse chatter fell silent.
> Later they turned into the Kings of the story.
> The wind, which was very cold
> Turned into the singing of angels.
> Of the hole in the roof that let in the frost nothing remained
> But the star that looked through it.
> All this was due to the vision of her son, who was easy
> Fond of singing
> Surrounded himself with poor folk
> And was in the habit of mixing with kings
> And of seeing a star above his head at night-time.[3]

Thousands heard this on the BBC World Service and TV. In *Christmas Legend* (1923)[4] it's the voice of the social unconscious, which permeates his work: "Come in dear wind and be our guest/You too have neither home nor rest."

There's a special charge in this writing. Philosophers have called Brecht "a philosopher among the poets," even that "daring poet-philosopher" Friedrich Nietzsche dreamt of.[5] Distrusting abstractions, Brecht was attracted to practical Chinese thought, in the spirit of Wang Yangming's saying: "Knowledge is the beginning of action and action the completion of knowledge."[6] Knowledge is only acquired through practice. If action fails, what does that say about your knowledge?

The 1968-generation idolized Brecht, but their faith in the political efficacy of his work diminished when the social system did not collapse. Three responses were possible: abandon, situate, and/or re-read it. The Heirs forbade deviations from their view of his intention. Rehearsing *The Threepenny Opera* in the Berliner Ensemble, Dario Fo heard a voice in the stalls: "But where is Papa's text?" Pretending to throw it over his shoulder, he replied: "Papa's text?" They fired him. Productions beyond Europe and America were not beholden to this writ.

The narrowly interpreted plays, hardly performable in Germany, have a certain cachet elsewhere. The poetry still astonishes. His innovative dramatic theory was faithfully misunderstood. Brecht's views on language—for example, *Fetischismus der Begriffe*—scarcely registered.[7] Some re-reading fantasizes, like Stephan Bock's onomantic, kabbalistic chinoiserie, in which *The Good Person of Szechwan* encodes virtually all East Asian culture and the future of international theater. But productive re-reading must uncover a neglected responsibility *in* the text.

Brecht read the *Daodejing* in 1920. His work reached Japan in 1932. The dancer Ito Michio's younger brother, Ito Kunio (1904-1994), returned from Berlin in 1931, where he had seen *Man is Man* and *The Measures Taken* as well as *The Threepenny Opera*. After seeing Alexander Tairow's Moscow production on the way home, he thought he could do better.[8] Said to have constructed the text from memory, he told me he had G. W. Pabst's film scenario. Playing Macheath, he called it *Beggars' Theater*, set in Tokyo at the start of Meiji Era. The artist's name he took describes him: Senda Korea. Koreans were blamed for causing the 1923 earthquake. Mistaken for one, he was chased and beaten up in Sendagaya, a district of Tokyo.

After prison and the War, Senda, helped by Iwabuchi Tatsuji, performed and published virtually all of Brecht, the outstanding Asian achievement. His model productions provoked the experimental "Black Tent" reaction, but I found some among the very best: his 1980 *Caucasian Chalk Circle*, and *The Good Person of Szechwan* in 1986 with Komaki Kurihara's subtle narrative acting and credible *doubleness* of voice, speaking *through*—not instead of—the other self, interweaving—not separating—identities, as no Western production I've seen ever quite managed.

Huang Zuolin's six-hour lecture introduced Brecht to China in 1951. Stimulated by Senda, his 1959 anti-war *Mother Courage* in Shanghai "failed," he told me, after eleven performances, though I don't really believe in failure. Many left, but Ba Jin stayed to the end.⁹ But *Life of Galileo*, staged with Chen Rong en suite for six weeks in 1979, sold out in the large China Youth Arts Theater in Beijing, now symptomatically replaced by a larger shopping mall. This was the longest run of any Western play, translated by Ding Yangzhong on paper given him to write his confession in detention during the Cultural Revolution. When a prelate waved his little black book, everyone knew what was meant.

Brecht was seriously discussed in China in the early 1980s, just as German directors abandoned him. They said the problem was not the model, which could be changed, but the figures, who can't. They were too constructed and can't be questioned.¹⁰ That became the default response. Roland Barthes linked Brecht's social gestus with Denis Diderot's tableau, as an ideal meaning is "contained under a single point of view."¹¹ However, Jean-Paul Sartre suggested a more striking analogy in the 1950s. He argued that Brecht's plays were like Jean Racine's, not on account of a comparable distancing but, as its consequence, of the reverse, namely a more intense engagement between audience and characters, for "we find ourselves in them without diminishing our stupefaction."¹² Brecht's audience was like a group of ethnographers approaching a foreign tribe, and exclaiming in astonishment: "those savages, that's us!"¹³

The audience then *produces itself*, if shocked into an auto-ethnographic experience more complex than either current extreme, scientific certainty or empathetic identification, can furnish since both, though differently, inhibit self-examination. Without some empathy — "that's us" — there is no impulse to question the self. But only then do we realize that "we are victims and accomplices at the same time."¹⁴

In 1941 Brecht described the traps within two instrumentalizing social theories: Behaviorism and Marxism. If Behaviorism encouraged the subject to believe in its freedom to choose between material goods, Marxism justified political control, because the ultimate subject of history was still creating the conditions for an as yet imperfectly realized universal freedom. He remarked: "the demolition, explosion, atomization of the individual psyche is a fact, so it's not a false, conventional observation if one discerns in individuals a strange lack of center. But lack of center does not mean lack of substance."¹⁵

We think of substance as centering, so what does this unusual distinction imply? The most quoted line of modern German poetry — "Erst kommt das Fressen, dann kommt die Moral" (Food comes first, then comes morality) — echoes Alfred Forke's paraphrase of Mencius (Mengzi).¹⁶

Mengzi distinguished between a *desire* for action and the possibility of *realizing it*. Conditions permitting, ordinary people will do what is right. So it is incumbent upon the ruler to create those conditions. He discusses this situational morality in the vivid anecdotal manner Brecht admired. A philosopher says "man's nature is indifferent to good and evil, just as water is indifferent to east and west." Mengzi replies it is not indifferent to up and down. If you use force, water will go uphill, and when men do what is not good, their nature is treated in this way.[17]

That is perhaps one source, though not the only basis, for the distinction between absence of center and presence of substance. Here substance is the precipitate of desire, a somatically discernible psychological phenomenon and moral possibility, at times only visible by its absence, in depression and, sometimes, in rage. It can't create the world to its liking. Centerlessness is the lack of focus or ability, not just a matter of individual choice, to realize what is substantial. That this can be achieved by an exercise of will, or by declaring it should be so, is the illusion of every orthodox moral system, philosophical or religious, Eastern or Western, as it was the illusory hope of the expressionists in Brecht's generation.[18] In Erich Fromm's analytic social psychology, necessary conformity to *social character* also forms the *social unconscious*, the repository of unrealized substantial desire, hence the divergence between "substance" and "center," as Chinese social and moral philosophy supposed.[19]

Brecht avoided the language of psychoanalysis. Emotions are deemed distractions from the main event: we should rather watch what the characters do, or what is done to them. But marginalizing, or decentering, the emotions increases their force. Any putative rejection of psychology needs situating. Brecht refused ego-psychology, not the unconscious, which is pivotal to his work. When asking in 1938 whether he really wanted "to do away with the space where the unconscious, half conscious, uncontrolled, ambiguous, multipurposed could play itself out" the unstated answer is obviously: No![20]

Ego-psychology encourages the individual to accept normative social character. But if society has gone mad, deviation may signify sanity. An assumed normalization operates well in a naturalist aesthetic, *even* where the audience sympathizes with the resisting character, since the *frame* of normality remains unquestioned. Turning away from naturalism or forestalling empathy in order to inhibit identification seems to de-psychologize and thereby to de-*problematize* the subject. But the reverse is true.

Because de-psychologizing *re*-problematizes the subject, since it creates the conditions for formulating a halfway adequate theory of subjectivity upon the stage. The audience are not confirmed in their possession of a *certain* truth or, alternatively, justified in its rejection, but must rather question the relationship between ego and other, self and certainty, practice and theory, and confront the problematic nature of their *own* identity. This is what energizes Brecht's theater.[21]

It does not, of course, reject emotions, but enquires into their origin. It abandons an emotional style, since identificatory presuppositions determine the response. In anthropological distancing, strangers estrange us from ourselves. If not somehow distanced, they offer psychological escape through an empathy, which *appears* to share their burden, but in reality amounts to self-exculpation, sustaining a repression, as we project onto others what we hide from ourselves. The moment we "identify" with them, secretly pleased by our own sensitivity, we paradoxically both lose our self and sever ourselves from them. We effectively scapegoat them and they suffer for us. Then the actual *inter*relationship between audience and character, reader and read, remains opaque.

Brecht did not always manage to inhibit this escape. One reason may have been a way of talking about *the* alienation effect. Singularized, it created the expectation of a recognizable method, an applicable technique, enabling the audience to see through whatever estrangement has singled out for observation. Not only Barthes equated this with a correct perspective. Simplifications are easier to remember.

But estranging may have divergent consequences. All estrangements depend on realizing that, for whatever reason, a conventional response is no longer adequate. An imperfectly known reveals a lack of understanding, which lies either inside or outside us. Separating them distinguishes between alienating to clarify and explain, or to question and explore. Either ignorance is replaced by knowledge, or superficial understanding points to a deeper ignorance. One offers knowledge, the other confronts us with uncertainty. Theory either explains estrangement, or estrangement reveals an insufficient theory. The effect of this distinction is far reaching, since the consequences are psychologically, epistemologically, and politically different.

The alienation effect is mostly equated with instruction. The other estrangement, less discussed, or even discounted, perhaps because "self"-questioning seems to turn towards the so-called "Aristotelian" theater and needless self-preoccupation, offers nothing instructional, and draws us into a more troubling analysis. If we recognize our doubleness as victim and accomplice, we both participate and separate from ourselves. What matters is to interrupt any self-*retraction* or, as Brecht remarked, the audience's tendency to believe in its *own* indestructibility, to assume "this could never happen to me."[22] The solution for what looks like a dilemma—to both identify and not identify—is not to simplify but to complicate the figure. The emphasis is not on the certainty of the observed but on awakening uncertainty in the observer. What matters is not that the character learns, and we too should mark and inwardly digest this, but that "the spectator should see," or confront his own repressions.²³

Brecht became an expert in counter-discourses: philosophical, ethical, political, psychological, metaphorical, linguistic, and dramaturgical. Not only East Asia helped formulate them, but there are numerous echoes. The less proof positivist for such echoes, the more interesting they are. Herr Keuner remarks: whoever boasts of writing long books all by themselves has lost the mental ability of Zhuangzi, nine-tenths of whom consists of quotations.²⁴ We have heard the *ethical* counter-discourse in *The Threepenny Opera*, mediating Mencius, and the *psychological* counter-discourse about substance and center.

Brecht's early diaries allude to Chinese thought: "A Chinese sentence: If the grains of sand turn against people, people must go away" (September 1920).²⁵ The encounter with Laozi occurred in the same month. Richard Wilhelm's translation adjusted the *Daodejing* to salvationist expectations, even including the forgiveness of sins.²⁶ Unlike Alfred Döblin or Klabund, Brecht reflected none of this. A comment in July 1921 suggests how he then read it: "I am too lazy for childish battles and too Asiatic to perish at the stake for truth."²⁷ His central metaphor, the flux of things, feeds on this Daoist tributary, on Nietzsche and, later, on Karl Marx's "flow of movement."²⁸ Daoism expresses the Chinese social unconscious. A *pro memoria* note I found in the Archives interprets this *integrative* metaphor from Heraclitus to Marx: "their teaching of the flow of things/not just that everything flows/but how it flows/and can be made to flow."²⁹ In his Laotse poem hope is possible when it appears least justified. The Dao and Marxist thought, far from opposing each other, in fact interpenetrate.

The *philosophical* counter-discourse stretches across cultures, theories and religions and though the object of attention changes, there are constants in the questioning. Brecht complains in 1929 about "world systematizers," who pretend to conduct their politics entirely for the working classes: when they "refer to the proletariat, it's only customer service." His German words now sound impeccably Neu-Deutsch: "Dass diese Weltbildhauer sich auf das Proletariat berufen, das ist nur Service (Kundendienst)."³⁰ He adds: "There are some people who are suspected of only wanting to make revolution in order to bring about dialectical materialism." In other words, they are idealists without regard for real people or practical consequences. At the time he was reading Mozi (Me Ti), a contemporary of Socrates, who furnished his Me-ti persona and says virtually the same about the Confucian scholars.³¹

Brecht's Me-ti was "against constructing too complete images of the world."³² Transferred into *aesthetic* counter-discourse, this explains his admiration for Chinese painting, whose empty spaces remind us of nature's irreducibility, never submitting everything to one single point of view or accomplishing "the thorough subjugation of the viewer."[33] "This order," he remarked, "requires no force." The same attitude guides in 1955 his *critical* response, another counter-discourse, to Ernst Schumacher's reading of the early plays. Brecht tells him: "You could drop some evaluations and instead leave some questions open. That's always productive. Why put everything into one category, even if it's the most attractive?"[34]

In his study, Brecht hung two pictures of Confucius.[35] We shouldn't sentimentalize this, for the respected teacher served as a warning that you may cease to learn. V. I. Lenin argued that matter is independent of consciousness, and historical materialism independent of social consciousness.[36] Josef Stalin administered this as "revolution from above." Brecht invokes the silence of Buddha, who refused metaphysical disputes with his students about the nature of nirvana instead of getting out of the burning house.[37] Buddhism criticized the effect of concepts, and anti-essentialism links Brecht with a philosophy of practice: "The theory of knowledge must above all be a critique of language," and "philosophy should be more concerned with the language of people than with the language of philosophers."[38] That could be Ludwig Wittgenstein. Brecht pasted a "Song Guanyin Boddhisatva" opposite the title page of his own Lutheran Bible, turning its back on the written word, on absolutes and dreams of transcendence.[39]

The *metaphorical* counter-discourse in *Terzinen über die Liebe* (also called *Die Liebenden/The Lovers*, or *Song of the Cranes*)[40] rejects transcendence, and counters metaphysical longings with East Asian metaphors of life's flight through time.[41] Among the early *Psalms* are what one might call Schopenhauerian haiku.[42] Other poems remind critics of tanka, though I am more struck by the differences. A tanka version of *Die Maske des Bösen*[43] would imply everything in half as many words.[44] But when his Chinese poems differ from their source, they often resonate with the originals he did not know.[45]

As for dramaturgical counter-discourse, Brecht adopted Japanese and Chinese plots, and learnt from their acting. The evidence is incontrovertible, but there is disagreement about the consequences. Elizabeth Hauptmann told me he read Arthur Waley's Introduction to the *Noh* plays. Seami describes how representing a state or emotion involves its opposite, something Brecht also noted in Chinese technique. As Seami said: "in matter there is also emptiness, in emptiness there is also matter."[46] Due to this commonality, I called a section in *Brechts Ost Asien* "Alienation Effects in Japanese Acting." Of course they were very different, though there is a visual analogy in *Man is Man*, but he was stimulated by their practices.

Though it also looks, sounds, and seems different, Chinese theater had a conscious social component and sometimes even a political effect, and Brecht was also impressed by its aesthetic quality. Reading one through the other is perhaps not as unproductive as it may first seem to Western and Eastern scholars.[47] It is said that Chinese theater expresses a character's emotional life, which Brecht's actor critiques. Brecht says of Chinese acting:

> The performer's self-observation, an artful and artistic act of self-alienation, stopped the spectator from losing himself in the character completely, *i.e. to the point of giving up his own identity*, and lent a splendid remoteness to the events. *Yet the spectator's empathy was not entirely rejected*. The audience identifies itself with the actor as being an observer, and accordingly develops his attitude of observing or looking on.[48]

That Mei Lanfang demonstrated acting techniques is thought to explain why Brecht missed the full evocation of the character's emotions. Self-observation is considered more obviously a consequence of demonstration than of performance and it cannot be extended to suggest the self-*alienation* Brecht advocates. But Mei Lanfang corroborates Brecht's admiration for what demonstrating can achieve, recording his own astonishment at the dramatic and psychological effect of watching another actor's "mere" demonstration without costume. Demonstration heightens the distancing, which in Chinese aesthetics brings things closer, creating, on another level, as Brecht understood, a more powerful and penetrating, hence memorable, effect of reality.[49] By "self-alienation" (*Selbstentfremdung*) Brecht meant a contrary effect, both *preventing* a *complete* loss of spectatorial identity and *encouraging* a degree of empathy through the skillfully represented complexity of the character's position, which is too subtle for easy identification.

Brecht's essay on Chinese acting is often read in translation with consequences for its interpretation.[50] Where John Willett's version speaks of the *coldness* with which the Chinese actor "holds himself remote from the character portrayed," Brecht says *Durchkältung*. Willett says that gestures representing emotions are "decorously expressed," though Brecht meant and also wrote *sparsam dargestellt*,[51] which means "sparingly" represented, not overdone. *Durchkältung* refers to a style that chills, cools down, understates or underplays, in the sense of "less is more." The consequence, however, is something like the opposite, not freezing, but rather increasing emotional effect. At issue is *how* emotions are shown.

Brecht does not say Chinese acting is cold, only that it seems so when measured by Western conventions. He says:

To the Western actor the Chinese artist's playing appears in many respects cold. That does not mean the Chinese theater does without the representation of emotions. The artist performs events of great passion but his presentation is unheated. At moments of intense excitation for the character the artist takes a strand of hair between his lips and bites it in two.[52]

When Brecht speaks of the actor "quoting the character played," the evidence for many critics of Brecht's misrepresentation, he adds: "But with what art he does this!"[53] At issue is not the style as such, but what that style achieves: the clarity of an aesthetically satisfying externalized representation of intense emotions and complex, contradictory situations that took Brecht's breath away. As for the style, which of course he never copied but whose effect he wished to emulate, he was still talking about it twenty years later to the doubtlessly bemused actors in the Berliner Ensemble.

Some critics argue that the sophisticated Chinese audience holds back, not simply identifying with the character but taking in the whole sequence of events. That is why Brecht wanted to develop the art of spectating (*Zuschaukunst*), adequate to the art of acting (*Schauspielkunst*) in Chinese theater. If Chinese actors stress and Brecht downplays emotions, that does not mean he misunderstood Chinese theater or that the effect is essentially different. In some respects it may be, but I am arguing one central point. He was struck by the difference between comparatively crude Western and sophisticated Chinese acting. Apart from taste or preference, the Chinese method distances or stylizes in order to intensify. Emotional excitation in conventional Western theater was directly expressed by yelling and waving your arms. In Chinese theater it is *symbolized* as the actor bites through an imagined hair (though Willett says "chews" it), one of the imaginative externalizations Brecht mentions.

The effect is so powerful because, while apparently doing less, it *shows* the discerning spectator more: we *see* a figure driven by passion and frustration, *and* we *see* the repression that is still in command. Aware of this doubleness when playing Yang Guifei in *The Drunken Concubine*, Mei Lanfang offered a contradictory emotional engagement, not release. Brecht saw a style that clarified his intentions by externalizing complex events gesture by gesture, step by step, sentence by sentence with a gracefulness that affected his later aesthetic, the opposite of the German uncorporeal lack of clarity he criticizes in the *Short Organon*.

As for events in East Asia, a Hong Kong Seminar in 1981 brought first accounts of East Asian productions from those directly involved, also from Indian practitioners and Westerners.[54] The discussion centered on whether traditional forms would evolve or Marxism change. I specially

The Visions of Simone Machard: refugees seek shelter at the inn. Photo Courtesy of Fredric Mao and Antony Tatlow.

remember Huang Zuolin's observation of a gap between emotion and gesture in traditional Chinese acting, denied by some critics. The challenge, he said, was to show the drunk Li Bai on a sober horse.

Encouraged in 1983 to organize an International Brecht Society (IBS) Symposium in Beijing, I was asked not to mention Marxism. But it was frustrated anyway by the *Campaign against Spiritual Pollution*. The *People's Daily* had published an article in March 1983 by Central Committee member Zhou Yang suggesting that "alienation," not only a capitalist phenomenon, was also possible under Communism: not the best time to discuss the A-Effect!

During the 1985 *Brecht in China* Conference in Beijing and Shanghai there were notable productions, including a shortened version of *The Good Person of Szechwan* in the Central Academy of Drama, distanced into the old Chinese society and developing a Chinese style, played very fast with clever pantomime, especially from the scroungers and hangers-on, who lost that phoney strangeness they can have in Europe or America. An Academy Shakespeare expert said to me: "I didn't realize how well Brecht understood China. That's what China was like!" Many said: only after the Cultural Revolution could they really understand Brecht. In comparison, the visually innovative Sichuan opera adaptation of the play seemed abstract and unsure of itself. In Lin Zhaohua's *Schweyk*, a huge rope net hung over Schweyk's encounter with Bullinger. Lin and Gao Xingjian were both working in the People's Art Theater, and in *The Other*

Shore Gao uses a rope to suggest various human relationships including an enmeshing spider's web. At the Beijing Brecht conference Gao said: "Brecht was the first to make me understand…that the rules of this art could be reconstructed completely anew…So my own dramatic writing, all that I know, and all that I've written from my knowledge, has drawn a lot of courage from his work on this point."[55]

Of the performances presented at the 7th IBS Symposium in Hong Kong (1986), these re-readings of Brecht's plays deserve special mention:

a) The Haiyuza Theater's *Der Jasager/Neinsager*, in which *He said Yes*, but *She said No*! In this imaginative and literally high-wire production, the chorus of men and women in both plays wore dark green jackets and black trousers, but the all male performers in *Jasager* wore blue and white horizontally striped smocks over blue trousers and leggings and carried grey rucksacks, while the *Neinsager* were all female, wearing similar but now red and white striped smocks, with red rucksacks and red leggings, vividly stressing the interpretively significant gender difference.

b) The Philippine Educational Theater Association's *The Caucasian Chalk Circle*, set in Mindanao, adapted to an indigenous style, soldiers with machine guns among the spectators, the child taken from the crowd, an example of vibrant community theater acting out their daily experience.

Simone's brother apears as messenger. Transition to the dream sequences. Photo Courtesy of Fredric Mao and Antony Tatlow.

c) The Hong Kong Academy of Performing Arts' *The Visions of Simone Machard*. A Brecht Handbook spoke of its "very strange, unrealistic dream sequences" and "absolutely puzzling dream scenes."[56] But they are central to the play. The director, Fredric Mao, set it in China during the 1930s Japanese invasion, drawing on the heritage of the Chinese imagination. Ah Sei (Simone) dreams that she is one of the well-known women generals of the Yang Family, who resisted the 13th century Mongol invasion. As her daydreams begin, the acting gradually moves towards Chinese opera style. The pictures show three stages: the inn during the occupation; the transition to the dream sequences when her brother appears as a messenger; the counter world in the social unconscious unfolding as a dream of opera. (Illustrations 1-3)

I mentioned Ba Jin's interest in Brecht's Gao Qipei (1672-1734) painting, which hung behind his bed. His programmatic 1937 poem, *The Doubter*, describes the consequences of looking at this blue-black ink picture in the vigorous finger-painting style, depicting a man on a bench whose shoulders are hunched in thought.[57] The painting itself contains a poem, which explores in a Buddhist context the relationship between mind and universe, and the problem of distinguishing between good and evil men. The ontological vision in the words is offset by the earthiness of the portrait. Text and picture qualify and contradict each other, suggesting fissures within the text and in the portrait. No dignified visionary in the tradition of Buddhist iconography, this man wrestles with a problem, as can be seen from the positioning of the feet and the tension between them and the hunched shoulders.

The gap between practice and theory is a very Chinese theme, and his picture-poem suggests the inevitable ambiguity of all practice. Both poem and painting are in some sense self-portraits. There is no record of how much Brecht knew about the Chinese painting: the less, the better. But the analogies do not come from nowhere. The other resonates within ourselves, and we then glimpse the unconscious of a culture. Like the painting, Brecht's poetic self-portrait questions the "ontological" vision, the theory that is never, as contemporary convention decreed, scientifically correct, that cannot be taken for granted and must always be tested and changed through practice.

Our problem now is not how to realize the future but how to avoid it. Western culture has been defined by teleological models, whether religious, metaphysical, or economic: the Day of Judgment, absorption into some Absolute, the realization of Communism, or so-called globalization. If Marx turned G. W. F. Hegel upside-down to stand him on his feet, Arthur Schopenhauer transformed Hegel's ultimately benevolent World Spirit into a malevolent Will. His equally metaphysical model now seems a better way of concentrating minds. What we now need is

a relational, cybernetic, anti-teleological catastrophe avoidance theory. Vital to Brecht's legacy is what he called "interventionary thought."[58]

In Forke's *Me Ti* translation, Brecht marked this passage: "If you tell bad people that Heaven acts justly, their character, even if capable of improvement, will not be changed. You must cheerfully announce to them that Heaven behaves badly."[59] Friedrich Engels once remarked that we should not "flatter ourselves overmuch on account of our human conquest over nature. For each such conquest nature takes its revenge upon us…Thus at every step we are reminded that we by no means rule over nature like a conqueror over a foreign people."[60]

And that may well be the ultimate, self-alienating anthropological encounter.

The dream of victory in the counter world of opera. Photo Courtesy of Fredric Mao and Antony Tatlow.

Endnotes

1 Invited to "wrap-up" the International Brecht Society's 13th Symposium in Honolulu 2010, I here retain the direct address of that event.
2 Bertolt Brecht, *Werke: Große kommentierte Berliner und Frankfurter Ausgabe*, Vol. 13, ed. Werner Hecht (Berlin, Frankfurt/Main: Aufbau and Suhrkamp, 1987-2000), p. 243.
3 Bertolt Brecht, *Poems 1913-1956*, Michael Hamburger, trans. (London: Methuen, 1976), p. 98, modified.
4 BFA 13, p. 271.
5 The first comment I heard from Gerd Irrlitz, Humboldt University Professor of Philosophy, during a Berlin Seminar. The second is by Wolfgang Fritz Haug, Free University, Berlin Professor of Philosophy and editor of the *Historical-Critical Marxism Dictionary*, in Wolfgang Fritz Haug, ed., *Philosophieren mit Brecht und Gramsci* (Berlin: Argument Verlag, 1966), p. 10. The quotation comes from Friedrich Nietzsche, *Sämtliche Werke. Kritische Studien-Ausgabe*, Vol. 12 (Berlin: de Gruyter, 1988), p. 240.
6 Wing-Tsit Chan, comp. and trans., *A Source Book in Chinese Philosophy* (Princeton: Princeton University Press, 1963), pp. 669-670.
7 BFA 21, pp. 761-762.
8 Koreya Senda, *Wanderjahre* (Berlin: Henschelverlag, 1985), p. 145. In 1930 *Drums in the Night* was translated, see Antony Tatlow and Tak-Wai Wong, eds., *Brecht and East Asian Theatre* (Hong Kong: Hong Kong University Press, 1982), p. 111.
9 Forced to kneel on broken glass during the Cultural Revolution, Ba Jin cried out to his tormentors: "No matter what you do to me, it will not change the truth." When I met him in 1984 (22 October), he was most interested to hear about Brecht's painting by Gao Qipei.
10 Jürgen Flimm said this to me in Cologne (8 September 1980). Likewise, Volker Hesse (Düsseldorf) told me he couldn't direct the late plays. *The Good Person of Szechwan* was unperformable (30 June 1984). Directing *The Caucasian Chalk Circle* in Singapore in 1989, Markwart Müller-Elmau (Ulm) spoke of Brecht's "ideological puppet theater," whose final act must take place outside the theater. He put "simplicity on stage." His "typified characters" particularly appealed to Asian actors and directors because they expect first of all "clear unambiguous statements that do not require reading between the lines" (16 December 1989). For Peter von Becker, Brecht could *only* be performed in Asia, where the fairy-tale quality of his work could be realized. Von Becker, "Wo Märchen wieder wahr werden," *Theater Heute* 2 (1987): pp. 15-19.
11 Roland Barthes, "Diderot, Brecht, Eisenstein," in Roland Barthes, *Image, Music, Text* (London: Fontana, 1977), p. 71.
12 Jean-Paul Sartre, "Brecht et les classiques," in Jean-Paul Sartre, *Un théâtre de situations* (Paris: Gallimard, 1973), pp. 90-91. This first appeared in a brochure, "Hommage international à Bertolt Brecht," in April 1957 in a programme of the *Théâtre des Nations* for which the Berliner Ensemble performed *Life of Galileo* and *Mother Courage*.
13 Ibid., p. 110.
14 Ibid., p. 91.
15 BFA 26, p. 476.
16 "Hunger und Durst...sind Feinde jeder Moral." Alfred Forke, *Geschichte der alten chinesischen Philosophie* (Hamburg: Kommissionsverlag L. Friederichsen & Co., 1927), p. 212. Brecht had this book as well as Richard Wilhelm's Mencius translation, Richard Wilhelm, *Mong Dsi* (Jena: Eugen Dietrichs, 1916).
17 See James Legge, *The Chinese Classics*, Vol. 2 (Hong Kong: University of Hong Kong Press, 1960), pp. 395-396. This theme recurs in Brecht's writing. See Antony Tatlow, *The Mask of Evil* (Bern, Frankfurt/Main, Las Vegas: Peter Lang, 1977), pp. 469-475.
18 The questions raised by this distinction between "substance" and "center" occur throughout Brecht's work. Their formulation depends on the socio-political context. A later version of this dilemma appears around 1945, connected with an unfinished poem, "Lehrgedicht von der Natur der Menschen," itself related to *De rerum natura* by

Lucretius: "So auch der tapfere Mensch ist nicht ganz tapfer: manchmal versagt er./In ihm liegt Feigheit und Mut und der Mut triumphiert, doch nicht immer./Und wenn er einmal versagt, dann listet ihn nicht bei den Feigen" (BFA 15, p. 172).

19   Erich Fromm, *The Erich Fromm Reader,* ed. Rainer Funk (New Jersey: Humanities Press, 1994), p. 9; originally in Erich Fromm, *The Crisis of Psychoanalysis* (New York: Henry Holt, 1955).

20   BFA 22/1, p. 468.

21   Anyone doubting that Brecht's theater is still equated with the rationalizations of an instructional style, might look at some responses during the Brecht Centennial. See *Brecht 100 <=> 2000, The Brecht Yearbook* 24 (1999): pp. 1-3.

22   BFA 25, p. 241.

23   BFA 24, p. 264.

24   BFA 18, p. 441.

25   BFA 26, p. 167.

26   Laotse, *Tao Te King. Das Buch vom Sinn und Leben* (München: Eugen Dietrichs Verlag, 1996), p. 105.

27   BFA 26, p. 232.

28   "In ihrer mystifizierten Form ward die Dialektik deutsche Mode, weil sie das Bestehende zu verklären schien. In ihrer rationalen Gestalt ist sie dem Bürgertum und seinen doktrinären Wortführern ein Ärgernis und ein Greuel, weil sie in dem positiven Verständnis des Bestehenden zugleich auch das Verständnis seiner Negation, seines notwendigen Untergangs einschließt, jede gewordene Form im Flusse der Bewegung, also auch nach ihrer vergänglichen Seite auffasst, sich durch nichts imponieren lässt, ihrem Wesen nach kritisch und revolutionär ist." Karl Marx, Friedrich Engels, *Werke* (Berlin: Dietz Verlag, 1972), p. 28, dated 24 January 1873 in the *Afterword* to the 2nd edition of *Das Kapital.*

29   Bertolt Brecht Archiv (BBA) 328/10.

30   BFA 21, p. 349.

31   *Mê Ti des Sozialethikers und seiner Schüler philosophische Werke,* Alfred Forke, trans. (Berlin: Kommissionsverlag der Vereinigung wissenschaftlicher Verleger, 1922).

32   BFA 18, p. 60.

33   BFA 22, pp. 133-134.

34   BFA 30, p. 329.

35   The text above one of these portraits reads: xīan shī kŏng zĭ xíng jiāo xiàng (a picture of the first teacher Confucius on his way to educate).

36   V. I. Lenin,"Materialism and Empirio-criticism," *Collected Works,* Vol. 14 (Moscow: Progress Publishers, 1968), p. 326.

37   BFA 12, p. 36.

38   BFA 21, pp. 413, 402.

39   This figure is sometimes described as a water-moon type, gazing on the moon's reflection.

40   BFA 14, p. 15.

41   See Jan Knopf, *Brecht-Handbuch,* Vol. 2 (Stuttgart: Metzler Verlag, 2001), pp. 168-172.

42   BFA 11, p. 30.

43   BFA 12, p. 124.

44   See Antony Tatlow, *Brechts Ost Asien* (Berlin: Parthas-Verlag, 1998), p. 36.

45   Ibid., pp. 30-35.

46   Ibid., pp. 17-22.

47   For Min Tian, Brecht's response is an orientalizing imposition and an example of "prescribed superiority." Min Tian, "'Alienation-Effect' for Whom? Brecht's (Mis) interpretation of the Classical Chinese Theatre" *Asian Theatre Journal,* 14.2 (Fall 1997): pp. 200-222. Ronnie Bai gives a more differentiated reading, but stresses Brecht's words and not the practice that followed. He sets out to prove the sole impulse from Chinese theater. Ronnie Bai, "Dances with Mei Lanfang: Brecht and the Alienation Effect," *Comparative Drama* 32 (1998): p. 3.

48 BFA 22, p. 202, I quote John Willett's version in Bertolt Brecht, *Brecht on Theater*, John Willett, trans. (New York: Hill & Wang, 1964), p. 93. I have italicized what Min Tian omits from this passage in presenting Brecht's views.
49 Mei Lanfang, "Reflections on my stage life," in Wu Zuguang, Huang Zuolin, Mei Shaowu, eds., *Peking Opera and Mei Lanfang* (Beijing: New World Press, 1980), p. 44.
50 Brecht, *Brecht on Theater*, pp. 91-99. The cited quotations are on p. 93.
51 BFA 22, p. 203.
52 Ibid., pp. 202-203.
53 Ibid., p. 204.
54 Tatlow and Wong, *Brecht and East Asian Theatre* and *Communications from the International Brecht Society*, Vol. 10, No. 3 (July 1982), pp. 3-14.
55 Gao Xingjian, *Wo yu Bulaixite* (Me and Brecht), *Qingyi* (1985), pp. 52-56.
56 Jan Knopf, *Brecht-Handbuch*, Vol. 1 (Stuttgart: Metzler Verlag, 1980), pp. 240-241.
57 I have discussed in detail this fascinating relationship in German in Tatlow, *Brechts Ost Asien*, pp. 13-16, and in English in Antony Tatlow, "Unconscious Documents. Brecht and East Asia," in Paolo Amalfitano, *L'Oriente. Storia di una figura nelle arti occidentali (1700-2000)*, Vol. 2 (Roma: Bulzoni Editore, 2007), pp. 215-232.
58 BFA 21, p. 524.
59 "Wenn man zu schlechten Menschen sagt, dass der Himmel gerecht handelt, so lässt sich ihr Charakter, auch wenn er verbesserungsfähig, nicht ändern. Man muß ihnen frohlockend verkünden, dass der Himmel schlecht handelt." Me Ti, p. 505. Brecht also marked this short sentence — "Generosität schließt das eigene Selbst nicht aus." (p. 510) — whose doubleness resonates throughout his work and corroborates what is so succinctly formulated, and problematized, in this last poem: "Dauerten wir unendlich/ So wandelt sich alles./Da wir aber endlich sind,/Bleibt vieles beim Alten" (BFA 15, p. 294).
60 Karl Marx and Friedrich Engels, *Selected Works* (London: Lawrence & Wishart, 1968), p. 365, from *The Dialectics of Nature*, first published in 1925 in German in the USSR.

Book Reviews

Joachim Lang. *Neues vom alten Brecht: Manfred Wekwerth im Gespräch.* Valentin F. Lang and Karoline Sprenger. Berlin: Aurora, 2010. 192 Seiten.

The full title of this book contains a contradiction in that new material is promised from someone who has already spoken and written at length about Brecht. This is acknowledged by Manfred Wekwerth's interlocutor, Joachim Lang, in his introduction when he references a volume of interviews with Hans-Dieter Schütt of 1995 (*Manfred Wekwerth*) and Wekwerth's autobiography of 2000 (*Erinnern ist Leben*). He also acknowledges that he has previously published an interview with Wekwerth, together with Jürgen Hillesheim, in a collection that marked Brecht's centenary in 1998 (*Denken heisst verändern*). Nonetheless, he notes that he considers this book worth printing "weil es Gespräche mit einem seiner [Brecht's] engsten Mitarbeiter gibt, der sagt, so hätte er noch nicht über Brecht geredet" (7). In addition, he writes that it is important to correct misconceptions or indeed prejudices about Brecht. The two primary ones that he lists are that Brecht was a cold rationalist theatermaker and that he exploited his co-workers, the women in particular. One could argue that bringing up the charge of exploitation once again gives John Fuegi's unscholarly claims of 1994 additional credence. The irony is that they had been well and truly put to bed many years beforehand, not least by the testimonies of Lang and Hillesheim's interview partners in their highly informative collection of interviews.

The text on the book's back cover does not bode well for a reader hoping to find something new. The "Unentdecktes" that is to be found within is listed as: "die Faszination des Naiven bei der ersten Begegnung mit dem Dramatiker, den Mut zum Genuss im Brechtschen Theater, Brechts Kunst des Vergessens beim Inszenieren, seine Ästhetik des Gebrauchtseins angesichts seiner verbeulten Autos, Brecht-Frisuren in Sibirien, Brechts Haltung zum 17. Juni und eine Angst vor dem Scheintod." I have given this list in its entirety to note that there was only one feature of which I was not aware, having reread the Wekwerth books mentioned above, and that was the detail about imitations of Brecht's haircut in Siberia, which, suffice it to say, is an amusing detail at most. Wekwerth brought the category of the naive to scholarship's attention in his notes on working with Brecht; *Mut zum Genuss* is the title of Wekwerth's latest book on Brecht (German: 2009; English, *Daring to Play*: 2011). Wekwerth addresses all the other issues in his previous works, often using very similar formulations. In short, the reader is prepared for disappointment in advance.

The book itself is one long series of questions and answers, edited down from several interviews. Consequently, there are no chapter divisions to help the reader navigate the various periods or topics covered, only short phrases on the top right corner of every odd-numbered page. On occasion they offer information, as in "Bechts Filmprojekte" (97), but mostly they leave the reader wondering to what they might be referring: "Neigung zu Mumpitz" or "Befreiungsakte" (41 and 143 respectively). For the most part, the text takes a chronological approach, although it starts with Wekwerth's experience of and responses to Brecht's death (something he has already discussed in *Manfred Wekwerth* and *Denken heisst verändern*). There are occasional jumps in time, but these are more the exception than the rule. Lang takes the reader through Brecht in Augsburg, Berlin, and exile, periods about which Wekwerth can only speculate or offer information gleaned from other works or people. When, for example, he says that in his opinion Margarete Steffin was not a great actress (85), it can only be in his opinion, to which he is entitled, but which offers the reader nothing "Neues." It is only on page 110 that Lang says: "Jetzt kommen wir in die Zeit, als Sie Brecht kennengelernt haben."

This is the point at which the book could have radically changed. Lang, whom one presumes has read the books he referenced in his introduction, proceeds, however, to ask questions already asked and receives answers already known. The stories about how Wekwerth came to the Berliner Ensemble, Helene Weigel buying up meters of green corduroy for the theater and the staff, Brecht's initial inability to take criticism and then later to accept it, and many, many others are neither new nor told in novel ways that shed additional light on matters. Indeed, so slack is the editing that Wekwerth is allowed to quote Peter Palitzsch's view on why Wekwerth was employed at the BE at all in two separate places (31 and 113). The quotations in inverted commas are lexically different while remaining semantically identical.

Wekwerth is an extremely valuable resource. He is one of the few people left who worked with Brecht in the theater and, as opposed to the actors still alive, he can give insights into Brecht's working methods from the perspective of the auditorium, the much disputed relationship between theory and practice in rehearsal, and the ways in which Brecht conferred with his assistants at the regular meetings that took place after rehearsals, to name but three areas. Lang could also have asked specific questions about the productions on which Wekwerth assisted or directed while Brecht was still alive. Instead, Lang treads familiar ground and elicits very little that is not already known to readers and scholars.

When interesting points do arise, Lang fails to pursue them. For example, Wekwerth comments that he found the BE's *Urfaust* "nicht gut" (151) but the reader is none the wiser as to the reasons why. That Brecht wanted his "Schüler" to run the BE after his death is, to my knowledge, a new assertion and one worthy of closer attention. And when Wekwerth posits the idea that Brecht was keen to expand the BE's fame in order to reach more spectators, I would have hoped for a challenge to this formulation. After all, popularity and populism are two separate categories with different effects on theatrical efficacy.

The text itself is also amply supported by footnotes that mostly help the reader with biographical or factual information. Here there are occasional errors. One footnote puts *Der Kaukasische Kreidekreis* "im Mittelpunkt" (15) of the London tour of 1956 when really all three productions had similar status (*Courage*: 9 performances; *Kreidekreis*: 8; *Pauken und Trompeten*: 7); a reference to Wittgenstein (101) draws the reader to the *Tractatus*, while Wekwerth is referring to positions taken from *Philosophical Investigations*; and Käthe Reichel is said to have played Grusche (149), although the note fails to mention that this was in the film and not in the BE production.

The new discoveries are sadly few. That there was a discussion about whether to call the BE "Neues Berliner Ensemble" (118) on its transfer to the Theater am Schiffbauerdamm is interesting, as are answers given to questions about the mood at the BE in the immediate wake of 17 June 1953. Unfortunately, there is little more that has not already been said. One has to conclude that the title of this book is what the Germans would call "Etikettenschwindel," false labeling. And while one can accuse Wekwerth of using environmentally friendly strategies in recycling anecdotes from *Manfred Wekwerth* and *Erinnern ist Denken*, here, I would suggest, he is the innocent or at least the considerably less guilty party. Yes, he retells many familiar tales and gives many familiar opinions, but it is the responsibility of the author and the editors to publish a book that delivers on its very marketable title. Lang may well delegate this responsibility to his interview partner in the line quoted from his introduction at the top of this review, but he has sabotaged this potentially fascinating book by focusing on periods to which Wekwerth was not witness and by raising issues already well dealt with by Wekwerth and other contemporaries.

David Barnett
University of Sussex

John J. White and Ann White. *Bertolt Brecht's "Furcht und Elend des Dritten Reiches:" A German Exile Drama in the Struggle against Fascism*. Rochester: Camden House, 2010. 262 pages.

The title of this English language monograph refers to *Furcht und Elend des Dritten Reiches* rather than to the English version *The Private Life of the Master Race*, produced by Brecht and Eric Bentley during Brecht's exile in the United States. A "Textual Note" lists various extant versions and suggests that the one in the BFA may not be the preferred one. The authors nevertheless use it as a basis for their monograph, reasoning that "this is now the standard edition" (ix). It is difficult to evaluate this decision since the authors do not provide a substantive comparison of the versions. As a consequence references to the various versions, in the authors' discussions of individual scenes of *Furcht und Elend*, are somewhat confusing, as in the passages on "Die Kiste" (89 ff) or "Die Internationale" (122-23). This vagueness is signaled already in the book's title, which refers to Brecht's play as *des Dritten Reiches*. The actual title is *des III. Reiches*. Brecht's use of Roman numerals is not insignificant: they serve as a visual reminder that the Roman Empire, like other empires implied in the Nazis' grandiose attempt at genealogy, has perished.

The book is organized into five chapters. Chapters 1 and 2 present the historical context of the play and Brecht's reflections on fascism both in his non-fictional and fictional works. Chapters 3 and 4 look at the depiction of Nazi Germany and the forms of opposition depicted in *Furcht und Elend*. Chapters 5 and 6 focus on formal aspects. The first two chapters situate Brecht and the play within the political and cultural context of the time. While the authors refer to a multitude of sources, their discussions are rarely sustained and the references to fascism, Nazism, and Stalinism do not seem to be guided by any theory or theories. Cases in point are the frequent references to Marxism-Leninism, usually with the qualifier "orthodoxy" (31, 55). What is meant by Marxism-Leninism? Is it synonymous with Soviet communism? With Stalinism? Is there, for the Whites, a Marxism-Leninism that is not orthodox? Do they consider it a valid political theory or is their use of the term ironic? Absent any differentiation, we are left with non-verifiable statements such as: Brecht "unerringly based his antifascist campaign on a rigorously class-oriented Marxist-Leninist analysis" (9). This seems both simplistic and redundant. In addition to adhering to "Marxism-Leninism," Brecht supposedly also follows the directives of the Comintern (64), he illustrates its concepts (90), and he makes "respectful bows in the Comintern's direction" (34). The Comintern here appears as a kind of sinister bogey controlling Brecht in secret ways. What is missing is a discussion of the Comintern as a historical organization, of its structures, its policies, its influence (or lack thereof) on various national sections (of which Brecht was never a member). Another bogey of the Whites is Georg Lukács; for example, he is referred to in formulaic phrases such as "Lukács and his acolytes" (184) or "Lukács and his camarilla" (207). "Acolytes" suggests a cult with Lukács as its leader, "camarilla" a monarch. There is no attempt at discussing either his status or his stature. A reference to Lukács's "antimodernist revisionism" (225) is at a minimum superficial, considering his admiring essays on modernist writers such as Thomas and Heinrich Mann, Feuchtwanger, and Arnold Zweig.

A lack of theoretical engagement and sustained argument also afflicts the passage in the historical chapters where the Whites discuss Brecht's

"Application of the Base-Superstructure Model to the Third Reich" (53). The authors wish to show that he uses Marx's model to explain why the German proletariat did not rise up, once the Nazis went to war against the Soviet Union. Their discussion is based on a passage in Brecht's journals. In thinking about the Nazi invasion of the Soviet Union, Brecht argues that, by destroying the institutions of the working class, the Nazis destroyed the workers' ability to resist Hitler. This proves, according to Brecht, "daß das gesellschaftliche Sein das Bewußtsein bestimmt" (53). In Marx this dictum serves as a kind of preamble to the base-superstructure model (MEW 13, 8-9). The model itself is concerned with the dialectical relationship between *Produktivkräfte* (productive forces) and *Produktionsverhältnisse* (relations of production) as the mechanism that drives history. While the Whites refer to this as "the textbook Marxist model" (54), they provide no discussion of it. There is no evaluation of its significance for Brecht beyond the claim that he uses it "in a mechanistically determinist way" (56) and that he fails to deploy it "with sufficient rigor" (59). Whatever such judgments may be based on, they overlook the fact that in his journal Brecht never refers to *Produktivkräfte* or *Produktionsverhältnisse*. By the time he quoted Marx's dictum about being and consciousness, it had acquired a status independent of the base-superstructure model, and that is how Brecht uses it.

In the opening chapter and throughout their monograph the Whites discuss *Furcht und Elend* as a documentary play. The German version that is the focus of the monograph suggests no such thing. The authors' categorization is based on the subtitle of the US-version ("A Documentary Play"). It was added under entirely different circumstances; most likely, as the Whites themselves suggest (25), with a view toward its marketability in the US. The Whites draw their understanding of the genre from the German Documentary Theater of the 1960s (25 ff.) without, however, referring to any of its theoretical texts. This leads to a reinvention of its categories far removed from the strategic and aesthetic concepts famously formulated in Peter Weiss's "Notizen zum dokumentarischen Theater." As a consequence, the authors conclude that a play such as Weiss's *Viet Nam Discourse* is "*entirely fictional*" (ibid., original emphasis). This in spite of the fact that the play closely adheres to a key concept of the Documentary Theater, which postulates that historical sources – newspapers, speeches, proclamations, and other historical documents – should be quoted as much as possible in their unaltered form. Already the word "Discourse" in the title signals a critical distance from fiction.

To emphasize the documentarism of *Furcht und Elend*, the authors quote from a letter in which Brecht recommends the use of a montage of documents with the intent of making them speak for themselves without recourse to emotions (24). In Brecht's letter, however, the passage refers to non fictional texts such as the *Braunbuch* of 1933. While *Furcht und Elend* indeed cites facts and figures, its predominant mode is fiction. Its meaning or meanings are not brought out through a presentation of facts but rather through Brecht's artful and highly artificial use of language and dramatic devices, as well as through the centrality of the *Gestus*. And unlike Brecht's recommendation for non-fictional interventions against fascism, his play uses – and is meant to produce in the audience – emotions. The fact that authentic material underlies the scenes does not make *Furcht und Elend* a documentary play, any more than, say, *Galileo*.

As a consequence of their categorization, the Whites, in evaluating Brecht's depiction of the Third Reich, approach the play more as historiography than as literature. Their interpretation is based on what they consider likely behavior by real people at the time. This leads them to the conclusion that the actions of the Jewish wife are "unlikely" in "real-life" (208, 211). In focusing on the psychology and believability of individual characters' words and actions, the authors take the scenes at their face value, treating them as naturalistic depictions. In this they unwittingly follow Lukács, whose reading of some of the scenes is in line with the socialist realism they reject. What they overlook in such a reading is that the scenes are calculated for the effect they have on the *audience* rather than on the characters on stage. The significance of a scene such as "Dienst am Volke" is not whether the behavior it depicts may believably boost the morale of concentration camp inmates (123) but whether it may boost insight in the audience. In the same way *Die Physiker* is not about denouncing the two scientists as "cowering academics" or "archetypal 'Tuis'" (203; I find no such characterizations in this scene) but about making visible to the audience the system that deforms them. Rather than naturalistic "textbook illustration[s]" (122), the scenes in *Furcht und Elend* are stylized, abstracted, and compressed.

In discussing the formal aspects of *Furcht und Elend*, the authors argue that Brecht uses "covert estranging strategies" (190) and "covert defamiliarization devices" (213). This, according to the Whites, is at odds with Brecht's "customary assumption" that "effective alienation goes hand in hand with ostentatious anti-illusionism" (190). The argument lacks clarity. What are Brecht's "customary assumptions" about his work? What is meant by "effective" alienation or "ostentatious" anti-illusionism? Do the authors mean to say that the distancing effects are less visible in *Furcht und Elend* than in other plays? To the contrary, the play deploys quite "overtly" various devices of the Epic Theater such as poems, songs, placards, the freezing of action into tableaux, and so on. While one may argue that some of the (communist) political arguments in *Furcht und Elend* are camouflaged – for obvious reasons – that is not the case with the distancing devices.

Overall the Whites' terminology – they refer to "*illusion-based* alienation" (220), to "Brecht's *mainstream* anti-illusionist Epic Theater" (222), and to "*genuine* Epic Theater" (227; emphases added) – remains confusing. They claim that the stanzas about the relationship between parents and children at the beginning of "Der Spitzel" offer "a defamiliarizing picture" when they merely offer an "unfamiliar" picture (216). The Whites' understanding that in Brechtian theater "the whole is greater than the sum of its parts" (227) seems to miss what is new in Epic Theater: that each scene stands for itself and the whole is simply the addition of its parts.

>Robert Cohen
>New York University

Frank Raddatz: *Der Demetriusplan: Oder wie sich Heiner Müller den Brechtthron erschlich*. Berlin: Theater der Zeit, 2010. 235 pages.

"Aber es kommt wenig dabei heraus, wenn man sich absolut auf Brecht konzentriert."

Heiner Müller wrote these words in connection with his work on Shakespeare later in his career, summarizing how this encounter enriched his appreciation of Brecht's work. For Frank Raddatz this remark is symptomatic for Müller's use of Brecht as author and icon. If we follow this argument, then Shakespeare marks one of the turning points in the Müller-Brecht relationship, a move that Raddatz calls the "Demetriusplan," which can be roughly described as Müller's "zig zag" movement toward and away from Brechtian poetics and politics, until his final occupation of Brecht in the context German unification. *Der Demetriusplan*, appearing 15 years after Müller's death, offers an initial long term retrospective on Heiner Müller's work.

The polemical title sets the tone for the book as a whole. What's more, the suggestion that Müller was after what some might consider the Brecht-Throne and could not manage to reach it through his own accomplishments, thus had to use methods of "erschleichen," suggests something sinister in Müller's intentions. In the introduction Raddatz invites his readers to employ any "kriminelle Energie" they might have to follow conventional and unconventional traces through the landscape between Müller and Brecht. Brecht is introduced as Müller's "obsession" and the book is supposed to find out what drove Müller to and away from Brecht. In particular, Raddatz is interested in the twenty years of Müller's writing life marked by his abandonment of politically explicit plays such as *Der Lohndrücker* and *Zement*, the last of which was *Traktor* (1975). In the mid-seventies Müller began producing dense metaphorical texts for the theater, which represented a move away from Brecht. Müller explicitly publicized this rejection in texts such as "Verabschiedung des Lehrstücks."

According to Raddatz "Der Demetriusplan setzt da ein, wo Müller nach einer äußerst erfolgreichen Periode der Revision und Abkopplung, sich urplötzlich wieder in das Fahrwasser des Gründungsheros begibt, ohne dass die Motive, welche die Korrektur veranlassten, einsichtig werden" (Raddatz, 18). Examining the reasons for Müller's u-turn toward Brecht—from embrace of Brecht, to his mid-career rejection of his legacy and then to his re-embrace at the end of his career—is what Raddatz sets out to do. The result reads partly like a mystery novel, partly like a theoretical treatise. Whereas the book's concluding insight might seem unsurprising—it was Müller's writer's block at the end of his career that made him turn toward Brecht, which did not help because Brecht kept his throne—that story is interestingly and idiosyncratically told, and the theoretical insights into Brecht's epic theater and Nietzsche's concept of tragedy make the book as valuable as it is enjoyable.

In his introduction Raddatz discusses Rainer Nägele's groundbreaking essay on Brecht in which Nägele declares the conventionally assumed opposition of Brecht and Antonin Artaud to be misguided and instead presents his findings of the theater of cruelty in Brecht's work. Raddatz returns to Nietzsche to take issue with that approach, formulating a position that guides his reading of the Brecht – Müller constellation: "Apollo und Dionysos—die bipolare Welt des Tragöden: alles eins? Ist es nicht weiser, das heißt tragödiennäher die Unvereinbarkeit zu akzeptieren, wenn nicht zu feiern?" (10). Raddatz is committed to keep the bi-polar structure that sees Brecht as the proponent of a theater of distance and recognition in opposition to Müller as the proponent of *Rauschästhetik*.

According to Raddatz, Nietzsche's *Birth of Tragedy* provides a "Negativfolie" to epic theater (49). Nietzsche saw in Wagner's *Gesamtkunstwerk* the resurrection of Dionysian tragedy and Raddatz builds his definition of Brecht's epic theater in strict opposition if not to Nietzsche, then to Wagner. Even where Brecht the philosopher is engaged with Nietzsche, Brecht the playwright from 1930 on fought passionately against Wagner and the revival of Dionysian tragedy. The ingredients of epic theater such as disruption, separation between actor and character, and signification culminate in a theater of distance that places the audience in a relaxed state of critical awareness. Raddatz concludes that Brecht's theater is one of "Heiterkeit," designed to promote a theater of *Lebenskunst* that should enable the audience to master reality. Interesting here is the parallel that Raddatz draws between Brecht and Freud concluding that both are engaged in a "Erziehung zur Realität" that has a concrete political goal, that of limited human happiness (27). These unconventional insights are the result of Raddatz's straightforward and detailed reading of Brecht's theories.

The rift between Müller and Brecht unfolds along the Dionysian aspects of tragedy. Brecht's maxim of critical disposition in theater aesthetics as well as in politics and history, "halte der Tragödie, die ein Menschenbild der Geworfenheit zeichnet, wo Schicksalsmächte dominieren und der Tod durch heroisches Pathos golorifiziert wird, eine auf Wissenschaft fundierte Welt der Heiterkeit entgegen" (92). Whereas Brecht considers Theater the art form to foster "Lebenskunst," Müller seeks a theater against the denial of death (93). This opposition becomes most pointed in the theatrical treatment of German fascism particularly with regard to Auschwitz. Critics have often decried Brecht's blind spot with regard to Auschwitz, saying that he reduced the complexities of the Holocaust to a political phenomenon with roots in fascism as an extreme form of capitalism. Raddatz rightly observes: "Für die verstörenden Aspekte der Geschichte bietet Brecht's Ästhetik keine Form"(73). The disturbing aspects of history are exactly what Müller seeks to present in his model of tragedy. "Müller's originäre Leistung besteht darin, seinen Entwurf des Tragischen sowohl in einem dionysisch inspirierten Denkens wie im apokalyptischen Szenario Benjamins zu verwurzeln." Here Raddatz carefully examines Müller's works on fascism, predominantly *Die Schlacht*, but he also rightly notes Müller refusal to treat the topic directly when he says: "Ich kann kein Stück über Auschwitz schreiben. Wo der Schrecken versteint, hört das Spiel auf"(102). As horror turns to stone, tragedy looses one of its formative forces. In regard to Auschwitz, Müller insists on what Adorno calls "Bilderverbot," the claim that the horror of the event defies representation.

Instead of representing Auschwitz as event Müller sets out to examine fascist subjectivity as one form of historical occurrence inside of what Raddatz calls the "Spannungsfeld des Subjekts" (112), producing scenes that alternate between tragedy and clown shows such as in *Die Schlacht*. Müller rejects historical representation in favor of a micro-structure of subjectivity that is understood as a field of history. Raddatz observes: "Am Grund des Unbewussten haust die Unersättlichkeit der Gewalt, die ebenso im Faschismus an die Oberfläche tritt, wie sie zugleich Müllers literarische Produktivität antreibt" (76). While one should disagree with this parallel, it can be said the "Unersättlichkeit der Gewalt" is what Nietzsche's Dionysus celebrates and what Müller's texts seek to capture in subjectivity and history.

The exploration of subjectivity coincides with Müller's abandonment of Brechtian poetics, because Müller sought to reach what cannot be represented: "Die ganze Anstrengung des Schreibens ist, die Qualität die eigenen Träume zu erreichen, auch die Unabhängigkeit von Interpretation"(125). Reaching one's dreams has never been a concern of Brechtian theater, which seeks to examine human action as social acts. Müller on the other hand moves from play to text, from writing as exploration to writing as revelation. Works such as *Leben Grundlings* present what Raddatz calls "Theater als Störfall." The literary figure of disturbance is the metaphor which Raddatz defines with Hans-Christoph Blumenberg "Störung des Zusammenhangs, der Homogenität…as Die Metapher blockiert die Flüssigkeit der Rezeption des Textes" (155). While frustrating provides freedom from interpretation as Müller intended, it also hinders theatrical representation and opens up new approaches to performance.

Müller's desire to reach his own dreams through highly metaphorical texts creates his need for new imagery. Raddatz concludes: "Die Entnabelung von Brecht führt zur Allianz mit dem Surrealismus" (125). To assign causality here might be premature, yet it does enable Raddatz to place Müller in an interesting relation to the American director Robert Wilson whose performance productions often ignore the semantic quality of the text and whose structuring of space often takes the place of the plot. It was on Wilson's stage that Müller's metaphorical texts such as *Hamletmaschine* could unfold.

While these works, as Raddatz readily admits, are of astonishing quality, they were all produced in a single short period of Müller's life. During that period Müller developed a new notion of art, one that withdrew from what Raddatz calls "hermeneutisch eindeutigen Zugriffen" (125). Müller's theatrical work culminates in speechlessness, while the author himself engaged in numerous interviews announcing future plays that never materialized. Raddatz juxtaposes both authors against each other, granting Brecht's concept of epic theater as "eine umfassenden Wandel antreibende Kraft" (224) with a specific Brechtian form of critique that includes both art and science. Whereas Brecht's approach guaranteed lasting productivity, Müller experienced a "Nachlassen des Schreibdrangs" (227). His writer's block was intensified by the fall of the wall, which removed the immediate source of the collective trauma he had been exploring—the failure of the GDR to emerge as a humane socialist system.

It is then during German unification that Müller repositions himself relative to Brecht. Raddatz concludes: "Die Grundfigur des Demetriusplans besteht darin, die Grenzlinien der Tragödie in die antiaristotelischen Zentren des epischen Theaters zu verschieben" (222). It is within this discourse on tragedy that Raddatz locates the difference between Müller and Brecht: "Das Axiom der Distanz, Voraussetzung von Brecht's gesamtem Theaterbau, meint eben nicht den Schrecken, der vom Dargestellten ausgeht, sondern einen Schrecken, der über das Dargestellte einsetzt, weil die szenische Apparatur bereits Distanz geschaffen hat" (213). For Raddatz this difference not only determines the content and representations of each playwright's theatrical work, but also determined their lives. Brecht with his theater of critical distance kept accumulating resources from social reality, whereas Müller's theater of disturbance suffered what Raddatz calls a "Resourcenschwund." Brecht's concept of distance has proven to be the more successful strategy for a canonical author. Brecht remained a productive author until the end of his life—Müller did not. What's more, the historical reality of political movement and change, which showed that the GDR was not frozen in the political status quo, led Müller's approach to history into a dead end. The "tragic" outcome of the Demetriusplan, as Raddatz sees it, is the amazing success of *Der aufhaltsame Aufstieg des Arturo Ui* at the Berliner Ensemble under the direction of Heiner Müller, a success that reaffirmed Brecht's superior position in twentieth century German theater. While Brecht's overall productivity is beyond doubt, this particular performance of *Arturo Ui* owes much to Müller as its director. Martin Wuttke's acrobatic presentation of Hitler from dog to human swastika revealed history less as subjectivity than as flesh, producing a new take on the theater of cruelty.

Astrid Oesmann
The University of Iowa, Iowa City

Jost Hermand. *Die Toten schweigen nicht.* Frankfurt am Main: Peter Lang, 2010. 195 pages.

In his brief introductory remarks to this intriguing collection of Brecht essays, Jost Hermand notes that Brecht never lost, "die konkrete gesellschaftliche Situation aus dem Auge"(7). Fittingly, Hermand's thirteen essays accomplish the same feat. While he certainly offers insightful analysis of Brecht's literary works and personal writings, the true value of the collection lies in Hermand's ability to place Brecht's works in both cultural and historical contexts. Those looking for close literary analysis of Brecht's texts may find themselves disappointed, as Hermand instead elects to investigate the circumstances surrounding the creation of many influential and some less-influential Brecht works. This emphasis on Brecht as writer, teacher, and political activist provides the reader with an understanding of the man himself, his reasoning, and his motivation.

While the essays focus on Brecht as a person, they are by no means purely biographical. It is in the context of Brecht's life and experiences that Hermand integrates his literary analysis. Brecht, perhaps more than most other authors, used his surroundings and the then-current political/cultural environment to inspire his works. The true value of the collection is Hermand's overarching theme, namely that Brecht's works, to a profound extent, reflected Brecht's own life experiences, and resulted from his direct encounters with capitalism and socialism as well as with democracy and Hitler's national socialism. This knowledge, not only of the background for the inception of Brecht's works, but of Brecht's thoughts and feelings as well, allows for a fuller understanding of Brecht as a person, and as a literary artist.

Hermand goes to extensive lengths to portray Brecht as a teacher whose ideas remain valid today. Indeed, Brecht himself wanted to be, "ein Lehrer, ein Wissender, wenn nicht gar ein 'Weiser'"(9). The collection chronicles Brecht's struggles to rouse the masses through his prose, poetry and works for the stage. With time, Brecht came to understand that catchy songs and lyrics were simply incapable of spurring a revolution in and of themselves, and he designed not only dialogue and lyrics to open the mind, but the music of his plays as well. Brecht designed all of these elements to come together to inspire the audience towards social change through "Spaß an der Veränderung"(104). Hermand effectively describes Brecht's general rejection of genre borders, in favor of involving every viewer and reader in the discussion of the work. And while Brecht occasionally included the genre-identifying label "Lehrstück" to his titles, Hermand notes that Brecht could have applied the same term to every one of his works after 1930 (100).

Yet, while Hermand occasionally overdoes his praise of Brecht, he explicitly recognizes what Brecht was not: a politician or a martyr. Brecht's involvement in politics stretched only as far as the edge of the stage, or the final sentence of a poem. By refraining from official membership in any political party, Brecht may have attained greater autonomy to shake the masses in his own way through the use of "Vernunft" in both text and music. While Brecht's ideal tombstone would have read, "Er hat Vorschläge gemacht. Wir haben sie angenommen," he wanted to contribute by opening the minds of the proletariat through his writings and plays, not through expressing his opinion in a local party meeting (94). Additionally, Hermand's collection includes an entire essay on Brecht's phobia of martyrdom; the phrase "lieber nützlich leben als heroisch sterben," is peppered throughout the volume (22). Hermand's account of Brecht's time in exile illustrates Brecht's idea of weathering the storm in order to rekindle the fire afterwards. Much of Brecht's life typified the notion of working "für die kommenden, besseren Zeiten." Indeed, after the fall of the Third Reich, Brecht returned to Germany in the hopes of establishing influence in the theater and with the East German government. Hermand's analysis suggests that Brecht's own "Vernunft" dictated his actions in fleeing Germany and eventually Europe, but that his survival and desire to stoke the fire of revolution from abroad was revolutionary in and of itself.

Hermand also elaborates extensively on the dichotomies of Brecht's life, in particular his relationship to the proletariat. Despite Brecht's sympathies for the working classes, he generally found himself frustrated by their unwillingness to organize and bring about a revolution. Hermand chronicles Brecht's struggle to effectively communicate with the working classes by mixing the proper amount of teaching/encouragment with entertainment. One such example came in the general misunderstanding of *Aufstieg und Fall der Stadt Mahagonny*. As Hermand notes, "(Die Zuschauer) fragten sich meist umsonst: Handelte es sich...um die Utopie einer Paradiesstadt, wo man sich jeden Wunsch erfüllen kann, oder um die Dystopie einer untergehenden Welt, die von vornherein so verrottet ist, daß es aus ihr keinen Ausweg mehr gibt"(46)? Obviously the potential messages of these two readings are starkly different. While Brecht later integrated placards on stage, as well as music specifically composed to bring the audience into the discussion, he struggled to share his greater political vision with the working classes. Indeed, Brecht occasionally mused that the proletariat's more unseemly qualities (he uses the words "Phlegma" and "Freßlust") might end up being the ones that could eventually fuel Hitler's ouster (78). Brecht's troubled relationship with the masses as well as his faith in their ability to rise up runs from one essay to another, regardless of topic. Hermand also captures Brecht's dichotomous political views, which influenced his future more than perhaps any other element of his life, and he portrays Brecht as a "bürgerlicher Sympathisant des Sozialismus" who remained unswayed by the "verblendeter Mitläufer" of Stalinist doctrine (12). This stance often left Brecht a political vagrant who never fell sufficiently in step with any political party to become an official member.

The volume's most insightful essay, "Brecht in Hollywood," skillfully articulates Brecht's struggles in Los Angeles during his exile. Hermand's description of Brecht captures the image of a man both comically and tragically displaced—the ultimate outsider. Indeed it is hard to imagine a less harmonious match of person and city than Brecht and Los Angeles. Brecht not only abhorred the city's "quick buck" mentality (he admitted seeing tiny price tags attached to everything in his mind's eye) but also the superficial and transitory nature of Americans in general (108). Los Angeles had neither a reading/working class that could be swept up into socialist fervor, nor did it have the cultural forums in which Brecht traditionally felt welcome, such as a theater in which he could produce his works. As Hermand notes, Brecht portrayed Hollywood in *Liefere die Ware* as "eine Hölle, die sich als Himmel ausgibt, das heißt als einen Ort der Korruption, in dem keinerlei soziales Verantwortungsgefühl herrscht"(117). At the same time, Brecht somehow had to earn money in this otherworldly place, and Hermand details the struggles of Brecht in composing what he considered meaningful work that still had enough popular appeal to bring in an income. Here Hermand's praise of Brecht briefly borders on glorification. He describes Brecht's general lack of assimilation (which ran counter to what many of his contemporary fellow Germans participated in during their exile) in terms of turning into a

Schnellamerikaner: "Brecht war einfach zu widersetzlich und begabt"(115). There is no questioning Brecht's social contrariness in America, but this stubbornness probably had more to do with Brecht retaining his ideals.

If there is a recurring weakness in the collection it comes in the brief moments when Hermand strays from solid analysis, or from historical discourse, and moves to political commentary. For nearly the entire collection, Hermand acts as a trusted guide into Brecht's mind and intentions, yet at points he conflates his own political preferences with the explication of Brecht's ideas. It is unclear if Hermand's reference to the bombings of Hiroshima and Nagasaki as "sinnlos" is the opinion of himself, Brecht or of possibly both men. Either way, the term "sinnlos" conveys a personal opinion that needs extra clarification. Brecht did not associate war with socialist societies, but rather with "Lebensweise und mitunter Sterbensweise der kapitalistischen Länder"(141). In this context it seems that Hermand's credibility takes a small hit at the sake of expressing his opinion. In a collection that does not feature much in the way of Hermand's own opinions, the few passages where he inserts them are stark.

Additionally, Hermand tends to assume more previous knowledge from his readers than may be warranted. Hermand notes in the introduction that while Brecht conferences and speeches are good for scholarship, such meetings and exchanges of ideas need to be held outside of academic settings as well, so that people and groups not already heavily laden with theory can engage in the discussion. In short, Hermand seeks to include people who know little of Brecht in the discussion of his works and ideas. Clearly, one of the main goals of these essays is to begin a dialogue about Brecht's ideas with people now unfamiliar with the playwright. The collection will certainly interest scholars and Brecht-enthusiasts, but its dense language and content are less likely to engage a wider non-academic audience.

Regardless of the level of a given reader's Brecht-fluency, Hermand effectively maintains a positive, occasionally humorous tone. This is particularly important when writing about an author who, while generally respected amongst his peers, was nearly universally seen as being difficult to work with. Hermand manages to allow the reader to peer into Brecht's often-frustrated mind, briefly engage in his thought processes, and yet emerge without feeling discouraged. In this, Hermand's writing mimics Brecht's. Just as Brecht abhorred the idea of mankind's tragic "Grundsituation" (and instead focused on enlightening the minds of his audience), so too does Hermand favor insightful discussion over an obsession with the more tragic and depressing elements of Brecht's life (99).

Brecht did not view the world in terms of good and bad as much as he did in terms of "'nützlich' oder 'unnützlich'"(93). Similarly, Hermand's collection of Brecht essays is not just good in terms of quality, but serves to be useful through informing and inspiring his readers. The essays contained in the volume not only examine Brecht's writing, the reception of his work, and his ideology, but also the nature of his relationships with other artists. As with his work, it is clear that Brecht viewed these relationships in terms of usefulness. That is not to say that Brecht simply used those around him to satisfy his own wishes, but that he constantly pushed his working partners to greater heights, and to the limits of their own particular skill sets (39). Brecht did this in an effort to awaken the masses and create societal change. This insight provides the reader with a deeper appreciation of Brecht as a writer and teacher, as well as providing a vision of his social goals. Brecht joined the argument for the use of unconventional methods of knowledge-sharing to counter unconventional weapons (142). This legacy remains relevant for modern society and Hermand's volume fully articulates Brecht's efforts to educate and broaden the mind. This is a highly insightful volume and an excellent reference for scholars as well as those wishing to learn more about Brecht's life and works.

Carl R. Follmer
The University of Iowa, Iowa City

Hanns Eisler. *Briefe 1907–1943*. Herausgegeben von Jürgen Schebera und Maren Köster. *Schriften*. Band 4.1. Herausgegeben von der Internationalen Hanns Eisler Gesellschaft. Wiesbaden, Leipzig, Paris: Breitkopf & Härtel, 2010. 532 Seiten.

Fünfzig Jahre nach Eislers Tod im Jahr 1962 erscheint nun endlich – nach der höchst verdienstvollen von Manfred Grabs edierten *Werkausgabe* und der von Günter Meyer reichlich kommentierten Ausgabe der *Schriften* – eine historisch-kritische *Gesamtausgabe* aller von Eisler komponierten Werke sowie sämtlicher von ihm publizierten Essays sowie unpublizierten Gespräche, Interviews, Notizen, Dichtungen und Briefe, die in neun Serien herauskommen sollen. Das klingt auf Anhieb exorbitant, ist aber bei einem so bedeutsamen Komponisten und Essayisten wie Eisler mehr als gerechtfertigt. Die Briefe werden in dieser Gesamtausgabe vier Bände umfassen, von denen der erste – hier zur Besprechung anstehende – die Jahre 1907 bis 1943 umfaßt. Herausgegeben wurde er von Jürgen Schebera, der allen Eisler-Freunden schon durch sein Buch *Hanns Eisler im USA-Exil* (Berlin: Akademie-Verlag, 1978), seine Eisler-Biographie (Mainz: Schott-Verlag, 1998) sowie viele, stets Neuland erschließende Aufsätze zu diesem Komponisten wohlvertraut ist, sowie von Maren Köster, die in den letzten

15 Jahren mehrere Publikationen zu Eisler, darunter zum *Faustus*, zum *Höllenangst*-Projekt und zu Remigrationsproblemen, herausgebracht hat.

Aus Eislers frühen Jahren haben sich – außer einigen Briefen an engste Jugendfreunde wie Heinrich Burkard und Rudolf Kolisch – fast nur Briefe an seinen "hochverehrten Meister" Arnold Schönberg sowie dessen Schüler Alban Berg erhalten. Daher erfahren wir zwar aus ihnen einiges über Eislers frühe "modernistische" Kompositionsversuche und dann sein sich gegen Mitte der zwanziger Jahre allmählich abkühlendes Verhältnis zu den höchst elitären Kompositionsweisen der sogenannten Zweiten Wiener Schule (welch ein Euphemismus!), aber kaum etwas über Eislers politische Aktivitäten im Dienst der kommunistischen Arbeiterbewegung in Berlin. Erst ab 1930 tauchen auch Briefe an den Deutschen Arbeiter-Sängerbund und die sowjetische Filmgesellschaft Mežrabpom auf, in denen sich Eislers Anteilnahme an den damaligen sozialistischen Kulturbestrebungen zu erkennen gibt.

An Brecht hat sich aus dieser Zeit, in der beide zusammen in Berlin an der *Maßnahme*, der *Mutter* und *Kuhle Wampe* arbeiteten, nur eine nichtssagende Postkarte erhalten. Erst ab 1933, als sich Eisler und Brecht plötzlich an verschiedenen Exilorten befanden, wird der Briefwechsel zwischen ihnen plötzlich rege. Inhaltlich handelt es sich dabei zumeist um kurzgefaßte Mitteilungen, in denen es vor allem um die von ihnen gemeinsam in Paris veranstaltete Ausgabe der *Gedichte Lieder Chöre* und die Zusammenarbeit an den *Rundköpfen und Spitzköpfen* geht, die allerdings für Brecht-Kenner kaum Neues bieten. Ab 1935, dem Jahr ihres gemeinsamen New York-Besuchs, bei dem sie Einfluß auf eine Aufführung von Brechts *Mutter* zu nehmen versuchten, stellt sich zwischen beiden erstmals das kameradschaftliche "Du" ein. Wichtig sind in diesem Zusammenhang Eislers Bemerkungen über die äußerst brutale Form, in der sich in diesem Land – ohne den in Europa üblichen "Überbau" – der Kampf zwischen den Reichen und den Armen abspiele. Um an diesen Kämpfen teilnehmen zu können, wünscht sich Eisler in seinen Briefen an Brecht immer wieder neue diesbezügliche Liedtexte und läßt dabei nebenher seine Wut über George Grosz aus, der in New York zu einem "abscheulichen Spießbürger" geworden sei. Um so mehr wünscht sich Eisler endlich wieder "bei Dir zu sitzen und zu arbeiten". Daß Brecht ihm so selten auf seine dringlichen Bitten antwortete, schmerzte Eisler offenbar sehr. Mehrfach heißt es in diesem Zusammenhang: "Leider hast Du mir auf meinen letzten Brief nicht geantwortet und auch nichts geschickt."

Nach 1938 überwiegen dann Briefe, in denen sich Eisler vor allem um Aufenthaltsgenehmigungen und Anstellungschancen in den USA bemühte. Vor allem die Briefe an die häufig von ihm getrennte "Lou" legen ein beredtes Zeugnis dafür ab, wie mühsam die meisten dieser

Bemühungen waren. Selbst als Eisler von April bis Anfang August 1942 in Hollywood, wo andere Exilanten zum Teil recht erfolgreich waren, irgendwelche Filmmusikaufträge zu ergattern suchte, "flutschte" es nicht. Erst als er von Fritz Lang das Angebot erhielt, die Musik zu dem Film *Hangmen Also Die* zu komponieren, atmete er wieder auf. Doch ein geregeltes Einkommen – nach langen Jahren der finanziellen Unsicherheit – bot ihm erst das Stipendium der Rockefeller Foundation, mit Theodor W. Adorno ein Buch über Filmkompositionen zu schreiben. An Brecht finden sich nach 1941 keine Briefe mehr, da sie nach langen Jahren der Trennung endlich wieder in Hollywood zusammentrafen. Daher erfahren wir aus den Briefen dieser Zeit weder etwas über ihre Zusammenarbeit an den *Hollywood Elegien* noch über Brechts Reaktion auf Eislers Komposition *Vierzehn Arten, den Regen zu beschreiben*, mit der Brecht offenbar überhaupt nichts anfangen konnte. Interessant aus diesem Zeitabschnitt sind nur die höchstpersönlich gehaltenen Briefe an den Dramatiker Clifford Odets sowie an Eduard Steuermann und Rudolf Kolisch, Eislers alte Freunde aus der frühen Wiener Zeit, die wie Schönberg und er ebenfalls in Los Angeles Zuflucht gesucht hatten. Anschließend folgt auf den Seiten 275 bis 513 (!) ein überaus sorgfältiger Kommentar zu jedem Brief, der nicht nur die gewohnten positivistischen Belege bietet, sondern auch höchst aufschlußreiche persönliche, politische und kulturgeschichtliche Hintergrundserläuterungen liefert.

Seien wir ehrlich: alles in allem ist dieser Briefband weder musiktheoretisch noch politisch besonders aufregend. Dafür sind die meisten Briefe – trotz mancher witzigen Pointen, die für Eisler allgemein bezeichnend sind – viel zu kurz und karg. Wie fast alle Briefe Brechts sind auch die Briefe Eislers keine Zeugnisse eines großen Briefschreibers. Dennoch sind sie wichtige Dokumente aus dem Leben eines sich erst mühsam durchschlagenden jungen Komponisten und dann nach 1933 für einen von Land zu Land gehetzten Exilanten ("Öfters die Länder als die Schuhe wechselnd"), in denen sowohl das politische Engagement eines auf bürgerliche Erfolge weitgehend verzichtenden jungen Komponisten als auch die gleiche nicht nachlassende Widerborstigkeit im Exil zum Ausdruck kommen. Ich weiß, es gibt bedeutendere Briefausgaben aus diesen Jahren. Aber da es sich um Eisler, den "großen Eisler," einen der wenigen sozial engagierten deutschen Komponisten dieser Jahre handelt, ist schließlich doch *alles* wichtig, was wir selbst in diesen Briefen über ihn, seine Biographie, seine vielfältigen Bemühungen um die Durchsetzung nichtelitärer Musikkonzepte und sein nicht nachlassendes Eintreten für die von Brecht stets betonte "dritte Sache" erfahren können. Wir dürfen daher gespannt auf die nächsten drei Bände sein.

Jost Hermand
University of Wisconsin, Madison

Bertolt Brecht, *Notizbücher 24 und 25 (1927-1930)*. Notizbuch-Ausgabe Bd. 7. Herausgegeben von Martin Kölbel und Peter Villwock. Berlin: Suhrkamp Verlag, 2010. 539 Seiten.

Among the heterogeneous material housed in the Bertolt Brecht Archive of the Akademie der Künste in Berlin there are 54 notebooks of varying formats and number of leaves and 2 address books that Brecht filled with jottings between 1918 and 1956. Like his other unauthorized but carefully preserved writings – the diaries (*Tagebücher*, covering the years 1913 to 1922), the work journals (*Arbeitsjournale*, covering the years 1919 to 1955), and the selected letters that are available in the thirty volumes of the *Werke* edition (specifically in vols. 26-30), these notebooks were never intended for a reading public, even though about one-third of the jottings was selectively smuggled into or referenced in this edition. The *Notizbücher* consist of thin sketchbooks or writing pads that fit in coat or jacket pockets and that Brecht kept at hand while sitting in a train or at a café to jot down fragmentary thoughts, quotes, lines of text for current projects, telephone numbers, reading notes, doctors' advice, etc. Taken as whole, they document the development and continuities of his thematic interests, revealing the balance or tension between order and chaos that characterized his work process. The volume under review is the first to appear in what is projected as a fourteen volume, complete edition of the *Notizbücher*. What do they contain and what use are they to those interested in Brecht? (Reviewer's disclaimer: I wrote two letters of support to granting agencies for the initial funding of this edition and interviewed the editors at its presentation in the Brecht-Haus in Berlin on December 2, 2010.)

The idea for the edition goes back to a proposal by Peter Villwock and Erdmut Wizisla (director of the Brecht Archive) in 2005. Funded by the Deutsche Literaturfonds in Darmstadt, the complete set of original notebooks, which were decaying in the Archive (fading ink and pencil lead, disintegrating bindings, and damage from adhesive tape, glue, and metal paper clips used to file the fragile leaves), were professionally restored and digitized – in itself an important undertaking for Brecht scholarship; in addition, the two notebooks in this volume 7, covering the three critical years of 1927 to 1930 in Brecht's development as a writer and thinker, were transcribed and edited by Villwock as a model for the entire planned edition. Completed and scheduled for publication by Suhrkamp in spring 2008, it was delayed until late 2010, when the Otto Wolff-Stiftung (Cologne) guaranteed funding for ongoing editing of the next volumes.

Villwock and Kölbel are experienced editors, having both worked on projects of the Institut für Textkritik in Heidelberg (www.textkritik.de). For readers familiar with the editions published by Stroemfeld Verlag in cooperation with the Heidelberg Institut (e.g., Hölderlin, Kafka, Keller,

Kleist, Trakl, Robert Walser), the volume under review has a familiar layout and design. Three-quarters of the bulky volume consists of black-and-white facsimiles and facing-page transcriptions of the two notebooks with brief marginal notes and footnotes for clarifications and cross-referencing, while one-quarter comprises the apparatus that includes a detailed description of the respective notebook (contents, physical makeup, binding, missing pages), page-by-page commentaries that not only offer explanations and possible interpretations of individual notes but also seek to situate them within the larger context of Brecht's productivity, a timetable of the years covered by the respective notebooks, a bibliography of cited works, and four separate indices covering titles of Brecht's works, institutions, and names, practically providing a concordance to the entire volume. While the amount of layered information, the numerous abbreviations and distinctive typefaces, and the need to page between the facsimiles and the back material create at first a cumbersome and disorientating obstacle to the reader, with practice the entire system begins to make sense and actually becomes quite efficient. Users beware: there is a steep learning curve! In fact, this is not intended as a user-friendly edition that smoothes the way to easy comprehension of a stable text; it is rather a "basis" edition, as Villwock has elaborated at great length in a "Prolegomena" to the project (*editio* 23/2009: 71-108), committed to the principles of reproduction, description, transcription, and commentary so that future scholars have a point of departure for their scholarship on Brecht.

The notebooks contain neither texts in a conventional sense nor works-in-progress but rather casual and even idiosyncratic thoughts and reminders, raw material that supplements and also leaves room for speculation. Moreover, unlike 90 percent of Brecht's other writings that were produced on a typewriter or by dictation, these are handwritten in his more or sometimes less legible script. While both Elisabeth Hauptmann and Hertha Ramtun transcribed these notes after Brecht's death, the editors are verifying their originals and correcting mistakes or highlighting ambiguities where their predecessors made calls that are not obvious or correct. Finally, Brecht (mis)used his notebooks, tearing out pages and placing leaves in other files so that almost none of the 54 notebooks are complete, just as several other notebooks are apparently missing; here the editors rely on the forensic tools of detectives in examining paper quality and calligraphy to identify placement and sequencing of orphan pages strewn through other Archive files (these will be collected and reproduced in the final volume 14 of the edition).

So what do we gain from reading Brecht's jotted notes? In a general sense they reveal – like the *Modellbücher*, the *Versuche* series, and the *Arbeitsjournale* – the experimental character of this writer's workshop, and with careful attention they may actually help document the process of how texts evolved, how words, sentences, and entire projects preoccupied him or were rejected. In this volume, for example, we find notes on Brecht's automobile (his Steyr) that gradually meld into a never realized plan for a collaborative comedy with Kurt Weill (working title: "Der Moabiter Pferdehandel"). We also find jottings and a chorus for a Rosa Luxemburg play ("Die letzten Wochen der Rosa Luxemburg"). The notebooks functioned for Brecht like a storehouse or a portable memory bank; for us they have the potential of becoming a quarry, especially for those interested in biographical aspects of Brecht's creativity and in the genealogy of his texts and ideas. *Notizbuch* 24 includes variants and ideas for *Fatzer*, *Die Dreigroschenoper*, and *Lehrstücke*; *Notizbuch* 25 has (unpublished) Keuner anecdotes, entries on *Mahagonny*, concept pieces on "Haltung" and "Gestus," thoughts on Marxism, and reflections about a new journal ("Krise und Kritik") that never came to fruition. It is unlikely that the material in the two notebooks of volume 7 or any of the other projected volumes will change our image of Brecht, but they will certainly help answer some hypotheses and correct some questionable identifications in the *Werke* edition. In the 103-page "Einführung in die Edition (NBA)," available separately at the Suhrkamp website installed for the edition of the *Notizbücher*, the editors summarize 42 different numbered examples of what one might learn from the *Notizbücher* 24 and 25 (pp. 47-70) – from relatively major corrections to poetic texts such as "Das Zehnte Sonett" or verses in *Fatzer* to minor quibbles about Ramthun's deciphering of illegible handwriting.

I note finally that the physical design of the printed volumes is handsome: a large-size format on good quality paper; and the paper binding helps keep the price manageable (€ 24,90) both for individual and library purchase. In addition, Suhrkamp is offering through partner e-book distributors a downloadable version of each volume, priced similarly to the print edition. A definite advantage of the electronic version is the inclusion of color facsimiles of the original *Notizbuch* leaves. I could imagine the entire 14-volume edition as a DVD publication when it is completed. As mentioned, Suhrkamp Verlag has established a supplementary website for the NBA or *Notizbuch-Ausgabe* at: http://www.suhrkamp.de/bertolt_brecht_notizbuecher_einfuehrung_559.html. As of this writing (May 2011) the left-hand menu of options includes the 51-page introduction to the entire project (also in the print edition), the complete appendices for the *Notizbücher* 24 and 25 (as published in the print edition), a "forum" with notes and additions to the printed volume(s) as the editors continue to make discoveries in the Archive, a cumulative index of the volumes as they are published, and two sections with scans of related original documents from the Brecht Archive. The electronic supplement is a first for Suhrkamp Verlag, as it gradually moves into the digital age; currently access is free, not based on a subscription, and will become an important supplement to the printed version as material is added. Both in print and online the *Notizbuch-Ausgabe* is an important contribution to Brecht scholarship and a model for future editing practices of the Archive's manuscripts.

>   Marc Silberman
>   University of Wisconsin, Madison

J. Chris Westgate, ed. *Brecht, Broadway and United States Theatre.* Newcastle, UK: Cambridge Scholars Publishing, 2007. xxix + 196 pages.

This inconsistently edited and uneven collection of nine essays ostensibly on Brecht on Broadway and the American stage more generally (if you believe the book's title) was stimulated by a belief that U.S. producers (and especially critics) of Brechtian plays since *The Mother* in 1935 (presented in New York by The Theatre Union) have failed to understand the playwright's concepts (starting with epic theater) and have thus offered distorted presentations of those few plays actually given a professional production in the U.S. The book's title is misleading, since there is little on Brecht as produced throughout the country; rather, the focus, what there is of it, is on Broadway and, to a lesser extent, other venues in New York. In fact, one of the most successful (critical and popular) of Brechtian productions was the 1955 staging of *The Threepenny Opera* Off-Broadway at the Theatre de Lys, now the Lucille Lortel, yet this volume, due to its imprecision, would lead you to believe that it was produced on Broadway!

One of the problems with a study that intends to confront the inability – or the purposeful incongruities – of professional productions to come to terms with Brecht's theater theories (which, as the editor acknowledges, changed over time) as applied to actual staging is that the history of professional Brecht production on Broadway (and throughout New York City for that matter) is a scant one, with a small body of insightful criticism for these productions. The result in too many of these essays is, therefore, too much generalization, hyperbole, and bias (the editor and several authors display a pronounced anti-Broadway attitude). I for one would have welcomed a collection that actually did examine Brechtian production throughout the U.S., including the large number of academic and professional regional examples that might have provided some useful conclusions and insights regarding how Brecht has been treated in a commercial or academic setting outside of New York.

So what *does* this collection offer? It is divided into three parts, following a lengthy introductory essay by the editor ("A Dialectical History"): "The History of Brecht on Broadway," "Brecht on Broadway Today" (there is another title in the text!), and "The Future of Brecht on Broadway" (there are two variants titles of this part as well). Westgate's introduction is often aggravating. The prose is awkward, the ideas confusing, and the progression of thought too often lacking in clarity. Moreover, it is rife with careless errors: Circle in the Square is cited as Circle on the Square; the House UnAmerican Activities Committee is called a Commission; it describes the 1955 *Threepenny* as a Broadway run (inexplicably the editor states that Brecht would "have perhaps disowned this production," certainly not my sense of this fine production, which I saw in 1957); the same subheading is, confusingly, used twice; references to The Theatre Union consistently omit "The," although the article is part of its proper name. Other peeves are too numerous to mention, although I do confess that the editor's discussion of Brechtian criticism has some merit. The objective of the collection as stated in the introduction is "to consider the many encounters between Brecht and Broadway... in terms of dramaturgy, performance, and reception." It hardly accomplishes this, even given that there are only a dozen or so Broadway Brecht productions on record. It is quickly clear in this essay that Brecht – and by extension more serious playwrights – were doomed to be "inhibited" by the "superstructure of commercialized escapism." If this was true of the Broadway of the 1930s, it must be that today's Broadway provides an impossible environment for any serious effort (and especially one with Marxist notions)! Or so is the editor's implication.

Part I includes three essays. There is a useful review and analysis of that 1935 production of *The Mother* by Anne Fletcher, the author of a useful new study of the Brecht collaborator, designer Mordecai Gorelik (reviewed in the last volume of *The Brecht Yearbook*). Her effort gets Part I off to a strong start (my only quibble is citing *Mise en scene* [without an accent] as *mis en scene*, an editorial gaffe throughout the book). The second essay, by Arminda Apgar, strikes me as both naïve and overly judgmental of America's professional theater's objective ("sheer entertainment"). The purpose of her essay is to examine "Misconception & Misunderstanding: Brecht & American Theatre," according to its title. The author states that America "neither recognizes nor understands the intent of his [Brecht's] work, and is ideologically incapable of doing so due to the requirements of capitalist cultural logic." Really! For me, Apgar depends too much on inconsequential reviews (few real critics are cited) to reach her damning conclusions, and she focuses too much on the "commercialism" of American theater, which she believes prevents its audience from any true critical thought. Her essay is unnecessarily repetitive. The final essay in Part I – Ilka Saal's "Broadway & the Depoliticization of Epic Theatre: The Case of Erwin Piscator"– is one of the better contributions, though veering away from Brecht to a focus on Erwin Piscator. Regardless, the essay is critically astute, well informed, and provides an excellent explanation of two views of epic theater by looking at Piscator's directorial projects in

New York during the 1940s and 1950s (in particular *Case of Clyde Griffiths* in 1936). An exceptionally good bibliography completes her essay.

Part II (in the text called "In The Shadow of September 11th: Renewed Interest in Brecht on Broadway") also contains three essays, only one of which deals directly with a Brechtian text: Norman Roessler's "dialectical" casebook of the 2002 National Actors Theatre staging, with Al Pacino, of *The Resistible Rise of Arturo Ui*. In this poorly proofed essay (errors are too plentiful to enumerate here; they definitely serve as a detriment to the essay's credibility) the author, though noting the minute number of Brecht productions on Broadway, underscores that his usage of the word Broadway is "a synonym for commercial American Theater," yet this production of *Arturo Ui* was presented by a theater company that had ambitions of becoming America's national theater and, though leasing Broadway theaters (the Belasco and later the Lyceum), never thought of itself as a "commercial" operation. Roessler does admit this in his good analysis of the production; so why the statement on Broadway = commercial? The second essay in Part II (by Kathryn A. Edney) is a quite thorough analysis of the unique 2001 musical *Urinetown* as Brechtian. I found her arguments quite persuasive. The final essay by David Kornhaber reaches for an example of a Brechtian tradition in the solo work of actress Sarah Jones (*Bridge and Tunnel*, Off-Broadway, 2004; transferred to Broadway in 2006), who specializes in presenting multiple roles (in this case fourteen immigrant characters). Kornhaber sees "Brecht's idea of *gestus*. . . a key tool in Jones' arsenal." Perhaps so, though I could suggest an even closer model – but from the distant past – in the English actor/mimic Charles Mathews (1776-1835), who annually (from 1818 until late in his life) offered "Mr. Mathews at Home" with a protean presentation of multiple characters. I am honestly not sure why the *gestus* model was pursued here (the case is tenuous at best), yet I applaud the attention it brings to Jones, one of America's immensely and uniquely talented actors/authors.

The final section ("The Future of Brecht on Broadway" in the table of contents and "The Future of Brecht & Broadway" in the text) hardly does either. The first of two essays (by Dominic Symonds) actually pays more attention to Brecht in recent British theater and specifically to the production of *Jerry Springer: The Opera* (2003), which in the introduction is called *Jerry Springer: The Musical*! Granted, it is not really an opera but calling it one is part of its point, an ironic aspect of this unusual event that is explored in some detail by Symonds, along with other techniques within this hybrid. The essay is certainly entertaining (oops!) and poses a number of issues within the text that could be considered Brechtian. The final offering in Part III by William J. Burling is titled "Brecht's 'U-Effect:' Theorizing the Horizons of Revolutionary Theatre," and provides a good summary of Brecht's idea of epic theater as defined and illuminated by

Umfunktionierung (refunction, among its several translations), a complex and little-understood ("epecially by Americans") example of Brecht's many theoretical concepts. Like the first essay in this section, Burling's prime examples of the "U-Effect" are from non-American productions: Brecht's adaptation of *Coriolanus* (*Coriolan*), not staged until 1964, and *My Name is Rachel Corrie*, based on the diary and other writings of an American peace activist (killed in Gaza by an Israeli bulldozer) and first presented in London in 2005. A great controversy ensued over its scheduled U.S. premiere (set for October 2006). Alas, its New York staging occurred after this essay was written and thus Burling was unable to follow the history to its rather unsensational and anti-climactic conclusion. Regardless, Burling's essay is the most intellectually stimulating in this oddly conceived and presented collection.

Don B. Wilmeth, emeritus
Brown University

Lothar van Laak. *Medien und Medialität des Epischen in Literatur und Film des 20. Jahrhunderts. Bertolt Brecht – Uwe Johnson – Lars von Trier*. München: Fink, 2009. 376 Seiten

Lothar van Laaks Habilitationsschrift *Medien und Medialität des Epischen* nimmt sich Gewichtiges vor: Sie fragt nach der grundlegenden Qualität unseres Erzählens in und für die Medien. Das ist nun eine tatsächlich fundamentale Frage, auf die van Laak eine systematische Antwort aus nicht weniger als vier Perspektiven verspricht, nämlich der Erzählanthropologie, der Narratologie, der Gattungs- und der Medientheorie. Der kleinste gemeinsame Nenner dieser Perspektiven ist, in einem Wort: das Epische. Für dieses sind, wie in den ersten beiden Kapiteln ausgeführt wird, wiederum Medialität und Medien konstitutiv (vgl. etwa S. 14).

Schon hier wird das Problem offenbar, dass der komplexe und deutungsoffene Begriff des Epischen durch einen zweiten komplexen und viel diskutierten begründet wird, den des Mediums. Bei dessen Bestimmung gibt es in der aktuellen medienphilosophischen Debatte nur einen einzigen Konsens, dass, wie Stefan Münker es pointiert ausgedrückt hat, jenseits des Trivialen jeder Konsens aufhört und dessen Deutungsversuche so verschiedenartig sind, dass Lorenz Engell resümiert: "Wenn schlicht alles Medium wäre, dann wäre Medium nichts."[1] Damit nicht genug, zieht van Laak noch einen weiteren komplexen Begriff zur

---

1 Stefan Münker, "Was ist ein Medium?" in Münker and Alexander Roesler, Hrsg., *Was ist ein Medium?* (Frankfurt/Main: Suhrkamp, 2008), 247-61; and Lorenz Engell, "Wege, Kanäle, Übertragungen," in Engell et al., Hrsg., *Kursbuch Medienkultur. Die maßgeblichen Theorien von Brecht bis Baudrillard* (Stuttgart: DVA, 1999), 127.

Vermittlung heran: den der Leiblichkeit. Denn schon der Leib selbst wird als Medium vorgestellt, in dem sich "funktionale Vermitteltheit *und* konkrete historische Vermittlung" (53) verbinden. Das Beispiel für diesen Konnex gibt bei van Laak die Figur des Rhapsoden: die Gestalt des Sängers, die im Vortrag dem Publikum leibhaftig gegenübersteht.

Begründet wird das Epische zudem aus einer anthropologischen Ursituation, der Erfahrung des leiblichen In-der-Welt-Seins, wenn das Kind sich dem Erzählen der Eltern bewusst wird: "Denn, wenn dem Kind von seinen Eltern erzählt wird, vernimmt es nicht nur eine Geschichte. Es macht die konkret spürbare Erfahrung der Stimme, die sie ihm vermittelt, mit ihr der Medien, die das Erzählen gestalten, und es erfährt auch sich selbst als Teil einer, ihm erzählten Welt. So realisiert sich das Epische in seiner Medialität" (9). Solche Initialszenen sind als Theorie-Gründungsmodelle nicht ohne Vorbild (man denke an Lacans Spiegelstadium oder Kittlers Begründung des Aufschreibesystems von 1800), jedoch bleibt es dabei nicht. Das Epische wird darüber hinaus bestimmt als "Modus der Weltzugewandtheit," also: als eine besondere narrative Qualität, die die Welt sinnvoll einzurichten in der Lage ist, und als "zentrales und für die Moderne grundlegend zu reflektierendes Phänomen des Erzählens," in dem sich eine gelingende Erfahrung von Leiblichkeit in der Geschichtenhaftigkeit der Wahrnehmung von Welt äußert (17). Das Epische à la van Laak wird so zum Mittel, den Dualismus von Körper und Seele "zumindest deutlich zu relativieren" (ebd.).

Glaubt man nun, als Erklärung des Epischen eine entpolitisierte und anthropologisch überhöhte Funktion dessen ausgemacht zu haben, was Lukács als das Erzählen beschrieb: nämlich die Wiedergewinnung einer verlorenen Dimension ursprünglicher Körperlichkeit in einem sinnproduzierenden narrativen Verfahren, wird man enttäuscht, denn andererseits bringt das Epische nun auch "Subjektivität und Individualität als ein In-der-Welt-sein" (341) zum Ausdruck, also, *cum grano salis*, gerade das, was Lukács als das Beschreiben gedeutet hatte. Wenn dann noch die Arbeit am Mythos und die großen Erzählungen bemüht werden und über die einhundert Seiten des dritten Kapitels die—durchaus mit Gewinn zu lesenden—Begriffsgeschichten von Herder bis Hegel, Lukács bis Lugowski, Wagner bis Waldenfels, Emil Staiger, Wolfgang Kayser und Käte Hamburger, Balázs, Benjamin und Adorno ihr Sediment auf der Bestimmung des Epischen hinterlassen, scheint verständlich, was van Laak so vehement kritisiert: dass in den einschlägigeren Narrationstheorien "das Epische aus der Beschreibung und Erklärung des Erzählens ausgeschlossen" (80) bleibt, weil es eben kaum auf den Begriff zu bringen, mithin schwer anschlussfähig ist. Diese Problematik wird auch durch die Summenbildung des Autors nicht ausgeräumt, der die Qualität des Epischen "vorläufig zusammengefasst" so umreißt: "Das Epische realisiert sich als 'große Erzählung' bzw. genauer und—

wenn es seine 'Arbeit am Mythos' auch mitleistet—weniger mythisch verstanden: als ein an der Leiblichkeit ansetzender Erzählprozess und in seiner Gestalt als ein Erzählen offenen Anfangs, von großer oder langer Dauer, sich vervielfältigender Struktur mit Verweisungscharakter und tendenzieller Unabschliessbarkeit...Dieses Erzählen also eröffnet uns, wenn nicht Totalität an Sinn, so doch ein gedeutet-deutbares Panorama der Welt" (83).

Das dank zweier Exkurse längste vierte Kapitel des Buchs forscht den Gestaltungen des Epischen im 20. Jahrhundert nach und untersucht dabei die Positionen Brechts, Fritz Langs, Uwe Johnsons und Lars von Triers. Auch hier kommt das Epische nicht auf einen Begriff, sondern wird mit Blick auf ganz unterschiedliche Bereiche operationalisiert: bei Brecht material- und produktionsästhetisch, bei Lang werkästhetisch, bei Johnson mit Bezug auf die Rezeptionsproblematik und anhand "bestimmte[r] Synthesen der Medienreflexion" (186) bei von Trier. Die forschungsleitende Implikation der Analysen von Brecht und Lang ist dabei die Konstatierung eines Bewusstseinswandels, der der Entstehung der technischen Massenmedien Film und Rundfunk parallel geht. Für die Analyse der Entwicklung des Epischen werden als Anfangs- und Endpunkt *Mann ist Mann* und *Der kaukasische Kreidekreis* sowie der *Dreigroschen*-Komplex untersucht. Zusammengefasst beschreibt das Kapitel die Verdichtung des Epischen zu einem Gestus und zu einer spezifischen Wirklichkeitsorientierung der Bühne Brechts; damit würde es produktiv für seine Modernisierung des Theaters und die Neukonzeption des Dramas, das sich in den medialen Schüben des 20. Jahrhunderts neu ausrichten muss.

Fritz Lang wird demgegenüber im ersten Exkurs zugestanden, mit den Nibelungenfilmen dem Stummfilm selbst epische Qualität verliehen zu haben, dadurch nämlich, dass der Film selbst zu einem "neuen Rhapsoden" würde. Denn, und das folgende Zitat mag auch den Stil des Buchs belegen, der "Film, die Kamera und ihre Bilder lösen den Erzähler ab, heben ihn auf oder haben ihn eliminiert....Der Rhapsode ist tot, es lebe der 'neue Rhapsode:' der Film, der im Ausmalen seiner Bilder, im Verweilen auf den epischen Blöcken seiner Erzählung, epischer als das Epos selbst zu sein scheint" (235f.). Statt des distanzierenden Kommentars (wie bei Brecht) findet sich hier eine Bewegung ins Mythische. Lang "bringt so ein totalisierendes Episches des Films hervor, das den spezifischen Charakter der doppelten Medialität des eigenen Mediums durch Überwältigung zu überspielen versucht" (236f.).

An Uwe Johnsons "Schreibweise des Epischen" wird anhand der Romane *Jahrestage* und *Das dritte Buch über Achim* vor allem die durchgehende erzählerische Selbst- und Medienreflexivität des eigenen Erzählens herausgestellt. Sie wird im zweiten Exkurs kontrastiert mit der Verfilmung der *Jahrestage* durch Margarethe von Trotta, die die komplexe Rekursivität der literarischen Vorlage melodramatisch in eine Familiengeschichte auflöst. Lars von Triers Schaffen wird über das Gruppenmanifest "Dogma 95" und anhand der Filme *Breaking the Waves*, *Dancer in the Dark* und *Dogville* in den Blick genommen. Es wird herausgestellt als "ein episches Kino der Leiblichkeit, das die Erzählgesten selbstkritisch erprobt und die Stimme des Leibs bildlich zur Darstellung bringt" (303).

Insgesamt ist dies also ein weitgefächertes, selbst episch zu nennendes Buch über die Konjunkturen des Epischen im 20. Jahrhundert. Dabei macht Lothar van Laak es dem Leser nicht leicht. Einerseits liegt das an einem auf stringenten Satzbau und Thesenhaftigkeit zuweilen verzichtenden, ausufernd philosophesken Stil; andererseits hat es wohl auch eine systematische Ursache: Bei aller Hochachtung vor dem hohen Anspruch, der Komplexität des Themas und der Fülle von Texten, die der Autor in seine Untersuchung einarbeitet, bleibt letztlich schwer auszumachen, inwiefern das Epische, das immer wieder und höchst unterschiedlich operationalisiert wird, letztlich als systematischer Leitbegriff dienen kann, um die grundlegende Qualität des Erzählens in der Moderne (das, wie der Autor sehr zu Recht vermerkt, im 20. Jahrhundert durch verschiedene Medialisierungsschübe gegangen ist) auf einen gemeinsamen Nenner zu bringen.

Henning Wrage
Haverford College, Philadelphia

Books Received

Bertolt Brecht. *Notizbücher 24-25 (1927-1930). Notizbücher* Bd. 7. Hrsg. von Martin Kölbel und Peter Villwock. Berlin: Suhrkamp, 2010.

Wolfgang Conrad, Ernst Ullrich-Pinkert und Erich Unglaub. *Brechts Söhne: Topographie, Biographie, Werk*. Frankfurt am Main: Peter Lang, 2010.

Hanns Eisler. *Briefe 1907-1943*. Hrsg. von Jürgen Schebera und Maren Köster. Wiesbaden: Breitkopf & Härtel, 2010.

Simone Finkele. *Substrat antiker Tradierung: Brechts Feldherrenmodell Lukullus*. Würzburg: Koenigshausen und Neumann, 2011.

Hans Wilmer Geppert. *Bert Brechts Lyrik: Aussenansichten*. Tübingen: Francke Verlag, 2011.

Najat E. Hassan. *Brecht-Rezeption im Irak, in Syrien und Ägypten seit den sechziger Jahren*. Berlin: Logos Verlag, 2010. [dissertation Rostock]

Phoebe von Held. *Alienation and Theatricality: Diderot after Brecht*. Oxford: Legenda, 2011.

Sebastian Kleinschmidt, Hrsg. *Das Angesicht der Erde: Brechts Ästhetik der Natur. Brecht-Tage 2008*. Berlin: Theater der Zeit, 2009.

Karl Köhler, Hrsg. *Gute Leute sind überall gut: Hacks und Brecht. Zweite wissenschaftliche Tagung der Peter-Hacks-Gesellschaft*. Berlin: Aurora Verlag, 2010.

Denise Kratzmeier. *Es wechseln die Zeiten: Zur Bedeutung von Geschichte im Werk und Ästhetik Bertolt Brechts*. Würzburg: Königshausen und Neumann, 2010

Joachim Lang. *Neues vom alten Brecht: Manfred Wekwerth im Gespräch*. Hrsg. von Valentin F. Lang und Karoline Sprenger. Berlin: Aurora, 2010.

Emily Lecouvey. *Témoignages de Brecht sur la musique, 1920-1955*. Editions universitaires européennes, 2011. [print on demand]

Mathias Mayer, Hrsg. *Der Philosoph Bert Brecht*. Würzburg: Koenigshausen und Neumann, 2011.

Anneliese Penzendorfer. *Lars von Triers "Dogville:" eine Fusion Film vs. Brechts episches Theater. Eine Filmanalyse in 13 Kapiteln und einem Prolog*. Saarbrücken: VDM Verlag Dr. Müller, 2010. [dissertation]

Brecht in/and Asia // Brecht in/und Asien
Friedemann Weidauer et al., eds., *The Brecht Yearbook / Das Brecht-Jahrbuch* Volume 36 (Storrs, CT: The International Brecht Society, 2011)

Contributors

Farzana Akhter is an Assistant Professor in the Department of English at East West University, Dhaka. She also works as an Adjunct Professor at the University of Dhaka. She has been awarded an M. Phil. degree from the University of Dhaka for her research on Bertolt Brecht and his influence on Bangladeshi drama.

Amal Allana is a theater director and a chairperson of the National School of Drama (NSD) in New Delhi. Trained in direction at NSD, she studied Brecht's work in the GDR from 1969 to 1971. Here she was privy to rehearsals of Brecht productions by Benno Besson, Ruth Berghaus, Manfred Karge, Matthias Langhoff and Fritz Bennewitz, who also happened to be her tutor. In 1970 she assisted Bennewitz on *The Threepenny Opera* in India. Japanese traditional theater was her next major influence. These intercultural influences impacted critically on her directorial projects. Working with classical and contemporary texts, both Indian and foreign, and devising her own texts, she scrutinizes India's contemporary history — whether political, sociological or autobiographical — in an attempt to trace the formation of a postcolonial cultural identity. Central to this project is the role of women. Allana has staged over 60 productions and received several national awards for her contributions to Indian theater.

Andreas Aurin holds a BA in Musicology and Cultural Studies from Humboldt-University Berlin and a BA (Hons) in Theater Studies from the University of New South Wales, Sydney (UNSW). Aurin is a PhD candidate at UNSW investigating the dialectical relationship between text and music in all six of Brecht's *Lehrstücke*. His interest in the music-text relationship in the *Lehrstück* started in 2003 when he met East German composer Kurt Schwaen, with whom he collaborated as a performer in numerous recitals until Schwaen passed away in 2007. Aurin's first scholarly engagement with the dialectical relationship between music and text is entitled *"Viele Dinge sind in einem Ding." Zur Dialektik im Lehrstück "Die Horatier und die Kuriatier,"* which was published on the occasion of Schwaen's 100th birthday at the Kurt-Schwaen-Archive in Berlin, 2009.

Dennis Carroll recently retired as Professor and Chair of Theatre and Dance, University of Hawai'i at Mānoa. He is the author of eight produced plays, many articles on contemporary American, Finnish and Australian theater and two books, *Australian Contemporary Drama* (rev. ed., Sydney: Currency Press, 1995) and *David Mamet* (Houndmills: Macmillan, 1987).

Jan Creutzenberg, M.A., studied theater studies, cultural studies and philosophy in Berlin and Paris. He graduated in 2010 from the Free University with a thesis on performative processes in Korean *pansori*, a form of singing-storytelling music theater. His research interests include the history, politics and practices of the performing arts in Korea, with a special focus on the use of traditional techniques in contemporary performances as well as on cross-cultural adaptations of Western classics. On the latter, he presented a paper at the German Shakespeare Society's 2009 conference: "To Be or Not to Be (Korean): Lee Youn-taek's *Hamlet* and the Reception of Shakespeare in Korea" (available for download at <http://shakespeare-gesellschaft.de/publikationen.seminar.ausgabe2009.htm>).

Boris Daussà-Pastor is a theater PhD student at The Graduate Center, City University of New York, and a Teaching Fellow at Brooklyn College. Originally from Barcelona, he has traveled regularly to Kerala for *kathakali* training and field research since 2004. He has published some articles on this subject as well as a book-length practical training guide in collaboration with his *kathakali* teacher Kalamandalam KM John. Boris also conducts workshops using principles of *kathakali* training to develop the creativity and artistic skills of non-*kathakali* actors. His other areas of expertise include Hispanophone Caribbean theater (Cuba, Dominican Republic, and Puerto Rico) and the theorization of theater and culture from post-national perspectives.

Melissa Dinsman is a doctoral candidate in the PhD in Literature Program at the University of Notre Dame. Her main area of study is global modernism, with an emphasis on British, Irish, American and German literature. She is currently writing a dissertation on the use of radio by literary modernists for both pedagogical and propagandistic purposes.

Joerg Esleben is Associate Professor of German at the University of Ottawa, Canada. His primary research interests include intercultural theater, cultural relations between Germany and India, travel writing, and the Faust theme. He is a co-editor of *Mapping Channels between Ganges and Rhein: German-Indian Cross Cultural Relations* (Newcastle: Cambridge Scholars, 2008) and the author of numerous articles, for example, on the work of Georg Forster, the early German response to Kalidasa's drama *Sakuntala*, and the reception of Goethe's *Faust* in Canada.

Eberhard Fritz has served as archivist of the House of Württemberg in Altshausen near Ravensburg since 1987. He has published several books and numerous essays on the history of the State of Württemberg, especially on the history of the Court of Württemberg and on local and regional history. His focus is on researching German pietism from a socio-historical point of view. He received his doctorate from the University of Paderborn in 2001 with a thesis on *Radikaler Pietismus in Württemberg. Religiöse Ideale im Konflikt mit gesellschaftlichen Realitäten*. Sinced then, he has published additional papers on this topic that also treat pietism in Southwestern German Free Cities and in Alsace. In addition he has researched the influence of pietism on people such as Bertolt Brecht, Friedrich Engels, Johann Friedrich Oberlin, Albert Schweitzer, Gustav Werner and other less famous figures. These micro studies resulted in the thesis that numerous public figures who grew up in this kind of religious environment and became well known on the basis of their social and cultural accomplishments in some way had been influenced by radical pietist convictions.

Günther Heeg is Professor of Theater Studies at the University of Leipzig and Vice President of the International Brecht Society (IBS). He has written books and numerous articles on Bertolt Brecht, Heiner Müller, the intermediality of arts, and contemporary theater. Recent research projects include: "Encountering the Other. Cultural Inflexions of Space and Time," "Shared/Divided Community–Collective Creativity," and "The Presence of the Past." His publications include: *Das Phantasma der natürlichen Gestalt: Körper, Sprache und Bild im Theater des 18. Jahrhunderts* (2000); *Klopfzeichen aus dem Mausoleum. Brecht-Schulung am Berliner Ensemble*; (2000), *Stillstand und Bewegung. Intermediale Studien zur Theatralität von Text, Bild und Musik, München* (co-ed., 2004); *Mind the Map–History Is Not Given* (co-ed., 2006); *Theatrographie. Heiner Müllers Theater der Schrift* (ed., 2009); *Globalizing Areas. Kulturelle Flexionen von Raum und Zeit* (co-ed., 2011).

Akira Ichikawa is a professor of media studies and aesthetics at Osaka University. From 2005 to 2009 he was the director of a German-Japanese research project on "Brecht and Music," the findings of which were recently published in Japan. Ichikawa is also the editor and translator of the Japanese publications of *Brecht. Poems and Songs* (Tokyo 2008), *Brecht. Music and* Stage (Tokyo 2009), and *Brecht. Plays* (Tokyo 2009). In 2010 he started a new project on "Brecht/Weigel and the Berlin Ensemble," with the participation of Jan Knopf, Joachim Lucchesi, and Hirokazu Akiba. In addition to his research, Ichikawa has not only translated many German plays into Japanese but also initiated their first Japanese stage productions.

Zheng Jie is a PhD candidate of the Division of English at Nanyang Technological University. She is completing her dissertation on Brecht and China.

David G. John received his doctorate in German from the University of Toronto in 1975. Since 1974, with the exception of one year at McGill University in Montreal, he has been a professor of German at the University of Waterloo, Ontario, Canada. During this time he has held numerous senior administrative positions in the Faculty of Arts and the Canadian Association of University Teachers of German, and is founder of the Waterloo Centre for German Studies (www.wcgs.ca). His research interests and major publications include a critical edition of the works of

Johann Christian Krüger (Tübingen: Niemeyer, 1986) and monographs on the German *Nachspiel* (University of Toronto Press, 1991), Goethe and Schiller (McGill-Queen's UP, 1998), and German intercultural stagings of Goethe's *Faust* (University of Toronto Press, to appear 2011). He is currently working with a team of researchers on Fritz Bennewitz's directing activity in India, with a principal focus on Brecht.

Parichat Jungwiwattanaporn is an Assistant Professor at Thammasat University. A researcher and writer on theater history and criticism in Thailand, she has participated in a national research project on "Criticism as an Intellectual Power in Contemporary Thai Society" since 1999. After earning her PhD in Asian Theater at the Department of Theater and Dance at the University of Hawai'i at Mānoa in 2010, she has been the chair of this research project, in which criticism of various art forms in Thailand (theater, film, music, dance, and visual arts) intersects with a multidisciplinary theoretical framework (aesthetics, philosophy, anthropology, and sociology). Parichat Jungwiwattanaporn's academic interests include political theater, theater for social change, and contemporary theater in Asia. Her publications include three co-authored books and two books on Thai contemporary theater and criticism as well as a number of articles for Asian Theater Journal, the SPAFA journal (a publication of the SEAMEO Regional Centre for Archaeology and Fine Arts in Southeast Asia), and various newspapers.

Weijia Li is Assistant Professor of German at Western Illinois University. Li received his PhD in Germanic Languages and Literatures from The Ohio State University in 2009. His teaching and research interests include German contemporary literature and minority literature, German cinema, and Chinese-German cultural encounters. Li's first book, *China und China-Erfahrung in Leben und Werk von Anna Seghers*, was published in 2010. His current research focuses on Chinese left-wing political activists during the Weimar Republic.

Joachim Lucchesi studied musicology at the Humboldt-Universität in Berlin. He has taught and worked at various universities in Germany, Japan, and the United States, and in 1997-1998 he was a musical dramaturge at the Berliner Ensemble. Lucchesi has published widely on the history of music, theater and literature. He is also the author of several standard works on Brecht and music: *Musik bei Brecht* (1988, together with Ronald K. Shull); *Das Verhör in der Oper: Die Debatte um Brechts/Dessaus 'Lukullus' 1951* (1993), and *Die Dreigroschenoper: Der Erstdruck 1928 – Text und Kommentar* (2004). He is a member of the presidium of the Kurt Weill society in Dessau, and he also serves on the editorial board of the Augsburg-based Brecht journal *Dreigroschenheft*.

Martin Revermann is Associate Professor of Classics and Theatre Studies at the University of Toronto, with research interests in Greek drama (including its reception), Brecht, theater iconography, theater theory and theater sociology. He is the author of *Comic Business: Theatricality, Dramatic Technique and Performance Contexts of Aristophanic Comedy* (Oxford 2006), the editor of the *Cambridge Companion to Greek Comedy* (Cambridge forthcoming), and the co-editor of *Performance, Iconography, Reception: Studies in Honour of Oliver Taplin* (Oxford 2008) as well as *Beyond the 5th Century: Interactions with Greek Tragedy from the Fourth Century BCE to the Middle Ages* (Berlin, New York 2010).

Rolf Rohmer was Professor of Theater History at the Theater Academy Leipzig until his retirement in 1995. He also served as the Vice Chancellor of the Academy (1969-1982) and is a former Artistic Director of Deutsches Theater Berlin (1982-1984). Since 1995 he has been in charge of the Fritz Bennewitz Archive in Leipzig. His main research centers on dramaturgy and on international relationships in the field of modern theater. He led various commissions of the International Theatre Institute (ITI) and was the President of the International Federation of Theatre Research (FIRT/IFTR) from 1979 to 1983. He has also been involved in related international projects such as *The International Bibliography of Theatre* and *The World Encyclopedia of Contemporary Theatre*.

Richard Schechner has pioneered environmental theater and audience participation in plays he has directed in the United States, Taiwan, mainland China, India, and the Republic of South Africa. His productions have won major awards such as the BITEF (Belgrade International Experimental Theatre Festival) Prize, two OBIEs (New York off-Broadway prize), as well as the Mondello Prize (Italy). His productions include *Dionysus in 69, Commune, Mother Courage and Her Children, Three Sisters, Faust/gastronome, Oresteia, Hamlet: That Is the Question, Yokastas Redux,* and *Swimming to Spalding*. He has radically reinterpreted and deconstructed canonical texts of the Western repertory as well as directed new plays and devised performances. In addition to his directing, Schechner is a leading performance theorist, author, University Professor and Professor of Performance Studies (New York University), editor of the Enactments book series (Seagull), and editor of *TDR*.

Marc Silberman is Professor of German Studies and Affiliate Professor of Theater/Drama and of Film Studies at the University of Wisconsin, Madison. He received his PhD from Indiana University in 1975 and taught at the University of Texas in San Antonio until 1988 and as guest professor at UCLA, the Freie Universität Berlin and the Universität Freiburg/Br. He has published, co-edited, and translated material in a number of scholarly domains: GDR novels, Heiner Müller, Bertolt Brecht, German film history, traditions of political theater. He has been active in the International Brecht Society since the early 1980s, editing the journal *Communications* (1982-86) as well as the *Brecht Yearbook* (1989-1995), overseeing the *Yearbook*'s book review section (1986-), and co-organizing several of the IBS symposia over the past 15 years.

Gudrun Tabbert-Jones is an Associate Professor of German at Santa Clara University. She was born and raised in Germany. After her *Abitur* she studied at the *Pädagogische Hochschule* Darmstadt, Germany, and in Paris, France. Subsequently she taught French and English at a German secondary school. After her emigration to the United States she completed her M.A. and her PhD at Stanford University. She wrote her dissertation on *Die Funktion der liedhaften Einlage in den frühen Stücken Brechts* (The Function of the Songs in Bertolt Brecht's Early Plays), and has given papers and written articles on Brecht. From 1995 to 2003 she was the editor of *Communications from the International Brecht Society*.

Yuan Tan, PhD in German literature from Göttingen University (Germany), is associate professor in the German Department, Huazhong University of Science and Technology (Wuhan 430074, China). His academic fields are German literature and translation history.

Michiko Tanigawa is a Professor emeritus of German Culture Studies at Tokyo University of Foreign Studies. Her research focus is on modern German theater (Heiner Müller, Elfriede Jelinek, Pina Bausch, and Brecht). She has published many books on German contemporary theater, including Brecht, translated many texts from German into Japanese, and is often involved in theater productions.

Antony Tatlow: University of Hong Kong 1965-96, Founding Professor of Comparative Literature Department; Professor of Comparative Literature, University of Dublin 1996-2005; Honorary Professor, Drama Department, University of Dublin 2006-. International Brecht Society President 1982-90; Consultant to the Central Academy of Drama, Beijing 1985-; Editorial Board *Brecht Yearbook* 1991- . Relevant books: *Brechts chinesische Gedichte*. Frankfurt: Suhrkamp 1973; *The Mask of Evil. Brecht's Response to the Poetry, Theatre & Thought of China & Japan*. Berne: Peter Lang 1977; (ed.) *Brecht and East Asian Theatre*, Hong Kong: HKU Press 1982; (ed.) *Brecht in Asia & Africa*, Brecht Yearbook 14, 1989; *Benwen Renleixue*. (*Textual Anthropology. A Practice of Reading*). Beijing: Peking University Press 1996; *Brechts Ost Asien—ein Parallog*. Berlin: Parthas 1998; *Shakespeare, Brecht and the Intercultural Sign*. Durham NC: Duke University Press 2001; (ed.) *Where Extremes Meet, Rereading Brecht & Beckett*, Brecht Yearbook 27, 2002.

Friedemann Weidauer is Associate Professor of German at the University of Connecticut. He has served as the editor of the Brecht Yearbook since fall 2008. Recent publications include articles on Brecht, Christoph Hein, and Jurek Becker.

Markus Wessendorf holds a PhD in Applied Theater Studies from the University of Giessen and is currently Associate Professor at the Department of Theatre and Dance at the University of Hawai'i at Mānoa. His publications include a monograph on Richard Foreman's Ontological-Hysteric Theater and a co-edited volume on interdisciplinary relationships between theater and the other arts. He has also written essays and articles on Brecht, The Wooster Group, Richard Maxwell, and various other theater artists and dramatists. As a director, he has staged Heiner Müller's *Germania Death in Berlin* (New York 1989), Norman Price's *Barking Dogs* (Brisbane 1998), Laurent Gaudé's *Battle of Will* (Honolulu 2005), Will Eno's *Thom Pain (Based on Nothing)* (Honolulu 2006), and Samuel Beckett's *Waiting for Godot* (Honolulu 2010). He has also translated Brecht's *Die Judith von Shimoda* into English, and he was the main organizer of the 13th IBS Symposium on "Brecht in/and Asia" in Honolulu.

General note

p.161? from 34 bottom: FB gets too much credit: 1) success due to being part of broader plan. 2) didn't preach Socialist/Communist message.
 — Motivation? Personal advantage? → Fame in India + GDR; escape from GDR; freer sexual life?